LEARNING AND MEMORY:

The Behavioral and Biological Substrates

LEARNING AND MEMORY:

The Behavioral and Biological Substrates

Edited by

ISIDORE GORMEZANO
EDWARD A. WASSERMAN
University of Iowa

LEA

1992

LAWRENCE ERLBAUM ASSOCIATES, PUBLISHERS

Hillsdale, New Jersey   Hove and London

Lawrence Erlbaum Associates, Inc., Publishers
365 Broadway
Hillsdale, New Jersey 07642

Library of Congress Cataloging-in-Publication Data

Learning and memory : the behavioral and biological substrates /
    edited by Isidore Gormezano, Edward A. Wasserman.
        p.   cm.
    Includes bibliographical references and indexes.
    ISBN 0-8058-0888-4
    1. Learning. 2. Memory. I. Gormezano, Isidore. II. Wasserman,
Edward A.
    [DNLM: 1. Behavior, Animal—physiology. 2. Conditioning
(Psychology)—physiology. 3. Learning—physiology. 4. Memory—
physiology.   WL 102 L436]
QP408.L435 1992
156'.31—dc20
DNLM/DLC
for Library of Congress   91-46937
                                                               CIP

OCLC: 25049422

Printed in the United States of America
10 9 8 7 6 5 4 3 2 1

Contents

Preface

This volume presents contributions made at The University of Iowa's biennial symposia on *Learning and Memory: The Behavioral and Biological Substrates.* Initiation of the symposium was made possible by Professor John H. Harvey's (Chair, Department of Psychology, 1986–1989) leadership and sustained efforts in obtaining the financial support of the College of Liberal Arts (Professor Gerhard Loewenberg, Dean). Additional support was generously provided by the College of Medicine (Dean John W. Eckstein), through the Departments of Pharmacology (Professor P. Michael Conn, Head) and Physiology and Biophysics (Professor Robert E. Fellows, Head). Finally, we gratefully acknowledge the support of the Neuroscience Program (Professor Joe D. Coulter, Chair).

It is proper also to acknowledge that the success of the symposia depended upon the capable assistance of several staff members at The University of Iowa: most noteworthy, Ms. Terry Powell, Program Associate, Conferences and Institutes, Ms. Jean Jensen, Ms. Pamela Young, and Mr. André Mallie. In addition, we acknowledge the air transportation arrangements for participants provided by Travel Concepts, Iowa City, IA.

Introduction

Isidore Gormezano
University of Iowa

This volume presents the views and findings of behaviorally and biologically oriented investigators invited to participate in the University of Iowa's biennial learning and memory symposium. In recent years, a number of edited volumes have appeared in learning and memory. However, we believe that few of them involve as balanced a set of behavioral and biological contributions as presently achieved. Whereas the present chapters vary in their scope and depth of coverage, they are all amply referenced so that the researcher, teacher, and student can obtain the background information appropriate to their respective needs. It should also be noted that editors of multiauthored volumes sometimes face the unpleasant choice of waiting or not waiting for the very last contributors to proceed with publication. As a consequence, several topics originally planned for inclusion in this volume are absent. In any event for purposes of discussion, the content of the present contributions can be categorized in three groups, as detailed next.

Chapters 1 to 3 reveal the scientific maturing of ecological, ethiological and comparative perspectives in the study of learning and memory, whereas Chapters 4 and 5, employing the more traditional paradigms of matching-to-sample and partial reinforcement, respectively, provide an expanded view of basic learning and memory processes. Collectively, Chapters 1 to 5 provide sets of learning and memory data that offer interesting challenges to their biological analysis. At present, the principle impediment to meeting this challenge lies in the need to develop the appropriate reductionistic methodologies. Hopefully, these chapters will stimulate the biologically oriented readers to such an undertaking.

Roberts (Chapter 1) illustrates the maturing analysis of foraging from an anthropomorphic perspective, to biological models appealing to evolutionary processes, to his radial maze analysis of such patch-related variables as the density, location, number, and size of food items. The accumulation of data indicating the importance of memory to foraging led Roberts to select the radial maze as a particularly useful paradigm for the experimental study of foraging. Moreover, in reviewing the results of a series of his radial maze experiments, Roberts demonstrates the paradigm's ecological validity and power to investigate the role of memory in foraging as well as for the study of memory per se.

Shettleworth (Chapter 2), starting from a comparative and ecological perspective, presents the results of a program of research directed at comparing the memory of birds for stored and encountered food in storing and nonstoring bird species under several experimental paradigms. In one procedure, for example, each bird is tested in an aviary with holes drilled in tree branches providing food storage sites. After eating a few seeds, the bird proceeds to store up to a dozen seeds individually, among as many as 97 holes. Subsequently, the holes are covered with a small flap of cloth and after various retention intervals, the bird is permitted to recover the seeds. At a procedural level, at least, the bird food-storing paradigm differs substantially from the memory paradigms employed with other species (e.g., pigeon, rat). Nevertheless the food-storing paradigm reveals the extraordinary ability of the birds to retrieve stored food at very extended retention intervals, after only a single learning trial. In brief, Shettleworth's studies constitute an eloquent testimonial to the power of a comparative and ecological framework to provide new insights and challenges to the study of memory mechanisms.

Wright (Chapter 3) advances the unassailable position that failures to observe higher mental processes in animals may reflect the employment of inappropriate apparatus and paradigms. In operational terms, Wright draws our attention to the need to employ experimental protocols whose stimulus dimensions and response demands take advantage of the organism's innate characteristics while minimizing incompatibilities. Wright supports his view with studies in which modest changes in traditional training and testing situations yielded substantial gains in ability of monkeys to perform list memory tasks, and in the success of pigeons and monkeys to learn abstract concepts.

Chatlosh and Wasserman (Chapter 4) describe the results of a series of pigeon short-term memory experiments with matching-to-sample procedures. The reported studies are concerned with determining the role of anticipatory responses on memory under prolonged retention intervals. In one experiment, they reported that manipulating the probability of reinforcement following different sample stimuli markedly reduced the rate of forgetting compared to a fixed probability of reinforcement following the test stimuli. These and other results are interpreted by the authors to provide strong support for the view that expectancies of different trial outcomes have stimulus properties that can serve a mnemonic function.

Daly (Chapter 5), starting with the seminal paper by Wyckoff (1952), critically reviews the appetitive-observing response literature that meet her criteria of being "pure" observing response experiments (i.e., control for response cost, response competition, response changeover, and response choice). Considering experimental outcomes for studies meeting such criteria, Daly illustrates the power of her linear operator model, DMOD, to predict the conditions under which subjects will reveal a preference for unpredictable appetitive rewards—a possible outcome not addressed by any previous theoretical account. The predictive power of Daly's model rests upon her quantitative formalizing of constructs incorporating: (a) Amsel's (1958) frustration account of the aversive consequences of the unexpected omission of reward; and (b) the consequences of reintroducing reward. Collectively, these constructs provide a model whose ability to integrate a large body of data is impressive.

In Chapters 6 to 8 as elaborated next, the authors have provided contributions revealing the harmonious wedding of behavioral paradigms with well-delineated biological methodologies for a reductionistic analysis of behaviorally defined constructs (e.g., "internal" clock, sensitization, fear). On the other hand, Chapters 9 and 10 reveal the maturing of methodological and conceptual developments in the behavioral and biological analysis of teratogens and environmental variations on brain functioning and development, respectively,.

Church et al. (Chapter 6) detail the functioning of the internal clock, memory, and decision-processing components of an information-processing model of timing. In this theory of timing, the internal clock, postulated to be composed of a pacemaker, switch, and accumulator, has the status of a hypothetical construct whose surplus meaning readily suggests experimental interventions for effective time perception and time production. In particular, the internal clock, as a hypothetical construct, suggests a variety of interventions that might be expected to alter the internal state of the organism, for example, and as they demonstrate, a variety of drugs would be expected to affect the operating characteristics of the clock (e.g., clock speed).

Stewart (Chapter 7) presents a series of experiments designed to determine the conditions under which repeated exposure to opiate and stimulant drugs leads to: (a) sensitization of their behavioral activating effects (i.e., increased locomotor responsiveness to repeated drug injection), and (b) conditioned stimuli gaining control over the expression of that sensitization. In brief, Steward presents a provocative set of experiments indicating that the development of locomotor sensitization in rats is correlated with increases in the extracellular concentration of dopamine (DA) in the gomatodendritic region of the mesolimbic DA neurons, whereas CS control appears to be correlated with the release of the DA from both cell body and terminal regions of the neurons. Although only correlative in nature, Stewart's findings suggest where in the nervous system (and by what mechanism) learned changes in the ability of sensory stimuli to modulate activity might take place.

Davis et al. (Chapter 8), employing the fear-potentiated startle paradigm for the study of learning and memory in vertebrates, provide a review of their efforts, and those of others, in determining the neural pathways involved. In particular, they detail their efforts at delineating the role of the central nucleus of the amyglada and its possible connections to the acoustic startle pathway and to visual structures carrying information about the visual conditioned stimulus. These investigators join a small but growing group of behavioral neuroscientists who have targeted simple and robust learning paradigms tractable to their neural substrates and sites of neural change.

Goodlett et al. (Chapter 9) review the results of a series of anatomical and behavioral studies attesting to the power of their animal model to experimentally delineate the causes and consequences of the fetal alcohol syndrome (FAS). Although FAS has been long recognized as a clinical syndrome, there has been a paucity of evidence of its behavioral effects. Employing an elegant maintenance paradigm involving gastric feedings, these investigators have been able to deliver doses of alcohol during a postnatal period of rapid brain growth. As a consequence, their FAS model has unfolded anatomical damage and behavioral dysfunctions ordinarily related to alcohol dosage and the postnatal period of exposure. In addition to their clinical significance, the elucidation of the factors mediating teratogenic effects of alcohol will also enhance our general understanding of brain-behavior relationships.

Greenough et al. (Chapter 10) summarize more than two decades of their research on the anatomical effects of environmental complexity. In addition, they present their most recent findings on research directed at isolating learning-dependent anatomical changes in the mammalian brain arising from the effects of early sensory experience on brain information storage. They also provide evidence to suggest three dissociable aspects of brain information storage: (a) overproduction of synapses followed by selective preservation; (b) activity dependent synaptogenesis; and (c) altered metabolic capacity. Of considerable theoretical interest is their assertion that different neural processes may mediate experience-induced synaptogenesis during development versus adulthood. They speculate that, from an evolutionary perspective, some aspects of the rearing environment remain invariant and, thereby, permit the stabilizing of certain associative connections and synaptogenesis. In contrast, the authors suggest that in later development and in adulthood varied experience drives synaptogenesis.

In Chapters 11 to 16, the authors, following in a tradition pioneered by Pavlov (1927) and Lashley (1929, 1950), employ a variety of behavioral techniques to advance an understanding of the biological basis of learning and memory. Specifically, these authors present findings that reveal major advances in our understanding of the functional role of anatomically distinct structures, synaptogenic changes, and, with the use of model systems, the loci of neural and biophysical changes in learning and memory.

LoTurco et al. (Chapter 11) review their striking findings on the biophysical and biochemical correlates of associative learning in the in vitro brain slice preparation of the rabbit hippocampal CA1 neurons and Hermissenda B cells.

Specifically, they have identified increases in the excitability of both CA1 and B cells with associatively induced long-term biochemical change mediated by protein kinase C (PKC). Accordingly, they propose that a general mechanism of neural plasticity, related to associative learning, may be the activation of PKC and the consequent modification of potassium currents. Interestingly, their biochemical model of associative learning allocates a central role to the behavioral associative principle of contiguity.

Kesner and Jackson-Smith (Chapter 12) assume that specific neural regions (like the hippocampus) selectively participate in such psychological processes as the discrimination of time and space, the experience of affect, and the generation of responses. The interplay of these psychological processes in learning and memory and the neural regions that mediate successful performance is the focus of their research program. Taking their lead from clinical and experimental findings with human beings, Kesner and Jackson-Smith report a series of systematic investigations with rats, which suggest that analogous neural regions in these two species serve similar mnemonic functions. These findings thus constitute broad support, indeed, for their attribute model of memory.

Berger and Bassett (Chapter 13) discuss the function of the hippocampus in the modulation of learned behaviors. They give special consideration to the functional correlates of single-unit activity and to the activity of larger collections of spatially contiguous hippocampal cells. Berger and Bassett further urge that a proper picture of hippocampal function must also consider the interface between the hippocampus and other regions of the brain more specifically tuned to coordinating motor activity. Failure to consider the interplay between the hippocampus and other brain structures may greatly distort our understanding of how the hippocampus influences the performance of learned behaviors.

McCabe et al. (Chapter 14) describe a systematic series of studies using a wide range of behavioral, physiological, and pharmacological methods to elucidate the neural mechanisms of heart rate conditioning in rabbits. Especially noteworthy is their use of differential conditioning as a basic behavioral paradigm; this method sheds considerable light on the role of excitation and inhibition in controlling cardiac responses, and it also allows one to pinpoint associative changes in both CS and US processing. Although much remains to be learned about the involved neural circuitry, the plan of attack outlined by these authors appears to be particularly promising.

Moore and Desmond (Chapter 15) describe a hypothetical neural network that shows promise in explaining *whether* and *when* an organism predicts US occurrence from presentation of the CS. This computational model was developed to explain several details of rabbit nictitating membrane conditioning including inhibition of delay, blocking, and the intermixture of interstimulus intervals. Furthermore, by taking into account known facts of cerebellar function and anatomy, the model of Moore and Desmond strove to be physiologically plausible. The heuristic value of the model will be determined by how effective it is in stimulating new lines of behavioral and physiological inquiry into the neural locus of conditioning.

Thompson and Steinmetz (Chapter 16) review an extensive series of behavioral and physiological investigations leading them to conclude that classical conditioning of the rabbit's nictitating membrane response establishes multiple memory traces in a very localized region of the cerebellum, the dentate interpositus. Damage to the site is observed to eliminate conditioned responses, but to spare unconditioned responses. Thompson and Steinmetz express their surprise with having found the cerebellum as the locus of engram formation. Moreover, they acknowledge that other brain regions, such as the hippocampus, surely participate in performance of the conditioned response in more complex behavioral tasks.

1 Foraging by Rats on a Radial Maze: Learning, Memory, and Decision Rules

William A. Roberts
University of Western Ontario

The research I discuss represents a blending of two areas of investigation, spatial memory and foraging. Beginning with the seminal article of Olton and Samuelson (1976), a number of experiments have been carried out on the radial maze to find out how rats and other animals remember and forget spatial information. This research has revealed that rats can remember a large number of locations visited (Olton, Collison, & Werz, 1977; Roberts, 1979) and that the format of memory is maplike and based on extramaze visual cues (Mazmanian & Roberts, 1983; Suzuki, Augerinos, & Black, 1980). Although rats can remember locations visited on the radial maze over several hours (Beatty & Shavalia, 1980), forgetting can arise from both proactive and retroactive interference caused by other spatial experiences (Roberts, 1981; Roberts & Dale, 1981).

If one reflects on the functional role of spatial memory, it seems clear that spatial memory promotes fitness in rats and other animals (Shettleworth, 1983). Specifically, spatial memory allows animals to remember where in space a number of places are located that are vital to survival, such as food locations, the location of home base, and the locations of potential predators and conspecifics. Spatial memory also allows an organism to keep track of its own movements through a spatial landscape and prevents redundant visits to locations recently visited. Finally, animals not only remember locations in their environment but also remember the contents of those locations or important events that occurred at those locations.

Much of this concern with the functional role of spatial memory is incorporated within the second area of investigation, foraging theory. Spatial memory may be seen to be at the service of foraging strategies that tend to maximize the survival of an organism or its genes. Thus, spatial knowledge informs decisions that tend to maximize energy gained over time by a forager and its offspring and to minimize exposure to predation.

Shettleworth (1989) has recently stressed the distinction between *functional* and *mechanistic* foraging questions. Many models of foraging advanced by biologists have addressed functional questions about the way in which evolutionary processes would shape optimal foraging behavior. Psychologists, on the other hand, have tended to focus on proximal questions about the more immediate mechanisms that govern foraging decisions in existing animals. Presumably, these two approaches to the study of foraging go hand in hand; that is, mechanisms of foraging evolved to serve functions that tend to optimize foraging behavior. For example, if it is optimal for a forager to visit environmental locations containing food and to avoid ones not containing food, there should be evolutionary pressures for the selection of organisms that can learn and remember food locations.

Much of the foraging work in psychology has been carried out in Skinner boxes, with animals working for reinforcements on concurrent and multiple schedules that deliver reinforcement at different rates on a random or quasi-random basis. The question usually asked in such experiments is whether an animal will learn to switch between keys or schedules at times that tend to maximize the overall energy gain (e.g., Bhatt & Wasserman, 1987; Dow & Lea, 1987; Fantino & Abarca, 1985; Kamil, Yoerg, & Clements, 1988). Relatively few experiments have been carried out in the psychology laboratory to investigate what may be a relatively more realistic situation of animals foraging across a spatial field in which food may be found in different locations. Further, few experiments have been done to study foraging when the forager may have complete or nearly complete knowledge of an environment and its contents.

Within natural settings or seminatural environments constructed in the laboratory, evidence of the important functional use of spatial memory in foraging has begun to accumulate. Menzel (1973, 1978) allowed chimpanzees to observe as many as 18 food items being hidden at different locations in an open outdoor field. When released, the chimpanzees foraged in a least-distance-traveled pattern and thus minimized the time and effort required to accumulate all the available food. When confronted with an abundance of food that cannot be consumed at the moment, some species of birds hoard available food and recover it at a later time. In both the field and the laboratory, it has been shown that Clark's nutcrackers can remember a vast number of locations where pinyon pine seeds have been buried days before (Balda, 1980; Balda & Turek, 1984; Kamil & Balda, 1985). Marsh tits and chickadees allowed to hide food in a natural setting or in holes in trees in a laboratory show foraging efficiency by selectively returning to those places where food was hidden (Sherry, 1987; Shettleworth & Krebs, 1982, 1986). By using spatial memory for the location and contents of food sites, foraging birds save valuable time and energy that would be lost if a search not informed by memory were used.

A few recent laboratory studies with rats suggest foraging efficiency. Mellgren and his associates examined the foraging patterns of rats confronted with food items buried in boxes of sand that were dispersed about a large room (Mellgren, 1982; Mellgren & Brown, 1987; Mellgren, Misasi, & Brown, 1984). Rats searched longer in patches as patch density and travel time between patches increased and showed the most efficient foraging when patch density was unpredictable and patches were difficult to reach. Several radial maze studies suggest that rats are very sensitive to the contents of maze arms and tend to prioritize their visits to arms on the basis of their contents. Hulse and O'Leary (1982) placed different quantities of reward pellets in food cups at the ends of the arms of a four-arm radial maze and found that rats came to enter the arms with the largest amounts before the arms with the smaller amounts. In other experiments, water-deprived rats have encountered water or other liquid substances placed on the arms of a radial maze. Rats learned to avoid an arm that did not contain water and to prefer one that contained chocolate milk (Batson, Best, Phillips, Patel, & Gilleland, 1986). When consumption of saccharin was followed by lithium chloride poisoning, rats avoided any arm of a radial maze that contained saccharin (Batson et al., 1986; Melcer & Timberlake, 1985).

In the experiments reported here, I show that rats foraging on a radial maze are sensitive to several variables that are directly relevant to foraging in a natural setting. These variables include structural aspects of the foraging situation, such as differences in density of food among patches, location of food within a patch, travel time between patches, and ease of access to food placed in feeders, and properties of food items, such as number and size. In several cases, rats' behaviors will appear illogical or unnecessary within the laboratory context. However, consideration of this behavior from an evolutionary point of view suggests that it has definite survival value. It is argued that the radial maze has considerable ecological validity for the study of foraging in rats, and that this ecological validity may be a result of the radial maze mimicking to a certain extent the burrow system of wild rats.

OPTIMAL FORAGING BY RATS

In several experiments my students and I have carried out recently, we have extended the use of the radial maze for studying foraging in rats by adding certain constraints on foraging. In Fig. 1.1, a top diagram is shown of a four-arm radial maze used in my laboratory. Notice that each arm contains four feeding stations or food cups attached to a platform on the side of the arm. In the experiment depicted in the figure, the arms of the maze were defined as patches, and the patches contained 0 (0% patch), 1 (25% patch), 2 (50% patch), or 3 (75% patch)

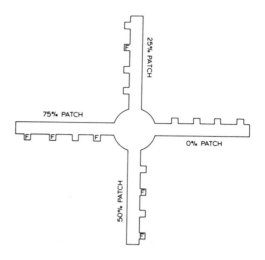

FIG. 1.1. Diagram of a four-arm radial maze with four feeding stations on each arm (patch). Patch density was varied by placing food (F) in 0 (0% patch), 1 (25% patch), 2 (50% patch), or 3 (75% patch) of the feeders in each patch. (From Roberts & Ilersich, 1989. Copyright 1989 by American Psychological Association. Reprinted by permission.)

baited feeders. The baited feeders (F) each contained a pellet of General Mill's Count Chocula breakfast cereal. Information was varied in this experiment. One group of rats was allowed to forage with the food locations remaining fixed throughout 24 foraging sessions. This group then had the opportunity to learn food locations and to make use of reference memory to forage efficiently. A second group of rats had food locations varied randomly from one session to the next; the four patches always contained 0, 1, 2, or 3 baited feeders, but patch density and the specific locations of baited feeders within patches varied randomly between daily sessions. Two other constraints on foraging were manipulated. Travel time between patches was manipulated by requiring rats to climb over wooden barriers placed at the entrance to each arm. On alternate daily sessions, barriers were either present or absent. As a third constraint, the time and effort required to gain access to feeders was raised by requiring rats to push metal covers off the feeders to get at their contents. One subgroup of rats within

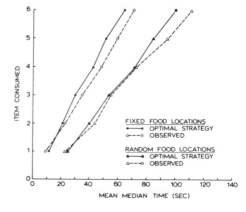

FIG. 1.2. Gain functions showing mean median times at which successive food items were consumed. The optimal strategy curves are based on computer simulations, and the observed curves are based on rats foraging for food in fixed or random locations on a four-arm maze.

each of the fixed and random food location conditions was tested with covered feeders, and another subgroup was tested with open feeders.

In Fig. 1.2, two fixed food location curves and two random food location curves are shown for animals foraging with barriers placed at patch entrances and covers placed over feeders. One curve represents optimal foraging as determined by a computer simulation. The simulations were done by using average times for different components of foraging taken from the final sessions of testing (see Roberts & Ilersich, 1989) and computing the times at which food items 1–6 would be consumed if an optimal strategy were used. In the case of fixed food locations, the optimal strategy was entering patches in decreasing order of density and visiting only baited feeders within each patch. With random food locations, the optimal strategy was to enter four different patches and exhaustively visit all four feeders within the patch. The observed curves represent the actual times at which rats consumed items on the final sessions of testing. Note that the fixed food location group collected all food items substantially sooner than the random food location group. An important observation to be made is that both groups' curves are only slightly below the optimal foraging curves. The observed points were generally within 10% of the times generated for the optimal curves. In other words, rats were making foraging decisions that kept their rate of food accumulation near optimality.

FORAGING DECISION RULES

We may inquire about the mechanisms or decision rules rats used in this experiment to stay near optimal foraging. All three of the constraining variables manipulated had an effect on foraging decisions.

The Effect of Travel Time

When travel time between patches was raised by placing barriers at patch entrances, rats in the random food location condition stayed in patches longer and visited all the feeders in the patch before leaving. The rate of patch reentry then was low. Without barriers, rats stayed for a shorter time in patches, less frequently visited all the feeders within a patch, and more frequently revisited patches. These findings suggest that rats were willing to abandon patches without exhaustively searching them when the price of a revisit was low, but not when the price of a revisit was high.

Discrimination Among Patches

The difference between fixed and random observed curves seen in Fig. 1.2 suggests that rats were using reference memory to locate food items sooner in the fixed food location group. Evidence for food location learning can be sought at two levels of choice decisions: choice among patches varying in food density and choice between baited and unbaited feeders within patches. Discrimination among patches is examined in Fig. 1.3, in which the mean rank of entry into patches varying in food density is plotted across blocks of two daily sessions. Lower ranks indicate early patch entrance, and higher ranks indicate late patch entrance. The data from the random food location group are shown in the left panel and indicate that rats never discriminated among patches. This finding is important because it indicates that rats could not detect patch density by the use of odor cues. In the right panel, rats developed a strong tendency to enter the 0% patch late in the sequence of patch visits. In many cases, rats simply did not enter the 0% patch. Although there is some average tendency for rats to enter the 75% patch before the 50% and 25% patches, the differences among these three patches were not statistically significant. These findings indicate that rats strongly discriminated between patches with food and a patch without food. The finding that they did not discriminate strongly among patches with different numbers of baited feeders suggests that decisions among these patches might have been based on a decision process in which an entry decision was made whenever a scan of reference memory yielded at least one baited feeder.

Discrimination Among Feeders

Rats tested with fixed food locations came to discriminate well between baited and unbaited feeders within patches. Selective foraging between feeders appeared, however, only if feeders were covered. As a measure of feeder discrimination, it was determined whether the first feeder visited upon entry into patches

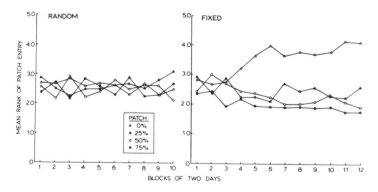

FIG. 1.3. Mean ranks of first entry into patches varying in density plotted over blocks of 2 days. Data for the random food locations condition are shown in the left panel, and data for the fixed food locations condition are shown in the right panel. (From Roberts & Ilersich, 1989. Copyright 1989 by American Psychological Association. Reprinted by permission.)

of different density was baited or unbaited. The percentage of baited feeders visited was calculated for each patch over the final sessions of testing. When rats had to remove a cover from each feeder to reach its contents, the percentages of baited feeders visited were 70%, 81%, and 95% in the 25%, 50%, and 75% density patches, respectively, and each of these percentages significantly exceeded patch density. When the feeders were open, the percentages of initial visits to baited feeders were 20%, 52%, and 74% in the 25%, 50%, and 75% density patches, respectively, and none of these percentages differed significantly from patch density.

To understand this difference between covered and open feeders, the difference in foraging patterns between groups of rats must be described. Without covers on the feeders, rats foraged in a linear fashion; that is, a rat entered a patch and visited the feeders in order from the first feeder on the arm, systematically poking its nose into each feeder. This pattern led to visits to a number of unbaited feeders and meant that the likelihood of making an initial visit to a baited feeder would be no better than chance or patch density. When the feeders were covered, rats showed much greater selectivity by bypassing empty feeders and going to baited feeders. Further, these rats typically left a patch after visiting baited feeders, with few visits to unbaited feeders. These findings suggest that rats become much more selective in their foraging decisions among feeders when a price of extra time and effort to reach food is introduced.

Rats trained with random food locations tended to forage linearly within patches, both with covered and open feeders, and percentages of initial visits to a baited feeder did not significantly exceed patch density. This finding suggests that rats were not using odor cues to locate baited feeders within patches. The accuracy shown by rats in the fixed food location and covered feeder condition can be attributed to reference memory for the contents of feeders placed within different patches.

Foraging for Different Numbers of Food Pellets

In some recent experiments, the four-arm radial maze was used to examine foraging through patches within which the feeders contained different numbers of food pellets (Ilersich, Mazmanian, & Roberts, 1988). A depiction of this maze is shown in Fig. 1.4, with the numbers on each feeder indicating the number of 45-mg food pellets placed in each feeder. Each patch contained a total of 20 pellets, but the pellets were unevenly distributed among feeders. The first feeder in each patch contained 1 pellet, and the remaining three feeders contained 1, 5, and 13 pellets; the order in which the latter three quantities occurred varied from patch to patch.

Two groups of rats were allowed to forage for 10 sessions, one group with the feeders covered and the other group with the feeders open. The results were in striking agreement with those obtained in the preceding experiment in which

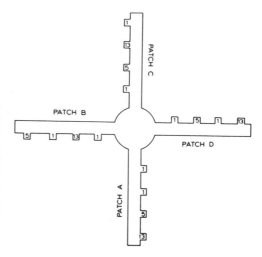

FIG. 1.4. Diagram of a four-arm radial maze with 20 45-mg food pellets distributed among the feeders in each arm. The first feeder in each arm contains 1 pellet, and the remaining feeders contain, 1, 5, and 13 pellets. (From Ilersich, Mazmanian, & Roberts, 1988. Copyright 1988 by the Psychonomic Society. Reprinted by permission.)

patch density was manipulated. The group foraging with covered feeders tended to make initial visits to the feeders containing 5 and 13 pellets in each patch. After visiting these feeders, they ate the pellets in the 1-pellet feeders on some occasions and simply left the patch on other occasions. On some sessions, a subject would visit all the 5- and 13-pellet feeders on the maze before returning to patches to eat from the single pellet feeders. The rats tested with open feeders foraged linearly by visiting feeders in order from each alley's entrance to its end. The effect of these different foraging patterns on pellets consumed can be seen in Fig. 1.5. Mean pellets consumed are plotted across the four feeders visited within patches for the covers and open groups. The covers group clearly consumed far more pellets than the open group at the first feeder visited, and this difference was reversed at the final feeder visited in the patch.

FIG. 1.5. Curves showing the mean pellets consumed at the first, second, third, and fourth feeder visited by rats in the covers and open feeders groups. Each point represents mean pellets consumed over all four patches and over Days 2–10 of testing. (From Ilersich, Mazmanian, & Roberts, 1988. Copyright by the Psychonomic Society. Reprinted by permission.)

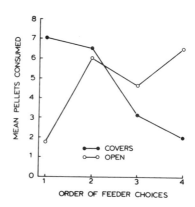

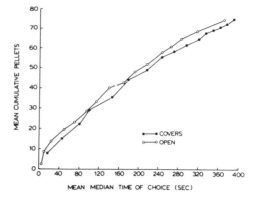

FIG. 1.6. Mean cumulative pellets consumed as a function of mean median time of arrival at successive feeding stations. (From Ilersich, Mazmanian, & Roberts, 1988. Copyright by the Psychonomic Society. Reprinted by permission.)

Once again, it appears that rats forage selectively when accessibility of food is made difficult but show simple linear foraging when little effort is required to attain food. The impact of selective foraging versus linear foraging can be seen in Fig. 1.6. Cumulative pellets consumed is plotted against the mean median time of a visit to each of the 16 feeders on the maze. If rats in both groups foraged using the same pattern, we would expect the curve for the covers group to be lower than that for the open group, because these animals required extra time to uncover food. The observation that the curves for the covers and open groups are very close to one another suggests that selective foraging by the covers group allowed them to acquire food at the same rate as the open group did while using a linear foraging strategy.

A subsequent experiment showed that the use of foraging strategies is quite flexible. A single group of rats was tested on alternate days with covered and open feeders. On covered-feeder days, rats foraged selectively by visiting the 5- and 13-pellet feeders first in each patch. On open-feeder days, rats visited feeders in a linear sequence. A distinction between knowledge and performance seems clear from this finding. Rats appear to have stored the contents of different feeders in reference memory, but their foraging strategy and hence their use of this information is dependent on the open or covered feeders testing conditions.

CENTRAL PLACE FORAGING

In the experiments thus far discussed, the arms of the radial maze have been treated as patches, and we have studied how rats choose between patches and selectively consume food located within patches. An alternate form of foraging practiced by many species of animals is called central place foraging. Central place foragers tend to collect food found in patches and carry it back to a home base to feed offspring or to eat in safety (Bryant & Turner, 1982; Carlson &

Moreno, 1981; Covich, 1987; Kacelnik, 1984; Orians & Pearson, 1979). Wild rats have been observed carrying pieces of food into their burrow system or to a protected place near the burrow, such as a tree trunk or a cluster of rocks (Barnett, 1975; Lore & Flannely, 1978; Neider, Cagnin, & Parisi, 1982).

In some recent experiments with grey squirrels (*Sciurus carolinensis*), Lima and his colleagues have observed that these animals sometimes eat food items where they are found in the patch and sometimes carry them to a central place of safety (Lima & Valone, 1986; Lima, Valone, & Caraco, 1985). Two factors appear to determine which decision a squirrel will make. One factor is the size of a food item; squirrels eat small items in the patch and carry larger items to safety before consuming them. Distance of the food from the central place is the second factor; squirrels are less likely to carry a food item to safety if it is a long distance from the home cover than if it is a short distance.

As a theoretical account of these observations, it has been suggested that squirrels and other central place foragers make food-carrying decisions that strike an optimum tradeoff between foraging efficiency and minimizing risk of predation (Lima, 1985; Lima & Valone, 1986; Lima et al., 1985). A concern only with foraging efficiency suggests that all food items should be eaten where they are encountered in order to maximize energy consumed over time spent foraging. On the other hand, consuming food in the open is dangerous because the forager is exposing itself and its food to possible predation from other species or con-specifics. As an optimal tradeoff between these concerns, animals may decide to eat small items, which can be consumed rapidly, in the patch but carry larger items, that require longer handling time, back to safety. As the distance of items encountered from the central place increases, the round-trip time increases. Decisions may then more often favor eating in the patch, because the trip to home and back may take more time than that required to eat the food item.

Measurements of the travel time and handling or eating time taken by grey squirrels supported the idea that food carrying was motivated by avoidance of predation (Lima et al., 1985). Squirrels ate food items faster in the patch than they did after carrying them to the safety of a tree. Consuming food faster in the open would reduce time exposed to predators. When a decision to carry food was made, the travel time to carry food to safety was much shorter than the travel time required to cover the same distance when not carrying food. This behavior suggests a strong imperative not to be intercepted while carrying food.

Recent research with rats suggests that many of these central place foraging behaviors observed in wild rodents may be seen in the laboratory. Laboratory rats display different motor behaviors when consuming food of different sizes; very small items are eaten as they are received, but rats sit on their haunches to eat intermediate size pellets and hoard large pellets (Whishaw, Nicholson, & Oddie, 1989). On the radial maze, large items are carried to the center of the maze for consumption, and small items are eaten on the arms (Phelps & Roberts, 1989; Whishaw & Tomie, 1989).

CENTRAL PLACE FORAGING ON A RADIAL MAZE

The next experiment demonstrates a number of foraging strategies used by rats and in particular suggests that rats show central place foraging on the radial maze under certain conditions. The apparatus used was a six-arm radial maze; it consisted of six open elevated alleys, each 76 cm long and 9 cm wide, that radiated outward at equal angles from one another from a circular central platform that was 35 cm in diameter. The major independent variable studied in the experiment was the amount of food placed at the end of each arm of the maze. Hulse and O'Leary (1982) investigated arm choice when different numbers of 45-mg pellets were placed on the arms of a radial maze. This experiment was similar in design, with the important difference that quantity of food was varied by placing single pieces of food varying in weight and size on the ends of each arm of the maze. Cubes of Kraft's American processed cheese (mild cheddar) were cut that weighed 0.05, 0.45, 0.90, 1.80, and 2.70 g. On each testing session, one cube of each size was placed on the end of each of five arms of the maze. The sixth arm contained no food. Thirty-six male hooded rats, kept at 85% of free-feeding weight, were allowed to forage for these food items once a day for 18 days. The locations of food items of different weight were assigned randomly to each rat at the beginning of the experiment, and each rat was then tested over the 18 days with the same item sizes always placed in each arm location. An exact record of each rat's foraging behavior was kept on a computer.

Discrimination Among Food Items

Rats initially chose arms on the maze in an order that was unrelated to the size of food items. As sessions progressed, however, they progressively came to enter the alleys with the larger cubes of cheese before those with smaller cubes of cheese. The alley containing no food was often entered last or not at all. The acquisition of selective foraging among alleys can be seen in Fig. 1.7. For each

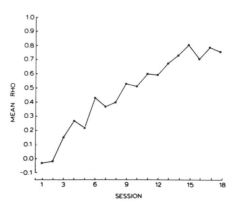

FIG. 1.7. Mean Rho plotted as a function of 18 sessions of testing on a six-arm radial maze. Mean Rho indicates the degree of correlation between food item size and rank order of alley choice.

rat on each daily session, the rank order correlation (Rho) was calculated between rank of item weight and rank of alley entrance; the 2.70-g item was rank 1,
the 1.80-g item rank 2, and so forth, in order to yield a positive correlation as
alley discrimination occurred. The mean Rho rose from around 0 on initial
sessions to between 0.70 and 0.80 over sessions 14–18. Rats appear to organize
their foraging choices among arms in descending order of item size, just as Hulse
and O'Leary (1982) found was the case with different numbers of food pellets.

Food Carrying as a Function of Item Size

Rats made different decisions about where to eat food items that depended on an
item's size. This decision process is shown in Fig. 1.8; one curve plots the
proportion of opportunities on which items of different sizes were eaten where
they were found on the end of an arm, and the other curve plots the proportion of
opportunities on which items were carried to the central platform of the maze for
consumption. Items weighing only 0.05 g almost always were eaten on the arm,
whereas large items weighing 1.80 g and 2.70 g almost always were carried to
the center. At the intermediate quantities of 0.45 g and 0.90 g, rats both carried
and ate on the arm. Similar functions have been generated when all the arms of
the maze contained the same item size, but size was varied between sessions
(Phelps & Roberts, 1989).

These data suggest two important things. First, rats appear to treat the center
of the radial maze as a central place where food items may be consumed in
safety. They treat the arms of the maze as a place where predation or food
thievery is probable, much as a grey squirrel treats an open patch. Second, food
carrying decisions are strong controlled by item size, and the tendency to increase carrying with increases in item size agrees with Lima's model of central
place foraging.

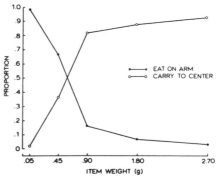

FIG. 1.8. Proportion of items
eaten on an arm of the maze or
carried to the center plotted as a
function of item weight.

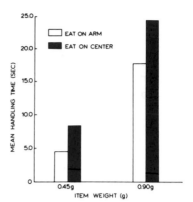

FIG. 1.9. Mean handling times for 0.45- and 0.90-g items eaten on an arm or on the center of the radial maze.

Temporal Components of Central Place Foraging

The handling time or length of time required by rats to eat food items was measured. Because 0.45-g ad 0.90-g items were both eaten on the arms and in the center of the maze, it was possible to compare handling times for items of identical sizes eaten in different places. In Fig. 1.9, mean handling times are shown for each of these items when eaten on an arm and in the center. Not surprisingly, rats took longer to eat 0.90-g items than 0.45-g items. Of more importance, rats consistently ate both sizes of food faster when eating on an arm than when eating in the center of the maze. These results further reinforce the notion that rats treat the arms as patches and the center of the maze as a haven. Just as grey squirrels eat faster in the patch where predation is likely, rats eat faster on the arms of the maze.

Two travel time components were measured. The travel time out to a patch was the time that elapsed between the moment a rat left the central platform and the time it reached a food item. The travel time return was the time between the moment an animal either finished eating an item on an arm or picked up the item

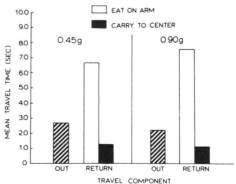

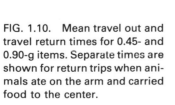

FIG. 1.10. Mean travel out and travel return times for 0.45- and 0.90-g items. Separate times are shown for return trips when animals ate on the arm and carried food to the center.

to carry it and the time the animal returned to the central platform. Mean travel times taken with 0.45-g and 0.90-g items are shown in Fig. 1.10. The travel time patterns are very similar for both item sizes. The travel times required to travel out to a food item are between 2 and 3 s. When returning, travel time varies markedly between instances when food is and is not carried. After eating an item on an arm, rats return slowly, taking around 7 s and stopping to groom, sniff the alley, or visually explore the environment. When rats choose to carry a food item, however, they race back to the center in just over 1 s. Once again, the rat's behavior on the maze mirrors behavior seen in wild rodents and suggests a strong imperative to avoid predation or thievery while on the arm of the maze.

CONCLUSIONS

These experiments indicate that a number of foraging decision mechanisms in rats may be revealed on a radial maze. These findings particularly reveal how hard-wired or instinctual mechanisms interact with experience to determine foraging decisions. Although these decision mechanisms appear to be genetically based and shaped by the rat's evolutionary history, they are often informed by learning and memory. A good example is the way rats deal with different quantities of food placed at the ends of the arms of a radial maze. Both the current experiment with food items of different weight and the Hulse and O'Leary (1982) experiment with different numbers of food pellets show that rats gradually form reference memory for the locations of different amounts of food and then use memory to order their foraging choices within a session from largest food source to smallest. A good question is why rats should bother to enter alleys according to amount of food they contain. Because the rat is left on the maze until it collects all the available food, it will collect the same amount of food on the maze in the same total length of time with any order of arm entries. The key to understanding a rat's behavior is to ask what foraging strategies a rat in a natural setting would have evolved in order to maximize its fitness. Wild rats must forage within the context of predators and conspecifics that compete for food. In such a setting, the best strategy is to go for the largest possible energy sources first; if a forager must flee or fight for food at some point in a foraging bout, it will have accumulated more energy up to that point if it first went for the largest food source. Laboratory rats then are demonstrating evolved strategies that may seem inappropriate in the laboratory but make considerable sense from an evolutionary perspective.

The rule that a rat will learn always to go for the largest food sources first does not always hold and may be dependent on other foraging constraints. When rats foraged in patches with multiple feeders, they showed a preference for feeders that contained food over those that contained no food only when the feeders were covered and the rat had to work to get at the food. Similarly, when feeders contained different numbers of pellets, rats chose those with the largest quantities of food first only when the feeders had covers. When access to food was made easy by leaving feeders open, rats fell back on a linear strategy of visiting every feeder in spatial order. A strategy of sampling all food sources may be the rat's default option unless access to food is made difficult. From this point of view, the selective foraging seen when different quantities of food are placed on the ends of a radial maze may arise from the travel time required to run up and down the arms of the maze.

A final example of what appears to be hard-wired decision rules is found in central place foraging on the radial maze. Rats begin to carry large food items to the center of the maze on the first day of testing. After as many as 50 days of testing, food-carrying functions like that seen in Fig. 1.8 are still found. Although rats are never interrupted during testing sessions and certainly no predators appear, rats continue to behave as if the center of the maze is a place of safety to which large pieces of food must be carried. One evolutionary basis for this behavior may be the wild rat's burrow structure, in which central chambers are built with a number of escape routes or bolt holes (Pisano & Storer, 1948). The center of the maze may be a preferred place to consume food because it offers the greatest number of escape routes. Both the difference in handling times for food eaten on an arm and in the center and the difference in return travel times when carrying and not carrying food reinforce the conclusion that rats perceive the center of the maze as considerably safer than the arms.

The radial maze appears to have considerable ecological validity for the study of foraging in rats. Although it has traditionally been used as a tool for the investigation of memory (Olton, 1978; Roberts, 1984), it appears that its use can now be extended to the study of several kinds of foraging in rats. Further, experiments on the radial maze appear to be providing us with considerable information about the functional use of memory in animal foraging.

ACKNOWLEDGMENT

Preparation of this chapter was supported by Grant A7894 from the National Sciences and Engineering Research Council of Canada.

REFERENCES

Balda, R. P. (1980). Recovery of cached seeds by a captive *Nucifraga caryocactes*. *Zeitschrift fur Tierpsychologie, 52*, 331–346.

Balda, R. P., & Turek, R. J. (1984). The cache-recovery system as an example of memory capabilities in Clark's nutcracker. In H. L. Roitblat, T. G. Bever, & H. S. Terrace (Eds.), *Animal cognition* (pp. 513–532). Hillsdale, NJ: Lawrence Erlbaum Associates.

Barnett, S. A. (1975). *The rat*. Chicago: Chicago University Press.

Batson, J. D., Best, M. R., Phillips, D. L., Patel, H., & Gilleland, K. R. (1986). Foraging on the radial-arm maze: Effects of altering the reward at a target location. *Animal Learning & Behavior, 14*, 241–248.

Beatty, W. W., & Shavalia, D. A. (1980). Spatial memory in rats: Time course of working memory and effect of anesthetics. *Behavioral and Neural Biology, 28*, 454–462.

Bhatt, R. S., & Wasserman, E. A. (1987). Choice behavior of pigeons on progressive and multiple schedules: A test of optimal foraging theory. *Journal of Experimental Psychology: Animal Behavior Processes, 13*, 40–51.

Bryant, D. M., & Turner, A. K. (1982). Central place foraging by swallows (*Hirundinidae*): The question of load size. *Animal Behaviour, 30*, 845–856.

Carlson, A., & Moreno, J. (1981). Central place foraging in the wheatear (*Oenanthe oenanthe*): An experimental test. *Journal of Animal Ecology, 50*, 917–924.

Covich, A. P. (1987). Optimal use of space by neighboring central place foragers: When and where to store surplus resources. In L. Green & H. Kagel (Eds.), *Advances in behavioral economics* (pp. 249–294). Norwood, NJ: Ablex.

Dow, S. M., & Lea, S. E. G. (1987). Foraging in a changing environment: Simulations in the operant laboratory. In M. L. Commons, A. Kacelnik, & S. J. Shettleworth (Eds.), *Quantitative analyses of behavior: Foraging* (Vol. 6, pp. 89–113). Hillsdale, NJ: Lawrence Erlbaum Associates.

Fantino, E., & Abarca, N. (1985). Choice, optimal foraging, and the delay-reduction hypothesis. *The Behavioral and Brain Sciences, 8*, 315–330.

Hulse, S. H., & O'Leary, D. K. (1982). Serial pattern learning: Teaching an alphabet to rats. *Journal of Experimental Psychology: Animal Behavior Processes, 8*, 260–273.

Ilersich, T. J., Mazmanian, D. S., & Roberts, W. A. (1988). Foraging for covered and uncovered food on a radial maze. *Animal Learning & Behavior, 16*, 388–394.

Kacelnik, A. (1984). Central place foraging in starlings (*Sturnus vulgaris*). I. Patch residence time. *Journal of Animal Ecology, 53*, 283–299.

Kamil, A. C., & Balda, R. P. (1985). Cache recovery and spatial memory in Clark's nutcracker. *Journal of Experimental Psychology: Animal Behavior Processes, 11*, 95–111.

Kamil, A. C., Yoerg, S. I., & Clements, K. C. (1988). Rules to leave by: Patch departure in foraging blue jays. *Animal Behaviour, 36*, 843–853.

Lima, S. L. (1985). Maximizing feeding efficiency and minimizing time exposed to predators: A trade-off in the black-capped chickadee. *Oecologia, 66*, 60–67.

Lima, S. L., & Valone, T. J. (1986). Influence of predation risk on diet selection: A simple example in the grey squirrel. *Animal Behaviour, 34*, 536–544.

Lima, S. L., Valone, T. J., & Caraco, T. (1985). Foraging efficiency-predation risk trade-off in the grey squirrel. *Animal Behaviour, 33*, 155–165.

Lore, R., & Flannely, K. J. (1978). Habitat selection and burrow construction by wild *Rattus norvegicus* in a landfill. *Journal of Comparative and Physiological Psychology, 92*, 888–896.

Mazmanian, D. S., & Roberts, W. A. (1983). Spatial memory in rats under restricted viewing conditions. *Learning and Motivation, 14*, 123–139.

Melcer, T., & Timberlake, W. (1985). Poison avoidance and patch (location) selection in rats. *Animal Learning & Behavior, 13*, 60–68.

Mellgren, R. L. (1982). Foraging in a simulated environment: There's a rat loose in the lab. *Journal of The Experimental Analysis of Behavior, 38*, 93–100.

Mellgren, R. L., & Brown, S. W. (1987). Environmental constraints on optimal-foraging behavior. In M. L. Commons, A. Kacelnik, & S. J. Shettleworth (Eds.), *Quantitative analyses of behavior: Foraging* (Vol. 6, pp. 133–151). Hillsdale, NJ: Lawrence Erlbaum Associates.

Mellgren, R. L., Misasi, L., & Brown, S. W. (1984). Optimal foraging theory: Prey density and travel requirements in *Rattus norvegicus*. *Journal of Comparative Psychology, 98*, 142–153.

Menzel, E. W. (1973). Chimpanzee spatial memory organization. *Science, 182*, 943–945.

Menzel, E. W. (1978). Cognitive mapping in chimpanzees. In S. H. Hulse, H. Fowler, & W. K.

Honig (Eds.), *Cognitive processes in animal behavior* (pp. 375–422). Hillsdale, NJ: Lawrence Erlbaum Associates.

Neider, L., Cagnin, M., & Parisi, L. (1982). Burrowing and feeding behavior in the rat. *Animal Behaviour, 30*, 837–844.

Olton, D. S. (1978). Characteristics of spatial memory. In S. H. Hulse, H. Fowler, & W. K. Honig (Eds.), *Cognitive processes in animal behavior* (pp. 341–373). Hillsdale, NJ: Lawrence Erlbaum Associates.

Olton, D. S., Collison, D., & Werz, M. A. (1977). Spatial memory and radial arm maze performance of rats. *Learning and Motivation, 8*, 289–314.

Olton, D. S., & Samuelson, R. J. (1976). Remembrance of places passed: Spatial memory in rats. *Journal of Experimental Psychology: Animal Behavior Processes, 2*, 97–116.

Orians, G. H., & Pearson, N. E. (1979). On the theory of central place foraging. In D. J. Horn, R. D. Mitchell, & G. R. Stairs (Eds.), *Analysis of ecological systems* (pp. 154–177). Columbus: Ohio State University Press.

Phelps, M. T., & Roberts, W. A. (1989). Central place foraging by *Rattus norvegicus* on a radial maze. *Journal of Comparative Psychology, 103*, 326–338.

Pisano, R. G., & Storer, T. I. (1948). Burrows and feeding of the Norway rat. *Journal of Mammalogy, 29*, 374–383.

Roberts, W. A. (1979). Spatial memory in the rat on a hierarchical maze. *Learning and Motivation, 10*, 117–140.

Roberts, W. A. (1981). Retroactive inhibition in rat spatial memory. *Animal Learning & Behavior, 9*, 566–574.

Roberts, W. A. (1984). Some issues in animal spatial memory. In H. L. Roitblat, T. G. Bever, & H. S. Terrace (Eds.), *Animal cognition* (pp. 425–443). Hillsdale, NJ: Lawrence Erlbaum Associates.

Roberts, W. A., & Dale, R. H. I. (1981). Remembrance of places lasts: Proactive inhibition and patterns of choice in rat spatial memory. *Learning and Motivation, 12*, 261–281.

Roberts, W. A., & Ilersich, T. J. (1989). Foraging on the radial maze: The role of travel time, food accessibility, and the predictability of food location. *Journal of Experimental Psychology: Animal Behavior Processes, 15*, 274–285.

Sherry, D. F. (1987). Foraging for stored food. In M. L. Commons, A. Kacelnik, & S. J. Shettleworth (Eds.), *Quantitative analyses of behavior: Foraging* (pp. 209–227). Hillsdale, NJ: Lawrence Erlbaum Associates.

Shettleworth, S. J. (1983). Memory in food-hoarding birds. *Scientific American, 248*, 102–110.

Shettleworth, S. J. (1989). Animals foraging in the lab: Problems and promises. *Journal of Experimental Psychology: Animal Behavior Processes, 15*, 81–87.

Shettleworth, S. J., & Krebs, J. R. (1982). How marsh tits find their hoards: The roles of site preference and spatial memory. *Journal of Experimental Psychology: Animal Behavior Processes, 8*, 354–375.

Shettleworth, S. J., & Krebs, J. R. (1986). Stored and encountered seeds: A comparison of two spatial memory tasks in marsh tits and chickadees. *Journal of Experimental Psychology: Animal Behavior Processes, 12*, 248–257.

Suzuki, S., Augerinos, G., & Black, A. H. (1980). Stimulus control of spatial behavior on the eight-arm maze in rats. *Learning and Motivation, 11*, 1–18.

Whishaw, I. Q., Nicholson, L., & Oddie, S. D. (1989). Food-pellet size directs hoarding in rats. *Bulletin of the Psychonomic Society, 27*, 57–59.

Whishaw, I. Q., & Tomie, J-A. (1989). Food-pellet size modifies the hoarding behavior of foraging rats. *Psychobiology, 17*, 93–101.

2 Spatial Memory in Hoarding and Nonhoarding Tits (*Paridae*)

Sara J. Shettleworth
University of Toronto

Some birds and mammals store food in scattered locations and find it again days, weeks, or even months later using memory (Sherry, 1985). The analysis of their memory incorporates the methods and insights of natural history, behavioral ecology, animal cognition, comparative psychology, and neuroscience. I begin this chapter by briefly reviewing what we know about memory in food-storing birds, particularly the chickadees and titmice (*Paridae*). The importance of good spatial memory for a food-storing way of life raises the question whether memory for stored food is in some sense an adaptive specialization (Rozin & Kalat, 1971). The main part of the chapter describes some results from a program of research that has tackled this question by comparing memory for stored and encountered food in storing species and by comparing memory of storing and nonstoring species in a variety of tasks.

FOOD STORING AND THE SYNTHETIC APPROACH TO ANIMAL INTELLIGENCE

The study of memory in food-storing birds is one of the best examples of how a naturally occurring memory phenomenon can be analyzed with all the tools behavioral biology has at its disposal in what Kamil (1987) has termed the synthetic approach to animal intelligence. To begin with, formal modeling has been used to argue that food storing will only evolve if individuals have either highly specific site preferences or memory for the locations of their own hoards (Andersson & Krebs, 1978). Otherwise, "cheaters" who pilfer others' stores without investing any effort in storing themselves will have an evolutionary advantage over those who store. Thus, food storing provides a rare example in which the existence of a specific cognitive capacity can be predicted from evolutionary first principles. Evidence for the use of memory can then be sought for birds recovering their stores in the field. Although some of this evidence is indirect, taken all together it points quite convincingly to the conclusion that food-storing parids and corvids (jays, crows, and nutcrackers) do indeed use memory to recover their stores under natural conditions (reviews in Balda, Bunch, Kamil, Sherry, & Tomback, 1987; Shettleworth, 1990). Thus, in principle at least, laboratory studies of memory in these birds can be guided by information about the functions their memory serves in natural conditions. Indeed, most of our detailed knowledge about the properties of memory for stored food has come from laboratory studies with Clark's nutcrackers (*Nucifraga columbiana*) and various tit species (reviews in Balda et al., 1987; Sherry, 1985; Shettleworth, 1990). Here I emphasize the work with tits, which has been done mainly in Oxford and Toronto by Krebs, Sherry, me, and our students. Clark's nutcrackers and the other corvids are the subjects of a parallel research program, also involving collaboration between psychologists and zoologists, principally Balda, Kamil, and Vander Wall.

A study by Shettleworth and Krebs (1982), using marsh tits (*Parus palustris*), illustrates some of the important features of laboratory tests of memory for stored food in parids. The birds were tested individually in a large aviary furnished with tree branches. These provided 97 storage sites in the form of holes drilled at 8–12-inch intervals, each one the right size to hold a single hemp seed. So that birds could not see the seeds from a distance, a small flap of black cloth hung down over each hole. This also meant that we could easily score "looks" for seeds by recording when a bird lifted the cloth over a hole.

Four birds each had a series of daily trials in which they were food deprived overnight and allowed into the aviary in the morning with a bowl of hemp seeds. After eating a few seeds, a bird would begin to store, taking seeds from the bowl one by one and pushing and tapping them into the holes under the cloths. Each bird was allowed to store 12 seeds, which usually took less than 20 minutes. It was then returned to its home cage, where it remained without food for a retention interval of 2 hours. Phase 2 of the trial, the recovery or test phase, consisted of allowing the bird back into the aviary with the bowl of seeds absent and seeds in the places where they had been stored in the first phase. The locations of holes the bird inspected were recorded. Performance was very accurate, especially at the beginning of each trial. Random search would have required about eight (97/12) looks to find each seed, but on average the birds took not much more than one look per seed at the beginning of trials (Fig. 2.1).

To control for the possibility that the birds were using cues emanating from the seeds themselves, at the end of the experiment we gave them a few trials in which the seeds they stored were moved to different sites between the two phases of the trial. They continued to visit the sites they had used for storage and

FIG. 2.1. Errors per seed encountered for four marsh tits recovering 12 seeds stored among
97 holes. Means of individual bird
medians. "Regular trials" (dashed
line): 12 trials in which the birds
found seeds in the holes where
they had stored them 2 hours earlier. "Transplanted seeds": en-
counters with seeds on two control trials per bird when the experimenter moved the stored seeds
to different holes before the bird
was allowed to search for them.
"Own storage sites": performance
on control trials with visits to
holes where the bird had not
stored a seed that day counted as
errors and visits to the now-emp-
ty storage sites counted as correct looks. Data from Shettleworth
and Krebs (1982), Experiment 1.

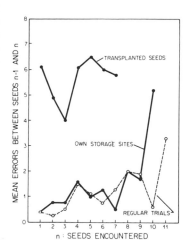

encountered the relocated seeds at a rate a little above chance (Fig. 2.1). The rate
was above chance because most birds did not ever use, or even visit, all the
potential storage sites. The distribution of seeds in the control trials took this into
account by using only sites that the individual being tested had used for storage
on earlier trials in the experiment. Thus, the effective chance rate was actually
better than 1 seed in 8.1 looks (12 seeds in 97 sites).

Other ways of assessing memory and controlling for cues from the seeds have
been used in other experiments. For example, numbers of visits to storage sites
and times spent there in the recovery phase with all seeds removed have been
compared to those same measures in a separate prestorage phase (Sherry, Krebs,
& Cowie, 1981). In our recent work with black-capped chickadees (*Parus
atricapillus,* Shettleworth & Krebs, 1986; Shettleworth, Krebs, Healy, & Thomas, 1990), we have used "partial reinforcement." During the recovery phase, a
randomly chosen 50% of the stored seeds are present in the holes where they
were stored; the other storage sites are empty. Accuracy is compared for sites
with seeds remaining versus emptied sites. This method permits continuous
assessment of any cueing on holes with seeds. Both methods indicate that cues
from the seeds themselves are rarely used, if ever.

The role of the site preferences just mentioned and ways in which they can be
taken into account in tests of memory are discussed further in a later section. In
our study with marsh tits (Shettleworth & Krebs, 1982, Experiment 2), we
provided a fairly direct demonstration that the birds do not achieve accurate
performance merely by visiting the same preferred places every time they go into

the aviary. Rather, memory of seed locations guides their behavior in a flexible way. Marsh tits were given a series of trials in which they were allowed to store more seeds after the 2-hr retention interval. We instructed them to do this simply by leaving the bowl of seeds in the room for their second visit of the day. Now if the birds remember where they have stored seeds in the first phase of the trial, they should visit different sites in the second phase rather than going back to the same sites, as they would if they were recovering seeds. This is what happened. The birds visited the already-filled holes at the rate that would be expected by chance or slightly below this. They stored their seeds in the still-empty holes.

The list of what else we know about memory for storage sites in tits, chiefly black-capped chickadees and marsh tits, includes the following:

1. In the field, hundreds of items may be stored in a single day (Cowie, Krebs, & Sherry, 1981). They are recovered within 2 or 3 days, if at all (Stevens & Krebs, 1986). This short-term storage contrasts with what is found in some of the corvids, which store thousands of items for periods of months (cf. Balda et al., 1987). In both groups of birds, food storing is seasonal in the wild and in laboratory conditions (Ludescher, 1980, for willow tits).

2. Parids' memory for storage sites is more persistent than memory of other species in typical laboratory tasks testing memory for an event that has occurred on a single trial. Recovery of stored seeds is as good after 24 hours as after 3 (Sherry et al., 1981). Seeds stored 48 hours ago are treated no differently than seeds stored 24 hours ago (Sherry, 1984). However, recovery accuracy in black-capped chickadees does decline after 14–28 days (Hitchcock & Sherry, 1990).

3. Besides remembering the locations of stored items, birds recovering their stores keep track of where they have already searched, as evidenced by the fact that they do not revisit these sites (Sherry & Vaccarino, 1989; Shettleworth & Krebs, 1982). However, when chickadees are tested for recovery of stored seeds with half the stored items removed, as in the "partial reinforcement" control procedure referred to earlier, they make by far the majority of their revisits to the emptied sites (Shettleworth & Krebs, unpublished data). In contrast to the tits, nutcrackers do revisit already-emptied sites in laboratory tests (Balda, Kamil, & Grim, 1986). In the wild, nutcrackers store several seeds in each cache, and they can rely on a visible record of what sites they have visited in the form of digging marks and seed husks. Thus, they might not need to use memory to avoid revisits.

4. Chickadees tend to recover preferred items (sunflower seeds) before less preferred items (safflower seeds; Sherry, 1984). Thus, they remember something about the contents of the caches, not merely their locations.

5. Marsh tits use information about which types of sites are "safe" for storage and which types are pilfered. For example, over trials they shift their storing effort from moss to bark if stored items are systematically removed from

moss by an experimenter (Stevens, 1984). In our laboratory we routinely remove any seeds stored in "illegal" sites outside the sites we provide. This effectively trains the chickadees not to use illegal sites, and one can trace a steady decline in illegal site use over sessions (unpublished data).

6. As might be expected from its role in mammalian spatial memory (cf. Berger this volume; Kesner, this volume), an intact hippocampus is necessary for successful recovery of stored food, although it is not necessary for storing in the first place (Krushinskaya, 1966; Sherry & Vaccarino, 1989). The lesioned chickadees in Sherry and Vaccarino's study not only failed to find their stores, but they revisited sites already searched much more than control birds.

Food-Storing Memory as an Adaptive Specialization

Rozin and Kalat (1971) introduced the notion that some kinds or aspects of learning and memory might be adaptively specialized for tasks the species possessing them confront in natural conditions. Adaptive specializations of learning or memory are quantitative or (as is more usually implied) qualitative differences in the properties of learning or memory that parallel differences in functional requirements for that memory. A familiar example from associative learning is that of conditioned taste aversion. Although conditioned taste aversion appears to have the same properties as other forms of associative learning, the delay between CS and US that can be sustained is much great than in, say, fear conditioning (Rescorla, 1988). This quantitative difference parallels a difference in requirements for learning about food, where consequences of ingestion may be delayed, as compared to learning about the consequences of signals for immediate danger.

In their further development of the idea of adaptive specialization, Sherry and Schacter (1987) pointed out that separate learning or memory systems having different rules of operation might be expected to evolve when a species must solve learning or memory problems that have functionally incompatible requirements. They cited, as an example, the apparently very different requirements of song learning and food storing. In song learning (at least in some species), a highly specific class of inputs is encoded permanently on the basis of more or less passive exposure during a restricted period early in life, whereas in food storing the bird must remember an ever-changing set of information throughout its adult life. However, as Sherry and Schacter pointed out, it is not clear that the memory used in recovering stored food need have qualitatively different characteristics from the memory necessary in normal foraging or, indeed, in remembering the locations of rivals, territorial boundaries, mates, or other resources (cf. Sherry, 1987). Nevertheless, remembering locations of stored food does appear to require that more items be remembered for longer and perhaps with greater accuracy than is otherwise necessary in foraging. After all, the whole point of storing food is to place it somewhere inaccessible to competitors who might otherwise remove it before the storer can return to eat it. Storing food is not worthwhile unless it makes remembering the location of that food more valuable than remembering its original location or the locations of similar items. This kind of argument suggests that food-storing memory should be adaptively specialized in a quantitative manner to retain considerable amounts of accurate information for a long time.

For the past few years, John Krebs and I have been collaborating on a research program designed to discover whether memory of food-storing tits is in fact adaptively specialized. We have looked at the problem in two ways. First, we have compared memory for locations of stored food with memory for other kinds of items *within* storing species. Memory for stored items might be more accurate, capacious, or long lasting than memory for items encountered under similar circumstances. Second, we have compared memory in a variety of tasks *between* storing and nonstoring tit species. Our hypothesis here is that food-storing tits should perform better than their nonstoring relatives in tasks with similar memory requirements to storing, whereas species should not differ, or should differ less, on tasks unrelated to storing. The morphological and behavioral specializations of storing species (especially the corvids; Vander Wall & Balda, 1981) ought to be accompanied by specializations of memory. This hypothesis is encouraged by neuroanatomical work showing that storing species have a larger hippocampus relative to brain and body weight than nonstoring species (Krebs, Sherry, Healy, Perry, & Vaccarino, 1989; Sherry, Vaccarino, Buckenham, & Herz, 1989).

Memory for Stored and Encountered Food in Food-Storing Tits

The performance of birds recovering stored food, in the laboratory or in the field, seems at first glance to be very much better than the performance of rats or pigeons on standard laboratory tests of memory like delayed matching to sample or radial mazes (cf. Shettleworth, 1985). At second glance, however, it is clear that there are so many differences among the tasks involved as to make a comparison virtually meaningless (for further discussion, see Shettleworth, 1985). For example, in storing, a bird visits sites that differ from each other spatially and perhaps in other ways, and it places food *in* the site. Different sites are used in different storing episodes, even to some extent in laboratory tests where the choice of sites is much more limited than it would be in the field (see following). In contrast, delayed matching to sample and radial maze tasks are basically recency discriminations (Staddon, 1983). Correct performance depends on remembering which of a small set of samples was presented most recently or which arms of the maze were visited most recently. In the spatial delayed matching task used with pigeons (Wilkie & Summers, 1982), the stimuli are very close together and the animal does not move about in space to get to them. In the spatial delayed matching test developed for rats by Roitblat and Harley (1988), the rat does visit the locations, but there are only three of them and they are used repeatedly within each session. Pigeons, at least, can remember the significance of hundreds of photographic slides for over a year (Vaughn & Greene, 1984), but they have to be trained for hundreds of trials in the first place, whereas a food hoarder must remember whether or not food is in a site on the basis of a single brief visit. Pigeons can remember the features of a novel slide after one or two exposures (Bhatt, Wasserman, Reynolds, & Knauss, 1988; Macphail & Reilly, 1989), but how long these memories last has not yet been established. Single-trial memory tasks are discussed further at the end of this chapter.

The considerations just outlined make clear that to properly compare memory for locations of stored food and food not stored within a storing species it is necessary to use a task that is like storing in every respect except that of requiring the bird to store. We can then ask, does storing food give its location a special status in memory, as if the bird has a special memory store for memories of hoarded food? Alternatively, is it the favorable procedural aspects of storing (e.g., visiting spatially separated sites and seeing the food in them) that makes memory for stored items so good? An affirmative answer to this question would mean that the food storer remembers the locations of its stores in the same way as it remembers the locations of other food items. However, its memory might still be quantitatively specialized in capacity or persistence when compared to that of nonstorers. Cross-species comparisons like those described later in the chapter are required to examine this possibility.

We have compared memory for stored food and food not stored in two ways: by allowing birds to encounter items placed by the experimenter in potential storage sites while they were trying to store food themselves, and by testing birds on a task we call "window-shopping." In window-shopping (Shettleworth & Krebs, 1986), a bird first visits a number of sites and sees food in some of them behind a small window. Inspecting the sites is encouraged by having an accessible crumb of seed for the bird to eat in front of each window that covers a seed. Then, in phase 2 of each trial, after a retention interval, the windows are opened and the bird is allowed to return and eat food in the sites where it saw food in phase 1. This task is similar to the spatial delayed matching task for rats described by Roitblat and Harley (1988), but their task involved only three different possible locations (arms of a maze). On phase 1 of each trial, the rat ate some food in one arm, where there was some more food under a screen (analogous to the window in our task). It was rewarded for returning to the same arm later on.

Our first comparisons of memory for stored seeds and seeds merely seen (Shettleworth & Krebs, 1986) did not give a clear answer to the question whether these two kinds of seeds are remembered equally well. In the first experiment, marsh tits encountered seeds hidden in potential storage sites while they were storing seeds themselves. Because each of the holes we provided could hold only one seed, when a marsh tit lifted the cloth flap covering a hole and found a seed there already, it had to store the seed it was carrying in another site. However, at the end of the storing episode it potentially had information about both the storage sites and the sites where it had encountered seeds. Indeed, when tested 2 hours later, the birds recovered the same proportions of encountered as stored seeds. We could find no evidence, for example in the sequence of stored and encountered seeds recovered, that the birds remembered these two types of items differently.

In contrast to these results were the results of window-shopping tests with black-capped chickadees (Shettleworth & Krebs, 1986, Experiments 2 and 3). Here, the same individuals were tested in storing trials and window-shopping trials in the same environment. The results established that chickadees *could* recover seeds they had seen behind windows after a retention interval of 2 hours when they had seen six seeds in phase 1. Performance was worse than with storing, but only two birds both window-shopped and stored within the same experiment. Moreover, the window-shopping and storing tasks differed in potentially important ways. In storing, the birds could use any of the holes, but only some of the holes were baited with seeds in the window-shopping trials. This meant that to recover stored seeds effectively, the birds had only to remember where they had been in phase 1 of a trial (each time a seed was taken from the bowl, it was usually placed in the first hole the bird visited). However, to recover window-shopped seeds, they had to discriminate between holes visited in phase 1 that held seeds and holes visited and found to be empty. Arguably, the latter is a more difficult task.

We therefore conducted a further series of experiments designed to compare window-shopping and storing under conditions as similar as possible to each other. Our first approach was to make window-shopping like the storing trials in the previous study by baiting all the holes with seeds in phase 1 of each trial and allowing the bird to store in any hole in the matched storing trials. Four black-capped chickadees stored 5–7 seeds on 10–14 trials each and then window-shopped 5–7 seeds on 8–12 trials in the same environment. The retention interval for both types of trials was about 90 minutes. Otherwise the procedure was as in Experiment 1 of Shettleworth et al. (1990).

To analyze the data we divided the holes into preference classes according to the proportion of trials on which they had been visited in phase 1 of trials of a given type. Within each preference class, the probability of visiting sites in phase 2 of trials when a seed had been seen or stored there was compared to the probability of a visit in phase 2 when there had been no visit in phase 1. To the extent the birds remember where seeds are (and/or, in this design, where they went in phase 1), they should show good discrimination between the two classes of sites, unvisited versus visited and containing a seed. They did discriminate significantly in both conditions, but they discriminated better when they had stored the seeds than when they had window-shopped (i.e., there was a significant interaction of experience by type of trial; Fig. 2.2).

FIG. 2.2. Mean (+ standard error) performance of four black-capped chickadees that stored food and window-shopped in the same environment. The probability of visiting holes in the first 10 looks of phase 2 of trials is shown as a function of the experience of those same holes on phase 1 (storing or seeing a seed, or not visiting the hole). Data are the means of "high preference" holes (visited during phase 1 on more than 30% of trials) and "low preference" holes (those visited during phase 1 at least once but on not more than 30% of trials).

The same birds performed very accurately when recovering stored seeds in a second experiment (Shettleworth et al., 1990, Experiment 1A), so it is unlikely that the difference between window-shopping and storing was due to the window-shopping trials following the storing trials. However, a closer inspection of the data brings the whole comparison of memory in the two tasks into question because it suggests that the birds were solving them in different ways. The chickadees had strong site preferences when they were window-shopping. Each bird had a few favorite sites that it visited on many of the window-shopping trials whereas never visiting a large proportion of other sites (Fig. 2.3). In effect, the birds were treating window-shopping as a kind of reference memory task, in which food was to be found in some of the same places on every trial. During recovery the birds also tended to go to some sites almost regardless of whether a seed had been seen there in phase 1 of that trial. When the birds were storing, on the other hand, preferences were much less marked, with fewer never-visited sites and less extreme favorite sites. Chi-square tests on the data in Fig. 2.3 were significant in every case. Just as when storing in the wild (Sherry, Avery, & Stevens, 1982), the birds tended to store in different places from day to day.

In further experiments (Shettleworth et al., 1990, Experiments 1A and 1B), we were able to make chickadees and coal tits (*Parus ater*, a Eurasian food-storer) treat window-shopping more as a working memory task by allowing them only to store or see seeds in a different random half of the sites on each trial. This procedure generally abolished the difference in site preferences between the two tasks, but the difference in performance during phase 2 remained.

The foregoing studies established more clearly than those of Shettleworth and Krebs (1986) that food-storing tits can recover seeds they have seen behind windows at well above chance and, unlike the rats studied by Roitblat and Harley

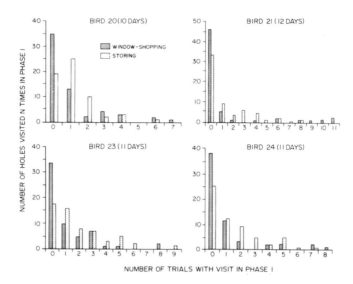

FIG. 2.3. Distributions of numbers of sites visited on different numbers of trials for each of four chickadees. Data include only the first five holes visited on each trial while the bird was storing or window-shopping. The birds had stronger site preferences when they were window-shopping than when they were storing in that they had more holes with 0 visits as well as more holes visited on a large number of trials.

(1988), with relatively little training. However, they leave unresolved the issue of why recovery accuracy differs between storing and window-shopping, whereas recovery of stored seeds and seeds encountered during storing does not differ. Are seeds seen without windows somehow more memorable or more attractive than seeds seen behind windows, or is the bird perhaps in some special state while it is storing that makes everything memorable? To answer this question, we exposed four chickadees to a series of three intermixed types of trials in which they always stored five seeds but while doing so they encountered seeds without windows, saw seeds behind windows, or encountered sites blocked off with a paper sticker (Shettleworth et al., 1990, Experiment 2). The results (Fig. 2.4) confirmed those of Shettleworth and Krebs (1986) for marsh tits: After a 90-min retention interval, stored seeds and seeds encountered without windows while storing were recovered equally well. However, seeds seen behind windows were recovered less well than seeds stored in the same episode. Nevertheless, the birds were more likely to return to the window-shopping sites than to holes merely covered with a paper sticker.

These results clearly establish that, when a bird sees seeds behind windows while it is storing, it does not return to these locations as accurately as to the locations of stored seeds. Thus, to answer one of the questions with which we began the experiment, chickadees are apparently not in some special state while storing that makes all food locations equally memorable. However, the reasons why birds perform less accurately when recovering window-shopped than when recovering encountered seeds are not yet clear. One possibility is that the birds do not actually see all the seeds we record as seen. This would mean that from their point of view they are rewarded in phase 2 of window-shopping trials for visiting some sites that they merely visited in phase 1. This perceived contingency could well result in poorer discrimination of the kind documented in Fig. 2.4. On the other hand, the birds might see all the seeds we think we do but treat seeds that are inaccessible in phase 1 as less valuable or less worth returning to than stored seeds. Indeed, one important question about the window-shopping test is why should the birds return at all to seeds that were seen as inaccessible? One might expect them to treat seeds behind windows no differently from blocked, empty holes. The fact is, however, that they do return to window-shopped seeds at above-chance levels from the very first trials. We have never found significant evidence of improvement in window-shopping over trials, although improvement might be expected if the birds had to be taught that seeds inaccessible in phase 1 become accessible later (Shettleworth & Krebs, 1986; Krebs, Healy, & Shettleworth, 1990).

A second unanswered question is, do the birds treat stored seeds and seeds encountered without windows in the same way under all conditions? Although the evidence cited earlier shows that food-storing tits remember a number of subtle details of a storing episode, do they nevertheless encode stored and encountered seeds in the same way? On both functional and causal grounds one might expect some discrimination between these two classes of items. Items stored by the bird ought to be safer and therefore remembered better than items

FIG. 2.4. Mean performance (+ standard error) of four chickadees that stored five seeds in each of a series of trials. On each trial they also saw five seeds not behind windows (encountered seeds, E), five seeds behind windows (window-shopped seeds, W), or five holes blocked with a sticker (blocked holes, B). Probability of a visit in the first 15 visits of phase 2 is shown as a function of experience in phase 1. S = stored seed; U = visited but empty (unseeded) site; N = site not visited on that trial. Data for each bird are means of high and low preference holes, as in Fig. 2.2. Data from Shettleworth et al. (1990).

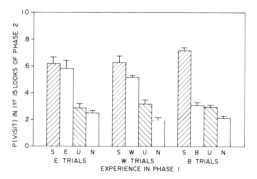

just found lying around or stored by another bird. Moreover, birds appear to spend longer times at storage sites, poking the seed into place, than at sites where they simply see seeds. Longer exposure to storage sites might be expected to favor memory for them.

The most direct way to ask if the birds discriminate stored and encountered seeds is to make it worth their while to do so, for example, by pilfering encountered seeds while allowing stored seeds to be recovered, and vice versa. This we plan to do in the future. However, we have tested the notion that encountered seeds ought eventually to be remembered less well than stored seeds by comparing recovery of the two types of items after 2-hour and 26-hour retention intervals (Shettleworth et al., 1990, Experiment 3). There was no differential forgetting of the two types of items and indeed, in line with the results reviewed earlier, there was no significant decrement in performance after 26 hours.

Cross-Species Comparisons

Some tit species store and others do not. In Britain and Europe, food-storing coal tits and marsh tits can be found in similar areas to nonstoring blue tits (*Parus caeruleus*) and great tits (*P. major*). Among the corvids, most species store, but they vary in the extent to which their life is organized around storing (Vander Wall & Baldà, 1981). For example, among species found in the American Southwest, Clark's nutcracker has a long sharp beak for prying out seeds from unripe pine cones and a large sublingual pouch for carrying seeds. It is an exceptionally strong flier and it uses this capacity to transport seeds to slopes kilometers away from where it gathers them. It breeds early in the spring, before most other species in the area, and feeds its young on stored pine seeds. In contrast, pinyon jays (*Gymnorhinus cyanocephalus*) and scrub jays (*Aphelocoma coerulescens*) are morphologically less specialized and do much less storing.

The question naturally arises whether species differences in storing behavior are accompanied by species differences in memory (i.e., are any aspects of memory in storing species adaptively specialized for recovery of stored food?). One can imagine a number of answers to this question. At one extreme, it might be that there are no differences among tit or among corvid species in accuracy, capacity, or persistence of memory. Food storers might remember the locations of their caches well simply because visiting a site and placing food in it provides favorable conditions for memory. At the other extreme, food storers might have better memory in general than nonstorers. In between is the possibility that food storers are especially good at just those things required in food storing, such as remembering features of a large number of different locations on the basis of a single brief visit to each one. The comparisons of memory for stored and encountered food reviewed in the preceding section are consistent with any of these possibilities.

The speculation that food storers might have better spatial memory in some sense than nonstorers is encouraged by the results of neuroanatomical work. Storing species have a larger hippocampus relative to brain and body size than nonstorers (Krebs, Sherry, Healy, Perry, & Vaccarino, 1989; Sherry et al., 1989). The lesion studies already mentioned (Sherry & Vaccarino, 1989) show that the hippocampus is not necessary for storing behavior itself, because chickadees with hippocampal lesions stored normally. Rather, the hippocampus is involved in some way in memory. Exactly how it is involved and what the cross-species differences in size means can only be resolved by further behavioral and neurobiological work (cf. Krebs, Hilton, & Healy, 1990; Krebs, 1990).

Comparative behavioral studies of memory are ongoing with both tits and corvids (Balda & Kamil, 1989; Krebs, Healy, & Shettleworth, 1990; Krebs, Hilton, & Healy, 1990; review in Krebs, 1990). Our strategy with the tits is to look at performance in a range of tasks with different degrees of similarity to food storing. Species differences ought to be most marked in tasks most similar to storing. In one series of studies, performance of coal tits and great tits was compared in two versions of window-shopping (Krebs, Healy, & Shettleworth, 1990). In a simplified version of the task, the aviary held only seven potential sites for seeds. In phase 1 of each daily trial, a different site held a piece of peanut behind a window, and the bird also found a small piece of peanut to eat there. The windows were all covered with small curtains, to the birds had to look under them to find the peanut. Both species looked in about four holes in this phase, the average to be expected from random search (Fig. 2.5). However, if they remembered where the peanut was that day, in phase 2, half an hour later, performance should have been better than chance, which it was for both species. However, coal tits visited significantly fewer sites to find the peanut than did great tits. Other measures of performance taking into account site preferences also revealed slightly better performance by the storing coal tits. Moreover, neither quicker learning of the task by the coal tits nor lower motivation in the great tits appeared to be involved in the differences in performance in window-shopping.

FIG. 2.5. Mean number of visits to find one seed hidden among seven possible sites. Subjects were four coal tits and four great tits. Phase 2 (PH 2) was a test of memory for the seed's location 30 minutes after phase 1 (PH 1). (The standard error is 0 for great tits in phase 2). Data from Krebs, Healy, and Shettleworth (1990).

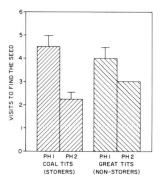

One noteworthy feature of the data depicted in Fig. 2.5 is that, in phase 1, when they should have been searching at random for the peanut, the coal tits appear to take slightly more looks than the great tits. Although it was not significant, part of the reason for the difference was revealed by analyzing where the birds looked in phase 1 as a function of where the peanut had been on previous days. The coal tits' search was influenced by previous locations: They were significantly more likely to go to sites rewarded in the preceding three trials than to sites rewarded in still earlier trials. The great tits showed no such tendency. This can be seen as a case where better memory actually leads to worse performance, a kind of case that might repay further investigation in our comparative studies (Staddon, 1985).

In a second experiment, we attempted to see whether the species differences in simple window-shopping would be exaggerated in the more complex version of the task where items are to be found in several of 60 possible sites and the retention interval is longer (Krebs, Healy, & Shettleworth, in press, Experiment 2). However, although there was again a significant difference in performance in favor of the coal tits, the species difference was still not very large.

Of course, all we can really say so far is that these results are consistent with the hypothesis of species differences in memory related to storing. One of their limitations is that they compare just one storing and one nonstoring species. Clearly, we need to increase the number of species of each kind in the sample. It should be noted, however, that unlike many conventional studies of possible species differences in learning and memory (e.g., Macphail, 1987), the comparisons of storing and nonstoring species are based on an explicit hypothesis about the direction of difference to be expected (cf. Kamil, 1987, for further discussion).

It is also important to note that coal tits are not simply better in general at laboratory food-finding tasks. This is shown by some work by Susan Hilton in Oxford (Krebs, Hilton, & Healy, 1990). Hilton compared the performance of two storing and two nonstoring species (coal tits and marsh tits; great tits and blue tits) in two reference memory tasks and one working memory task. In the reference memory tasks, the birds found food on each trial in six of many possible sites in a large aviary. The sites were holes in sections of tree branches, covered with small cloth curtains. The spatial version of the task required them to learn six locations that were the same each day. The cue version required them to locate the baited sites by means of colored cards. Here the correct sites were in different locations each day. Performance in both tasks was measured as number of errors in the first six holes inspected. All four species learned both tasks quickly. Within 30 trials they were performing nearly perfectly, making only one error on average in the first six looks. Most important for our purposes, the species did not differ on the color task, and on the spatial task the food-storing coat tits performed slightly worse than the other species.

In another experiment, Hilton compared the same four species, as well as greenfinches, an unrelated species, on a working memory task like a radial maze (Hilton & Krebs, 1990). Eight feeders were located in a circle in a large room with a perch in the center that had a lamp over it. The birds were trained to collect food from the feeders and return to the lighted central perch to eat each piece. The experimenter encouraged them to do this by turning out the lights in the room each time a seed was collected, then turning them on again when the bird had finished eating at the central perch. This neat trick allowed Hilton to circumvent the problems that have arisen in other "open field" radial maze tests with birds in which the subjects have tended simply to go round the aviary visiting feeding sites in order (Balda & Kamil, 1988; Spetch & Edwards, 1986).

All the birds learned to perform the task (i.e., to visit all eight baited feeders without revisiting emptied ones) at above chance within about 15 trials, and performance did not appear to improve beyond about 24 trials. There were no species differences in this training phase, with all free choices. Then, the birds were tested with four forced choices followed by four free choices after retention intervals of 30 seconds, 2 hours, and 24 hours. Forced choices were run by electronically locking the doors to four feeders and unlocking them for the free-choice phase. Birds spent the retention intervals in their home cages. When percent-correct choices in choices 5–8 were analyzed, there was a significant interaction of species with retention interval. The storing species performed slightly less well than the nonstoring tits at the 30-second retention interval, but better at 24 hours. Thus, they were affected less by lengthening the retention interval than the nonstoring species. All the birds, however, performed above chance after 24 hours.

Similar kinds of comparisons between tasks and species have been made with corvids. Balda and Kamil (1988) trained nutcrackers in an open-field analogue of the radial maze with eight holes in which seeds could be buried. The birds performed well with four forced followed by four free choices at retention intervals up to 6 hours, but they were close to chance after 24 hours. Thus, in this task the birds appear to forget where they have already retrieved seeds within about a day. In contrast, in laboratory tests in a similar environment (e.g., Kamil & Balda, 1985), nutcrackers remember the locations of many caches for at least 14 days. It is not yet clear what differences between the tasks are responsible for the differences in the results. Recovering caches involves memory for where food is, whereas performing well in a radial maze requires remembering where food is not or what locations have already been visited. As Balda and Kamil (1988) pointed out, it may be relevant that, unlike tits, nutcrackers also seem to have trouble avoiding sites from which caches have been recovered.

Among the corvids, species that rely to different degrees on food storing can be compared in hoarding tasks. Balda and Kamil (1989) compared the accuracy with which nutcrackers, pinyon jays, and scrub jays recovered caches of pine seeds made in a large aviary 7 days earlier. Scrub jays, which rely least on caching in the wild, performed significantly worse than pinyon jays or nutcrackers, but the latter two species did not differ. However, the behavior of the three species also differed in a number of ways during the caching phase, and these differences, rather than species differences in spatial memory, might have been responsible for the differences in recovery performance. For example, when they were allowed to, the scrub jays tended to place their caches much closer together than did the other birds, giving themselves a different spatial memory problem. The scrub jays and pinyon jays often made several visits to each cache site, taking seeds there one by one, whereas the nutcrackers buried several seeds at once. If they had also made several visits to each site, their memory might have been better than that of the other species. Nevertheless, just as in the comparative studies with tits, the results, though limited, are consistent with the hypothesis that there are species differences in memory correlated with hoarding behavior, and they encourage further research.

CONCLUSIONS AND PROSPECTS FOR THE FUTURE

The last few years have seen considerable progress in understanding the properties of memory in food-storing birds in laboratory and field studies of food storing. However, it is still not possible to give a definite answer to the question is the memory of food-storing birds adaptively specialized? The results of our within-species comparisons do not indicate that locations of stored seeds are remembered any better than locations of seeds encountered by the bird under similar circumstances. However, it is still possible that the two kinds of items would prove to be remembered differentially under conditions that we have not yet tested, for example, with retention intervals of longer than a day. In contrast, the results of the cross-species comparisons are consistent with the hypothesis that aspects of memory important to successful recovery of stored food are adaptively specialized, at least in a quantitative way, in storing species. However, this type of work is only just beginning. One long-term aim of research with both tits and corvids is to characterize the similarities and differences, if any, between storing and nonstoring species in a variety of tests of memory and to relate these to the requirements of food storing.

Tests similar to the radial maze tasks, like those described earlier, are an obvious choice for comparing storing species with their relatives. Behavior of other species on the radial maze is reasonably well understood, and memory for locations of stored food is in some sense spatial. However, the radial maze captures only one aspect of the food-storer's task, remembering what hoards have been emptied and therefore should not be revisited. Chickadees, nutcrackers, and other food-storing birds also have to remember where they put food in the first place. A task like window-shopping provides a better test of this ability than does the radial maze. However, storing food in the wild has one important feature lacking in our window-shopping tests, and indeed in most laboratory tests of food storing reported so far; that is, as far as we know, the birds use different sites all the time. Thus they must be very good at encoding the features of many unique storage sites on the basis of a single brief visit to each one. Laboratory tests of memory for stored food, particularly those I have described with the parids in which each bird has many trials in the same restricted environment, are instead recency discriminations. What the bird has to remember is "Where are the seeds today?". David Brodbeck, working in my laboratory, has begun to look at how chickadees perform when food is in a unique site on each trial (Brodbeck, Burack, & Shettleworth, 1992). In his task, every trial has three new, differently decorated feeders in different locations. On phase 1 of a trial, the bird is allowed to eat part of a peanut wedged into one feeder. It is allowed to return and finish the peanut after a retention interval. With a retention interval of 5 minutes, the birds perform almost perfectly, finding the peanut on the first look, within about 15 trials. It will be interesting to see how other tit species perform on such a task, which is similar to tasks with trial-unique stimuli that produce very good performance in monkeys (Mishkin & Delacour, 1975) and rats (Aggleton, 1985; see also Wright, this volume).

A long-term aim of the comparative behavioral studies is to relate them to the ongoing neuroanatomical work referred to earlier. The differences in hippocampal volume documented so far are exciting, but much more needs to be done before we understand what they mean (cf. Krebs, 1990; Krebs, Hilton, & Healy, 1990). Spatial memory and hippocampal function in mammals are comparatively well studied (Berger, this volume; Kesner, this volume), so it may be possible for the work on food-storing birds and the work on these species to enrich each other. In other areas, there has been considerable success in relating brain structure and function to aspects of naturally occurring learning and memory (e.g., Horn, 1985; Konishi, 1985). Memory for stored food is attractive to approach in this way because we know it is used in the wild to different degrees by different species, and it promises a rich body of comparative behavioral and neuroanatomical data. The research reviewed in this chapter is just a beginning.

ACKNOWLEDGMENTS

Preparation of this chapter and the research from my laboratory described in it were supported by operating grants from the Natural Sciences and Engineering Research Council of Canada (NSERC). Collaboration with John Krebs has been supported in succession by a Guggenheim Fellowship, a NATO Grant for International Collaboration in Research, and the international programs of NSERC. The idea for window-shopping arose in a conversation with Larry Squire at a Dahlem Conference, and David Sherry suggested the name for it. I thank Erik Mathon and Rick Westwood for help in preparing the manuscript and David Brodbeck for comments.

REFERENCES

Aggleton, J. P. (1985). One-trial object recognition by rats. *Quarterly Journal of Experimental Psychology, 37B,* 279–294.

Andersson, M., & Krebs, J. R. (1978). On the evolution of hoarding behaviour. *Animal Behaviour, 26,* 707–711.

Balda, R. P., Bunch, K. G., Kamil, A. C., Sherry, D. F., & Tomback, D. F. (1987). Cache site memory in birds. In A. C. Kamil, J. R. Krebs, & H. R. Pulliam (Eds.), *Foraging behavior* (pp. 645–666). New York & London: Plenum Press.

Balda, R. P., & Kamil, A. C. (1988). The spatial memory of Clark's nutcrackers (*Nucifraga columbiana*) in an analogue of the radial-arm maze. *Animal Learning and Behavior, 16,* 116–122.

Balda, R. P., & Kamil, A. C. (1989). A comparative study of cache recovery by three corvid species. *Animal Behaviour, 38,* 486–495.

Balda, R. P., Kamil, A. C., & Grim, K. (1986). Revisits to emptied cache sites by Clark's nutcrackers (*Nucifraga columbiana*). *Animal Behaviour, 34,* 1289–1298.

Bhatt, R. S., Wasserman, E. A., Reynolds, W. F., & Knauss, K. S. (1988). Conceptual behavior in pigeons: Categorization of both familiar and novel examples from four classes of natural and artificial stimuli. *Journal of Experimental Psychology: Animal Behavior Processes, 14,* 219–234.

Brodbeck, D. R., Burack, O. R., & Shettleworth, S. J. (1992). One-trial associative memory in black-capped chickadees. *Journal of Experimental Psychology: Animal Behavior Processes, 18,* 12–21.

Cowie, R. J., Krebs, J. R., & Sherry, D. F. (1981). Food storing by marsh tits. *Animal Behaviour, 29,* 1252–1259.

Hilton, S. C., & Krebs, J. R. (1990). Spatial memory of four species of *Parus:* Performance in an open-field analogue of a radial maze. *Quarterly Journal of Experimental Psychology, 42B,* 345–368.

Hitchcock, C. L., & Sherry, D. F. (1990). Long term memory for cache location in the black-capped chickadee (*Parus atricapillus*). *Animal Behaviour, 40,* 701–712.

Horn, G. (1985). *Memory, imprinting, and the brain.* Oxford: Clarendon Press.

Kamil, A. C. (1987). A synthetic approach to the study of animal intelligence. *Nebraska Symposium on Motivation,* 257–308.

Kamil, A. C., & Balda, R. P. (1985). Cache recovery and spatial memory in Clark's nutcrackers (*Nucifraga columbiana*). *Journal of Experimental Psychology: Animal Behavior Processes, 11,* 95–111.

Konishi, M. (1985). Birdsong: From behaviour to neuron. *Annual Review of Neuroscience, 8,* 125–170.

Krebs, J. R. (1990). Food-storing birds. Adaptive specialization in brain and behaviour? *Philosophical Transactions of the Royal Society (London) B, 329,* 153–160.

Krebs, J. R., Healy, S. D., & Shettleworth, S. J. (1990). Spatial memory of Paridae: Comparison of a storing and non-storing species, *Parus ater* and *Parus major. Animal Behaviour, 39,* 1127–1137.

Krebs, J. R., Hilton, S. C., & Healy, S. D. (1990). Memory in food-storing birds: Adaptive specialization in brain and behavior?. In G. M. Edelman, W. E. Gall, & W. M. Cowan (Eds.), *Signal and sense: Local and global order in perceptual maps* (pp. 475–498). New York: Springer.

Krebs, R. K., Sherry, D. F., Healy, S. D., Perry, H. P., & Vaccarino, A. L. (1989). Hippocampal specialization of food-storing birds. *Proceedings of the National Academy of Sciences, 86,* 1388–1392.

Krushinskaya, N. L. (1966). Some complex forms of feeding behaviour of nutcrackers after removal of their old cortex. *Journal of Evolutionary Biochemistry and Physiology, 11,* 564–568.

Ludescher, F. B. (1980). Fressen und verstecken von samereien bei der Weidenmeise *Parus mon-*

tanus in jahresverlauf unter konstanten ernahrungsbedingungen. *Okologie der Vogel, 2,* 135–144.

Macphail, E. M. (1987). The comparative psychology of intelligence. *Behavioral and Brain Sciences, 10,* 645–695.

Macphail, E. M., & Reilly, S. (1989). Rapid acquisition of a novelty versus familiarity concept by pigeons (*Columba livia*). *Journal of Experimental Psychology: Animal Behavior Processes, 15,* 242–252.

Mishkin, M., & Delacour, J. (1975). An analysis of short-term visual memory in the monkey. *Journal of Experimental Psychology: Animal Behavior Processes, 1,* 326–334.

Rescorla, R. A. (1988). Behavioral studies of Pavlovian conditioning. *Annual Review of Neuroscience, 11,* 329–352.

Roitblat, H. L., & Harley, H. E. (1988). Spatial delayed matching-to-sample performance by rats: Learning, memory, and proactive interference. *Journal of Experimental Psychology: Animal Behavior Processes, 14,* 71–82.

Rozin, P., & Kalat, J. W. (1971). Specific hungers and poison avoidance as adaptive specializations of learning. *Psychological Review, 78,* 459–486.

Sherry, D. (1984). Food storage by black-capped chickadees: Memory for the location and contents of caches. *Animal Behaviour, 32,* 451–464.

Sherry, D. (1985). Food storage by birds and mammals. *Advances in the Study of Behavior, 15,* 153–188.

Sherry, D. (1987). Foraging for stored food. In M. L. Commons, A. Kacelnik, & S. J. Shettleworth (Eds.), *Quantitative analyses of behavior. Vol VI: Foraging* (pp. 209–227). Hillsdale, NJ: Lawrence Erlbaum Associates.

Sherry, D., Avery, M., & Stevens, A. (1982). The spacing of stored food by marsh tits. *Zeitschrift fur Tierpsychologie, 58,* 153–162.

Sherry, D. F., Krebs, J. R., & Cowie, R. J. (1981). Memory for the location of stored food in marsh tits. *Animal Behaviour, 29,* 1260–1266.

Sherry, D. F., & Schacter, D. L. (1987). The evolution of multiple memory systems. *Psychological Review, 94,* 439–454.

Sherry, D. F., & Vaccarino, A. L. (1989). Hippocampus and memory for caches in black-capped chickadees. *Behavioral Neuroscience, 103,* 308–318.

Sherry, D. F., Vaccarino, A. L., Buckenham, K., & Herz, R. S. (1989). The hippocampal complex of food-storing birds. *Brain, Behavior, and Evolution, 34,* 308–317.

Shettleworth, S. J. (1985). Food storing by birds: Implications for comparative studies of memory. In N. M. Weinberger, J. L. McGaugh, & G. Lynch (Eds.), *Memory systems of the brain* (pp. 231–250). Guilford: New York.

Shettleworth, S. J. (1990). Spatial memory in food-storing birds. *Philosophical Transactions of the Royal Society (London) B, 329,* 143–151.

Shettleworth, S. J., & Krebs, J. R. (1982). How marsh tits find their hoards: The roles of site preference and spatial memory. *Journal of Experimental Psychology: Animal Behavior Processes, 8,* 354–375.

Shettleworth, S. J., & Krebs, J. R. (1986). Stored and encountered seeds: A comparison of two spatial memory tasks in marsh tits and chickadees. *Journal of Experimental Psychology: Animal Behavior Processes, 12,* 248–257.

Shettleworth, S. J., Krebs, J. R., Healy, S. D., & Thomas, C. M. (1990). Spatial memory of food-storing tits (*Parus ater* and *P. atricapillus*): Comparison of storing and non-storing tasks. *Journal of Comparative Psychology, 104,* 71–81.

Spetch, M. L., & Edwards, C. A. (1986). Spatial memory in pigeons (*Columba livia*) in an open-field feeding environment. *Journal of Comparative Psychology, 100,* 266–278.

Staddon, J. E. R. (1983). *Adaptive behavior and learning.* New York: Cambridge University Press.

Staddon, J. E. R. (1985). Inference, memory, and representation. In N. M. Weinberger, J. L. McGaugh, & G. Lynch (Eds.), *Memory systems of the brain* (pp. 287–295). Guilford: New York.

Stevens, T. A. (1984). *Food storing by marsh tits*. Unpublished doctoral thesis, Oxford University.

Stevens, T. A., & Krebs, J. R. (1986). Retrieval of stored seeds by marsh tits *Parus palustris* in the field. *Ibis, 128,* 513–525.

Vander Wall, S. B., & Balda, R. P. (1981). Ecology and evolution of food-storage behavior in conifer-seed-caching corvids. *Zeitschrift fur Tierpsychologie, 56,* 217–242.

Vaughan, W. Jr., & Greene, S. L. (1984). Pigeon visual memory capacity. *Journal of Experimental Psychology: Animal Behavior Processes, 10,* 256–271.

Wilkie, D. M., & Summers, R. J. (1982). Pigeons' spatial memory: Factors affecting delayed matching of key location. *Journal of the Experimental Analysis of Behavior, 37,* 45–56.

3

Testing The Cognitive Capacities of Animals

Anthony A. Wright
University of Texas Health Science Center at Houston
Graduate School of Biomedical Sciences

Comparative animal cognition often involves the inability as well as the ability of animals to perform cognitive tasks. The question and the theme of this chapter is, are these inabilities a limitation of the capacity of the animal or are they a limitation of the experimenter's ability to design the tests such that the animals can express their ability (e.g., to learn abstract concepts)? There are many things that each animal species (including humans) cannot do; each species has its limitations. But when cognitive capacities are considered, we should be asking whether or not animals can perform such cognitive tasks under conditions best suited for them to reveal these capacities.

We as experimenters spend a great deal of time constructing elaborate explanatory mechanisms (e.g., encoding, storage, retrieval, and rehearsal) without questioning the basic task itself. We stick our animals in a Skinner Box that is basically of a half-century old design. The stimuli we use are, more often than not, ones chosen by engineers for stimulus projector units to be sold with the Skinner Boxes. And not all too infrequently we go into the laboratory and maybe ask, "Let's see, what experiment can I do with this apparatus?" The apparatus is driving our research.

What we need to do is to continuously question the procedures we use with regards to this question of suitability and continuously refine our procedures. Sometimes refinements will be simply an optimization of a parameter (e.g., stimulus exposure duration or retention interval). Other times the apparatus may require a complete redesign and an entirely different procedure. This question of suitability only becomes an issue when the requirements of the experiment taxes the subjects' abilities; and such is the nature of many animal cognition experiments. Perhaps this is the reason why "functional compatibility" (cf. Sherry & Schacter, 1987) has not hithertofore been an issue in animal learning research.

The purpose of this chapter is to present three examples from my laboratory that demonstrate certain animal cognitive abilities, where in each case it had been thought that the task was beyond the capability of the particular animal species. In all these cases, slight changes in the training and testing situation produced substantial performance changes: The first example concerns animals being able to perform list memory tasks; the second is the pigeon's ability to learn abstract concepts, and the third is the monkey's ability to learn the abstract concept of same/different with auditory stimuli.

MEMORY PROCESSING OF LISTS BY MONKEYS

In 1980, Steve Sands and I showed that monkeys could be trained to accurately perform list memory tasks with lists of 10 and 20 items (Sands & Wright, 1980a, 1980b). In this list memory task, the list items were successively presented on a upper rear projection screen. Following the list, a single probe or test item was presented on a lower rear projection screen. Half the time the probe matched one of the list items and half the time it matched none of them. The monkey moved a lever in one direction to indicate that the probe was in the list and moved it in the other direction to indicate that it was not in the list. Prior to this work, other researchers (Devine & Jones, 1975; Eddy, 1973; Gaffan, 1977) had attempted to train monkeys in list memory tasks, but their monkeys only performed at 65%—70% correct with short lists of three items, and performance deteriorated rapidly for longer list lengths.

We showed that with a large collection of distinctly different slide-picture stimuli that the monkey performed 93% correct with 3-item lists, 86% correct with 10-item lists, and even 83% correct with 20 item lists.

These U-shaped serial position functions indicate process-separation and dual memory processes much as these are for humans (Glanzer, 1972; Tulving, 1987). The recency effect, the comparatively good performance for the last list items, is the primary memory component. The primacy effect, the comparatively good performance for the first list items (and the middle portion of the serial position function), is the secondary memory component. This was the first clear evidence, of which we are aware, of a primary effect for an infrahuman animal species. There has since been additional demonstrations of primacy effects for rhesus and other primate species (Buchanan, Gill, & Braggio, 1981; Roberts & Kraemer, 1981; Wright, Santiago, & Sands, 1984; Wright, Santiago, Sands, Kendrick, & Cook, 1985), pigeons (Santiago & Wright, 1984; Wright et al., 1985) and rats (Bolhuis & van Kampen, 1988; Kesner, 1985; Kesner & Novak, 1982). Most memory researchers seem to agree that the primary–secondary

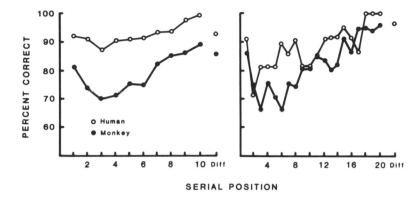

FIG. 3.1. Performance by a rhesus monkey on a serial probe recognition task with 10 items per list and 20 items per list. The broken-line functions show performance on Same trials, for each serial position, where the probe items matched one of the list items. Performance on Different trials (Diff) is shown to the right of each panel and is for trials where the probe items matched no list item.

memory process separation is an important one, but notwithstanding the vast amount of theorizing, the relationship between primary and secondary memory has been elusive.

The reason that monkeys were able to perform well with these long lists of 10 and 20 items appears to be that the experiments were conducted in such a way that proactive interference in the task was minimized. Originally we did not set out to minimize PI, but PI was minimized, nevertheless, in the process of doing something else. Our original hypothesis was that other researchers had had trouble obtaining good performance from their monkeys because the memory items were too abstract and unfamiliar to the monkeys. Thus, we set out to train monkeys with pictures of familiar items. In order to test whether or not familiarity was important, we used a collection of 211 different pictures, some of familiar items and some of unfamiliar items. The familiarity variable had no discernible effect on performance, but the PI variable did have a large effect.

Proactive interference (PI) is created when items are repeated. Take the case where a few items are reused many times in the course of a daily session. On trials where the probe test item does not match any of the list items, having seen the probe item many times prior, possibly just in the immediately preceding list, tends to confuse the subject that maybe it was in the test list. This PI effect is shown in Fig. 3.2. The better performance is with 211 different items, the ones used in the previous 10- and 20-item list studies. In this condition these items were presented only once in a daily session—trial unique. The poorer performance is with a collection of only 6 items. Hence, these 6 items were repeated many times. This item repetition produces PI and lowers performance. Overall

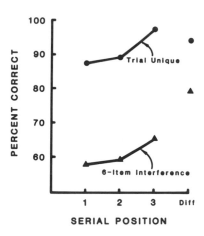

FIG. 3.2. Performance by a monkey with 3-item lists where the picture stimuli were selected (without replacement) from a 211 item pool (trial unique) or were selected from a small pool of only 6 items (6-item interference).

performance was 93% with trial-unique item presentations and 70% with the 6-item repetition condition. This performance with the 6-item set is identical to that obtained by other investigators (e.g., Gaffan, 1977, who used a small pool of only 6 items to test monkeys in a 3-item SPR task).

In the same year that our experiments on the effects of PI in monkey list memory were published, another experiment was published showing the effects of PI on monkey matching to sample performance (Overman & Doty, 1980). In matching to sample, a sample is presented and the subject is reinforced for choosing the comparison stimulus that matches the sample stimulus. Overman and Doty showed that with a large collection of slides, presented trial unique, monkeys learned the matching-to-sample concept and could accurately perform the MTS task with delays of 24 hours.

The effects of PI can even extend across sessions. In a recent experiment, we showed that repeated presentation of the same 320 stimuli (in a 4-item list memory task) produced a performance deterioration (Jitsumori, Wright, & Cook, 1988). Over a period of several months of testing, performance dropped by more than 15%. Testing with novel stimuli (some were not novel but had not been seen for more than 2 years) produced a marked increase in performance as shown in Fig. 3.3.

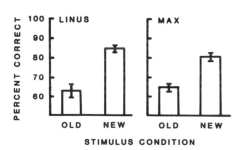

FIG. 3.3. SPR performance by two monkeys (Linus & Max) with stimuli that had been repeatedly seen (but scrambled in order) over several months (Old), and performance upon the introduction of novel or very unfamiliar stimuli (New).

High PI clearly lowers learned performance, and it also seems to interfere with acquisition. Tasks and concepts that have seemed beyond the capabilities of certain species may be within their capability once interference is removed from the learning and test situations.

ABSTRACT CONCEPT LEARNING BY PIGEONS

The second example concerns the apparent inability of pigeons to learn abstract concepts. Abstract concepts are ones that depend on relations between two or more stimuli. Examples would be same/different concept (where two stimuli are identical half the time and nonidentical half the time), matching-to-sample concept (as described in the Overman and Doty experiment aforementioned), or oddity from sample concept (like matching but the correct choice is the one that does not match). Abstract concepts, also referred to as relational concepts, higher level/order concepts, rules, or simply concepts, are to be distinguished from natural concepts (e.g., Herrnstein, Loveland, & Cable, 1976; Medin & Schaffer, 1978), class concepts (Bourne, 1970), and property sets (Hayes-Roth & Hayes-Roth, 1977). In all these latter situations there is a category, bound by some specific stimulus features (e.g., person, water, or tree; see Herrnstein et al., 1976), that unifies the category, whereas with abstract concepts a relationship among stimuli (e.g., same/different, matching to sample, oddity from sample) transcends individual stimuli and individual features.

Here too, with attempts to test for pigeons' capacity for concept learning, investigators have used only small numbers of training stimuli. The color circles, lines, and shapes of the in-line projector unit have been used over and over again with the same result—pigeons do not show any evidence of concept learning (Berryman, Cumming, Cohen, & Johnson, 1965; Cumming & Berryman, 1961; Cumming, Berryman, & Cohen, 1965; Farthing & Opuda, 1974; Holmes, 1979; Santi, 1978, 1982). We conducted a matching-to-sample concept learning experiment (Wright, Cook, Rivera, Sands, & Delius, 1988) but were not bound by the Skinner Box or the IEE stimulus in-line projector units.

A diagram of the apparatus is shown in Fig. 3.4. The stimuli were projected on a video monitor turned on its back so that the stimuli projected from the floor of the apparatus. The reasoning was that pigeons forage for seeds and grains on the ground so that the stimulus-reinforcer associations might be better formed by stimuli projected from the ground. An observation that lends some support for this reasoning is that the pigeons in this apparatus were somewhat more deliberate in their inspections of the individual stimuli, in their looking back and forth between the comparison stimuli, and in their eventual choice response than in a traditional Skinner Box. In a Skinner Box with the stimuli projected onto pecking keys mounted on a vertical stimulus panel, the choice responses are lightning quick, and all of us who have worked with pigeons have marveled at how

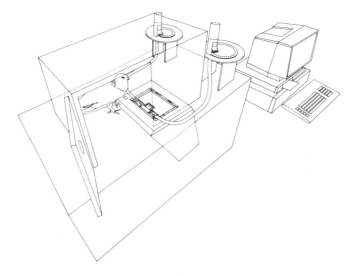

FIG. 3.4. Drawing of the apparatus showing a pigeon, the video display from the floor of the chamber, and the grain feeders to dispense grain on top of the video picture stimuli.

accurate they can be with such short response times. In our apparatus, responses were recorded by an infrared LED matrix touch screen.

Another novelty of this apparatus was that a large number of different stimuli were used in the training of one group of pigeons, and these stimuli were cartoons, drawn in full color, and stored in the computer memory. Examples of some of the stimuli as they appeared on a MTS trial are shown in Fig. 3.5.

The final novelty of this apparatus that is mentioned was the way in which the pigeons in this apparatus were reinforced. The grain delivery mechanisms are shown mounted on the outside and toward the rear of the apparatus in Fig. 3.4. They were a modification of a rat feeder with a shaving brush used as a grain reservoir (see Wright et al., 1988 for details). Grain reinforcement, for correct choice responses, was placed on top of the picture stimulus, and the pigeons actually ate off of the stimulus. This method of delivering reinforcement was different from the traditional way of reinforcing pigeons in a Skinner Box. In a Skinner Box, pigeons turn away from the stimulus (i.e., they take themselves out of the stimulus) and stick their heads into a lighted opening in order to eat from a briefly presented grain hopper.

Other experimental details included a FI 2-sec requirement before a sample peck response was effective in turning on comparison stimuli. Following a correct response the correct comparison stimulus remained on for 10 seconds so that the pigeons would eat the grain off of the stimulus picture, and with the sample also remaining on (1 s) the pigeons would have additional opportunities to notice and possibly learn the identity relationship. The incorrect comparison was turned off immediately following correct comparison choices. Following incorrect choices, the incorrect comparison was turned off immediately, the sample remained for 1 second, the correct comparison remained for 2 seconds, and the trial was repeated (correction procedure).

The ceiling was lowered over the video screen, which is distinct from what is called a ceiling effect. The lowering of the ceiling prevented the pigeons from walking on the pictures and dirtying them, which is distinct from what is called a floor effect.

Two groups of pigeons were trained in this apparatus. One group was trained with 152 different stimuli. For this group, each 76-trial session was composed from all 152 stimuli. No stimulus was repeated within a daily session (trial-

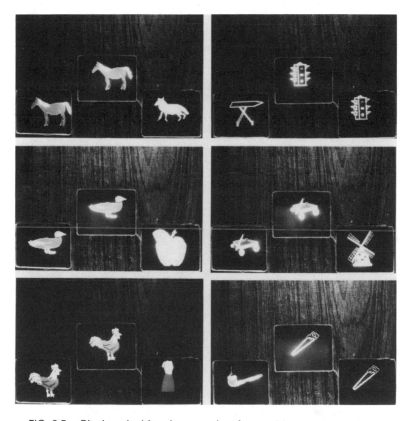

FIG. 3.5. Black and white photographs of a matching-to-sample stimulus display showing two training stimuli. The middle cartoon is the sample stimulus, and the other two are the comparison stimuli. The correct response is a choice (peck) of the comparison that matches the sample.

unique stimulus presentations). The stimuli and pairings were randomly selected for each daily session. The other group was trained with only two stimuli. After each group learned the discrimination to a performance criterion of 75% correct, transfer testing was conducted to see whether or not any of the pigeons had learned the concept of matching to sample.

Verifying that a concept has been learned is not an easy matter, and there is by no means complete agreement as to the requirements that must be met in order to demonstrate concept learning. This lack of agreement among researchers over what constitutes concept learning led us (and others) to take a comparatively conservative stance (Premack, 1978; Wright et al., 1988; Wright, Santiago, & Sands, 1984; Wright, Santiago, Urcuioli, & Sands, 1984). The first, and most important, requirement was to establish procedures from which results could be interpreted unambiguously by separating the effect of training from transfer. To this end, procedures were adopted where: (a) The novel transfer stimuli were chosen to be distinctly different from the training stimuli and from each other. This requirement necessitated that the stimuli be complex and multidimensional, particularly in this case where a comparatively large number of training and test stimuli were used; (b) transfer testing was limited to a single presentation of each novel stimulus so that the results would not be confounded by a history of reinforcement and possible learning. This procedural aspect required a large number of training stimuli, but it nevertheless seemed the most straightforward way to conduct the experiment. The procedure of testing in extinction was rejected because we have found that highly trained subjects quickly learn to discriminate training from test stimuli, and even in such situations the most important datum is also the first trial performance. Even though these two guiding principles of the procedure would probably insure a clear evaluation of transfer performance, they would not in themselves insure a clear interpretation of concept learning. The level of transfer performance that constitutes concept learning is not a matter that is easily settled. It is unlikely today that a simple difference from chance performance would, in itself, be seriously considered as evidence for concept learning. At the other extreme, one might discover transfer that showed no performance drop relative to training performance. In the experiment reported in this chapter, we were fortunate to obtain such high performance, and this made the task of arguing for concept learning considerably easier.

Ten transfer trials were intermixed with 66 regular training trials. If the pigeons were correct on a transfer trial, then they were reinforced. Incorrect choices were not rewarded. There was no correction procedure for training or transfer trials. Four such transfer sessions were conducted. Fig. 3.6 shows that the group trained with 152 trial-unique stimuli performed as well (80%) with novel stimuli as they did with the training stimuli and hence had learned the matching to sample concept. Those pigeons trained with only two stimuli did not show any significant transfer (transfer was not different from chance performance) and hence showed no abstract concept learning.

FIG. 3.6. Left: Average baseline and transfer performance
for the group trained with 152
different visual stimuli with
each stimulus presented on
only one trial (trial-unique) during each daily training session.
Right: Average baseline and
transfer performance for the 2-
stimulus group trained with
only 2 different stimuli with
both stimuli presented on all 76
trials of each daily session. In
each case, transfer was to 40
novel stimulus pairs presented
only once. Error bars are standard errors of the mean for the
subjects in each group combined.

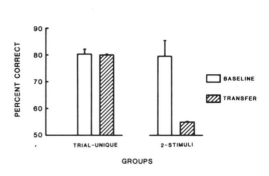

It is clear from the results of this experiment that pigeons do have the capacity
to learn some abstract concept—in this case the matching-to-sample concept. It
is also clear that a substantial set of training stimuli is a necessary requirement for
such concept learning. It remains to be seen whether or not other aspects of this
experiment (stimuli from the floor, reinforcement in the stimulus) are critical to
the abstract concept learning.

Experiments with humans have also shown that the degree of concept learning
varies directly with the number of training exemplars (Homa & Chambliss, 1975;
Homa, Cross, Cornell, Goldman, & Schwartz, 1973; Homa, Sterling, & Treple,
1981; Omohundro, 1981). Similarly, experiments with monkeys in visual concept learning have shown the importance of a large number of exemplars: Moon
and Harlow (1955, oddity-from-sample: 512 exemplars); Overman and Doty
(1980, matching-to-sample: 100 exemplars); Wright, Santiago, and Sands (1984,
210 exemplars). Thus, evidence from these primate experiments shows a strong
correlation between concept learning and the number of exemplars. In addition,
we have recently shown the importance of a large number of exemplars, as well
as some other procedural requirements, in monkey concept learning with auditory stimuli.

CONCEPT LEARNING WITH AUDITORY
STIMULI BY MONKEYS

The third example from our laboratory that is discussed in this chapter concerns
what was the apparent inability of monkeys to learn concepts with auditory
stimuli. Concept learning research with monkeys has suffered from some of the
same problems previously discussed with pigeon concept learning. The verifica-

tion of concept learning is not an easy matter, and this is why the conservative approach was chosen to: select distinctly different stimuli, test the stimuli only once, and obtain transfer performance equivalent to baseline performance. Other approaches can result in uncertain interpretation of the results and leaves one unsure about whether or not any concept learning has occurred. For example, in one monkey experiment on auditory concept learning (D'Amato & Colombo, 1985), only 2 auditory training stimuli were used, only 2 to 6 new auditory transfer stimuli were tested (the number is difficult to determine because familiar stimuli were pulsed, alternated with other familiar stimuli, or pulsed and alternated following an octave frequency change), only 1 of 4 trial types contained all novel stimuli, only averages for 24 and 48 trials over all 4 trial types were presented (1 of the 4 trial types actually contained no new stimuli and 2 others contained only 1 new stimulus), and only 4 out of 8 monkeys learned the task. Occasionally, these concept learning requirements have been fulfilled using monkeys as subjects, but only previously with visual stimuli (Moon & Harlow, 1955; Overman & Doty, 1980; Wright, Santiago, & Sands, 1984).

Even attempts to train simple auditory discriminations with monkeys have encountered difficulties (see Cowey, 1968; D'Amato, 1973; D'Amato & Salmon, 1982; Dewson & Cowey, 1969; Dewson, Wertheim, & Lynch, 1968; Thompson, 1980, 1981; Wegener, 1964). This is all somewhat strange because the monkey's hearing is well developed (Fobes & King, 1982; Stebbins, 1970, 1971, 1973). Furthermore, monkeys readily respond to conspecific vocalizations in the wild and in the laboratory (Beecher, Petersen, Zoloth, Moody, & Stebbins, 1979; Green, 1975; Green & Marler, 1979; Masataka, 1983, 1985; Seyfarth, Cheney, & Marler, 1980; Waser, 1975, 1977; Waser & Waser, 1977; Zoloth, Petersen, Beecher, Green, Marler, Moody, & Stebbins, 1979).

Initially, we assumed that researchers who had had trouble training their monkeys with auditory stimuli had simply used too few stimuli, and the resulting proactive interference had prevented learning the task. Although this may have been true and a large item pool may be necessary, it was, however, in itself not sufficient.

We translated our visual same/different task directly into an auditory task. An upper pair of speakers played the first sound (in stereo); a lower pair of speakers played the second or probe sound. The monkey being trained in this task, BW, manipulated a 3-position level: down to begin the trial, right for "same" responses, and left for "different" responses. We used environmental sounds (mostly from sound effects records), for example: ping pong, walking on gravel, Big Ben strikes, school bell rings, rooster crows, typing on manual typewriter, owl hoots, marching band, fire engine siren, stage coach and yells, telephone busy signal, coyote howls, etc. We trained our monkey in this task for a year and a half, with not even the slightest hint of learning. We even tried fading from a visual task (with this monkey and another one that was well trained in the visual SPR task) to the auditory task with no success.

We completely redesigned the task in an attempt to try to train this performance (see Shyan, Wright, Cook, & Jitsumori, 1987). Two elements of this design were probably crucial in our finally being able to train this performance. The first was that the monkeys now had to touch the speaker from which the sound emanated; they had to make contact with the stimulus source. Contact with the sound source has been shown to be important in other monkey auditory discrimination tasks (e.g., Downey & Harrison, 1972, 1975; Harrison, 1984; Harrison, Downey, Iverson, & Pratt, 1977; Harrison, Downey, Segal, & Howe, 1971; Harrison, Iverson, & Pratt, 1977; Segal & Harrison, 1978).

Three speakers were positioned on three sides of the experimental cage. Touch responses to the speakers were electrically monitored via copper screens positioned in front of the speakers. A trial began with a sample sound (natural and manmade sounds) played from the center speaker (13 s). A "touch" to the center speaker played a probe sound from both side speakers. A right side speaker "touch" was correct (banana pellet) when the probe sound matched the center one, a left touch was correct (Tang orange juice) when the two were different. Incorrect responses were followed by a 25-s time out. Time out or reward was followed by a 25-s ITI.

The second aspect that was probably crucial to training the monkeys with auditory stimuli was a special fading procedure. When fading began, the side sound was played only from the correct side speaker: from the right-hand one if it matched the sample sound, or from the left-hand one if it did not match. Thus, the two monkeys being trained had only to localize the sound. Once learned (approximately two, 25 trial sessions), the intensity from the incorrect speaker was gradually increased (approximately eight, 25-trial sessions) until the sound from both side speakers was of equal intensity.

Once performance was better than 80% correct, the 38 training sounds were reshuffled. After 6 different acquisitions, the 2 monkeys could perform at the criterion performance level upon the first presentation of new mixtures of the 38 stimuli. Transfer was then conducted. Novel sound pairs, intermixed with regular training trials, were presented only once, and correct choices rewarded on transfer as well as training trials as per the previously mentioned requirements for transfer testing.

The results from the transfer tests showed 78.8% correct performance, which was not different from the monkeys' training trial performance of 77.3% correct. This complete transfer shows that the monkeys had learned the same/different concept with auditory stimuli.

The evidence converges on the importance of a large number of exemplars being necessary for monkey auditory concept learning. But a large number of stimuli is probably only part of the total requirement. As previously mentioned, one monkey, BW, had been trained prior to the experiment with 72 different sound stimuli; this monkey did not acquire the task even after more than 17,000 trials over more than a year's training.

From this discussion of animal concept learning it should be clear that there may be a number of different procedural requirements for concept learning to

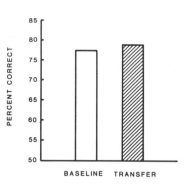

FIG. 3.7.   Baseline and transfer performance by two rhesus monkeys, BW and FD, in an auditory same/different task where the auditory items were natural and environmental sounds. Transfer performance was from only one exposure to each pair of novel stimuli.

occur. A substantial number of exemplars is probably a universal requirement. Other requirements will likely depend on the concept to be learned and the particular species learning the concept. In the case of monkeys learning a same/different concept with auditory stimuli, contact with the sound source and possibly the fading procedure may have been crucial in addition to the large number of exemplars.

CONCLUDING REMARKS

The message here is that we need to be more docile to any specific cognitive requirements of our species. We need to try out different procedures, and even different species. The pigeon, for example, may have been a bad choice of species to explore cognitive and memory tasks. In our well-controlled experimental environments the pigeon readily develops adverse reactions to changes, and one of these changes is novel transfer stimuli. Pigeons seem to be predisposed to learning responses to the absolute properties of individual stimuli rather than to the relative properties among stimuli. Many, or even most, cognitive tasks are relational ones that require training and learning against the predispositions of the pigeon. As our animal cognitive/memory tasks become better tuned to take advantage of the species predispositions and functional incompatibilities from procedures are minimized (Sherry & Schacter, 1987), notions of capacity limitation for certain types of cognitive learning such as concepts may all but disappear, which should put even more pressure on the question of species' cognitive/intelligence differences.

ACKNOWLEDGMENTS

Preparation of this article was supported in part by grants MH 35202 and MH 42881 to the author.

REFERENCES

Beecher, M., Petersen, M., Zoloth, S., Moody, D., & Stebbins, W. (1979). Perception of conspecific vocalizations by Japanese monkeys (*Macaca fuscata*). *Brain, Behavior and Evolution, 16*, 443–460.

Berryman, R., Cumming, W. W., Cohen, L. R., & Johnson, D. F. (1965). Acquisition and transfer of simultaneous oddity. *Psychological Reports, 17*, 767–775.

Bolhuis, J. J., & van Kampen, H. S. (1988). Serial position curves in spatial memory of rats: Primacy and recency effects. *The Quarterly Journal of Experimental Psychology, 40*, 135–149.

Bourne, L. E., Jr. (1970). Knowing and using concepts. *Psychological Review, 77*, 546–556.

Buchanan, J. P., Gill, T. V., & Braggio, J. T. (1981). Serial position and clustering effects in chimpanzee's "free recall." *Memory and Cognition, 9*, 651–660.

Cowey, A. (1968). Discrimination. In L. Weiskrantz (Ed.), *Analysis of behavioral change* (pp. 189–238). New York: Harper & Row.

Cumming, W. W., & Berryman, R. (1961). Some data on matching behavior in the pigeon. *Journal of the Experimental Analysis of Behavior, 4*, 281–284.

Cumming, W. W., Berryman, R., & Cohen, L. R. (1965). Acquisition and transfer of zero delay matching. *Psychological Reports, 17*, 435–445.

D'Amato, M. R. (1973). Delayed matching and short-term memory in monkeys. In G. H. Bower (Ed.), *The psychology of learning and motivation: Advances in theory and research* (Vol. 7, pp. 227–269). New York: Academic Press.

D'Amato, M. R., & Colombo, M. (1985). Auditory matching-to-sample in monkeys (*Cebus apella*). *Animal Learning and Behavior, 13*, 375–382.

D'Amato, M. R., & Salmon, D. P. (1982). Tune discrimination in monkeys (*Cebus apella*) and rats. *Animal Learning & Behavior, 10*, 126–134.

Devine, J. V., & Jones, L. C. (1975). Matching-to-successive samples: A multiple-unit memory task with rhesus monkeys. *Behavior Research Methods and Instrumentation, 7*, 438–440.

Dewson, J. H., III, & Cowey, A. (1969). Discrimination of auditory sequences by monkeys. *Nature, 222*, 695–697.

Dewson, J. H., III, Wertheim, G. A., & Lynch, J. C. (1968). Acquisition of successive auditory discrimination in monkeys. *Journal of the Acoustical Society of America, 43*, 162–163.

Downey, P., & Harrison, J. M. (1972). Control of responding by location of auditory stimuli: Role of differential and non-differential reinforcement. *Journal of the Experimental Analysis of Behavior, 18*, 453–463.

Downey, P., & Harrison, J. M. (1975). Control of responding by sound location in monkeys: Rapid acquisition in darkness. *Journal of the Experimental Analysis of Behavior, 23*, 265–276.

Eddy, D. R. (1973). *Memory processing in Macaca speciosa: Mental processes revealed by reaction time experiments.* Unpublished doctoral dissertation, Carnegie-Mellon University.

Farthing, G. W., & Opuda, M. J. (1974). Transfer of matching-to-sample in pigeons. *Journal of the Experimental Analysis of Behavior, 21*, 199–213.

Fobes, J. L., & King, J. E. (1982). Auditory and chemoreceptive sensitivity in primates. In J. L. Fobes & J. E. King (Eds.), *Primate behavior* (pp. 245–270). New York: Academic Press.

Gaffan, D. (1977). Recognition memory after short retention intervals in fornix-transected monkeys. *Quarterly Journal of Experimental Psychology, 29*, 557–588.

Glanzer, M. (1972). Storage mechanisms in recall. In G. H. Bower (Ed.), *The psychology of learning and motivation* (Vol. 5, 129–193). New York: Academic Press.

Green, S. (1975). The variation of vocal pattern with social situation in the Japanese monkey (*Macaca fuscata*): A field study. In L. Rosenblum (Ed.), *Primate behavior*, (Vol. 4, pp. 1–102). New York: Academic Press.

Green, S., & Marler, P. (1979). The analysis of animal communication. In P. Marler & J. G Vandenbergh (Eds.), *Social behavior and communication* (Vol. 3). New York: Plenum Press.

Harrison, J. M. (1984). The functional analysis of auditory discrimination. *Journal of the Acoustical Society of America, 75,* 1848–1854.

Harrison, J. M., Downey, P., Iverson, S. D., & Pratt, S. R. (1977). Control of responding by location of auditory stimuli: Adjacency of sound and response. *Journal of the Experimental Analysis of Behavior, 28,* 243–251.

Harrison, J. M., Downey, P., Segal, M., & Howe, M. (1971). Control of responding by location of auditory stimuli: Rapid acquisition in monkey and rat. *Journal of the Experimental Analysis of Behavior, 15,* 379–386.

Harrison, J. M., Iverson, S. D., & Pratt, S. R. (1977). Control of responding by location of auditory stimuli: adjacency of sound and response. *Journal of the Experimental Analysis of Behavior, 28,* 243–251.

Hayes-Roth, B., & Hayes-Roth, F. (1977). Concept learning and the recognition and classification of exemplars. *Journal of Verbal Learning and Verbal Behavior, 16,* 321–338.

Herrnstein, R. J., Loveland, D. H., & Cable, C. (1976). Natural concepts in pigeons. *Journal of Experimental Psychology: Animal Behavior Processes, 2,* 285–302.

Holmes, P. W. (1979). Transfer of matching performance in pigeons. *Journal of the Experimental Analysis of Behavior, 31,* 103–114.

Homa, D., & Chambliss, D. (1975). The relative contributions of common and distinctive information on the abstraction from ill-defined categories. *Journal of Experimental Psychology: Human Learning and Memory, 1,* 351–359.

Homa, D., Cross, J., Cornell, D., Goldman, D., & Schwartz, S. (1973). Prototype abstraction and classification of new instances as a function of number of instances defining the prototype. *Journal of Experimental Psychology, 101,* 116–122.

Homa, D., Sterling, S., & Treple, L. (1981). Limitations of exemplar-based generalization and the abstraction of categorical information. *Journal of Experimental Psychology: Human Learning and Memory, 7,* 418–439.

Jitsumori, M., Wright, A. A., & Cook, R. G. (1988). Long-term proactive interference and novelty enhancement effects in monkey list memory. *Journal of Experimental Psychology: Animal Behavior Processes, 14,* 146–154.

Kesner, R. P. (1985). Correspondence between humans and animals in coding of temporal attributes: Role of hippocampus and prefrontal cortex, *Annals of the New York Academy of Sciences, 444,* 122–136.

Kesner, R. P., & Novak, J. M. (1982). Serial position curve in rats: Role of the dorsal hippocampus. *Science,* 173–175.

Masataka, N. (1983). Categorical responses to natural and synthesized alarm calls in Goeldi's monkeys (*Callimico goeldii*). *Primates, 24,* 40–51.

Masataka, N. (1985). Development of vocal recognition of mothers in infant Japanese macaques. *Developmental Psychobiology, 18,* 107–114.

Medin, D. L., & Schaffer, M. M. (1978). Context theory of classification learning. *Psychological Review, 85,* 207–238.

Moon, L. E., & Harlow, H. F. (1955). Analysis of oddity learning by rhesus monkeys. *Journal of Comparative and Physiological Psychology, 48,* 188–195.

Omohundro, J. (1981). Recognition vs. classification of ill-defined category exemplars. *Memory and Cognition, 9.* 324–331.

Overman, W. H., Jr., & Doty, R. W. (1980). Prolonged visual memory in macaques and man. *Neuroscience, 5,* 1825–1831.

Premack, D. (1978). On the abstractness of human concepts: Why it would be difficult to talk to a pigeon. In S. H. Hulse, H. Fowler, & W. K. Honig (Eds.), *Cognitive processes in animal behavior.* Hillsdale, NJ: Lawrence Erlbaum Associates.

Roberts, W. A., & Kraemer, P. J. (1981). Recognition memory for lists of visual stimuli in monkeys and humans. *Animal Learning and Behavior, 9,* 587–594.

Santi, A. (1978). The role of physical identity of the sample and correct comparison stimulus in matching-to-sample paradigms. *Journal of the Experimental Analysis of Behavior, 29,* 511–516.

Santi, A. (1982). Hue matching and hue oddity in pigeons: Is explicit training not to peck incorrect hue combinations a sufficient condition for transfer? *The Psychological Record, 32,* 61–73.

Shyan, M. S., Wright, A. A., Cook, R. G., & Jitsumori, M. (1987). Acquisition of the auditory same/different task in a rhesus monkey. *Bulletin of the Psychonomic Society, 25(1),* 1–4.

Sands, S. F., & Wright, A. A. (1980a). Primate memory: Retention of serial list items by a rhesus monkey. *Science, 209,* 938–940.

Sands, S. F., & Wright, A. A. (1980b). Serial probe recognition performance by a rhesus monkey and a human with 10- and 20-item lists. *Journal of Experimental Psychology: Animal Behavior Processes, 6,* 386–396.

Santiago, H. C., & Wright, A. A. (1984). Pigeon memory: Same/different concept learning, serial probe recognition acquisition and probe delay effects in the serial position function. *Journal of Experimental Psychology: Animal Behavior Processes, 10,* 498–512.

Segal, M., & Harrison, J. M. (1978). The control of responding by auditory stimuli: Interactions between different dimensions of the stimuli. *Journal of the Experimental Analysis of Behavior, 30,* 97–106.

Seyfarth, R. M., Cheney, D., & Marler, P. (1980). Monkey responses to different alarm calls: Evidence of predator classification and semantic communication. *Science, 210,* 801–803.

Sherry, D. F., & Schacter, D. L. (1987). The evolution of multiple memory systems. *Psychological Review, 94,* 439–454.

Stebbins, W. C. (1970). Studies of hearing and hearing loss in the monkey. In W. C. Stebbins (Ed.), *Animal psychophysics: The design and conduct of sensory experiments* (pp. 41–66). New York: Appleton-Century-Crofts.

Stebbins, W. C. (1971). Hearing. In A. M. Schrier & F. Stollnitz (Eds.), *Behavior of nonhuman primates* (Vol. 3, pp. 159–192). New York: Academic Press.

Stebbins, W. C. (1973). Hearing of Old World monkeys (*Cerecopithecinae*). *American Journal of Physical Anthropology, 38,* 357–364.

Thompson, R. K. R. (1980). Auditory cued reversal and matching-to-sample learning by rhesus monkeys. *Antropologia Comtemporanea, 3,* 284–292.

Thompson, R. K. R. (1981). *Follow-up to the auditory matching by a monkey paper.* Unpublished manuscript.

Tulving, E. (1987). Introduction: Multiple memory systems and consciousness, *Human Neurobiology, 6,* 67–80.

Waser, P. M. (1975). Experimental playbacks show vocal mediation in intergroup avoidance in forest monkeys. *Nature, 255,* 56–58.

Waser, P. M. (1977). Sound localization by monkeys: A field experiment. *Behavioral Ecology and Sociobiology, 2,* 427–431.

Waser, P. M., & Waser, M. S. (1977). Experimental studies of primate vocalization: Specializations for long-distance propagation. *Zietchrift fur Tierpsychology, 43,* 239–263.

Wegener, J. G. (1964). Auditory discrimination behavior of normal monkeys. *Journal of Auditory Research, 4,* 81–106.

Wright, A. A., Cook, R. G., Rivera, J. J., Sands, S. F., & Delius, J. D. (1988). Concept learning by pigeons: Matching to sample with trial-unique video picture stimuli. *Animal Learning & Behavior, 16,* 436–444.

Wright, A. A., Santiago, H. C., & Sands, S. F. (1984). Monkey memory: Same/different concept learning, serial probe acquisition, and probe delay effects. *Journal of Experimental Psychology: Animal Behavior Processes, 10,* 513–529.

Wright, A. A., Santiago, H. C., Sands, S. F., Kendrick, D. F., & Cook, R. G. (1985). Memory processing of serial lists by pigeons, monkeys, and people. *Science, 229,* 287–289.

Wright, A. A., Santiago, H. C., Urcuioli, P. J., & Sands, S. F. (1984). Monkey and pigeons acquisition of same/different concept using pictorial stimuli. In M. L. Commons & R. J. Herrnstein (Eds.), *Quantitative analysis of behavior* (Vol. IV, pp. 295–317).

Zoloth, S., Petersen, M., Beecher, M., Green, S., Marler, P., Moody, D., & Stebbins, W. (1979). Species-specific perceptual processing of vocal sounds by Old World monkeys. *Science, 204,* 870–873.

4 Memory and Expectancy in Delayed Discrimination Procedures

Diane L. Chatlosh
California State University, Chico

Edward A. Wasserman
University of Iowa

In a delayed conditional discrimination task, an organism must base its responses on previously presented stimuli. For example, consider a typical delayed matching-to-sample (MTS) task for pigeons. The occurrence of a red or a green center keylight signals whether a peck to a red or a green side keylight will later produce food. The red or green center keylight is the sample stimulus for the trial. The offset of the sample stimulus is followed by a brief delay during which no events are scheduled. Once this retention interval has elapsed, red and green test stimuli are simultaneously presented on the two side keys. The red and green side keylights are the test stimuli; their locations (left and right) are reversed on a random half of the trials. The bird's task is simply to peck the red test stimulus after a red sample and to peck the green test stimulus after a green sample, regardless of their locations on the side keys on a particular trial. Performance on a delayed MTS task is thought to be a reflection of pigeons' short-term memory; elucidating the nature of this short-term memory is the goal of many studies of animal cognition.

RETROSPECTION AND PROSPECTION

What kind of memory mechanism is it that makes it possible for subjects to respond correctly during the choice test of a delayed discrimination task? According to one view of short-term memory, a sample stimulus forms a memory trace, which is thought to be an isomorphic representation of the actual stimulus (e.g., Roberts & Grant, 1976; for a somewhat different interpretation, see Roitblat, 1980). The trace is thought to grow while the stimulus is presented and

61

gradually to decay when the stimulus is withdrawn. It is assumed that test performance is a function of the strength of the remaining trace. Thus, trace decay theories espouse a retrospective explanation of animal short-term memory. When confronted with the test, the animal looks back upon the sample stimulus for clues about how to behave.

Trace decay theories nicely accommodate two well-established memory phenomena. First, as the retention interval in a memory task is lengthened, discriminative performance typically worsens (e.g., Kraemer & Roberts, 1984; Nelson & Wasserman, 1978). Presumably, the decline in stimulus control is due to a progressive weakening of the stimulus trace. Second, as the sample duration in a memory task is increased, discriminative performance typically improves (e.g., Nelson & Wasserman, 1978; Roberts, 1972; Roberts & Grant, 1974). This heightened stimulus control is presumably due to the progressive strengthening of the stimulus trace.

However, further research has indicated that, although these retention interval and sample duration effects do occur with some types of conditional discrimination tasks, there are important exceptions. Specifically, for discrimination tasks in which it is possible to anticipate, at the time of the sample, which of two responses (or whether or not a single response) will be reinforced during the test, performance does not always simply worsen with increasing retention intervals and improve with increasing sample durations (e.g., Honig & Wasserman, 1981; Smith, 1967; Wasserman, 1986). Moreover, not only do trace decay theories fail to account for the absence of retention interval and sample duration effects in these particular situations, but as we see later, such theories also cannot easily explain the presence of certain other memory phenomena. These and other shortcomings of trace decay theories suggest that not all short-term memory is retrospective. Instead, investigations of the role of anticipation in animal memory suggest that, at least some of the time, a prospective process may underlie performance on short-term memory tasks. In other words, the animal may look ahead toward future events for clues about how to behave in delayed discrimination procedures.

LEARNED EXPECTANCIES

One kind of anticipatory mechanism that may aid performance is a learned expectancy. Tolman (1932) was the first to introduce the concept of expectancy as an intervening variable. He believed that learning consists of acquiring the expectancy that in the presence of a particular event, a particular response will result in a particular outcome. Although Tolman's ideas about learned expectancies were not popular among his contemporaries, 40 years later the general gist of his ideas was revived and adopted by several learning theorists. For instance, Trapold and Overmier (1972) hypothesized that each type of reinforcer elicits specific feedback stimuli that support the acquisition of specific learned expectancies. The learned expectancies then become part of the stimulus complex that controls behavior. Bolles (1972), on the other hand, suggested that learning consists of the development of two expectancies: one resulting from environmental stimulus–outcome contingencies and the other representing response–outcome contingencies. Current investigators, in their attempts to expand and refine these views of anticipatory memory processes, have developed new techniques that provide a more detailed and incisive look at the nature of expectancies and the means by which they may help mediate delays in discrimination tasks.

Differential Outcomes Effect

In an innovative pair of experiments, Trapold (1970) provided direct evidence that two different positive reinforcers can produce discriminably different expectancies that function as additional cues in a discrimination task. In the first experiment, rats were required to make one response (R1) in the presence of one set of stimuli (S1) and to make a second response (R2) in the presence of a second set of stimuli (S2). Subjects that received a food pellet (O1) after one stimulus–response sequence (S1–R1–O1) and a shot of sucrose after the other stimulus–response sequence (S2–R2–O2) learned faster than subjects that either always received a food pellet (S1–R1–O1 and S2–R2–O1) or always received a shot of sucrose after both stimulus–response sequences (S1–R1–O2 and S2–R2–O2). Trapold's explanation for this effect was that different learned expectancies developed with differential outcomes, so that when either set of stimuli was presented a specific outcome expectancy was evoked. Differential outcome expectancies thereby facilitated discriminative performance by providing the subject with an additional source of information.

In Trapold's (1970) second experiment, all subjects were again required to make one response in the presence of one set of stimuli to obtain a food pellet (S1–R1–O1) and to make a second response in the presence of a second set of stimuli to obtain a shot of sucrose (S2–R2–O2). But, in this investigation, subjects were first exposed to stimulus–outcome sequences. Subjects pretrained with stimulus–outcome sequences that were consistent with the subsequent discrimination task (i.e., S1–O1 and S2–O2) learned faster than subjects pretrained with inconsistent stimulus–outcome sequences (S1–O2 and S2–O1). Thus, Trapold concluded that the two kinds of pretraining produced discriminably different learned expectancies.

Subsequent to Trapold's (1970) groundbreaking experiments, much additional research has attested to the generality of what has come to be called the differential outcomes effect; that is, performance on delayed discrimination tasks is superior when different trial outcomes are associated with each sample stimulus than when the same outcome is associated with each sample or when different outcomes are randomly associated with the samples. Since Trapold first reported the differential outcomes effect, it has been further investigated in several species, with an assortment of differential outcomes, and using a variety of discrimination procedures. For example, Brodigan and Peterson (1976) studied the effect with pigeons given food and water reinforcers. Other differential outcomes that have been used include corn and wheat (Edwards, Jagielo, Zentall, & Hogan, Experiment 1, 1982), peas and wheat (Edwards, et al., Experiment 2, 1982), and food and a tone (Peterson & Trapold, 1980, 1982; Peterson, Wheeler, & Trapold, 1980). And, Fedorchak and Bolles (1986) used a single outcome (water) that was presented with and without a biologically neutral stimulus (light flash).

The occurrence of the differential outcomes effect also is not restricted to appetitive reinforcers. Overmier, Bull, and Trapold (1971) found that differential locations (left and right hind legs) and qualities (constant and pulsating shock) of aversive outcomes facilitated discriminative performance in dogs. Moreover, it is not even necessary for the outcomes to be qualitatively different from one another. Reinforcers that differ on quantitative dimensions such as magnitude (Carlson & Wielkiewicz, 1976), delay (Carlson & Wielkiewicz, 1972), and spatial location (Williams, Butler, & Overmier, 1990) are also effective in producing the differential outcomes effect. Furthermore, the delayed discrimination task can involve identity matches (e.g., Edwards et al., 1982; Peterson & Trapold, Experiments 1 and 2b, 1980, 1982), mismatches (e.g., Peterson & Trapold, 1980), or symbolic matches (e.g., Brodigan & Peterson, 1976; Peterson & Trapold, Experiments 2a and 3, 1980, 1982; Peterson, Wheeler, & Armstrong, 1978; Peterson, Wheeler, & Trapold, 1980).

Strength of Expectancy Cues

Not only has the existence of learned expectancies received broad empirical support, but there are also data to suggest that learned expectancies may be exceptionally durable and potent memory cues. First, there is evidence that learned expectancy cues are especially effective when a choice test is delayed after the sample stimulus. Brodigan and Peterson (1976) used pigeons that were simultaneously food and water deprived. For half the birds, each sample stimulus was associated with a unique outcome, either food or water; for the other half of the birds, both sample stimuli were equally associated with both food and water. Although the two groups performed similarly when there was no delay between the sample and the test stimuli, the group that received consistent differential outcomes performed more discriminatively than the control group when the choice test was delayed for 3 or 15 s. These and similar findings (e.g., Edwards et al., 1982; Honig, Matheson, & Dodd, 1984; Linwick, Overmier, Peterson, & Mertens, 1988; Peterson et al., 1978, 1980; Williams et al., 1990) imply that learned expectancy cues may persist longer than more conventional cues.

Second, Peterson (1984) compared the extent of the advantage afforded by learned expectancies in a color MTS task and a line MTS task with pigeons.

Using nondifferential reinforcement for matches, the color discrimination was learned more quickly than the line discrimination, and performance reached a higher asymptote on the color problem than on the line problem. In addition, a 1-s delay between the sample and test stimuli more seriously disrupted performance on the line task than on the color task. These findings are consistent with previous research indicating that, for pigeons, lines are more difficult to remember than are colors (e.g., Carter & Eckerman, 1975; Farthing, Wagner, Gilmour, & Waxman, 1977; Nelson & Wasserman, 1981; Urcuioli & Zentall, 1986; Wasserman, Bhatt, Chatlosh, & Kiedinger, 1987). However, when differential outcomes were scheduled in the line matching task, so that learned expectancies could function as discriminative stimuli, the performance differences reported by Peterson disappeared. The fact that learned expectancies were most effective with difficult discriminations suggests that these cues are sometimes stronger than more conventional cues (also see Edwards et al., 1982).

The third kind of evidence for the strength of expectancy cues comes from experiments with various transfer tests. These tests have revealed that discriminative performance is disrupted when the outcomes for previously learned expectancies are reversed, even though the more conventional cues remain intact; conversely, discriminative performance is enhanced when outcome expectancy cues are suddenly made available to subjects whose performance had previously depended solely on more conventional cues (e.g., Honig et al., 1984; Peterson & Trapold, 1982; Peterson et al., 1978).

Fourth, by manipulating both prechoice and postchoice events, Peterson, Linwick, and Overmier (1987) were able to compare directly the effectiveness of learned expectancies and memory traces. When accurate discriminations could be based on either the memory traces of color cues or on differential outcome expectancies, pigeons performed better than when accurate discriminations could be based on either the memory traces of colors or on the memory traces of food and no-food prechoice events. Thus, the authors concluded that outcome expectancies make better mnemonic aids than do additional memory traces.

Further Issues

Although numerous recent findings give credence to the "outcome expectancy theory" (Peterson & Trapold, 1982, p. 572), a myriad of questions remain unanswered. We have not yet fully described the characteristics of learned expectancies nor have we completely specified the conditions favoring their usage. What's more, we cannot yet predict all their behavioral effects, nor can we even be certain whether learned expectancies are behavioral or cognitive mediators of animals' performances on delayed discrimination tasks (but see later discussion). We have addressed some of these issues in our own research, which corroborates and extends several previously reported expectancy effects.

Differential Outcome Probability Expectancies

General Procedure.   The procedures we have used to study learned expectancies with pigeon subjects differ in several ways from those that have thus far been described. Most investigators of the differential outcomes effect have used delayed two-choice discriminations and MTS procedures; however, we used delayed successive MTS procedures (Wasserman, 1976). With two-choice procedures, the subject determines, by its response, whether or not a particular trial ends with a reinforcer; but with successive procedures, the experimenter, not the subject, directly controls the probability of reinforcement on a particular trial. Because of this special feature of successive MTS tasks, we could manipulate outcome probabilities to generate differential learned expectancies and to test subjects' performances on subsequent transfer tasks. Whereas the percentage of correct choices is the typical dependent measure with two-choice procedures, response rates to the singly presented test stimuli are the dependent measures with successive MTS procedures. These response rates are used to form conditional discrimination ratios (DRs) that can range from .5, indicating indiscriminate performance, to 1.0, indicating perfect discrimination.

Symbolic MTS Experiments.   In a prior series of studies, DeLong and Wasserman (1981), using a successive symbolic MTS task, demonstrated that the probability of the occurrence of a single outcome (i.e., food) is yet another quantitative dimension along which differential expectancies can be learned (also see Santi, 1989; Santi & Roberts, 1985a, 1985b; Urcuioli, 1990; Urcuioli & Zentall, 1990). In each of their first pair of experiments (1A and 1B), the typical differential outcomes procedure was used, so that the discriminative performance of four pigeons trained with differential outcome probabilities (Group D) was compared to that of four pigeons trained with nondifferential outcome probabilities (Group ND) across several retention intervals. In Experiment 1A (C–L), the sample stimuli were colors (green and red) and the test stimuli were lines (vertical and slanted). Green-vertical and red-slanted sample-test sequences were designated as positive; thus, green-slanted and red-vertical sequences were negative. In Experiment 1B (L–C), the lines were the sample stimuli and the colors were the test stimuli. Vertical-green and slanted-red sequences were designated as positive; thus, vertical-red and slanted-green sequences were negative.

In both experiments, the conditions for Groups D and ND were exactly the same, except for the different probabilities of reinforcement associated with each positive trial type. For both groups, positive trials sometimes ended in reinforcement and negative trials never did. For Group ND, the individual reinforcement probabilities associated with each positive trial type were both equal to .6. Thus, there was no opportunity for differential outcome expectancies to develop in Group ND. But, for Group D, each of the positive trial types was associated with a different outcome probability, .2 or 1.0. As a result, in Group D, each sample and test stimulus was also associated with a specific outcome probability, either

.1 or .5 (one-half of the trials with a particular stimulus were negative and, thus, never ended in reinforcement). Therefore, it was possible for differential outcome expectancies to develop in Group D. Also, note that the average probability of reinforcement across all trials was the same in both groups (.3).

In accordance with outcome expectancy theory, DeLong and Wasserman (1981) predicted that, because of their association with differential outcome probabilities in Group D, each sample stimulus would come to evoke a specific learned expectancy. This expectancy would then provide subjects in Group D with an extra cue for solving the discrimination. Because of the advantage afforded by this additional redundant cue, Group D was expected to acquire the conditional discrimination faster than Group ND. Indeed, with the more difficult L–C task of Experiment 1B (see previous discussion), the manner in which outcome probabilities were scheduled might even mean the difference between learning the discrimination and not learning the discrimination at all. Moreover, given the prior evidence of the enduring nature of learned expectancies, it was hypothesized that the performance difference between Groups D and ND would expand as the retention interval increased from 0 to 10 s.

Analyses of the conditional DRs revealed the typical differential outcomes effect. When the individual sample stimuli were uniquely associated with different outcome probabilities (Group D), acquisition proceeded more quickly than when the sample stimuli were both associated with the same outcome probability (Group ND; see Fig. 4.1, 4.2). Furthermore, the differential outcomes condition resulted in higher terminal levels of discriminative control than did the non-differential condition. These results suggest that outcome probabilities in a suc-

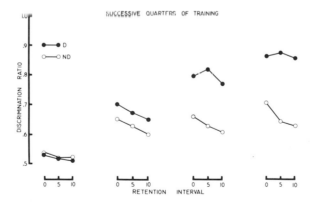

FIG. 4.1. Conditional discrimination performance for differential (D) and nondifferential (ND) reinforcement groups at 0-s, 5-s, 10-s retention intervals across successive quarters of color-line training in Experiment 1A of DeLong and Wasserman (1981). (Each quarter represents a 12-day period.) Copyright (1981) by the American Psychological Association. Reprinted by permission of the publisher.

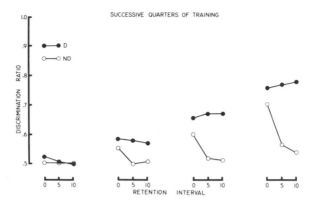

FIG. 4.2. Conditional discrimination performance for differential (D) and nondifferential (ND) reinforcement groups at 0-s, 5-s, and 10-s retention intervals across successive quarters of line-color training in Experiment 1B of DeLong and Wasserman (1981). (Each quarter represents a 30-day period.) Copyright (1981) by the American Psychological Association. Reprinted by permission of the publisher.

cessive symbolic MTS task function much like other properties of reinforcers in choice MTS tasks and thereby extend the generality of the differential outcomes effect to another quantitative dimension of outcomes as well as to another discrimination task. In addition, and again consistent with the results of prior studies, the difference between the discriminative performance of Groups D and ND tended to increase as the retention interval lengthened. This effect was most notable in Experiment 1B due to the particularly poor discriminative performance of Group ND on the L–C task at all but the 0-s retention interval.

In the second experiment, Group D from Experiment 1A (C–L task) received further differential training, but with the outcome probabilities for the two positive sample-test sequences reversed. In prior studies, conditional discrimination performance was seriously disrupted when qualitatively different reinforcers were similarly reversed under two-choice discrimination procedures (e.g., Peterson et al., 1978; Peterson & Trapold, 1982). According to outcome expectancy theory, subjects originally trained with differential outcomes come to rely on cues provided by learned expectancies; when the outcomes are reversed, these learned expectancies are no longer useful cues, and thus, conditional discrimination performance deteriorates. The theoretical impact of this outcome reversal effect lies in the fact that alternative explanations for the differential outcomes effect do not predict a disruption of performance. For example, if discriminative performance relies only on retrospective memory, reversing outcomes should have little influence on responding because during both original training and reversal training the same sample-test sequences are followed by reinforcement.

Consistent with outcome expectancy theory, DeLong and Wasserman (1981) found that not only did discriminative performance rapidly decrease immediately following the outcome reversal, but also that the amount of the decrease grew with longer retention intervals (see Fig. 4.3). Moreover, as reversal training progressed and new expectancies were supposedly being learned, discriminative performance improved, but the longer the retention interval, the slower the recovery.

The third experiment in the series was designed primarily to pursue the possibility that overt response mediation, in the form of sample-specific responding, was responsible for the differential outcomes effect. DeLong and Wasserman (1981) observed that, quite separate from their differential test keypeck rates, and although not required, subjects trained with differential outcome probabilities also exhibited differential sample keypeck rates; that is, subjects responded more to the sample stimulus associated with the higher outcome probability than to the sample stimulus associated with the lower outcome probability. We already know that specifically training animals to respond differentially to the sample stimuli in a conditional discrimination task facilitates their performance (e.g., Cohen, Looney, Brady, & Aucella, 1976; Lydersen & Perkins, 1974; Urcuioli & Honig, 1980; Zentall, Hogan, Howard, & Moore, 1978). Thus, it was certainly possible that the sample-specific behavior that spontaneously developed in groups trained with differential outcome probabilities in Experiments 1 and 2 mediated the retention intervals and enhanced discriminative performance.

The training conditions for Groups D and ND of Experiment 3 were identical to those of Experiment 1A, with the exception of 20 trials added to each session during which sample responses were occasionally immediately reinforced with

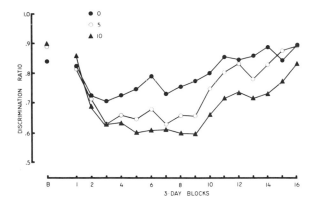

FIG. 4.3. Conditional discrimination performance in Experiment 2 of De Long and Wasserman (1981) at 0-s, 5-s, and 10-s retention intervals over 3-day training blocks. (Baseline [B] corresponds to performance on the 3 days just prior to the reversal of reinforcement probabilities.) Copyright (1981) by the American Psychological Association. Reprinted by permission of the publisher.

food. This manipulation minimized the difference between sample response rates in Group D. Yet, despite the lack of sample-specific responding, Group D consistently performed better than Group ND at 5-s and 10-s retention intervals, a finding that implies that sample-specific response rates were, at least, not critical to the general differential outcomes effect (see Fig. 4.4). Of course, whether or not other unobserved sample-specific responses mediated the delays of the conditional discrimination in Group D could not be determined.

To recapitulate, DeLong and Wasserman's (1981) experiments demonstrated that: (a) the differential outcomes effect generalizes to a successive symbolic MTS task; (b) outcome probabilities can be used to produce differential training conditions; (c) like other learned expectancies, differential outcome probability expectancies are most effective as sources of stimulus control when there is a delay between sample and test stimuli; (d) like outcome qualities, reversal of outcome probabilities following differential training temporarily disrupts conditional discrimination performance; and (e) at least with the successive symbolic MTS paradigm, sample-specific response rates do not fully explain the differential outcomes effect. All these findings are consistent with outcome expectancy theory.

Identity MTS Experiments. In a recent series of experiments, we replicated some of DeLong and Wasserman's (1981) findings with an identity MTS procedure, and we tested several other predictions of outcome expectancy theory by examining performance on additional transfer tasks. Again, a successive MTS

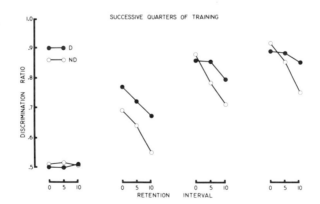

FIG. 4.4. Conditional discrimination performance for differential (D) and nondifferential reinforcement groups at 0-s, 5-s, and 10-s retention intervals across successive quarters of color-line training with reinforced sample key pecking in Experiment 3 of DeLong and Wasserman (1981). (Each quarter represents a 9-day period.) Copyright (1981) by the American Psychological Association. Reprinted by permission of the publisher.

procedure was used, in which matches were probabilistically reinforced and nonmatches were never reinforced. However, in these experiments, both the sample and the test stimuli were blue (B) and violet (V) keylights. Positive trials involved sample-test identity matches (i.e., B–B and V–V); negative trials involved nonmatches (i.e., B–V and V–B).

In the first experiment, we were primarily interested in extending the generality of the differential outcomes effect to the successive identity MTS procedure. Given that DeLong and Wasserman's (1981) symbolic MTS task involved both color and line stimuli, which are not equally discriminable for pigeons (see previous discussion), we felt it was important to replicate their findings using all color stimuli. Thus, other than using a slightly different set of retention intervals (i.e., 1-s, 5-s, and 10-s rather than 0-s, 5-s, and 10-s), different colors as sample stimuli (blue and violet rather than green and red), and the same colors as test stimuli, the procedure essentially duplicated that of Experiment 1A in the DeLong and Wasserman (1981) series (see Table 4.1).

Eight naive pigeons were divided into two groups: Group D and Group ND. Group D was trained under differential outcome conditions and Group ND was trained under nondifferential outcome conditions. Food reinforcement probabilities following the two types of positive trial sequences (i.e., B–B and V–V) in Group D were .2 and 1.0. (These outcome probabilities were counterbalanced for positive trial types.) Thus, each sample stimulus was uniquely associated with a different probability of reinforcement, .1 or .5. In Group ND, the probability of reinforcement for both positive trial types was again .6, so that the overall probability of reinforcement was the same (.3) in the two groups.

At the start of each trial, a flash of the houselight signaled the onset of a B or V sample stimulus presented on the center response key of a standard pigeon chamber. The first keypeck after 5 s terminated the sample stimulus and was followed by a 1–s, 5–s, or 10–s retention interval, during which no events were scheduled. When the retention interval timed out, a B or V test stimulus was

TABLE 4.1
Trial Sequences in Successive Matching-to-Sample Task

Trial Sequence/Trial Possibilities	1	2	3	4
Sample stimulus (5 s)	B	B	V	V
Retention interval (1, 5, or 10 s)	-	-	-	-
Test stimulus (5 s)	B	V	B	V
Probability of reinforcement				
Group D[a]	.2	0	0	1.0
Group ND	.6	0	0	.6

Note. B = blue, V = violet
[a]The probability of reinforcement for positive trial sequences 1 and 4 was counterbalanced within Group D. From DeLong and Wasserman (1981) by the American Psychological Association. Reprinted by permission of the publisher.

presented on the center response key. On positive trials, the first peck to the test stimulus after 5 s terminated it and was sometimes followed by 3-s access to mixed grain, according to the preset probabilities. On negative trials, the test stimulus was automatically terminated after 5 s and was followed by a 3-s blackout. The four trial types (B–B, B–V, V–B, V–V) were presented with each of the three retention intervals (1-s, 5-s, 10-s) five times per session. Conditional discrimination ratios were computed with response rates during the first 5 s of test stimulus presentations for successive 3-day blocks of training. Overall conditional DRs were obtained for each retention interval by averaging across two component ratios that represent performance on each positive trial type. For example, the component DR for B–B positive sequences was the test response rate on B–B trials divided by the sum of the test response rates on B–B and V–B trials, and the component DR for V–V positive sequences was the test response rate on V–V trials divided by the sum of the test response rates on V–V and B–V trials. The mean of these two component DRs was used as an overall measure of discriminative performance. As usual, these DRs could range from .5, indicating indiscriminate performance, to 1.0, indicating perfect discrimination.

The DRs indicated that, whereas Group D acquired the MTS task at all three retention intervals, Group ND showed little evidence of acquisition with 5-s and 10-s retention intervals, and only moderate increases in discriminative control with 1–s retention intervals (see Fig. 4.5). As was true of prior findings, these results are also compatible with the idea that in Group D the sample stimuli

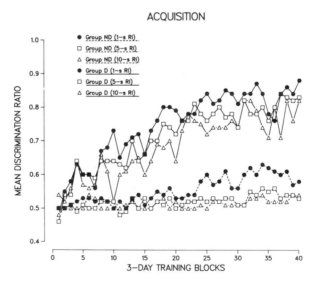

FIG. 4.5. Conditional discrimination performance for differential (D) and nondifferential (ND) reinforcement groups at 1-s, 5-s, and 10-s retention intervals (RIs) over 3-day training blocks in Experiment 1.

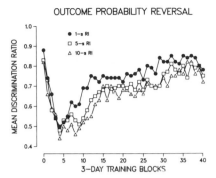

FIG. 4.6. Conditional discrimination performance in Experiment 2 at 1-s, 5-s, and 10-s retention intervals (RIs) over 3-day training blocks. (Block O represents performance on the 3 days just prior to the reversal of reinforcement probabilities.)

activated specific learned expectancies that functioned as supplementary cues, giving these subjects a distinct advantage over subjects in Group ND.

Experiment 2 replicated the outcome reversal effect that DeLong and Wasserman (1981) obtained with the symbolic MTS task; that is, Group D of Experiment 1 received further differential training, but with the outcome probabilities for B–B and V–V trials reversed. Once again, the data were consistent with outcome expectancy theory. Reversing the reinforcement probabilities associated with the sample stimuli initially had a debilitating effect on discriminative performance, but as new expectancies were learned, there was a gradual return of stimulus control (see Fig. 4.6). Thus, subjects in Group D were, indeed, relying on cues provided by learned outcome expectancies. In addition, overall conditional discrimination performance was worse at longer retention intervals. This retention interval effect is especially interesting in light of the fact that no reliable retention interval differences existed in the last block of training in Experiment 1. Thus, specific learned expectancies may well exert more stimulus control at longer retention intervals.

If learned expectancies truly function in a manner similar to more conventional external cues in controlling behavior, then we would expect the effects of nondifferential pretraining to be comparable to those of irrelevancy pretraining (Mackintosh, 1973); that is, subjects might learn to ignore expectancy cues when they provide no predictive information. If subjects receiving nondifferential pretraining are later switched to a training condition in which sample stimuli are now differentially correlated with reinforcement, learned irrelevancy of expectancy information might impede their utilization of these new cues in solving the discrimination. Experiment 3 addressed this issue by giving Group ND of Experiment 1 continued training, but now with different reinforcement probabilities associated with each of the sample stimuli. Because these were the same probabilities as those for Group D of Experiment 1, a comparison of the performances of these two groups would indicate whether nondifferential pretraining produced any proactive interference. Conditional DRs indicated that, although performance generally improved across blocks of training, the rate of improvement was slower for animals with prior nondifferential training than for animals that had not received prior training (see Fig. 4.7). Overall, there was a tendency for the 5-s and 10-s retention intervals to control lower levels of performance for only the pretrained subjects.

Thus, prior experience with nondifferential reinforcement probabilities retarded the rate of conditional discrimination improvement. Moreover, this is a particularly cogent demonstration of negative transfer, given that the pretrained group received twice as many training sessions as did the group exposed to differential reinforcement probabilities from the outset. These results, too, are difficult to explain without appealing to outcome expectancy theory.

According to outcome expectancy theory, once subjects have learned to capitalize on differential expectancy cues, altering these expectancies should disrupt discriminative performance. We demonstrated this predicted disruption in Experiment 2 by reversing the different outcome probabilities associated with the individual sample stimuli. In Experiment 4, instead of reversing the differential expectancy cues, we eliminated them. Following the differential training phase

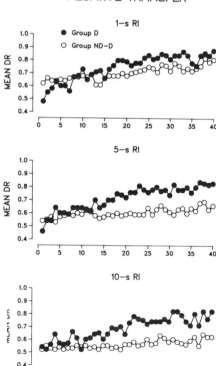

FIG. 4.7. Conditional discrimination performance during differential reinforcement training for groups receiving prior nondifferential reinforcement training (ND-D) or no prior training (D) at 1-s, 5-s, and 10-s retention intervals (RIs) over 3-day training blocks in Experiment 3.

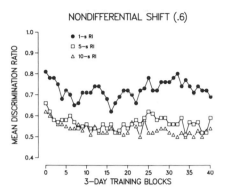

FIG. 4.8. Conditional discrimination performance in Experiment 4 at 1-s, 5-s, and 10-s retention intervals (RIs) over 3-day training blocks. (Block O represents performance on the 3 days just prior to the shift to nondifferential reinforcement.)

of Experiment 3, Group ND was returned to its original training conditions, in which both positive trial sequences produced reinforcement with a probability of .6. As expected, conditional DRs indicated an initial loss of discriminative control, and that test performance was generally worse at longer retention intervals (see Fig. 4.8).

Finally, because our data thus far had consistently demonstrated the beneficial effects of differential reinforcement probability cues, we decided to investigate their efficacy more directly in Experiment 5. A very stringent test of the effects of differential expectancy cue elimination would be to increase the overall probability of reinforcement for positive trial sequences. Group D, originally given differential training and then exposed to the outcome reversal manipulation, was now shifted to a nondifferential training condition in which reinforcement was delivered after all positive trial sequences. Thus, this training procedure entailed an increase in the probability of reinforcement from .2 to 1.0 for one positive trial type, whereas for the other positive trial type the probability of reinforcement remained 1.0. Although the average probability of reinforcement for positive trials increased by 67% with this manipulation, the extra reinforcement was ineffective in overcoming the detrimental effects of eliminating the differential expectancy cues (see Fig. 4.9). Conditional discrimination performance worsened when subjects were shifted to nondifferential training, with performance particularly poor at 5-s and 10-s retention intervals.

To summarize, our recent series of results support the assertion that differential reinforcement probabilities produced learned expectancies that helped to mediate the delays in the successive identity MTS task on four counts. First, when sample stimuli were differentially correlated with reinforcement, acquisition of the discrimination was facilitated. Second, reversing the differential reinforcement probabilities associated with the two sample stimuli disrupted discriminative performance. Third, experience with nondifferential reinforcement probabilities produced negative transfer when subjects were subsequently trained with differential reinforcement probabilities. And fourth, eliminating differential

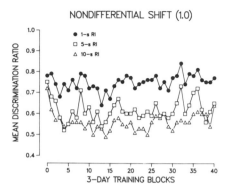

FIG. 4.9. Conditional discrimination performance in Experiment 5 at 1-s, 5-s, and 10-s retention intervals (RIs) over 3-day training blocks. (Block O represents performance on the 3 days just prior to the shift to nondifferential reinforcement.)

reinforcement cues caused a loss of discriminative control, notwithstanding an increase in the overall reinforcement rate.

CONCLUDING REMARKS

An abundance of evidence from differential outcome experiments suggests that outcome expectancy cues appreciably enhance the memorability of significant stimuli. Not only has the differential outcomes procedure been instrumental in the substantiation of the potency and durability of outcome expectancy cues, but researchers continue to incorporate the basic procedure into more complex experimental designs. For example, Santi and Roberts (1985a) recently examined performance differences with differential and nondifferential outcomes on "many-to-one" and "one-to-many" MTS tasks. One of the things they discovered was that the typical differential outcomes effect generalized to the atypical "one-to-many" discrimination. This result suggests that outcome expectancies may mediate responding to more than one correct test stimulus. As previously mentioned, Peterson and his colleagues (Linwick et al., 1988; Peterson, Linwick, & Overmier, 1987) have also used the differential outcomes procedure in novel ways. By manipulating both prechoice and postchoice events, they were able to compare the extent to which expectancies and memories acquire and maintain control over behavior on a delayed discrimination task. Although expectancies were more effective discriminative stimuli than were memories, both cues were thought to be simultaneously influencing discriminative performance. However, the precise nature of this influence has yet to be determined (e.g., see Santi, 1989; Urcuioli, 1990). In any case, research on the differential outcomes effect is likely to continue to provide provocative information about short-term memory processes.

Yet, outcome expectancies are not the only anticipatory processes that may mediate delayed discrimination performance. Prior research indicates that response expectancy cues can also facilitate short-term retention (e.g., Chatlosh & Wasserman, 1987; Honig & Dodd, 1983; Honig & Wasserman, 1981; Smith, 1967; for an alternative explanation under successive discrimination procedures, see Urcuioli & Zentall, 1990). And, it is likely that anticipation of other trial characteristics, such as the duration of the retention interval (Wasserman, Grosch, & Nevin, 1982), influence discriminative performance as well (for a review, see Honig & Dodd, 1986). All these anticipatory mechanisms presumably reflect prospective memory processes.

Thus, we are no longer inquiring whether short-term memory is a prospective or a retrospective process. Clearly, both memory mechanisms are important to delayed discrimination performance. Indeed, as others have suggested (e.g., Grant, 1982; Urcuioli & Zentall, 1986), it is probable that animals, like people, are flexible information processors and that they use the most reliable and simple means available to remember significant stimuli. Therefore, the task that lies ahead involves specifying the conditions that give rise to each individual memory process or to both memory processes. Although we may or may not ultimately determine that one process is more important than the other, we must surely conclude that animal short-term memory is much more flexible and complex than was once thought.

REFERENCES

Bolles, R. C. (1972). Reinforcement, expectancy, and learning. *Psychological Review, 79,* 394–409.

Brodigan, D. L., & Peterson, G. B. (1976). Two-choice conditional discrimination performance of pigeons as a function of reward expectancy, prechoice delay, and domesticity. *Animal Learning and Behavior, 4,* 121–124.

Carlson, J. G., & Wielkiewicz, R. M. (1972). Delay of reinforcement in instrumental discrimination learning of rats. *Journal of Comparative and Physiological Psychology, 81,* 365–370.

Carlson, J. G., & Wielkiewicz, R. M. (1976). Mediators of the effects of magnitude of reinforcement. *Learning and Motivation, 7,* 184–196.

Carter, D. E., & Eckerman, D. A. (1975). Symbolic matching by pigeons: Rate of learning complex discriminations predicted from simple discriminations. *Science, 187,* 662–664.

Chatlosh, D. L., & Wasserman, E. A. (1987). Delayed temporal discrimination in pigeons: A comparison of two procedures. *Journal of the Experimental Analysis of Behavior, 47,* 299–309.

Cohen, L. R., Looney, T. A., Brady, J. H., & Aucella, A. F. (1976). Differential sample response schedules in the acquisition of conditional discriminations by pigeons. *Journal of the Experimental Analysis of Behavior, 26,* 301–314.

DeLong, R. E., & Wasserman, E. A. (1981). Effects of differential reinforcement expectancies on successive matching-to-sample performance in pigeons. *Journal of Experimental Psychology: Animal Behavior Processes, 7,* 394–412.

Edwards, C. A., Jagielo, J. A., Zentall, T. R., & Hogan, D. E. (1982). Acquired equivalence and distinctiveness in matching to sample by pigeons: Mediation by reinforcer-specific expectancies. *Journal of Experimental Psychology: Animal Behavior Processes, 8,* 244–259.

Farthing, G. W., Wagner, J. M., Gilmour, S., & Waxman, H. M. (1977). Short-term memory and information processing in pigeons. *Learning and Motivation, 8,* 520–532.

Fedorchak, P. M., & Bolles, R. C. (1986). Differential outcome effect using a biologically neutral outcome difference. *Journal of Experimental Psychology: Animal Behavior Processes, 12,* 125–130.

Grant, D. S. (1982). Prospective versus retrospective coding of samples of stimuli, responses, and reinforcers in delayed matching with pigeons. *Learning and Motivation, 13,* 265–280.

Honig, W. K., & Dodd, P. W. D. (1983). Delayed discriminations in the pigeon: The role of within-trial location of conditional cues. *Animal Learning and Behavior, 11,* 1–9.

Honig, W. K., & Dodd, P. W. D. (1986). Anticipation and intention in working memory. In D. F. Kendrick, M. E. Rilling, & M. R. Denny (Eds.), *Theories of animal memory* (pp. 77–100). Hillsdale, NJ: Lawrence Erlbaum Associates.

Honig, W. K., Matheson, W. R., & Dodd, P. W. D. (1984). Outcome expectancies as mediators for discriminative responding. *Canadian Journal of Psychology, 38,* 196–217.

Honig, W. K., & Thompson, R. K. R. (1982). Retrospective and prospective processing in animal working memory. In G. H. Bower (Ed.), *The psychology of learning and motivation* (pp. 239–283). New York: Academic Press.

Honig, W. K., & Wasserman, E. A. (1981). Performance of pigeons on delayed simple and conditional discriminations under equivalent training procedures. *Learning and Motivation, 12,* 149–170.

Kraemer, P. J., & Roberts, W. A. (1984). Short-term memory for visual and auditory stimuli in pigeons. *Animal Learning and Behavior, 12,* 275–284.

Linwick, D., Overmier, J. B., Peterson, G. B., & Mertens, M. (1988). Interaction of memories and expectancies as mediators of choice behavior. *American Journal of Psychology, 101,* 313–334.

Lydersen, T., & Perkins, D. (1974). Effects of response-produced stimuli upon conditional discrimination performance. *Journal of the Experimental Analysis of Behavior, 21,* 307–314.

Mackintosh, N. J. (1973). Stimulus selection: Learning to ignore stimuli that predict no change in reinforcement. In R. A. Hinde & J. Stevenson-Hinde (Eds.), *Constraints on learning* (pp. 75–96). London: Academic Press.

Nelson, K. R., & Wasserman, E. A. (1978). Temporal factors influencing the pigeon's successive matching-to-sample performance: Sample duration, intertrial interval, and retention interval. *Journal of the Experimental Analysis of Behavior, 30,* 153–162.

Nelson, K. R., & Wasserman, E. A. (1981). Stimulus asymmetry in the pigeon's successive matching-to-sample performance. *Bulletin of the Psychonomic Society, 18,* 343–346.

Overmier, J. B., Bull, J. A., III, & Trapold, M. A. (1971). Discriminative cue properties of different fears and their role in response selection in dogs. *Journal of Comparative and Physiological Psychology, 76,* 478–482.

Peterson, G. B. (1984). The differential outcomes procedure: A paradigm for studying how expectancies guide behavior. In H. L. Roitblat, T. G. Bever, H. S. Terrace (Eds.), *Animal cognition* (pp. 135–148). Hillsdale, NJ: Lawrence Erlbaum Associates.

Peterson, G. B., Linwick, D., & Overmier, J. B. (1987). On the comparative efficacy of memories and expectancies as cues for choice behavior in pigeons. *Learning and Motivation, 18,* 1–20.

Peterson, G. B., & Trapold, M. A. (1980). Effects of altering outcome expectancies on pigeons' delayed conditional discrimination performance. *Learning and Motivation, 11,* 267–288.

Peterson, G. B., & Trapold, M. A. (1982). Expectancy mediation of concurrent conditional discriminations. *American Journal of Psychology, 95,* 571–580.

Peterson, G. B., Wheeler, R. L., & Armstrong, G. D. (1978). Expectancies as mediators in the differential-reward conditional discrimination performance of pigeons. *Animal Learning and Behavior, 6,* 279–285.

Peterson, G. B., Wheeler, R. L., & Trapold, M. A. (1980). Enhancement of pigeons' conditional discrimination performance by expectancies of reinforcement and nonreinforcement. *Animal Learning and Behavior, 8,* 22–30.

Roberts, W. A. (1972). Short-term memory in the pigeon: Effects of repetition and spacing. *Journal of Experimental Psychology, 94,* 74–83.

Roberts, W. A., & Grant, D. S. (1974). Short-term memory in the pigeon with presentation time precisely controlled. *Learning and Motivation, 5,* 393–408.

Roberts, W. A., & Grant, D. S. (1976). Studies of short-term memory in the pigeon using the delayed matching-to-sample procedure. In D. L. Medin, W. A. Roberts, & R. T. Davis (Eds.), *Processes of animal memory* (pp. 79–112). Hillsdale, NJ: Lawrence Erlbaum Associates.

Roitblat, H. L. (1980). Codes and coding processes in pigeon short-term memory. *Animal Learning and Behavior, 8,* 341–351.

Santi, A. (1989). Differential outcome expectancies and directed forgetting effects in pigeons. *Animal Learning and Behavior, 17,* 349–354.

Santi, A., & Roberts, W. A. (1985a). Prospective representation: The effects of varied mapping of sample stimuli to comparison stimuli and differential trial outcomes on pigeons' working memory. *Animal Learning and Behavior, 13,* 103–108.

Santi, A., & Roberts, W. A. (1985b). Reinforcement expectancy and trial spacing effects in delayed matching to sample by pigeons. *Animal Learning and Behavior, 13,* 274–284.

Smith, L. (1967). Delayed discrimination and delayed matching in pigeons. *Journal of the Experimental Analysis of Behavior, 10,* 529–533.

Tolman, E. C. (1932). *Purposive behavior in animals and men.* New York: Appleton-Century.

Trapold, M. A. (1970). Are expectancies based upon different positive reinforcing events discriminably different? *Learning and Motivation, 1,* 129–140.

Trapold, M. A., & Overmier, J. B. (1972). The second learning process in instrumental learning. In A. H. Black & W. F. Prokasy (Eds.), *Classical conditioning II: Current research and theory* (pp. 427–452). New York: Appleton-Century-Crofts.

Urcuioli, P. J. (1990). Some relationships between outcome expectancies and sample stimuli in pigeons' delayed matching. *Animal Learning and Behavior, 18,* 302–314.

Urcuioli, P. J., & Honig, W. K. (1980). Control of choice in conditional discrimination by sample-specific behaviors. *Journal of Experimental Psychology: Animal Behavior Processes, 6,* 251–277.

Urcuioli, P. J., & Zentall, T. R. (1986). Retrospective coding in pigeons' delayed matching-to-sample. *Journal of Experimental Psychology: Animal Behavior Processes, 12,* 69–77.

Urcuioli, P. J., & Zentall, T. R. (1990). On the role of trial outcomes in delayed discriminations. *Animal Learning and Behavior, 18,* 141–150.

Wasserman, E. A. (1976). Successive matching to sample in the pigeon: Variations on a theme by Konorski. *Behavior Research Methods and Instrumentation, 8,* 278–282.

Wasserman, E. A. (1986). Prospection and retrospection as processes of animal short-term memory. In D. F. Kendrick, M. E. Rilling, & M. R. Denny (Eds.), *Theories of animal memory* (pp. 53–75). Hillsdale, NJ: Lawrence Erlbaum Associates.

Wasserman, E. A., Bhatt, R. S., Chatlosh, D. L., & Kiedinger, R. E. (1987). Discrimination of and memory for dimension and value information by pigeons. *Learning and Motivation, 18,* 34–56.

Wasserman, E. A., Grosch, J., & Nevin, J. A. (1982). Effects of signalled retention intervals on pigeon short-term memory. *Animal Learning and Behavior, 10,* 330–338.

Williams, D. A., Butler, M. M., & Overmier, J. B. (1990). Expectancies of reinforcer location and quality as cues for a conditional discrimination in pigeons. *Journal of Experimental Psychology: Animal Behavior Processes, 16,* 3–13.

Zentall, T. R., Hogan, D. E., Howard, M. M., & Moore, B. S. (1978). Delayed matching in the pigeon: Effect on performance of sample-specific observing responses and differential delay behavior. *Learning and Motivation, 9,* 202–218.

5
Preference for Unpredictability is Reversed When Unpredictable Nonreward is Aversive: Procedures, Data, and Theories of Appetitive Observing Response Acquisition

Helen B. Daly
State University of New York College at Oswego

Pretend that you buy a lottery ticket every Friday. You soon discover that there are two types of tickets: a blue one and an orange one. Both types have a label that you can peel off. The words, YOU WIN, or the words, YOU LOSE, are written under the label on the blue ticket. The word, MAYBE, is written under the label on the orange ticket. Both tickets cost the same amount, the size of the prize is the same, the probability of winning is the same (e.g., 50%), and if you win you do not receive the prize until the following Friday for either ticket. Which ticket would you buy? Now pretend that one of your parents has died of Huntingston's chorea. This is an incurable disease that occurs in middle age and leads to a slow and agonizing death. If one of your parents had Huntingston's chorea, you have a 50% chance of carrying the gene and definitely becoming ill. There is a test to determine if you carry the gene. Would you take the test and ask for the results?

What these two examples have in common is a choice between an unpredictable versus a predictable situation. The first is an example of an appetitive reward, the second of an aversive reward. Wyckoff (1952) was one of the first to study these preferences and called them observing response experiments, because he showed that pigeons would step on a pedal to "observe" the stimuli that predicted reward outcome. Several hundred studies have been done to determine the variables that influence the magnitude of the preference, and at least 11 theories have been developed to account for the preference. The purpose of this chapter is to provide a partial review of the appetitive observing response literature,[1] and discuss the shortcomings of many of the experimental procedures used to study preference for predictability. A theory (DMOD) that predicts that subjects will prefer unpredictable appetitive rewards under certain conditions is also reviewed. Studies that support these predictions, as well as how other theories have trouble integrating these results, are described.

Experimental Analogs of the Lottery Example

There are four experimental observing response procedures that are similar to the lottery example: the E maze for rats developed by Perkins (1955; Prokasy, 1956), a two-key choice procedure for pigeons developed by Bower (Bower, McClean, & Meacham, 1966), the three-lever procedure for rats used by McMichael, Lanzetta, and Driscoll (1967), and a three-key nose-poke procedure for rats developed by Daly (unpublished). Of these four procedures the E maze is the most used, and a diagram appears in Fig. 5.1. The hungry rat is placed into the startbox and has a choice of turning right or left at the choice point. Following either choice, a black or a white insert (floor and side walls) is present in the delay chamber. These colors are not visible until the choice is made, and a door is closed behind the rat to prevent selection of the other choice once a color has been seen. On one side of the maze, the colors predict the reward outcome: Black is paired with food in the goalbox (called the S+ stimulus), white is paired with no food (called the S− stimulus), and each color is presented on 50% of the trials (predictable reward side, a simple discrimination schedule). On the other side both colors are followed by food on 50% of the trials (unpredictable reward side, a partial reinforcement schedule). In this procedure, the rat must learn that black on the right means food, black on the left means maybe food, white on the right means no food, white on the left means maybe food. This is called the difficult observing response discrimination procedure or configure condition. In some studies, the unpredictable reward side is gray on every trial, and food is given on a random half of the trials (called the S+/− stimulus). This is the simple observing response discrimination procedure. Which side has the predictable stimuli, and which color is associated with reward are counterbalanced across subjects. In some experiments, subjects are delayed in the delay chamber for 15 seconds; in other experiments, all the doors are open and the subject can run straight into the goalbox. The doors are closed behind the rat to prevent retracing. The rats are typically given eight trials per day,

---

[1]I apologize to those researchers whose studies I had to omit due to space limitations.

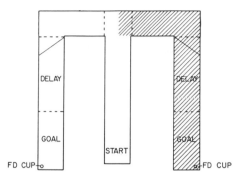

FIG. 5.1. Floorplan of the E-maze apparatus (---- represents doors; //// represents wire mesh floor). Black, white, or gray inserts are placed into the delay and goalboxes, which are not visible at the choice-point.

where the first four are free-choice trials, and on the fifth trial they are forced to the side not selected on the first trial, on the sixth trial to the side not selected on the second trial, etc. The forced trials are given to equate experience with reward and nonreward in the predictable and unpredictable situation. The probability of reward is equal on both sides (50%), the size of the reward is the same, the amount of effort required to go to the predictable or unpredictable reward side is equal, and the choice cannot be reversed. The only difference between the sides is whether the stimuli present predict reward outcome or not (see Daly, 1985, 1989, for additional details).

In the Daly three-key nose-poke computer-controlled procedure for rats, a center key (a 2.6 cm diameter Coulbourn pigeon key) must be pressed once to turn on the two side keys. One press on one side key results in a click or tone, and these stimuli are correlated with reward outcome. A press on the other side key results in a bright or dim light, and these stimuli are both uncorrelated with reward outcome. Food pellets are delivered 2 (immediate) or 15 (delayed) seconds later, independent of any response. The same combination of free- and forced-choice trials are given as in the E maze procedure (on forced trials only one side key is turned on), and which side and which stimuli are correlated with reward are totally counterbalanced across subjects.

In the Bower keypeck procedure for pigeons, two side keys with a horizontal or vertical bar are turned on (side is random on each trial). A peck on one key turns on either a green or a red light, and these stimuli are correlated with reward delay (fixed interval 40 or 10 seconds). A peck on the other key turns on a yellow light, and reward delay is unpredictable (in Experiment 4 they used the configure condition, and the green and red lights were used in the uncorrelated condition also). Bower et al. equated experience with both choices by giving all forced trials until the final free-choice test phase.

There are three retractible levers in the McMichael procedure. The rat first has a choice of two levers. A press on one lever turns on either a bright or a dim light, and these stimuli are correlated with reward outcome. A press on the other lever turns on a noise that is uncorrelated with reward outcome. The rat must then press a bar on the other side of the chamber to obtain the reward. On forced trials, only one choice lever is introduced, and a combination of free and forced trials are used to equate reward experience in the predictable and unpredictable situation.

Control of the Four RCs

The important aspect of the four observing response procedures just described is that all conditions are the same following the two choices, except whether the stimuli are correlated with reward outcome or not. As Bower et al. (1966) pointed out, "the advance information is 'useless' in the sense that the delivery time is predetermined and S [subject] can do nothing to modify it" (p. 184). Wyckoff (1952) said "we adopt the term 'observing response' (Ro) to refer to any response which results in exposure to the pair of discriminative stimuli involved" (p. 431). Hirota (1974) stated that "observing responses are defined as those that result in exposure to discriminative stimuli but that have no effect on the probability of reinforcement" (p. 259).

There are additional procedures that researchers call observing response experiments, but one must be careful not to classify them all into one category: Different processes may be involved in the choice behavior, and there may be simpler explanations for the preferences obtained in some of these procedures. To be a "pure" observing response experiment, I argue that the four RCs must be controlled for: response cost, response competition, response changeover, and response choice. The four "pure" procedures described earlier control for the four RCs. Some of the other "observing response" procedures do not control for them.

1. Response Cost.   This refers to the effort required to obtain the stimuli correlated or not correlated with reward outcome. Response cost is equal in the four "pure" procedures: A turn to the left or right in the E maze, a press on the right or left key, requires the same effort. There are some procedures where a response is required to turn on the stimuli correlated with reward outcome. If no response is made, the subject remains in the unpredictable situation; there is zero response cost to remain in the unpredictable situation. For example, if the subject does not step on a pedal in the Wyckoff (1969) procedure, the response key remains white and rewards are unpredictable, but if the pigeon steps on a pedal, then the light changes to red or green (see also Hirota, 1972; Zeigler & Wyckoff, 1961).

Some procedures require several responses to obtain the stimuli correlated with reward outcome, and it is especially important to control for response cost when effort is high. For example, Wilton and Clements (1971) required pigeons to complete a fixed interval (FI) 15-second schedule to obtain the stimuli, but no response to remain in the unpredictable situation. Kelleher, Riddle, and Cook (1962) required pigeons to complete a fixed ratio (FR) schedule. Response rate on the observing response key was high on an FR 1 schedule but decreased as the FR requirement was increased. The concurrent chains procedure (e.g., Fantino, 1977, pp. 327–328) requires the subject to complete a variable interval (VI) schedule to obtain the stimuli correlated or uncorrelated with reward outcome. Hursh and Fantino (1974) showed that response cost, even if it is equal, is important, because preference for predictability was higher on a VI 60-second than on a VI 15-second schedule.

One can also have differential response cost in the presence of the stimuli correlated and uncorrelated with reward outcome. For example, Kelleher et al. (1962) reinforced subjects on a VR 100 schedule. They noted that pecks occurred when the stimulus signaling reinforcement on the VR 100 schedule was on, but "if observing responses produced the negative stimulus, the bird paused until the red stimulus went off" (p. 6). Therefore, if the response cost to obtain food is high, one can reduce this cost by choosing predictable rewards and not respond on S− trials (see also Fantino & Case, 1983). The Daly nose-poke procedure does not have this second type of response cost confound, because there is no response required. In the E maze, rats are required to enter the goalbox on all trials, so response cost is equal.

2. Response Competition. This refers to the competition between making the response to obtain the stimuli correlated with reward outcome and the response to obtain food. There is no response competition in the four "pure" procedures, because the observing response choice is made before the response to obtain food. Some procedures require the subject to choose between responding on a key that results in food and responding on a key that turns on the stimuli. If the subject responds on the stimulus key, the reinforcement could be delayed. Kelleher et al. (1962) noted that "in the presence of the mixed stimulus, the disposition to respond to the observing key was in competition with the disposition to respond on the food-producing key" (p. 12).

One must also be careful that the opposite problem does not occur. Hirota (1972) replicated Wyckoff's procedure and showed that Wyckoff had placed the pedal (observing response) so close to the food key that if the pigeon pressed the key he had to step on the pedal: "The correlation between key-response rates and pedal standing time occurs as a result of the physical relationship between key and pedal" (p. 275).

3. Response Choice. This refers to a possible inbalance in experiences with reward and nonreward in the predictable and unpredictable situation. If the absolute number of rewarded and nonrewarded trials is not equated, then slight preferences for either the predictable or unpredictable choice could be magnified into large ones because the subject is receiving most of its rewards following that choice. Unfortunately, most procedures used to study preference for predictability do not control for response choice. Response choice is equated in the four "pure" procedures by using forced trials to equate experience with reward and nonreward on the predictable and unpredictable reward side.

4. Response Changeover.   This refers to the procedure that allows the subject to escape from the stimulus correlated with nonreward in the predictable situation and to return to the unpredictable situation. The four "pure" procedures control response changeover: Subjects cannot escape from the stimulus correlated with nonreward and return to the side where rewards are unpredictable. If response changeover is allowed, then the subject can avoid all nonreinforced trials on the predictable side, thus creating an imbalance in the number of rewarded and nonrewarded trials experienced in the predictable and unpredictable sides. The Wyckoff procedure and similar techniques used by Dinsmoor (1983) allow the subject to escape from the stimulus correlated with nonreward and return to the unpredictable stimuli. Harsh, Badia, and Ryan (1983) showed that response changeover (noncommitment procedure) results in opposite results from the commitment procedure where subjects cannot escape from the stimuli.

Lack of control of one RC may cause additional problems. For example, if response cost is not equated and subjects prefer not to make a response to obtain the stimuli correlated with reward outcome, then they will receive more rewards in the unpredictable than predictable reward situation and response choice is not equated. Response competition may lead to the same problem.

In the real world, the four RCs are probably rarely controlled, and research must be done to determine the variables that influence preference for predictability when these factors are not controlled. If, however, one wants to develop a theoretical explanation for the results, one must be able to eliminate simpler explanations such as would be possible if one or more of the RCs are not controlled. Control over the RCs is especially important if one wants to determine if unpredictable rewards are ever preferred over predictable rewards, because response competition and unequal response cost could lead to preference for unpredictability.

DMOD Predicted Preference for Unpredictability

Since the 1950s when Wyckoff began research in preference for predictability, both research and theory focused on variables that influence the strength of the preference for predictability. Theories did not address the possibility that, under certain conditions, a preference for unpredictability could develop. DMOD is the only exception, and this theory predicted the conditions under which subjects would prefer unpredictability.

DMOD is a mathematical/computer simulation[2] model that can account for behavior in over 60 learning situations (see Daly & Daly, 1982, 1987, 1991). The model was developed to account for behavior in simple learning situations and was subsequently applied to preference of predictability experiments without modification. Three important goal events are assumed to occur in complex appetitive learning experiments. The *first of these goal events* is the occurrence of a *reward* (e.g., food). Reward is assumed to condition approach (Vap) toward the goal. The Rescorla and Wagner (1972) modification of the Bush and Mosteller (1955) linear operator equation is used to calculate the trial-by-trial change in Vap: $\triangle \text{Vap} = \alpha \beta (\lambda - \bar{V}\text{ap})$. $\triangle V$ represents the change in learning on a trial, and $\bar{V}$ represents the amount already learned to all stimuli present on that trial (e.g., $\bar{V} = Va + Vx$, if cues a and x are present). The three parameters, α, β, and λ, are fixed by the experimental procedures. Alpha (α) represents the salience (intensity) of the stimulus present ($0 < \alpha \leq 1$). Beta (β) represents the learning rate, which in appetitive learning is assumed to be determined in part by the drive level associated with the reward (.15 is used for a subject deprived to 80%–85% of its ad lib. body weight). Lambda (λ) represents the size of the goal event, and 1 is used for a very large reward, .1 for a very small reward, and 0 when no reward is given. Vap is larger the larger the reward, the greater the number of trials, and the larger the percentage of reinforcement. Vap is identical to the V value in the Rescorla and Wagner (1972) model.

In the framework of DMOD, the *second important goal event* that occurs in observing response experiments is the *unexpected omission of the reward.* Nonreward is assumed to be an aversive experience, which becomes associated with the stimuli present (e.g., Amsel, 1958; Daly & Daly, 1991). The same linear operator equation is used to calculate changes in the aversiveness expected, Vav. The λ value, however, is the difference between the reward received (0 on a nonrewarded trial) and the reward expected, which is indexed by the $\bar{V}$ap value. It is further assumed, based on the work of Kahneman and Tversky (1982), that the omission of a reward is more important than its presence, so the discrepancy between obtained and expected reward is a value greater than 1 and is currently assumed to be 2. Therefore, the λ value on a nonreinforced trial is $2(0-\bar{V}\text{ap})$, and $\triangle \text{Vav} = \alpha \beta[2(0-\bar{V}\text{ap}) - \bar{V}\text{av}]$. Vav is conditioned when nonreward occurs after Vap has been conditioned. Vav is a negative number, and the larger the Vap value, the larger the negative Vav value.

The *third goal event* that occurs in observing response experiments is *reintroduction of the reward.* Once Vav is conditioned and an aversive event in the goalbox is expected, the presence of the reward conditions courage to approach the aversive goal (also called counterconditioning, e.g., Amsel, 1958). The same

---

[2]The DMOD computer program and instruction manual can be obtained from the author. A user-friendly, menu-based version of the program, written in C, will run on UNIX-based micro and minicomputers (VAXs and the AT&T UNIX PC), and under DOS (IBM PC/AT/XTs and compatibles). An older version written in BASIC (see Daly & Daly, 1984) is also still available.

linear operator equation is used to calculate the amount of counterconditioning (Vcc), except the λ value is the discrepancy between the amount of aversiveness obtained (0 on a rewarded trial) and the amount expected, which is indexed by $\bar{V}$av. The λ value is (0-$\bar{V}$av) and △Vcc = αβ[(0-$\bar{V}$av) − $\bar{V}$cc]. The absence of any goal event results in a reduction in the V value; on nonrewarded trials Vap and Vcc decline, and on rewarded trials Vav becomes less negative.

A description of how computer simulations are done to obtain DMOD's predictions for the E maze is given in Daly (1985, Appendix). Observing response experiments are basically choice experiments, with the choice being between receiving rewards in a discrimination (predictable) or partial reinforcement (unpredictable) situation. The parameter values and which cues are present on which trials is determined by the experimental procedures (e.g., reward magnitude determines λ, drive level determines β). To predict behavior, all three V values are added to obtain the total V (Vt) value: Vt = $\bar{V}$ap + $\bar{V}$av + $\bar{V}$cc. The preference is measured by the difference between the Vt values of the stimuli on the right versus left side of the choice point. The choice-point stimuli receive secondary reinforcement from the stimuli after the choice (e.g., black or white inserts). DMOD makes ordinal predictions because scaling of parameter values and response mapping rules have not been worked out. Like other similar models, it is called quasi-quantitative (Hilgard & Bower, 1975), and predictions are assessed by correct ordering of groups and within-group reversals across trials, not by curve-fitting techniques (see Daly & Daly, 1991). DMOD simulations show that Vav is conditioned in observing response experiments, but only on the unpredictable reward side, where rewards are presented on a partial reinforcement schedule. DMOD simulations show that predictable nonreward is aversive only early in training and that Vav decreases to zero with extended simple discrimination training. There is much empirical support for this prediction (see Daly & Daly, 1982, pp. 460–461, and Daly & Daly, 1991). Vcc is conditioned only when Vav has also been conditioned. Vcc is therefore conditioned on the unpredictable reward side only, because there is no Vav on the predictable reward side.

DMOD simulations show that in experimental conditions under which there is only Vap, subjects should prefer the unpredictable reward side (due to a blocking phenomenon, see Daly, 1985). This preference is reversed only when the experimental conditions allow Vav to be conditioned. Vav on the unpredictable reward side makes subjects avoid that choice and select the predictable reward side. Vcc only partially counteracts the Vav value on the unpredictable side, and therefore, when Vav is large, subjects are expected to prefer the predictable reward side. Subjects should prefer unpredictability if Vav is small.

What are the conditions where little, if any, Vav is conditioned and subjects should prefer unpredictability? Nonreward is not very aversive if one only expects a *small reward:* Being runner up in a 10 cent lottery is not nearly as aversive as being runner up in a million dollar lottery. Simulations of DMOD show that when a small one-pellet reward is given ($\lambda = .1$) and there is no delay of reinforcement, the Vav value is so low that it is below threshold (see Daly, 1989, footnote 3), and the Vt value is larger on the unpredictable than on the predictable reward side. When a large 15-pellet reward is given ($\lambda = 1$), Vav is large on the unpredictable side and the Vt value is therefore small. DMOD's predictions were supported by the results of a study in the E maze. The only difference between the groups was that, on rewarded trials on both the predictable and unpredictable reward side, one group received 1 pellet and the other group received 15 pellets. Figure 5.2 shows the results. A 50% preference is chance performance, below 50% is a preference for unpredictability, and above 50% is a preference for predictability. The 15-pellet group learned to prefer the predictable reward side, whereas the 1-pellet group preferred the unpredictable reward side. The preference for unpredictable rewards is not because of a lack of discrimination on the predictable reward side: Subjects ran faster toward the goal in the presence of the color associated with reward than in the presence of the color associated with nonreward (see Daly, 1985, Fig. 1).

Figure 5.3 shows the asymptotic preferences of experiments we have run in the E maze. The mean preferences across experiments that tested the same groups are presented. Negative percentages indicate a preference for unpredictability, positive percentages a preference for predictability. Under all conditions, even when unpredictability was preferred, subjects learned to discriminate between S+ and S-; they entered the "delay" box more quickly when the S+ color was present than when the S- color was. Figure 5.3 includes the preference values at asymptote for not only the 1- and 15-pellet conditions (1P and 15P) tested under the no-delay condition, but also for a medium 5-pellet (5P) reward condition that resulted in a small preference for predictability. What these results suggest is that choices can vary from a preference for unpredictability to predictability and that variables can increase or decrease this preference. Reward magnitude appears to a be a powerful variable and can cause preferences to vary from one extreme to the other.

Simulations show that Vav is small when there are *few nonrewarded trials*.

FIG. 5.2. Percent choice of observing response (obs. resp.) side (50% is chance, below 50% is a preference for unpredictability) in blocks of 16 trials (8 free-choice trials), in the no-delay, simple observing response E maze procedure. From Daly (1985). Copyright (1985) by The American Psychological Association. Reprinted by permission of the author.

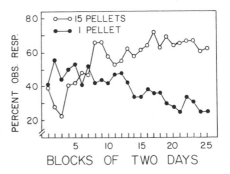

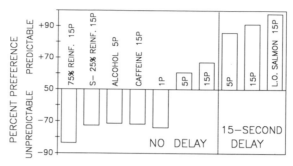

FIG. 5.3. Summary of percent preference on the last day of training in nine experiments run in the Oswego laboratory. Positive numbers represent preference for predictability, and negative numbers a preference for unpredictability. All experiments used the simple discrimination observing response procedure with a gray insert on the unpredictable side (p = pellets; L.O. SALMON = Lake Ontario salmon; see text for explanation of conditions).

This can be done by presenting the color associated with reward on 75% of the trials and the color associated with nonreward on 25% of the trials, and rewarding subjects on a random 75% of the trials on the unpredictable side. The decrease in the number of nonrewarded trials results in an increase in the number of rewarded trials, which increases the size of Vcc relative to Vav. Vav is not below threshold, as in the small reward case, but it is the large Vcc value that counteracts Vav and results in a preference for unpredictability. Therefore, DMOD simulations show that a lenient schedule of reinforcement should result in a preference for the unpredictable reward side. A 75% reinforcement schedule resulted in a strong preference for the unpredictable reward side (see Fig. 5.3, 75% REINF.), just as DMOD had predicted (see Daly, 1989, Experiment 1).

One can also increase the number of reinforced trials by occasionally rewarding subjects in the presence of the stimulus associated with nonreward on the predictable reward side, and by increasing the number of rewarded trials on the unpredictable reward side by the same amount. Simulations indicate that this not only decreases Vav and increases Vcc on the unpredictable side, but it conditions Vav on the predictable side, because nonreward is no longer entirely predictable. DMOD predicts that subjects should prefer the unpredictable reward side, and they did (see Fig. 5.3, S- 25% REINF., and Daly, 1989, Experiment 2).

Alcohol is a drug known to decrease the aversiveness of both electric shock and aversive nonreward (Daly, 1989). If the dose is sufficient to drop the Vav value below threshold, then rats given alcohol should prefer unpredictable rewards. Vav is large in the large, 15-pellet reward condition, and the alcohol dose (0.75 cc/100 kg of a 20% solution) should decrease Vav but not be sufficient to drop Vav below threshold: Preference should decrease to chance only, and did

(Daly, 1989, Fig. 4). Vav should be smaller in the medium-sized, 5-pellet reward condition, alcohol should drop Vav below threshold, and subjects should prefer unpredictability. They did. The results appear in Fig. 5.3 (see also Daly, 1989, Experiments 4 and 5).

Caffeine decreases the rate of extinction in a runway (Joyce & Daly, 1987; Miller & Miles, 1935). It therefore appears that one effect caffeine has is to decrease conditioning of Vav. If true, then subjects should prefer unpredictable rewards. Rats injected with a 10 mg/kg dose of caffeine preferred unpredictability (see Fig. 5.3), whereas the control rats injected with saline behaved like the 15-pellet group in Fig. 5.2 and preferred predictability.

Previous research had shown preference for unpredictability, but few took notice of these results. For example, Lutz and Perkins (1960) tested rats in the E maze with no delay of a 5-pellet reinforcement. Subjects showed a decline in preference from chance level, but Perkins did not mention it. McMichael, Lanzetta, and Driscoll (1967) noted a decline in preference when a small reward was given on 80% of the trials but did not analyze if the decrease was significant.

Hershiser and Trapold (1971) obtained a preference for unpredictable rewards in three experiments. Their procedure did not control for response changeover and tested for preferences in the presence of S− in a shuttle box. When response changeover was not allowed in the same procedure, subjects preferred predictability (Harsh et al., 1983). Marcucella and Margolius (1978) and Harsh, Badia, and Ryan (1984) showed preference for unpredictability in the changeover lever press procedure, but this procedure is not a true observing response experiment because there is no real S−. Subjects can switch from either a light to a dark condition or vice versa. The dark condition results in food on a variable time (VT) 60-second schedule (unpredictable), and the light condition results in a 5-second flashing light followed by food (predictable). There is, however, no S−, a signal that predicts no food.

All Theories (Except DMOD) Have Difficulty Accounting for Preference for Unpredictability

Wyckoff's (1969) mathematical model uses the *secondary reinforcing* value of the stimuli present during the delay interval to calculate preferences, but unfortunately he could not derive the direction of the inequality independently of the data. He had no mechanism to determine when the inequality would be in the opposite direction and a preference for unpredictability should occur. The *utility analysis* of *Bower* et al. (1966) extended Wyckoff's secondary reinforcement model to include different delays of reward but stated: "Wyckoff's utility analysis appears to account parsimoniously for most of the results . . . an annoying feature is that the concave utility curve . . . is inferred from the data in a post hoc manner. An important question is whether more elementary considerations (theoretical assumptions) can be found which . . . imply the concave utility curve" (p. 191). One of their suggestions was frustration. Because Vav can be considered similar to the concept of frustration, DMOD appears to include the "elementary consideration" Bower et al. were looking for.

The reduction in time-to-reinforcement a stimulus signals provides the conditioned or secondary reinforcement value in *Fantino's delay-reduction* hypothesis (1977). It is again the balance between the positive value of the stimulus correlated with reduction in the time to reinforcement and the possible conditioned negative or punishment value of the stimulus correlated with nonreward (Fantino, 1981) that determines the size of the preference. Fantino (1983), like Wyckoff and Bower, assumed that "positive events are more effective in establishing behavior than comparable negative events are in weakening it" (p. 707). Because the basis for this assumption is not worked out, this theory also has no way of independently predicting conditions under which a preference for unpredictability should occur. A similar assumption within DMOD is based on independent data. DMOD has two β values. β_I is the incremental learning rate and is determined by drive level in the appetitive case. A .15 value is used for a high drive state, and .05 for a very low drive state. β_D is the decremental learning rate, or rate of unlearning and growth of inhibition. A .05 values is used in all simulations (value taken from the Rescorla and Wagner model). When subjects are hungry (high drive), the β_I value is higher than the β_D value. Although this is similar to the assumption made by Wyckoff and by Fantino, it is not based on results of preference for predictability studies but is independently determined in simple studies involving drive level. As a consequence of the assumption, however, DMOD predicts that a low hunger drive decreases preference for predictable food rewards (Daly & Daly, 1982), which matches the data (Wehling & Prokasy, 1962).

Berlyne's (1960) *uncertainty-reduction* analysis assumes that "the white key induced a conflict between pecking and not pecking, expecting and not expecting food, excitation and inhibition. The coloring of the key that resulted from stepping on the pedal must then have attenuated the conflict by strengthening one of the competing tendencies and weakening the others" (pp. 205–206). This theory would have to make the unlikely assumption that uncertainty reduction is punishing under some conditions to be able to account for those conditions that results in a preference for unpredictability.

Hendry (1969) applied *information theory* and uncertainty-reduction analyses to preference for predictability. "Information is something we get when some person or machine tells us something we did not know before" (Garner, 1962, p. 2). Both the stimulus signaling reward and the stimulus signaling nonreward provide information and are therefore both reinforcing. Information of the former stimulus is $p \log(1/p)$, and by the latter stimulus is $(1-p) \log 1/(1-p)$, where p is the relative frequency with which reward follows the stimulus. It appears impossible for this theory to account for the preference for unpredictability—information would have to be punishing.

The major assumption of *Perkin's* (1955) *preparatory response theory* is that "the occurrence of salivary conditioning when the US is food implies that a situation consisting of context, food, and saliva is more reinforcing than a situation consisting of context, food, and absence of saliva" (p. 344). Subjects prefer predictability because they can maximize the reward value of the food by salivating before receipt of food on rewarded trials and refrain from salivating on nonrewarded trials. Although this analysis has been able to account for much of the data, it does not seem able to account for the conditions when unpredictability is preferred: When would salivating the correct amount be less reinforcing than not knowing how much to salivate?

The *selective-observing hypothesis* of *Dinsmoor* (1983) assumes that subjects prefer predictability because they escape from the stimulus associated with nonreward (S−), thereby minimizing their exposure to that stimulus. His research shows that subjects will make a response to turn off S−, which provides support for the hypothesis. If subjects cannot escape S−, they should probably show indifference and not prefer unpredictability.

Zeaman and House (1963) extended their model of intra and extradimensional shifts in retardates to observing response experiments. They assumed that subjects observe the dimensions (e.g., color, form, position) and then make instrumental responses to the stimuli (e.g. red–green, circle–triangle, right–left). Their analysis, however, applies only to procedures that allow subjects to choose between the stimuli correlated with reward outcome, such as the green versus the red stimuli. When this is permitted, however, the subject can decrease "the number of times it selects the stimulus associated with nonreward (S−), that is, it chooses S+ (the stimulus associated with reward) and avoids S−, thus increasing the number of reinforced trials to the correct stimulus dimension" (Daly, 1985, p. 297). This model would predict indifference and not predict a preference for unpredictability, if subjects are forced to experience S−.

One attempt has been made to use *Staddon* and *Simmelhag's* (1971) *interim response theory* to account for preference for predictability. Green and Rachlin (1977) assumed that the "value of informative stimuli may be in their function as discriminative stimuli for interim activities and terminal response . . . noninformative stimuli do not permit such differentiation of behavior" (pp. 255, 262). Many of the variables that influence preference for predictability have not been incorporated into interim response theory, and details of the predictions of this theory need to be worked out. It would, however, appear difficult to determine which variables should result in a preference for unpredictability.

Hershiser and Trapold (1971) developed a *discriminated $\overline{CS}$ hypothesis* to account for the preference for unpredictability they found in the shuttlebox procedure. In this procedure, the subject chooses between one side where for 55 seconds no food is delivered and then a 5-second tone is followed by food, and the other side where the tone occurs after the food reward. They state that "on the signalled side a discrimination forms between background stimuli (including side color) which were not reinforced and the compound stimulus of background stimuli plus tone which was reinforced" (p. 327). This procedure not only does not control for response changeover, but it also requires subjects to choose in the presence of the predictable stimuli: S− (the background stimulus) is on for the longer time, and therefore subjects prefer unpredictability. The discriminated $\overline{CS}$ analysis does not apply to the four "pure" observing response procedures, where subjects must choose prior to obtaining the stimuli correlated with reward outcome.

DMOD also uses secondary reinforcement to calculate the Vt values for predictable versus unpredictable rewards: the Vap, Vav, and Vcc values of the stimuli present following a choice provide secondary reinforcement for the stimuli present before the choice. It is the Vav value conditioned by unpredictable nonreward that lowers the Vt value on the unpredictable side. Variables that reduce Vav (small reward, high percentage of reinforced trials, alcohol, immediate rewards, low drive level) all increase the relative size of Vt on the unpredictable side and result in less avoidance for that side or even a preference for it. DMOD allows the levels of input variables to determine parameter values that in turn influence the magnitude of the preference. Figure 5.3 shows the conditions where a preference for unpredictability occurred and confirms DMOD's predictions.

Additional Results That Theories Must Account for

There are several replicable results that current theories of observing response acquisition must be able to account for. A brief review of these follow.

1. Delayed Versus Immediate Reinforcement.   Figure 5.3 shows that with a large reward and a 15-second delay preference for the predictable side is over 90%. Many of the subjects we have run under this condition show a 100% preference for predictable rewards. Lutz and Perkins (1960) obtained the same results using the E maze, showing that if delays were 3, 9, 27, or 81 seconds rats showed a strong preference for predictable rewards. The group given no delay dropped their preference from chance to about 30%, which is a 70% preference for unpredictability. This drop, however, was not noted by the authors.

Both DMOD and Fantino's delay-reduction theory predict that the delay of reinforcement should be important. The latter theory assumes that the secondary reinforcing value of the stimulus is larger the greater the reduction in time to reinforcement it signals. Simulations of DMOD show that unpredictable delays are aversive. The longer the delay, the larger the increase in Vav on the unpredictable reward side and the more that side is avoided.

2. Reward Magnitude.   Reward magnitude is one variable previously reviewed that influences preference greatly, and subjects prefer unpredictability with a small reward and predictability with a large reward (see Fig. 5.2). This was true when rewards are not delayed. If they are delayed, then preference for predictability is increased and small rewards result in chance preference and large rewards result in almost a 100% preference for predictability (see Mitchell, Perkins, & Perkins, 1965, 25, 5, and 1 pellet; Levis & Perkins, 1965, 2 cc and .4 cc of water, both in the E maze).

Preliminary data from the Daly three-key nose-poke procedure replicated the reward magnitude and delay of reward results obtained in the E maze. We ran four rats in the 1-pellet condition with no delay of reinforcement, followed by the 15-pellet condition with no delay, the 15-pellet condition with a 15-second delay, and the 15-pellet, no-delay condition again, each for 25 days (32 trials per day, 16 free-choice trials). Figure 5.4 shows the data for the last 5 days under each condition. The percent preference on free-choice trials appears in the left panel, and DMOD simulation results appear in the right panel. Negative percent preferences and negative DMOD difference scores indicate a preference for unpredictability. Just as in the E maze and predicted by DMOD, the 1-pellet, no-delay condition resulted in a preference for unpredictability: Subjects began at a 50% (chance) preference level on the first block of 5 days and dropped to a −65% preference (preference for the unpredictable side). The 15-pellet, 15-second delay condition resulted in a strong preference for predictability. The 15-pellet, no-delay condition showed a strong order effect. It was tested first after the subjects developed a preference for unpredictability in the 1-pellet, no-delay condition, and preferences rose from −65% to −58%. It was then tested after the subjects had developed a preference for predictability in the 15-pellet, 15-second delay condition, and preference dropped from 91% to 80%. It is not surprising that the 15-pellet, no-delay condition is so influenced by the previous condition: This condition has always shown the most variability between subjects in pre-

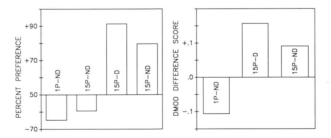

FIG. 5.4. Percent preference for Trials 641–800, and DMOD simulations for asymptote ($\alpha s = 1$, $\beta_I = .15$, $\beta_D = .05$, $\lambda = 1.0$, .1, and 0 for 15, 1, and 0 pellets; see Daly, 1985, Appendix for simulation details), in the three-key nose-poke observing response procedure. The order of testing was: 1-pellet and no delay, 15 pellets and no delay, 15-pellets and 15-second delay, and 15 pellets and no delay again (P = pellets; ND = no delay of reinforcement; D = 15-second delay of reinforcement).

vious E maze studies (Daly & Daly, 1982, p. 470; Daly, 1989, footnote 2). These data, however, show, in a within-subject design, what was shown in between-subject designs in the E maze: Reward magnitude and delay are both powerful variables, and only when a small reward is given in the no-delay condition does a strong preference for unpredictability occur.

Many theories can account for the result that larger rewards result in stronger preferences for predictability: Uncertainty is greater the larger the reward; preparatory responses enhance the reinforcing properties of large but not small rewards; large rewards result in larger Vav on the unpredictable reward side, and therefore large rewards increase the preference for predictability.

3. Drive Level.   High drive levels increase preference for predictability. Wehling and Prokasy (1962), using the E maze, showed that rats deprived of food for 20 hours preferred predictability, whereas rats deprived for only 12 hours showed indifference. They tested rats in the delay condition only.

Not many theories have incorporated drive within their framework. Simulations of DMOD match these results. The β_I value is determined by the drive level. Lower β_I values result in smaller Vav values and therefore smaller preferences for predictability.

4. Consumption of Environmentally Contaminated Lake Ontario Salmon.   We have shown that consumption by laboratory rats of a 30% diet of Lake Ontario salmon for 20 days increases their reactivity to aversive events such as reward reductions, mild shocks, and novel situations (Daly, in press). This increase in reactivity is presumably due to the toxic chemicals found in the fish (e.g., PCBs, dioxin, mirex, cadmium, lead, mercury), because the same effect does not occur in rats fed uncontaminated Pacific Ocean salmon: The group fed Pacific Ocean salmon does not differ from a no-salmon control group. Because rats fed Lake Ontario salmon are hyper-reactive to aversive events, it is not surprising that this diet increases their preference for predictable rewards (see Fig. 5.3 and Daly, Hertzler, & Sargent, 1989). DMOD simulations for all effects of ingestion of Lake Ontario salmon are done by increasing the λ value for Vav. Simulations show that Vav is larger on the unpredictable reward side, and therefore subjects fed Lake Ontario salmon have a greater preference for predictability.

5. Drugs.   Few studies have tested the effects of drugs on preference for predictability. As noted earlier, alcohol decreases the preference for predictability. If a medium-sized reward is given, alcohol results in a preference for unpredictable rewards. If a large reward is given, preference is reduced to chance (Daly, 1989), presumably because the larger reward resulted in a larger Vav value, and the alcohol dose was not sufficient to drop the Vav value below threshold. Caffeine also decreases preference for predictability. In the no-delay condition, even with a large reward, a preference for unpredictability develops. In the delay condition, however, caffeine reduces preference to chance (Joyce & Daly, 1987). Both of these drugs produce a variety of behavioral effects consistent with the assumption that they decrease the rate of conditioning of Vav, and simulations varying the rate parameter (β_I for Vav) show that preference for predictability should be reduced.

Kelleher et al. (1962) showed that observing by pigeons was increased by chlorpromazine even though overall response rate decreased. Their procedure did not control for three RCs. They used the two-key procedure where one key turned on the stimuli correlated with reward outcome and the other was the food key. Hence, response competition was a potential problem. They also did not equate response cost or balance number of rewards (response choice). It is impossible to determine how lack of control of three RCs might interact with the effects of chlorpromazine.

6. Complex Configural Discrimination. The simple observing response discrimination procedure—where a single stimulus is present on the unpredictable side on every trial—results in faster acquisition than when the same two stimuli are present in both the predictable and unpredictable situation (e.g., black and white stimuli on both the unpredictable and predictable side), but they are correlated with reward outcome on the predictable side only (configural condition). The differences are small when large rewards are delayed, but subjects in the configure condition prefer unpredictability when rewards are not delayed (Daly, 1985, Fig. 2, E maze). DMOD simulations match the results (see Daly & Daly, 1982, Figs. 2 and 3).

7. Escape from Stimuli Associated with Unpredictability. When rewards are large and delayed, rats show a strong preference for predictability, even in the configural condition. If the preference is due to aversiveness on the unpredictable side, then subjects should learn a new response to escape from the stimuli associated with the unpredictable side. If there is no aversiveness on the predictable side, then they should not learn to escape from the stimuli associated with a choice to the predictable side. Daly (1974; see also Daly & Daly, 1991) tested the aversiveness of these stimuli by allowing rats to jump over a hurdle into a neutral box to escape these stimuli. In the E maze, the floor texture on the right and left sides of the maze differ: The floor is wire mesh on the right side and smooth metal on the left side. Following acquisition of the observing response, the doors at the choice point and into the delay box were closed, and subjects were placed into the gray boxes with the different floor texture. A door over a hurdle was opened into boxes attached to the E maze, and speed of jumping the hurdle into these neutral boxes was measured. Previous research using the hurdle-jump escape response to measure aversiveness of stimuli associated with shock (e.g., McAllister & McAllister, 1972) and omission of food rewards (e.g., Daly, 1974) has shown that variables known to result in large amounts of aversiveness result in faster hurdle-jump speeds. Speeds to jump the hurdle after E-maze acquisition showed that subjects placed on the floor texture associated with the unpredictable side learned to jump the hurdle, but subjects placed on the floor texture associated with the predictable side jumped at the same slow speed as the control subjects who had never been rewarded in the E maze (see Daly, 1974, Fig. 21, and Daly & Daly, 1991). These results match DMOD simulations that show that aversiveness (Vav) is conditioned only on the unpredictable reward side. It is unclear how other theories could account for these results.

8. Decreasing Percentage of Reinforced Trials Increases Preference for Predictability.   The maximum preference for predictability occurs when S+ is presented on less than 50% of the trials (e.g., Eckerman, 1973; Kendall, 1973; McMichael et al., 1967; McMillan, 1974; Steiner, 1970; Wilton & Clements, 1971; see Fantino, 1977, pp. 322–325, for a review). Only when preferences are close to 100% in all groups, or if variability is high, has this result not occurred (Bower et al., 1966; Daly, 1989; Hendry, 1969). The opposite result has been obtained only once (Green & Rachlin, 1977), but a high response cost was required and a within-subject design was used where order effects may have occurred.

One prediction of information theory is that, as one increases or decreases the number of reinforced trials, one decreases the difference in amount of information in the predictable and unpredictable reward conditions, and subjects should decrease their preference for predictability. The vast majority of results contradict this prediction. Wilton and Clements (1971) attempted to salvage information theory by stating that it is the information for good news and not bad news that is important: "only information in the positive signal is reinforcing" (p. 162). Some have questioned whether this modification is permissible within information theory: Eckerman (1973) argued that "they have left information theory with only one theoretical hand clapping" (p. 46).

DMOD simulations match the results: Increasing nonreinforced trials increases Vav in the unpredictable situation and preference for predictability should be greater.

9. Increasing Percentage of Reinforcement Decreases Preference for Predictability.   The decrease in preference when reward percentage increases has been shown by many (see reference in previous section). This result is predicted by most theories. Figure 5.3 shows that, when 75% of the trials are reinforced and there is no delay of reward, rats prefer unpredictability. Only DMOD can apparently account for this result (see previous section on DMOD). When rewards are delayed, a 75% schedule still results in a lower preference than a 50% schedule, but choice is now at chance level (Daly, 1989, Fig. 2). This result was also predicted by DMOD, because delay is aversive and increases Vav, and Vav cannot be counteracted by Vcc to result in a preference for unpredictability.

10. Changing Predictive Validity of S+ and S−.   Ward (1971) showed that, the greater the decrease in predictive validity between S+ and reward and between S− and nonreward, the greater the decrease in preference for predictability in the E maze (4-pellet reward and a 10-second delay): Group 100–0 (S+ and S− correlation with reward) showed a strong preference for predictability, and Group 50–50 was indifferent, with Groups .875–.125, .75–.25, and .625–.375 ordering themselves nicely in between. Deich (1977), in an unpublished MA thesis at the University of Iowa, showed that Group 100–0 had a stronger preference for predictability than Groups 100–50 and 50–0. Figure 5.3 shows that Group 100–25 (S− 25% REINF.), in a no-delay condition, had a strong preference for unpredictability.

These results can be accounted for by assuming that decreasing the predictive validity decreases uncertainty reduction, information, or secondary reinforcing properties, but only DMOD can account for the preference for unpredictability in Group 100–25 when there is no delay of reward. If Vav is substantially reduced relative to Vcc in the unpredictable situation, then a preference for unpredictability occurs, especially when Vav is increased on the predictable side by making S− an unreliable predictor of nonreward. Ward's and Deich's data can easily be accounted for by this analysis.

11. Relative Values of the S+ and S− (Predictive) and S+/− (Unpredictive) Stimuli.   Bower et al. (1966) tested response strength in the presence of S+, S−, and S+/− after acquisition of the observing response. Response strength was strongest to S+, weakest to S−, and S+/− was in between. Jenkins and Boakes (1973) showed similar results. Daly (1985, Experiment 3) tested the effects of these stimuli present at the choice point in the E maze. Subjects learned to go to S+ if it was present, and to S+/− if S− was present.

DMOD simulations match these results, in that the Vt values of the stimuli are ranked S+ > S+/− > S− (Daly, 1985, Table 4). These data contradict predictions of uncertainty reduction and information theories. S− is informative and reduces uncertainty and should be preferred over S+/−.

One variation of the observing response procedure is to have the observing response turn on only S− and see if the observing response is made, as information and uncertainty theories predict. Although there have been a few results that support this prediction (e.g., Perone & Baron, 1980, using humans), Fantino and Case (1983) pointed out that these results may be due to the unequal response cost in the presence of S+ and S− versus S+/−. Fantino and Case also tested humans using a low effort task and found that S+/− was preferred over S−.

Dinsmoor (1983) showed that subjects escape from $S-$ to $S+/-$, and his results are the basis of his selective-observing hypothesis. All secondary reinforcement theories can account for these results, including DMOD. The interesting question for the selective observing hypothesis is whether escape from $S-$ is the only reason for preferences for predictability. Clearly not, because there are experiments in which escape from $S-$ is not possible and a strong preference for predictability occurs. If the RCs called response choice and response changeover are controlled, the subject experiences nonreward and reward an equal number of times in the predictable and nonpredictable situation. This is true in the standard E maze procedure, as well as in Bower's key-poke, McMichael's three-lever, and Daly's nose-poke procedure. In the Daly nose-poke procedure, exposure time to all stimuli is fixed by the experimenter and is not under the control of the subject; no food response is required after the subject makes a choice of the predictable or unpredictable reward situation. In the E maze, the exposure time to the stimuli is, in part, under the control of the subject, because he must enter the delay chamber before the delay period begins. Subjects frequently do not enter the chamber immediately after seeing $S-$, thus increasing their exposure to the stimulus. The conditions that increase time to enter $S-$ (high rewards, high drive, long delays) are the same variables that increase the preference for the predictable side. These results contradict the predictions of the selective-observing hypothesis. Dinsmoor (personal communication) has argued that subjects may escape $S-$ by closing their eyes. This argument may be valid when there are visual stimuli but is more difficult to make when auditory stimuli are used (see Badia, Ryan, & Harsh, 1981, and Harsh et al., 1984). In the Daly nose-poke procedure, subjects show a strong preference for predictability when the $S+$ and $S-$ stimuli are tones or clicks. It is therefore doubtful that the selective-observing hypothesis can account for all situations where subjects prefer predictability and cannot account for when unpredictability is preferred when the choice is made before $S-$ appears (see Daly, 1986).

CONCLUSIONS

There are many variables that influence preference for predictability, and preferences range from strong preferences for unpredictability to strong preferences for predictability. It appears that the sole theory not only able to integrate the variables that influence preferences but to predict the conditions when a preference for unpredictability should occur is DMOD. This mathematical/computer simulation model was developed to account for behavior in simple learning situations and was then applied without modification to observing response experiments. The primary basis for the prediction is Vav, the conditioned anticipation of aversive nonreward, and to a smaller degree blocking and Vcc (courage to approach aversive events). Variables that decrease Vav on the unpredictable side (e.g., small reward magnitude, no delay, alcohol, few nonreinforced trials) decrease preference for predictability. If Vav is low enough, then unpredictability is preferred (see Fig. 5.3). The combination of variables is important. For example, when rewards are not delayed, small rewards result in a preference for unpredictability, a medium reward results in a small preference for predictability, and a large reward results in a medium preference for predictability. If rewards are delayed, then a small reward results in indifference, but a large reward results in a very strong preference for predictability. No other theory applied to observing response acquisition can account for this range of results without making some unlikely assumptions (uncertainty is rewarding, information is punishing), or they have no mechanism to decide the value of the secondary reinforcement. Other theories have trouble accounting for the increase in preference as the percentage of rewards decrease, and that the unpredictable situation is preferred over the stimulus correlated with the absence of reward.

There are several experimental procedures that are called observing response experiments that do not control for one or more of the four RCs: response cost, response competition, response choice, and response changeover. Therefore, simpler explanations of preference for predictability are possible in these experiments (e.g., escape from S−). The challenge is to develop a theoretical account of the variables that influence preference for predictability and unpredictability when the four RCs are controlled. DMOD appears to be a big step in this direction.

REFERENCES

Amsel, A. (1985). The role of frustrative nonreward in continuous reward situations. *Psychological Bulletin, 55,* 102–119.

Badia, P., Ryan, K., & Harsh, J. (1981). Choosing schedules of signalled negative events over schedules of unsignalled ones. *Journal of the Experimental Analysis of Behavior, 35,* 187–195.

Berlyne, D. E. (1960). *Conflict, arousal and curiosity.* New York: McGraw-Hill.

Bower, G., McLean, J., & Meacham, H. (1966). Value of knowing when reinforcement is due. *Journal of Comparative and Physiological Psychology, 62,* 184–192.

Bush, R. R., & Mosteller, F. (1955). *Stochastic models for learning.* New York: Wiley.

Daly, H. B. (1974). Reinforcing properties of escape from frustration aroused in various learning situations. In G. H. Bower (Ed.), *The psychology of learning and motivation* (Vol. 8, pp. 187–231). New York: Academic Press.

Daly, H. B. (1985). Observing response acquisition: Preference for unpredictable appetitive rewards obtained under conditions predicted by DMOD. *Journal of Experimental Psychology: Animal Behavior Processes, 11,* 294–316.

Daly, H. B. (1986). Dinsmoor's selective observing hypothesis probably cannot account for preference for unpredictable rewards: DMOD can. *The Behavioral & Brain Sciences, 9,* 365–370.

Daly, H. B. (1989). Preference for unpredictable rewards occurs with high proportion of reinforced trials or alcohol if rewards are not delayed. *Journal of Experimental Psychology: Animal Behavior Processes, 15,* 3–13.

Daly, H. B. (in press). The evaluation of behavioral changes produced by consumption of environmentally contaminated fish. In R. L. Isaacson & K. F. Jensen (Eds.), *The vulnerable brain and environmental risks, Vol. 1: Malnutrition and hazard assessment.* New York: Plenum Press.

Daly, H. B., & Daly, J. T. (1982). A mathematical model of reward and aversive nonreward: Its application in over 30 appetitive learning situations. *Journal of Experimental Psychology: General, 111,* 441–480.

Daly, H. B., & Daly, J. T. (1984). DMOD—A mathematical model of reward and aversive nonreward in appetitive learning situations. Program and instruction manual. *Behavior Research Methods, Instruments, & Computers, 16,* 38–52.

Daly, H. B., & Daly, J. T. (1987). A computer simulation/mathematical model of learning. Extension of DMOD from appetitive to aversive situations. *Behavior Research Methods, Instruments, & Computers, 19,* 108–112.

Daly, H. B., & Daly, J. T. (1991). Value of mathematical modeling of appetitive and aversive learning: Review and extension of DMOD. In M. R. Denny (Ed.), *Fear, avoidance, and phobias: A fundamental analysis.* Hillsdale, NJ: Lawrence Erlbaum Associates.

Daly, H. B., Hertzler, D. R., & Sargent, D. M. (1989). Ingestion of contaminated Lake Ontario salmon by laboratory rats increases their reaction to aversive nonreward and mild shock. *Behavioral Neurosciences, 103.*

Deich, J. D. (1977). *The acquisition and maintenance of observing behavior in pigeons.* Unpublished masters thesis, The University of Iowa.

Dinsmoor, J. A. (1983). Observing and conditioned reinforcement. *The Behavioral and Brain Sciences, 6,* 693–704.

Eckerman, D. A. (1973). Uncertainty reduction and conditioned reinforcement. *The Psychological Record, 23,* 39–47.

Fantino, E. (1977). Conditioned reinforcement: Choice and information. In W. K. Honig & J. E. R. Staddon (Eds.), *Handbook of operant behavior* (pp. 313–339). Englewood Cliffs, NJ: Prentice-Hall.

Fantino, E. (1981). Contiguity, response strength, and the delay-reduction hypothesis. In P. Harzem & M. H. Zeiler (Eds.), *Advances in analysis of behavior: Predictability, correlation, and contiguity* (Vol. 1, pp. 169–201). New York: Wiley.

Fantino, E. (1983). Observing and the delay-reduction hypothesis. *The Behavioral and Brain Sciences, 6,* 707–708.

Fantino, E., & Case, D. A. (1983). Human observing maintained by stimuli correlated with reinforcement but not extinction. *Journal of the Experimental Analysis of Behavior, 40,* 193–210.

Garner, W. R. (1962). *Uncertainty and conflict as psychological concepts.* New York: Wiley.

Green, L., & Rachlin, H. (1977). Pigeons' preference for stimulus information: Effects of amount of information. *Journal of the Experimental Analysis of Behavior, 27,* 255–263.

Harsh, J., Badia, P., & Ryan, K. (1983). Factors affecting choice of signaled or unsignaled food schedules. *Journal of the Experimental Analysis of Behavior, 40,* 265–273.

Harsh, J., Badia, P., & Ryan, K. (1984). Signal modality and choice between signaled and unsignaled food. *Journal of the Experimental Analysis of Behavior, 42,* 279–289.

Hendry, D. P. (1969). Reinforcing value of information: Fixed ratio schedule. In D. P. Hendry (Ed.), *Conditioned reinforcement* (pp. 300–334). Homewood, IL: Dorsey.

Hershiser, D., & Trapold, M. A. (1971). Preference for unsignaled over signaled direct reinforcement in the rat. *Journal of Comparative and Physiological Psychology, 77,* 323–328.

Hilgard, E. R., & Bower, G. H. (1975). *Theories of learning.* Englewood, NJ: Prentice-Hall.

Hirota, T. T. (1972). The Wyckoff observing response—A reappraisal. *Journal of the Experimental Analysis of Behavior, 18,* 263–276.

Hirota, T. T. (1974). The relationship between observing behavior and food-key response rates under mixed and multiple schedules of reinforcement. *Journal of the Experimental Analysis of Behavior, 21,* 259–266.

Hursh, S. R., & Fantino, E. (1974). An appraisal of preference for multiple versus mixed schedules. *Journal of the Experimental Analysis of Behavior, 22*, 31–38.

Jenkins, H. M., & Boakes, R. A. (1973). Observing stimulus sources that signal food or no food. *Journal of the Experimental Analysis of Behavior, 20*, 197–207.

Joyce, H. L., & Daly, H. B. (1987). *Caffeine decreases preference for predictable rewards.* Paper presented at the Eastern Psychological Association Convention, Arlington, VA.

Kahneman, D., & Tversky, A. (1982). The psychology of preferences. *Scientific American, 246*, 160–173.

Kelleher, R. T., Riddle, W. C., & Cook, L. C. (1962). Observing responses in pigeons. *Journal of the Experimental Analysis of Behavior, 5*, 3–13.

Kendall, S. B. (1973). Effects of two procedures for varying information transmission on observing responses. *Journal of the Experimental Analysis of Behavior, 20*, 73–83.

Levis, D. J., & Perkins, C. C., Jr. (1965). Acquisition of observing responses (Ro) with water reward. *Psychological Reports, 16*, 114.

Lutz, R. E., & Perkins, C. C., Jr. (1960). A time variable in the acquisition of observing responses. *Journal of Comparative and Physiological Psychology, 53*, 180–182.

Marcucella, H., & Margolius, G. (1978). Time allocation in concurrent schedules: The effect of signalled reinforcement. *Journal of the Experimental Analysis of Behavior, 29*, 419–430.

McAllister, W. R., & McAllister, D. E. (1972). Behavioral measurement of conditioned fear. In F. R. Brush (Ed.), *Aversive conditioning and learning.* New York: Academic Press.

McMichael, J. S., Lanzetta, J. T., & Driscoll, J. M. (1967). Infrequent reward facilitates observing responses in rats. *Psychonomic Science, 8*, 23–24.

McMillan, J. C. (1974). Average uncertainty as a determinant of observing behavior. *Journal of the Experimental Analysis of Behavior, 22*, 401–408.

Miller, N. E., & Miles, W. R. (1935). Effect of caffeine on the running speed of hungry, satiated, and frustrated rats. *Journal of Comparative Psychology, 20*, 397–412.

Mitchell, K. M., Perkins, N. P., & Perkins, C. C., Jr. (1965). Conditions affecting acquisition of observing responses in the absence of differential reward. *Journal of Comparative and Physiological Psychology, 60*, 435–437.

Perkins, C. C. Jr. (1955). The stimulus conditions which follow learned responses. *Psychological Review, 62*, 341–348.

Perone, M., & Baron, A. (1980). Reinforcement of human observing behavior by a stimulus correlated with extinction or increased effort. *Journal of the Experimental Analysis of Behavior, 34*, 239–261.

Prokasy, W. F. (1956). The acquisition of observing responses in the absence of differential external reinforcement. *Journal of Comparative and Physiological Psychology, 49*, 131–134.

Rescorla, R. A., & Wagner, A. R. (1972). A theory of Pavlovian conditioning: Variations in the effectiveness of reinforcement and nonreinforcement. In A. H. Black & W. F. Prokasy (Eds.), *Classical conditioning II: Current research and theory.* New York: Appleton-Century-Crofts.

Steiner, J. (1970). Observing responses and uncertainty reduction: II. The effects of varying the probability of reinforcement. *Quarterly Journal of Experimental Psychology, 22*, 592–599.

Staddon, J. E. R., & Simmelhag, V. L. (1971). The "superstition" experiment: A reexamination of its implications for the principle of adaptive behavior. *Psychological Review, 78*, 3–43.

Ward, E. F. (1971). Acquisition and extinction of the observing response as a function of stimulus predictive validity. *Psychonomic Science, 24*, 139–141.

Wehling, H. E., & Prokasy, W. F. (1962). Role of food deprivation in the acquisition of the observing response. *Psychological Reports, 10*, 399–407.

Wilton, R. N., & Clements, R. O. (1971). Observing responses and informative stimuli. *Journal of the Experimental Analysis of Behavior, 15*, 199–204.

Wyckoff, L. B. (1952). The role of observing responses in discrimination learning. I. *Psychological Review, 59*, 431–442.

Wyckoff, L. B. (1969). The role of observing responses in discrimination learning. II. In D. P. Hendry (Ed.), *Conditioned reinforcement* (pp. 237–259). Homewood IL: Dorsey Press.

Zeaman, D., & House, B. J. (1963). The role of attention in retardate discrimination learning. In N. R. Ellis (Ed.), *Handbook of mental deficiency* (pp. 159–223). New York: McGraw-Hill.

Zeigler, H. P., & Wyckoff, L. B. (1961). Observing responses and discrimination learning. *The Quarterly Journal of Experimental Psychology, 13,* 129–140.

6

Biological and Psychological Description of an Internal Clock

Russell M. Church
Hilary A. Broadbent
Brown University

John Gibbon
New York State Psychiatric Institute and Columbia University

Studies of time perception demonstrate that animals can discriminate the duration of external stimuli. For example, an animal can be trained to make different responses depending on the duration of a stimulus (Church, 1989; Gibbon & Allan, 1984). An animal can also be trained to respond at regular intervals (Weiss & Laties, 1965).

The data of time perception and time production experiments can be described without postulating an internal clock or any intervening variables. With such an approach, functional relationships between independent variables and the behavior of the animal can be established and general principles, such as Weber's law, can be applied to animal timing (Gibbon, 1977). But to explain the psychophysical data, many investigators have found it useful to assume the existence of an internal timing mechanism and other processes intervening between the input and output variables. One goal is to use the postulated intervening processes to obtain a greater understanding of time discrimination and timed performance. At a minimum, intervening variables have provided convenient metaphors to guide thinking about the influence of the conditions of stimulation and reinforcement on responding. An alternative goal is to use information about time discrimination and timed performance to obtain a greater understanding of fundamental psychological processes. These intervening variables may represent psychological processes that translate the input into behavior. A still more ambitious goal is to describe the biological realization of these mental processes. A quantitative specification of the intervening variables may provide a needed roadmap for identifying the biological basis of timing.

The concept of an internal clock was used by Hoagland (1933) as a physiological concept to account for changes in human time discrimination as a function of internal temperature. The psychological reality of the concept was clarified by the introduction of additional psychological modules, such as memory and decision processes, that translate a clock reading into behavior (Treisman, 1963). And the testability of the concept was greatly increased by quantitative specification of the characteristics of the internal clock and the accumulation process (Creelman, 1962). Recent analyses of animal timing have extended both the psychological and the mathematical specification of the concept of an internal clock (Gibbon, Church, & Meck, 1984).

TIMING OF CONTINUOUS EXTERNAL STIMULI

An Information-Processing Description

One information-processing model of timing consists of three main parts: a clock (consisting of a pacemaker, switch, and accumulator), a memory, and a decision process (comparator) (see Fig. 6.1.) The pacemaker emits pulses at some rate (λ) and these pulses may be sent into an accumulator by closing a switch. If the sum in the accumulator is close enough to a sample value in reference memory, a response occurs. If a response is reinforced, the value in the accumulator is transferred to reference memory, with some error if k* is not equal to 1.0.

For such an information-processing model to be testable, it is necessary to specify the distribution form and parameter values of the random variables and the quantitative rule for a response decision (Gibbon & Church, 1984). The random variables are clock speed (λ) in pulses per second, the latency in seconds to close the switch at the beginning of an interval and to open it at the end of an interval, the memory storage constant (k*), and the response decision threshold. Clock speed may be a random variable with some distribution form (such as Poisson), and its parameter values may vary in some manner within and across trials. The latency to close the switch at the beginning of an interval and the latency to open the switch at the end of an interval may be a random variable unrelated to the duration being timed (Meck, Church, & Gibbon, 1985). The memory storage constant may be a random variable so that the value stored in

FIG. 6.1. An information-processing model of timing that includes a clock, reference memory, and comparator. The clock consists of a pacemaker that emits pulses that may be sent into an accumulator by closing a switch. The speed of the clock is λ pulses per second; the memory storage constant is k*.

An Information–Processing Model

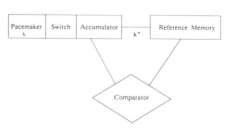

reference memory is not exactly the value in the accumulator. Finally, the decision to respond is based on some comparison between the perceived value and a remembered value, and the response threshold for this decision may be a random variable. A decision rule is necessary to specify the meaning of a value in the accumulator being "close enough" to a value in reference memory to produce a response. A ratio of these values may be compared to a variable threshold to determine whether or not a response will be made. The distribution of these random variables determines the predicted performance (Gibbon, Church, & Meck, 1984). Experimental conditions control the operation of the switch, and they may affect one or more of the random variables.

Three Procedures

For the study of timing, a response can be reinforced if it occurs at a particular time, or a particular response can be reinforced depending on the duration of a signal (Catania, 1970; Church, 1989). The peak procedure (Roberts, 1981) is an example of reinforcement of a response that occurs at a particular time. In this procedure, a signal goes on at the beginning of each trial and continues to the end of the trial. Two trial types are randomly interspersed. On approximately half the trials, reinforcement is primed at some particular time after the onset of the signal. On the other half of the trials, the signal continues considerably beyond the expected time of reinforcement, and no reinforcement is primed. The animal is free to respond at all times during these nonreinforced trials, and the pattern of responding provides a measure of the animal's ability to estimate the expected time of reinforcement. The top left panel of Fig. 6.2 shows data from 10 sessions of one rat in a peak procedure using white noise as the signal, lever pressing as the response, and 20 s as the expected time of food reinforcement (Church, Miller, Meck, & Gibbon, 1991). In this experiment, a limited hold was in effect on reinforced trials such that only responses between 18.5 and 22.5 s since the beginning of the trial were reinforced. On these trials, responses before 18.5 s had no consequences, and responses after 22.5 s terminated the trial without reinforcement. The function relating response rate to time since the signal began on the nonreinforced trials increased to a maximum near the time that food was sometimes available and then decreased in a nearly symmetrical way.

The bisection procedure (Church & Deluty, 1977; Stubbs, 1976) is an example of reinforcement of a particular response depending on the duration of a signal. Stimuli in this procedure consist of signals of various durations. Typically, the animal is trained to make one response following a short-duration signal (to press the left of two levers following a 2-s white noise signal, for example) and a different response following a signal of a longer duration (to press the right lever following an 8-s signal). Correct responses following these two signals are reinforced. After differential responding to these signals has been established, nonreinforced trials with signals of intermediate durations are presented. The proba-

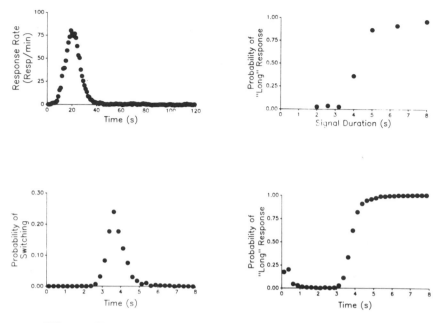

FIG. 6.2. Temporal discrimination procedures. In the peak procedure (upper left panel), the mean response rate is shown as a function of time since the trial began. In the bisection procedure (upper right panel), the mean probability of a "long" response is shown as a function of time since the trial began. In the continuous bisection procedure, the mean probability of switching from the "short" to the "long" response is shown as a function of time since the trial began (lower left panel), and the mean probability of a "long" response is shown as a function of time since the trial began (lower right panel).

bilities of left and right responses following each of the signal types are calculated. The point at which the probability of a right response equals that of a left response is called the point of bisection. It has been considered to be a measure of the time that is judged by the animals to be equally similar to the two criterion signals. The top right panel of Fig. 6.2 shows data from five sessions of one rat in a bisection procedure.

A third procedure, which is referred to as continuous bisection, combines aspects of both the peak procedure and the bisection procedure (Platt & Davis, 1983). On half the trials the first left response after a short duration (such as 40 s) was reinforced; on the other half the first right response after a longer duration (such as 120 s) was reinforced. Trials were terminated by reinforcement (or, rarely, by a 240-s criterion of nonresponse) and were separated by an intertrial interval. The response keys were available at all times, and a record was kept of the time of each left and right response. The pigeon usually began responding on the left response key. If it did not receive food, it would, after some period of time, begin responding on the right key and receive food. The time of switching is defined as the mean of the time of the last left response and the time of the first right response.

A similar procedure has been used with rats with left- and right-lever responses. The bottom left panel of Fig. 6.2 shows the probability of switching (on trials with a single switch from the left lever to the right lever) as a function of time since the trial began for a single rat. The probability of switching at a given time, like the response rate in the peak procedure, increased to a maximum and then decreased in a slightly asymmetrical manner. The bottom right panel of Fig. 6.2 shows the probability of a right-lever response as a function of time since the trial began for the same rat. This function, like the bisection function, increased as an S-shaped function, and it provides a measure of the subjective middle of the interval.

The operation of the internal clock is assumed to be similar in all three procedures. At the onset of the signal, the switch is closed, permitting pulses from the pacemaker to be summed in the accumulator. In the peak procedure, if the value in the accumulator is close enough to a sample of a value from reference memory, then a response will be made. In the continuous bisection procedure, if the value in the accumulator is close enough to a sample of a value in reference memory associated with a left response, then a left response will be made; if the value in the accumulator is close enough to a sample of a value in reference memory associated with a right response, then a right response will be made. If there were nonreinforced trials, the decision during a trial would go from "neither" to "left" to "right" to "neither." Between the "left" and "right" decision, there could be either a "both" or "neither" decision. In the standard bisection procedure, the same psychological processes may occur, but the animal has the opportunity to execute a single response only after a signal has terminated.

Two Patterns of Effect

There are two important and separable concepts, clock speed (λ) and memory storage constant (k^*). Clock speed is the pacemaker rate in pulses per second. The memory stage constant transforms the perceived number of pulses in the accumulator into the remembered number of pulses in memory. The distinction between clock speed and the memory constant is essential for understanding the effects of various independent variables on timing (Meck, 1983).

Figure 6.3 shows what would happen if an independent variable affected clock speed. The horizontal axis is time since the trial began (physical time), and the vertical axis is the accumulator value (subjective time). The diagonal line shows the accumulator value as a function of time. The top panel shows the relationship between time since the trial began and accumulator value before a treatment that

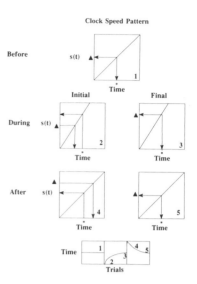

FIG. 6.3. The clock speed pattern. The effect of a treatment that affects clock speed is shown before the treatment is introduced (top panel), during the treatment (second row of panels), and after the treatment is terminated (third row of panels). This phasic pattern is shown in the bottom panel. See text for details.

affected clock speed. The second row of panels illustrates the changes that occur during a treatment that increases clock speed: The initial effect on the first sessions is shown on the left and the final effect is shown on the right. The third row of panels illustrates changes after the treatment was no longer applied: The initial effect on the first sessions is shown on the left and the final effect on the last sessions is shown on the right. The clock speed, as shown by the slope of the diagonal line, was normal before and after the treatment (first and third rows) and was increased during the treatment (second row). The asterisk marks the time of reinforcement and the arrow on the vertical axis points to the accumulator value that corresponds to this physical time. The triangle marks the accumulator value associated with the expected time of reinforcement and the arrow on the horizontal axis points to the physical time that corresponds to this accumulator value.

Before treatment, the expected time of reinforcement corresponds to the physical time of reinforcement. The initial effect of a treatment that increases clock speed is that the expected time of reinforcement occurs earlier than the actual time of reinforcement (the initial effect during treatment). Eventually, the expected time of reinforcement adjusts to correspond to the actual time of reinforcement (the final effect during treatment). After the treatment is discontinued, the initial effect is that the expected time of reinforcement occurs later than the actual time of reinforcement (the initial effect after treatment). Eventually, the expected time of reinforcement again adjusts to correspond to the actual time of reinforcement (the final effect after treatment). This phasic effect at the transition from one condition to another is summarized in the bottom panel (the numbers correspond to the panels above).

Drugs such as amphetamine and methamphetamine increase the level of dopamine in the synaptic cleft by increasing the release of dopamine and inhibiting its reuptake. These drugs lead to changes in behavior that can be interpreted as an increase in clock speed. When methamphetamine was first administered, the time of the maximum response rate in the peak procedure occurred earlier, and the duration that the animal was equally likely to report as short or long in the bisection procedure was shorter (Maricq & Church, 1983, Maricq, Roberts, & Church, 1981). When animals that had been trained on temporal discrimination with methamphetamine were first tested on days on which a saline control injection was given, the time of the maximum response rate occurred later and the duration that the animal was equally likely to report a stimulus as short or long occurred later (Meck, 1983). All these results suggest methamphetamine increased the speed of the internal clock, probably by increasing the effective level of brain dopamine. This may also be the mechanism that leads to an increase in clock speed by electric footshock (Meck, 1983) and by electrical stimulation of the medial forebrain bundle (MFB) (Meck, 1988). The magnitude of the effect of methamphetamine was increased by morphine (Meck & Church, 1984). (See Stewart, this volume, for description and interpretation of the relationship between opiate and stimulant drugs.) A snack of protein had a similar effect, but the mechanism presumably involves changes in the ratio of various amino acids that are transported through the blood-brain barrier (Meck & Church, 1987b).

In contrast, neuroleptic drugs, such as haloperidol, that decrease the effective level of dopamine by blocking dopamine receptors, lead to changes in behavior that can be interpreted as a decrease in clock speed. When haloperidol was first administered, the duration that the animal was equally likely to report as short or long in the bisection procedure was longer (Maricq & Church, 1983). When animals trained on temporal discrimination with haloperidol were first tested on days on which a saline control injection was given, the time that the animal was equally likely to report as short or long occurred earlier (Meck, 1983). In a test of five different neuroleptic drugs (spiroperidol, pimozide, haloperidol, chlorpromazine, and promazine), the correlation between the binding affinity of these drugs to the D_2 dopamine receptors and to the dose of the drug required to shift the psychophysical function rightward by 15%–20% was .98 (Meck, 1986). A snack of carbohydrate had a similar effect (Meck & Church, 1987b).

The pattern of transient behavior changes provides evidence for a change in clock speed, and the magnitude of the transient provides a quantitative estimate of the magnitude of the change in speed, but it does not provide an estimate of absolute clock speed. Treatments that have reversible effects, such as low doses of stimulants or neuroleptics, allow multiple measures of the changes in clock speed so that reliable estimates can be made. Treatments that have permanent effects on the nervous system, such as lesions and neurotoxins, permit, at best, only a single measure of a transient change.

Figure 6.4 shows what would happen if an independent variable affected the

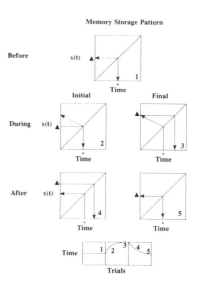

FIG. 6.4. The memory storage pattern. The effect of a treatment that affects the memory storage constant is shown before the treatment is introduced (top panel), during the treatment (second row of panels), and after the treatment is terminated (third row of panels). This gradual pattern is shown in the bottom panel. See text for details.

memory storage constant. The horizontal axis is time since the trial began and the vertical axis is the accumulator value. The diagonal line shows the accumulator value as a function of time. The top panel shows the relationship between the time since the trial began and the accumulator value before a treatment that affected the memory storage constant. The second row of panels illustrates the changes that occur during a treatment that increased memory storage constant: The initial effect on the first sessions is shown on the left and the final effect is shown on the right. The third row of panels illustrates changes after the treatment was no longer applied: The initial effect on the first sessions is shown on the left and the final effect on the last sessions is shown on the right. The memory storage constant was normal before and after the treatment (the first and third rows) and was increased during the treatment (in the second row). The asterisk marks the time of reinforcement and the arrow on the vertical axis points to the accumulator value that corresponds to this physical time. The triangle marks the accumulator value associated with the expected time of reinforcement, and the arrow on the horizontal axis points to the physical time that corresponds to this accumulator value.

Before treatment, the expected time of reinforcement corresponds to the physical time of reinforcement. There is no initial effect of a treatment that increases the memory storage constant because the expected time of reinforcement remains at the actual time of reinforcement (the initial effect during treatment). However, the value that is stored in memory on these trials is larger than the value in the accumulator. Eventually, the expected time of reinforcement adjusts to be later than the actual time of reinforcement (the final effect during treatment). Note that the animals never correct the expected time of reinforcement. After the treatment is discontinued, the initial effect is that the expected time of reinforcement remains later than the actual time of reinforcement (the initial effect after treatment). Eventually, the expected time of reinforcement adjusts to correspond to the actual time of reinforcement (the final effect after treatment). This gradual effect at the transition from one condition to another is summarized in the bottom panel (the numbers correspond to the panels above).

Because the functions produced by changes in clock speed and changes in the memory constant are so different, they are readily distinguished. Changes in clock speed produce the abrupt "on" and "off" effects, whereas changes in the memory constant produce gradually learned effects. Changes in the memory constant affect storage, not retrieval, because the treatment during training, not testing, has been found to be critical.

Drugs, such as physostigmine, that decrease the acetylcholine-degrading enzyme cholinesterase, decrease the memory constant (Meck & Church, 1987a). A snack of choline also decreases the memory constant (Meck & Church, 1987b). Vasopressin has a similar effect, although a common biological mechanism has not been identified (Meck, 1983; Meck, Church, & Wenk, 1986). Lesions of the fimbria fornix, a major extrinsic pathway of the hippocampus, or ibotenic acid lesions of the septal area, which has cell bodies that project to terminal fields in the hippocampus, decreased the memory constant (Meck, Church, & Olton, 1984; Meck, Church, Wenk, & Olton, 1987; Olton, Meck, & Church, 1987).

In contrast, drugs such as atropine that block acetylcholine receptors increase the memory constant (Meck & Church, 1987a). The magnitude of the effect depends on the dose of the drug. An increase in the memory constant has also been observed in aged rats, although repeated administration of vasopressin to rats when they were 10 months old appeared to inoculate them against these age-related effects (Meck, Church, & Wenk, 1986). Lesions of the frontal cortex, or ibotenic acid lesions of the nucleus basalis magnocellularis that has cell bodies that project to terminal fields in the cerebral cortex, increased the memory constant (Meck, Church, Wenk, & Olton, 1987; Olton, Wenk, Church, & Meck, 1988).

Table 6.1 provides a list of treatments that appear to increase or decrease clock speed and that appear to increase or decrease the memory constant.

TABLE 6.1
Treatments Affecting Clock Speed and the Memory Storage Constant

Direction	Clock	Memory
Left	Methamphetamine Footshock MFB Stimulation Protein	Physostigmine Choline Vasopressin Fimbria Fornix lesion Septal lesion
Right	Haloperidol Other neuroleptics Carbohydrate	Atropine Age Frontal corex lesion Nucleus Basalis lesion

TIMING OF THE INTERVAL BETWEEN SUCCESSIVE
RESPONSES

Drinking

For timing of external stimuli, we have postulated the existence of an internal clock and described some of its characteristics. For timing the interval between successive responses, especially when the responses occur at fairly regular intervals, one may also postulate the existence of an internal clock and describe its characteristics. It is possible that properties of the clock used for timing external stimuli and for timing the interval between successive responses are the same.

When a rat drinks water, it does so in a stereotyped rhythmic fashion. The tongue moves out to the tube of the water bottle and then up and back into the mouth. When the rat is drinking, the tongue touches the tube about seven times per second and this rate is relatively constant (Stellar & Hill, 1952). The distribution of the interlick interval is smooth and nearly symmetrical with a mean of about 150 msec and a standard deviation of only about 15 msec (Corbit & Luschei, 1969). Investigators have been impressed by this regularity and have noted that all rats tested had similar functions, and that these functions are not much (if at all) affected by conditions that affect the total water consumption, such as water deprivation or the presence of saccharin. The typical function was found to be somewhat more peaked than a normal curve.

The probability distribution of interlick intervals is shown for three rats in Fig. 6.5. The rats received a daily ration of about 15 g of dry food and water in the home cage from 4 to 7 pm and then were water deprived for 17 hours. At that time, they were placed in the testing cage with 100 45-mg food pellets and, after 1 hour, a water bottle was made available. Each interlick interval was recorded to the nearest millisecond during the 30-minute period that the water was available and the data were averaged over five sessions.

The data are similar to those previously reported by others. The mean interlick interval was 146, 152, and 143 ms, with standard deviations of 13.5, 15.8, and 11.0 ms. Thus, the ratio of the standard deviation to the mean was 9.3%, 10.3%, and 7.7%. The function was quite symmetrical and its asymptotic value was near zero. Most of the interlick intervals were between 100 and 200 ms (83%, 88%, and 94%). Most responses outside the limits shown on this figure were indicative of the beginning of a new burst of responding.

One approach to understanding the relatively regular interlick interval distribution is to determine the biological mechanism involved in the production of the response. Cells in the reticular formation of the medulla project to the hypoglossal nuclei. Each nucleus contains about 3,500 motor neurons in longitudinally oriented cell columns. The cells in the dorsal region of the nucleus have axons that project to the tongue retractor muscles and the cells in the ventral region of the nucleus have axons that project to the tongue protruder muscles

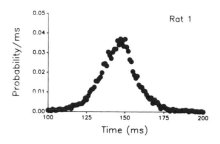

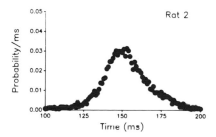

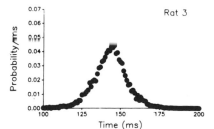

FIG. 6.5. Frequency distribution of interlick intervals. Probability per millisecond as a function of time in milliseconds for
three rats.

(Travers, 1985). The nature of the oscillatory circuit might be described on the
basis of analysis of single unit activity of the motor neurons.

Another approach to understanding the relatively regular interlick interval
distribution is to develop a psychological model of the time of occurrence of each
lick that accounts for the form and spread, as well as the mean, of the distribution
of interlick intervals. Figure 6.6 shows several possible psychological models:

One possibility is that each response reflexively elicits the next response. If
the time required for a response to drive the next response were a constant, then

the interlick interval would be a constant. In fact, as we have noted, there is some variability in the interval between licks. If the probability of an event at each instant were constant, and thus independent of the time of occurrence of the previous event, then the distribution of interevent intervals would be an exponential waiting-time distribution. The three left panels of Fig. 6.6 show three ways in which variability between responses might occur if each response were timed from a previous one. The top left panel (exponential) involves a single random variable with an exponential waiting-time distribution; the middle left panel (gamma) involves two random variables, each with an exponential waiting-time distribution; and the bottom left panel (normal) involves many random variables, each with an exponential waiting-time distribution. Responses are shown by the solid circles, hypothetical intervening events are shown by the open circles, and random waiting-time intervals are shown by horizontal lines. For example, in the middle left panel a response elicits an intervening event after one random waiting-time interval, and then this intervening event elicits a response after a second random waiting-time interval. The interresponse interval (r) equals the sum of two exponential waiting times ($a_1 + b_1$). The first might represent a random neural time and the second might represent a random motor time.

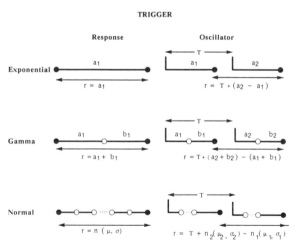

FIG. 6.6. Six models of the time interval between successive responses. For the models in the left column, each response serves as a trigger for the next response; for the models in the right column, a regular clock pulse serves as a trigger for the next response. In the exponential models, there is one random exponential waiting time between trigger and response; in the gamma models, there is a sequence of two random exponential waiting times between trigger and response; and in the normal models, there is a very long sequence of random exponential waiting times between trigger and response.

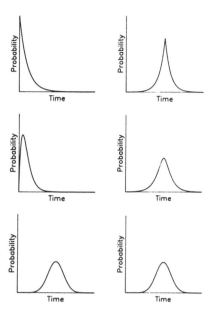

FIG. 6.7. Distribution of the interresponse times for the six models. An exponential waiting-time distribution (top left panel), a two-fold general-gamma distribution (middle left panel), and a normal distribution (bottom left panel); a LaPlace distribution (top right panel), a difference between two two-fold general-gamma distributions (middle right panel), and a normal distribution (bottom right panel).

An alternative possibility is that each response is triggered by a clock pulse that occurs at a constant interval (T). The three panels on the right show three ways in which variability between responses might occur if each response is timed from a clock pulse. The top right panel involves a single random variable with an exponential waiting-time distribution; the middle right panel involves two random variables, each with an exponential waiting-time distribution; and the bottom right panel involves many random variables, each with an exponential waiting-time distribution. For example, in the middle right panel a clock pulse (vertical line) elicits an intervening event after one random waiting-time interval, and this intervening event elicits a response after a second random waiting-time interval. In this case, the measured interresponse interval is a constant (T) plus a difference between two random variables ($a_2 + b_2$ and $a_1 + b_1$).

The form of the expected distribution of interresponse intervals can be described based on the assumed generating process (Luce, 1986). The observed distributions exclude all but one of these six processes from further consideration. The forms of the distribution are shown on the left side for the three cases in which a response is triggered by the previous response. If the variability were characterized by a single random waiting-time distribution, the interlick interval would be an exponential distribution (as shown in the top left panel). If the variability were characterized by two serial random waiting-time distributions, the interlick would be a two-fold general-gamma distribution (as shown in the middle left panel). (It is called two-fold because it is the sum of two independent random variables, and it is called a general-gamma distribution because the rate parameter of each of the exponential variables is not necessarily the same; see McGill & Gibbon, 1965.) If the variability were characterized by many serial random waiting-time distributions, the interlick interval would approximate a normal distribution (as shown in the bottom left panel).

The forms of the distribution are shown on the right side for the three cases in which a response is triggered by an accurate clock. If the variability between clock and response were characterized by a single random waiting-time, the interlick interval would be the difference between two exponential waiting times (the LaPlace distribution as shown in the top right panel). If the variability were characterized by two serial waiting-times initiated by a clock, the interval would be the difference between two two-fold general-gamma variables, as shown in the middle right panel. (See Appendix for the derivation of this distribution.) If the variability were characterized by many serial waiting-times initiated by a clock, the interval would be approximately normal as shown in the bottom right panel.

The symmetry of the distribution of interlick intervals rules out the processes leading to a single exponential or a two-fold general-gamma distribution. (In some cases that are not shown here, there were asymmetries in the distribution presumably due to gradual drifts in the mean interlick interval and to flatter center portions of the distribution presumably due to changes in the mean interlick interval that is influenced by the distance between the tube and the cage.) The remaining three distribution forms are plotted along with the data in Figure 6.8. The mean interresponse interval was estimated from the data and used to fit all three distributions. In addition, the standard deviation of the interresponse interval was used to fit the LaPlace distribution and the normal distribution; the two parameters of the distribution of the difference between two two-fold general-gamma distributions were estimated from the data with an iterative procedure.

If the random delay following each clock pulse were an exponential waiting time, a LaPlace distribution of interresponse times would result. Although the LaPlace distribution (left panels of Fig. 6.8) accounted for a high percentage of the variance (92%, 87%, and 92%), the systematic deviations of the data from the theory clearly indicate that the interlick interval was not produced by the mechanism that produces a LaPlace distribution. In each case, the theory was more peaked than the data. Thus, the response was not produced by a single clock-driven waiting-time distribution.

The normal distribution (right panels of Fig. 6.8) also accounted for a high percentage of the variance (96%, 93%, and 97%), but again the systematic deviations of the data from the theory clearly indicate that the interlick interval was not produced by a mechanism that produces a normal distribution. In each case, the data were more peaked than the theory. Thus, the response was not produced by many response-driven or clock-driven waiting-time distributions.

The remaining possibility is that the process is a clock-driven one with two exponential waiting times (center panels of Fig. 6.8). The clock drives one

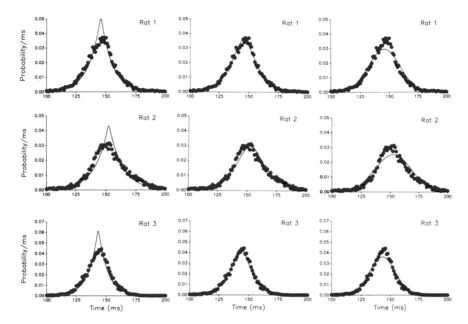

FIG. 6.8. Comparison of interlick interval distributions of the three rats with the theoretical distributions based on the three clock-driven models: LaPlace (left column), Tau–Gamma (center column), and Normal (right column).

process (perhaps neural) that drives a second process (perhaps motor). The estimates of the means of the exponentials for Rat 1 was 6.9 and 6.9 ms, for Rat 2 was 6.9 and 9.5 ms, and for Rat 3 was 6.9 and 4.4 ms. This distribution accounted for a high percentage of the variance (99%, 96%, and 99%), and there were no large systematic deviations of the data from the theory.

The differences in the probability of response predicted by the model and observed in the data are shown in Figure 6.9 for each of the three subjects with each of the clock-driven models. This plot of residuals emphasizes any systematic deviation of the data from the model. There were regular systematic deviations of the data from the LaPlace and normal distributions, but any systematic deviations of the data from the difference between two two-fold general-gamma distributions were small. The quality of the fit is noteworthy because there are 100 data points. Many function forms can fit a small number of data points, but systematic deviations become readily apparent when the data points are finely spaced. We refer to this as the Tau–Gamma hypothesis, a function that can be obtained from a fixed interval between clock pulses and two serial exponential waiting-time intervals.

McGill (1962, 1963) has derived the LaPlace distribution and a variety of others associated with a correction for missed trigger intervals. For our present

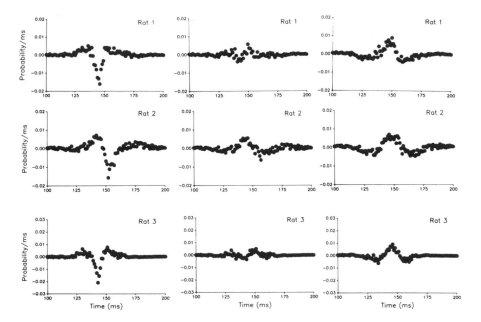

FIG. 6.9. Difference between interlick interval distributions of the three rats and the theoretical distributions base on the three clock-driven models: LaPlace (left column), Tau–Gamma (center column), and Normal (right column).

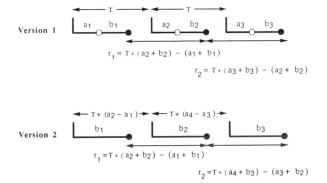

FIG. 6.10. Two versions of the Tau–Gamma hypothesis: A fixed clock and a two-fold general-gamma delay (top panel), and a clock with LaPlace variability and an exponential delay (bottom panel).

purposes, the period between triggers is large relative to the delay from trigger to response, and we ignore these complications. Our Tau–Gamma hypothesis is a straightforward extension of McGill's LaPlace derivation and represents a generalization that may be reinterpreted to accommodate variance in the clock system as well. For example, if we regard "true" triggers as being comprised of τ + a, then the mean periodic component becomes τ + $1/\alpha$, and the response component remains as our b in the second row in Fig. 6.6. The mathematics, of course, are precisely the same as behavior, and hence this interpretation is more in the spirit of the Wing–Kristofferson account, in which they posit a trigger with a triangular distribution (drawn from a difference of two uniformly distributed variates).

The Wing and Kristofferson analysis (Wing, 1980; Wing & Kristofferson, 1973) includes an analysis that McGill's did not, namely, an autocorrelation function of some importance. When successive interresponse times are correlated, the result is a negative correlation from the common negative component, as is evident in Fig. 6.6. Importantly, this negative correlation disappears at lags greater than 1, and the strength of the negative correlation may be used to measure the difference between variances associated with the clock and with the response component. Thus, in our reinterpretation of the Tau–Gamma hypothesis, if effective triggers include some variance with resulting LaPlace distribution, then the difference between that variance and variance associated with b, the final response path is reflected in the squared lag 1 correlation. Pittendrigh and Daan (1976) rediscovered this kind of analysis in a circadian context, where it has precisely the same form and the same underlying rationale, but with triggers in the 24-hr range.

The two-process model for repetitive responding has been developed without any specific assumption about the distribution forms of the random sources of variance. If they are assumed to be exponential, however, the two-process model and the Tau–Gamma hypothesis can be directly compared.

The first version of the Tau–Gamma hypothesis, as shown in Fig. 6.6, is redrawn in Fig. 6.10 and compared to a second version of the Tau–Gamma hypothesis in which one source of variance is associated with the clock and another source of variance is associated with the response. The two models make identical predictions about the distribution of interresponse intervals and for the autocorrelations between all interresponse intervals except adjacent ones. The two models make difference predictions about the autocorrelation functions at lag 1. According to the first version of the Tau–Gamma hypothesis, it should be $-.5$. According to the second version, it should be between $-.5$ (if all the variability were in the motor delay) and 0 (if all the variability were in the clock). The essential difference is that successive interresponse intervals are composed of two common elements in Version 1 (a_2 and b_2) and of only one common element in Version 2 (b_2).

The comparison of oscillator models with one, two, or many random variables has demonstrated that two is better than one or many. The distribution forms have shown that the exponential waiting times are a reasonable approximation. Both versions of the Tau–Gamma hypothesis have these characteristics, but the second version also makes use of the major feature of the two-process models—the separation of the sources of variance into those associated with excitatory event and delay from event to response.

A biological mechanism sufficient to produce the reported results would be one with a constant oscillator and two serial processes between the oscillator and the observed response. Each of these serial processes would be a random waiting-time distribution. Alternatively, there may be a variable oscillator and a single process between the oscillator and the observed response. Oscillator variability would reflect the difference between two random waiting-time distributions (perhaps to the lower and upper bound of a tendency to respond) and variability from event to response would be a random waiting-time distribution. Of course, it is possible there are other formal mechanisms sufficient to produce this result. An ex-Gaussian is defined as a normal distribution followed by an exponential (Burbeck & Luce, 1982). One might consider the possibility that the clock is Gaussian followed by a single random waiting-time distribution. The difference between two ex-Gaussian variables might be similar to the data. The data, however, rule out many other possibilities and encourage a direct identification of the processes involved. This could be feasible because only two sources of variance, each with a simple form, appear to be sufficient to account for the data.

The information-processing model that has been applied to timing of external stimuli may also be appropriate for timing of the interval between successive responses. For licking, the value in reference memory is a relatively fixed value of about 150 milliseconds. When the number of pulses in the accumulator approximate the number in reference memory, a response will be initiated and the accumulator reset to zero. There are two sources of variability: (a) the time required for the comparison process, and (b) the time required for the execution of the response. If these are both exponential waiting-time distributions and the comparison is completed before the execution begins, then the form of the distribution would be as observed.

Tapping

Of course, it is critical to know whether the Tau–Gamma hypothesis that appears to account for the distribution of interlick intervals can also account for other examples of repetitive behavior. It is possible that specialized mechanisms would be used for specialized functions, like control of the tongue in drinking. But evolution is thought to be conservative and opportunistic so that a successful mechanism would be reused for many purposes. To test this possibility in a very different situation, human subjects attempted to tap a microswitch in synchrony with a tone that occurred every 500 msec. The tone lasted for 50 msec (10 ms risetime), and it was delivered binaurally through earphones. The session lasted for 30 m with 12 two-m periods with the periodic tones separated by 30-s periods of rest. The results for three subjects are compared with the three clock-driven models in Fig. 6.11.

The Tau–Gamma hypothesis (center panels of Fig. 6.11) accounted for over 99% of the variance in the distribution of interresponse time of each of the three subjects, and any systematic deviations for the data from the theory are subtle. The estimates of the means of the exponentials for Subject 1 was 10.0 and 16.7 ms, for Subject 2 was 11.1 and 16.7 ms, and for Subject 3 was 11.1 and 9.1 ms. The LaPlace distribution (left panels of Fig. 6.11) accounted for a high percentage of the variance (86%, 84%, and 95%), but the theory was more peaked than the data in all cases. The normal distribution (right panels of Fig. 6.11) also accounted for only a little less of the variance than the Tau–Gamma hypothesis in each case (99%, 95%, and 99%), but in two of the three cases the data were more peaked than the theory.

The differences between theory and data are shown in Fig. 6.12. These data are inconsistent with a response-triggered response, no matter how many exponential waiting times are introduced. They are consistent with a clock-triggered response with exactly two exponential waiting times, but not with fewer or more. Perhaps the generality of the Tau–Gamma mechanism is that, on many different

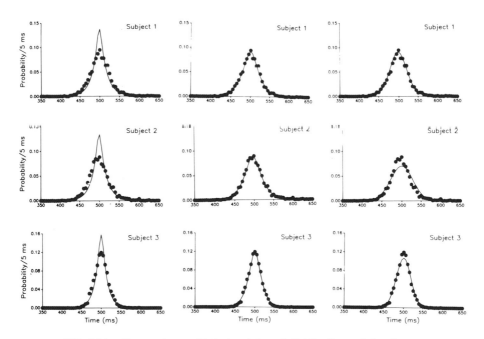

FIG. 6.11. Comparison of intertap interval distributions of the three subjects with the theoretical distributions based on the three clock-driven models: LaPlace (left column), Tau–Gamma (center column), and Normal (right column).

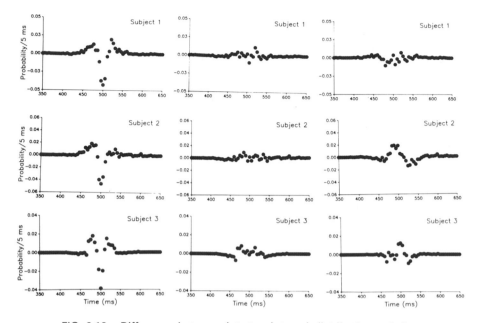

FIG. 6.12. Difference between intertap interval distributions of the three subjects and the theoretical distributions based on the three clock-driven models: LaPlace (left column), Tau–Gamma (center column), and Normal (right column).

scales, there are random waiting-time processes that can be labeled as *decision* and *execution*.

In the tapping procedure, the pacemaker emits pulses that are switched into an accumulator. When the number of pulses in the accumulator approximate the number in reference memory, a response will be initiated and the accumulator reset to zero. Because the tones occur at regular 500-msec intervals, the representation of the number of pulses in memory can be maintained quite accurately. There are, however, two sources of variability: (a) the time required for the comparison process, and (b) the time required for the execution of the response. If these are both exponential waiting-time distributions and the comparison is completed before the execution begins, then the form of the distribution would be as observed.

CONCLUSION

The information-processing model of timing is useful for understanding time perception and timed performance. The same information-processing model may apply to time perception and to the timing of repetitive motor responses. In this chapter we have reviewed the previous analyses of time perception and the influence of various treatments on the speed of the internal clock involved in such time perception. Then we attempted to extend this analysis to the timing of repetitive responses (drinking by rats and tapping by people).

The major strength of the physiological analysis of clock speed is that it provides explicit predictions of the effect of various treatments (such as injection of methamphetamine) on the intervening variable. The major strength of the cognitive model is that it provides explicit predictions of the effects of changes in the intervening variable (such as clock speed) on behavior. It appears that dopaminergic drugs affect the internal clock, and that the internal clock is a critical module in temporal perception and timed performance.

ACKNOWLEDGMENTS

The authors express appreciation to J. Michael Walker, Jeffrey Winter, and Jennifer Horne for contributions to the collection and interpretation of the drinking behavior of the animals, to Charles Collyer for helpful comments on the Tau–Gamma model, and to Stephen Fairhurst and Nick Staddon for programming contributions. This research was supported in part by a Grant from the National Institute of Mental Health, R01-MH44234.

REFERENCES

Burbeck, S. L., & Luce, R. D. (1982). Evidence from auditory simple reaction times for both change and level detectors. *Perception & Psychophysics, 32,* 117–133.

Catania, A. C. (1970). Reinforcement schedules and psychophysical judgments: A study of some temporal properties of behavior. In W. N. Schoenfeld, *The theory of reinforcement schedules* (pp. 1–42). New York: Appleton-Century-Crofts.

Church, R. M. (1989). Theories of timing behavior. In S. B. Klein & R. R. Mowrer (Eds.), *Contemporary learning theory* (Vol 2, pp. 41–71). Hillsdale, NJ: Lawrence Erlbaum Associates.

Church, R. M., & Deluty, M. Z. (1977). Bisection of temporal intervals. *Journal of Experimental Psychology: Animal Behavior Processes, 3,* 216–228.

Church, R. M., Miller, K. D., Meck, W. H., & Gibbon, J. (1991). Symmetrical and asymmetrical sources of variance in temporal generalization. *Animal Learning & Behavior, 19,* 207–214.

Corbit, J. D., & Luschei, E. S. (1969). Invariance of the rat's rate of drinking. *Journal of Comparative and Physiological Psychology, 69,* 119–125.

Creelman, C. D. (1962). Human discrimination of auditory duration. *Journal of the Acoustical Society of America, 34,* 582–593.

Gibbon, J. (1977). Scalar expectancy theory and Weber's law in animal timing. *Psychological Review, 84,* 279–325.

Gibbon, J. & Allan, L. G. (Eds.). (1984). Timing and time perception. *Annals of the New York Academy of Sciences* (Vol. 423). New York: New York Academy of Sciences.

Gibbon, J., & Church, R. M. (1984). Sources of variance in information processing theories of timing. In H. L. Roitblat, T. G. Bever, & H. S. Terrace (Eds.), Animal cognition (pp. 465–488). Hillsdale, NJ: Lawrence Erlbaum Associates.

Gibbon, J., Church, R. M., & Meck, W. H. (1984). Scalar timing in memory. In J. Gibbon & L. G.

Allan (Eds.), *Annals of The New York Academy of Sciences: Timing and time perception* (pp. 52–77). New York: New York Academy of Sciences.

Hoagland, H. (1933). The physiological control of judgments of duration: Evidence for a chemical clock. *Journal of General Psychology, 9,* 267–287.

Luce, R. D. (1986). *Response times.* New York: Oxford University Press.

Maricq, A. V., & Church, R. M. (1983). The differential effects of haloperidol and methamphetamine on time estimation in the rat. *Psychopharmacology, 79,* 10–15.

Maricq, A. V., Roberts, S., & Church, R. M. (1981). Methamphetamine and time estimation. *Journal of Experimental Psychology: Animal Behavior Processes, 7,* 18–30.

McGill, W. J. (1962). Random fluctuations of response rate. *Psychometrica, 27,* 3–17.

McGill, W. J. (1963). Stochastic latency mechanisms. In R. D. Luce, R. R. Bush, & E. Galanter. *Handbook of mathematical psychology* (Vol. 1, pp. 309–360). New York: Wiley.

McGill, W. J., & Gibbon, J. (1965). The general-gamma distribution and reaction times. *Journal of Mathematical Psychology, 2,* 1–18.

Meck, W. H. (1983). Selective adjustment of the speed of internal clock and memory processes. *Journal of Experimental Psychology: Animal Behavior Processes, 9,* 171–201.

Meck, W. H. (1986). Affinity for the dopamine D_2 receptor predicts neuroleptic potency in decreasing the speed of an internal clock. *Pharmacology Biochemistry & Behavior, 25,* 1185–1189.

Meck, W. H. (1988). Internal clock and reward pathways share physiologically similar information-processing stages. In M. L. Commons, R. M. Church, J. R. Stellar, & A. R. Wagner (Eds.), *Quantitative analyses of behavior: Biological determinants of reinforcement* (Vol. 7). Hillsdale, NJ: Lawrence Erlbaum Associates.

Meck, W. H., & Church, R. M. (1984). Opioid effects on timing behavior in the rat: Possible actions on dopaminergic and GABAergic neurons. *Society for Neuroscience Abstracts, 10,* 1103.

Meck, W. H., & Church, R. M. (1987a). Cholinergic modulations of the content of temporal memory. *Behavioral Neuroscience, 101,* 457–464.

Meck, W. H., & Church, R. M. (1987b). Nutrients that modify the speed of internal clock and memory storage processes. *Behavioral Neuroscience, 101,* 465–475.

Meck, W. H., Church, R. M., & Gibbon, J. (1985). Temporal integration in duration and number discrimination. *Journal of Experimental Psychology: Animal Behavior Processes, 11,* 591–597.

Meck, W. H., Church, R. M., & Olton, D. S. (1984). Hippocampus, time, and memory. *Behavioral Neuroscience, 98,* 3–22.

Meck, W. H., Church, R. M., & Wenk, G. L. (1986). Arginine vasopressin inoculates against age-related increases in sodium-dependent high affinity choline uptake and discrepancies in the content of temporal memory. *European Journal of Pharmacology, 130,* 327–331.

Meck, W. H., Church, R. M., Wenk, G. L., & Olton, D. S. (1987). Nucleus Basalis Magnocellularis and Medial Septal Area lesions differentially impair temporal memory. *The Journal of Neuroscience, 7,* 3505–3511.

Olton, D. S., Meck, W. H., & Church, R. M. (1987). Separation of hippocampal and amygdaloid involvement in temporal dysfunctions. *Brain Research, 404,* 180–188.

Olton, D. S., Wenk, G. L., Church, R. M., & Meck, W. H. (1988). Attention and the frontal cortex as examined by simultaneous temporal processing. *Neuropsychologia, 26,* 307–318.

Pittendrigh, C. S., & Daan, S. (1976). A functional analysis of circadian pacemakers in nocturnal rodents. *Journal of Comparative Physiology, 106,* 223–252.

Platt, J. R., & Davis, E. R. (1983). Bisection of temporal intervals by pigeons. *Journal of Experimental Psychology: Animal Behavior Processes, 9,* 160–170.

Roberts, S. (1981). Isolation of an internal clock. *Journal of Experimental Psychology: Animal Behavior Processes, 7,* 242–268.

Stellar, E., & Hill, J. H. (1952). The rat's rate of drinking as a function of water deprivation. *Journal of Comparative and Physiological Psychology, 45,* 96–102.

Stubbs, D. A. (1976). Scaling of stimulus duration by pigeons. *Journal of the Experimental Analysis of Behavior, 26,* 15–25.

Travers, J. B. (1985). Organization and projections of the orofacial motor nuclei. In G. Paxinos, *The rat nervous system: Vol. 2. Hindbrain and spinal cord* (pp. 111–128). New York: Academic press.

Treisman, M. (1963). Temporal discrimination and the indifference interval: Implications for a model of the "internal clock." *Psychological Monographs, 77,* 1–31 (Whole No. 576).

Weiss, B., & Laties, V. G. (1965). Reinforcemenet schedule generated by an on-line digital computer. *Science, 148,* 658–661.

Wing, A. M. (1980). The long and short of timing in response sequences. In G. E. Stelmach & J. Requin (Eds.), *Tutorials in motor behavior.* Amsterdam: North-Holland.

Wing, A. M., & Kristofferson, A. B. (1973). Response delays and the timing of discrete motor responses. *Perception and Psychophysics, 14,* 5–12.

APPENDIX A: *TAU–GAMMA HYPOTHESIS*

We require the distribution of

$$r_n = \tau + t_{n+1} - t_n, \tag{A1}$$

where the t_i are 2-fold general gamma variates, $t = a + b$, with

$$f(a) = \alpha e^{-\alpha a} \quad \text{and} \quad f(b) = \beta e^{-\beta b}, \quad \alpha \neq \beta. \tag{A2}$$

McGill and Gibbon (1965) have analyzed this convolution in some detail. For two components, it has density

$$g_2(t) = c_1 \alpha e^{-\alpha t} + c_2 \beta e^{-\beta t} \tag{A3}$$

where

$$c_1 = 1/(1-\alpha/\beta), \quad c_2 = 1/(1-\beta/\alpha). \tag{A4}$$

To find the t_i difference distribution in (A1), let $x = t_{n+1} - t_n$ and consider the event $x > T$, $T > 0$. We fix t_n, and

$$1 - F_x(T) \equiv P(x > T) = P(t_{n+1} > T + t_n) \equiv 1 - G_2(T + t_n),$$

known to be given by

$$1 - G_2(y) = c_1 e^{-\alpha y} + c_2 e^{-\beta y}.$$

Setting $y = T + t_n$ and integrating,

$$1 - F_x(T) = \int_0^\infty [1 - G_2(T + t)] \, g_2(t) \, dt,$$

which gives

$$1 - F_x(T) = c_1^2 e^{-\alpha T} [(1/2) - \alpha/(\alpha+\beta)] + c_2^2 e^{-\beta T} [(1/2) - \beta/(\alpha+\beta)].$$

Some algebraic simplification shows

$$1 - F_x(T) = (1/2)(c_1 d_1 e^{-\alpha|T|} + c_2 d_2 e^{-\beta|T|}), \tag{A5}$$

where the c_i are as above (A4), and

$$d_1 = 1/(1 + \alpha/\beta), \quad d_2 = 1/(1 + \beta/\alpha). \tag{A6}$$

But a strictly symmetrical argument for $x < T < 0$ shows the same forms, (A5,6), justifying $|T|$ in A5. Equations A5 and A6 were used to define the time bins for the data fits.

Differentiating A5, x is seen to have density

$$f(x) = (1/2)(c_1 d_1 \alpha e^{-\alpha|x|} + c_2 d_2 \beta e^{-\beta|x|}), \tag{A7}$$

with, of course, $F_r(T) = F_x(T-\tau)$ and $f_r(r) = f_x(r-\tau)$.

7

Conditioned Stimulus Control of the Expression of Sensitization of the Behavioral Activating Effects of Opiate and Stimulant Drugs

Jane Stewart
Concordia University
Montreal, Quebec, Canada

Sensitization is a ubiquitous biological phenomenon, seen in the long-lasting increase in response to same or weaker stimuli following presentation of a strong stimulus. Sensitization has been used to describe the enhancement of reflexive responses following their repeated elicitation (e.g., Groves & Thompson, 1970), the increased behavioral and biochemical responsiveness to drugs (e.g., Robinson & Becker, 1986) and stressors (e.g., Anisman & Sklar, 1979) following their initial presentation, the growth in the response to repeated epileptic discharge (e.g., Post, Weiss, & Pert, 1988), and the increased responsivity of the immune system following initial exposure to an antigen (e.g., Cooper, 1980). Antelman (1988) has argued that sensitization may be a property of cells, a simple form of memory that is manifested as a more rapid and larger response to a strong stimulus following its intermittent exposure.

USES OF THE TERM SENSITIZATION

Neurophysiologists have used the term sensitization, as opposed to habituation, to refer to the long-lasting increment in response occurring upon repeated presentation of a stimulus that at its initial presentation reliably elicits a response (Groves & Thompson, 1970). Based on studies of the mammalian spinal flexion reflex (Spencer, Thompson, & Neilson, 1966; Thompson & Spencer, 1966), Groves and Thompson argued that the processes in the central nervous system underlying such response sensitization must involve interneuronal plasticity. The fact that, following the repeated presentation of a strong stimulus, sensitization of response is seen to stimuli other than the originally eliciting stimulus makes this appear likely.

In the field of Pavlovian conditioning, response sensitization of this latter type is a well-recognized phenomenon. The changed ability of a provisional "conditional" stimulus (CS) to elicit a response following repeated presentations of the unconditioned stimulus (UCS) alone (i.e., in the absence of CS–UCS pairings), is known as sensitization or pseudoconditioning and is considered to be a form of nonassociative learning (see Mackintosh, 1974). This phenomenon has been shown from studies in aplysia to be due to a form of heterosynaptic facilitation of potential CS neural elements having access to the neural elements mediating the unconditioned response (UR) that requires only repeated presentation of the UCS. Conditioning is thought to be "pairing specific enhancement of sensitization" that appears to develop from the co-occurrence of cellular processes produced by the firing of the CS and the UCS stimulated elements (Kandel, Abrams, Bernier, Carew, Hawkins, & Schwartz, 1983). Interestingly, studies on the ontogenetic development of the phenomenon of sensitization in aplysia have shown it to be a process that emerges after habituation relatively late in the juvenile period (Rankin, Nolen, Marcus, Stopfer, & Carew, 1988), suggesting that it may coincide with the addition of facilitatory units to the neural circuitry.

In the psychopharmacological literature, the term sensitization has come to refer to the increased response to a drug that follows its repeated intermittent presentation. First used to describe the increased motor excitation produced by a given dose of a stimulant drug such as amphetamine after repeated injection, the term sensitization is now used more generally to describe the phenomenon of increased responsiveness to a drug, as opposed to decreased responsiveness or "tolerance" that follows repeated drug administration (Eikelboom & Stewart, 1982; Robinson & Becker, 1986; Siegel, 1977).

One question that arises about these various uses of the term sensitization is whether there is any common basis for the phenomena being described. It seems possible, for example, that drugs that act in the central nervous system to facilitate or mimic neuronal firing would produce effects similar to those produced by external stimuli. When such drugs are given repeatedly, sensitization of these effects might come about via processes similar to those underlying the sensitization brought about by repeated presentation of an external stimulus. Drugs, or their effects, can serve as UCSs to promote conditioned drug effects (Stewart & Eikelboom, 1987), and sensitization to drugs, as in the other cases of sensitization described, arises from repeated presentation of the UCS alone. Knowledge of where or how a drug acted to produce any particular unconditioned effect might provide a clue to the neural processes mediating sensitization of that effect. In the case of stimulant and opiate drugs such as amphetamine and morphine, there is strong evidence that the unconditioned excitatory effects on locomotor activity are mediated by their actions on the mesolimbic and striatal DA neurons.

And although the expression of the sensitized drug effects could result from many factors such as changes in metabolism or receptor availability and sensitivity, there is growing evidence that sensitization of the behavioral activating effects of these drugs results from changes in neuronal functioning within these midbrain dopamine (DA) systems and their related circuitry.

Sensitization to Opiate and Stimulant Drugs

Repeated intermittent systemic injections of amphetamine, cocaine, or morphine lead, to, among other things, sensitization of the behavioral activating effects of these drugs. For example, the enhancement in locomotor activity that occurs following initial exposure to relatively low doses of these drugs increases with repeated exposure, and animals repeatedly preexposed to a given dose show enhanced locomotor activity compared to animals given the same dose for the first time.

Two features of sensitization of the locomotor activating effects of stimulant and opiate drugs are discussed in this chapter. The first is that functional changes in mesolimbic and striatal DA neurons appear to mediate the behavioral sensitization found after repeated intermittent administration of both stimulant and opiate drugs such as amphetamine, cocaine, and morphine. This is of particular interest because there is reason to think that the mesolimbic DA system is a behavioral facilitatory system. Activity in this system promotes forward locomotion and approach, enhances the effectiveness of positive incentive stimuli, and appears to underlie the motivational or rewarding properties of stimulant and opiate drugs as well as those of more natural positive incentives (Iversen, 1983; Stewart, de Wit, & Eikelboom, 1984; Taylor & Robbins, 1984, 1986; Wise & Bozarth, 1987). For this reason, sensitization of activity in this system could serve to enhance the response of animals to stimuli having neural access to it (e.g., Keller, Striker, & Zigmond, 1983; Louilot, LeMoal, & Simon, 1986). A second important feature of the sensitization of the behavioral activating effects of opiate and stimulant drugs is that its expression can readily come under control of environmental stimuli. When exposure to these drugs is paired exclusively with one set of environmental stimuli, sensitization to the locomotor stimulant effects is manifested only in the presence of these stimuli (i.e., the sensitization of responding to the drugs comes under CS control and stimuli paired with these drugs come to elicit conditioned increases in activity; see Stewart & Vezina, 1988). These observations may have significance for an understanding of how environmental stimuli play a part in drug seeking and in the nature and intensity of responses to drugs of abuse. In this chapter, experiments designed to determine the conditions under which exposure to opiate and stimulant drugs leads to sensitization of their behavioral activating effects, and experiments aimed at clarifying how CSs gain control of the expression of sensitization are described.

Changes in the Functioning of Dopamine Neurons Accompany Behavioral Sensitization

Locomotor stimulant effects of both stimulant and opiate drugs appear to be mediated by the mesolimbic and striatal dopamine (DA) neurons. When these drugs are given systemically, DA is increased in the extracellular space, both at terminals and in the somatodendritic region. In the case of stimulants, extracellular DA is increased either by direct transmitter release or re-uptake blockade (Kuczenski, 1983) and is accompanied by reduced cell firing (Wang, 1981; White, Wachtel, Johansen, & Einhorn, 1987); in the case of opiates, extracellular DA is increased by increased neuron firing (see Gysling & Wang, 1983; Matthews & German, 1984). When morphine and certain other opioid peptides are given by microinjection into the cell body region of DA neurons in the ventral tegmental area (VTA), where morphine increases firing in DA neurons, enhanced locomotor activity is seen in the absence of the initial behavioral depression found after systemic injections (Joyce & Iversen, 1979; Kalivas, 1985a; Vezina & Stewart, 1984). As described previously, repeated intermittent injections of these drugs lead to long-lasting sensitization of their behavioral stimulant effects (e.g., Babbini, Gaiardi, & Bartoletti, 1975; Kalivas, Taylor, & Miller, 1985; Post, 1980; Segal & Mandell, 1974; Vezina & Stewart, 1984). Animals showing sensitized responding to systemic morphine (Vezina, Giovino, Wise, & Stewart, 1989) or intra-VTA opioids (Kalivas, 1985b) display cross-sensitization to amphetamine and vice versa (Stewart & Vezina, 1987), a finding that suggests that similar neurobiochemical changes might underlie the observed behavioral changes in response to the drugs. It has been found, in fact, that behavioral sensitization to these drug effects is accompanied by long-lasting functional modifications in DA neurons. Several studies have provided evidence for enduring enhancement of drug-stimulated DA release in terminal regions following preexposure to amphetamine and cocaine (Peris & Zahniser, 1987; Robinson & Becker, 1986). Animals showing sensitization of behavioral responses to morphine show greater turnover of DA in nucleus accumbens (NAC) in response to morphine challenge than previously untreated animals (Kalivas, 1985b). In the case of both opiate and stimulant drugs, little if any evidence has been found for changes in steady-state metabolism in terminal regions; the changes seen are in response to pharmacological challenge. Another interesting accompaniment of behavioral sensitization reported for both morphine and cocaine is decreased release of DA from cell body regions of the neurons in response to drug challenge (Duffy & Kalivas, 1988; Kalivas & Duffy, 1987). Decreased release from somatodendritic regions has important implications for impulse regulation. As noted elsewhere (Kalivas, Duffy, Dilts, & Abhold, 1988; Stewart & Vezina, 1988), reduced DA release from somatodendritic regions would mean reduced autoreceptor stimulation and, therefore, increased cell excitability, making the neurons more easily fired by excitatory influences. Such changes may account for the enhanced behavioral excitation seen in response to environmental stressors such as electric shock and tail pinch that accompanies sensitization to these drugs (Antelman & Chiodo, 1983; Kalivas, Richardson-Carlson, & van Orden, 1986). The accumulated evidence suggests that repeated intermittent exposure to either opiate or stimulant drugs leads to enduring changes in the functioning of the mesolimbic and striatal DA neurons, or in the local circuitry controlling their responsiveness, that could account for their increased sensitivity to challenge both by drugs and environmental stimuli.

Conditions for the Development of Sensitization to Stimulant and Opiate Drugs

The knowledge that both stimulant and opiate drugs act to increase DA in the extracellular space, and the finding that changes in the mesolimbic and striatal DA system accompany sensitization of the behavioral activating effects has led to more specific investigations of the mechanisms through which DA neurons might mediate the development of sensitization to the locomotor activating effects of these drugs. One approach has been to study the effect of blocking specific DA receptor types during the initial preexposure to the drug on the development of sensitization. A second approach has been to study the site of action of the drugs critical for the development of sensitization by injecting drugs intracranially at specific target areas. In these experiments and those described in later sections, animals repeatedly exposed to a drug during a *Preexposure Phase* were compared in a *Test Phase* to animals not previously exposed to the drug or to animals preexposed while undergoing an experimental manipulation.

In one set of experiments concerned with the role of D–1 and D–2 DA receptor activation, Vezina and Stewart (1989) pretreated rats with systemic injections of either the D–1 DA receptor antagonist, SCH–23390, the D–2 DA antagonists, pimozide and Ro22–2586, or saline prior to each of five preexposures to amphetamine given systemically, every other day. During the preexposure phase, all three antagonists completely blocked the locomotor effects of amphetamine, but only the D–1 DA antagonist blocked the development of sensitization to amphetamine. Figure 7.1 shows the activity scores of the animals on the test for sensitization when all animals received amphetamine only. It can be seen in the left panel that animals previously exposed to amphetamine in the presence of the D–1 antagonist (SCH–23390) were no more active on this test than animals never previously given amphetamine (group SAL–SAL). On the other hand, animals preexposed to amphetamine in the presence of either of the two D–2 antagonists were as active as animals that received repeated injections of amphetamine alone (SAL–AM).

Systemically administered SCH–23390 could have acted to interfere with the effects of DA released either from terminals in the NAC, where both D–1 and D–2 DA receptors are situated on postsynaptic neurons, or from somatodendritic regions, where D–1 receptors have been found on the terminals of non-DA

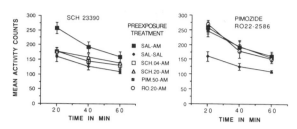

FIG. 7.1.   Test for Sensitization. The effect of D–1 (SCH-23390) and D–2 (Pimozide and Ro22–2586) DA receptor blockade during the preexposure period on the development of sensitization to the locomotor activating effects of amphetamine. No antagonists were administered on the test when all animals received 0.5 mg/kg amphetamine, i.p. Data are shown as groups means (± S.E.M.). (Adapted with permission from Vezina & Stewart, 1989.)

neurons in substantia nigra pars reticulata (SNr) and VTA (Altar & Hauser, 1987). In a second set of experiments, we have shown that bilateral microinjections of SCH–23390 given directly into the VTA or SNr are sufficient to block the development of sensitization to systemic injections of amphetamine (Stewart & Vezina, 1989). During a preexposure phase, different groups of animals received four amphetamine injections, once every other day, immediately following the intracranial injection of either SCH–23390 or vehicle. Group VEH–SAL received injections of the vehicle and saline only. Figure 7.2 shows the behavior of animals on a test for sensitization when animals in all treatment groups were given amphetamine only. These data suggest that the changes underlying the

FIG. 7.2.   Test for Sensitization. The effect of D–1 (SCH–23390) DA receptor blockade given into the VTA and SNr during the pre-exposure period on the development of sensitization to the locomotor activating effects of amphetamine. All animals received only amphetamine (0.5 mg/kg, i.p.) on this test. The data are shown as group means (± S.E.M.). The numbers at the base of each bar indicate the number of animals per group. (Reproduced with permission from Stewart & Vezina, 1989.)

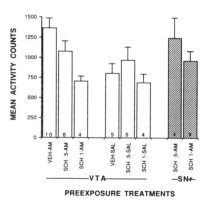

development of sensitization to amphetamine are due to the effects of DA released in the somatodendritic regions. Other data make this seem likely. In an experiment reported by Kalivas and Weber (1988), it was found that microinjections of amphetamine directly into the somatodendritic region of DA neurons in either VTA or SN were sufficient to sensitize animals to later systemic injections of amphetamine, as well as to cross-sensitize to systemic cocaine, even though these central injections did not cause behavioral activation. Vezina and Stewart (1988, 1990) have found that intra-VTA injections of amphetamine sensitizes animals to later systemic injections of morphine and have also confirmed the previous observations of Dougherty and Ellinwood (1981) and Kalivas and Weber (1988), that repeated injections of amphetamine to the terminal regions of DA neurons in NAC and striatum do not lead to sensitization of the behavioral effects of systemic amphetamine even though animals are extremely active following these central injections.

Taken together, the findings discussed in this section lend support to the idea that excessive DA release from the somatodendritic region of the DA neurons can bring about changes in the DA neurons themselves, or in the local circuitry controlling these neurons, and that these changes underlie the sensitized responding to amphetamine as well as the cross-sensitization seen to opiate drugs and to stressors and other environmental stimuli. The additional findings that sensitization to amphetamine developed even when the behavioral activating effects of the drug were blocked during the preexposure phase, as in the experiments with the D–2 DA antagonists, or were not induced, as in the experiment in which amphetamine was applied directly to the cell body region of the DA neurons, would seem to imply that direct activation of response production systems is not required to bring about the neural changes that underlie behavioral sensitization.

Conditioned Stimulus Control of Sensitization to Drugs

CS control of the expression of sensitization to a drug effect refers to the fact that animals preexposed to a drug repeatedly in the presence of one set of environmental stimuli, when given a test for sensitization, will show a greater response to the drug than animals not preexposed to the drug, or animals preexposed to the drug in an environment different from the test environment. In the terminology of conditioning this would be a case in which a CS, the environment, affected the magnitude of the response to the UCS, the drug. This method of testing for the effects of a CS, and the nature of the results obtained, has parallels in conditioning experiments in which brain stimulation was used to elicit the UR. Thomas (1972), for example, described a set of experiments in which a technique taken from neurophysiology, called the conditioning-test technique, was used to study both facilitation and inhibition by external CSs of the responses elicited by electrical brain stimulation. In one set of experiments tones and lights were used as CS+ and CS− in a discrimination experiment, and electrical stimulation of hypothalamic areas capable of eliciting "fear" or "rage" responses was used as the UCS. Following discriminative conditioning, presentation of the CS+, which had been paired with the brain stimulation (the UCS), augmented responding to threshold levels of brain stimulation. The CS−, which had always been presented in the absence of the UCS, was capable of inhibiting responding even when no response to the CS− alone was observed. Clearly, the presentation of the CSs had profound effects on responsivity to the electrical stimulation, effects that resemble in some respects the effects of CS environments on the response to centrally acting drugs. Modulating effects of CSs on the magnitude and intensity of responses to natural UCSs have been found in other experiments in which the CS is presented just prior to or in conjunction with the UCS (Hollis, 1982; Rescorla, 1969; Zamble, Hadad, Mitchell, & Cutmore, 1985). In all these situations the magnitude and intensity of the response to the UCS is modulated by stimuli that have been explicitly paired or unpaired with UCS presentations. Note that in these cases the effects of the previous pairings are assessed by studying the effects of the CS on the response to the UCS, and not by studying the response to the CS in the absence of the UCS. It can be asked, in this context, whether the processes that underlie the modulatory effects of the CS on the response to the UCS are the same as those that underlie the conditioned responses (CR) to the CS in the absence of the UCS; that is, does the CS elicit a single effect that is responsible both for the conditioned response and for the modulation of the response to the UCS?

Evidence for Conditioned Stimulus Control of Sensitized Responses to Stimulant and Opiate Drugs

CS control of sensitization has been found to develop following systemic injections of amphetamine (Tilson & Rech, 1973), morphine (Mansfield, Wenger, Benedict, Halter, & Woods, 1981), and cocaine (Hinson & Poulos, 1981; Post, 1980; Post, Lockfeld, Squillace, & Contel, 1981).

In an initial experiment to determine whether the locomotor activity elicited and the sensitization that develops when morphine is applied directly into the VTA could be brought under CS control, Vezina and Stewart (1984) found that animals given repeated applications of morphine into the VTA just before being placed into a distinctive environment (group PAIRED) were much more active on a later test for sensitization in that environment than animals given the same repeated applications of morphine, but in another environment (group UNPAIRED), or than animals never previously exposed to morphine (group CTL). The test for sensitization, in which all animals received intra-VTA morphine just prior to being placed in the activity boxes, following five treatment blocks during which group PAIRED was given morphine on five occasions prior to being placed in activity boxes, and a sham injection in the home cage; group UNPAIRED received a sham injection prior to being placed in the activity boxes,

FIG. 7.3. Test for Sensitization. Mean activity counts (± S.E.M.) on the test for conditioned environmental control of sensitization following preexposure to VTA morphine in the activity boxes (PAIRED), in the home cage (UNPAIRED), or not at all (CTL) (Group n's = 8). On this test all animals received morphine in the VTA prior to being placed in the activity boxes. (Adapted with permission from Vezina & Stewart, 1984.)

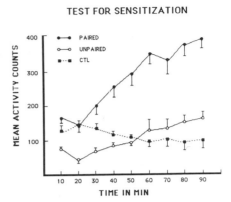

and morphine in the home cage; and Group CTL received sham injections in both environments. Figure 7.3 shows the behavior of the three groups of animals on the test for sensitization. Group PAIRED, which received morphine associated with the activity box for the sixth time, on this test, was much more active than either group CTL, which had never had morphine before, or group UNPAIRED, which, though it had received morphine on five previous occasions, had never before received morphine in the activity boxes. In fact, in the initial 50 min of the test for sensitization, the activity of group UNPAIRED was significantly suppressed compared to that of group CTL, suggesting that activity was inhibited in the presence of environmental cues that reliably predicted the absence of drug. Animals in these latter two groups were, however, significantly more active after morphine than they were following sham treatments. This can be seen by comparing their behavior on the test for conditioning (Fig. 7.4) when all animals received sham treatments. In this test, animals in group PAIRED were significantly more active in the environment previously paired with drug than were animals in the other two groups. Thus, it appeared that repeated activation of the mesolimbic DA in the presence of a specific set of environmental stimuli was a

FIG. 7.4. Test for Conditioning. Mean activity counts (± S.E.M.) on the test for conditioning following preexposure to VTA morphine in the activity boxes (PAIRED), the home cages (UNPAIRED), or not at all (CTL). On this test all animals received sham administrations in the VTA. These are the same animals as those shown in Fig. 7.3. (Adapted with permission from Vezina & Stewart, 1984.)

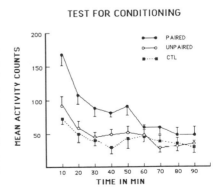

sufficient condition for the development of the drug-induced conditioned activity. The next set of experiments was designed to determine whether the stimuli that control the expression of sensitization to either morphine or amphetamine could control the expression of cross-sensitization to the other drug.

Conditioned Stimulus Control of Cross-Sensitization Between Opiate and Stimulant Drugs

In a first set of experiments on conditioned control of cross-sensitization, Stewart and Vezina (1987) found that groups of animals preexposed to systemic injections of amphetamine in the distinctive environment of the activity boxes were significantly more active in this environment on a test for cross-sensitization to morphine than animals preexposed to amphetamine in the home cage or animals not preexposed to amphetamine. Animals were preexposed every other day for 5 days to systemic injections of amphetamine in either the activity boxes (group PAIRED) or the home cage (group UNPAIRED) and given saline injections in the other environment on alternate days, or given saline in both places (group CTL). Figure 7.5a shows the mean activity counts of three such groups that were preexposed to amphetamine and tested for cross-sensitization to morphine given systemically. Notice that animals previously exposed to amphetamine in the activity boxes (PAIRED) were significantly more active when given morphine

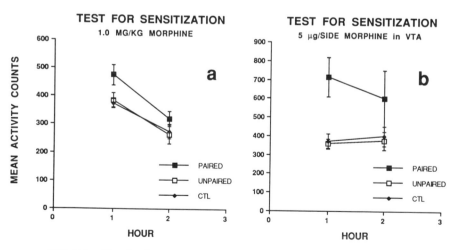

FIG. 7.5.   Test for Cross-Sensitization. Mean activity counts (± S.E.M.) on the test for conditioned environmental control of cross-sensitization to morphine following preexposure to 1.0 mg/kg amphetamine, i.p. in the activity boxes (PAIRED); the home cages (UNPAIRED) or not at all (CTL). On this test all animals were given 1.0 mg/kg morphine, i.p., only (a); or 5 µg/0.5 µl saline/side morphine in the VTA, only (b). (Adapted with permission from Stewart & Vezina, 1987.)

FIG. 7.6. Test for Cross-Sensitization. Mean activity counts (± S.E.M.) on the test for conditioned environmental control of cross-sensitization to amphetamine in animals preexposed to 10 mg/kg morphine, i.p., in the activity boxes (PAIRED); the home cages (UNPAIRED); or not at all (CTL). On this test all animals were given 1.0 mg/kg amphetamine, i.p. (Adapted with permission from Vezina, Giovino, Wise & Stewart, 1989.)

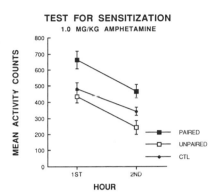

than animals in the other two groups. This CS control of cross-sensitization to morphine is even more clear in groups of animals that were given intra-VTA injections of morphine on the test for sensitization (Fig. 7.5b). Animals were much more active when given morphine directly into the cell body region of the VTA than when morphine was administered systemically. But what is most striking is that animals in the group UNPAIRED showed no evidence for sensitization to the effects of morphine when compared to animals that had never previously received amphetamine, even though they had received amphetamine on five previous occasions.

A similar experiment was carried out to assess CS control of cross-sensitization between morphine and amphetamine given systemically (Vezina, Giovino, Wise, & Stewart, 1989). Figure 7.6 shows the behavior of animals on a test for sensitization to the effects of amphetamine after previous exposure to morphine. Groups were treated as in the previous study, but the drug was given on only four occasions. Again the environmental specificity of the expression of cross-sensitization is clear. What is not clear is how or where this stimulus control is exerted. Stimuli (CSs+ or CSs−), previously paired with drug or with the absence of drug, might act to facilitate or inhibit firing of DA cells or to facilitate or inhibit DA release. Either action could serve to modulate the effects of opiate and stimulant drugs, even though the drugs have very different mechanisms of action.

In an attempt to specify where the effects of the CS might interact with the unconditioned effects of the drug to allow for CS control of sensitization, we studied the development of sensitization to the effects of amphetamine injected directly into the VTA, or the NAC, using a conditioning paradigm (Vezina & Stewart, 1988, 1990). As mentioned earlier, it was known that animals given repeated intra-VTA injections of amphetamine would show sensitization to subsequent systemic injections of either amphetamine or morphine, whereas animals given injections of amphetamine into the NAC would not. We wanted to determine whether the sensitization from VTA injections could come under CS control. During the preexposure phase, groups of rats were given bilateral injections of amphetamine either into the VTA or the NAC prior to being placed in the activity boxes and saline in the home cages (PAIRED), saline in the activity boxes and amphetamine in the home cages (UNPAIRED), or saline in both environments (CTL). On subsequent tests for sensitization and conditioning, all animals were placed in the activity boxes following systemic injections of morphine and saline, respectively. Figure 7.7 shows the behavior of animals on the test for sensitization. Animals that had previously received amphetamine in the VTA (7a) showed sensitized responding to morphine, but there was no evidence for CS control of sensitization; both group PAIRED and group UNPAIRED were more active than group CTL, but they were not different from each other. As reported previously, sensitization did not develop following repeated administration of amphetamine to the NAC (7b). Figure 7.8 shows the results from the test for conditioning when all animals were treated with saline only. Note that in neither case was there any evidence for conditioning.

In this experiment, DA release and reuptake blockade from the somato-dendritic region of the neurons, though sufficient for the development of sensitization, appeared not to engage the neural circuitry in a manner that allowed the integration of sensory information necessary for the development of CS control. It was also shown that excessive postsynaptic DA receptor stimulation,

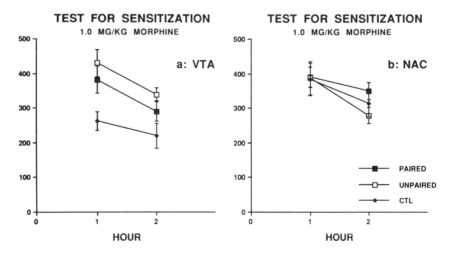

FIG. 7.7.   Test for Cross-Sensitization. Mean activity counts (± S.E.M.) on the test for conditioned environmental control of cross-sensitization to morphine in animals preexposed to injections of 2.5 µg/0.5 µl saline/side amphetamine into either the VTA (a), or the NAC (b). During preexposure animals were given amphetamine in the activity boxes (PAIRED), the home cages (UNPAIRED), or not at all (CTL). On this test all animals were given 1.0 mg/kg morphine, i.p., only. (Adapted with permission from Vezina & Stewart, 1990.)

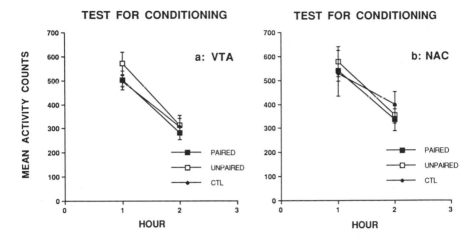

FIG. 7.8. Test for Conditioning. Mean activity counts (± S.E.M.) on the test for conditioned activity following preexposure to 2.5 μg/0.5 μl saline/side amphetamine into either the VTA (a), or the NAC (b). On this test animals were given injections of saline only. (Adapted with permission from Vezina & Stewart, 1990.)

at least in the NAC alone, led neither to sensitization nor to conditioning of activity, even though animals were very active during the preexposure period. As we have suggested elsewhere (Stewart & Vezina, 1988), it may be that only when these DA neurons are activated in their entirety, allowing for feedback from their own projections or from those of other DA neurons projecting to other limbic or cortical areas, does the possibility exist for sensory interactions to take place.

The Effects of Extinction on the Conditioned Control of Sensitization to Drugs

In another attempt to determine the nature of CS control of the expression of sensitization to drugs, we studied the effects of extinction training on previously established CS control of sensitization of the locomotor effects of amphetamine (Stewart & Vezina, 1991). Animals were divided into three groups as in the conditioning experiments previously described, group PAIRED, UNPAIRED, and CTL. During the preexposure phase, animals were given the appropriate systemic injections of amphetamine or saline in the activity boxes and in the home cages. Following the preexposure phase, evidence for both conditioned activity and CS control of sensitization to amphetamine was found in tests when all animals were administered saline and amphetamine, respectively. A series of extinction sessions followed during which all groups were tested repeatedly in the activity boxes as before, but during which all animals were given only saline injections both in the activity boxes and in the home cages. By the last day of extinction training, there were no differences in activity between the groups. On the test for sensitization to amphetamine that followed, however, activity levels in group PAIRED and group UNPAIRED did not differ and were significantly higher than in the saline control group. Thus, after the extinction sessions, sensitization was evident in both groups that had been preexposed repeatedly to amphetamine; whereas, in the test for sensitization given prior to extinction, animals in group UNPAIRED had been no more active than animals in the saline control group. It appears that the extinction sessions had eliminated the inhibition of the expression of sensitization previously seen in group UNPAIRED when tested in the CS- environment. These data provide another example of drug-induced sensitization in the absence of conditioned effects, suggesting again that any account of the development of CS control of the expression of sensitization to stimulant and opiate drugs must provide an explanation for the changes underlying sensitization to the drug effects that are independent of conditioning.

A Test of the Effects of Conditioned (Drug-Paired) Stimuli on the Response to a Nondrug Unconditioned Stimulus

The data from our studies on conditioning presented earlier suggest to us that, when environmental stimuli are paired with activation of mesolimbic DA neurons or with DA release from somatodendritic and terminal regions, these stimuli gain the power both to control the behavioral expression of sensitization within the system and to bring about conditioned facilitation of locomotor behavior in the absence of drugs. We (Vezina & Stewart, 1987) and others (see Carr, Fibiger, & Phillips, 1989) have shown elsewhere that environmental stimuli previously paired with morphine not only facilitate locomotion and exploratory behavior, but, in addition, induce approach and maintenance of contact with them, suggesting that such CSs might bring about changes in neural systems mediating appetitive behaviors in general. As mentioned previously, activity in the meso-limbic DA system facilitates locomotion and approach and enhances the effectiveness of positive incentive stimuli. It might be expected, therefore, that CSs previously paired with drug-induced activity in this system could facilitate the expression of behaviors elicited by other primary incentive stimuli or UCSs. We have tested this idea by studying sexual responsiveness of male rats presented with an estrous female in an environment previously paired with morphine (Mitchell & Stewart, 1990). We chose to study the facilitation of male sexual behavior because activation of the mesolimbic DA system has been directly implicated in the mediation of sexual arousal in the male rat (Alderson & Baum, 1981; Mitchell & Stewart, 1989). In these experiments we have found that the elicitation of the conditioned drug effect by the environmental stimuli previously associated with morphine can facilitate sexual arousal in the presence of a sexually receptive female.

Male rats were initially screened for sexual behavior prior to the drug preexposure phase of the experiment. During the preexposure phase in which no female rats were present, one group of male rats (PAIRED) was injected with morphine on four occasions, once every other day, and placed into a distinctive box later to be used as a mating arena; on alternate days they were given saline injections in the home cage. An UNPAIRED group received saline in the box and morphine in the home cage. A CONTROL group received saline in both environments. Two days following the fourth morphine treatment, all animals were tested in the mating arenas for 30 min with a sexually receptive female. A second test was given 2 weeks later. In both tests, animals in the PAIRED group displayed significantly greater and more persistent female-directed behavior than animals in both the UNPAIRED and CONTROL groups. Figure 7.9 shows that group PAIRED had significantly shorter latencies to mount than the other two

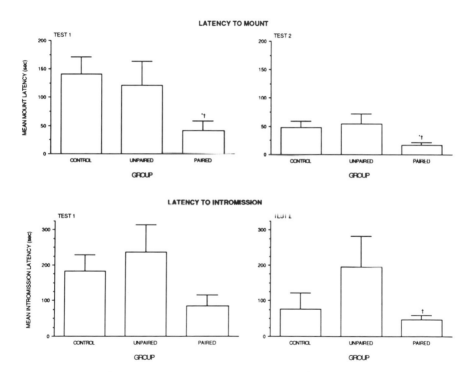

FIG. 7.9.   Test for Conditioned Facilitation of Mating. Mean (± S.E.M.) mount and intromission latencies of animals that had previously received 10.0 mg/kg morphine, i.p., paired with the mating arena (PAIRED), the home cage (UNPAIRED), or not at all (CONTROL). On this test all animals received injections of saline only. *Significantly different from CONTROL, $p < .05$; †significantly different from UNPAIRED, $p < .05$. (Reproduced with permission from Mitchell & Stewart, 1990.)

groups in both tests and a shorter intromission latency than the UNPAIRED group in the second test. These data showing that a CS previously paired with morphine can facilitate sexual behaviors elicited by a sexually receptive female are consistent with the view that a CS previously paired with enhanced responding within the mesolimbic DA system can facilitate the expression of behaviors elicited by other primary incentive stimuli or UCSs, stimuli that presumably also enhance activity within that system.

SUMMARY

The findings of the experiments discussed in this chapter can be summarized as follows:

1. Repeated intermittent systemic injections of either amphetamine or morphine lead to sensitization of the behavioral activating effects of these drugs, and sensitization to one of these drugs leads to cross-sensitization to the other.
2. The development of sensitization to systemic amphetamine can be blocked by concurrent injections of a D–1 receptor antagonist, given either systemically or into the VTA/SNr region, suggesting that activation of D–1 receptors in the somatodendritic region of the DA cells is critical for the development of sensitization.
3. Intra-VTA injections of amphetamine or morphine lead to the development of sensitization of locomotor activity, but intra-NAC injections do not, suggesting that development of sensitization occurs through the local circuitry in the VTA region.
4. Conditioned stimulus control of sensitization develops when amphetamine or morphine are given systemically, and when morphine is given intra-VTA. When sensitization is produced by intra-VTA amphetamine injections, however, CS control does not develop.

It may be possible on the basis of the data presented here to sketch out a preliminary account of the actions of stimulant and opiate drugs necessary for the development of sensitization and for the development of CS control of the expression of sensitization. Table 7.1 summarizes the data from sensitization experiments using both systemic and intracranial injections of amphetamine and morphine. Note that the development of sensitization, itself, is associated in all cases with increases in extracellular concentration of DA in the somatodendritic region of the mesolimbic DA neurons. When the drug acts only to cause release in the terminal regions of the DA neurons in the NAC, neither sensitization nor CS control develops. DA release from somatodendritic regions is not, however, a sufficient condition for the development of conditioned stimulus control of sen-

TABLE 7.1
Summary of Data from Sensitization Experiments Using Systemic and Intracranial Injections of
Amphetamine and Morphine

Preexposure Drug	DA Release Cell Body	Terminal	Animal Active	Behavioral Sensitization	Conditioned Stimulus Control
AMPH I. P.	+	+	+	+	+
AMPH VTA	+	-	-	+	-
AMPH NAC	-	+	+	-	-
MOR I. P.	+	+	+	+	+
MOR VTA	+	+	+	+	+
MOR NAC	NON-DA DEPENDENT		+	-	?

sitization. The table shows that CS control only develops when the drug acts to bring about release of DA from both cell body and terminal regions of the neurons. Neither in itself is sufficient.

Figure 7.10 is a schematic diagram depicting a set of DA neurons (hatched) and some of their interconnections. Drugs acting to increase extracellular DA in the somatodendritic region would allow for activation of both D–2 DA receptors on the DA neurons themselves (autoreceptors) and D–1 DA receptors on non-DA axon terminals. Our experiments have shown the blockade of the D–1 receptor in this region blocks the development of sensitization of the behavioral effects of amphetamine. These data suggest, therefore, that it is via the local circuit in the VTA cell body region that sensitization is triggered. If sensitization develops as a result of repeated exposure to increased extracellular DA in the cell body region, it might be that CSs could come to exert their control over the expression of sensitization by interacting in this region with the UCS actions of drugs.

Figure 7.11 depicts two possible ways in which a CS might have access to and

FIG. 7.10. Diagrammatic representation of mesolimbic DA neurons (hatched) and some of their possible interconnections. In the cell body region, DA neurons release DA from cell bodies and dendritic processes that can act at D–2 autoreceptors to inhibit DA cell firing. DA released from cell bodies and dendrites is also shown to act on D–1 receptors located on non-DA neurons to reinforce activity within a local circuit. In the terminal region, released DA can act on D–2 autoreceptors and on postsynaptic D–1 and D–2 receptors.

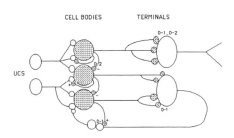

FIG. 7.11. Diagrammatic representation of CS input at the level of the DA cell bodies: (1) shows a CS unit with direct access to the DA neuron and capable of being influenced by locally released DA; (2) shows a CS unit with direct access to a non-DA neuron that is capable of being reinforced by locally released DA (see Fig. 7.10). The CS unit, itself, however, is capable of being reinforced indirectly by DA released in the terminal region.

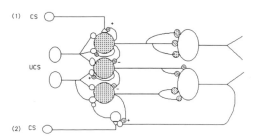

thus come to influence the firing of DA cells. At the top of the diagram is a CS unit (1) that has a direct connection to the DA cell. If activity in this CS unit were to co-occur with activity in the DA cell, the potential would exist for the firing of the DA unit to influence activity in the terminals of the CS unit. This arrangement, although providing the possibility for conditioning to take place, is unlikely to be one that could account for CS control over the expression of sensitization to amphetamine and morphine. Remember that CS control does not develop when environmental stimuli are paired with increased extracellular DA in the somatodendritic region alone. A second arrangement is shown at the bottom of the figure. Here the CS unit (2) has access to the somatodendritic region of the DA neuron via an interneuron that, in turn, is influenced by the output of cells having their origins in the terminal regions of the DA neurons. In this case, DA release in the terminal region is able to influence cells in the cell body region. The cells in the somatodendritic region, activated by the CS neuron, are in turn influenced by the somatodendritic release of DA. This arrangement would require increased extracellular DA in both terminal and cell body regions in order for the effectiveness of the CS to be affected by pairings with the drug effect, and, as we have seen, is the condition that leads to CS control of

FIG. 7.12. Diagrammatic representation of additional CS inputs that interact with the DA neuron at the terminal region: (3) shows the CS unit terminating on a DA neuron terminal and having the potential to influence the release of DA from the terminal; (4) shows a CS unit ending on a postsynaptic neuron and capable of being reinforced by release of DA from neuron terminals.

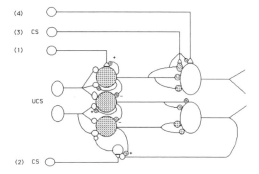

sensitization. Note also that both of these arrangements would permit a CS alone to elicit conditioned activation of the system in the absence of a drug.

Shown in Fig. 7.12 are two other configurations that would allow for a CS paired with increased extracellular DA in both somatodendritic and terminal regions of the neuron to gain control over the expression of sensitization. In these cases, the CS unit interacts with the DA neuron only in the terminal regions. The CS unit (3) is shown to have access to the terminals where it could gain control over the release of DA. In this case, CS control would develop at terminal sites independently from the development of sensitization, itself, and would act there to influence the expression of sensitization. This possibility is based on recent studies by Glowinski and colleagues and by Phillipson and colleagues, both of whom have evidence for modulation of release of DA from terminals in the striatum via activation of a thalamo–cortico–striatal neuronal loop (Cheramy, Romo, Godeheu, Baruch, & Glowinski, 1986; Kilpatrick, Jones, Johnson, Cornwall, & Phillipson, 1986; Kilpatrick, Jones, Pycock, Riches, & Phillipson, 1986; Kilpatrick & Phillipson, 1986; Romo, Cheramy, Godeheu, & Glowinski, 1986a, 1986b). Pharmacological and electrical stimulation of certain thalamic nuclei induce the release of DA from striatal neuron terminals, and there is evidence to suggest that these effects are due to presynaptic facilitation. Cheramy et al. (1986) also found indirect presynaptic inhibitory control over DA release from terminals. Although less is known about similar effects in the thalamo–limbic cortex–accumbens–VTA loop, Jones, Kilpatrick, & Phillipson (1987) have found that stimulation of the dorsomedial nucleus of the thalamus can regulate DA release from terminals in frontal cortex. The arrangement shown (3) would allow the CS to facilitate or inhibit the release of DA from terminals, both in the presence of drug where it could modulate the expression of sensitization, and in the absence of drug. In arrangement (4), the CS unit is shown to interact directly with the postsynaptic neuron and to be influenced presynaptically by the DA neuron. In this case, DA would be involved in the development of conditioning, but the CS would not come to have any direct facilitatory control over activity within the DA system itself. Whether such an arrangement would allow for the conditioned control of sensitization is unclear.

These attempts to model the various ways in which concurrent activity in systems carrying information about the CS might interact with drug-induced changes in the DA systems are preliminary and clearly simplistic. They do force us, however, to think about how and where in the nervous system the learned changes in the ability of sensory stimuli to modulate activity might take place.

ACKNOWLEDGMENTS

This chapter was supported by grants from the Medical Research Council of Canada and Fonds pour la Formation de Chercheurs et l'Aide à la Recherche.

REFERENCES

Alderson, L. M., & Baum, M. J. (1981). Differential effects of gonadal steroids on dopamine metabolism in mesolimbic and nigrostriatal pathways of male rat brain. *Brain Research, 218,* 189–206.

Altar, C. A., & Hauser, K. (1987). Topography of substantia nigra innervation by D_1 receptor-containing striatal neurons. *Brain Research, 410,* 1–11.

Anisman, H., & Sklar, L. S. (1979). Catecholamine depletion in mice upon reexposure to stress: Mediation of the escape deficits produced by inescapable shock. *Journal of Comparative and Physiological Psychology, 93,* 610–625.

Antelman, S. M. (1988). Stressor-induced sensitization to subsequent stress: Implications for the development and treatment of clinical disorders. In P. W. Kalivas & C. D. Barnes (Eds.), *Sensitization in the nervous system* (pp. 227–254). Caldwell, NJ: Telford Press.

Antelman, S. M., & Chiodo, L. A. (1983). Amphetamine as a stressor. In I. Creese (Ed.), *Stimulants: Neurochemical, behavioral, and clinical perspectives* (pp. 269–299). New York: Raven Press.

Babbini, M., Gaiardi, M., & Bartoletti, M. (1975). Persistence of chronic morphine effects upon activity in rats 8 months after ceasing the treatment. *Neuropharmacology, 14,* 611–614.

Carr, G. D., Fibiger, H. C., & Phillips, A. G. (1989). Conditioned place preference as a measure of drug reward. In J. M. Liebman & S. J. Cooper (Eds.), *The neuropharmacological basis of reward* (pp. 264–319). Oxford: Clarendon Press.

Cheramy, A., Romo, R., Godeheu, G., Baruch, P., & Glowinski, J. (1986). In vivo presynaptic control of dopamine release in the cat caudate nucleus. II. Facilitatory or inhibitory influence of l-glutamate. *Neuroscience, 19,* 1081–1090.

Cooper, E. L. (1980). Cell-mediated memory in invertebrates. In M. J. Manning (Ed.), *Phylogeny of immunological memory* (pp. 35–46). Amsterdam: Elsevier/North Holland.

Dougherty, G. G., Jr., & Ellinwood, E. H. (1981). Chronic d-amphetamine in nucleus accumbens: Lack of tolerance or reverse tolerance of locomotor activity. *Life Sciences, 28,* 2295–2298.

Duffy, P., & Kalivas, P. W. (1988). Inhibition of endogenous dopamine release from the ventromedial mesencephalon after daily cocaine or morphine. In P. W. Kalivas & C. B. Nemeroff (Eds.), *The mesocorticolimbic dopamine system. Annals of the New York Academy of Sciences, 537,* 475–477.

Eikelboom, R., & Stewart, J. (1982). The conditioning of drug-induced physiological responses. *Psychological Review, 89,* 507–528.

Groves, P. M., & Thompson, R. F. (1970). Habituation: A dual-process theory. *Psychological Review, 77,* 419–450.

Gysling, K., & Wang, R. Y. (1983). Morphine-induced activation of A10 dopamine neurons in the rat. *Brain Research, 277,* 119–127.

Hinson, R. E., & Poulos, C. X. (1981). Sensitization to the behavioral effects of cocaine: Modification by Pavlovian conditioning. *Pharmacology Biochemistry & Behavior, 15,* 559–562.

Hollis, K. L. (1982). Pavlovian conditioning of signal-centered action patterns and autonomic behavior: A biological analysis of function. In J. S. Rosenblatt, R. H. Hinde, C. Beer, & M. Busnel (Eds.), *Advances in the study of behavior* (Vol. 12, pp. 1–64). New York: Academic Press.

Iversen, S. D. (1983). Brain endorphins and reward function: Some thoughts and speculations. In J. E. Smith & J. D. Lane (Eds.), *The neurobiology of opiate reward processes* (pp. 439–468). Amsterdam: Elsevier/North Holland Biomedical Press.

Jones, M. W., Kilpatrick, I. C., & Phillipson, O. T. (1987). Regulation of dopamine function in the prefrontal cortex of the rat by the thalamic mediodorsal nucleus. *Brain Research Bulletin, 19,* 9–17.

Joyce, E. M., & Iversen, S. D. (1979). The effect of morphine applied locally to mesencephalic dopamine cell bodies on spontaneous motor activity in the rat. *Neuroscience Letters, 14,* 207–212.

Kalivas, P. W. (1985a). Interactions between neuropeptides and dopamine neurons in the ventromedial mesencephalon. *Neuroscience and Biobehavioral Reviews, 9,* 573–587.

Kalivas, P. W. (1985b). Sensitization to repeated enkephalin administration into the ventral tegmental area of the rat. II. Involvement of the mesolimbic dopamine system. *Journal of Pharmacology and Experimental Therapeutics, 235,* 544–550.

Kalivas, P. W., & Duffy, P. (1987). Sensitization to repeated morphine injection in the rat: Possible involvement of A10 dopamine neurons. *Journal of Pharmacology and Experimental Therapeutics, 241,* 204–212.

Kalivas, P. W., Duffy, P., Dilts, R., & Abhold, R. (1988). Enkephalin modulation of A10 dopamine neurons: A role in dopamine sensitization. In P. W. Kalivas & C. B. Nemeroff (Eds.), *The mesocorticolimbic dopamine system. Annals of the New York Academy of Sciences, 537,* 405–414.

Kalivas, P. W., Richardson-Carlson, R., & van Orden, G. (1986). Cross-sensitization between foot shock stress and enkephalin-induced motor activity. *Biological Psychiatry, 21,* 939–950.

Kalivas, P. W., Taylor, S., & Miller, J. S. (1985). Sensitization to repeated enkephalin administration into the ventral tegmental area of the rat. I. Behavioral characterization. *Journal of Pharmacology and Experimental Therapeutics, 235,* 537–543.

Kalivas, P. W., & Weber, B. (1988). Amphetamine injection into the ventral mesencephalon sensitizes rats to peripheral amphetamine and cocaine. *Journal of Pharmacology and Experimental Therapeutics, 245,* 1095–1102.

Kandel, E. R., Abrams, T., Bernier, L., Carew, T. J., Hawkins, R. D., & Schwartz, J. A. (1983). Classical conditioning and sensitization share aspects of the same molecular cascade in Aplysia. *Cold Spring Harbor Symposium on Quantitative Biology, 48,* 821–830.

Keller, R. W., Striker, E. M., & Zigmond, M. J. (1983). Environmental stimuli but not homeostatic challenges produce apparent increases in dopaminergic activity in the striatum: An analysis by in vivo voltammetry. *Brain Research, 279,* 159–170.

Kilpatrick, I. C., Jones, M. W., Johnson, B. J., Cornwall, J., & Phillipson, O. T. (1986). Thalamic control of dopaminergic functions in the caudate-putamen of the rat. II. Studies using ibotenic acid injection of the parafascicular-intralaminar nuclei. *Neuroscience, 19,* 979–990.

Kilpatrick, I. C., Jones, M. W., Pycock, C. J., Riches, I., & Phillipson, O. T. (1986). Thalamic control of dopaminergic functions in the caudate-putamen of the rat. III. The effects of lesions in the parafascicular-intralaminar nuclei on D2 dopamine receptors and high affinity dopamine uptake. *Neuroscience, 19,* 991–1005.

Kilpatrick, I. C., & Phillipson, O. T. (1986). Thalamic control of dopaminergic functions in the caudate-putamen of the rat. I. The influence of electrical stimulation of the parafascicular nucleus on dopamine utilization. *Neuroscience, 19,* 965–978.

Kuczenski, R. (1983). Biochemical actions of amphetamine and other stimulants. In I. Creese (Ed.), *Stimulants: Neurochemical, Behavioral and Clinical Perspectives* (pp. 31–61) New York: Raven Press.

Louilot, A., LeMoal, M., & Simon, H. (1986). Differential reactivity of dopaminergic neurons in the nucleus accumbens in response to different behavioral situations: An in vivo voltammetric study in the free moving rat. *Brain Research, 397,* 395–400.

Macintosh, N. J. (1974). *The psychology of animal learning.* New York: Academic Press.

Mansfield, J. G., Wenger, J. R., Benedict, R. S., Halter, J. B., & Woods, S. C. (1981). Sensitization to the hyperthermic and catecholamine-releasing effects of morphine. *Life Sciences, 29,* 1697–1704.

Matthews, R. T., & German, D. C. (1984). Electrophysiological evidence for excitation of rat ventral tegmental area dopamine neurons by morphine. *Neuroscience, 11,* 617–628.

Mitchell, J. B., & Stewart, J. (1989). Effects of castration, steroid replacement, and sexual experience on mesolimbic dopamine and sexual behaviors in the male rat. *Brain Research, 491,* 116–127.

Mitchell, J. B., & Stewart, J. (1990). Facilitation of sexual behaviors in the male rat in the presence of stimuli previously paired with systemic injections of morphine. *Pharmacology Biochemistry & Behavior, 35,* 367–372.

Peris, J., & Zahniser, N. R. (1987). One injection of cocaine produces a long-lasting increase in (^{3}H)-dopamine release. *Pharmacology Biochemistry & Behavior, 27,* 533–535.

Post, R. M. (1980). Intermittent versus continuous stimulation: Effect of time interval on the development of sensitization or tolerance. *Life Sciences, 26,* 1275–1282.

Post, R. M., Lockfeld, K. M., Squillace, K. M., & Contel, N. R. (1981). Drug-environment interaction: Context dependency of cocaine-induced behavioral sensitization. *Life Sciences, 28,* 755–760.

Post, R. M., Weiss, S. R. B., & Pert, A. (1988). Cocaine-induced behavioral sensitization and kindling: Implications for the emergence of psychopathology and seizures. In P. W. Kalivas & C. B. Nemeroff. *The mesocorticolimbic dopamine system. Annals of the New York Academy of Sciences, 537,* 292–308.

Rankin, C. H., Nolen, T. G., Marcus, E. A., Stopfer, M., & Carew, T. J. (1988). The development of sensitization in aplysia. In P. W. Kalivas & C. D. Barnes (Eds.), *Sensitization in the nervous system* (pp. 1–25). Caldwell, NJ: Telford Press.

Rescorla, R. A. (1969). Pavlovian conditioned inhibition. *Psychological Bulletin, 72,* 77–94.

Robinson, T. E., & Becker, J. B. (1986). Enduring changes in brain and behavior produced by chronic amphetamine administration: A review and evaluation of animal models of amphetamine psychosis. *Brain Research Review, 11,* 157–198.

Romo, R., Charamy, A., Godeheu, G., & Glowinski, J. (1986a). In vivo presynaptic control of dopamine release in the cat caudate nucleus. I. Opposite changes in neuronal activity and release evoked from thalamic motor nuclei. *Neuroscience, 19,* 1067–1079.

Romo, R., Cheramy, A., Godeheu, G., & Glowinski, J. (1986b). In vivo presynaptic control of dopamine release in the cat caudate nucleus. II. Further evidence for the implication of corticostriatal glutamatergic neurons, *Neuroscience, 19,* 1091–1099.

Segal, D. S., & Mandell, A. J. (1974). Long-term administration of d-amphetamine: Progressive augmentation of motor activity and stereotypy. *Pharmacology, Biochemistry and Behavior, 2,* 249–255.

Siegel, S. (1977). Learning and psychopharmacology. In M. E. Jarvik (Ed.), *Psychopharmacology in the practice of medicine* (pp. 59–70). New York: Appleton–Century–Crofts.

Spencer, W. A., Thompson, R. F., & Neilson, D. R., Jr. (1966). Decrement of ventral root electrotonus and intracellularly recorded post-synaptic potentials produced by iterated cutaneous afferent volleys. *Journal of Neurophysiology, 29,* 253–274.

Stewart, J., de Wit, H., & Eikelboom, R. (1984). The role of unconditioned and conditioned drug effects in the self-administration of opiates and stimulants. *Psychological Review, 91,* 251–268.

Stewart, J., & Eikelboom, R. (1987). Conditioned drug effects. In L. L. Iversen, S. D. Iversen, & S. H. Snyder (Eds.), *Handbook of psychopharmacology* (Vol. 19, pp. 1–57). New York: Plenum Press.

Stewart, J., & Vezina, P. (1987). Environment-specific enhancement of the hyperactivity induced by systemic or intra-VTA morphine injections in rats preexposed to amphetamine. *Psychobiology, 15,* 144–153.

Stewart, J., & Vezina, P. (1988). Conditioning and behavioral sensitization. In P. W. Kalivas & C. D. Barnes (Eds.), *Sensitization in the nervous system* (pp. 207–224). Caldwell, NJ: Telford Press.

Stewart, J., & Vezina, P. (1989). Microinjections of SCH–23390 into the ventral tegmental area and substantia nigra pars reticulata attenuate the development of sensitization to the locomotor activating effects of systemic amphetamine. *Brain Research, 495,* 401–406.

Stewart, J., & Vezina, P. (1991). Extinction procedures abolish conditioned stimulus control but spare sensitized responding to amphetamine. *Behavioural Pharmacology, 2,* 65–71.

Taylor, J. R., & Robbins, T. W. (1984). Enhanced behavioural control by conditioned reinforcers following microinjections of d-amphetamine into the nucleus accumbens. *Psychopharmacology, 84,* 405–412.

Taylor, J. R., & Robbins, T. W. (1986). 6-hydroxydopamine lesions of the nucleus accumbens, but not of the caudate nucleus, attenuate enhanced responding with reward-related stimuli produced by intra-accumbens d-amphetamine. *Psychopharmacology, 90,* 390–397.

Thomas, E. (1972). Excitatory and inhibitory processes in hypothalamic conditioning. In R. A. Boakes & M. S. Halliday (Eds.), *Inhibition and learning* (pp. 359–380). New York: Academic Press.

Thompson, R. F., & Spencer, W. A. (1966). Habituation: A model phenomenon for the study of neuronal substrates of behavior. *Psychological Review, 73,* 16–43.

Tilson, H. A., & Rech, R. H. (1973). Conditioned drug effects and absence of tolerance to d-amphetamine induced motor activity. *Pharmacology Biochemistry & Behavior, 1,* 149–153.

Vezina, P., Giovino, A. A., Wise, R. A., & Stewart, J. (1989). Environment-specific cross-sensitization between the locomotor activating effects of morphine and amphetamine. *Pharmacology Biochemistry & Behavior, 32,* 581–584.

Vezina, P., & Stewart, J. (1984). Conditioning and place-specific sensitization of increases in activity induced by morphine in the VTA. *Pharmacology Biochemistry & Behavior, 20,* 925–934.

Vezina, P., & Stewart, J. (1987). Conditioned locomotion and place preference elicited by tactile cues paired exclusively with morphine in an open field. *Psychopharmacology, 91,* 375–380.

Vezina, P., & Stewart, J. (1988). Amphetamine injected repeatedly into the VTA or the N. accumbens does not produce environment-specific sensitization or conditioning of its locomotor activating effects. *Society for Neuroscience Abstracts, 14,* 221.

Vezina, P., & Stewart, J. (1989). The effect of dopamine receptor blockade on the development of sensitization to the locomotor activating effects of amphetamine and morphine. *Brain Research, 499,* 108–120.

Vezina, P., & Stewart, J. (1990). Amphetamine administered to the ventral tegmental area but not to the nucleus accumbens sensitizes rats to systemic morphine: Lack of conditioned effects. *Brain Research, 516,* 99–106.

Wang, R. Y. (1981). Dopaminergic neurons in the rat ventral tegmental area. III. Effects of d- and l-amphetamine. *Brain Research Reviews, 3,* 123–140.

White, F. J., Wachtel, S. R., Johansen, P. A., & Einhorn, L. C. (1987). Electrophysiological studies of the rat mesoaccumbens dopamine system: Focus on dopamine receptor subtypes, interactions, and the effects of cocaine. In L. A. Chiodo & A. S. Freeman (Eds.), *Neurophysiology of dopaminergic systems* (pp. 317–365). Grosse Pointe, MI: Lakeshore Publishing.

Wise, R. A., & Bozarth, M. A. (1987). A psychomotor stimulant theory of addiction. *Psychological Review, 94,* 469–492.

Zamble, E., Hadad, G. M., Mitchell, J. B., & Cutmore, T. R. H. (1985). Pavlovian conditioning of sexual arousal: First- and second-order effects. *Journal of Experimental Psychology (Animal Behavior), 11,* 598–610.

8 A Neural Analysis of Fear Conditioning

Michael Davis
Janice M. Hitchcock
Jeffrey B. Rosen
Ribicoff Research Facilities of the Connecticut Mental Health Center
Yale University School of Medicine

A major challenge in neuroscience is to understand the biological substrates of learning and memory. Eventually this will involve a detailed cellular and biochemical description of the events in the nervous system that result in a relatively permanent change in neural transmission that allows a formerly neutral stimulus to produce or affect some behavioral response. The most definitive work on the cellular and biochemical analysis of learning and memory has been carried out in invertebrate nervous systems (Alkon, 1979; Carew, 1984; Castellucci, Pinsker, Kupfermann, & Kandel, 1970; Crow & Alkon, 1980; Hawkins, Abrams, Carew, & Kandel, 1983, Walters & Byrne, 1985). A major advance in the analysis of these questions was to choose a simple reflex behavior that could be modified by experience and then determine the neural circuit that mediated the behavior being measured. Once this was done it was possible to isolate where different types of plasticity occurred and then determine how these changes were brought about at the cellular level.

Comparably detailed biochemical analyses of learning and memory that relate directly to behavioral output have not been possible in vertebrate nervous systems. In large part this is because it has been very difficult to isolate where plastic changes take place in complex vertebrate nervous systems. Thus at this stage it is important to develop simple models of learning and memory in complex vertebrates that can be used to isolate loci within the nervous system where plastic changes take place that allow a conditioned stimulus to induce or affect behavior. The short-latency acoustic startle reflex enhanced by prior classical fear conditioning may be an especially promising model system with which to carry out this type of analysis.

The purpose of this chapter is to describe the fear-potentiated startle paradigm and the advantages it provides for a neuroanatomical analysis of fear conditioning. The neural pathways involved in the startle reflex are described. The role of the amygdala in fear-potentiated startle and its possible connections to the startle pathway and critical visual structures that carry information about the conditioned stimulus are reviewed. Finally, the importance of the central nucleus of the amygdala and its efferent projections to several brainstem target areas for the expression of fear are outlined.

THE FEAR-POTENTIATED STARTLE PARADIGM

Brown, Kalish, and Farber (1951) demonstrated that the amplitude of the acoustic startle reflex in the rat can be augmented by presenting the eliciting auditory startle stimulus in the presence of a cue (e.g., a light) that has previously been paired with a shock. This phenomenon has been termed the *fear-potentiated startle effect* and has been replicated using either an auditory or a visual conditioned stimulus and when startle has been elicited by either a loud sound or an airpuff (Albert, Dempesy, & Sorenson, 1985; Anderson, Johnson, & Kempton, 1969a, 1969b; Berg & Davis, 1984, 1985; Cassella & Davis, 1985, 1986a; Cassella, Harty, & Davis, 1986, Chi 1965; Davis, 1979a, 1979b; Davis & Astrachan, 1978; Davis, Redmond, & Baraban, 1979; Galvani, 1970; Hitchcock & Davis, 1986a, 1987; Kurtz & Siegel, 1966; Leaton & Borszcz, 1985; Siegel, 1967; Tischler & Davis, 1983; Wagner, Siegel, & Fein, 1967).

In this test a central state of fear is considered to be the conditioned response (cf. McAllister & McAllister, 1971). Conditioned fear is operationally defined by elevated startle amplitude in the presence of a cue previously paired with a shock (see Fig. 8.1). Thus, the conditioned stimulus does not elicit startle. Furthermore, the startle-eliciting stimulus is never paired with a shock. Instead, the conditioned stimulus is paired with a shock, and startle is elicited by another stimulus either in the presence or absence of the conditioned stimulus. Fear-potentiated startle is said to occur if startle is greater when elicited in the presence of the conditioned stimulus. Potentiated startle only occurs following paired, rather than unpaired or "random," presentations of the conditioned stimulus and the shock, which indicates that it is a valid measure of classical conditioning (Davis & Astrachan, 1978). Discriminations between visual and auditory conditioned stimuli (Hitchcock & Davis, 1986b; see Fig. 8.2) or between auditory cues that differ in duration (Siegel, 1967) have also been demonstrated with potentiated startle. Generalization decrements resulting from a change in the frequency of a pure tone conditioned stimulus between training and testing have also been reported (Siegel, 1967). Increased startle in the presence of the conditioned stimulus still occurs very reliably at least 1 month after original training,

TRAINING: LIGHT and SHOCK PAIRED

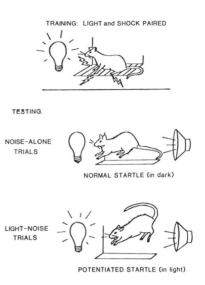

FIG. 8.1. Cartoon depicting the fear-potentiated startle paradigm. During training a neutral stimulus (conditioned stimulus) such as a light is consistently paired with a footshock. During testing startle is elicited by an auditory stimulus (e.g., a 100–dB burst of white noise) in the presence (Light–Noise trial type) or absence (Noise-Alone trial type) of the conditioned stimulus. This is simply a cartoon so that the positions and postures that are pictured may not mimic the actual behavior of the animals.

making it appropriate for the study of long-term memory as well (Cassella & Davis, 1985).

It has been suggested, however, that potentiated startle may not reflect increased fear in the presence of a conditioned fear stimulus but instead results from the animal making a postural adjustment (e.g., crouching) in anticipation of the impending footshock that is especially conducive to startle (Kurtz & Siegel, 1966). In support of this interpretation, these authors reported that startle was increased in the presence of a cue previously paired with a footshock, but not

FIG. 8.2. Discriminative conditioning measured by fear-potentiated startle. Mean amplitude startle response elicited by a noise burst in the absence of a conditioned stimulus (Noise-Alone trial type) or in the presence of a stimulus that has been consistently paired with a footshock (CS+, Noise trial type) or not paired with a footshock (CS−, Noise trial type) using either a light as the CS+ and a 75 dB, 4,000 Hz tone as the CS− (left bars), or a 75 dB, 4,000 Hz tone as the CS+ and a light as the CS− (right bars).

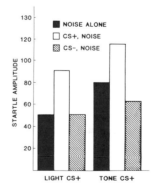

when the cue previously had been paired with a backshock, even though the shock levels at the two loci were adjusted to support equivalent avoidance responding in another situation. In examining this difference, we found that the magnitude of the potentiated startle effect was nonmonotonically related to the shock intensity used in training using either footshocks or backshocks (Davis & Astrachan, 1978). Hence, moderate levels of footshock or backshock produced robust potentiated startle, whereas low or high levels of shock did not. It is possible, therefore, that the failure to find potentiated startle using backshocks in the Kurtz and Siegel study resulted because the effective shock intensity was either too high or too low. Moreover, in spinally transected rats rigidly held in a modified stereotaxic instrument that prevented obvious postural adjustments, the pinna component of startle was found to be enhanced in the presence of a cue previously paired with a footshock (Cassella & Davis, 1986a). Potentiation of startle measured electromyographically in neck muscles also occurs in the absence of any obvious postural adjustment (Cassella, Harty, & Davis, 1986). In addition, the magnitude of potentiated startle correlates highly with the degree of freezing, a very common measure of fear (Leaton & Borszcz, 1985). Taken together, therefore, the data strongly suggest that potentiated startle is a valid measure of classical fear conditioning.

NEURAL SYSTEMS INVOLVED IN FEAR-POTENTIATED STARTLE

A major advantage of the potentiated startle paradigm is that fear is being measured by a change in a simple reflex. Hence, with potentiated startle, fear is expressed through some neural circuit that is activated by the conditioned stimulus and ultimately impinges on the startle circuit. We have begun to delineate these two neural pathways and to see how they interconnect to mediate potentiated startle.

The Acoustic Startle Pathway

In the rat the latency of acoustic startle is 6 msec recorded electromyographically in the foreleg and 8 msec in the hindleg (Ison, McAdam, & Hammond, 1973). This is an extraordinarily short latency and indicates that only a few synapses can be involved. Figure 8.3 illustrates the nuclei and fiber tracts we believe mediate the acoustic startle response in the rat (Davis, Gendelman, Tischler, & Gendelman, 1982).

The posteroventral cochlear nucleus (VCN) appears to be the first synapse in the primary acoustic startle circuit. Bilateral lesions of the VCN, but not the neighboring dorsal cochlear nuclei, abolish acoustic startle. In awake rats, bilateral, single-pulse stimulation of the VCN (1 ms pulse width, 10–25 μA) elicits startle-like responses with a latency of 7.0–7.5 ms (see Fig. 8.4).

FIG. 8.3. Schematic diagram of a primary acoustic startle circuit consisting of the ventral cochlear nucleus (VCN), an area just medial and ventral to the ventral nucleus of the lateral lemniscus (VLL), and the nucleus reticularis pontis caudalis (RPC). Other abbreviations used are: A, aqueduct; CNIC, central nucleus of the inferior colliculus; CU, cuneate nucleus; DCN, dorsal cochlear nucleus; DP, decussation of pyramids; DR, dorsal raphe nucleus; ENIC, external nucleus of the inferior colliculus; HRP, horseradish peroxidase; IO, inferior olive; LL, lateral lemniscus; LM, medial lemniscus; LV, lateral vestibular nuclues; MLF, medial longitudinal fasciculus; MTB, medial nucleus of the trapezoid body; MV, medial vestibular nucleus; nVII, nucleus of the seventh nerve; P, pyramids; RGI, nucleus reticularis gigantocellularis; RPO, nucleus reticularis pontis oralis; RST, reticulospinal tract; RSTm, medial reticulospinal tract; SO, superior olive; TSV, spinal tract of the fifth nerve; VAS, ventral acoustic stria; VII, seventh nerve. (From Davis et al., 1982, with permission of the Williams & Wilkins Co.)

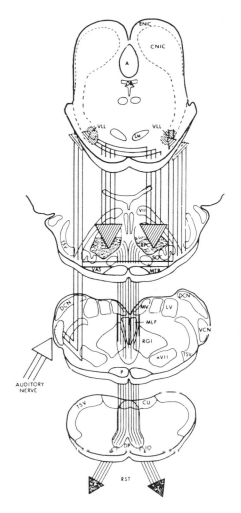

The next synapse appears to occur in an area just medial and ventral to the ventral nucleus of the lateral lemniscus (VLL). Bilateral lesions of the VLL eliminate acoustic startle and electrical stimulation of this area elicits startle-like responses with an average latency of about 6.0 ms (Fig. 8.4).

The next synapse may occur in a ventromedial region of the nucleus reticularis pontis caudalis (RPC). Bilateral lesions of this area abolish acoustic startle. Electrical stimulation of points within the RPC elicits startle-like responses with an average latency of about 5 msec. Cell bodies in the RPC send their axons to all levels of the spinal cord by way of the reticulo-spinal tract. This tract courses near or through the medial longitudinal fasciculus (MLF) on the midline and then bifurcates to form the ventral funiculi in the spinal cord. Complete lesions of the

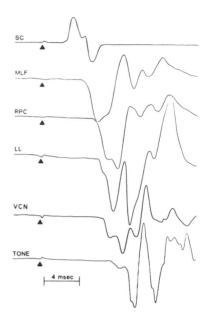

FIG. 8.4. Electromyographic recording from the quadriceps femoris muscle complex of the "startle" response elicited by electrical stimulation in the spinal cord (SC), medial longitudinal fasciculus (MLF), nucleus reticularis pontis caudalis (RPC), nuclei of the lateral lemniscus (LL), or ventral cochlear nucleus (VCN) or by a tone. (From Davis et al., 1982, with permission of the Williams & Wilkins Co.)

MLF eliminate acoustic startle, and electrical stimulation on the midline through the MLF elicits leg movements with a latency of about 4.0–4.5 ms (Fig. 8.4).

Fibers from the reticulo-spinal tract synapse in the spinal cord, forming the final synapse before the neuromuscular junction. Direct monosynaptic connections onto motorneurons as well as indirect ones through an interneuron in the cord are possible. To date we have not determined whether spinal interneurons are involved.

More recently, we have found that infusion of ibotenic acid, which destroys cell bodies without damaging fibers of passage (Schwarcz et al., 1979; Zaczek & Coyle, 1982), into either the VCN, the area near the VLL, or RPC, also eliminates acoustic startle (Cassella & Davis, 1986b).

Fear Potentiation of a Short-Latency Startle Response Measured Electromyographically

Like may measures of fear, such as the conditioned emotional response, potentiated startle represents a case in which the conditioned stimulus modulates an ongoing behavior. Because startle can be measured electromyographically with a latency of only 8 ms, the light should potentiate this 8-ms response. Typically, however, startle is not measured electromyographically but instead is measured as a movement of a cage over a relatively long interval after onset of the startle-eliciting stimulus (e.g., 200 ms). Hence it is possible that the visual conditioned stimulus does not actually alter the very short-latency startle response but instead might facilitate other auditory systems that could produce cage movements at longer latencies. If so, this might mean that the visual conditioned stimulus would not actually alter transmission along the short-latency pathway outlined in Fig. 8.3. On the other hand, if the light did increase the very short-latency startle reflex, one would have to conclude that it alters transmission at some point in the short-latency pathway. In fact, we found that a light previously paired with a footshock markedly potentiated the short-latency startle that is measured electromyographically in the neck muscles (Cassella et al., 1986; Fig. 8.5). In addition, there were high correlations within each rat between the degree of potentiation of startle measured electromyographically and by cage movement. Based on these data, the visual conditioned stimulus must ultimately alter neural transmission somewhere along the short-latency pathway outlined in Fig. 8.3 instead of recruiting other longer latency auditory pathways.

Determining the Point Within the Startle Pathway Where Fear Alters Neural Transmission

Having delineated the startle reflex circuit involved in fear-potentiated startle, the next task was to determine the point within the startle circuit where the visual conditioned stimulus modulates transmission following conditioning. To do this, startle-like responses were elicited electrically from various points along the startle pathway before and after presentation of a light that was either paired or not paired with a shock in different groups of rats (Berg & Davis, 1985). Startle elicited by electrical stimulation at or before the point in the startle circuit where the light modulates transmission should show potentiation, whereas startle elicited beyond this point should not (see Fig. 8.6). In this experiment, at least 24 hr

FIG. 8.5. Oscilloscope tracings of startle elicited in the absence (top panel) or presence of the light conditioned stimulus (lower panel). The top trace in each panel displays the output of a sound-level meter that measures the startle stimulus. The middle trace shows the electromyographic response measured from the neck muscles, and the lower trace shows the startle cage accelerometer output. (From Cassella et al., 1986, with permission from Pergamon Press.)

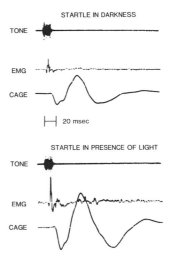

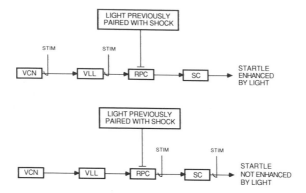

FIG. 8.6. Schematic diagram of modulation of electrically elicited startle by presentation of a light previously paired with a shock. The point of electrical elicitation of startle is indicated by the "stim" symbol. The model predicts that if the light ultimately modulates neural transmission at the RPC, then startle elicited electrically in the VCN or VLL will be enhanced by the light, because the signal produced by electrical stimulation must travel through the area where the light modulates neural transmission. In contrast, startle elicited electrically in the RPC beyond the area of modulation or startle elicited electrically in spinal motor neurons will not be enhanced by the light, because the signal produced by electrical stimulation will bypass the area where the light modulates neural transmission.

prior to training, separate groups of rats were implanted with bilateral monopolar electrodes (0.25 mm diameter, 0.5 mm uninsulated tip) in the ventral cochlear nucleus, ventral nuclei of the lateral lemniscus, or nucleus reticularis pontis caudalis. In addition, other groups were implanted with electrodes aimed at lateral as well as medial aspects of the ventral acoustic stria (VAS), the fibers that connect the VCN to the VLL. Following recovery, all groups were trained to be fearful of a light by pairing it with a footshock.

Figure 8.7 shows that potentiation of electrically elicited startle was equivalent to potentiation of acoustic startle at all locations up through the VLL. In contrast, startle elicited from the RPC was not potentiated. The difference in potentiation of electrically and acoustically elicited startle at sites beyond the VLL cannot be attributed to the extent of effective conditioning, because potentiation of startle elicited acoustically was just as great in the RPC group as it was in the VCN, VAS, and VLL groups. Furthermore, the potentiation of electrically elicited startle was specific to an explicit pairing of light and shock during training. Animals with electrodes implanted in the VCN and trained with a random temporal relation between light and shock showed no sign of potentiation of either electrically or acoustically elicited startle. Finally, other studies showed that drugs like diazepam, which are known to block fear-potentiated startle elicited acoustically, also block fear-potentiated startle elicited electrically through the VCN (Berg & Davis, 1984). Taken together, these data indicate that the VLL or the RPC is the point in the startle pathway where a visual conditioned stimulus ultimately modulates transmission following conditioning so as to affect the startle reflex.

Lesions of the Central Nucleus of the Amygdala Block Fear-Potentiated Startle

Recently, several studies have indicated that lesions of the cerebellum or lesions of efferents from the cerebellum to the red nucleus eliminate classically conditioned motor responses such as the nictitating membrane response and conditioned leg flexion (cf. Thompson et al., 1987). Interestingly, however, these lesions did not block heart rate conditioning (Lavond, Lincoln, McCormick, & Thompson, 1984), suggesting that the cerebellum may not be required for fear conditioning. On the other hand, lesions of the central nucleus of the amygdala block heart rate conditioning (Cohen, 1975; Gentile et al., 1986; Kapp, Frysinger, Gallagher, & Haselton, 1979) as well as blocking measures of conditioned fear in several other experimental paradigms (cf. Davis, 1992). Because

FIG. 8.7. Magnitude of fear-potentiated startle effect when startle was elicited either acoustically (white bars) or electrically (black bars) in different groups of rats that had electrodes implanted in the ventral cochlear nucleus (VCN), ventral acoustic stria (VAS), ventral lateral lemniscus (VLL) or nucleus reticularis pontis caudalis (RPC). The white bars represent the degree of potentiation of startle elicited acoustically in rats with electrodes implanted into different parts of the startle pathway. The black bars represent the degree of potentiation of startle elicited electrically through electrodes implanted in different parts of the startle pathway. Degree of potentiation is expressed as the mean difference in startle amplitude in the presence versus absence of the visual conditioned stimulus. (From Berg & Davis, 1985, with permission from the American Psychological Association.)

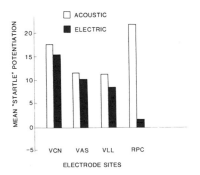

potentiated startle is a measure of fear, we hypothesized that lesions of the amygdala should block potentiated startle, whereas lesions of the cerebellum or red nucleus might not.

Lesions of the central nucleus of the amygdala following fear conditioning were shown to completely eliminate potentiated startle (Hitchcock & Davis, 1986a; Fig. 8.8). In contrast, transection of the cerebellar peduncles or lesions of the red nucleus had no effect on potentiated startle (see Fig. 8.8). Another experiment using a visual prepulse test indicated that the blockade of potentiated startle observed in animals with lesions of the amygdala could not be attributed to visual impairment. A third experiment indicated that the absence of potentiation in the amygdala-lesioned animals did not simply result from a lowered startle level ceiling, because the amygdala-lesioned animals could show increased startle with increased stimulus intensity and with administration of strychnine (see Fig. 8.9), a drug that reliably increases startle (Kehne, Gallager, & Davis, 1981). Taken together, the results of these experiments support the hypothesis that the amygdala is involved in potentiated startle—a measure of conditioned fear. The results are also consistent with the hypothesis that the cerebellum is involved in motor conditioning rather than fear conditioning (Thompson et al., 1987). It is still possible, however, that the cerebellum could modulate potentiated startle because electrical stimulation of the cerebellum has been reported to increase the magnitude of potentiated startle (Albert et al., 1985), and recent studies indicate that lesions of the vermis may alter heart rate conditioning in rats (Supple & Leaton, 1986).

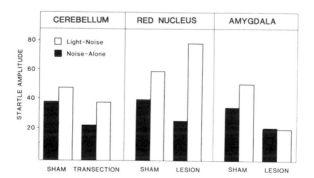

FIG.8.8. Mean amplitude startle on the Light–Noise or Noise-Alone trials in rats in which the cerebellum was surgically transected from the brainstem or in rats with electrolytic lesions of the red nucleus or the central nucleus of the amygdala. Sham animals for the cerebellar experiment had the transection knife inserted under the cerebellum but the fiber pathways were not cut. Sham animals for the other experiments had the electrodes lowered into the brain but no current was passed.

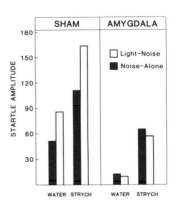

FIG. 8.9. Mean amplitude startle on the Light–Noise and Noise-Alone trials in rats with lesions of the central nucleus of the amygdala or sham lesions when testing was carried out after injection of either strychnine (0.75 mg/kg) or its vehicle, water. (From Hitchcock & Davis, 1986, with permission from the American Psychological Association.)

Enhancement of Acoustic Startle by Electrical Stimulation of the Amygdala

At the present time it is not clear how the amygdala participates in fear-potentiated startle. It is possible that the light, after being paired with shock, activates the amygdala that would then increase startle. Short-latency visual-evoked potentials have been recorded in the amygdala (Pollock, Bock, Fuchs, & Lohaus, 1976; Sanghera, Rolls, Roper-Hall, 1979), and electrical stimulation of the amygdala has been reported to produce fear-like behaviors in animals (Applegate, Kapp, Underwood, & McNall, 1983; Gloor, 1960), to mimic conditioned and unconditioned cardiac effects in rabbit heart rate conditioning (Kapp et al., 1982), and to elicit feelings of anxiety in humans (Chapman et al., 1954). Consistent with this, we have found that low-level electrical stimulation of the amygdala (e.g., 40–400 μA, 25 ms trains of 0.1 ms square wave cathodal pulses) markedly increases acoustic startle amplitude (Rosen & Davis, 1988). This excitatory effect has occurred in every rat that we have tested so far in which electrodes were found to be placed in the central, intercalated, or medial nucleus of the amygdala or in the area just medial to the amygdaloid complex (see Fig. 8.10).

Stimulation of the area just medial to the amygdala had the lowest threshold for increasing acoustic startle. This area coincides with the initial part of the ventral amygdalofugal pathway as it begins its projection to the lower brainstem (Krettek & Price, 1978; Post & Mai, 1980; Schwaber, Kapp, Higgins, & Rapp, 1982). Low-level electrical stimulation at this site would be expected to activate a large number of fibers projecting to the brainstem because they are highly concentrated at this part of the pathway. In contrast, stimulation of the amygdala nuclei themselves, where the neurons of these fibers originate, would require higher currents (i.e., more current spread) to activate the same number of brainstem projections because the neurons are dispersed throughout the nuclei. Further studies involving stimulation of the area just medial to the amygdala where the ventral amygdalofugal pathway begins, in combination with lesions of cell

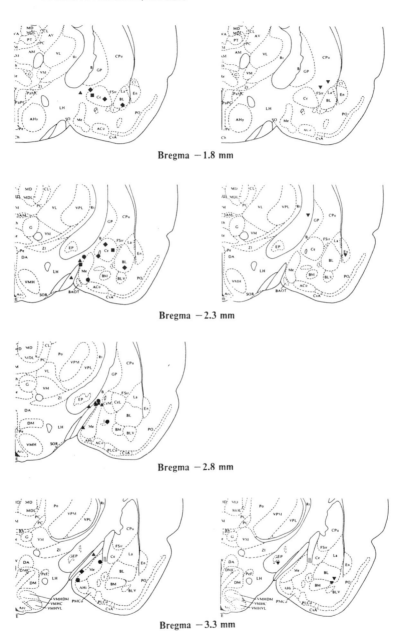

FIG. 8.10.   Schematic representation of effective and ineffective stimulation sites in the amygdala for enhancement of acoustic startle. Effective sites at currents below 100 μA (▲), at 100–200 μA (●), at 201–300 μA (■), and 301–400 μA (♦) are shown on the left. Ineffective sites (▼) are shown on the right.

bodies (e.g., ibotenic acid lesions) in the central, medial, intercalated or basolateral nucleus, would help clarify whether enhancement of startle by stimulation in this pathway actually results from activation of the axons originating from these amygdaloid nuclei.

Electrical stimulation of the amygdala did not produce any signs of behavioral activation except for an enhancement of startle at these stimulation currents and durations, indicating that startle is an extremely sensitive index of amygdala stimulation. Moreover, the duration of stimulation is well below that used to produce kindling in rats (Handforth, 1984), so that the effects on startle are not associated with convulsions.

The excitatory effect on startle occurs within a few milliseconds from the onset of amygdala stimulation. This rapidity of action means that the increase in startle is not secondary to autonomic or hormonal changes that might be produced by amygdala stimulation, because these would have a much longer latency. In addition, electrical stimulation of the amygdala alone does not elicit startle even at high currents. Finally, electrical stimulation of several other nearby brain areas such as the endopiriform nucleus, fundus striati, internal capsule, or some sites in the basolateral nucleus of the amygdala does not increase startle (see Fig. 8.10).

The Role of Different Amygdala Efferent Projections in Fear-Potentiated Startle

As mentioned earlier, lesions of the central nucleus of the amygdala block fear-potentiated startle (Fig. 8.11). Recently, we have been using the sensitive *Phaseolus vulgaris*-leucoagglutinin (PHA–L) anterograde tracing technique (Gerfen & Sawchenko, 1984) and lesion studies to delineate possible connections between the amygdala and the startle pathway in relation to fear-potentiated startle (Hitchcock & Davis, 1991; Rosen, Hitchcock, Sananes, Miserendino, & Davis, 1991). The central nucleus of the amygdala projects to a variety of brain regions via two major efferent pathways, the stria terminalis and the ventral amygdalofugal pathway. Lesions of the stria terminalis itself, or the bed nucleus of the stria terminalis, a major projection area of this pathway, do not block potentiated startle (see Fig. 8.12). Knife cuts of the rostral part of the ventral amygdalofugal pathway, which would interrupt its projections to the rostral lateral hypothalamus and substantia innominata, also fail to block potentiated startle (see Fig. 8.13). On the other hand, lesions of the caudal part of the ventral amygdalofugal pathway, at the point where it passes through the subthalamic area and cerebral peduncles, completely block potentiated startle (see Fig. 8.14). Interestingly, Jarrell et al. (1986) found that lesions of this area also block heart rate conditioning, another measure of fear conditioning. Finally, lesions of the substantia nigra, which receives central nucleus projections as well as fibers of passage from the central nucleus of the amygdala to more caudal brainstem

FIG. 8.11. Lower panel shows the mean amplitude startle response on Noise-Alone trials (black bars) and Light–Noise trials (white bars) in unoperated rats, rats given sham lesions, and rats given bilateral lesions of the central nucleus of the amygdala. The center panel shows a histological reconstruction of a representative lesion of the central nucleus of the amygdala. The black area represents the cavity produced by the lesion and the striped area represents the surrounding area of gliosis. The upper panel shows a schematic representation of a deposit of *Phaseolus vulgaris* leucoagglutinin (PHA-L) into the left central nucleus of the amygdala and PHA-L labeled fibers from the amygdala. Actual density of labeling is not accurately reflected in the schematics shown in Fig. 8.10–8.13.

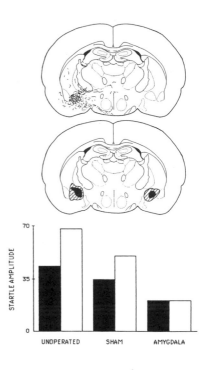

FIG. 8.12. Lower panel shows the mean amplitude startle response on Noise-Alone trials (black bars) and Light–Noise trials (white bars) in unoperated rats, rats given sham lesions, and rats given bilateral lesions of the bed nucleus of the stria terminalis. The center panel shows a histological reconstruction of a representative lesion of the bed nucleus of the stria terminalis. The upper panel shows a schematic representation of terminals and fibers in the bed nucleus of the stria terminalis after deposition of PHA–L into the left central nucleus of the amygdala as shown in Fig. 8.10.

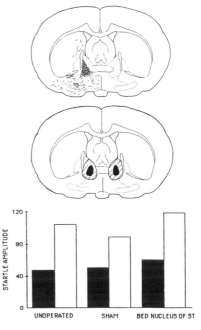

FIG. 8.13. Lower panel shows the mean amplitude startle response on Noise-Alone trials (black bars) and Light–Noise trials (white bars) in unoperated rats, rats given sham transections, and rats given bilateral transections in the rostral division of the ventral amygalofugal pathway that interrupted the connection between the central nucleus of the amygdala and the rostral hypothalamus and substantia innominata. The center panel shows a histological reconstruction of the transection. The upper panel shows a schematic representation of terminals and fibers in the rostral division of the ventral amygdalofugal pathway after deposition of PHA–L into the left central nucleus of the amygdala as shown in Fig. 8.10.

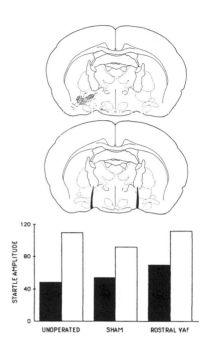

FIG. 8.14. Lower panel shows the mean amplitude startle response on Noise-Alone trials (black bars) and Light–Noise trials (white bars) in unoperated rats, rats given sham lesions, and rats given bilateral lesions of the caudal division of the ventral amygdalofugal pathway that interrupted the connection between the central nucleus of the amygdala and the brainstem. The center panel shows a representative lesion of the caudal ventral amygdalofugal pathway. The upper panel shows a schematic representation of terminals and fibers in the caudal division of the ventral amygdalofugal pathway after a deposit of PHA–L into the left central nucleus of the amygdala as shown in Fig. 8.10.

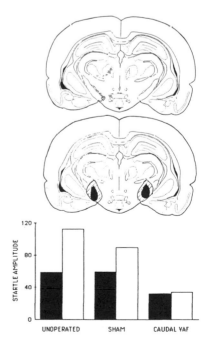

regions, also block potentiated startle. This blockade does not seem to involve dopamine cells in the zona compacta because infusion of the dopamine neurotoxin 6–OHDA into the substantia nigra did not block potentiated startle despite over a 90% depletion of dopamine in the caudate nucleus.

These lesion experiments indicate that the pathway from the central nucleus of the amygdala to the startle circuit travels through the caudal part of the ventral amygdalofugal pathway, which is known to project directly to many parts of the pons, medulla, and probably the spinal cord (Krettek & Price, 1978; Mizuno, Takahashi, Satoda, & Matsushima, 1985; Post & Mai, 1980; Price & Amaral, 1981; Sandrew, Edwards, Poletti, & Foote, 1986; Schwaber, Kapp, Higgins, & Rapp, 1982). In fact, Inagaki et al. (1983) have reported direct connections between the central nucleus of the amygdala and the exact part of the nucleus reticularis pontis caudalis (an area just dorsal to the superior olive) that is critical for startle. We have now confirmed this projection using both anterograde and retrograde tracing techniques (Rosen et al., 1991).

Relationship of the Amygdala to the Visual Structures Involved in Fear-Potentiated Startle

Thus far we have no direct information linking the amygdala to any visual structures that appear critical for fear-potentiated startle. The central nucleus of the amygdala is known to receive input from the lateral nucleus of the amygdala, which receives afferents from the insular cortex (Turner & Zimmer, 1984). The insular cortex receives visual information (Turner & Zimmer, 1984) through a pathway probably involving the lateral geniculate nucleus, visual cortex, and visual association cortex. Thus it is possible that the visual conditioned stimulus would activate the central nucleus of the amygdala after being relayed through these structures. Previous experiments in our laboratory found that lesions of the lateral geniculate nucleus and the visual cortex blocked fear-potentiated startle when testing occurred 1–2 days after these lesions. In contrast, lesions of superficial layers of the superior colliculus, the pretectal area, parietal cortex, or the dorsal lateral lemniscus did not block potentiated startle (Tischler & Davis, 1983). It was also reported in that study that lesions of deep and intermediate layers of the superior colliculus blocked fear-potentiated startle. Recently, we have replicated this result with testing 6–7 days after lesions of deep and intermediate layers of the superior colliculus (Hitchcock & Davis, 1986c). At this time, however, baseline levels of startle (i.e., on the Noise-Alone trials) were markedly elevated after lesions of the superior colliculus. In fact, when these animals were retested using a very weak, 75-dB startle stimulus, they each showed increased startle in the presence of the light. Hence, input from the deep and intermediate layers of the superior colliculus, which project directly to the ventral nucleus of the lateral lemniscus (Henkel, 1981; Henkel & Edwards, 1978), appear to tonically inhibit acoustic startle. This effect may interfere with the measurement of fear-potentiated startle unless special test conditions are arranged. However, the superior colliculus does not appear to be either an obligatory visual relay in startle potentiated by a visual conditioned fear stimulus or part of the pathway connecting the central nucleus of the amygdala to the startle circuit.

More recently, we have found that total removal of the visual cortex does not block fear-potentiated startle using a visual conditioned stimulus when testing occurs 1–2 wks after the ablation (Rosen et al., unpublished observations). In contrast, relatively small lesions of the perirhinal cortex do block fear-potentiated startle using a visual conditioned stimulus (Rosen et al., unpublished observations). Moreover, NMDA-induced lesions of the lateral and basolateral amygdaloid nuclei, which receive projections from the perirhinal cortex and project to the central amygdaloid nucleus, also completely block fear-potentiated startle (Sananes & Davis, in press). Hence, we now believe that visual information is relayed from the ventral lateral geniculate to the perirhinal cortex and into the central amygdaloid nucleus, via the lateral and basolateral nuclei of the amygdala. Currently, we are evaluating the role of various connections between the ventral lateral geniculate and perirhinal cortex in fear-potentiated startle.

ENHANCEMENT OF STARTLE BY FOOTSHOCKS

Effects of Footshocks on Acoustic Startle

Fear-potentiated startle is defined by an increase in startle in the presence of a cue previously paired with shock. One might expect, therefore, that shock itself should increase startle amplitude, so that fear-potentiated startle would reflect the familiar finding that the conditioned response mimics the unconditioned response. Curiously, however, Brown et al. (1951) reported that acoustic startle was actually depressed when elicited from 15 to 60 sec after a footshock, although longer intervals were not tested. Recently, Fanselow and colleagues (e.g., Fanselow, 1981, 1982, 1984; Fanselow & Bolles, 1979) have shown that shock leads to an increase in freezing, a traditional measure of fear in rats. Interestingly, however, freezing does not occur immediately after the shock but develops gradually over several minutes. The magnitude of fear-potentiated startle correlates highly with the amount of freezing measured in the same experimental situation (Leaton & Borszcz, 1985); therefore we reasoned that startle should increase for several minutes following footshock with a time course similar to that of freezing reported by Fanselow. Consistent with this expectation, Fig. 8.15 shows that a series of 10 shocks (0.6 ma, 0.5 sec in duration presented at a rate of 1 shock per sec) markedly increased startle measured over a 20-minute period after the shocks (Davis, 1989). Interestingly, this effect did not occur immediately but developed over several minutes, similar to the time course of freezing seen

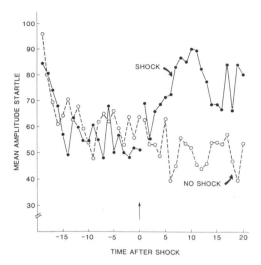

FIG. 8.15. Enhancemenet of startle by footshock. The figure shows the mean amplitude startle response prior to and following a series of five 0.6 mA, 500 msec footshocks (indicated by the arrow) presented once per second (solid), or no intervening shock (open). Forty 105-dB noise bursts were presented at a 30-sec interval both before and after the shocks.

by Fanselow. However, unlike Fanselow's results where freezing appears to be context specific, several experiments in our laboratory lead to the conclusion that this increase in startle does not result from a rapid conditioning to the context. Therefore, we think that the increase in startle seen after footshocks may represent the unconditioned effects of the shock on startle, and that this becomes conditioned to a light that is consistently paired with that shock.

The Role of the Amygdala in Footshock-Induced Enhancement of Startle

Because footshock is both aversive and fear producing, it is possible that footshock activates the amygdala, which then leads to an elevation of startle via connections between the amygdala and the startle pathway. In fact, lesions of the central nucleus of the amygdala or lesions of the ventral amygdalofugal pathway prevent footshocks from enhancing startle (Hitchcock & Davis, 1989).

If footshock enhances startle by activating the central nucleus of the amygdala, then interruption of the neural pathway that mediates footshock-induced activation of the amygdala should block shock-induced enhancement of startle. In addition, if activation of the amygdala by a footshock is critical for the acquisition of fear conditioning, then interruption of this pathway should also block the acquisition of fear-potentiated startle. Importantly, however, lesions made following acquisition should *not* block performance of fear-potentiated startle, because after acquisition the conditioned stimulus should now activate the amygdala thereby increasing startle, independent of the pathway connecting footshock to the amygdala.

The most direct way in which a footshock could activate the central nucleus of the amygdala would involve pain receptors in the footpads that would send information through the lateral spinothalamic tract to the intralaminar nucleus of the thalamus and the medial division of the medial geniculate nucleus (Lund & Webster, 1967; Mehler, 1969). These structures are known to have direct projections to the central nucleus of the amygdala (LeDoux, Ruggiero, & Reis, 1985; Ottersen & Ben-Ari, 1979). A more complex pathway would involve projections of the spinothalamic tract to the ventral posterolateral nucleus of the thalamus, to somatosensory cortex I and II, which then project to the insular cortex, which project to the central nucleus of the amygdala (cf. Turner & Zimmer, 1984). Finally, other inputs might involve spino-reticular pathways that would activate catecholamine-containing neurons of the lateral tegmentum or locus coeruleus (e.g., Guyenet & Byrum, 1985; McMahon & Wall, 1985), which would then project to the amygdala (cf. Moore & Card, 1984). Hence, future studies will evaluate the role of these various pathways in enhancement of startle by footshocks and their involvement in the acquisition of fear-potentiated startle.

THE ROLE OF THE AMYGDALA IN INNATE AND CONDITIONED FEAR

A variety of animal models have been used to infer a central state of fear or anxiety. In some models fear is inferred when an animal freezes, thus interrupting some ongoing behavior such as pressing a bar or interacting socially with other animals. In other models fear is measured by changes in autonomic activity, such as heart rate, blood pressure, or respiration. Fear can also be measured by a change in simple reflexes or a change in facial expressions and mouth movements. Thus fear appears to produce a complex pattern of behaviors that are highly correlated with each other.

Anatomical Connections Between the Amygdala and Brain Areas Involved in Fear

Similar to suggestions of several previous reviews (Gloor, 1960; Kapp & Pascoe, 1986; Kapp, Pascoe, & Bixler, 1984; Sarter & Markowitsch, 1985), Fig. 8.16 summarizes work done in many different laboratories indicating that the central nucleus of the amygdala has direct projections to a variety of brainstem areas that might be expected to be involved in many of the signs of fear. Thus the central nucleus of the amygdala projects to a region of the central grey (Beitz, 1982; Post & Mai, 1980) that has been implicated in fear in a number of behavioral tests (Fanselow, 1991; Le Doux, Iwata, Cicchetti & Reis, 1988; Liebman, Mayer, & Liebeskind, 1970). Direct projections to the dorsal motor nucleus of the vagus (Hopkins & Holstege, 1978; Schwaber, Kapp, Higgins, & Rapp, 1982; Takeuchi, Matsushima, Matsushima, & Hopkins, 1983; Veening, Swanson, & Sawchenko, 1984) may be involved in several autonomic measures of fear, because the vagus nerve controls many different autonomic functions. Projec-

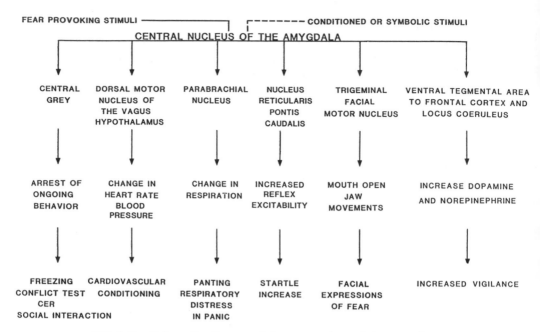

FIG. 8.16. Schematic diagram of the connections of the central nucleus of the amygdala to a variety of target areas that are probably involved in the pattern of behaviors that are typically associated with fear.

tions of the central nucleus of the amygdala to the parabrachial nucleus (Krettek & Price, 1978; Price & Amaral, 1981; Takeuchi, McLean, & Hopkins, 1982) may be involved in respiratory changes during fear, because electrical stimulation of the parabrachial nucleus is known to alter respiratory rate (Bertrand & Hugelin, 1971; Cohen, 1971). Direct projections to the trigeminal (Post & Mai, 1980) and perhaps the facial motor nuclei may mediate some of the facial expressions of fear. As outlined earlier, projections of the amygdala to the nucleus reticularis pontis caudalis (Inagaki et al., 1983) probably are involved in fear potentiation of the startle reflex. Finally, projections from the central nucleus of the amygdala to the ventral tegmental area (Phillipson, 1979) may mediate stress-induced changes in dopamine turnover in the frontal cortex (e.g., Thierry, Tassin, Blanc, & Glowinski, 1976). Moreover, this projection might also link the central nucleus of the amygdala to the locus coeruleus (Deutch, Goldstein, & Roth, 1986), which itself has been implicated in fear and anxiety (Redmond, 1977) or increased vigilance and attention (e.g., Aston-Jones & Bloom, 1981).

Fear Produced by Electrical Stimulation of the Amygdala

Importantly, it has also been shown that electrical stimulation of the central nucleus of the amygdala can produce a complex pattern of behavioral and autonomic changes that, taken together, constitute a state that highly resembles a state of fear. Thus, electrical stimulation of the central nucleus of the amygdala produces a cessation of ongoing behavior (Applegate, Kapp, Underwood, & McNall, 1983; Gloor, 1960). In fact, cessation of ongoing behavior is the critical measure of fear or anxiety in several animal models such as the operant conflict test (Geller & Seifter, 1960), the conditioned emotional response (Estes & Skinner, 1941), social interaction test (File, 1980), and freezing itself (e.g., Fanselow & Bolles, 1979). Stimulation of the amygdala can also alter heart rate (Applegate et al., 1983; Kapp, Gallagher, Underwood, McNall, & Whitehorn, 1982) and blood pressure (Morgenson & Calaresu, 1973), both measures used to study cardiovascular conditioning. Electrical stimulation of the central nucleus of the amygdala also alters respiration (Applegate et al., 1983; Harper, Frysinger, Trelease, & Marks, 1984), a prominent symptom of fear especially in panic disorders. Electrical stimulation of the amygdala also elicits jaw movements (Applegate et al., 1983; Gloor, 1960; Ohta, 1984), which often accompany the fear response. Amygdala stimulation can also produce gastric ulceration (Henke, 1980a, 1980b; Innes & Tansy, 1980; Sen & Anand, 1957), which may result from chronic fear or stress. As outlined earlier, electrical stimulation of specific parts of the amygdala increases the acoustic startle reflex, which is elevated during fear. Finally, it has been reported in humans that electrical stimulation of the amygdala elicits feelings of fear or anxiety as well as autonomic reactions indicative of fear (Chapman et al., 1954; Gloor, Olivier, & Quesney, 1981).

Taken together, the highly correlated set of behaviors seen during fear may result from activation of a single area of the brain (the central nucleus of the amygdala), which then projects to a variety of target areas that themselves are critical for each of the specific signs of fear. Moreover, it must be assumed that all these connections are already formed in an adult organism, because electrical stimulation produces these effects in the absence of prior explicit fear conditioning. Given this innate wiring diagram, it would seem most parsimonious to assume that a neutral stimulus will elicit a state of fear when that stimulus comes to activate the amygdala after being paired with an aversive stimulus. Thus plasticity following fear conditioning probably results from a change prior to or in the amygdala rather than a change in its efferent target areas.

The Role of the Amygdala in Fear Elicited by a Conditioned Stimulus

Consistent with this interpretation, several studies have shown that a neutral stimulus paired with aversive stimulation will now alter neural firing in the amygdala, especially the central nucleus of the amygdala (Henke, 1983; Pascoe & Kapp, 1985). Moreover, lesions of the central nucleus are known to eliminate or attenuate conditioned changes measured by a cessation of ongoing behavior such as freezing (Le Doux et al., 1988); reduced bar pressing in the operant conflict test (Shibata, Kataoka, Yamaskita, & Ueki, 1986) or the conditioned emotional response paradigm (Kellicut & Schwartzbaum, 1963; Spevack, Campbell, & Drake, 1975). Lesions of the central nucleus also block conditioned changes in heart rate (Cohen, 1975; Gentile, Jarrell, Teich, McCabe, & Schneidermen, 1986; Kapp, Frysinger, Gallagher, & Haselton, 1979), blood pressure (Iwata et al., 1986a), or ulceration induced by immobilization stress (Henke, 1980a, 1980b). Data outlined earlier indicate that lesions of the central nucleus of the amygdala block fear-potentiated startle (Hitchcock & Davis, 1986a). Lesions of the amygdala are known to block several measures of innate fear in different species (cf. Blanchard & Blanchard, 1972; Ursin, Jellestad, & Cabrera, 1981). This, with a large literature implicating the amygdala in many other measures of fear such as active and passive avoidance (for reviews see Kaada, 1972; Sarter & Markowitsch, 1985; Ursin, Jellestad, & Cabrera, 1981) and evaluation and memory of emotionally significant sensory stimuli (Bennett, Liang, & McGaugh, 1975; Handwerker, Gold, & McGaugh, 1974; Kesner, 1982; Liang, Bennett, & McGaugh, 1985; Bresnahan & Routtenberg, 1972; Ellis & Kesner, 1983; Gallagher & Kapp, 1981, 1978; Gold, Hankins, Edwards, Chester, & McGaugh, 1985; Liang, Juler, & McGaugh, 1986; Mishkin & Aggleton, 1981), compellingly indicate a crucial role of the amygdala in fear.

SUMMARY AND CONCLUSIONS

The potentiated startle paradigm measures conditioned fear by an increase in the amplitude of a simple reflex (the acoustic startle reflex) in the presence of a cue previously paired with shock. This paradigm offers a number of advantages as an alternative to most animal tests of fear or anxiety because it involves no operant and is reflected by an enhancement rather than a suppression of ongoing behavior. Lesion and electrical stimulation studies on fear-potentiated startle and startle increased by electrical stimulation of the amygdala are being used to define the neural pathways necessary for a visual conditioned stimulus to alter the acoustic startle reflex. The current working hypothesis is that the conditioned stimulus activates the central nucleus of the amygdala through a pathway involving the lateral geniculate nucleus perirhinal cortex and lateral and basolateral amygdaloid nuclei. The central nucleus of the amygdala then projects directly to the acoustic startle pathway, modulating the startle response. More work has to be done to define conclusively the relevant neural pathways involved in fear-potentiated startle. Nonetheless, we think that by combining behavioral, anatomical, physiological, and pharmacological approaches, it will be possible to determine each step along the pathway that mediates the ability of a stimulus signaling fear to alter behavior. Once the exact structures are delineated, it should be possible to determine the neurotransmitters that are released during a state of fear and how this chemical information is relayed along these pathways so as to affect behavior. Eventually, this approach should allow us to determine where plastic changes take place along these pathways to mediate the conditioned effects that are being measured and the biochemical processes that are involved.

ACKNOWLEDGMENTS

This research was supported by NSF Grant BNS–81–20476, NIMH Grant MH–47840 & MH–25642, NINCDS Grant NS–18033, Research Scientist Development Award MH–00004, a grant from the Air Force Office of Scientific Research and the State of Connecticut. Some of the results in this chapter were submitted to the Yale Graduate School in partial fulfillment of the requirement for a Ph.D. to Janice Hitchcock. Our sincere thanks are extended to Lee Schlesinger, who tested many of the animals used for these studies, to Bruce Kapp for helpful discussions about the brainstem projections of the amygdala, to Ariel Deutsch and Robert Roth for collaboration on the PHA–L studies, to James Cassella and John Kehne for comments on the manuscript, and to Leslie Fields for help in typing. Special thanks are extended to Don Weisz for alerting us some years ago to the importance of the amygdala in fear.

REFERENCES

Albert, T. J., Dempesy, C. W., & Sorenson, C. A. (1985). Anterior cerebellar vermal stimulation: Effect on behavior and basal forebrain neurochemistry in rat. *Biological Psychiatry, 20,* 1267–1276.

Alkon, D. L. (1979). Voltage-dependent calcium and potassium ion conductances: A contingency mechanism for an associative learning model. *Science, 205,* 810–816.

Anderson, D. C., Johnson, D., & Kempton, H. (1969a). Second-order fear conditioning as revealed through augmentation of a startle response: Part I. *Psychonomic Science, 16,* 5–7.

Anderson, D. C., Johnson, D., & Kempton, H. (1969b). Second-order fear conditioning as revealed through augmentation of a startle response: Part II. *Psychonomic Science, 16,* 7–9.

Applegate, C. D., Kapp, B. J., Underwood, M. D., & McNall, C. L. (1983). Autonomic and somatomotor effects of amygdala central n. stimulation in awake rabbits. *Physiology & Behavior, 31,* 353–360.

Aston-Jones, G., & Bloom, F. E. (1981). Norepinephrine-containing locus coeruleus neurons in behaving rats exhibit pronounced responses to non-noxious environmental stimuli. *Journal of Neuroscience, 1,* 887–900.

Beitz, A. J. (1982). The organization of afferent projections to the midbrain periaqueductal gray of the rat. *Neuroscience, 7,* 133–159.

Bennett, C., Liang, K. C., & McGaugh, J. L. (1985). Depletion of adrenal catecholamines alters the amnestic effect of amygdala stimulation. *Behavioral Brain Research, 15,* 83–91.

Berg, W. K., & Davis, M. (1984). Diazepam blocks fear-enhanced startle elicited electrically from the brainstem. *Physiology & Behavior, 32,* 333–336.

Berg, W. K., & Davis, M. (1985). Associative learning modifies startle reflexes at the lateral lemniscus. *Behavioral Neuroscience, 99,* 191–199.

Bertrand, S., & Hugelin, A. (1971). Respiratory synchronizing function of the nucleus parabrachialis medialis: Pneumotaxic mechanisms. *Journal of Neurophysiology, 34,* 180–207.

Blanchard, D. C., & Blanchard, R. J. (1972). Innate and conditioned reactions to threat in rats with amygdaloid lesions. *Journal of Comparative Physiological Psychology, 81,* 281–290.

Bresnaham, E., & Routtenberg, A. (1972). Memory disruption by unilateral low level, subseizure stimulation of the medial amygdaloid nucleus. *Physiology and Behavior, 9,* 513–525.

Brown, J. S., Kalish, H. I., & Farber, I. E. (1951). Conditioned fear as revealed by magnitude of startle response to an auditory stimulus. *Journal of Experimental Psychology, 41,* 317–328.

Carew, T. J. (1984). An introduction to cellular approaches used in the analysis of habituation and sensitization in *aplysia.* In H. V. S. Peeke & L. Petrinovich (Eds.), *Habituation, sensitization, and behavior* (pp. 205–249). New York, Academic Press.

Cassella, J. V., & Davis, M. (1985). Fear-enhanced acoustic startle is not attenuated by acute or chronic imipramine treatment in rats. *Psychopharmacology, 87,* 278–282.

Cassella, J. V., & Davis, M. (1986a). Habituation, prepulse inhibition, fear conditioning, and drug modulation of the acoustically elicited pinna reflex in rats. *Behavioral Neuroscience, 100,* 39–44.

Cassella, J. V., & Davis, M. (1986b). Neural structures mediating acoustic and tactile startle reflexes and the acoustically-elicited pinna response in rats: Electrolytic and ibotenic acid studies. *Society for Neuroscience Abstracts,* 1273.

Cassella, J. V., Harty, P. T., & Davis, M. (1986). Fear conditioning, pre-pulse inhibition and drug modulation of a short latency startle response measured electromyographically from neck muscles in the rat. *Physiology & Behavior, 36,* 1187–1191.

Castellucci, V., Pinsker, H., Kupfermann, I., & Kandel, E. R. (1970). Neuronal mechanisms of habituation and dishabituation of the gill-withdrawal reflex in *Aplysia. Science, 167,* 1745–1748.

Chapman, W. P., Schroeder, H. R., Guyer, G., Brazier, M. A. B., Fager, C., Poppen, J. L., Solomon, H. C., & Yakolev, P. I. (1954). Physiological evidence concerning the importance of the amygdaloid nuclear region in the integration of circulating function and emotion in man. *Science, 129,* 949–950.

Chi, C. C. (1965). The effect of amobarbital sodium on conditioned fear as measured by the potentiated startle response in rats. *Psychopharmacologia, 7,* 115–122.

Cohen, D. H. (1975). Involvement of the avian amygdalar homologue (archistriatum posterior and mediale) in defensively conditioned heart rate change. *Journal of Comparative Neurology, 160,* 13–36.

Cohen, M. I. (1971). Switching of the respiratory phases and evoked phrenic responses produced by rostral pontine electrical stimulation. *Journal of Physiology (London), 217,* 133–158.

Crow, T. J., & Alkon, D. L. (1980). Associative behavior modification in *Hermissenda:* Cellular correlates. *Science, 209,* 412–414.

Davis, M. (1979a). Diazepam and flurazepam: Effects on conditioned fear as measured with the potentiated startle paradigm. *Psychopharmacology, 62,* 1–7.

Davis, M. (1979b). Morphine and naloxone: Effects on conditioned fear as measured with the potentiated startle paradigm. *European Journal of Pharmacology, 54,* 341–347.

Davis, M. (1989). Sensitization of the startle reflex by footshock. *Behavioral Neuroscience, 103,* 495–503.

Davis, M. (1992). The role of the amygdala in fear & anxiety. *Annual Review of Neuroscience, 15,* 353–375.

Davis, M., & Astrachan, D. I. (1978). Conditioned fear and startle magnitude: Effects of different footshock or backshock intensities used in training. *Journal of Experimental Psychology: Animal Behavior Processes, 4,* 95–103.

Davis, M., Gendelman, D. S., Tischler, M. D., & Gendelman, P. M. (1982). A primary acoustic startle circuit: Lesions and stimulation studies. *Journal of Neuroscience, 6,* 791–805.

Davis, M., Redmond, D. E., Jr., & Baraban, J. M. (1979). Noradrenergic agonists and antagonists: Effects on conditioned fear as measured by the potentiated startle paradigm. *Psychopharmacology, 65,* 111–118.

Deutch, A. Y., Goldstein, M., & Roth, R. H. (1986). Activation of the locus coeruleus induced by selective stimulation of the ventral tegmental area. *Brain Research, 363,* 307–314.

Ellis, M. E., & Kesner, R. P. (1983). The noradrenergic system of the amygdala and aversive information processing. *Behavioral Neuroscience, 97,* 399–415.

Estes, W. K., & Skinner, B. F. (1941). Some quantitative properties of anxiety. *Journal of Experimental Psychology, 29,* 390–400.

Fanselow, M. S. (1981). Naloxone and pavlovian fear conditioning. *Learning and Motivation, 12*, 398–419.

Fanselow, M. S. (1982). The postshock activity burst. *Animal Learning and Behavior, 10*, 448–454.

Fanselow, M. S. (1984). Shock-induced analgesia on the formalin test: Effect of shock severity, naloxone, hypophysectomy, and associative variables. *Behavioral Neuroscience, 98*, 79–95.

Fanselow, M. S. (1991). The midbrain periaqueductal gray as a coordinator of action in response to fear and anxiety. In A. Depaulis & R. Bandler (Eds.), *The midbrain periaqueductal grey matter: Functional, anatomical and immunohistochemical organization*. New York: Plenum.

Fanselow, M. S., & Bolles, R. C. (1979). Naloxone and shock-elicited freezing in the rat. *Journal of Comparative and Physiological Psychology, 93*, 736–744.

File, S. E. (1980). The use of social interaction as a method for detecting anxiolytic activity of chlordiazepoxide-like drugs. *Journal of Neuroscience Methods, 2*, 219–238.

Gallagher, M., & Kapp, B. S. (1978). Manipulation of opiate activity in the amygdala alters memory processes. *Life Sciences, 23*, 1973–1978.

Gallagher, M., & Kapp, B. S. (1981). Effect of phentolamine administration into the amygdala complex of rats on time-dependent memory processes. *Behavioral and Neural Biology, 31*, 90–95.

Galvani, P. F. (1970). Air-puff-elicited startle: Habituation over trials and measurement of a hypothetical emotional response. *Behavioral Research Methods & Instrumentation, 2*, 232–233.

Geller, I., & Seifter, J. (1960). The effects of memprobamate, barbiturates, d-amphetamine and promazine on experimentally induced conflict in the rat. *Psychopharmacologia, 1*, 482–492.

Gentile, C. G., Jarrel, T. W., Teich, A., McCabe, P. M., & Schneiderman, N. (1986). The role of amygdaloid central nucleus in the retention of differential pavlovian conditioning of bradycardia in rabbits. *Behavioral Brain Research, 20*, 263–273.

Gerfen, C. R., & Sawchenko, P. E. (1984). An antegrade neuroanatomical tracing method that shows the detailed morphology of neurons, their axons and terminals: Immunohistochemical localization of an axonally transported plant lectin, *phaseolus vulgaris* leucoagglutinin (PHA-L). *Brain Research, 290*, 219–238.

Gloor, P. (1960). Amygdala. In J. Field (Ed.), *Handbook of physiology: Sec. I. Neurophysiology* (Vol. 2, pp. 1395–1420). Washington, DC: American Physiological Society.

Gloor, P., Olivier, A., & Quesney, L. F. (1981). The role of the amygdala in the expression of psychic phenomena in temporal lobe seizures. In Y. Ben-Ari (Ed.), *The amygdaloid complex*. New York: Elsevier/North-Holland.

Gold, P. E., Hankins, L., Edwards, R. M., Chester, J., & McGaugh, J. L. (1975). Memory inference and facilitation with posttrial amygdala stimulation: Effect varies with footshock level. *Brain Research, 86*, 509–513.

Guyenet, P. G., & Byrum, C. E. (1985). Comparative effects of sciatic nerve stimulation, blood pressure, and morphine on the activity of A5 and A6 pontine noradrenergic neurons. *Brain Research, 327*, 191–201.

Handforth, A. (1984). Implications of stimulus factors governing kindled seizure threshold. *Experimental Neurology, 86*, 33–39.

Handwerker, M. J., Gold, P. E., & McGaugh, J. L. (1974). Impairment of active avoidance learning with posttraining amygdala stimulation. *Brain Research, 75*, 324–327.

Harper, R. M., Frysinger, R. C., Trelease, R. B., & Marks, J. D. (1984). State-dependent alteration of respiratory cycle timing by stimulation of the central nucleus of the amygdala. *Brain Research, 306*, 1–8.

Hawkins, R. D., Abrams, T. W., Carew, T. J., & Kandel, E. R. (1983). A cellular mechanism of classical conditioning in *Aplysia*: Activity-dependent amplification of presynaptic facilitation. *Science, 219*, 400–405.

Henke, P. G. (1980a). The centromedial amygdala and gastric pathology in rats. *Physiology & Behavior, 25*, 107–112.

Henke, P. G. (1980b). The amygdala and restraint ulcers in rats. *Journal of Comparative and Physiology Psychology, 94,* 313–323.

Henke, P. G. (1983). Unit-activity in the central amygdalar nucleus of rats in response to immobilization-stress. *Brain Research Reviews, 10,* 833–837.

Henkel, C. K. (1981). Afferent sources of a lateral midbrain tegmental zone associated with the pinnae in the cat as mapped by retrograde transport of horseradish peroxidase. *Journal of Comparative Neurology, 203,* 213–226.

Henkel, C. K., & Edwards, S. B. (1978). The superior colliculus control of pinna movements in the cat: Possible anatomical connections. *Journal of Comparative Neurology, 182,* 763–776.

Hitchcock, J. M., & Davis, M. (1986). Lesions of the amygdala, but not of the cerebellum or red nucleus, block conditioned fear as measured with the potentiated startle paradigm. *Behavioral Neuroscience, 100,* 11–22.

Hitchcock, J. M., & Davis, M. (1986b). *Discrimination between visual and auditory stimuli demonstrated in the fear-potentiated startle paradigm.* Unpublished raw data.

Hitchcock, J. M., & Davis, M. (1986c). *Lesions of deep layers of the superior colliculus do not block fear-potentiated startle when very weak stimulus intensities are used to elicit acoustic startle.* Unpublished raw data.

Hitchcock, J. M., & Davis, M. (1991). The efferent pathway of the amygdala involved in conditioned fear as measured with the fear-potentiated startle paradigm. *Behavioral Neuroscience.*

Hitchcock, J. M., & Davis, M. (1987). Fear-potentiated startle using an auditory conditioned stimulus: Effect of lesions of the amygdala. *Physiology & Behavior, 39,* 403–408.

Hitchcock, J. M., Sananes, C. B., & Davis, M. (1989). Sensitization of the startle reflex by footshock: Blockade by lesions of the central nucleus of the amygdala or its efferent pathway to the brainstem. *Behavioral Neuroscience, 103,* 509–518.

Hopkins, D. A., & Holstege, G. (1978). Amygdaloid projections to the mesencephalon, pons and medulla oblongata in the cat. *Experimental Brain Research, 32,* 529–547.

Inagaki, S., Kawai, Y., Matsuzak, T., Shiosaka, S., & Tohyama, M. (1983). Precise terminal fields of the descending somatostatinergic neuron system from the amygdala complex of the rat. *Journal Hirnforch, 24,* 345–356.

Innes, D. L., & Tansy, M. F. (1980). Gastric mucosal ulceration associated with electrochemical stimulation of the limbic system. *Brain Research Bulletin, 5,* 33–36.

Ison, J. R., McAdam, D. W., & Hammond, G. R. (1973). Latency and amplitude changes in the acoustic startle reflex of the rat produced by variation in auditory prestimulation. *Physiology & Behavior, 10,* 1035–1039.

Iwata, J., LeDoux, J. E., Meeley, M. P., Arneric, S., & Reis, D. J. (1986). Intrinsic neurons in the amygdala field projected to by the medial geniculate body mediate emotional responses conditioned to acoustic stimuli. *Brain Research, 383,* 195–214.

Jarrell, T. W., McCabe, P. M., Teich, A., Gentile, C. G., VanDercar, D. H., & Schneidrman, N. (1986). Lateral subthalamic area as mediator of classically conditioned bradycardia in rabbits. *Behavioral Neuroscience, 100,* 3–10.

Kaada, B. R. (1972). Stimulation and regional ablation of the amygdaloid complex with reference to functional representations. In B. E. Eleftheriou (Ed.), *The neurobiology of the amygdala* (pp. 205–281). New York: Plenum Press.

Kapp, B. S., Frysinger, R. C., Gallagher, M., & Haselton, J. R. (1979). Amygdala central nucleus lesions: Effects on heart rate conditioning in the rabbit. *Physiology & Behavior, 23,* 1109–1117.

Kapp, B. S., Gallagher, M., Underwood, M. D., McNall, C. L., & Whitehorn, D. (1982). Cardiovascular responses elicited by electrical stimulation of the amygdala central nucleus in the rabbit. *Brain Research, 234,* 251–262.

Kapp, B. S., & Pascoe, J. P. (1986). Correlation aspects of memory: vertebrate model systems. In J. L. Martinez & R. P. Kesner (Eds.), *Learning and Memory: A Biological View* (pp. 473–488). New York: Academic Press.

Kapp, B. S., Pascoe, J. P., & Bixler, M. A. (1984). The amygdala: A neuroanatomical systems approach to its contribution to aversive conditioning. In N. Butters & L. S. Squire (Eds.), *The neuropsychology of memory* (pp. 473–488). New York: The Guilford Press.

Kehne, J. H., Gallager, D. W., & Davis, M. (1981). Strychnine: Brainstem and spinal mediation of excitatory effects on acoustic startle. *European Journal of Pharmacology, 76*, 177–186.

Kellicut, M. H., & Schwartzbaum, J. S. (1963). Formation of a conditioned emotional response (CER) following lesions of the amygdaloid complex in rats. *Psychological Review, 12*, 351–358.

Kesner, R. P. (1982). Brain stimulation: Effects on memory. *Behavioral and Neural Biology, 36*, 315–367.

Krettek, J. E., & Price, J. L. (1978). Amygdaloid projections to subcortical structures within the basal forebrain and brainstem in the rat and cat. *Journal of Comparative Neurology, 178*, 225–254.

Kurtz, K. H., & Siegel, A. (1966). Conditioned fear and magnitude of startle response: A replication and extension. *Journal of Comparative and Physiological Psychology, 62*, 8–14.

Lavond, D. G., Lincoln, J. S., McCormick, D. A., & Thompson, R. F. (1984). Effect of bilateral lesions of the lateral cerebellar nuclei on conditioning of heart-rate and nictitating membrane/eyelid responses in the rabbit. *Brain Research, 305*, 323–330.

Leaton, R. N., & Borszcz, G. S. (1985). Potentiated startle: Its relation to freezing and shock intensity in rats. *Journal of Experimental Psychology: Animal Behavior Processes, 11*, 421–428.

LeDoux, J. E., Ruggiero, D. A., & Reis, D. J. (1985). Projections to the subcortical forebrain from anatomically defined regions of the medial geniculate body in the rat. *Journal of Comparative Neurology, 242*, 182–213.

LeDoux, J. E., Iwata, J., Cicchetti, P., & Reis, D. J. (1988). Different projections of the central amygdaloid nucleus mediate autonomic and behavioral correlates of conditioned fear. *Journal of Neuroscience, 8*, 2517–2529.

Liang, K. C., Bennett, C., & McGaugh, J. L. (1985). Peripheral epinephrine modulates the effects of post-training amygdala stimulation on memory. *Behavioral Brain Research, 15*, 93–100.

Liang, K. C., Juler, R. G., & McGaugh, J. L. (1986). Modulating effects of posttraining epinephrine on memory: Involvement of the amygdala noradrenergic systems. *Brain Research, 368*, 125–133.

Liebman, J. M., Mayer, D. J., & Liebeskind, J. C. (1970). Mesencephalic central gray lesions and fear-motivated behavior in rats. *Brain Research, 23*, 353–370.

Lund, R. D., & Webster, K. E. (1967). Thalamic afferents from the spinal cord and trigeminal nuclei. *Journal of Comparative Neurology, 130*, 313–328.

McAllister, W. R., & McAllister, D. E. (1971). Behavioral measurement of conditioned fear. In F. R. Brush (Ed.), *Aversive conditioning learning* (pp. 105–179). New York: Academic Press.

McMahon, S. B., & Wall, P. D. (1985). Electrophysiological mapping of brainstem projections of spinal cord lamina I cells in the rat. *Brain Research, 333*, 19–26.

Mehler, W. R. (1969). Some neurological species differences—A posteriori. *Annual New York Academy Science, 167*, 424–468.

Mishkin, M., & Aggleton, J. (1981). Multiple functional contributions of the amygdala in the monkey. In Y. Ben-Ari (Ed.), *The amygdaloid complex.* New York: Elsevier/North-Holland.

Mizuno, N., Takahashi, O., Satoda, T., & Matsushima, R. (1985). Amygdalospinal projections in the macaque monkey. *Neuroscience Letters, 53*, 327–330.

Moore, R. Y., & Card, J. P. (1984). Noradrenaline-containing neuron systems. In A. Bjorklund, & T. Hokfelt (Eds.), *Handbook of chemical neuroanatomy.* Amsterdam: Elsevier.

Morgenson, G. J., & Calaresu, F. R. (1973). Cardiovascular responses to electrical stimulation of the amygdala in the rat. *Experimental Neurology, 39*, 166–180.

Ohta, M. (1984). Amygdaloid and cortical facilitation or inhibition of trigeminal motoneurons in the rat. *Brain Research, 291*, 39–48.

Ottersen, O. P., & Ben-Ari, Y. (1979). Afferent connections to the amygdaloid complex of the rat and cat. I. Projections from the thalamus. *Journal of Comparative Neurology, 187*, 401–424.

Pascoe, J. P., & Kapp, B. S. (1985). Electrophysiological characteristics of amygdaloid central nucleus neurons during Pavlovian fear conditioning in the rabbit. *Behavioral Brain Research, 16,* 117–133.

Phillipson, O. T. (1979). Afferent projections to the ventral tegmental area of Tsai and intrafascicular nucleus: A horseradish peroxidase study in the rat. *Journal of Comparative Neurology, 187,* 117–143.

Pollock, B., Bock, P. R., Fuchs, A. M., & Lohaus, R. (1976). Visually evoked potentials in cortical and subcortical brain structures of conscious rabbits with chronically implanted electrodes. *Arzneim-Forsch (Drug Research), 26,* 327–334.

Post, S., & Mai, J. K. (1980). Contribution to the amygdaloid projection field in the rat: A quantitative autoradiographic study. *Journal of Hirnforsch, 21,* 199–225.

Price, J. L., & Amaral, D. G. (1981). An autoradiographic study of the projections of the central nucleus of the monkey amygdala. *Journal of Neuroscience, 1,* 1242–1259.

Redmond, D. E. Jr. (1977). Alteration in the function of the nucleus locus coeruleus: A possible model for studies on anxiety. In Hanin (Ed.), *Animal models in psychiatry and neurology* (pp. 293–304). Oxford, Pergamon Press.

Rosen, J. B., & Davis, M. (1988). Enhancement of acoustic startle by electrical stimulation of the amygdala. *Behavioral Neuroscience, 102,* 195–202.

Rosen, J. B., Hitchcock, J. M., Sananes, C. B., Miserendino, M. J. D., & Davis, M. (1991). A direct projection from the central nucleus of the amygdala to the acoustic startle pathway: Anterograde and retrograde tracing studies. *Behavioral Neuroscience.*

Rosen, J. B., Hitchcock, J. M., Miserendino, M. J. D., Falls, W. A., Campeau, S., & Davis, M. Lesions of the perirhinal cortex, but not of the frontal, medial pre-frontal, visual or insular cortex block fear-potentiated startle using a visual conditioned stimulus (unpublished observations).

Sananes, C. B., & Davis, M. (in press). NMDA lesions of the lateral and basolateral nuclei of the amygdala block fear-potentiated startle and shock sensitization of startle. *Behavioral Neuroscience.*

Sandrew, B. B., Edwards, D. L., Poletti, C. E., & Foote, W. E. (1986). Amygdalospinal projections in the cat. *Brain Research, 373,* 235–239.

Sanghera, M. K., Rolls, E. T., & Roper-Hall, A. (1979). Visual responses of neurons in the dorsolateral amygdala of the alert monkey. *Experimental Neurology, 63,* 610–626.

Sarter, M., & Markowitsch, H. J. (1985). Involvement of the amygdala in learning and memory: A critical review, with emphasis on anatomical relations. *Behavioral Neuroscience, 99,* 342–380.

Schwaber, J. S., Kapp, B. S., Higgins, G. A., & Rapp, P. R. (1982). Amygdaloid and basal forebrain direct connections with the nucleus of the solitary tract and the dorsal motor nucleus. *Journal of Neuroscience, 2,* 1424–1438.

Schwarcz, M., Hokfelt, T., Fuxe, K., Jonsson, Goldstein, M., & Terenius, L. (1979). Ibotenic acid-induced neuronal degeneration: A morphological and neurochemical study. *Experimental Brain Research, 37,* 199–216.

Sen, R. N., & Anand, B. K. (1957). Effect of electrical stimulation of the limbic system of brain ('visceral brain') on gastric secretory activity and ulceration. *Indian Journal of Medical Research 45,* 515–521.

Shibata, K., Kataoka, Y., Yamashita, K., & Ueki, S. (1986). An important role of the central amygdaloid nucleus and mammillary body in the mediation of conflict behavior in rats. *Brain Research, 372,* 159–162.

Siegel, A. (1967). Stimulus generalization of a classically conditioned response along a temporal dimension. *Journal of Comparative and Physiological Psychology, 64,* 461–466.

Spevack, A. A., Campbell, C. T., & Drake, L. (1975). Effect of amygdalectomy on habituation and CER in rats. *Physiology & Behavior, 15,* 199–207.

Supple, W. F., & Leaton, R. N. (1986). Cerebellar vermis: Essential for classically conditioned bradycardia in rats. *Eastern Psychological Association* (p. 65).

Takeuchi, Y., Matsushima, S., Matsushima, S., & Hopkins, D. A. (1983). Direct amygdaloid projections to the dorsal motor nucleus of the vagus nerve: A light and electron microscopic study in the rat. *Brain Research, 280,* 143–147.

Takeuchi, Y., McLean, J. H., & Hopkins, D. A. (1982). Reciprocal connections between the amygdala and parabrachial nuclei: Ultrastructural demonstration by degeneration and axonal transport of HRP in the cat. *Brain Research, 239,* 583–588.

Thierry, A. M., Tassin, J. P., Blanc, G., & Glowinski, J. (1976). Selective activation of the mesocortical DA system by stress. *Nature, 263,* 242–244.

Thompson, R. F., Donegan, N. H., Clar, G. A., Lavond, D. G., Lincoln, J. S., Madden, J. IV, Mamounas, L. A., Mauk, M. D., & McCormick, D. A. (1987). Neuronal substrates of discrete, defensive conditioned reflexes, conditioned fear states, and their interactions in the rabbit. In I. Gormezano, W. F. Prokasy, & R. F. Thompson (Eds.), *Classical conditioning III: Behavioral, neurophysiological and neurochemical studies in the rabbit* 371–400. Hillsdale, NJ: Lawrence Erlbaum Associates.

Tischler, M. D., & Davis, M. (1983). A visual pathway that mediates fear-conditioned enhancement of acoustic startle. *Brain Research, 276,* 55–71.

Turner, B. H., & Zimmer, J. (1984). The architecture and some of the interconnections of the rat's amygdala and lateral periallocortex. *The Journal of Comparative Neurology, 227,* 540–557.

Ursin, H., Jellestad, F., & Cabrera, I. G. (1981). The amygdala, exploration and fear. In Y. Ben-Ari (Ed.), *The amygdaloid complex.* Amsterdam: Elsevier North Holland.

Veening, J. G., Swanson, L. W., & Sawchenko, P. E. (1984). The organization of projections from the central nucleus of the amygdala to brain stem sites involved in central autonomic regulation: A combined retrograde transport-immunohistochemical study. *Brain Research, 303,* 337–357.

Wagner, A. R., Siegel, L. S., & Fein, G. G. (1967). Extinction of conditioned fear as a function of percentage of reinforcement. *Journal of Comparative and Physiological Psychology, 63,* 160–164.

Walters, E. T., & Byrne, J. H. (1985). Long-term enhancement produced by activity-dependent modulation of Aplysia sensory neurons. *Journal of Neuroscience, 5,* 662–672.

Zaczek, R., & Coyle, J. T. (1982). Excitatory amino acid analogues: Neurotoxicity and seizures. *Neuropharmacology, 21,* 15–20.

An Animal Model of Central Nervous System Dysfunction Associated with Fetal Alcohol Exposure: Behavioral and Neuroanatomical Correlates

9

Charles R. Goodlett
Daniel J. Bonthius
Edward A. Wasserman
James R. West
University of Iowa

Experimental approaches to the psychobiology of learning and memory typically divide behavior into various functional components, then evaluate the neural substrates of those components through correlation with specific neural events, or through selective manipulation of identified cell populations or synapses. In contrast, when considering the effects of a teratogen such as alcohol on the developing central nervous system (CNS), it should be clear that exposure of the CNS to alcohol is a general rather than a selective event and is subject to individual variation in pharmacokinetics and pharmacodynamics (Goldstein, 1983). Whereas many fundamental properties of neurons are disrupted by alcohol, the mechanisms of alcohol's effects on the nervous system, including its toxicity on the developing nervous system, are not known (Michaelis & Michaelis, 1986).

On face value, then, it does not appear that alcohol would be a particularly useful tool for investigating brain development and behavioral function. However, because of its enormous potential for abuse by humans, and the now overwhelming documentation of birth defects induced by alcohol abuse during pregnancy, the need to characterize and to understand the effects of alcohol on the developing brain has become a priority for research in neurotoxicology and behavioral teratology. The expanding number of experimental studies of alcohol and brain development demonstrate that questions concerning the fundamental principles of brain development can also be framed in the context of studies regarding neuroteratological effects of alcohol.

CHARACTERISTICS OF THE HUMAN FETAL ALCOHOL SYNDROME (FAS)

The impetus for studies of alcohol and development arose from the formal description in 1973 of the Fetal Alcohol Syndrome (or FAS) by researchers in Seattle, Washington (Jones & Smith, 1973; Jones, Smith, Ulleland, & Streissguth, 1973). FAS is a constellation of clinical features in offspring of women with a history of alcohol abuse during pregnancy. The syndrome includes prenatal and postnatal growth deficiencies, a set of mild facial anomalies, and CNS dysfunction (Jones & Smith, 1973). Malformations of major organs are often but not always associated with the syndrome. Whereas any one of these effects could have various other causes, the constellation has only been observed in association with heavy prenatal alcohol exposure (Clarren & Smith, 1978). The worldwide incidence rate has been recently estimated at 1.9 per 1,000 live births (Abel & Sokol, 1987). Among alcoholic women, the incidence increases to 60 per 1,000 births. From such estimates, FAS is now recognized as one of the leading known causes of mental retardation (Abel & Sokol, 1987).

In the past, much emphasis has been placed on the relatively minor facial anomalies, primarily because of their necessity in making the diagnosis of FAS. Together these anomalies can be classified as a flattened, underdeveloped mid-face with one or more of the following: short palpebral fissures, hypoplastic philtrum, and thin upper vermillion. Sulik and her associates have shown that similar facial dysmorphology can be produced in a mouse animal model (Sulik, Johnston, & Webb, 1981). Administration of alcohol to pregnant dams in a narrow window of time around gestational day 7 produces comparable facial anomalies, including short palpebral fissures, joined maxillary prominences with an absent midline notch (comparable to the hypoplastic philtrum), and a small midface.

Although the facial dysmorphology is critical for diagnosing FAS, it is the CNS dysfunction associated with the syndrome that is of serious medical and social significance. A set of several major behavioral effects has been described for children diagnosed as having FAS (Streissguth, 1986; Streissguth, Clarren, & Jones, 1985). The most deleterious feature is a mild to moderate mental retardation, with IQs averaging between 65–70. Because the first formally diagnosed cases are only now reaching adulthood, the long-term effects are just now becoming evident, but it does not appear that the low IQs and mental retardation are improved with age (Streissguth, 1986; Streissguth, Clarren, & Jones, 1985). Other cognitive deficits are present, even in those not frankly retarded (Streissguth, Clarren, & Jones, 1985). There are deficiencies in many realms of learning, and classroom performance is below normal. There are anecdotal observations of attentional deficits or short attention spans, some of which have now been documented on laboratory vigilance tasks (Streissguth et al., 1984). FAS children tend to show strong perseverative tendencies and difficulty in shifting responses. They also exhibit classic signs of hyperactivity. They are impulsive and have lack of normal inhibitions, including lack of concern for personal safety in dangerous situations and lack of fear of strangers (Streissguth, 1986). In addition, motor deficits, gait abnormalities, sleep disturbances, perceptual problems, and autonomic dysfunction are often apparent.

There is little neuropathological data available on FAS because FAS usually is not fatal. Despite the larger clinical literature, fewer than 20 FAS cases have come to autopsy, with death usually due to other medical complications. Neuropathological evaluations have indicated gross and microscopic abnormalities in the brain (Clarren, 1986; Clarren & Smith, 1978; Majewski, 1981; Peiffer et al., 1979; Wisniewski, Drambska, Shar, & Qazi, 1983). There is usually a severe reduction in brain weight—or microencephaly—with obvious malformations of the gyri of the cortical mantle. Reductions in white matter and increased ventricular size are frequently seen as well. The neuropathological findings summarized across all autopsied cases, which likely represent the most severe end of the FAS spectrum, indicate that heavy prenatal alcohol exposure can induce microencephaly, cell loss, dysgenesis of the cerebrum, cerebellum, and corpus callosum, reduced white matter with corresponding increases in ventricular size, and neuroglial heterotopias and errors of migration (Clarren, 1986).

Although brain damage and behavioral dysfunction are the hallmarks of FAS, the use of the formal FAS criteria may discriminate only a minority of children adversely affected by prenatal alcohol exposure. The appearance of the constellation of effects may require heavy abuse over much of the pregnancy, and different symptoms may result from differences in the timing or pattern of exposure. For example, the facial anomalies and gross brain malformations may result from exposure during the first trimester, but other alcohol-related effects on CNS organization or fine structure, leading to behavioral dysfunction, may occur at other periods. The brain begins to develop early during gestation and continues over a more protracted period than other organs; therefore it may be vulnerable to different types of alcohol-induced damage at different stages (West, 1987).

It is suspected that the risk and severity of fetal alcohol effects are related to the timing and amount of alcohol consumption. However, because the actual level of drinking is difficult to document reliably, relationships between the occurrence of FAS and the level of drinking cannot readily be established (Earnhardt, Marrow-Tlucak, Sokol, & Martier, 1988; Little, Schultz, & Mandell, 1976; Rosett et al., 1983). However, in all FAS cases where the drinking history can be estimated, alcohol abuse is consistently present and is often spectacularly heavy. One example is a recent case report (Church & Gerkin, 1988) in which the woman engaged in binges over the last half of pregnancy, during which she drank two pints of vodka, one quart of wine, and 12 beers daily. At delivery, she had a blood alcohol level of 375 mg/dl.

Obviously, chronic and severe alcohol abuse is associated with many of the FAS cases, and tolerance to alcohol may be the best indictor of mothers carrying a fetus at risk (Earnhart et al., 1988). Even those who do respond to counseling and attempt to reduce drinking frequently lapse into binge drinking in the last trimester (Little & Streissguth, 1978; Stephens, 1985).

In summarizing the relevant characteristics of FAS, the following points indicate the need for experimental approaches using animal models:

The most devastating effects are the mental retardation and learning disabilities resulting from CNS damage.

There is considerable variation in the extent or severity of alcohol-induced birth defects.

The diagnosed cases of FAS may include only those with the most extreme effects of alcohol on the CNS.

Effects lasting into adulthood are only now being revealed in longitudinal studies.

Despite considerable publicity concerning the adverse effects of drinking during pregnancy (Surgeon General's Report, 1981), the incidence rate remains high.

USE OF ANIMAL MODELS IN STUDIES OF ALCOHOL AND DEVELOPMENT

In the wake of the initial description of FAS, 1½ decades of animal research on the effects of alcohol on development have produced literally hundreds of papers demonstrating that alcohol can alter behavioral development and can damage the brain (e.g., Abel, 1979; Barnes & Walker, 1981; Bauer-Moffett & Altman, 1977; Diaz & Samson, 1980; Reyes, Rivera, Saland, & Murray, 1983; Riley, Barron, & Hannigan, 1986; Riley, Lochry, & Shapiro, 1979; Samson & Diaz, 1982; West, 1986). Whereas these studies have provided a scientific confirmation of the observations of FAS in humans, the types of relevant research questions must now move beyond simple demonstrations that alcohol is harmful to the developing brain.

Progress is needed in four major areas. First, we need to focus on establishing correlations between behavioral effects and alterations in specific neural and hormonal substrates. Second, there is a need to examine carefully the changes in behavioral and neurological effects over the life-span, with an eye for neuroplasticity and compensatory changes as well as for permanent effects. Third, in deference to the wide range of variation of fetal alcohol effects, a better understanding of the factors affecting the risk for and severity of those effects is needed. Ultimately, animal research should bear on the mechanisms of CNS toxicity, with a goal of treatment or prevention. Evidence from our laboratory and from others has begun to address the first three issues. Less is known about the mechanisms (Michaelis & Michaelis, 1986), which will undoubtedly require complementary approaches combining *in vivo* and *in vitro* methods.

CHOOSING APPROPRIATE ANIMAL MODELS

In developing an animal model of FAS, there are two pressing issues that can be addressed only through the careful control of the model system. First, there must be control over the timing of the alcohol exposure relative to the development of the substrate. This addresses the basic question of whether temporal windows of vulnerability exist (West, 1987). Second, there should be control over, or at least knowledge concerning, the primary intervening variable—blood alcohol concentration (BAC). Questions concerning the correlation of effects with consumption level and BAC and questions of whether minimum threshold levels exist for risk of FAS are perhaps those most frequently asked, both by the public at large and by the medical community (Hanson, Streissguth, & Smith, 1976; Larsson, Bohlin, & Turell, 1985; Rosett et al., 1983).

With regard to the timing of alcohol exposure, the brain poses a difficult problem for comparative research. Whereas all mammals pass through the same stages of brain development, the timing of those stages *relative to birth* varies widely across species (Dobbing & Sands, 1979). If an animal model is to be used, the exposure must occur according to time scales relative to CNS development, rather than to time scales based on gestational length. For example, all mammals have a period of rapid brain growth, known as the brain growth spurt, which occurs relatively late in development and which includes dendritic growth, synaptogenesis, microneuron proliferation, glial proliferation, and myelination (Dobbing, 1981). In humans, this period of brain development encompasses the third trimester of pregnancy and the first few years of postnatal life (Dobbing & Sands, 1973) and is thought to be one of special vulnerability of the brain.

Dobbing and Sands (1979) have compared the timing of the brain growth spurt, relative to birth, across several species. These comparisons were performed by plotting the rate of brain growth (in percentage of adult weight) as a function of time scales appropriate for each species, but centered around birth. In the human, the brain growth spurt begins at the end of the second trimester, peaks around birth, and tapers over the first 2 years of life. For the rhesus monkey, the brain growth spurt is nearly over at the time of birth. For the rat, the comparable period of rapid brain growth occurs completely after birth, peaking at around postnatal day 10. Therefore, in order to compare the effects of alcohol exposure during the period of brain development that occurs during the third trimester in humans, the exposure of rats to alcohol must occur in neonates rather than *in utero*.

EARLY POSTNATAL ALCOHOL EXPOSURE AND
ARTIFICIAL REARING OF RATS

Methodologically, neonatal alcohol exposure in rats poses a difficult problem. Direct administration of alcohol to rat pups inevitably interferes with suckling and leads to effects due to undernutrition. One method that obviates this problem is to remove the pups from the dam and rear them artificially by feeding them through implanted gastrostomy tubes, through which milk formula can be infused (Diaz & Samson, 1980; Samson & Diaz, 1982; West, Hamre, & Pierce, 1984). The pups are placed in cups in a heated aquarium and connected to syringes that contain milk formula (see Kelly, Pierce, & West, 1987; West, Hamre, & Pierce, 1984). They are periodically infused with the formula via a timer-controlled infusion pump. The gastrostomized rats are assigned either to receive some infusions of milk formula that contain alcohol, or they may serve as artificially reared controls in which all their feedings are free of alcohol.

The pups typically are gastrostomized on the morning of postnatal day 4 and receive feedings every 2 hours until the morning of day 10. In some studies the pups are sacrificed on day 10 for evaluation of the brain; in others they are returned to lactating dams and weaned on day 21 for the studies at older ages. In addition to gastrostomy controls, normally reared suckle controls are included as an additional group to evaluate the effects of artificial rearing.

By using artificial rearing, we are able to satisfy the first requirement of controlling the timing of the exposure in rats in order to model alcohol exposure during the brain growth spurt of the human third trimester. What about the second requirement of control over BACs? By providing 12 feedings on each day of artificial rearing, we have the means for very precise control of the administration of alcohol to the pups. Simply by controlling the alcohol concentration in each feeding and the number of daily feedings that contain alcohol, we can examine the effect of variations in the pattern of alcohol consumption on brain development. For example, in one study (Bonthius, Goodlett, & West, 1988), the same daily amount of alcohol—6.6 g/kg/day—was given to different groups of neonatal rats from day 4 to the morning of day 10. One group got the daily dose spread over all 12 feedings; in a second group it was concentrated into 4 consecutive feedings of the 12 each day, and in the third it was concentrated into only 2 of the feedings. Not surprisingly, the BAC profiles were dramatically different. The uniform daily exposure produced low and stable BACs, and the concentrated exposures produced profiles with high peaks and low troughs, with the most concentrated treatment producing the highest peak BACs.

Importantly, these three exposures of the same daily amount of alcohol resulted in different effects on brain development. Whereas none of the alcohol treatments altered body growth relative to controls, brain weight was significantly reduced only in the two concentrated dosing regimens. Furthermore, the group given the most concentrated formula was the most severely affected. This clearly demonstrated that one of the factors that increases the severity of effects is the pattern of alcohol consumption. This implies that episodes of heavy drinking by pregnant women, in which high peak BACs are achieved, may be especially harmful to the fetus.

We have also examined the dose-response effects of alcohol exposure on neonatal brain growth, using the paradigm in which alcohol is included in four consecutive feedings each day, but in which the total amount of alcohol contained in the four daily feedings was systematically varied (Bonthius & West, 1988). The peak BACs produced by this paradigm using doses from 2.5 g/kg to 7.5 g/kg per day were a linear function of the daily dose of alcohol. The 6.6 g/kg dose and the 7.5 g/kg dose produced BACs above 300 and 400 mg/dl, respectively. In addition, an 8.5 g/kg dose was attempted but was uniformly lethal, indicating the 7.5 g/kg dose constituted an extreme treatment.

The brain weights on day 10 from these pups were reduced in a dose-dependent fashion, with the first statistically significant reduction occurring with the 4.5 g/kg dose, which produced a mean BAC of about 195 mg/dl. We have now seen across several studies that significant reductions in brain weight occur when peak BACs reach 160–190 mg/dl (Bonthius & West, 1988; Pierce & West,

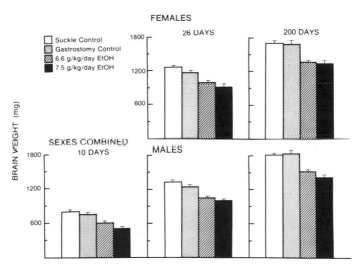

FIG. 9.1. Mean (±SEM) brain weights of suckle control, gastrostomy control, 6.6 g/kg/day, and 7.5 g/kg/day groups at three ages (10 days, 26 days, and 200 days). The rats were perfused with aldehyde fixatives. Significant reductions in whole brain weight of both alcohol groups were present at all three ages relative to each control group. No significant group differences in body weight were observed at 10 days or at 200 days; at 26 days, the 7.5 g/kg/day group had small but significant reductions of body weights compared to controls (90% of gastrostomy control body weights).

1986a, 1986b, 1987). More importantly, this study demonstrated a highly significant negative correlation between peak BAC and day 10 brain weight across all groups, with a correlation coefficient of -0.916. Thus, the brain growth deficits produced in this model are highly predicted by the peak BAC.

Using the 6.6 and 7.5 g/kg treatments, we have also examined brain growth restriction at later ages. As shown in Fig. 9.1., the brain weight deficits observed at 10 days remained significant at 26 days and at 200 days. This permanent deficit indicates the alcohol-induced brain growth restriction following neonatal exposure does not recover with termination of the alcohol treatment. In addition, the brain weight deficits occurred even though body growth was unaffected (6.6 g/kg dose) or only mildly retarded (7.5 g/kg dose), which is in contrast to other treatments such as malnutrition during similar periods of development (Dobbing, 1981).

USE OF THE RAT MODEL OF ALCOHOL EXPOSURE DURING THE BRAIN GROWTH SPURT

Presuming the validity of early postnatal alcohol exposure in rats as a model of third trimester exposure in humans, and given the advantages and experimental control it provides, what are the experimental goals in using this model? We have identified five goals roughly in descending order of progress or what has been attempted (see Table 9.1). Our first goal was to identify structures or cell populations vulnerable to damage. We have also examined some effects at different ages and have begun to test potential behavioral correlates. Most of the discussion relates to these first three goals, because we have not yet attempted to specify mechanisms or treatment strategies.

NEURONAL POPULATIONS VULNERABLE TO CELL LOSS

In choosing brain regions to evaluate, it is advantageous to use regions that have a relatively simple organization that is amenable to quantification, and in which the anatomy and development are reasonably well known. For these reasons, we have focused on the cerebellum and hippocampal formation. Both have discretely organized cell populations of large, prenatally generated projection neurons and small, postnatally generated local neurons (Altman, 1969, 1972; Altman & Bayer, 1978; Bayer, 1980a, 1980b). In the hippocampus, the large pyramidal cells are generated prenatally, whereas the granule cells of the dentate gyrus are generated postnatally. In the cerebellum, the large Purkinje cells are prenatally generated and lie superficial to the postnatally generated granule cells.

TABLE 9.1
Use of Animal Models of Alcohol-Induced Effects on CNS Development—Experimental Goals

1. To identify structures, regions, or cell populations at risk for cell loss, damage, or disruption.
2. To describe the developmental elaboration of the effects and the permanency of the effects.
3. To determine whether relationships can be established between behavioral changes and alterations in specific neural and hormonal mechanisms [brain-behavior relationships].
4. To provide insight into potential mechanisms of neurotoxicity.
5. To test treatments or intervention strategies for their potential to prevent or reverse alcohol-induced brain damage.

These spatial and temporal separations of cell populations in these two regions make them ideal for quantifying the effects of alcohol exposure on cell survival.

In the rat, the timing of neurogenesis puts different neuronal populations at different stages of development at the time of alcohol exposure in the early postnatal model (West, 1987). With neonatal alcohol exposure during postnatal days 4–10, many neurons, including cerebellar Purkinje cells and hippocampal pyramidal cells, are postmitotic and are undergoing differentiation. Other populations, including the cerebellar granule cells and dentate gyrus granule cells, are still proliferating. It is important to realize that with any alcohol-induced neuronal loss at this period, the postmitotic Purkinje and pyramidal cells cannot be replaced.

Several cell count studies on 10-day-old pups clearly show that alcohol-induced neuronal loss is not equal across the two regions, nor across cell populations (Pierce, Goodlett, & West, 1989; West, Bonthius, Hamre, & Pierce, 1988; see also Bauer-Moffett & Altman, 1977). Using 2-micron thick sections, we have quantified neuron numbers in the hippocampal formation, including CA1, CA3, CA4, and the granule cells of the dentate gyrus. In the hippocampus, the only significant reductions in regional area and in neuron numbers with the condensed dosing regimen (two to four alcohol-containing feedings per day) occurred in the pyramidal cells of field CA1. There was no significant cell loss in CA3 or CA4, nor in the dentate gyrus.

We have also quantified cerebellar Purkinje cells and granule cells in several studies in 10-day-olds (see Pierce, Goodlett, & West, 1989). We have consistently found large reductions in the number of Purkinje cells, with a smaller percentage loss of granule cells. The cerebellar granule cell loss appears correlated with the Purkinje cell loss across different lobules, suggesting the granule cell loss may be secondary to loss of their target population—the Purkinje cells. We have replicated these effects in another study of 10-day-old pups exposed to peak BACs of approximately 350 mg/dl. Compared to gastrostomy controls, the alcohol-treated pups had approximately a 40% reduction in the number of cerebellar Purkinje cells. These same alcohol-exposed rats had significantly fewer CA1 pyramidal cells (reduced by 15%), whereas neuron counts in CA3, CA4, and the dentate gyrus were unaffected relative to controls.

TABLE 9.2
Neuron Counts in 200-Day-Old Rats[a]

Group[b]	N	Hippocampus CA1	Pyramidal Cells CA3	CA4	Cerebellum Purkinje Cells
Suckle control	18	327 ±6	410 ±15	220 ±7	938 ±9
Gastrostomy control	16	323 ±7	386 ±9	211 ±6	933 ±12
6.6 g/kg/day Alcohol	16	272** ±7	397 ±12	209 ±6	660** ±19
7.5 g/kg/day Alcohol	14	260** ±10	384 ±9	200 ±10	602** ±19

[a]Values represent means (+ SEM) of counts of single horizontal hippocampal sections, and single sagital cerebellar sections (each 2 micrometers thick).
[b]Treatments were conducted during postnatal days 4 through 9; alcohol was given in four consecutive feedings each day.
**$p < .01$ compared to either control group, Newman-Keuls test.

We have recently completed counts from these same cell populations in 200-day-old rats from the early postnatal 6.6 and 7.5 g/kg alcohol treatments. These treatments yielded mean peak BACs during the treatment period of 335 and 415 mg/dl, respectively. The alcohol treatments resulted in significant, permanent reductions in pyramidal cells of hippocampal field CA1 and in cerebellar Purkinje cells (Table 9.2). Pyramidal cells in CA3 and CA4 were not reduced, which was the same pattern seen in 10-day-olds.

BEHAVIORAL STUDIES USING THE EARLY POSTNATAL EXPOSURE MODEL

The brain is clearly damaged by this early postnatal alcohol exposure, which encouraged us to initiate a series of behavioral studies to attempt to establish functional correlates of such damage. Because at least one subfield of the hippocampus suffers abnormal cell loss, and because the hippocampal formation is commonly linked to behavioral processes and learning capacities (Morris, 1983; O'Keefe & Nadel, 1978; Olton, 1983; Rawlins & Olton, 1981; Riley, Barron, & Hannigan, 1986; Zola-Morgan, Squire, & Amaral, 1986), conducting studies related to hippocampal function or sensitive to hippocampal damage is an appropriate initial step.

Before describing these studies, it is appropriate to acknowledge several caveats. First, as we have shown, the hippocampus is not the only brain structure disrupted by the early postnatal alcohol, nor is it even the most affected in terms of cell loss. Thus, we cannot easily dissociate behavioral dysfunction as a consequence of hippocampal damage from dysfunction resulting from damage in other brain regions. The best we can do is examine several tasks that are known to be sensitive to hippocampal damage and test whether other behaviors that are not altered by experimental hippocampal damage are affected by the early postnatal alcohol treatment. Second, we do not intend to imply that any observed effects are attributable solely to the neuron loss in CA1. Certainly, functional disruption can occur even in the absence of effects as extreme as neuronal death. In addition, considering the substantial cerebellar cell loss and given the recent demonstrations and emphasis on contributions of the cerebellum to learned performance (Ito, 1984; McCormick et al., 1982), including performance on tasks described later (Goldowitz & Koch, 1986; Lalonde, 1987), any behavioral effects may also relate to damage to that structure. Furthermore, we have not yet documented any effects in cortex, but they are likely to be present, given the large deficits in brain weight that we have observed. With these caveats in mind, the rest of the chapter describes three behavioral studies involving tasks historically linked to hippocampal function—activity, spatial navigation learning, and radial maze learning.

The first study (Kelly, Pierce, & West, 1987) examined activity in an open field, because hyperactivity is consistent both with hippocampal damage (O'Keefe & Nadel, 1978) and with FAS (Bond & DiGuisto, 1978; Streissguth, 1986). Rats of both sexes were given the 6.6 g/kg dose from days 4 through 9, either in a condensed dose paradigm (four consecutive feedings each day) or in the uniformly distributed paradigm (spread over the 12 feedings each day). Both male and female rats of the condensed alcohol treatment were hyperactive as adults in an open field, compared to the gastrostomy and suckle control groups. Rats given the uniform alcohol exposure, which produced low, constant BACs, were not different from controls

More recently, we have used several learning tasks sensitive to hippocampal damage, namely the Morris spatial navigation task (Morris, 1981, 1984) and a version of the radial maze developed by Olton (Olton, Collison, & Werz, 1977; Olton & Samuelson, 1976) and discussed extensively in other chapters of this book. We tested juvenile rats given the 6.6 g/kg dose, either in the condensed dose regimen or in the uniform exposure regimen, using the Morris navigation task (Goodlett, Kelly, & West, 1987). This task uses a 4-foot-wide diameter tank that is filled with opaque water, and a small platform is hidden just beneath the surface of the water. The rat is placed in the water at various locations around the tank and is allowed to swim around the tank until it finds the escape platform. There are no local cues to guide the rat to the platform, so it must use the constant visual spatial cues from outside the tank to triangulate and locate the platform. Starting from different locations from trial to trial, the most efficient means of finding the platform is through search patterns based on location relative to the external environment. Adult rats rapidly learn to swim directly to the platform (Morris, 1981), and lesions of the hippocampus severely disrupt this place navigation (Morris, 1983; Morris, Garrud, Rawlins, & O'Keefe, 1982; Kolb, Sutherland, & Whishaw, 1983; Sutherland, Kolb, & Whishaw, 1982; Sutherland, Whishaw, & Kolb, 1983). Development of this capacity also appears to coincide with maturation of the hippocampal formation (Dyck, Sutherland, & Buday, 1985; Rudy, Stadler-Morris, & Albert, 1988).

We first tested place navigation in rats from postnatal days 19–30, using four trials a day, with each trial within a session starting from a different compass point (Goodlett, Kelly, & West, 1987). The measures of learning included latency to escape and the distance traveled, which are usually highly correlated. Relative to controls, rats exposed to the high peak BACs of the condensed alcohol treatment were significantly impaired in acquisition of this learning as juveniles. The same dose given uniformly, which produced low, constant BACs, did not lead to a significant impairment in acquisition. The impairment of the condensed alcohol group is illustrated in Fig. 9.2, which shows examples of the

POSTNATAL DAY 27 ACQUISITION (9th TRAINING DAY)

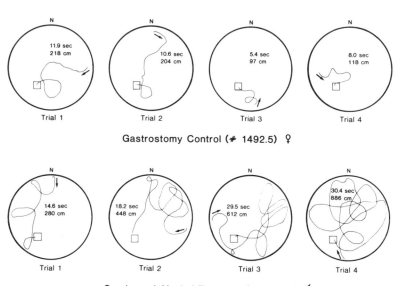

FIG. 9.2. Illustrations of the swimming paths taken to reach the submerged escape platform on the four trials on postnatal day 27 (the ninth training day). The subjects used in this example (gastrostomy control rat on top; 6.6 g/kg/day condensed dose treated rat on bottom) were near the group mean for average escape latency for the day. Note the relatively direct path on all four trials of the control, and the rapid correction when the platform was missed. Compare that to the looping search patterns of the alcohol-exposed rat, which had not developed strategies based on place navigation at this stage of training. From Goodlett, Kelly, and West (1987). Reprinted with permission.

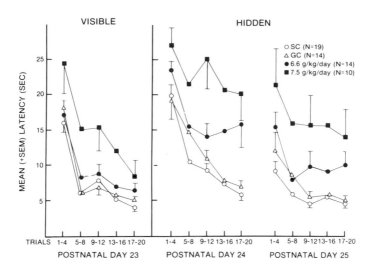

FIG. 9.3. Mean (±SEM) latency to reach the platform in the Morris navigation task incorporating 1 day (20 trials) of vision platform training (variable location) and 2 days (20 trials each) of hidden platform training (constant location). Training was conducted on postnatal days 23 (visible) and postnatal days 24 and 25 (hidden). Treatments (controls, 6.6 g/kg/day or 7.5 g/kg/day) were administered during postnatal days 4 through 9.

paths of an alcohol-treated rat compared to a control on the four trials on day 27. These two rats were near the group mean of the mean latency to escape over the four trials. Note the relatively direct path to the platform of the control on all four trials and immediate corrections on missed approaches, compared to the looping search pattern and absence of corrections of the alcohol-exposed animal. The condensed alcohol group also demonstrated impaired development of search patterns based on place strategies in "probe" trials, in which the platform was removed.

In a second experiment on juveniles, we tested two different daily doses of alcohol (given in four feedings each day)—the 6.6 g/kg per day treatment identical to that of the first study and a 7.5 g/kg per day treatment. Behavioral testing was restricted to 3 days, beginning on postnatal day 23. On the first day of testing the platform extended above the surface of the water, serving as a local visible guidance cue, and was moved randomly from place to place across the 20 trials given. On the next 2 days of testing (postnatal days 24 and 25), the platform was beneath the surface and was maintained in a constant location. As shown in Fig. 9.3, on the visible platform version all groups decreased their latencies to reach the platform, but the 7.5 g/kg group had a significant delay in their acquisition of this task. The 6.6 g/kg group was not different from controls on the visible problem. On the hidden problem, however, both alcohol-treated groups were impaired in their within-session learning of the spatial navigation task.

These data indicate that the types and severity of developmental learning impairments depend on the level of alcohol exposure during the brain growth spurt. The highest level of exposure produced acquisition impairments both on guidance learning and on spatial mapping, whereas the lower dose (which still produced BACs greater than 300 mg/dl) only affected the spatial mapping. This suggests the 6.6 g/kg treatment impairs the functional development of neural substrates necessary for place navigation, including the hippocampal formation, but the development of other neural systems is sufficient to support the simple guidance learning. In contrast, with the higher dose (producing higher BACs), even acquisition of the guidance task is disrupted at this postweaning age.

After finding navigation impairments in juveniles, we next examined acquisition of spatial navigation in adults in a new study, using behaviorally naive rats. There were only mild delays in the acquisition rate of females (Fig. 9.4), and no differences in the males, which replicated an earlier finding in our laboratory (Kelly, Goodlett, Hulsether, & West, 1988). Thus, in contrast to the severe deficits in juveniles on the navigation task, the adults have largely compensated for any disruption induced by the early alcohol exposure.

Early postnatal alcohol exposure did not produce severe learning impairments in this relatively simple navigation learning task in adults; therefore we examined learning in a more complex task—one that puts greater demands on use of spatial information. A 12-arm radial maze was employed, which in principle can yield data concerning two potentially separable functional domains of memory, and which may have different neural substrates (Olton, 1983). Olton and others have proposed that two interacting memory functions can be defined based on their operating characteristics. The first, termed *reference memory,* includes information that is maintained independent of the specific temporal or spatial context, and which generalizes across situations. Reference memory has a large capacity and is maintained over long periods of time. It is resistant to interference, and the information may be acquired slowly over many trials. The second domain, termed *working memory,* involves short-term, flexible utilization of information specific to a given temporal and spatial context. It has a limited capacity, is highly vulnerable to interference, and is operationally useful only in a given context.

In the version of the 12-arm radial maze task that we used, six of the arms were baited at the start of each training session, and six were left unbaited. Though three different configurations were used, the same configuration was employed across the 30 training trials for a given rat. The 6-baited/6-unbaited configuration affords assessment of the two operationally defined memory processes (Olton & Papas, 1979). The acquisition of discrimination between the arms of the baited set from the arms of the unbaited set leads to avoidance of the never-baited arms and reflects more reference memory processes. The recogni-

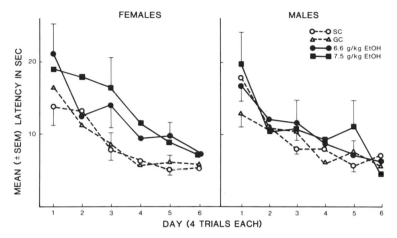

FIG. 9.4. Mean (±SEM) latency to reach the submerged platform in the Morris maze task in female and male adult rats (~90 days old) as a function of treatment. Effects of early postnatal alcohol treatment were present only in females, which took more trials to develop efficient spatial navigation. Nevertheless, these effects were mild and much less severe than those seen in both sexes in the studies on juvenile rats.

tion and avoidance of arms already entered within a given session reflects more working memory processes.

We tested 64 rats from 11 litters, divided into 4 treatment groups—suckle control, gastrostomy control, 6.6 g/kg, and 7.5 g/kg alcohol—with group numbers between 14 and 18. All testing was initiated after 100 days of age. They were dieted to 80%–85% free-feeding weight and pretrained for 8–10 days before the 6-baited/6-unbaited training procedure was instituted. Each rat was given 1 session per day for 30 days, and each session was terminated when the rat obtained food from all 6 baited arms. The sequence of arm entries and latency to complete the session were recorded by observers blind to the experimental treatment of the rats.

The radial maze is rich in the data it provides, so we have examined the data in a variety of ways. First, we analyzed learning curves based on the probability of making a correct choice on each of the first six choices of each session (from Olton, Collison, & Werz, 1977). The data were transformed to correct for chance performance on each choice, such that a score of 0 represents chance and a score of 1.0 represents perfect performance (i.e., each of the first six choices in the session were correct). As shown in Fig. 9.5, averaged across blocks of five sessions, both alcohol-exposed groups acquired the task at a significantly slower rate than the two control groups over the 30-day period. Though none of the groups approached perfect performance, which is reported to require 40–50 days

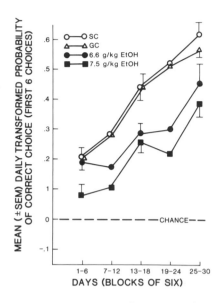

FIG. 9.5. Mean (±SEM) transformed probability of making a correct choice on each of the first six choices of each session, averaged across choices over blocks of 6 days. The transformed probabilities (modified from Olton, Collison, & Werz, 1977) were calculated for each choice as follows (p = probability): The numerator was defined as p(correct)observed − p(correct) expected, with p(correct)expected starting at 0.5 for each session and decreasing as a function of the number of correct arms entered over choices within a session. The denominator of the score for each trial was either 1-p(correct)expected [when p(correct)observed > p(correct) expected], or p(correct)expected-0 [when p(correct)expected > p(correct)observed]. This transformation results in scores that range from −1.0 to +1.0, with 0 reflecting chance performance and +1.0 reflecting perfect performance (correct on each of the six choices of each session). Note the significantly slower learning of the alcohol-exposed groups.

of training in these types of studies (Olton & Papas, 1979), the controls were superior in their rate of acquisition.

We then analyzed the group error rates over blocks of trials as a function of the types of errors. The first type of error, shown in the left panel of Fig. 9.6 and labeled *unbaited arm initial errors*, is the number of entries into arms that were never baited, provided each entry was the first into a given unbaited arm in a session. These errors correspond to measures that Olton and others designated as predominantly engaging reference memory processes (Olton, 1983; Olton, Becker, & Handelmann, 1979; Olton & Papas, 1979), because they involve the discrimination of the baited arm set from the unbaited arm set. With respect to these errors, although it is clear that none of the groups approached perfect performance, the controls did reduce their error rates significantly more rapidly than did the alcohol groups.

An even bigger group effect was seen in error rates that are thought to reflect aberrant working memory function, that is, those on the far right panel of Fig. 9.6 designated *repeated baited-arm entries*. These are the reentries within a session into arms that were baited, but from which the bait had already been retrieved. These repeated entries into baited arms occur at relatively low rates in normal rats and are the hallmark of rats with hippocampal damage (Becker,

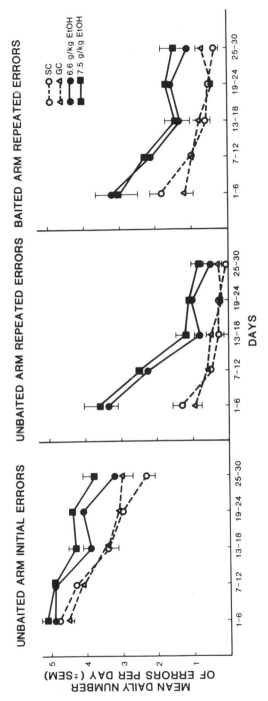

FIG. 9.6. Mean (±SEM) number of errors in the radial maze as a function of type of error, averaged over blocks of six trials. Left panel: errors resulting from entries into an unbaited arm, given that each of those entries was the first (to a given unbaited arm) of the session. These errors are taken as a measure of reference memory (Olton & Papas, 1979). Middle panel: errors resulting from repeated entries within a session into an unbaited arm, given that the unbaited arm had previously been entered during the session. These errors are taken as one measure of working memory. Right panel: errors resulting from entries within a session into an arm that initially was baited, but from which the bait had been retrieved earlier in the session. These errors are the traditional measure of working memory (Olton & Papas, 1979; Olton & Samuelson, 1976).

Walker, & Olton, 1980; Olton, Collison, & Wertz, 1977; Olton & Papas, 1979; Olton & Samuelson, 1976). Note the large effect of alcohol treatment on these types of errors, relative to controls.

Finally, an extraordinary effect of alcohol treatment was present in the third category of errors shown in the middle panel of Fig. 9.6 and designated *unbaited arm repeated errors,* which were repeated entries within sessions into unbaited arms. We interpret these errors as reflecting impaired working memory and indeed they are highly correlated ($r = +.96$) with the repeated within-session errors into baited arms (Fig. 9.6, right panel). Because these types of errors occur at very low rates in controls, the large differences between controls and alcohol-exposed rats indicate a major deficit in performance associated with working memory.

The effects on errors associated with working memory deficits were so large, that we examined the correlation between CA1 neuronal number and the total number of working memory errors (repeated errors into baited arms plus repeated errors into unbaited arms). As shown in Fig. 9.7, taken across all groups, there was a significant correlation between CA1 pyramidal cell number and the logarithmic transformation of the number of working memory errors. The logarithmic transformation was performed because the error scores were not normally distributed in the alcohol-treated groups. Interestingly, the deviations from the regression line got larger as the number of pyramidal cells decrease. There was also a single strongly aberrant point of zero errors for one alcohol-treated rat. Though this animal was not included in the regression analysis, it does provide an interesting exception discussed later.

The relevance of the association between CA1 loss and working memory errors is strengthened by the lack of any relationship of these errors to CA3 counts ($r = +.05$). This association between CA1 pyramidal counts and specific aspects of radial maze performance is consistent with the literature showing hippocampal involvement in working memory (Olton, 1983; Olton, Becker, & Handelmann, 1979). These findings also have an interesting parallel with studies that demonstrated transient working memory deficits in rats suffering ischemic hippocampal injury in adulthood, which causes selective CA1 pyramidal cell loss (Davis, Baranowski, Pulsinelli, & Volpe, 1987; Davis, Tribuna, Pulsinelli, & Volpe, 1986; Volpe, Pulsinelli, & Davis, 1986; Volpe, Waszek, & Davis, 1988; Gionet, Thomas, Warner, Goodlett, Wasserman, & West, 1991). Nevertheless, the residual variations in working memory errors in our alcohol-treated rats certainly indicate that CA1 neuronal number is not entirely predictive of these types of errors. In addition, there is a weaker association between CA1 neuron counts in these rats and reference memory errors ($r = -.29$), so the effect is only moderately selective. Finally, given the known and unknown effects of the alcohol treatment on other brain regions, it is not appropriate to attribute these working memory impairments solely to CA1 damage.

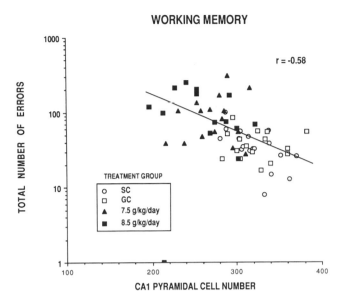

FIG. 9.7. Scatterplot of the log of the number of working memory errors against the number of CA1 pyramidal neurons counted in a single 2-micrometer-thick horizontal section through the mid-temporal hippocampal formation. The regression line is based on a least-squares analysis of the log scores. Group codes of the individual scores are indicated in the legend.

In fact, from some perspectives, deficits in working memory may not be the best characterization for these alcohol-treated rats. In several cases, their performance in the maze involved persistent use of response strategies instead of selective entry into various arms based on spatial information processing. These strategies are shown in Table 9.3 in examples from the last week of training from two alcohol cases, compared to a control. First, note the greater number of choices required for the alcohol-treated rats. More importantly, note the specific response strategies apparent in their choice sequences. The first case used an adjacent arm strategy on every day of testing (not just on the ones shown), and the rat was perfectly content to be 50% correct every day. This rat was the one that never committed a single working memory error, because such errors cannot occur with the adjacent arm strategy. The second made frequent use of an every-other-arm strategy throughout training. Several other alcohol-treated rats demonstrated this second type of strategy throughout the training period. Controls occasionally showed strategies similar to the every-other-arm example early in training, but they rarely maintained those strategies as training progressed and

TABLE 9.3

The Sequence of Arm Choices on Selected Trails in the Last Eight Days of Radial Maze Training

Trial	Arm Choices
SUB. 1892.8 7.5 g/kg ALCOHOL	
22	1 12 11 10 9 8 7 6 5 4 3
24	5 4 3 2 1 12 11 10 9 8 11 10
26	9 8 7 6 5 4 3 2 1 12 11 10
28	3 2 1 12 11 10 9 8 6 5 1 12
30	10 9 8 7 6 5 4 3 2 1
SUB. 1029.3 7.5 g/kg ALCOHOL	
22	12 2 4 6 8 10 12 2 4 6 8 11 10 12 8 2 9
24	5 7 9 11 1 3 5 4 6 11 12 8 3 2
26	1 3 5 7 9 11 1 3 12 9 7 5 3 2
28	5 7 9 11 1 3 7 2 4 8 10 5 4 12
30	12 2 4 6 8 10 12 3 5 7 9 7 5 9 3
SUB. 1029.4 GASTROSTOMY CONTROL	
22	12 4 1 5 7 9 12 2 2
24	6 4 12 9 7 12 8 5
26	12 2 4 9 2 10 3 5 7
28	11 4 5 2 1 12 7 3
30	7 2 9 1 12 5 4

Note. These examples demonstrate perseverative response strategies of two alcohol-exposed rats compared to a control. Bold numbers indicate the choices on which bait was obtained.

were not present in the last week of training. These types of behavioral effects suggest that, in the absence of efficient spatial information processing, some of the alcohol-treated rats resort to persistent response strategies, an effect that may best be characterized as perseverative tendencies.

SUMMARY

Several studies in our laboratory over the last 6 years have used exposure to alcohol during the early postnatal brain growth spurt of rats to model some of the effects of alcohol on the CNS of humans exposed to alcohol in utero. The effects documented to date include microencephaly that persists into adulthood, permanent neuronal loss that varies in extent with brain region and cell population, developmental delays in many aspects of behavior, as well as permanent dysfunction in several spheres of behavior.

With regard to neuronal loss, populations of large, postmitotic neurons undergoing differentiation are generally more vulnerable than the populations of small neurons that are still proliferating during the period of alcohol exposure. Nevertheless, there are differences between the hippocampus and cerebellum with respect to these effects. In the hippocampal formation, only the CA1 pyramidal cells had significant reductions, with no loss of pyramidal cells in CA3 and only rarely in CA4 (West, Hamre, & Cassell, 1986), and there was no significant loss of dentate gyrus granule cells. In the cerebellum, there were consistently large percent losses of Purkinje cells, and there was also a smaller but significant reduction in granule cells. Thus, these postnatally generated neurons (granule cells) were diminished, perhaps in concert with the loss of their targets (the Purkinje cells).

The behavioral effects have been most extensively examined in tasks sensitive to hippocampal damage. There was clear evidence of developmental delays in spatial navigation, a task known to depend on hippocampal development. More importantly, there were permanent effects in activity in a novel environment and in acquisition of a complex radial maze task. The working memory deficits and perseverative response strategies of alcohol-exposed rats may be associated with the CA1 neuron loss. The severity of the alcohol-induced effects was correlated with the peak blood alcohol concentration to which the neonatal rats were exposed. Brain weights were linearly related to peak BAC, and statistically significant reductions in brain weight were detectable when BACs reached 160–190 mg/dl. The permanent behavioral deficits and neuron loss were consistently present when BACs exceeded 300 mg/dl.

Many of the effects that we have documented in rats following alcohol exposure during the early postnatal brain weight spurt correspond to the major characteristics of CNS dysfunction in FAS. These include permanent restriction of brain weight, neuron loss, hyperactivity, learning deficits, deficiencies in memory function, and perseverative tendencies. These results encourage the further use of this animal model of FAS, particularly to specify better the relationship between alcohol-induced brain damage and behavioral dysfunction. In addition, the model affords the potential to evaluate CNS disruption that is less extreme than cell loss, which may have important implications for lower levels of prenatal alcohol exposure in humans that do not lead to a diagnosis of FAS, but which nevertheless may have adverse effects on the development of the nervous system.

ACKNOWLEDGMENTS

We thank Craig Pleggenkuhle and Bob Halloran for contributing to the behavioral testing, Blake Hamann for assisting with the cell counts, and Sara Hulsether, Jolonda Mahoney, and John Nichols for assisting with the artificial rearing. We also thank Keith Miller for constructing the radial maze.

REFERENCES

Abel, E. L. (1979). Prenatal effects of alcohol on adult learning in rats. *Pharmacology & Behavior, 10,* 239–243.

Abel, E. L., & Sokol, R. J. (1987). Incidence of fetal alcohol syndrome and economic impact of FAS-related anomalies. *Drug & Alcohol Dependence, 19,* 51–70.

Altman, J. (1969). Autoradiographic and histological studies of postnatal neurogenesis. III. Dating the time of production and onset of differentiation of cerebellar microneurons in rats. *Journal of Comparative Neurology, 136,* 269–294.

Altman, J. (1972). Postnatal development of the cerebellar cortex in the rat. II. Phases in the maturation of Purkinje cells and of the molecular layer. *Journal of Comparative Neurology, 145,* 399–464.

Altman, J., & Bayer, S. A. (1978). Prenatal development of the cerebellar system in the rat. I. Cytogenesis and histogenesis of the deep nuclei and the cortex of the cerebellum. *Journal of Comparative Neurology, 179,* 23–48.

Barnes, D. E., & Walker, D. W. (1981). Prenatal ethanol exposure permanently reduces the number of pyramidal neurons in rat hippocampus. *Developmental Brain Research, 1,* 333–340.

Bauer-Moffett, C., & Altman, J. (1977). The effect of ethanol chronically administered to preweanling rats on cerebellar development: A morphological study. *Brain Research, 119,* 249–268.

Bayer, S. A. (1980a). Development of the hippocampal region in the rat. I. Neurogenesis examined with ³H-thymidine autoradiography. *Journal of Comparative Neurology, 190,* 87–114.

Bayer, S. A. (1980b). Development of the hippocampal region in the rat. II. Morphogenesis during embryonic and early postnatal life. *Journal of Comparative Neurology, 190,* 115–134.

Becker, J. T., Walker, J. A., & Olton, D. S. (1980). Neuroanatomical bases of spatial memory. *Brain Research, 200,* 307–320.

Bond, N. W., & DiGuisto, E. L. (1978). Avoidance conditioning and Hebb-Williams maze performance in rats treated prenatally with alcohol. *Psychopharmacology, 58,* 69–71.

Bonthius, D. J., Goodlett, C. R., & West, J. R. (1988). Blood alcohol concentration and severity of microencephaly in neonatal rats depend on the pattern of alcohol administration. *Alcohol, 5,* 209–214.

Bonthius, D. J., & West, J. R. (1988). Blood alcohol concentration and microencephaly: A dose-response study in the neonatal rat. *Teratology, 37,* 223–231.

Church, M. W., & Gerkin, K. P. (1988). Hearing disorders in children with fetal alcohol syndrome: Findings from case reports. *Pediatrics, 82,* 147–154.

Clarren, S. K. (1986). Neuropathology in fetal alcohol syndrome. In J. R. West (Ed.), *Alcohol and brain development* (pp. 158–166). New York: Oxford University Press.

Clarren, S. K., & Smith, D. W. (1978). The fetal alcohol syndrome. *New England Journal of Medicine, 298,* 1063–1067.

Davis, H. P., Baranowski, J. R., Pulsinelli, W. A., & Volpe, B. T. (1987). Retention of reference memory following ischemic hippocampal damage. *Physiology & Behavior, 39,* 783–786.

Davis, H. P., Tribuna, J., Pulsinelli, W. A., & Volpe, B. T. (1986). Reference and working memory in rats following hippocampal damage induced by transient forebrain ischemia. *Physiology & Behavior, 37,* 1387–1392.

Diaz, J., & Samson, H. H. (1980). Impaired brain growth in neonatal rat pups exposed to alcohol. *Science, 208,* 751–753.

Dobbing, J. (1981). The later development of the brain and its vulnerability. In J. A. Davis & J. Dobbing (Eds.), *Scientific foundations of paediatrics* (pp. 331–336). London: Heinemann.

Dobbing, J., & Sands, J. (1973). Quantitative growth and development of human brain. *Archives of Diseases of Children, 48,* 757–767.

Dobbing, J., & Sands, J. (1979). Comparative aspects of the brain growth spurt. *Early Human Development, 3,* 79–83.

Dyck, R. H., Sutherland, R. J., & Buday, M. R. (1985). The ontogeny of mapping and nonmapping spatial strategies following neonatal hippocampal damage in rats. *Society for Neuroscience Abstracts, 11,* 832.

Earnhart, C. B., Marrow-Tlucak, M., Sokol, R. J., & Martier, S. (1988). Underreporting of alcohol use in pregnancy. *Alcoholism: Clinical and Experimental Research, 12,* 506–511.

Gionet, T. X., Thomas, J. D., Warner, D. S., Goodlett, C. R., Wasserman, E. A., & West, J. R. (1991). Forebrain ischemia induces selective behavioral impairments associated with hippocampal CA1 injury in the rat. *Stroke, 22,* 1040–1047.

Goldowitz, D., & Koch, J. (1986). Performance of normal and neurological mutant mice on radial arm maze and active avoidance tasks. *Behavioural & Neural Biology, 46,* 216–222.

Goldstein, D. B. (1983). *Pharmacology of alcohol.* New York: Oxford University Press.

Goodlett, C. R., Kelly, S. J., & West, J. R. (1987). Early postnatal alcohol exposure that produces high blood alcohol levels impairs development of spatial navigation learning. *Psychobiology, 15,* 64–74.

Hanson, J. W., Jones, K. L., & Smith, D. W. (1976). Fetal alcohol syndrome: Experience with 41 patients. *Journal of the American Medical Association, 235,* 1458–1460.

Hanson, J. W., Streissguth, A. P., & Smith, D. W. (1978). The effects of moderate alcohol consumption during pregnancy on fetal growth and morphogenesis. *Journal of Pediatrics, 92,* 457–460.

Ito, M. (1984). *The cerebellum and neural control.* New York: Raven Press.

Jones, K. L., & Smith, D. W. (1973). Recognition of the fetal alcohol syndrome in early infancy. *Lancet, 2,* 999–1001.

Jones, K. L., Smith, D. W., Ulleland, C. N., & Streissguth, A. P. (1973). Pattern of malformation in offspring of chronic alcoholic mothers. *Lancet, 1,* 1267–1271.

Kelly, S. J., Goodlett, C. R., Hulsether, S. A., & West, J. R. (1988). Impaired spatial navigation in adult female but not adult male rats exposed to alcohol during the brain growth spurt. *Behavioral Brain Research, 27,* 247–257.

Kelly, S. J., Pierce, D. R., & West, J. R. (1987). Microcephaly and hyperactivity in adult rats can be induced by neonatal exposure to high blood alcohol concentrations. *Experimental Neurology, 96*, 580–593.

Kolb, B., Sutherland, R. J., & Whishaw, I. Q. (1983). Comparison of the contributions of the frontal and parietal association cortex to spatial localization in rats. *Behavioral Neuroscience, 97*, 13–27.

Lalonde, R. (1987). Exploration and spatial learning in staggerer mutant mice. *Journal of Neurogenetics, 4*, 285–292.

Larsson, G., Bohlin, A. B., & Turell, R. (1985). Prospective study of children exposed to variable amounts of alcohol *in utero. Archives of Diseases of Children, 60*, 316–321.

Little, R. E., Schultz, F. A., & Mandell, W. (1976). Drinking during pregnancy. *Journal of Studies of Alcohol, 37*, 375–379.

Little, R. E., & Streissguth, A. P. (1978). Drinking during pregnancy in alcoholic women. *Alcoholism: Clinical and Experimental Research, 2*, 179–183.

Majewski, F. (1981). Alcohol embryopathy: Some facts and speculations about pathogenesis. *Neurobehavioral Toxicology and Teratology, 3*, 129–144.

McCormick, D. A., Clark, G. A., Lavond, D. G., & Thompson, R. T. (1982). Initial localization of the memory trace for a basis form of learning. *Proceedings of the National Academy of Sciences, USA, 79*, 2731–2735.

Michaelis, E. K., & Michaelis, M. L. (1986). Molecular events underlying the effects of ethanol on the developing central nervous system. In J. R. West (Ed.), *Alcohol and brain development* (pp. 277–309). New York: Oxford University Press.

Morris, R. G. M. (1981). Spatial localization does not require the presence of local cues. *Learning & Motivation, 12*, 239–260.

Morris, R. G. M. (1983). An attempt to dissociate spatial-mapping and working memory theories of hippocampal function. In W. Seifert (Ed.), *The neurobiology of the hippocampus* (pp. 405–432). London: Academic Press.

Morris, R. G. M. (1984). Developments of a water maze procedure for studying spatial learning in the rat. *Journal of Neuroscience Methods, 11*, 47–60.

Morris, R. G. M., Garrud, P., Rawlins, J. N. P., & O'Keefe, J. (1982). Place navigation impaired in rats with hippocampal lesions. *Nature, 297*, 681–683.

O'Keefe, J., & Nadel, L. (1978). *The hippocampus as a cognitive map.* Oxford: Oxford University Press.

Olton, D. S. (1983). Memory functions of the hippocampus. In W. Seifert (Ed.), *The neurobiology of the hippocampus* (pp. 335–373). London: Academic Press.

Olton, D. S., Becker, J. T., & Handelmann, G. E. (1979). Hippocampus, space and memory. *Behavior and Brain Sciences, 2*, 313–365.

Olton, D. S., Collison, C., & Werz, M. A. (1977). Spatial memory and radial arm maze performance of rats. *Learning & Motivation, 8*, 289–314.

Olton, D. S., & Papas, B. C. (1979). Spatial memory and hippocampal function. *Neuropsychologia, 17*, 669–682.

Olton, D. S., & Samuelson, R. J. (1976). Remembrance of places passed: Spatial memory in rats. *Journal of Experimental Psychology: Animal Behavioral Processes, 2*, 97–116.

Peiffer, J., Majewski, F., Fischbach, H., Bierich, J. R., & Volk, B. (1979). Alcohol embryo- and fetopathy. *Journal of the Neurological Sciences, 41*, 125–137.

Pierce, D. R., Goodlett, C. R., & West, J. R. (1989). Differential neuronal loss following early postnatal alcohol exposure. *Teratology, 40*, 113–126.

Pierce, D. R., & West, J. R. (1986a). Alcohol-induced microencephaly during the third trimester equivalent: Relationship to dose and blood alcohol concentration. *Alcohol, 3*, 185–191.

Pierce, D. R., & West, J. R. (1986b). Blood alcohol concentration: A critical factor for producing fetal alcohol effects. *Alcohol, 3*, 269–272.

Pierce, D. R., & West, J. R. (1987). Differential deficits in regional brain growth induced by postnatal alcohol. *Neurotoxicology & Teratology, 9,* 129–141.

Rawlins, J. N. P., & Olton, D. S. (1981). The septo-hippocampal system and cognitive mapping. *Behavioural Brain Research, 5,* 53–61.

Reyes, E., Rivera, J. M., Saland, L. C., & Murray, H. M. (1983). Effects of maternal administration of alcohol on fetal brain development. *Neurobehavioral Toxicology and Teratology, 5,* 263–267.

Riley, E. P., Barron, S., & Hannigan, J. H. (1986). Response inhibition deficits following prenatal alcohol exposure: A comparison to the effects of hippocampal lesions in rats. In J. R. West (Ed.), *Alcohol and brain development* (pp. 71–102). New York: Oxford University Press.

Riley, E. P., Lochry, E. A., & Shapiro, N. R. (1979). Lack of response inhibition in rats prenatally exposed to ethanol. *Psychopharmacology, 62,* 47–52.

Rosett, H. L., Weiner, L., Lee, A., Suckerman, B., Dooling, E., & Oppenheimer, E. (1983). Patterns of alcohol consumption and fetal development. *Obstetrics and Gynecology, 61,* 539–546.

Rudy, J. W., Stadler-Morris, S., & Albert, D. (1988). Ontogeny of spatial navigation behaviors in the rat: Dissociation of proximal and distal cue-based behaviors. *Behavioral Neuroscience, 101,* 141–143.

Samson, H. H., & Diaz, J. (1982). Effects of neonatal ethanol exposure on brain development in rodents. In E. L. Abel (Ed.), *Fetal alcohol syndrome, Vol. III, animal studies* (pp. 131–150). Boca Raton, FL: CRC Press.

Stephens, C. J. (1985). Alcohol consumption during pregnancy among southern city women. *Drug and Alcohol Dependence, 16,* 19–29.

Streissguth, A. P. (1986). The behavioral teratology of alcohol: Performance, behavioral and intellectual deficits in prenatally exposed children. In J. R. West (Ed.), *Alcohol and brain development* (pp. 3–49). New York: Oxford University Press.

Streissguth, A. P., Clarren, S. K., & Jones, K. L. (1985). Natural history of the fetal alcohol syndrome: A 10-year follow-up of eleven patients. *Lancet, 1,* 85–91.

Streissguth, A. P., Martin, D. C., Barr, H. M., Sandman, B. M., Kircher, G. L., & Darby, B. L. (1984). Intrauterine alcohol and nicotine exposure: Attention and reaction time in 4-year-old children. *Developmental Psychology, 20,* 533–541.

Sulik, K. K., Johnston, M. C., & Webb, M. A. (1981). Fetal alcohol syndrome: Embryogenesis in a mouse model. *Science, 214,* 936–938.

Surgeon General's Advisory on Alcohol and Pregnancy. (1981). *FDA Drug Bulletin, 11,* 9–10.

Sutherland, R. J., Kolb, B., & Whishaw, I. Q. (1982). Spatial mapping: Definitive disruption by hippocampal or medial frontal damage in the rat. *Neuroscience Letters, 31,* 271–276.

Sutherland, R. J., Whishaw, I. Q., & Kolb, B. (1983). A behavioural analysis of spatial localization following electrolytic, kainate- or colchicine-induced damage to the hippocampal formation in the rat. *Behavioural Brain Research, 7,* 133–153.

Volpe, B. T., Pulsinelli, W. A., & Davis, H. P. (1986). Rats with ischemic-induced hippocampal injury demonstrate dissociated memory impairments on 12-arm radial maze. *Annals of Neurology, 20,* 154.

Volpe, B. T., Waczek, B., & Davis, H. P. (1988). Modified T-maze training demonstrates dissociated memory loss in rats with ischemic hippocampal injury. *Behavioural Brain Research, 27,* 259–268.

West, J. R. (Ed.). (1986). *Alcohol and brain development.* New York: Oxford University Press.

West, J. R. (1987). Fetal alcohol-induced brain damage and the problem of temporal vulnerability: A review. *Alcohol and Drug Research, 7,* 423–441.

West, J. R., Bonthius, D. J., Hamre, K. M., & Pierce, D. R. (1988). Regional vulnerability of the developing brain to alcohol exposure. *Australian Drug and Alcohol Review, 7,* 65–68.

West, J. R., & Hamre, K. M. (1985). Effects of alcohol exposure during different periods of development: Changes in hippocampal mossy fibers. *Developmental Brain Research, 17,* 280–284.

West, J. R., Hamre, K. M., & Cassell, M. D. (1986). Effects of ethanol exposure during the third trimester equivalent on neuron number in rat hippocampus and dentate gyrus. *Alcoholism: Clinical and Experimental Research, 10,* 190–197.

West, J. R., Hamre, K. M., & Pierce, D. R. (1984). Delay in brain growth induced by alcohol in artificially reared rat pups. *Alcohol, 1,* 213–222.

Wisniewski, H., Drambska, M., Shar, J. H., & Qazi, Q. (1983). A clinical neuropathological study of the fetal alcohol syndrome. *Neuropediatrics, 14,* 197–201.

Zola-Morgan, S., Squire, L., & Amaral, D. G. (1986). Human amnesia and medial temporal region: Enduring memory impairment following a bilateral lesion limited to field CA1 of the hippocampus. *Journal of Neuroscience, 6,* 2950–2967.

10 Experience-Dependent Synaptogenesis as a Plausible Memory Mechanism

William T. Greenough
Ginger S. Withers
Brenda J. Anderson
University of Illinois at Urbana-Champaign

This chapter focuses on what might be going on at the relatively simple level of the individual neuron in the mammalian brain during memory formation. One of the things that is becoming increasingly clear is that, at the level of the cell, the brain may not have any very special understanding of a process equivalent to the one we term *memory;* that is, from the viewpoint of the individual neuron, processes that we define as memory may involve the same mechanisms that are used in other cellular processes that have little to do with what we call memory. One of the most obvious examples of this may be the type of information incorporation that appears to occur during the early development of mammalian sensory and motor systems. For example, the fine tuning of pattern vision requires visual experience in many, if not all, mammals (Tees, 1986). Although many of the details still remain to be specified, it is clear that a great deal of the shaping of fine perceptual and motor skills, the integration of these capacities, and the acquisition of knowledge of the physical world arise through interaction with the environment in early development. Because of the tendency for many of these phenomena to be limited by critical or sensitive periods in development, they have often been thought of as different from adult memory not only in degree of specificity but also in terms of the proposed mechanisms. At the same time, others have stressed possible similarities between developmental and adult forms of plasticity (e.g., Changeaux & Danchin, 1976; Cotman & Nieto-Sampedro, 1984; Greenough, 1978).

In this chapter, we begin by describing one line of research that we believe is beginning to point to aspects of the learning process that differentiate it from at least some cases of early sensory development and also to indicate aspects of development that do not appear to be present during information storage in later life. Specifically, there is evidence for three aspects of brain information storage that are dissociable from one another under various conditions: (a) the over-production of synapses followed by selective preservation and elimination of subsets of them; (b) activity-dependent synaptogenesis, which may or may not involve a similar overproduction and selection process; and (c) the alteration of associated metabolic capacity, as indicated by the extent of vascularization of the brain.

Differential Environmental Complexity

The key behavioral paradigm for much of this work is the complex (or "en-riched") environment design, originated by Hebb (1949). Hebb and his students demonstrated that animals raised as pets, or in a physically and socially complex laboratory environment (e.g., Forgays & Forgays, 1952; Hymovitch, 1952), were superior to those from standard laboratory housing on a variety of learning tasks, such as complex maze learning. Subsequently, in an extensive series of studies, Rosenzweig, Bennett, and Diamond (1972) and their co-workers determined that, as compared to animals reared individually or socially in standard laborato-ry cages, certain regions of the neocortex were heavier and thicker in animals from a complex environment similar to that described later. In addition, whereas there were some difficulties with the quantitative measurement techniques, the visual cortex (the area most affected by such environments) appeared to have larger neuronal nuclei and more or larger glial cells in the complex environment animals. Rosenzweig and colleagues proposed that, because these groups had differential opportunities to learn about objects and occurrences in their environ-ments, and because the groups performed differently on learning tasks, they presented an excellent opportunity to study phenomena in the brain associated with learning and memory.

Cellular Consequences of Differential Environmental Complexity and Training: Effects on Brain Synapse Numbers

Our approach to this issue has involved a series of experiments in which we explored the cellular consequences in the brain following the animal's exposure to one of these environments. Furthermore, we have utilized other paradigms to explore more thoroughly issues of the relationships of these phenomena to devel-opmental information storage and adult learning and memory. We began this work with the intention of testing both of the most popular synaptic hypotheses regarding the memory process, Tanzi's (1893) proposal that the circuitry of the brain might be altered through changes in the strength of pre-existing synaptic connections and Ramon y Cajal's (1893) proposal that altered circuitry might involve formation of entirely new connections. In both cases, it was theorized that information could be represented in the brain in the form of altered neural circuitry. Finding evidence of altered synaptic strength, or efficacy, has been the more complicated of the two hypotheses for reasons outlined elsewhere (Greenough & Chang, 1988) and is not detailed further, other than to note that there is considerable evidence that various structural characteristics of synapses may be altered by the organism's experience (Horn, 1990; Sirevaag & Greenough, 1985; Tieman, 1984). The search for the formation of new connections, or at least for differences in the numbers of connections per neuron, in the visual cortex of differentially reared animals has been more straightforward.

A number of early studies were directed at possible anatomical substrates of perceptual development. Evidence that visual deprivation impaired the development of visual ability led to a catalytic series of studies of the effects of deprivation that nearly simultaneously demonstrated (using various techniques) that visually deprived mammals had reduced numbers of synapses in visual cortex and other regions (Cragg, 1967; Fifkova, 1968; Globus & Scheibel, 1967; Valverde, 1967). Several of those involved suggested the potential for similar mechanisms to be involved in the adult memory process. At nearly the same time, reports that new synapses could form in the adult brain in regions deafferented by damage elsewhere gave new life to speculation that the adult brain might retain more structural plasticity than had been widely believed (Raisman, 1969). Finally, widely heralded evidence for synaptic "remodeling" in the brainstem of adult animals (Sotelo & Palay, 1971) suggested that such plasticity might not require damage for its expression.

Following in the footsteps of Holloway (1966), who first thought to examine dendritic fields in animals reared in complex environments, and Coleman and Riesen (1968), who demonstrated the power of the analyses we later borrowed in their study of visually deprived cats, we began the search for new connections by asking whether the amount of postsynaptic surface differed for neurons across three groups of animals reared with different levels of stimulation (or information) provided by their environments. The basic assumption was that, if the number of synapses per unit length of dendrite was about the same across the groups, the amount of dendrite per neuron would indicate how many synapses were made on each neuron. Environmental complexity (EC) involves housing rats or other animals in groups in large cages filled with an array of objects, such as commercial toys that are changed each day. EC rats, in our experiments, also receive the opportunity for exploration in a toy-filled "playbox" for ½ to 1 hour each day. Social condition (SC) subjects are housed in pairs in standard plastic tub-type cages with sawdust bedding, food, and water the only other items in the cage. Individual condition (IC) subjects are housed alone in similar cages. To assess postsynaptic surface, we used the Golgi staining procedure, a stain that has the property of impregnating entire neuronal dendritic fields such that their full extent (within limits established by the histological section) can be measured. Our initial studies involved the use of a camera lucida to make 2-dimensional projection tracings of neurons; more recently we have developed a computer-aided tracking system similar to that of Wann, Woolsey, Dierker, and Cowan (1973) that allows us to collect 3-dimensional data (DeVoogd, Chang, Floeter, Jencius, & Greenough, 1981). We have analyzed dendritic fields in a number of ways, but two quite simple ones have proven the most valuable. One involves simply measuring the total length of the dendritic field as if all the branch segments that make it up were laid end to end, as well as recording the lengths and numbers of the individual branches. The second type of analysis involves superimposing a series of concentric rings or spheres around the cell body and counting the number of occasions on which each sphere is intersected by a dendrite (Sholl, 1956). Both methods indicate the overall amount of dendrite, or postsynaptic surface that could contain synapses; the branch segment analysis additionally provides information regarding the location of group differences as a function of dendritic distance from the cell body, a rough equivalent to electrotonic distance; the ring or shell method indicates the absolute geometric location of dendrites with regard to the soma.

When Volkmar and Greenough (1972; Greenough & Volkmar, 1973) performed such analyses on a variety of cells from the occipital cortex of rats reared from weaning to late adolescence in one of the three environments described before, we found consistent differences across all cell types: Dendritic fields were larger in the EC animals. Averaged across three types of neurons in the upper four layers of occipital cortex, EC rats had approximately 20% more dendrite than IC rats. SC rats were intermediate between these groups but tended to be closer to the ICs. These results indicated that rats from more complex rearing conditions developed increased dendritic space for synapses.

These effects were not restricted to visual cortex, or to cerebral cortex in general. EC rats have been reported to exceed IC and/or SC rats in dendritic field dimensions in some temporal cortex neuron types (Greenough, Volkmar, & Juraska, 1973), as well as in the dentate gyrus of the hippocampal formation (Juraska, Fitch, Hendersen, & Rivers, 1985). Similar cerebellar cortex results have been reported for mice (Pysh & Weiss, 1979) and for monkeys (Floeter & Greenough, 1979). In addition, small differences in the density of spines along dendrites of occipital cortex pyramidal neurons favoring EC rats have been reported (Globus, Rosenzweig, Bennett, & Diamond, 1973). Such results suggest that the capacity of nerve cells to respond to appropriate afferent activity or other signals may be an ubiquitous feature of the mammalian brain.

There were two primary interpretational problems with the results for occipital cortex and other areas. First, because presynaptic innervation cannot be determined in Golgi-impregnated tissue, it was not clear whether the dendrites of the EC rats actually received more synaptic input than those of the other groups. Alternatively, synapses simply grew farther apart on the longer EC dendrites.

This seemed unlikely in light of the report by Globus et al. (1973) that the density of postsynaptic spines was in all cases either higher in EC than in IC rats or at least no lower, on one type of visual cortex pyramidal cell. However, electron microscopy was required to confirm that these spines actually were innervated. The second interpretational problem arose from the fact that Golgi stains are capricious. They impregnate only a small fraction of neurons in a given region, typically 1% to 5%. Whereas it is precisely this low density of impregnation that allows the processes of individual neurons to be followed and analyzed, the basis upon which this method selects particular neurons to be impregnated remains unclear. Because of this, it was conceivable that the Golgi procedure selected different types of neurons in the different experimental groups (e.g., neurons with larger dendritic fields in the EC rats) such that the differences reflected an environmental condition by histological stain interaction, rather than a true difference in the amount of dendrite per neuron.

A way of checking both of these possibilities involved a combination of light and electron microscopic quantification procedures (Turner & Greenough, 1983, 1985). The overall intent of the preceding Golgi stain dendritic field studies was to determine whether differential rearing conditions induced differences in the numbers of synapses per neuron. In these studies, the group differences in dendritic field size across the four different types of neurons were comparatively homogeneous. Thus in this special situation, in which the neurons in a region appear to be changing in the same general direction, an alternative way of asking this same question can be employed. The steps in this procedure were: (a) to calculate, for a specified tissue region, the number of synapses per unit tissue volume; (b) to similarly calculate, for the same tissue region, the number of neurons (neuronal nuclei) per unit tissue volume; and (c) to calculate the ratio of these two values, the number of synapses per neuron. In this calculation, the volume of the tissue drops out. This is important in comparisons between the differentially reared EC, SC, and IC animals; as is noted next, the volume of the tissue components other than neuronal nuclei and synapses differs among these groups. Thus, if we merely studied the density of synapses, the dilution of synapse density by these other tissue components (which result in the overall increase in tissue weight and volume reported by the Rosenzweig et al., 1972, group) could obscure any effects.

The results of such a study appear in Fig. 10.1 (Turner & Greenough, 1985). As the right-hand panel shows, the number of synapses per neuron is highest in the EC rats relative to the IC rats (which had the lowest number) by about 20%–25%, and intermediate in the SCs, as was the case for the data from the quantitative Golgi study. These data provide considerable confidence in the interpretation of quantitative Golgi studies as indicating real differences in synaptic numbers. This is important, because in brain regions where experience-induced changes may be very small and/or limited to a single type of neuron, the combined light-electron microscopic assessment of synapses per neuron, which averages all neurons in the tissue volume, might be subject to the effects of masking by unchanged neuronal

FIG. 10.1. Numerical density of synapses and neuronal nuclei and ratio of synapses to neurons in upper occipital cortex (layers I–IV) of rats reared from 23 to 55 days of age in environmental complexity (EC) in pairs in social cages (SC) or in individual cages (IC). Synapses were counted in conventionally stained electron micrographs and the counts corrected for differences in size using stereological formulae. Neuronal nuclei were estimated by point counting in toluidine blue stained light microscopic sections. Reduced neuronal density in more experienced animals presumably reflects the greater volume of neuronal processes, glia, and blood vessels, that have been previously reported. Data from Turner & Greenough (1985); figure from Greenough (1984). Copyright (1984) by permission of Elsevier Publications.

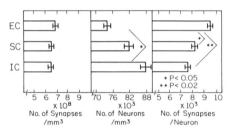

types. Our confidence in this finding is increased by two corroborative findings from independent laboratories: (a) Bhide and Bedi (1984) have similarly reported, for the occipital cortex of rats reared in a complex environment, a higher ratio of synapses to neurons than in rats reared in individual cages; and (b) Beaulieu and Colonnier (1987) have similarly reported an increased number of synapses per neuron in the visual cortex of cats reared in a complex environment, as compared with cats reared in individual cages. The consistency of the relative differences between these groups and the differences in the Turner and Greenough (1985) studies is particularly striking—both groups reported EC–IC differences of approximately 20%.

The environmental complexity paradigm is attractive for the study of learning and memory because differences in brain weight were found in adult animals as well (Bennett, Diamond, Krech, & Rosenzweig, 1964). Since that time, we have found that the effects of EC versus IC housing in previously socially housed rats on dendritic branching occurred, at least in upper visual cortex, in 4-month-old (Juraska, Greenough, Elliot, Mack, & Berkowitz, 1980) and 15-month-old (Green, Greenough, & Schlumpf, 1983) rats. Total dendritic length of neurons from the 15-month-old rats is presented in Fig. 10.2. In fact, in rats that are more than 2 years old (an age which is comparable to elderly humans) there are

FIG. 10.2. Mean total dendritic length per neuron for adult rats placed in complex or individual cage environments. Complete bifurcating and terminating branches are included in this measure. (When incomplete branches were included, as in other studies from this laboratory, nearly identical percentage differences between groups were obtained.) (From Green et al., 1983. c. 1983 Elsevier Science Publishers; by permission.)

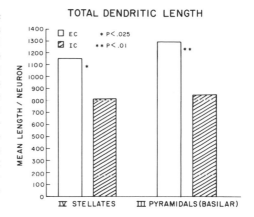

TOTAL DENDRITIC LENGTH

detectable effects of complex environmental housing upon dendritic fields in occipital (Isaacs, Black, Polinsky, & Greenough, 1986) and cerebellar cortex (Greenough, McDonald, Parnisari, & Camel, 1986), although the effects are much smaller and may sometimes occur against a backdrop of declining dendritic field size.

Preliminary data, using the combined light-electron microscopic quantification of the number of synapses per neuron, appears to confirm the results of these quantitative Golgi studies of mature animals. Hwang and Greenough (1986) found that adult rats reared in social conditions and placed in EC at about 4 months had a synapse per neuron ratio comparable to the data reported by Turner and Greenough (1985). This study also indicated that statistically significant increases in cortical depth had occurred in EC relative to SC and IC rats after just 10 days of housing in the complex environment.

If ultrastructural changes of this nature proposed to underlie long-term memory, or any form of long-lasting brain information storage, an important issue is whether, like long-term memory, the changes persist in the absence of continued immediate experience. Some of the early experiments on the persistence of increased brain weight (Bennett, Rosenzweig, Diamond, Morimoto, & Hebert, 1974; Klippel, 1978) indicated that not all of these changes were stable if the animals were removed from a complex environment for a period equivalent to the duration of exposure, whereas other measures (e.g., cortical thickness) indicated a relatively high degree of persistence (Katz & Davies, 1984). Recently, we have investigated this in animals placed in a "superenriched environment" at weaning, then rehoused for an equal period in IC, using light microscopy (see Fig. 10.3) (Camel, Withers, & Greenough, 1986), and in rats placed in our more typical complex environment for 30 days in young adulthood and similarly transferred to IC for another 30 days, using light-electron microscopic quantification of the number of synapses per neuron (Hwang & Greenough, 1986). In both cases, the dominant tendency was for most of the dendritic or synaptic

FIG. 10.3. Total length (within the thickness of the tissue section) of basilar dendrites of layer III pyramidal neurons for animals placed in superenriched (EC) or individual cage (IC) environment for 30 days; or superenriched environment for 30 days of individual caged environment (EC/IC); or individually caged environment for 60 days (IC/IC). Main effect of initial environment $p < .001$; no effect of duration or interactions. Adapted from Camel et al. (1986.)

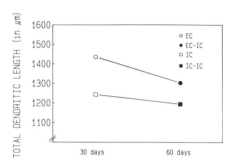

number per neuron differences induced by 30 days of differential housing to persist through an additional 30 days of individual cage housing. The small, often nonsignificant declines that were seen, however, suggest that these differences might well show substantial decay at longer periods following such exposure durations. This is, in fact, not particularly surprising, even if we assumed a direct correspondence between these changes and all memories acquired during a period of complex environment exposure. Certainly many memories, regardless of type (e.g., declarative vs. procedural; Squire & Cohen, 1984), will decay in the absence of regular use. Whether some baseline level of persistence above the level of the IC would be reached, as is suggested by experiments indicating relative stability in what might be termed really long-term memories (Squire, Slater, & Chace, 1975), or whether a relatively continuous decline occurs, remains a fascinating question.

Because of such findings, we reasoned that a somewhat more direct test of whether the same kinds of effects occurred when animals were trained on specific learning tasks was in order. Cummins, Walsh, Budtz-Olsen, Konstantinos, and Horsfall (1973) had reported that extensive Hebb–Williams (1946) maze training of 500-day-old IC rats increased forebrain weight (as well as a cerebral length × width measure) relative to groups that remained in IC cages. Our first experiment was similarly straightforward and similarly subject to a number of interpretations: Young adult rats were trained on a changing series of Hebb–Williams maze patterns over several weeks, and the visual cortex of these animals was compared with that of animals that had also been water deprived (water was the reward in the task) and given brief drinking bouts in the experimenter's hand at the time that the experimental rats received training trials. Whereas there were no group differences in some cell types that had been altered by exposure to a complex environment (e.g., layer IV stellate neurons), other cell types showed clear effects of the training. The branching of dendrites of the apical shafts of pyramidal neurons of layers IV and V was significantly greater in the trained

FIG. 10.4. Number of concentric sphere intersections beyond 250 μm of the cell body for split brain rats trained on a monocular maze task or controls. Group 1: Maze trained with alternate eyes occluded on successive days; Group 2: Maze trained with the same eye occluded each day; Group 3: Contact eye occluder placed in alternate eyes on successive days, but not trained; Group 4: Contact eye occluder in the same eye each day, but not trained. **, $p < 0.025$; ***, $p < 0.01$; n.s., statistically nonsignificant. Copyright (1984), by permission of Elsevier Science Publishers.

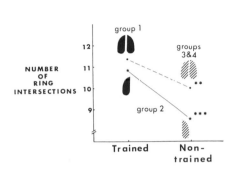

animals (Greenough, Juraska, & Volkmar, 1979). In a contemporary study, Bennett, Rosenzweig, Morimoto, and Hebert (1979) reported that rats reared such that they had to solve maze problems had increased tissue weight in the same general occipital area of the cortex. Our results indicated that the experience of maze training altered dendritic branching. However, for all three experiments, the alternative that the differences resulted from some nonlearning aspect of the training, such as metabolic or hormonal effects of stress, could not be ruled out.

An additional experiment has helped to rule out such alternatives, although neither, by any means, allows us to attribute the anatomical effects specifically to memorial aspects of training, and one of the two experiments clearly indicates that there may be nonspecific consequences of such training procedures. The first of these was a follow up of the maze training study, which used a split-brain procedure combined with unilateral eye occlusion to restrict visual input from maze training largely to the hemisphere contralateral to the open eye. The results of this study, as shown in Fig. 10.4, indicated that the effects of training could be seen in comparisons of the branching of dendrites between the two hemispheres within a unilaterally trained animal, a result not suggestive of general hormonal or metabolic causation, at least of the type carried by the circulation of the blood (Chang & Greenough, 1982).

CONCLUSIONS FROM STUDIES OF ENVIRONMENTAL COMPLEXITY AND TRAINING

The foregoing studies constitute the heart of the behaviorally based case that synaptogenesis, resulting in altered functional circuitry, are involved in mammalian long-term memory processes. In summary, the evidence indicates that:

1. Experience that alters later behavior alters the number of synapses in a given brain region.
2. These effects can be demonstrated throughout most of the life of the organism.
3. As with long-term memory, once induced, these effects tend to persist well beyond the specific events that induced them.
4. Similar effects occur in the brains of adults following training on learning tasks. In these cases, the effects occur in brain regions demonstrated by other means to be involved in the performance of the learned tasks.

Possible Alternative Sources of Altered Synapse Numbers

There are several alternative explanations that may account for the ultrastructural changes that are reported previously. Although none of them can be ruled out across all cases, there is experimental evidence in which each of these proposed causes has been shown to be unlikely.

One possible source of structural indicants of novel synapses in these situations deserves careful consideration. It is conceivable that new synapses form merely as a result of the physiological activity of neurons, either in direct proportion to nerve impulse activity or as a result of reaching or exceeding a threshold level of continuous activation. Whereas this certainly cannot be ruled out, a variety of results tend to argue against synaptogenesis occurring nonsystematically at the level of the individual neuron.

First, ultrastructural changes similar to those reported in the differential environment paradigm have been reported to occur following brief trains of high-frequency electrical stimulation of subfield CA1 of the hippocampal slice in vitro (Chang & Greenough, 1984; Lee, Oliver, Schottler, & Lynch, 1981; Lee, Schottler, Oliver, & Lynch, 1980). Slices receiving equivalent numbers of electrical pulses at lower frequencies do not show this synaptogenesis. This indicates that the pattern of stimulation, rather than the rate or merely the amount of stimulation alone, determines the lasting plastic response at the synaptic level.

Next, in response to differential environmental complexity, changes in dendritic fields of one neuronal population, the spiny branchlet region of cerebellar Purkinje neurons, occurred in the absence of changes in the dendritic fields of the granule cells that are the only afferents to these dendrites (Floeter & Greenough, 1979). Taken with the previous result, this indicates that the formation of synapses may be a highly specific response of a neuron to a particular afferent input pattern or configuration (e.g., conjoint activation of other Purkinje cell afferents or of a pattern of granule cells). More simply, changes in aggregate activity or input are not sufficient to alter synaptogenesis. The extent to which these two studies are generalizable is not clear; however, in these cases we can eliminate the suggestion that changes occur simply as a consequence of alterations in neuronal activity.

It has also been found that animals that are blinded, at least during early development, have more dendritic material in auditory regions of the cortex, compared to identically reared sighted animals (Burnstine, Beck, & Greenough, in prep.; Ryugo, Ryugo, Globus, & Killackey, 1975). (There is similar evidence for dark-reared animals and for animals housed in darkness in adulthood; Gyllensten, Malmfors, & Norrlin, 1966). This result indicates that differences in activity, at least of sensory afferents, are not necessary to alter synaptogenesis. The demand put on the auditory region by the organism's increased use of auditory information to perceive its surroundings seems to have been sufficient at least to set in motion the processes leading, ultimately, to synapse formation.

It has also been suggested that experience-associated synaptogenesis might be mediated via a change in neuromodulators or metabolic factors (e.g., cardiovascular changes) resulting from physical exercise. This is of particular concern in the case of complex environment studies, where the opportunity for and apparent involvement in physical activity appears far greater than in most learning tasks. Currently, the majority of the published work on this issue involves gross brain weight measures. Whereas there have been some indications that the opportunity for exercise (in a running wheel) may have small effects on such measures (Huntley & Newton, 1972), other reports have indicated that no effects could be detected (Krech, Rosenzweig, & Bennett, 1960; Zolman & Morimoto, 1965). Very preliminary results of quantitative Golgi measures in old rat occipital cortex (Black, Parnisari, Eichbaum, & Greenough, 1986) have indicated statistically reliable effects of running wheel exercise on a few dendritic field measures, but these effects were far smaller than those of a comparable period of exposure to a complex environment.

The possible contribution of hormonal and metabolic factors to the generation of these differences is unlikely to be of major significance given evidence discussed earlier (Chang & Greenough, 1984). If general or nonspecific consequences of training were mediating ultrastructural changes, then one would expect that using a within-subject control would result in no difference between trained and nontrained hemispheres. However, in the experiment using within-subject controls, trained hemispheres had significantly more dendritic material than nontrained hemispheres. Two additional findings should be mentioned. First, we often weigh peripheral organs of our subjects. In general, animals placed in these environments at postweaning display no differences in adrenal weights (Black, Sirevaag, Wallace, Savin, & Greenough, 1989). Thus in our studies, there is no indication of chronic stress, although higher adrenal weights have been reported by others in IC rats (Geller, Yuwiler, & Zolman, 1965). In any case, it seems unlikely that differential stress is responsible for the reduced dendritic and synaptic content of the IC rat's occipital cortex in the case of the studies of our laboratory, because just the opposite pattern, higher adrenal weights in the EC animals, occurred in the Hwang and Greenough study of adult synapses per neuron, in which the effects on the brain were in the same direction and of essentially the same magnitude as those seen in weanlings (Hwang & Greenough, 1986). Second, with regard to more general aspects of metabolism, it should be noted that IC rats typically weigh more than EC rats, probably at least in part because they consume more food (Fiala, Snow, & Greenough, 1977). This certainly suggests that IC rats are not suffering from malnutrition, although the possibility remains that there is some general difference in metabolic patterns in the two groups that is not mimicked by providing the opportunity for exercise.

A recently completed study makes a strong case for the independence of effects of neuronal activation from the effects of motor learning. Black, Isaacs, Anderson, Alcantara and Greenough (1990) compared four groups of adult female rats: 1) an acrobatic (AC) motor learning group that traversed a complicated and changing set of elevated pathways several times a day for 30 days, gradually becoming highly skilled at traversing objects such as loosely suspended ropes, narrow, obstacle-containing beams, link chains, and other difficult paths; 2) a forced exercise (FX) group that walked quickly at 10m/min on a treadmill for increasingly long periods until they were walking for 1 hour a day; 3) a voluntary exercise (VX) group that had free access to activity wheels attached to their cages and that ran almost twice as far as the forced exercise animals, and 4) an inactive condition (IC) in identical cages to the others and was handled briefly at the time that groups 1 and 2 were run. We quantified the density of blood vessels and the number of synapses per Purkinje neuron in the molecular layer of the cerebellar paramedian lobule, a region activated by motor tasks of this sort. Results appear in Fig. 5. Panel A shows that there is more molecular layer per Purkinje neuron—that is, that the volume of this layer, which contains most of the synapses on Purkinje neurons (as well as other neurons), has increased, similar to the cortical thickening that was seen in EC rats (Fig. 1). Panel B shows that the density of synapses did not differ statistically across groups. Panel C presents the number of molecular layer synapses per Purkinje neuron. There are more synapses in the AC motor learning group, while the "non-learning" groups do not differ. The addition of synapses thus appears restricted to those animals that underwent substantial amounts of learning. Panel D shows blood vessel density to be significantly elevated in the two exercise groups, with the AC group not different from the inactive controls. Apparently the neural activity in the paramedian lobule was sufficient to require capillary sprouting to support the exercise groups' physical activity, yet it did not alter the number of synapses. Clearly the effects of activity appear to be dissociable from the synapse addition that is seen exclusively in the motor learning group.

Thus, with regard to the effects of environmental complexity and of various training procedures upon synapse numbers, the evidence seems to be more compatible with the view that these effects are mediated via effects of learning-related activity of specific cells than it is with either a generally acting diffuse

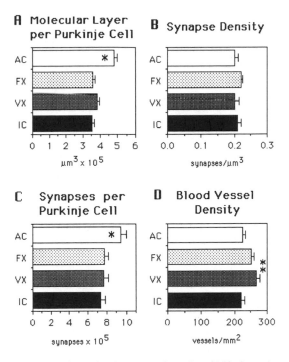

FIG. 10.5. Effect of acrobatic motor learning (AC), forced treadmill exercise (FX), voluntary activity wheel exercise (VX) and passive inactivity (IC) on cerebellar paramedian lobule in adult female rats. A. Volume of molecular layer per Purkinje neuron, calculated using the disector, an unbiased stereological method. B. Density of synapses in the molecular layer. C. Ratio of synapses to Purkinje neurons. (This includes, of course, many synapses that are not on Purkinje neurons, but serves to correct for changing volume per neuron.) D. Density of blood vessels in the molecular layer. General conclusion: Exercise, probably via related neuronal activity, alters the vascular system but not synaptic connectivity, whereas synapses are altered with learning. Adapted by permission from Black et al. (1990), p. 5571.

effect or a specific activity pattern that is unrelated to the information being stored by the nervous system. Put simply, the effects seem to arise more from learning than from other characteristics of physiological activity.

On the Relationships Between Developmental and Adult Information Storage Processes

An argument that has been made in some detail (Greenough, 1985, 1986) is that different processes may mediate experience-induced synaptogenesis during development versus adulthood. Specifically it was suggested that certain aspects of the environment (e.g., early visual experience) constitute sufficiently predictable (from an evolutionary perspective), or "expected," characteristics of the rearing environment. The organism's nervous system is programmed to take advantage of these stimuli. This "experience-expectant" aspect of development appears to ready the nervous system for the incorporation of environmental information by overproducing synaptic connections on a sensory system-wide basis. As proposed by many others (e.g., Changeaux & Danchin, 1976; LeVay, Weisel, & Hubel, 1980), the effect of early experience was to selectively stabilize certain connections that were activated by this experience, whereas others were either eliminated or allowed to passively deteriorate. As has been noted, such a process cannot solely account for all features of early visual system development (LeVay, Weisel, & Hubel, 1980), but the evidence is strong that such a process is involved.

It has been suggested that a similar process might continue into adulthood, and that information storage could depend on the chronic generation of comparatively small numbers of tentative synaptic connections. From this pool of generated synapses some proportion would be stabilized by ongoing neural events, forming the circuitry underlying aspects of adult memory (e.g., Changeux & Danchin, 1976; Cotman & Nieto-Sampedro, 1984; Greenough, 1978). However, there is experimental data that supports the alternative view of Ramon y Cajal (1893) and of Kappers (1917), that synapses might form actively and somewhat specifically in response to the neural activity associated with an event to be remembered. This is suggested by the rapidity with which new dendrites and synapses appear in plasticity paradigms. For example, Wallace, Kilman, Withers and Greenough (in prep.) detected significant increases in total dendritic length of visual cortex neurons after just four days of exposure to a complex environment. Moreover, in the long-term potentiation study noted earlier, Chang and Greenough (1984) had reported that new synapses appear to form within 10 to 15 minutes following a series of brief, high-frequency trains of electrical stimuli. This result has been repeated, using freeze-substitution procedures in place of the aldehyde fixatives used in the first study, indicating that the difference in the number of the two classes of synapses that are higher in the potentiated group, sessile spine and shaft synapses, was not the result of some artifact of the chemical fixation process (Chang, Hwang, Isaacs, & Greenough, 1986). The fact that synapses can form this rapidly in the hippocampus, even though the preparation is an artificial one, certainly suggests the possibility that synapses may form as rapidly in vivo in association with the memory process.

We are still trying to reinterpret another finding that we had initially viewed in support of active synapse formation, or "synapses on demand" associated with the adult form of memory storage. A report by Steward (1983) indicated that, during reactive synaptogenesis in the dentate gyrus, newly forming synapses appeared to be characterized by the presence of polyribosomal aggregates (PRAs) in the head and stem regions of their spines. Further evidence that PRAs might serve to mark new synapses came from developmental studies in which

PRAs were seen in the greatest numbers in spine head and stem regions during periods of high rates of synaptogenesis (Hwang & Greenough, 1984; Steward & Falk, 1986). Speculating from such findings that PRAs located in the spine head-stem region indicated new synapses, Greenough, Hwang, and Gorman (1985) reported that rats in EC housing had more synapses with PRAs in this region than SC or IC rats (in occipital cortex) and proposed this as evidence that synapses were forming in response to the greater information storage demands of the complex environment.

More recently, preliminary data has brought this interpretation into question. In an experiment already described (Hwang & Greenough, 1986), adult rats that had spent either 10 or 30 days in a complex environment were compared with those that, after 30 days in a complex environment, were placed in IC housing for an additional 30 days. At both the 10- and 30-day points, the EC rats had a greater number of synapses with PRAs in the head-stem spine region of occipital cortex synapses than corresponding SC and IC groups, as would have been expected from the preceding experiment and from the hypothesis that PRAs in this location indicate newly formed synapses. However, the group rehoused in the IC environment for an additional 30 days following EC exposure also had more head-stem PRAs than corresponding IC rats and did not differ statistically from the 10- and 30-day EC groups. Unless one assumes that the rats that have had the EC experience continue to think about such things and hence continue to form new synapses to encode whatever revelations transpire, it is difficult to conceive of what events would cause continuing synaptogenesis in these animals. Thus we should consider an alternative to the hypothesis that PRA location indicates synaptogenesis, at least exclusively. It may be, for example, that PRAs are translocated to spine head-stems to accommodate high levels of demand for a particular protein that is needed for both synaptogenesis and relatively high levels of synaptic activity following synapse formation or stabilization. It is even conceivable that the spine-situated PRAs translate synaptic constituents necessary for both synapse construction and later maintenance of an altered efficacy state, as could be the case for receptor or ion channel proteins.

Thus the finding that EC rats had a higher proportion of spines with PRAs located in the head-stem region (Greenough, Hwang, & Gorman, 1985) can no longer be taken as clear-cut support for the hypothesis that synapses are generated relatively rapidly in response to the demands of information storage. Nonetheless, the fact that (a) synapses can be generated in substantial numbers within minutes following appropriate patterns of electrical stimulation in vitro (Chang & Greenough, 1984; Chang, Hwang, Isaacs, & Greenough, 1986) and (b) significant increases in dendritic length occur after just 4 days in a complex environment (Wallace et al., in prep.), both argue strongly that active synaptogenesis constitutes at least a component of the adult memory storage process. Further work will be needed to examine this hypothesis in other ways. In particular, if antigens can be identified that are uniquely associated with the axonal or dendritic growth or synaptogenesis process, it should become possible both to more specifically examine the role of active synaptogenesis and to identify regions in which this occurs during learning or other conditions that activate brain information storage processes.

WHAT CHARACTERISTICS ARE UNIQUE
TO DEVELOPMENTAL INFORMATION
STORAGE PROCESSES?

We have argued that there appear to be two different conditions of experience-encoding synaptic mechanisms: the first tending to dominate in early development, in which synaptogenesis occurs largely independently of experience; the second tending to dominate in later development and adulthood, in which experience appears to drive aspects of synaptogenesis. Whether or not one accepts the premises of the foregoing discussion, one may still ask whether there are other features that tend to set developmental brain information storage processes apart from those of adulthood. We have recently begun to examine the response of nonsynaptic components of the cortical tissue to exposure to a complex environment at various ages. The results of these studies to date, which have focused on the vascular response, suggest that sizable differences may occur in the response of supportive tissue components between the ages of weaning and adulthood. Animals placed in EC housing at the age of weaning for 30 days have, in the upper 4 layers of occipital cortex, a higher concentration (volume fraction) of capillaries than animals reared in individual cages (Isaacs, Black, Polinsky, & Greenough, 1986). The difference exceeds that in synapses per neuron noted before, such that the EC rats have a greater vascular volume both per neuron and per synapse. At least a component of the brain's apparent need for this extra vascularization is indicated by the fact that the EC animals also have a greater volume of mitochondria per neuron (Sirevaag & Greenough, 1987). This result indicates that, in weanlings, non-neural supportive constituents apparently respond to the demand that the environment is placing upon the nervous system (beyond visual cortex, of course, we as yet have no idea of the response or any indication of a demand).

There are other indications of responsiveness of developing tissue, such as glial cells, to some aspect of environmental demand in animals exposed at weaning to the complex environment (Sirevaag & Greenough, 1991), but we do not have adult data, and we are still working out the developmental picture. What we do know is that, even in early adulthood, and especially as the animals grow older, this capacity appears to be increasingly diminished. At a year of age, when the brain is still very much capable of making new connections, the capacity to support those connections is diminished (Isaacs et al., 1986) but still responsive to sufficient demand (Black et al., 1990). The implication of these results is that, although the brain remains quite capable of adding synapses at this age, providing metabolic support for the massive numbers that are added as a result of exposure of individually reared animals to a complex environment at this age is no longer possible. The result could be what Smith (1984) termed a *power failure* under conditions of sufficiently great transient demand.

A great deal of detail remains to be filled in with regard to metabolic support, but one aspect seems clear: whereas the capacity to generate new synapses is not limited to early periods of development, there are critical periods for, or at least periods of differential ability of, the brain to provide other supporting aspects. To the extent that additional synapses represent either additional memory or additional capacities (alternatives not mutually exclusive), access to them might be more limited in the case of later acquisition, if the brain had not received the appropriate early experience.

ACKNOWLEDGMENTS

Preparation of this chapter and research not otherwise reported was supported by NIMH 35321 and 40631, NIH RR 07030, PHS 5 T-32EY07005, PHS 5 T-32GM7143, ONR N00014-85-K-0587, the Retirement Research Foundation, the System Development Foundation, and the University of Illinois Research Board.

REFERENCES

Beaulieu, C., & Colonnier, M. (1987). Effects of the richness of the environment on the cat visual cortex. *Journal of Comparative Neurology, 266,* 478–494.

Bennett, E. L., Diamond, M. C., Krech, D., & Rosenzweig, M. R. (1964). Chemical and anatomical plasticity of brain. *Science, 146,* 610–619.

Bennett, E. L., Rosenzweig, M. R., Diamond, M. C., Morimoto, H., & Hebert, M. (1974). Effects of successive environments on brain measures. *Physiology and Behavior, 12,* 621–631.

Bennett, E. L., Rosenzweig, M. R., Morimoto, H., & Hebert, M. (1979). Maze training alters brain weights and cortical RNA/DNA ratios. *Behavioral and Neural Biology, 26,* 1–22.

Bhide, P. G., & Bedi, K. S. (1984). The effects of a lengthy period of environmental diversity on well-fed and previously undernourished rats. II. Synapse to neuron ratios. *Journal of Comparative Neurology, 227,* 305–310.

Black, J. E., Isaacs, K. R., Anderson, B. J., Alcantara, A. A., & Greenough, W. T. (1990). Learning causes synaptogenesis, whereas motor activity causes angiogenesis, in cerebellar cortex of adult rats. *Proceedings of the National Academy of Sciences (USA), 87,* 5568–5572.

Black, J. E., Parnisari, R., Eichbaum, E., & Greenough, W. T. (1986). Morphological effects of housing environment and voluntary exercise on cerebral cortex and cerebellum of old rats. *Society for Neuroscience Abstracts, 12,* 1579.

Black, J. E., Sirevaag, A. M., Wallace, C. S., Savin, M. H., & Greenough, W. T. (1989). Effects of complex experience on somatic growth and organ development in rats. *Developmental Psychobiology, 22,* 727–752.

Burnstine, T., Beck, D., & Greenough, W., *in preparation.*

Camel, J. E., Withers, G. S., & Greenough, W. T. (1986). Persistence of visual cortex dendritic alterations induced by postweaning exposure to a "superenriched" environment in rats. *Behavioral Neuroscience, 100,* 810–813.

Chang, F.-L., & Greenough, W. T. (1982). Lateralized effects of monocular training on dendritic branching in adult split-brain rats. *Brain Research, 232,* 283–292.

Chang, F.-L. F., & Greenough, W. T. (1984). Transient and enduring morphological correlates of synaptic activity and efficacy change in the rat hippocampal slice. *Brain Research, 309,* 35–46.

Chang, F.-L. F., Hwang, H. M., Isaacs, K. R., & Greenough, W. T. (1986). Morphological effects of LTP studied with rapid freezing and freeze substitution in rat hippocampal slices. *Society for Neuroscience Abstracts, 12,* 506.

Changeux, J.-P., & Danchin, A. (1976). Selective stabilization of developing synapses as a mechanism for the specification of neuronal networks. *Nature, 264,* 705–712.

Coleman, P. D., & Riesen, A. H. (1968). Environmental effects on cortical dendritic fields. I. Rearing in the dark. *Journal of Anatomy (London), 102,* 363–374.

Colonnier, M., & Beaulieu, C. (1985). The differential effect of impoverished and enriched environments on the number of "round asymmetrical" and "flat symmetrical" synapses in the visual cortex of cat. *Society for Neuroscience Abstracts, 11,* 226.

Cotman, C. W., & Nieto-Sampedro, M. (1984). Cell biology of synaptic plasticity. *Science, 225,* 1287–1294.

Cragg, B. G. (1967). Changes in visual cortex on first exposure of rats to light. Effect on synaptic dimensions. *Nature, 215,* 251–253.

Cummins, R. A., Walsh, R. N., Budtz-Olsen, O. E., Konstantinos, T., & Horsfall, C. R. (1973). Environmentally-induced changes in the brains of elderly rats. *Nature, 243,* 516–518.

DeVoogd, T. J., Chang, F.-L. F., Floeter, M. K., Jencius, M. J., & Greenough, W. T. (1981). Distortions induced in neuronal quantification by camera lucida analysis: Comparisons using a semiautomated data acquisition system. *Journal of Neuroscience Methods, 3,* 285–294.

Fiala, B., Snow, F., & Greenough, W. T. (1977). "Impoverished" rats weigh more than "enriched" rats because they eat more. *Developmental Psychobiology, 10,* 537–541.

Fifkova, E. (1968). Changes in the visual cortex of rats after unilateral deprivation. *Nature, 220,* 379–381.

Floeter, M. K., & Greenough, W. T. (1979). Cerebellar plasticity: Modification of Purkinje cell structure by differential rearing in monkeys. *Science, 206,* 227–229.

Forgays, D. G., & Forgays, J. W. (1952). The nature of the effect of free-environmental experience in the rat. *Journal of Comparative and Physiological Psychology, 45,* 322–328.

Geller, E., Yuwiler, A., & Zolman, J. F. (1965). Effects of environmental complexity on constituents of brain and liver. *Journal of Neurochemistry, 12,* 949–955.

Globus, A., Rosenzweig, M. R., Bennett, E. L., & Diamond, M. C. (1973). Effects of differential experience on dendritic spine counts in rat cerebral cortex. *Journal of Comparative and Physiological Psychology, 82,* 175–181.

Globus, A., & Scheibel, A. B. (1967). The effect of visual deprivation on cortical neurons: A Golgi study. *Experimental Neurology, 19,* 331–345.

Green, E. J., Greenough, W. T., & Schlumpf, B. E. (1983). Effects of complex or isolated environments on cortical dendrites of middle-aged rats. *Brain Research, 264,* 233–240.

Greenough, W. T. (1978). Development and memory: The synaptic connection. In T. Teyler (Ed.), *Brain and learning* (pp. 127–145). Stamford, CT: Greylock.

Greenough, W. T. (1985). The possible role of experience-dependent synaptogenesis, or synapses on demand, in the memory process. In N. M. Weinberger, J. L. McGaugh, & G. Lynch (Eds.), *Memory systems of the brain* (pp. 77–103). New York: Guilford Press.

Greenough, W. T. (1986). What's special about development? Thoughts on the bases of experience-sensitive synaptic plasticity. In W. T. Greenough & J. M. Juraska (Eds.), *Developmental neuropsychobiology* (pp. 387–407). New York: Academic Press.

Greenough, W. T., & Chang, F.-L. F. (1988). Plasticity of synapse structure and pattern in the cerebral cortex. In E. G. Jones & A. Peters (Eds.), *Cerebral Cortex. Vol. 7* (pp. 391–440). New York: Plenum.

Greenough, W. T., Hwang, H.-M., & Gorman, C. (1985). Evidence for active synapse formation, or altered postsynaptic metabolism, in visual cortex of rats reared in complex environments. *Proceedings of the National Academy of Sciences, 82,* 4549–4552.

Greenough, W. T., Juraska, J. M., & Volkmar, F. R. (1979). Maze training effects on dendritic branching in occipital cortex of adult rats. *Behavioral and Neural Biology, 26,* 287–297.

Greenough, W. T., McDonald, J. W., Parnisari, R. M., & Camel, J. E. (1986). Environmental conditions modulate degeneration and new dendrite growth in cerebellum of senescent rats. *Brain Research, 380,* 136–143.

Greenough, W. T., & Volkmar, F. R. (1973). Pattern of dendritic branching in occipital cortex of rats reared in complex environments. *Experimental Neurology, 40,* 491–504.

Greenough, W. T., Volkmar, F. R., & Juraska, J. M. (1973). Effects of rearing complexity on dendritic branching in frontolateral and temporal cortex of the rat. *Experimental Neurology, 40,* 371–378.

Gyllensten, L., Malmfors, T., & Norrlin, M. L. (1966). Growth alteration in the auditory cortex of visually deprived mice. *Journal of Comparative Neurology, 126,* 463–470.

Hebb, D. O. (1949). *The organization of behavior.* New York: Wiley.

Hebb, D. O., & Williams, K. A. (1946). A method of rating animal intelligence. *Journal of Genetic Psychology, 34,* 59–65.

Holloway, R. L. (1966). Dendritic branching: Some preliminary results of training and complexity in rat visual cortex. *Brain Research, 2,* 393–396.

Horn, G. (1990). Neural bases of recognition memory investigated through an analysis of imprinting. *Philosophical Transactions of the Royal Society London B, 329,* 133–142.

Huntley, M. J., & Newton, J. M. (1972). Effects of environmental complexity and locomotor activity on brain change in the rat. *Physiology and Behavior, 8,* 725–727.

Hwang, H. M., & Greenough, W. T. (1984). Spine formation and synaptogenesis in rat visual cortex: A serial section developmental study. *Society for Neuroscience Abstracts, 10,* 579.

Hwang, H. M., & Greenough, W. T. (1986). Synaptic plasticity in adult rat occipital cortex following short-term, long-term and reversal of, differential housing environmental complexity. *Society for Neuroscience Abstracts, 12,* 1284.

Hymovitch, B. (1952). The effects of experimental variations on problem solving in the rat. *Journal of Comparative and Physiological Psychology, 45,* 313–321.

Isaacs, K. R., Black, J. E., Polinsky, M., & Greenough, W. T. (1986). Capillary morphology in visual cortex of middle-aged, but not old, rats is altered by housing environment. *Society for Neuroscience Abstracts, 12,* 1579.

Juraska, J. M., Fitch, J., Henderson, C., & Rivers, N. (1985). Sex differences in the dendritic branching of dentate granule cells following differential experience. *Brain Research, 333,* 73–80.

Juraska, J. M., Greenough, W. T., Elliott, C., Mack, K., & Berkowitz, R. (1980). Plasticity in adult rat visual cortex: An examination of several cell populations after differential rearing. *Behavioral and Neural Biology, 29,* 157–167.

Kappers, C. U. A. (1917). Further contributions on neurobiotaxis IX. An attempt to compare the phenomena of neurobiotaxis with other phenomena of taxis and tropism. The dynamic polarization of the neurone. *Journal of Comparative Neurology, 27,* 261–298.

Katz, H. B., & Davies, C. A. (1984). Effects of differential environments on the cerebral anatomy of rats as a function of previous and subsequent housing conditions. *Experimental Neurology, 83,* 274–287.

Klippel, J. A. (1978). Behavioral persistence following switchovers between environmental enrichment and impoverishment in mice. *Developmental Psychobiology, 11,* 541–557.

Krech, D., Rosenzweig, M. R., & Bennett, E. L. (1960). Effects of environmental complexity and training on brain chemistry. *Journal of Comparative and Physiological Psychology, 53,* 509–519.

Lee, K. S., Oliver, M., Schottler, F., & Lynch, G. (1981). Electron microscopic studies of brain slices: The effects of high-frequency stimulation on dendritic ultrastructure. In G. A. Kerkut & H. V. Wheal (Eds.), *Electrophsiology of isolated mammalian CNS preparations* (pp. 189–211). New York: Academic Press.

Lee, K. S., Schottler, F., Oliver, M., & Lynch, G. (1980). Brief bursts of high-frequency stimulation produce two types of structural change in rat hippocampus. *Journal of Neurophysiology, 44,* 247–258.

LeVay, S., Wiesel, T. N., & Hubel, D. H. (1980). The development of ocular dominance columns in normal and visually deprived monkeys. *Journal of Comparative Neurology, 191,* 1–51.

Pysh, J. J., & Weiss, G. M. (1979). Exercise during development induces an increase in Purkinje cell dendritic tree size. *Science, 206,* 230–232.

Raisman, G. (1969). Neuronal Plasticity in the septal nuclei of the adult brain. *Brain Research, 14,* 25–48.

Ramon y Cajal, S. (1893). New findings about the histological structure of the central nervous system. *Archiv fur Anatomie und Physiologie (Anatomie),* 319–428.

Rosenzweig, M. R., Bennett, E. L., & Diamond, M. C. (1972). Chemical and anatomical plasticity of brain: Replications and extensions. In J. Gaito (Ed.), *Macromolecules and behavior* (2nd ed., pp. 205–278). New York: Appleton-Century-Crofts.

Ryugo, D. K., Ryugo, R., Globus, A. & Killackey, H. P. (1975). Increased spine density in auditory cortex following visual or somatic deafferentation. *Brain Research, 90,* 143–146.

Sholl, D. A. (1956). *Organization of the cerebral cortex,* London: Methuen.

Sirevaag, A. M., & Greenough, W. T. (1985). Differential rearing effects on rat visual cortex synapses. II. Synaptic morphometry. *Developmental Brain Research, 19,* 215–226.

Sirevaag, A. M., & Greenough, W. T. (1987). Differential rearing effects on rat visual cortex synapses. III. Neuronal and glial nuclei, boutons, dendrites, and capillaries. *Developmental Brain Research, 424,* 320–332.

Sirevaag, A. M., & Greenough, W. T. (1991). Plasticity of GFAP-immunoreactive astrocyte size and number in visual cortex of rats reared in complex environments. *Brain Research, 540,* 273–278.

Smith, C. B. (1984). Aging and changes in cerebral energy metabolism. *Trends in Neuroscience, 7,* 203–208.

Sotelo, C., & Palay, S. L. (1971). Altered axons and axon terminals in the lateral vestibular nucleus of the rat. *Laboratory Investigation, 25,* 653–671.

Squire, L. R., & Cohen, N. J. (1984). Human memory and amnesia. In G. Lynch, J. L. McGaugh, & N. M. Weinberger (Eds.), *Neurobiology of learning and memory* (pp. 3–64). New York: Guilford Press.

Squire, L. R., Slater, P. C., & Chace, P. M. (1975). Retrograde amnesia: Temporal gradient in very long-term memory following electroconvulsive therapy. *Science, 187,* 77–79.

Steward, O. (1983). Polyribosomes at the base of dendritic spines of CNS neurons: Their possible role in synapse construction and modification. *Cold Spring Harbor Symposium on Quantitative Biology, 48,* 745–759.

Steward, O., & Falk, P. M. (1986). Protein-synthetic machinery at postsynaptic sites during synaptogenesis: A quantitative study of the association between polyribosomes and developing synapses. *Journal of Neuroscience, 6,* 412–423.

Tanzi, E. (1893). I fatti e le induzioni nell'odierna istologia del sistema nervosa. *Riv. Sperim. freniatria medic. leg, 19,* 419–472.

Tees, R. C. (1986). Experience and visual development: Behavioral evidence. In W. T. Greenough & J. M. Juraska (Eds.), *Developmental neuropsychobiology* (pp. 317–361). New York: Academic Press.

Tieman, S. B. (1984). Effects of monocular deprivation on geniculocortical synapses in the cat. *Journal of Comparative Neurology, 222,* 166–176.

Turner, A. M., & Greenough, W. T. (1983). Synapses per neuron and synaptic dimensions in occipital cortex of rats reared in complex, social, or isolation housing. *Acta Stereologica, 2* (Suppl. 1), 239–244.

Turner, A. M., & Greenough, W. T. (1985). Differential rearing effects on rat visual cortex synapses. I. Synaptic and neuronal density and synapses per neuron. *Brain Research, 329,* 195–203.

Valverde, F. (1967). Apical dendritic spines of the visual cortex and light deprivation in the mouse. *Experimental Brain Research, 3,* 337–352.

Volkmar, F. R., & Greenough, W. T. (1972). Rearing complexity affects branching of dendrites in the visual cortex of the rat. *Science, 176,* 1445–1447.

Wallace, C. S., Kilman, V. L., Withers, G. S., & Greenough, W. T. (in preparation). *Increases in dendritic length following four days of differential housing in weanling rats.*

Wann, D. F., Woolsey, T. A., Dierker, M. L., & Cowan, W. M. (1973). An on-line digital-computer system for the semiautomatic analysis of Golgi-impregnated neurons. *IEEE Transactions Biomedical Engineering, 20,* 233–247.

Zolman, J. F., & Morimoto, H. (1965). Cerebral changes related to duration of environmental complexity and locomotor activity. *Journal of Comparative and Physiological Psychology, 60,* 382 387.

11

Biophysical and Biochemical Records of Associative Memory in Rabbit CA1 Pyramidal Neurons and Hermissenda B Cells

Joseph L. Lo Turco
James L. Olds
Barry Bank
Daniel L. Alkon
National Institutes of Health

Associative memory, the storage of learned relationships, is a fundamental function of the central nervous system. Cellular correlates of learned behaviors are traces of associative memory, and as such represent elementary units of memory storage. Whereas there has been success in identifying elementary units of associative memory in mulluscan neurons, particularly in Hermissenda B cells (Alkon, 1984, Alkon et al., 1985, Lederhendeler & Farley, 1985, Nelson et al., 1990, Collin et al., 1991), technical limitations have impeded identification in mammalian neurons (Brons & Woods, 1980; Tsukahara et al., 1981). To overcome methodological difficulties presented by the mammalian brain, we have capitalized on inherent advantages offered by the in vitro brain slices technique (see Dingledine, 1982), the quantitative autoradiographic technique (see Pan, 1985), and a robust form of associative learning: classical conditioning of the rabbit eyeblink response (see Gormezano et al., 1986). By combining these methodologies, we have recently identified biophysical and biochemical correlates of associative learning in rabbit hippocampal CA1 neurons.

In this chapter we review the cellular correlates of classical conditioning that have been identified in rabbit hippocampal; CA 1cells and in Hermissenda B cells. The remarkable similarities between records of learning in these cell types are discussed. Based on these similarities we propose a general mechanism for the storage of associative information.

Classical Conditioning in Hermissenda and Rabbit

Classical conditioning, a prototypical form of associative learning is an ideal behavioral paradigm for the biological analysis of elementary learning processes.

One such advantage is that unlike nonassociative learning procedures (i.e., sensitization or habituation) classical conditioning affords the opportunity for rigorous control procedures. For example, explicitly unpaired control animals are exposed to environmental and stimulation conditions identical to conditioned animals with the exception that the CSs and USs are presented separately to the unpaired animals and in temporal contiguity to the conditioned animals. Thus, biophysical and biochemical effect of conditioning can be conclusively attributed to the temporal association of the CS and US and not to differences in the duration or amount of stimulation.

Classical or Pavlovian conditioning of Hermissenda has been demonstrated for one specific muscular response component of photoaxis (Lederhendler et al., 1986). Light (the CS) usually evokes a lengthening of the foot muscle (the single organ of locomotion), whereas rotation (the US) elicits a reflexive contraction of the same muscle. Following repeated pairing of light with rotation, light alone will elicit foot contraction (Lederhendler et al., 1986). This foot retraction is accompanied by an inhibition of phototaxis.

In rabbit eyeblink response conditioning, a CS (e.g., an auditory stimulus) is paired with a US (e.g., a mild electric pulse applied to the periorbital region of the face). The US elicits a reflexive eyeblink and a simultaneous sweep of the nictitating memebrane (the unconditioned response: UR). After repeated pairings the tone itself will come to elicit the eyeblink and nictitating membrane response (CR).

There are many similarities between Hermissenda and rabbit classical conditioning. The conditioned stimuli are both nonaversive sensory inputs, whereas the conditioned stimuli are aversive in nature. The unconditioned responses in each preparation are defensive muscular contractions (contraction of the foot muscle in Hermissenda and contraction of the ocular and facial muscles in rabbits; Lederhendler et al., 1986; Thompson et al., 1976). Most importantly, in both Hermissenda and rabbits the conditioned stimuli come to evoke new behavioral responses that resemble the unconditioned response. In other words, the CR is represented in the same effector system as the UR. This indicates that during conditioning the CS unequivocally acquires behavioral properties of the US, and thus has been associated with the US.

Identification of Neurons Involved in Conditioning

The B cells in Hermissenda and the hippocampal CA1 cells in rabbits have been shown to be involved in classical conditioning. In Hermissenda the neural network subserving the interaction of stimuli (CSs and USs) and the generation of responses has been delineated (Alkon, 1984, 1989; Matzel et al., in press; Alkon et al., in preparation). The B photoreceptors are inhibitory to the A photoreceptors, which in are in turn excitatory to motor neurons that control foot contraction and locomotion. During conditioning, increased excitability of the B cells, due to stimulus pairing of CS with US, results in a shortening of the foot and a decrease in phototactic behavior (Alkon, 1984).

Extracellular unit recordings made during rabbit eyeblink conditioning have shown that over 50% of CA1 pyramidal cells increase in firing frequency. This increased firing highly correlates with the topography of conditioned eyeblinks (Berger, Rinaldi, Weiz, & Thompson, 1983). Although ablation of the hippocampus does not disrupt the occurrence of conditioned responses (Shmaltz & Thios, 1972), ablation of the hippocampus has been shown to alter the latency (Port, Mikhail, & Patterson, 1985) and shape (Orr & Berger, 1985) of conditioned responses, and to severely impair performance in complex conditioning tasks (Berger & Orr, 1983; Port & Patterson, 1984; Solomon, 1977; Solomon & Moore, 1975). Figure 11.1 depicts the rabbit eyeblink conditioning tasks that are disrupted by the ablation of the hippocampus. In addition, pharmacological disruption of the hippocampus significantly impairs the acquisition of CRs (Solomon, Vander, Schaff, & Perry, 1983), and induction of long-term potentiation in the hippocampus greatly facilitates the acquisition of CR's (Berger, 1984). Taken

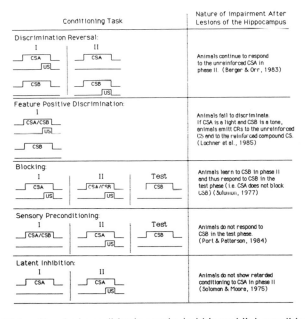

FIG. 11.1.   Classical conditioning tasks (rabbit eyeblink conditioning) that are disrupted after lesions of the hippocampus. The left column depicts the stimulus arrangements and trial types in the various conditioning tasks. The right column is a brief description of the nature of the impairment, relative to controls, caused by hippocampal lesions.

together, the increased unit activity in the hippocampus appears to encode information related to CS/US pairings that is important to optimal performance in classical conditioning tasks.

Cellular Records of Classical Conditioning

Once identified as involved in classical conditioning, to establish that particular neurons actually store information it must be determined that those neurons intrinsically change during conditioning. The only way to demonstrate such an intrinsic change is to make cellular measurements.

The first intrinsic cellular records of associative learning were identified in Hermissenda B cells (Alkon, 1982). Early and more recent studies all indicate that classical conditioning induces persistent (24 h) correlated reductions in the transient (IA) and calcium-dependent (IK-Ca^{++}) potassium currents in the B cells (Fig. 11.2; Alkon, 1985). In addition to the amplitudes of the currents, the

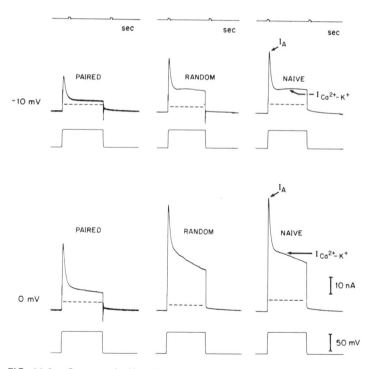

FIG. 11.2.   Currents in Hermissenda B cells are reduced by classical conditioning. Note that both of the major currents (IA and IK(Ca^{++})) in B cells from paired or conditioned animals (first traces in each row) are markedly reduced as compared to currents in B cells from the random group (middle traces: animals received explicitly inpaired CSs and USs in a random sequence) and B cells from naive animals.

kinetics also change with conditioning. Moreover, because induction of membrane changes in single B cells were found to cause behavior resembling associative learning (Farley et al., 1983) and fully account for increased activity in motor neurons responsible for generation of the conditioned response, the decrease in potassium currents in B cells are likely antecedents of the associatively learned decrease in phototactic behavior.

There is evidence that activation of GAB receptors on the B cell by statocyst presynaptic endings carrying US information in light-induced depolarization activates protein kinase C (PKC) which in turn phosphorylates a 20kD GTP-binding protein gating K^+ channels and thus causing changes in B cell excitability related to conditioning. Recently, it has been shown that the sign of the normally inhibitory GABA synapse between the presynaptic statocyst cells and post-synaptic B cells changes as a result of CS-US stimulus pairing (Alkon et al., In Preparation). This change in sign seems to be mediated by a GABA receptor. Additionally, IA and I (K-Ca^{++}) have been shown to be reduced by bath-applied phorbol ester (a PKC activator) particularly when combined with intracellular calcium loads (as would occur during CS/UCS stimulus pairing; Alkon et al., 1986). Furthermore, classical conditioning causes an increase in the in vivo phosphorylation of a 20kD GTP binding protein in eye cells (which include B cells and A cells) from classically conditioned animals as compared to eye cells from unpaired and naive controls (Neary, Crow, & Alkon, 1981; Nelson, Collin, & Alkon, 1990). These results, taken together suggest a complex chain of events that occur within the B cell as a result of stimulus paring. Thus, activation of the GABA receptors in combination with calcium loading of the B cell (as a result of the CS), causes a biphasic PSP in which a long lasting depolarization is manifested. As a result of these depolarization, and possibly mediated by GABA B receptor activation of PKC, the 20kD protein somehow interacts with potassium channels to cause an increase in electrical excitability in the B cell. It is this increase in electrical excitability which is the stored representation of the learned association.

In a series of recent studies we have identified biophysical and biochemical correlates of classical conditioning in rabbit hippocampal CA1 pyramidal cells. These biophysical and biochemical traces of associative learning have been identified by studying hippocampal slices that were isolated from rabbits 24 h following classical conditioning training, explicitly unpaired training, or no training.

The first conditioning-specific membrane change found in rabbit CA1 cells was a reduction in the hyperpolarization that follows action potentials (AHP; Disterhoft, Coulter, & Alkon, 1986). This pioneering study proved that biophysical correlates of learning are preserved and measurable in mammalian neurons maintained in vitro. Further analysis of the learning-specific reduction in the AHP has revealed that (a) the AHP is reduced in both amplitude and time course, (b) the AHP is most reduced for AHPs measured following four action potentials (c) the AHP reduction correlates with the acquisition of conditioned responses and (d) that a decrease in potassium current subserves the AHP reduction (Disterhoft et al., 1986; Coulter, Disterhoft, & Alkon, 1986; Sanchez-Andres & Alkon, 1991).

What makes the finding so remarkable is that both in Hermissenda and in the rabbit, a decrease in the same potassium current has been found to be the record of classical conditioning. This represents a compelling similarity in the biophysical substrates of classical conditioning between B cell in Hermissenda and the CA1 pyramidal neuron in rabbits.

The synaptic correlate that has been identified in CA1 cells is an increase in the summation of synaptic potentials (Lo Turco, Coulter, & Alkon, 1988). This synaptic difference, not apparent for single postsynaptic potentials, is characterized by increased depolarization to 50 Hz stimulation of the Schaeffer collaterals (Fig. 11.4). A change in any of several presynaptic or postsynaptic properties may account for the conditioning-specific increase in the summation of synaptic potentials. The possible changes include an increase in transmitter receptors (Mamounas, Thompson, Lynch, & Baudry, 1984), an increase in transmitter release, a decrease in synaptic inhibition and/or a decrease in dendritic potassium currents. Enhanced summation of synaptic potentials following conditioning did correlate with reduction of the post-synaptic K+ current, suggesting a post-synaptic mechanism for the enhanced summation.

PKC activation in CA1 cells has been directly related to eyeblink conditioning. Thus, a steady-state increase in PKC activity was found to be associated with the membrane in the CA1 hippocampal cell field of rabbits that had received 3 days of Pavolvian conditioning of the nictitating membrane (Bank et al., 1988).

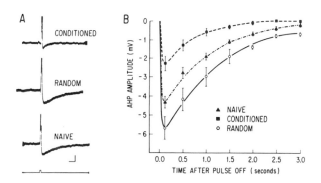

FIG. 11.3. The AHP in rabbit hippocampal CA1 cells are reduced by classical conditioning. A) representative recordings of hippocampal CA1 cells from conditioned, random (i.e., unpaired controls) or naive animals (calibration, 5mV & 500 msec); B) averages and SEM's pf AHP's recorded from cells of animals in the three behavioral conditions (N = 23). Measurements were made at isochronal points.

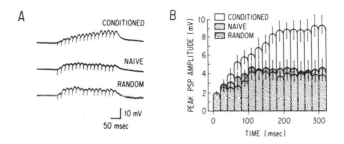

FIG. 11.4. Synaptic potential summation in rabbit CA1 cells is enhanced by classical conditioning. A) potentials to 300msec of 50Hz stimulation. The extracellular stimulation current needed to elicit a single 2 mV psp was approximately 1.0 uA and did not differ between groups. B) Profile of the peak psp amplitudes across 300 msec of 50Hz stimulation in cells from conditioned, random and naive animals (N = 15±SEM).

This sustained increase lasted as long as 24 h after the last training trial. These results taken together with the demonstration that a steady state decrease in the AHP in CA1 pyramidal cells occurs in similarly conditioned rabbits, but not in control animals (Disterhoft et al., 1986, Loturco et al., 1988, Coulter et al., 1989, Sanchez-Andres & Alkon, in press) and that PKC-activating phorbol esters can mimic the effect of Pavlovian conditioning on the AHP (Alkon et al., 1986), suggested an important role for PKC in associative memory storage within the hippocampus.

The advent of computerized image analysis and the development of high affinity radioligands for PKC (Worley et al., 1986a, 1986b), has made it possible to actually map the distributional changes in this enzyme after associative conditioning. In our laboratory, we have employed [³H]PDBU quantitative autoradiography to study membrane-associated PKC in rabbits that had also received 3 days of Pavlovian conditioning trials. Image analysis revealed a dramatic increase in membrane-associated PKC in the CA1 region of the hippocampus from conditioned animals but not control animals. This change in the distribution of the enzyme within the hippocampus was both long-lasting and dynamic (Fig. 11.5). While the increase was primarily localized in the area of the CA1 pyramidal cell somata 24 h after conditioning, the area of increased binding shifted to the basilar dendrites 72 h after conditioning (Olds et al., 1989).

In additional studies, the same methodology was used to study the initial acquisition of the conditioned response in rabbits. In contrast to the CA1 specific increase in membrane associated PKC seen 24 h and 72 h after 3 days of classical conditioning, rabbits studied after just 80 conditioning trials showed an increase in PKC membrane association specific to the stratum oriens of CA3 but not CA1 (Scharenberg et al., in press).

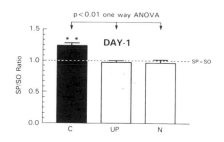

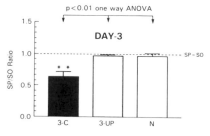

FIG. 11.5. (Top) Between-group comparisons of transept lines for 1-day retention animals. Normalization was accomplished with a ratio (SP:SO) obtained for each slice. Maximum (or minimum) binding values along transept-line portion within the cell body layer were divided by a binding value for the stratum oriens (measured on the transept line 7 pixels from the border between the stratim pyramidale and stratum oriens layers). When no obvious maximum or minimum values were apparent in the stratum pyramidale layer (as was usual for the controls) the average transept value within the stratum pyramidale layers provided the numerator of the ratio. This SP:SO ratio was then compared between groups by one way ANOVA. The bar graphs demonstrate a statistically significant change (35 ± 3% and 43 ± 5% increase in conditioned animals compared with unpaired controls or naives respectively (p < 0.01, N = 5 animals, 75 sections per group) in the pattern of PKC distribution within the hippocampus as a function of learning. (Bottom) Between-group comparisons of transept lines for 3-day retention animals and control groups (3-UP and N). The bar graphs show a statistically significant decrease in the SP:SO ratio (35 ± 2% and 30 ± 5%, respectively, compared with groups 3-UP and N, p < 0.01, N = 5 animals, 75 sections per group) calculated as for 1-day retention animals.

A hippocampal-specific change in PKC membrane association was also seen in rats that had received discrimination training in water maze procedure, but not in control animals (Olds et al., 1990). In this case, both spatial and cued discrimination procedures produced a significant decrease in [^{3}H]PDBU binding in the CA3 cell field. Both tasks required an intact hippocampus. What was extraordinary about this finding in relation to the previous result in rabbit hippocampus was the involvement of hippocampal PKC in a different species that was performing a completely different task. This suggests that the enzyme's role in memory storage is not simply an artifact of the learning task but reflects a more generalized involvement of PKC in a biological mechanism. This finding has recently been supported by work with inbred mouse mutants (Wehner et al., 1990a, 1990b) in which Mice with superior spatial-learning ability (as assessed by a water maze task) were shown to have significantly increased hippocampal PKC activity.

Cellular Records and Mnemonic Function

Biophysical records of classical conditioning may lend insight into how CA1 cells and B cells store and process information. In both cell types classical conditioning results in a sustained increase in excitability. In rabbit CA1 cells, enhanced summation of synaptic potentials and reduction in Ca^{++} dependent $K+$ conductance may be antecedant to the increases in within-trial firing frequency recorded during eye-blink conditioning (Berger, Alger, & Thompson, 1976; Berger et al., 1983). The enhanced summation of synaptic potentials would increase the probability of firing multiple action potentials. Thus, the biophysical alterations identified in vitro would enable cells in vivo to fire a burst of action potentials in response to synaptic input.

The conditioning-specific changes in CA1 cells may enable the hippocampus to process information about conditioned stimuli in a manner that is essential for its functioning. For example, because the enhanced psp summation is frequency dependent, only inputs that elicit a barrage of psps (perhaps conditioned or salient stimuli) would elicit a conditioning-specific response in CA1 pyramidal cells of conditioned animals. This dependence on input properties may endow the hippocampus with the ability to selectively process conditioned or salient stimuli. In fact, a general feature of both the AHP and psp summation change is that these conditioning-specific changes are greatest for strong stimuli. The AHP difference is present for AHP's following 1 spike and is greatest for AHP's following 4 spikes and the summation difference is greatest at the end of the 50 Hz stimulation. This may reflect a function of the hippocampus. After conditioning the CA1 pyramidal cells may serve as a filter for conditioned stimuli. This may serve to enhance performance or recall of such selectively gated stimuli. Consistent with this, animals without hippocampi are generally unable to reduce the excitatory strength of salient (Loechner, Lo Turco, & Weisz, 1985) or previously conditioned Css (Berger & Orr, 1983). The hippocampus may select such stimuli in the manner just discussed and then reduce the excitatory strength of these stimuli if they are not reinforced. This is quite consistent with attentional theories of hippocampal function (Moore & Stickney, 1980; Solomon & Moore, 1975).

The enhanced psp summation in cells from conditioned animals may enable the hippocampus to resolve differences in input strengths that previous to conditioning were unresolvable. The magniture of depolarization (see Fig. 11.3B) after 4 and 10 psps is significantly different in cells from conditioned animals, but in cells from controls the difference between 4 and 10 psps is not different. Thus, the conditioning-specific enhancement of psp summation would enable cells from conditioned animals to resolve a difference in stimuli. The AHP difference might further facilitate this resolution by enabling the conditioned cells to fire action potentials at different frequencies according to the magnitude of synaptic depolarization. Resolving such difference in input properties might be important for the role of the hippocampus during conditioning. For example, in both discrimination reversal and feature positive discrimination, animals without hippocampi are unable to discriminate between two conditioned stimuli (Berger & Orr, 1983; Loechner et al., 1985).

The B cells in Hermissenda are directly activated by the light CS. Thus, conditioning-specific enhancement of excitability in B cells, a consequence of decreased potassium conductances, results in enhanced B-cell responses to light. Through the neural network connecting visual and motor systems, the enhanced responses to light result in a contraction of foot muscles and an inhibition of phototaxis. A parallel between the behavioral significance of enhanced excitability of B cells in Hermissenda and of CA1 cells in rabbits appears to exist: increased neuronal excitability operating within neural circuitry to inhibit behavioral responding. This function is explicit for B cells and implicit for hippocampal CA1 pyramidal cells. The deficits in conditioning following lesions of the hippocampus (see Fig. 11.1) are characterized by an inability to inhibit inappropriate responses. Thus, the enhanced excitability of hippocampal cells may be necessary for inhibiting certain inappropriate responses. Whereas we caution that conclusively relating biophysical correlates of conditioning to behavior is premature and awaits further research, we are encouraged that the function of the hippocampus may begin to be understood in terms of biophysical and biochemical correlates of learning.

Similarities to Other Forms of Plasticity

The records of associative learning identified in B cells and CA1 pyramidal cells share features with other forms of neuronal plasticity. The decrease of potassium conductances has been proposed as the mechanism for activity-dependent facilitation in Aplysia (Hawkins, Abrams, Carew, & Kandel, 1982) and short-latency eye blink conditioning in the cat (Brons & Woods, 1980). Protein kinase C has been suggested to be involved in long-term potentiation (LTP). PKC is translocated to the plasma membrane in hippocampal dentate granule cells for at least one hr following induction of LTP (Akers et al., 1986). There is also a corresponding increase in the phorphorylation of the membrane-bound phosphoprotein F1 (or B-50), which lasts up to 3 days (Lovinger et al., 1986). In addition, activation of PKC by bath application of phorbol esters causes potentiation of synaptic transmission within the Shaeffer collateral-CA1 pathway (Malenka et al., 1986). This potentiation prevents further LTP produced by electrically induced synaptic input (Malenka et al., 1986).

Another form of LTP, associative LTP, is produced by pairing a weak synaptic input with a strong synaptic input. Wigstrom and colleagues have shown that the sufficient conditions for inducing associative LTP in hippocampal CA1 cells are a single volley briefly preceding or concurrent with strong post-synaptic depolarization (Gustaffson, Wigrstrom, Abrams, & Huang, 1987). Associative LTP, and particularly the conditions necessary for its induction, lend support to the model for associative plasticity that we propose next.

A Model for Induction of Persistent PKC Activation

Considering the similarities in cellular mechanism of plasticity in Hermissenda B cells and hippocampal pyramidal cells, we have constructed a general model for the persistent activation of PKC. This biochemical model of associative learning encompasses the cardinal feature of associative learning: temporal contiguity between two simuli. Basically, we propose that calcium-dependent second messenger systems function synergistically to activate PKC in a persistent manner (Fig. 11.6).

In many biological systems, the activation of PKC alone does not always elicit a physiological response. Usually, PKC activation has to be accompanied by intracellular calcium for full biological response (see Alkon & Rasmussen, 1988). The fact that bath application of phorbol ester or synthetic analogs of diacyglycerol (DG) only reduces IA and $IK(Ca^{++})$ if paired with a calcium load (Alkon et al., 1986) suggests a similar requirement in Hermissenda B cells. In the presence of DG or phorbol ester, basal levels of calcium are sufficient to fully activate PKC (Wolf, Cuatrecasas & Sahyoun, 1985) therefore a calcium load should not be necessary to reduce K+ currents. However, increased intracellular calcium is also necessary to reduce IA and $IK(Ca^{++})$ (Alkon et al., 1986). Therefore, the high levels of intracellular calcium required to reduce IA and $IK(Ca^{++})$ must be doing something in addition to directly activating PKC. This raises the possibility that there is a synergistic interaction between a calcium-dependent event and a DG/phorbol ester-dependent activation of PKC to yield complete reduction of the potassium currents. The synergistic requirement between calcium and PKC-mediated events for full biological activity has been observed in other systems such as platelet aggregation (Kaibuchi et al., 1983) and aldosterone secretion (Kojima, Kojima, Kreutter, & Rasmussen, 1984; Kojima, Kojima, & Rasmussen, 1985). PKC is particularly well suited to serve as a substrate for associatively induced alterations because there is an implicit requirement for an interaction between two inputs (Calcium and Diacyglycerol) that yield a biological response which neither one can yield a biological response that neither one alone can yield.

In the proposed model, the cellular CS-activated pathway is hypothesized to act through the glutamatergic synapse in the case of CA1 pyramidal cells, and through the light activation of rhodopsin in the B cell. Both of these pathways are likely to be coupled to G proteins that activated phospholipase C or A2 (Berrige, 1984). A product of this enzymatic reaction, DG, causes translocation of PKC

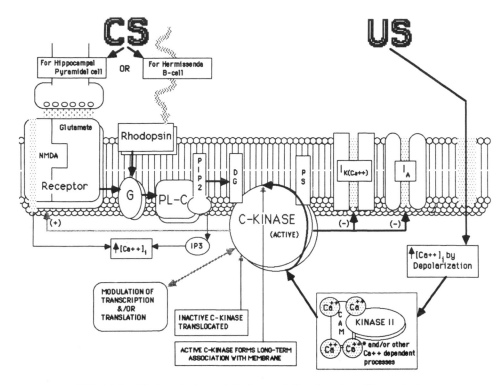

FIG. 11.6. Biochemical model of associative learning. The putative
CS-activated pathway acts through a glutamatergic synapse in the
case of CA1 cells and through light activation of rhodopsin in the B cell
to activate diacyglycerol (DG). DG causes translocation of PKC from
the cytosol to the membrane and IP3 increases intracellular calcium
concentrations. The CS-activated pathway causes a transient association of PKC with the membrane. The putative US-activated pathway,
causes an increase in internal calcium concentration in response to
depolarization. In Hermissenda this depolarization occurs as a result of
CS-US pairing and the switching of synaptic sign at the Hair Cell to B
cell GABAergic synapse. Concurrence of the CS- and US-activated
pathways leads to stable association of PKC with the membrane and
thereby to constituitive activation.

from the cytosol to the membrane. Another product of the same reaction, IP3,
acts on an intracellular smooth endoplasmic reticulum receptor to release inter-
cellular calcium stores. Therefore, the hypothesized CS-activated pathway
causes a transient association of PKC with the membrane. The US-activated
pathway, hypothesized to be an increase in internal calcium concentration in
response to depolarization, involves the activation of voltage-dependent calcium

channels in response to activation of the caudal hair cells. This increase in calcium partially results from the switch in the sign of the caudal hair cell to B cell GABAergic synapse (i.e., from hyperpolarization to depolarization) as a result of stimulus pairing. The GABAergic post-synaptic depolarization then opens voltage dependent calcium channels which in turn cause an enhanced depolarization and a sustained influx of calcium into the B cell (Alkon, Sanchez-Andres, and Collin, in preparation).

In hippocampal CA1 pyramidal cells the US-activated pathway is hypothesized to be calcium, because the US, unlike the CS, has been shown to elicit action potentials in approximately 30% of CA1 cells before conditioning (Berger et al., 1983) and this activation by the US increases greatly during the first 30 conditioning trials. Such activation likely causes a large influx of calcium into these cells via voltage-dependent calcium channels. In addition, associative LTP in CA1 cells has been shown to be induced by the forward pairing of a single synaptic volley with a depolarizing current pulse (Gustaffson et al., 1987) that triggers the influx of calcium into CA1 cells through NMDA channels.

In our model (see Fig. 11.6), concurrent stimulation of the CS- and US-activated pathways leads to a stable association of PKC with the membrane (either plasma, or intracellular). This stable association is presumed to occur via DG-dependent translocation of PKC. While PKC is associated with the membrane it becomes consituitively active and may modify membrane channels either by direct phosphorylation or via cp20 (Nelson et al., 1990).

Protein kinase C is also known to regulate the expression of gene products. For example, phorbol esters induce cellular growth, proliferation (see Blumberg, 1988), and more specifically accelerate protein and DNA synthesis. In support of this hypothesis, PKC activation has been shown to activate FOS/JUN binding to the AP1 promoter site on some genes (Auwerx et al., 1990). This property of PKC could serve to bridge the temporal domain between immediate and intermediate effects of conditioning (i.e., hours to months). Specifically, long term-translocation to the plasma membrane (hours to days) could underlie the immediate to intermediate effects of conditioning, whereas PKC activation of AP1 could trigger the genome to cause permanent neural alternations that underlie memories lasting from months to years.

SUMMARY

The hippocampal CA1 pyramidal cells and Hermissenda B cells change instrinsically during classical conditioning. The biophysical correlates that we have identified increase the excitability of both cell types and can be viewed as a manifestation of associatively induced long-term biochemical change mediated by a sequence of molecular events in which PKC plays a key role. At a cellular level, the correlates identified in rabbit CA1 cells are very similar to those identified in Hermissenda B cells: reduction of IK(Ca + +) that is mediated by long-term PKC activation. Thus, a general mechanism of neural modification related to associative learning may involve the activation of PKC and the consequent modification of potassium currents.

REFERENCES

Akers, R. F., Lovinger, D. M., Colley, P. A., Linden, D. J., & Routtenberg, A. (1986). Translocation of protein kinase C activity may mediate hippocampal long term potentiation.

Alkon, D. L. (1980). Membrane depolarization accumulates during acquisition of an associative behavioral change. *Science, 210,* 1375–1376.

Alkon, D. L. (1984). Changes of membrane currents during learning. *Journal of Experimental Biology, 112,* 95–112.

Alkon, D. L. (1989). Memory storage and neural systems. *Scientific American,* July, 42–50.

Alkon, D. L., Kubota, M., Neary, J. T., Naito, S., Coulter, D., & Rasmussen, H. (1986). C-kinase activation prolongs Ca2+-dependent inactivation of K+ currents [published erratum appears in *Biochem. Biophys. Res. Commun.,* 1986 Oct 30;140(2):774.] *Biochem. Biophys. Res. Commun., 134,* 1245–1253.

Alkon, D. L., Lederhendler, I., & Shoukimas, J. J. (1982). Primary changes of membrane currents during retention of associative learning. *Science, 215,* 693–695.

Alkon, D. L., Naito, S., Kubota, M. (1988). Regulation of Hermissenda K+ channels by cytoplasmic and membrane-associated C-kinase. *Journal of Neurochemistry, 51,* 903–917.

Alkon, D. L., & Rasmussen, H. (1988). A spatial-temporal model of cell activation. *Science, 239,* 998–1005.

Alkon, D. L., Sakakibara, M., Forman, R., Harrigan, J., Lederhendler, I., & Farley, J. (1985). Reduction of two voltage-dependent K+ currents mediates retention of a learned association. *Behav. Neural. Biol., 44,* 278–300.

Alkon, D. L., Blackwell, K. T., Barbour, G. S., Rigler, A. K., & Vogl, T. P. (1990). Pattern-recognition by an artificial network derived from biologic neuronal systems. *Biol. Cyber., 5,* 363–376.

Alkon, D. L., Sanchez-Andres, J. V., & Collin, C. (in preparation). Long-term transformation of an inhibitory into and excitatory GABA-ergic Response.

Baraban, J. M., Snyder, S. H., & Alger, B. E. (1985). Protein kinase C regulates ionic conductances in hippocampal neurons: electrophysiological effects of phorbol esters. *PNAS, USA, 82,* 2538–2342.

Bank, B., DeWeer, A., Kuzirian, A. M., Rasmussen, H., & Alkon, D. L. (1988). Classical conditioning induces long-term translocation of protein kinase C in rabbit hippocampal CA1 cells [published erratum appears in *Proc. Natl. Acad. Sci.,* USA, 1988 Jul;85(14):5344]. *Proceedings of the National Academy of Science, USA, 85,* 1988–1992.

Berger, T. W. (1984). Long-term potentiation of hippocamapal synaptic transmission accelerates behavioral learning. *Science, 224,* 627–630.

Berger, T. W., Alger, B., & Thompson, R. F. (1976). Neuronal substrate of classical conditioning in the hippocampus. *Science, 192,* 483–485.

Berger, T. W., Rinaldi, P. C., Weisz, D. J., & Thompson, R. F. (1983). Sinclye unit analysis of different hippocampal cell types during classical conditioning of rabbit nictitating membrane resoibse. *Journal of Neurophysiology, 50,* 1197–1219.

Berger, T. W., & Orr, B. W. (1983). Hippocampectomy selectively disrupts discrimination reversal conditioning of the rabbit nictitating membrane response. *Behav. Brain Res., 8,* 49–68.

Berrige, M. J. (1984). Ionositol triphosphate and diacylglycerol as second messengers. *Biochem. J., 220,* 345–360.

Blumberg, P. M. (1988). Protein kinase C as the receptor for the phorbol ester tumor promotors. *Cancer Research, 48,* 1–8.

Bliss, T. V. P., & Gardner-Medwin, A. R. (1973). Long-lasting potentiation of synaptic transmission in the dentate area of the unanaesthetized rabbit following stimulation of the perforant path. *Journal of Physiology (London), 232,* 357–374.

Brons, J. F., & Woods, C. D. (1980). Long-term changes in excitability of cortical neurons after Pavlovian conditioning and extinction. *Journal of Neurophysiology, 44,* 605–615.

Collin, C., Ikeno, H., Harrigan, J. F., Lederhendler, I., & Alkon, D. L. (1988). Sequential modification of membrane currents with classical conditioning. *Biophys. J., 54,* 955–960.

Collin, C., Papageorge, A. G., Lowy, D. R., & Alkon, D. L. (1990). Early enhancement of calcium currents injected into Hermissenda Neurons. *Science, 250,* 1743–1745.

Coulter, D. A., Lo Turco, J. J., Kubota, M., Disterhoft, J. F., Moore, J. W., & Alkon, D. L. (1989). Classical conditioning reduces amplitude and duration of calcium-dependent afterhyperpolarization in rabbit hippocampal pyramidal cells. *Journal of Neurophysiology, 61,* 971–981.

Dingledine, (Ed.). (1981). *Brain slices.* New York: Plenum Press.

Disterhoft, J. F., Coulter, D. A., Alkon, D. L. (1986). Conditioning-specific membrane changes of rabbit hippocampal neurons measured in vitro. *Proceedings of the National Academy of Science, U.S.A., 83,* 2733–2737.

El-Fakahany, E. E., Alger, B. E., Lai, W. S., Pitler, T. A., Worley, P. F., & Baraban, J. M. (1988). Neuronal muscarinic responses: role of protein kinase C. *FASEB.J., 2,* 2575–2583.

Farley, J., Richards, W. G., Ling, L., Linman, E., & Alkon, D. L. (1983). Membrane changes in a single photoreceptor during acquisition cause associative learning in Hermissenda. *Science, 221,* 1201–1203.

Farley, J., & Auerbach, S. (1986). Protein Kinase C activation induces conductance changes in Hermissenda photoreceptors like those seen in associative learning. *Nature, 319,* 220–223.

Gormezano, I., Prokasy, W. F., & Thompson, R. F. (1986). *Classical conditioning III. Behavioral, neurophysiological and neurochemical studies in the rabbit.* Hillsdale, NJ: Lawrence Erlbaum Associates.

Gustaffson, B., Wigstom, H., Abram, W. C., & Huang, Y. Y. (1987). Long-term potentiation.

Hawkins, R. D., Abrams, T. W., Carew, T. J., & Kandel, E. R. (1983). A cellular mechanism of classical conditioning Aplysia: activity-dependent amplification of presynaptic facilitation. *Science, 219,* 400–405.

Hannun, Y. A., Loomis, C. R., & Bell, R. M. (1985). Activation of protein kinase C by Triton X-100 mixed micelles containing diacylglycerol and phosphatidylserine. *J. Biol. Chem., 260,* 10039–10043.

Hashimoto, S., Suntoh, H., Taniyama, K., & Tanaka, C. (1988). Role of protein kinase C in the vesicular release of acetylcholine and norepinephrine from enteric neurons of the guinea pig small intestine. *Jpn J. Pharmacol., 48,* 377–385.

Hecker, E. (1978). *Carcinogenisis, A comprehensive survey.* In T. J. Slaga, A. Sivak, & R. K. Boutwell (Eds.) (Vol. 2, pp. 11–48). New York: Raven Press.

Hidaka, H., Tanaka, T., Onoda, K., et al. (1988). Cell type-specific expression of protein kinase C isozymes in the rabbit cerebellum. *J. Biol. Chem., 263,* 4523–4526.

Hotsin, J. R., & Prince, D. A. (1980). A calcium activated hyperpolarization follows repetitive firing in hippocampal neurons. *J. Neurophys., 43,* 409–419.

Huang, F. L., Yoshida, Y., Nakabayashi, H., Huang, K. P. (1987). Differential distribution of protein kinase C isozymes in the various regions of brain. *J. Biol. Chem., 262,* 15714–15720.

Huang, F. L., Yoshida, Y., Nakabayashi, H., Young, W. S. 3d, & Huang, K. P. (1988). Immunocytochemical localization of protein kinase C isozymes in rat brain. *J. Neurosci., 8*, 4734–4744.

Huang, F. L., Yoshida, Y., Nakabayashi, H., et al. (1989). Type I protein kinase C isozyme in the visual-information-processing pathway of monkey brain. *J. Cell Biochem., 39*.

Huang, K. P. (1989). The mechanism of protein kinase C activation. *Trends. Neurosci., 12*, 425–432.

Huang, K. P., Huang, F. L., Nakabayashi, H., & Yoshida, Y. (1988). Biochemical characterization of rat brain protein kinase C isozymes. *J. Biol. Chem., 263*, 14839–14845.

Huang, K. P., Huang, F. L., Nakabayashi, H., & Yoshida, Y. (1989). Expression and function of protein kinase C isozymes. *Acta Endocrinol. (Copenh.), 121*, 307–316.

Huynh, T. V., Cole, G., Katzman, R., Huang, K.-P., & Saitoh, T. (1989). Reduced PK-C immunoreactivity and altered protein phosphorylation in Alzheimer's disease fibroblasts. *Arch. Neurol, 43*, 1195–1199.

Kaibuchi, K., Takai, Y., Sawamura, M., Honshijima, M., Fujikura, T., & Nishizuka, Y. (1983). Synergistic functions of protein phosphorylation and calcium mobilization in platelet aggregation. *J. Biol. Chem., 258*, 6701–6704.

Katzman, R. (1986). Alzheimer's disease. *New England Journal of Medicine, 314*, 964–973.

Kojima, I., Kojima, K., Kreutter, D., & Rasmussen, H. (1984). The temporal integration of the aldosterone secretory response to angiotensin occurs via two intracellular pathways. *J. Biol. Chem., 259*, 14448–14457.

Kojima, I., Kojima, K., & Rasmussen, H. (1985). Role of calcium fluxes in the sustained phase of angiotensin II mediated aldosterone secretion from the adrenal glomerulosa cells. *J. Biol. Chem., 260*, 9177–9184.

Lancaster, B., & Adams, P. R. (1986). Single electrode voltage-clamp of slow AHP current in rat hippocampal cells. *J. Neurophys., 55*, 1268.

Lederhendler, I., Gart, S., & Alkon, D. L. (1986). Classical conditioning of Hermissenda: Origin of a new response. *Journal of Neuroscience, 85*, 1204–1211.

Lehman, J., Struble, R., Antuons, P., Coyle, J., Cork, L., & Price, D. (1984). Regional heterogeneity of choline acetyltransferase activity in the primate neocortex. *Brain Research, 322*, 361–364.

Lester, D. S., Orr, N., & Brumfeld, V. (1990). Structural distinction between soluble and particulate protein kinase C species. *J. Protein Chem., 9*, 209–220.

Levy, W. B., & Steward, O. (1979). Synapses as associative memory elements in the hippocampal formation. *Brain Research, 175*, 233–245.

Linden, D. J., & Routtenberg, A. (1989). The role of protein kinase C in long-term potentiation: a testable model. *Brain Research Brain Research Review, 14*, 279–296.

Loechner, K. J., Lo Turco, J. J., & Weisz, D. J. (1985). Effects of hippocampal lesions in feature-positive discrimination conditioning of the nictitating membrane response in the rabbit. *Soc. for Neurosci. Abstracts, 11*, 101.4.

Lo Turco, J. J., Coulter, D. A., & Alkon, D. L. (1988). Enhancement of synaptic potentials in rabbit CA1 pyramidal neurons following classical conditioning. *Proceedings of the National Academy of Science, U.S.A., 85*, 1672–1676.

Lovinger, D. M., Colley, P. A., Akers, R. F., Nelson, R. B., Routtenberg, A. (1986). Direct relation of long-term synaptic potentiation to phosphorylation of membrane protein F1, a substrate for membrane protein kinase C.

Lovinger, D. M., & Routtenberg, A. (1988). Synapse-specific protein kinase C activation enhances maintenance of long-term potentiation in rat hippocampus. *Journal of Physiology (London), 400*, 321–333.

Makowske, M., Ballester, R., Cayre, Y., & Rosen, O. M. (1988). Immunochemical evidence that three protein kinase C isozymes increase in abundance during HL-60 differentiation induced by dimethyl sulfoxide and retinoic acid. *J. Biol. Chem., 263,* 3402–3410.

Malenka, R. C., Ayoub, G. S., & Nicoll, R. A. (1987). Phorbol esters enhance transmitter release in rat hippocampal slices. *Brain Research, 403,* 198–203.

Malenka, R. C., Madison, D. V., Andrade, R., & Nicholl, R. A. (1986). Phorbol esters mimic some cholinergic actions in hippocampal pyramidal neurons. *Journal of Neuroscience, 6,* 475–480.

Mamounas, L. A., Thompson, R. F., Lynch, G., & Baudry, M. (1984). Classical conditioning of the rabbits eyelid response increases glutamate receptor bidning in hippocampal receptor membranes. *PNAS, USA, 81,* 2548–2552.

Masliah, E., Cole, G., Shimohama, S., Hansen, L., DeTeresa, R., Terry, R. D., & Saitoh, T. (1990). Differential involvement of protein kinase C isozymes in Alzheimer's Disease. *Journal of Neuroscience, 10,* 2113–2124.

Matzel, L. D., Schreurs, B., Lederhendler, I., & Alkon, D. L. (1989). Acquisition of conditioned associations in Hermissenda: Additive effects of contiguity and the forward interstimulus interval. *Behavioral Neuroscience.*

McPhie, D. L., Olds, J. L., Sanchez-Andres, J. V., & Alkon, D. L. (1989). Isolated pharmacological activation of three neurotransmitter systems produces differential translocation of PKC in the rabbit hippocampus. *Society for Neuroscience Meeting, 15,* 505–505. (Abstract)

McPhie, D. L., Matzel, L. D., Olds, J. L., Kuzirian, A. M., & Alkon, D. L. (in preparation). *Cell-specificity of molecular changes during memory storage.*

Mellonia, E., Pontremoli, S., Michetti, M., Sacco, O., Spartore, B., Salamino, F., & Horecker, B. L. (1985). Binding of protein kinase C to neurtrophil membranes in the presence of CA2+ requiring protease. *PNAS, USA, 82,* 6345–6349.

Moore, J. W., & Stickney, K. J. (1980). Formation of attentional-associative networks in real time: Role of the hippocampus and implications for conditioning. *Physiol. Psych., 8,* 207–217.

Morimoto, Y. M., Nobori, K., Edashige, K., Yamamoto, M., Kobayashi, S., & Utsumi, K. (1988). Activation of protein kinase C by fatty acids and its dependency on CA2+ and phospholipid. *Cell Struct. Funct., 13,* 45–49.

Nakabayashi, H., & Huang, K. P. (1988). Monoclonal antibodies against type II rat brain protein kinase C. *J. Biol. Chem., 263,* 298–304.

Neary, J. T., Crow, T., & Alkon, D. L. (1981). Change in a specific phosphoprotein band following associative learning in Hermissenda. *Nature, 293,* 658–660.

Neary, J. T., Naito, S., Dewer, A., & Alkon, D. L. (1986). Calcium/diacylglycerol activated phospholipid dependent protein kinase in the Hermissenda nervous system. *Journal of Neurochemistry, 47,* 1405–1411.

Nelsestuen, G. L., & Bazzi, M. D. (1989). In vitro properties of protein kinase C suggest and accumuating and long term regulation. In *Cell activation and signal initiation: Receptor and phospholipase control of Inositol Phosphate, PAF and Eicosanoid production* (pp. 253–266). New York: Alan R. Liss.

Nelson, R. B., Friedman, D. P., O'Neill, J. B., Mishkin, M., & Routtenberg, A. (1987). Gradients of protein kinase C substrate phosphorylation in primate visual system peak in visual memory storage areas. *Brain Research, 416,* 387–392.

Nelson, T. J., Collin, C., & Alkon, D. L. (1990). Isolation of a G Protein That is Modified by Learning and Reduces Potassium Currents in Hermissenda. *Science, 247,* 1479–1483.

Nishizuka, Y. (1988). The molecular heterogeneity of protein kinase C and its implications for cellular regulation. *Nature, 334,* 661–665.

Olds, J. (1972b). Learning and the hippocampus. *Rev. Can. Biol., 31,* Suppl: 215, Suppl: 238.

Olds, J. (1975). Unit recordings during Pavolvian conditioning. *UCLA Forum. Med. Sci.,* 343–371.

Olds, J., Disterhoft, J. F., Segal, M., Kornblith, C. L., & Hirsh, R. (1972a). Learning centers of rat brain mapped by measuring latencies of conditioned unit responses. *Journal of Neurophysiology, 35,* 202–219.

Olds, J. L., Anderson, M. L., McPhie, D. L., Staten, L. D., & Alkon, D. L. (1989). Imaging of memory-specific changes in the distribution of protein kinase C in the hippocampus. *Science, 245,* 866–869.

Olds, J. L., Golski, S., McPhie, D. L., Olton, D., Mishkin, M., & Alkon, D. L. (in press). Discrimination learning alters the distribution of protein kinase C in the hippocampus of rats. *Journal of Neuroscience.*

Onodera, H., Araki, T., & Kogure, K. (1989). Protein kinase C activity in the rat hippocampus after forebrain ischemia: autoradiographic analysis by [3H]phorbol 12,13-dibutyrate. *Brain Research, 481,* 1–7.

Orr, W. B., & Berger, T. W. (1985). Hippocampectomy disrupts the topography of conditioned nictitating response during reversal learning. *Behavioral Neuroscience, 99,* 33–45.

Ouimet, C. C., Wang, J. K., Walaas, S. I., Albert, K. A., & Greengard, P. (1990). Localization of the MARCKS (87 kDa) protein, a major specific substrate for protein kinase C, in rat brain. *Journal of Neuroscience, 10,* 1683–1698.

Pavlov, I. P. (1910). *Conditioned reflexes* (G. V. Anrep translator and ed.) London: Oxford University Press.

Port, R. L., Mikhail, A. A., & Patterson, M. M. (1985). Differential effects of hippocampectomy on classically conditioned rabbit nictitating membrane response related to interstimulus interval. *Behavioral Neuroscience, 99,* 200–208.

Port, R. L., & Patterson, M. M. (1984). Fimbrial lesions and sensory preconditioning. *Behavioral Neuroscience, 98,* 584–589.

Roth, B. L., Iadarola, M. J., Mehegan, J. P., & Jacobowitz, D. M. (1989a). Immunohistochemical distribution of beta-protein kinase C in rat hippocampus determined with an antibody against a synthetic peptide sequence. *Brain Research Bulletin, 22,* 893–897.

Roth, B. L., Mehegan, J. P., Jacobowitz, D. M., Robey, F., & Iadarola, M. J. (1989b). Rat brain protein kinase C: purification, antibody production, and quantification in discrete regions of hippocampus. *Journal of Neurochemistry, 52,* 215–221.

Routtenberg, A. (1986). Synaptic Plasticity and protein kinase C. In W. H. Gispen & A. Routtenberg (Eds.), *Progress in brain research* (pp. 211–234). New York: Elsevier Science Publishers.

Sanchez-Andres, J. V., & Alkon, D. L. (in press). Voltage-clamp analysis of the effects of classical conditioning in hippoakpus. *Journal of Neurophysiology.*

Saito, N., Kikkawa, U., Nishizuka, Y., & Tanaka, C. (1988). Distribution of protein kinase C-like immunoreactive neurons in rat brain. *Journal of Neuroscience, 8,* 369–382.

Saito, N., Kose, A., & Ito, A. (1989). Immunocytochemical localization of beta II subspecies of protein kinase C in rat brain. *Proceedings of the National Academy of Science,* U.S.A., *86,* 3409–3413.

Scharenberg, A. M., Olds, J. L., Schreurs, B. G., Craig, A. M., & Alkon, D. P. (in press). PKC redistribution within CA3 stratum oriens occurring during acquisition of NM conditioning in the rabbit. *Proceedings of the National Academy of Science, U.S.A.*

Schmaltz, L. W., & Theios, J. (1972). Acquisition and extinction of a classically conditioned response in hippocampectomized rabbits. *J. Comp. Physiol. Psych., 79,* 328–333.

Schwartz, J. H., & Greenberg, S. M. (1987). Molecular mechanisms for memory: second-messenger induced modifications of protein kinases in nerve cells. *Annual Review of Neuroscience, 10,* 459–476.

Solomon, P. R. (1977). Role of the hippocampus in blocking and conditioned inhibition of the rabbit's nictitating membrane response. *J. Comp. Physiol. Psych., 91,* 407–417.

Solomon, P. R., Solomon, S. D., Vander Schaff, E. R., & Perry, H. E. (1983). Altered activity in the hippocampus is more detrimental to classical conditioning than removing the structure. *Science, 220,* 329–331.

Solomon, P. R., & Moore, J. W. (1975). Latent inhibition and stimulus generalization of the classically conditioned nictitating membrane response in rabbits following hippocampal ablation. *J. Comp. Physiol. Psych.*, *89*, 1192–1203.

Stichel, C. C., & Singer, W. (1988). Localization of isoenzymes II/III of protein kinase C in the rat visual cortex (area 17), hippocampus and dentate gyrus. *Experimental Brain Research, 72*, 443–449.

Stopfer, M., & Carew, T. J. (1988). Development of sensitization in the escape locomotion system in Aplysia. *Journal of Neuroscience, 8*, 223–230.

Suzuki, T., & Siekevitz, P. (1989). Properties of a protein kinase C activity in synaptic plasma membrane and postsynaptic density fractions isolated from canine cerebral cortex. *Journal of Neurochemistry, 53*, 1751–1762.

Takeda, T., & Alkon, D. L. (1982). Correlated receptor and motorneuron changes during retention of associative learning of Hermissenda crassicornis. *Comp. Biochem. Physiol.* [A], *73*, 151–157.

Tsukuhara, N., Oda, Y., & Notsu, T. (1981). Classical conditioning mediated by the red nucleus in the cat. *Journal of Neuroscience, 1*, 72–79.

Van Lookeren, C., Campagne, M., Oestreicher, A. B., Van Bergen, e.n Henegowen, P. M., & Gispen, W. H. (1989). Ultrastructural immunocytochemical localization of B-50/GAP43, a protein kinase C substrate, in isolated presynaptic nerve terminals and neuronal growth cones. *J. Neurocytol., 18*, 479–489.

Wehner, J. M., Sleight, S., & Upchurch, M. (1990a). Relationship of hippocampal protein kinase C activity to spatial learning performance. *Society for Neuroscience Meeting, 15*, 1170–1170. (Abstract)

Wehner, J. M., Upchurch, M., & Sleight, S. (1990b). Correlation of hippocampal PKC activity with spatial learning ability. *Behavioral Genetics, 19*, 780–780. (Abstract)

Wolf, M., Cuatracasas, P., & Sahyoun, N. (1985). Interaction of protein kinase C with membranes is regulated by Ca2+, phorbol esters and ATP. *J. Biol. Chem., 260*, 15718–15722.

Wolf, M., & Sahyoun, N. (1986). Protein kinase C and phosphotidylserine bind to Mr 110,000/115,000 polypeptides enriched in cytoskeletal and postsynaptic density preparations. *J. Biol. Chem., 261*, 13327–13332.

Wong, K. L., Murakami, K., & Routtenberg, A. (1989). Dietary cis-fatty acids that increase protein F1 phosphorylation enhance spatial memory. *Brain Research, 505*, 302–305.

Wood, J. G., Girard, P. R., Mazzei, G. J., & Kuo, J. F. (1986). Immunocytochemical localization of protein kinase C in identified compartments of rat brain. *Journal of Neuroscience, 6*, 2571–2577.

Woodgett, J. R., & Hunter, T. (1987). Isolation and characterization of two distinct forms of protein kinase C. *J. Biol. Chem., 262*, 4836–4843.

Worley, P. F., Baraban, J. M., & Snyder, S. H. (1986a). Heterogeneous localization of protein kinase C in rat brain: autoradiographic analysis of phorbol ester receptor binding. *Journal of Neuroscience, 6*, 199–207.

Worley, P. F., Baraban, J. M., De Souza, E. B., & Snyder, S. H. (1986b). Mapping second messenger systems in the brain: differential localizations of adenylate cyclase and protein kinase C. *Proceedings of the National Academy of Science: USA, 83*, 4053–4057.

Yoshida, Y., Huang, F. L., Nakabayashi, H., & Huang, K. P. (1988). Tissue distribution and developmental expression of protein kinase C isozymes. *J. Biol. Chem., 263*, 9868–9873.

12

Neurobiology of an Attribute Model of Memory: Role of Prefrontal Cortex

Raymond P. Kesner
Pamela Jackson-Smith
University of Utah

There are many theoretical schemata one can select to organize the neu-robiological basis of the structure of memory. On a psychological level these schemata can vary from a single to a multiple task analysis, from a single or dual to a multiple memory analysis, and/or from a single to a multiple attribute analysis. On a neurobiological level these schemata can vary from a synapse, a single cell, or a neural region to the brain as a whole. We have decided that the best representation of memory might be in the form of multiple attributes, and that its neurobiological mediation is to be analyzed at the level of a neural region. Thus, the psychological unit of analysis is an attribute (e.g., space) and the neural unit of analysis is a neural region (e.g., hippocampus).

Based on earlier suggestions by Underwood (1969) and Spear (1976), I have proposed that any specific memory is composed of a set of features or attributes that are specific and unique for each learning experience (Kesner, 1980). In most animal experiments there are a set of at least five salient attributes that charac-terize mnemonic information. In humans one would also add a linguistic at-tribute. These are labeled space, time, affect, sensory perception, and response. A spatial attribute within this framework involves the coding and storage of specific stimuli representing places or relationships between places, which are usually independent of the subject's own body schema. It is exemplified by the ability to encode and remember maps and to localize stimuli in external space.

A temporal attribute involves the encoding and storage of specific stimuli or sets of spatially or temporally separated stimuli as part of an episode marking or tagging its occurrence in time, that is, separating one specific episode from previous or succeeding episodes.

251

An affect attribute involves the encoding and storage of reinforcement contingencies that result in positive or negative emotional experiences.

A sensory-perceptual attribute involves the encoding and storage of a set of sensory stimuli that are organized in the form of cues as part of a specific experience.

A response attribute involves the encoding and storage of information based on feedback from responses that occur in specific situations as well as the selection of appropriate responses.

These attributes are organized in both parallel and hierarchical systems and are likely to interact with each other in many combinations. For example, the interaction between spatial and temporal attributes can provide for the external context of a situation, which is important in determining when and where critical events occurred. Another important interaction involves the temporal and affective attributes. In this case the interaction can provide important information concerning the internal context (internal state of the organism), which is important in evaluating emotional experiences. There is also a possible interaction between spatial and response attributes that would result in the encoding and storage of responses that depend on accurate assessment of one's body orientation in space (egocentric localization). This interaction is influenced by vestibular and kinesthetic input that aids navigation in space relative to the animal. It is exemplified, for instance, by the ability to encode and remember right–left responses. Finally, there is an interaction between sensory-perception and response attributes. This interaction has been labeled S–R associations. In some tasks S–R associations are the most easily distinguishable attribute of a memory.

In this comprehensive model, Kesner (1980) has assumed that any specific memory is not only composed of a set of attributes but is further organized into a data-based memory and an expectancy- or knowledge-based memory system (see Fig. 12.1). The data-based memory system is biased towards the coding of incoming data concerning the present, with an emphasis on facts, data, and events that are usually personal and that occur within specific external and internal environmental contexts. To borrow a term from contemporary information-processing theory, the emphasis is on "bottom-up" processing. During initial learning there is a great emphasis on the data-based memory system, which will continue to be of importance even after initial learning in situations where trial unique or novel information needs to be remembered.

The expectancy- or knowledge-based memory system is biased towards previously stored information and can be thought of as one's general knowledge of the world. It can operate in the abstract in the absence of critical incoming data. From an informational-processing view, the emphasis is on "top-down" processing. The expectancy- or knowledge-based memory system would tend to be of greater importance after a task has been learned given that the situation is invar-

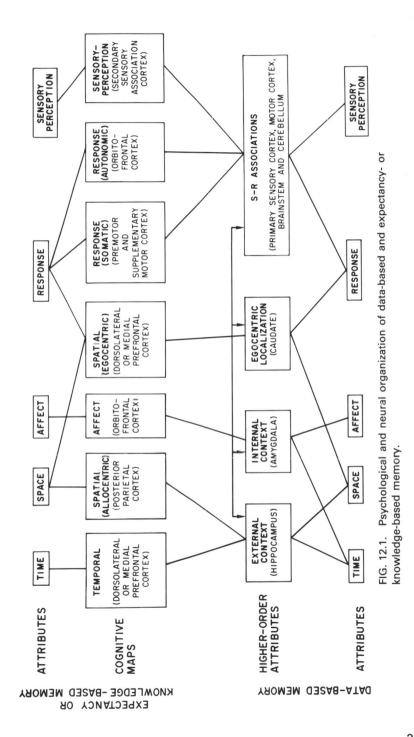

FIG. 12.1. Psychological and neural organization of data-based and expectancy- or knowledge-based memory.

253

iant and familiar. In most situations, however, one would expect a contribution of both systems with varying proportion of involvement of one relative to the other.

Memories within the expectancy- or knowledge-based memory system are assumed to be organized as a set of cognitive maps and their interactions that are unique for each memory. The exact nature and organization of knowledge structure within each cognitive map needs to be determined. The cognitive maps are labeled spatial (allocentric), temporal, affect, spatial (egocentric), response (somatic), response (autonomic), and sensory-perceptual and are influenced by a set of attributes such as space, time, affect, response, and sensory-perception as well as interactions between attributes such as space and response. Note that the same attributes are also associated with the data-based memory system. Of the many interactions between cognitive maps, a few appear to be of critical importance. They are labeled *scripts* representing the interaction between temporal and spatial cognitive maps, *schemata* representing the interaction between spatial and sensory-perceptual cognitive maps, *moods* representing the interaction between temporal and affect-laden cognitive maps, and *skills* representing the interaction between sensory-perceptual and response cognitive maps.

The structural organization of these attributes and their interactions with higher order levels of organization (e.g., internal and external contexts, egocentric localization, S–R associations as well as cognitive maps, scripts, schemata, moods, and skills) needs to be determined. As an initial attempt it is assumed that interactive patterns of independently operating attributes provide the organizational framework for the existence of each unique memory. At the neurobiological level it is assumed that specific brain regions code or store the aforementioned attributes and cognitive maps as well as their specific interactions. Furthermore, relative amounts of neural activity within each critical brain region that codes a critical attribute, a cognitive map, or a set of attributes and cognitive maps provides for the total neuronal substrate associated with each unique memory.

Which neural regions can be considered as candidates for the mediation of the attribute-based structure of memory? Within the model presented in Fig. 12.1, it is proposed that for the data-based memory system the hippocampus mediates the external context, the amygdala the internal context, the caudate nucleus egocentric localization, the primary-sensory cortex, motor cortex, brainstem, and cerebellum circuit the S–R association system. Within the expectancy- or knowledge-based memory system, it is proposed that the dorsolateral or medial prefrontal cortex mediates the temporal and spatial (egocentric) cognitive maps, the posterior parietal cortex the spatial (allocentric) cognitive maps, the orbito-frontal cortex the affect and response (autonomic) cognitive maps, the secondary sensory association cortex the sensory-perceptual cognitive maps, and the premotor and supplementary motor cortex the response (somatic) cognitive maps.

Furthermore, it is assumed that neural regions subserving higher order attributes and neural regions subserving cognitive maps can operate independently of each other, even though many interactions exist. Given that this latter assumption has empirical support, this attribute model would provide for both a psychological and neural foundation for neural network models, because a large number of neural network models assume a parallel-distributed memory system.

Finally, it is assumed that there is evolutionary continuity between animals and humans not only in terms of mnemonic function, but also in terms of brain–memory function relationships. Given that this assumption has empirical support, one can devise neural networks in animals that have validity for human brain function and memory. The attribute model differs from previously proposed models in that it is more comprehensive and incorporates most of the critical features of other models. There is also a suggestion of greater anatomical functional specificity as it relates to memory organization.

It is not possible in this chapter to provide empirical support and to discuss in detail each component of this multidimensional model of memory; therefore, we only concentrate on an analysis of the contribution of the prefrontal cortex. First, we elaborate on the unique and different functions of the prefrontal cortex and provide empirical support for the role of the prefrontal cortex in animals and humans in representing temporal and egocentric spatial information. Second, an attempt is made to demonstrate that the prefrontal cortex is part of the expectancy- or knowledge-based memory system.

DORSOLATERAL OR MEDIAL PREFRONTAL CORTEX AND TEMPORAL MAPS

The prefrontal cortex in humans is part of the frontal lobe and includes areas 8, 9, 10, 11, 12, 44, 45, 46, and 47 (see Fig. 12.2). It is defined as the projection area of the mediodorsal thalamic nucleus (MDN). Based mostly on anatomically distinct MDN projections to prefrontal cortex in primates (Rose & Woolsey, 1948), Kolb and Whishaw (1985) suggested that the prefrontal cortex be divided into a dorsolateral region roughly including areas 9, 10, 44, 45, and 46, an orbital-frontal region including areas 11, 12, and 47, and a frontal eye field region including areas 8 and 9. The prefrontal cortex has, in addition to the MDN, many afferents from visual, auditory, and somatosensory association cortex, the olfactory system, hypothalamus, hippocampus, locus coeruleus, and raphe nuclei, as well as many efferent connections to hypothalamus, central gray, putamen, caudate, motor cortex, and visual, auditory, and somatosensory association cortical regions. Thus, the prefrontal cortex can easily serve as a higher order integrative center.

Rose and Woolsey (1948) suggested that the mammalian prefrontal cortex, like other cortical divisions, can be defined with respect to its thalamic projection field (in this case nucleus medialis dorsalis), and that comparisons of the appropriate thalamic nuclei could be used in the determination of cortical homologies.

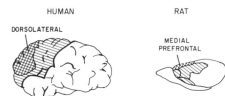

FIG. 12.2. A schematic representation of frontal cortex in the
human and rat. Adapted from
Kolb and Whishaw (1985).

Of particular importance is the observation that the pattern of MDN subdivisions and projections to prefrontal cortex in rats, monkeys, and perhaps humans are strikingly similar. In primates, the lateral, parvocellular segment of the MDN projects to the dorsolateral prefrontal cortex, and the central, magnocellular component of the MDN projects to the orbital-frontal region (Kievet & Kuypers, 1977). In rats, a histologically distinct lateral segment of the MDN projects preferentially to the medial prefrontal cortex, which includes the medial pre-central area, anterior cingulate cortex, and prelimbic, infralimbic, and taenia tecta regions, and the central subnucleus of the MDN selectively projects to the frontal cortex along the dorsal bank of the rhinal sulcus (orbital-agranular insular cortex) (Domesick, 1972; Krettek & Price, 1977; Leonard, 1969). More recently, Groenewegen (1988) has shown that the lateral component can be subdivided into a lateral and paralamellar segment of the MDN with the lateral segment projecting to the anterior cingulate cortex and the paralamellar segment project-ing to the medial precentral area. Furthermore, he has shown that the central component can be subdivided into a medial and central segment of the MDN with the medial segment projecting mostly to the prelimbic area and the dorsal agranular insular area and the central segment projecting to the ventral agranular insular and the lateral orbital areas. A schematic of prefrontal cortex in rats and humans is shown in Fig. 12.2. The possibility exists that the dorsolateral prefron-tal area in monkeys, and possibly in humans, and the medial prefrontal area in rats might subserve similar functions.

Humans

The attribute model suggests that the dorsolateral prefrontal cortex in humans and monkeys and medial prefrontal cortex in rats, in conjunction with their thalamic projection, stores and retrieves information in reference to a temporal cognitive map within the expectancy- or knowledge-based memory system. This neural region also receives critical inputs from sensory-perceptual cognitive maps, as mediated by secondary sensory association cortex, and influences the response cognitive map system, as mediated by the premotor and supplementary motor cortex. Support for this hypothesis can be found in the clinical literature dealing with human patients with prefrontal cortex lesions. In addition to prob-lems with lack of initiative or spontaneity, poor movement programming and reduced corollary discharge, there is often a deficit for information concerning temporal aspects of their environment. They cannot remember the order in which information was experienced, plan and create a complex set of motor movements, or program a temporally ordered set of activities. Frontal-cortex-damaged patients can remember that certain words or pictures have been presented but cannot discriminate the more from the less recent. Thus, memory for item information is intact, but memory for order information is impaired (Lewinsohn, Zieler, Libet, Eyeberg, & Nielson, 1972; Milner, 1971).

Recently, Milner's and Lewinsohn's et al. findings have been replicated and extended to spatial location and hand position information (Kesner & Fineman, 1989). Sixteen college students and 11 subjects with either unilateral (N = 8) or bilateral (N = 3) prefrontal cortex lesions were presented with a 6-item list of words, easily labeled pictures, abstract pictures, X's in specific spatial locations or hand positions, and tested for item recognition memory or order memory. The procedures used for the item recognition and order memory tests were first developed for the assessment of list learning for spatial location information in rats and were then adapted for use with brain-damaged patients. Because in rats only one test was given for each serial list, the same procedure was adopted for humans. This procedure has the advantage of minimizing response interference. Because the set size is only 6 items, normal subjects perform well on all the item recognition and order memory tests (see Table 12.1). Subjects received 24 item recognition memory tests and 20 order memory tests. The results for the patients with prefrontal lobe lesions are shown in Table 12.1 and indicate a clear item-order dissociation for all modalities.

In another experiment, frontal-cortex-damaged patients were impaired in their ability to self-order a sequence of stimuli presented one at a time (Petrides & Milner, 1982). Additional evidence comes from the finding that frontal-lobe-damaged patients are very poor at copying a series of facial movements. These patients have difficulty in ordering the various components of the sequence. The

TABLE 12.1
Mean Percent Correct

	Bilateral		Frontals Right		Left		Controls	
	Item	Order	Item	Order	Item	Order	Item	Order
Spatial locations	89	73	85	66	93	88	90	90
Words	89	60	90	75	94	71	98	96
Pictures	90	63	87	73	93	81	96	94
Abstract pictures	76	67	82	63	84	74	92	89
Hand positions	72	58	75	64	84	73	88	82

components are remembered correctly but are expressed in the incorrect order (Kolb & Milner, 1981). Frontal-lobe-damaged patients are also impaired in estimating the frequency of occurrence of specific items within a list (Milner, Petrides, & Smith, 1985). It has been suggested that frequency judgments require a search through memory for temporal information (Hintzman, Grandy, & Gold, 1981; Hintzman, Nozawa, & Irmscher, 1982; Milner et al., 1985; i.e., one needs to search one's memory for each specific instance of a specific item).

Animals

In monkeys, dorsolateral-prefrontal cortex lesions result in deficits in temporal ordering of events comparable to what has been described in humans. This temporal ordering deficit is evidenced by deficits in delayed response, delayed alternation, and delayed matching-to-sample tasks as well as self-ordering of a sequence of responses (Petrides & Milner, 1982; Pinto-Haumy & Linck, 1965). Even though no experiment comparable to Milner's (1971) observation of item-order dissociation has been carried out in monkeys, one experiment by Pribram and Tubbs (1967) can be interpreted in a somewhat similar vein. They showed that monkeys with prefrontal cortex lesions could not perform a 5-s right–left delayed alternation task (order deficit), but with a 15-s delay between a right–left couplet of responses no deficit was found. In this latter condition the animal could chunk, or categorize, each couplet as an item of information and would not need to remember the order of a right–left response. In delayed response, delayed alternation, or delayed matching-to-sample tasks, there are a large number of neurons in the dorsolateral prefrontal cortex that increase their firing rates only during the delay period. In many of these cells the increased discharge occurs only when the animal experiences cues that have to be remembered for subsequent accurate performance (Fuster, 1984). Based on the aforementioned findings, it has been suggested that the prefrontal cortex is primarily involved in temporal structuring of information in short-term memory (Fuster, 1980) or "noticing order in working memory" (Pribram, Ahumada, Hartog, & Ross, 1964).

In rats, lesions of the medial prefrontal cortex produce, in most studies, a deficit in DRL performance as well as deficits in a temporal go/no-go alternation task and a delayed alternation task (Johnston, Hart, & Howell, 1974; Rosenkilde & Divac, 1975). Deficits have also been observed in tasks in which rats emit a specific sequence of behavioral responses requiring temporal organization (Barker, 1967; Slotnick, 1967; Stamm, 1955).

In order to test further whether there is a correspondence in function of prefrontal cortex in rats and humans, rats were tested for item and order memory for a list of items (places on a maze; Kesner & Holbrook, 1987). Rats were trained on an eight-arm radial maze for Front Loop reinforcement. After extensive training each animal was allowed to visit four arms on each trial (one per day) in an order that was randomly selected for that trial (study phase). The sequencing of the four arms was accomplished by sequentially opening Plexiglas doors (one at a time) located at the entrance of each arm. Immediately after the animal had received reinforcement from the last of the four arms, the test phase began. During the test phase the animal was given two tests—one to test order memory and one to test item memory. The test for order memory consisted of opening the first and second, second and third, or third and fourth door that occurred in the sequence. The rule to be learned leading to an additional reinforcement was to choose the arm that occurred earlier in the sequence. The test for item memory consisted of opening of a door that was previously visited for that trial and a door that was not. The rule to be learned resulting in an additional reinforcement was to choose the arm previously visited during the study phase of the trial (win-stay rule). The order of presentation of the two tests was varied randomly.

Following extensive training, animals performed better than chance for each item or order position on both tests (Fig. 12.3). The animals then received medial-prefrontal cortex aspiration lesions. After recovery from surgery animals were given an additional 32 tests. Results are shown in Fig. 12.3 and indicate that medial-prefrontal cortex lesioned animals had an order memory deficit for all spatial locations but had excellent item memory for the first spatial location of

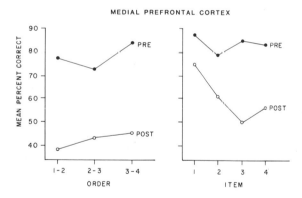

MEDIAL PREFRONTAL CORTEX

FIG. 12.3. Mean percentage correct responses as a function of serial order memory for spatial locations and item memory for spatial locations before (pre) and after (post) medial-prefrontal cortex lesions. During the study phase animals were exposed to a variable set of 4 spatial locations. During the test phase animals were given an order or item memory test. For the order memory test, the animals had to select of any two spatial locations, the location that occurred earlier in the study-phase sequence in order to receive an additional reinforcement. For the item memory test, the animals had to select of any two spatial locations, the spatial location that had been previously visited in the study phase sequence in order to receive an additional reinforcement.

the list with impaired item memory for the remaining spatial locations of the list. The possibility exists that poor performance for item information was due to the variable temporal-spatial sequences presented during the study phase. To test this possibility the lesioned animals were trained with a constant sequence (e.g., the same four arms were always selected), followed by tests of item and order memory. The results indicate that prefrontal-cortex lesioned animals had excellent item memory for all spatial locations of the list but had no memory for the order of presentation of the spatial locations (see Fig. 12.4). In additional tests this order deficit appeared even when the animals were allowed to self-order the spatial locations during the study phase or when the list length was only two spatial locations (Kesner & Holbrook, 1987). Thus, rats can remember the occurrence but not the temporal ordering of spatial events, suggesting that there is a correspondence between rats and humans with respect to the mnemonic functions of prefrontal cortex.

To what extent are the observed deficits due to direct damage of the medial prefrontal cortex or due to a diaschesis or mass action effect? Since recovery of function has not been observed in the above mentioned tasks, the deficits are probably not due to diaschesis. In order to test whether the observed deficits might be due to a mass action effect, animals with a comparable size lesion of another brain region, namely the parietal cortex, were tested in the same item and order and recognition memory task for spatial location information. The results indicated that animals with parietal cortex lesions are impaired for all events

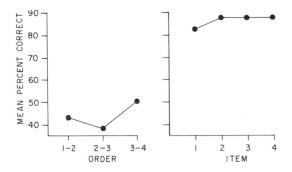

FIG. 12.4.   Mean percentage correct as a function of serial order and item memory using an invariant order for the study phase in animals with medial-prefrontal cortex lesions. During the study phase animals were exposed to a fixed set and order of 4 spatial locations. During the test phase, the animals were given an order or item memory test. For the order memory test, animals had to select of any two spatial locations, the spatial location that occurred earlier in the study phase sequence in order to receive an additional reinforcement. For the item memory test, animals had to select of any two spatial locations, the spatial location that had been previously visited in the study phase sequence in order to receive an additional reinforcement.

within the list on the item recognition task, as well as the last event or choice order on the order recognition task. These animals displayed normal memory for the first choice order within the list. Thus, for the first events within the list, there is a double dissociation effect with impaired performance on item recognition memory only for animals with parietal cortex lesions and impaired performance on order recognition memory only for animals with medial–prefrontal cortex lesions (Kesner & Gray, 1989). These results not only support the idea of functional specificity, but rule out a mass action interpretation of the deficits observed in animals with medial-prefrontal cortex lesions.

Are there any experiments in which memory for sequential presentation of nonspatial cues is critical for excellent performance within a task? In one experiment (Kesner & Allen, 1989), rats were required to enter one arm of an eight-arm radial maze containing a box with patterns painted on the walls and different somatosensory cues on the floor. This procedure was repeated until three different patterns (visual and somatosensory cues) had been presented for the trial. Each visual and somatosensory cue was presented in the same spatial location. Following the cue presentation phase, the rat was presented with an order memory probe. The probe consisted of the first and second, second and third, or first and third cues presented during the study phase. The animal was rewarded for entering the box containing the cue that occurred earlier in the sequence. Most rats were capable of learning to correctly respond to at least 1, and sometimes 2, of the memory probes (see Pre-level in Fig. 12.5). The data are based on the last 24 trials with 8 trials for each choice order. The best performance is represented as choice order 1. The animals then received large lesions of the medial prefrontal cortex or sham operations followed by 2 sets of 24 trials. Control animals maintained the same performance level and, thus, showed stable responding. In contrast, rats with medial-prefrontal cortex lesions performed at chance levels for all 3 choice orders (Fig. 12.5; Kesner & Allen, 1989). The data from this experiment suggest that the medial prefrontal cortex mediates some aspect of memory for sequential presentation of visual and somatosensory cues.

One shortcoming of any experiment with a sequential memory component is that the sequence is inherently confounded with the type of cue (e.g., spatial, visual, somatosensory, auditory, etc.) that is used. In order to answer this question, Hunt, Kesner, and DeSpain (1986) trained animals on a one-item delayed spatial matching-to-sample task. The animals were first trained in an eight-arm maze to enter a randomly selected arm in order to obtain reinforcement (study phase). Ten seconds after finding the food, the animal was removed from the maze for either a 0 sec-, 1 min-, or a 10-min delay period. Following the delay period all the doors were opened, and the animal was returned to the maze and given a retention test (test phase). Correct performance during the test phase required the animal to select among the eight arms the previously reinforced arm (i.e., the animal had to use a "win-stay" rule in order to receive an additional reinforcement). After extensive training rats made few errors. All rats received

FIG. 12.5. Mean percentage correct as a function of choice orders ranked from high to low before the lesion (Pre) and after medial-prefrontal cortex lesions (Post 1 & 2). During the study phase animals were exposed to a variable set of 3 visual and somatosensory cues. During the test phase animals had to select of any two sensory cues, the sensory cue that occurred earlier in the study phase sequence in order to receive an additional reinforcement.

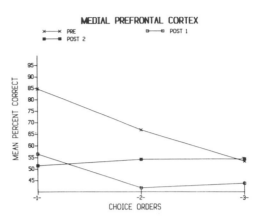

medial-prefrontal cortex or control lesions following training. After a 1-week recovery period, the rats were retested at each delay. The results are shown in Fig. 12.6 and indicate that, relative to controls, there are no deficits across any of the delays in animals with medial-prefrontal cortex lesions.

In another experiment, preliminary data indicate that animals with medial-prefrontal cortex lesions are also able to remember one visual and somatosensory cue at short retention delays (Kesner & Allen, 1989). Thus, the medial prefrontal cortex does not appear to mediate the memory representation of a single stimulus during the delay period, only the temporal order of a number of stimuli. These observations parallel the findings reported for frontal-lobe-damaged humans, in that memory at brief delays for tests of visual or tactile memory as well as digit and nonverbal object span is not impaired relative to control subjects (Ghent, Mishkin, & Teuber, 1962).

The possibility exists, however, that order memory was impaired in the Kesner and Holbrook (1987) and Kesner and Allen (1989) experiments because only

FIG. 12.6. Mean number of errors for animals with medial-prefrontal cortex (mpf) or sham-operated control (con) lesions as a function of delay in a delayed spatial matching-to-sample task. During the study phase animals were exposed to a single varied spatial location. During the test phase, following specific delays, animals were required to select the same spatial location (win-stay rule) among 8 possible spatial locations in order to receive additional reinforcement.

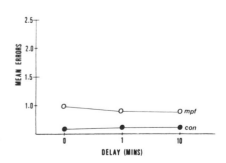

temporally adjacent items were selected. This is especially a problem because Estes (1986) has summarized data in humans demonstrating that order or sequential information is remembered better when more items (lag) occur between any two items to be tested. Thus, an experiment was designed to test order memory for items that were further apart temporally in the to-be-remembered sequence. Rats were initially trained on an eight-arm maze as described for the order recognition memory task. After extensive training, the rats were allowed on each trial (one per day) to visit all eight arms in an order that was randomly selected for that trial. This constituted the study phase. Immediately after the animal had received reinforcement from the last of the eight arms (i.e., completed the study phase), the test phase began. Only one test was given for each trial and consisted of opening two doors simultaneously. On a random basis, lags of 0, 1, 2, 3, 4, 5, or 6 were selected for the test. In the case of a lag of 0, the arms followed each other in the study phase; in the case of a lag of 6, in the study phase 6 items occurred between the two selected arms. The rule to be learned leading to an additional reinforcement was to choose the arm that occurred earlier in the sequence. The animals received a total of 56 trials with 8 tests randomly selected for each lag condition. In order to make comparisons with humans, the identical procedure was used for college students, but in this case spatial locations were presented one at a time as X's on a grid of 16 squares. The study phase consisted of the presentation of X's in 8 different locations. During the test phase subjects had to select from two X's that occurred during the study phase and that varied in terms of lag. There were 56 trials with 8 tests randomly selected for each lag condition. The results are shown in Fig. 12.7 and indicate that both rats and college students perform poorly for lag 0 but perform well for lags 1–6. College students, however, continue to improve with longer lags, whereas rats do not show such an improvement. Nevertheless, there appear to be comparable memory functions for rats and humans.

FIG. 12.7. Mean percentage correct as a function of lag between occurrences of items selected for the test phase in college students and rats. During the study phase college students or rats were exposed to a variable set of 8 spatial locations. During the test phase college students or animals had to select from any two spatial locations with a lag [number of spatial locations (0–6) between the previously visited spatial locations], the spatial location that occurred earlier in the study phase sequence.

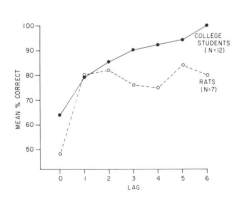

A subset of the animals then received lesions of the medial prefrontal cortex and after recovery from surgery were given an additional 56 trials. Results are shown in Fig. 12.8 and indicate that animals with medial-prefrontal cortex lesions could not remember order information even at the longest lag, even though there appeared to be some improvement with the longer lags. Recently, one patient with bilateral prefrontal cortex damage has been tested on the temporal lag task. Again, there was a marked impairment of order memory across lags.

To what extent are temporal organizational strategies mediated by the medial prefrontal cortex? The deficits seen in the variable item list task in comparison with the constant item list task suggest that the medial prefrontal cortex may indeed mediate temporal strategies. In order to test this idea more directly, Kesner and Allen (1989) trained animals on a list of four conditional discriminations or paired associates. In this case, a unique food item was presented in the center of an eight-arm maze and was always paired with the opening of a door in one of four spatial coordinates (e.g., Froot Loop cereal was paired with North, Cocoa Puff with South, etc.). The list of four paired associates was always presented sequentially, but in a random order with a 15-s intertrial interval in between presentations of each list. Prior to opening of the correct door leading to an additional piece of food, orienting responses (OR) were measured. A correct

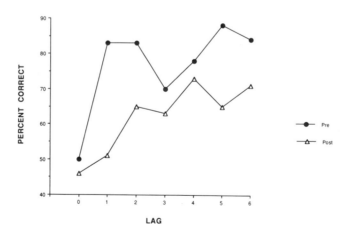

Medial Prefrontal Cortex Lesioned Animals

FIG. 12.8.   Mean percentage correct as a function of lag between occurrences of items selected for the test phase before (Pre) and after (Post) medial-prefrontal cortex lesions. During the study phase rats were exposed to a variable set of 8 spatial locations. During the test phase, rats had to select from any two spatial locations with a lag [number of spatial locations (0–6) between the previously visited spatial locations], the spatial location that occurred earlier in the study phase sequence.

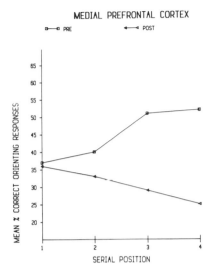

FIG. 12.9. Mean percentage correct orienting responses as a function of serial position within the list of presentation of four paired associates before (pre) and after (post) medial-prefrontal cortex lesions.

OR was defined as an orientation toward the appropriate door (e.g., North) for the specific food (e.g., Froot Loop) that was presented in the center of the maze. The correct door leading to the same food reinforcement was opened regardless of the location of the OR. Based on a variety of manipulations (changing extramaze cues, rotating the maze), it was concluded that animals use intramaze (i.e., nonspatial) visual and egocentric cues to perform correctly. Performance in this task is shown in Fig. 12.9 as a function of serial order of presentation of each paired associate. Note that there is a clear temporal structure with better performance on the later items within the list. Chance performance on this task is 25%. Support for the importance of generating a temporal structure comes from the observation that 15-s delays between each paired associate within the list attenuated the improved performance for the later items within the list. A retroactive analysis of relative frequency of errors revealed that animals made more errors the earlier the paired associate occurred within the list (Fig. 12.9). They made very few, if any, errors for the immediately preceding paired associate.

Animals with medial-prefrontal cortex lesions did not show improved performance across serial positions as shown in Fig. 12.9. A retroactive analysis of relative frequency of errors revealed that animals with lesions made many errors for paired associates that occurred throughout the list (Fig. 12.10).

Thus, the medial prefrontal cortex appears to play an important role in a task that involves the use of temporal strategies for adequate performance. These lesioned animals, however, could learn the task if only one paired associate item (minimizing the need for temporal organization) was used, demonstrating that they could use appropriate OR strategies and that they could learn a single paired associate based on nonspatial cues. Thus, only when sequential coding of infor-

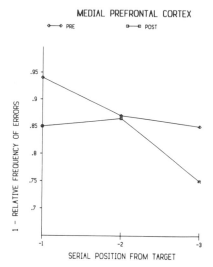

FIG. 12.10. Mean [1-(relative frequency of errors)] as a function of serial position (distance) from target before (pre) and after (post) medial-prefrontal cortex lesions.

mation is employed in this task does one observe impaired performance following medial-prefrontal cortex lesions.

Temporal organization is required for frequency memory (repetition), so it is not surprising that patients with prefrontal cortex damage are impaired in judgment for frequency of occurrence of specific items within a list. In order to elaborate further on possible correspondence in function of prefrontal cortex in rats and humans, a test was devised to study frequency memory in rats. The animals were tested on an 8-arm radial maze. On each trial (one per day) each animal was allowed to visit 4 arms to receive reinforcement in an order that was randomly selected for that trial. One of the arms was repeated with a lag of 1, 2, or 3 arms in between the repetition. The sequencing of the four arms and the

FIG. 12.11. Mean percentage correct as a function of repetition lag before (pre) and after (post) medial–prefrontal cortex lesions. During the study phase rats were exposed to a variable set of 4 spatial locations with one of the 4 spatial locations repeated a second time. During the test phase rats were required to choose between a once and twice presented spatial location. The correct response resulting in an additional reinforcement was to select the repeated spatial location.

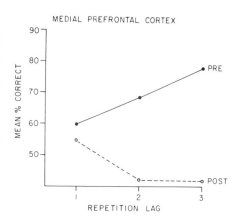

repetition of one of the arms was accomplished by sequentially opening Plexiglas doors to each arm (one at a time). This constituted the *study phase*. Within 20 seconds after entry into the last (fifth) arm of the study phase, the door in front of the repeated arm and the door in front of a nonrepeated arm were opened simultaneously. This constituted the *test phase*. The rule to be learned leading to an additional Froot Loop reinforcement was to choose the arm that had been *repeated* in the study phase sequence.

After extensive training, and based on at least 8 observations per lag, animals showed excellent memory for the repetition with a lag of 3 arms between a repetition (Fig. 12.11) but performed poorly for a lag of 1 or 2 arms, even when the data were analyzed separately for those trials on which the repetition occurred in the last serial position. This repetition lag effect (i.e., better retention with more items between a repetition) has also been reported for humans (Estes, 1986). The animals then received medial-prefrontal cortex aspiration lesions or served as sham-operated controls. After recovery from surgery, animals were given an additional 24 tests with 8 tests for each lag condition. Sham-operated animals showed no significant changes in performance. In contrast, animals with medial-prefrontal cortex lesions displayed a deficit for all lag conditions (see Fig. 12.11). The results, therefore, indicate that rats with medial-prefrontal cortex lesions have, like humans with prefrontal cortex damage, a similar deficit in performance of frequency memory. In summary, it appears that the dorsolateral cortex in humans and medial prefrontal cortex in the rat mediate temporal coding and temporal organization of information, supporting the idea that this neural region might represent information in the form of temporal attributes.

DORSOLATERAL OR MEDIAL PREFRONTAL CORTEX AND SPATIAL (EGOCENTRIC) MAPS

In addition to mediating a temporal map, the dorsolateral frontal cortex might also code, store, and retrieve information in reference to an egocentric spatial cognitive map within the expectancy- or knowledge-based memory system. Support for this hypothesis comes from the following studies. Monkeys with dorsolateral-frontal cortex lesions have deficits in delayed response, delayed alternation, and conditional response tasks (Fuster, 1980). In these tasks there are critical spatial and response components. For example, in the delayed response task, the correct spatial position is always relative to the animal's body position. Furthermore, in a delayed response task many prefrontal cortex cells fire differentially to cues that signal right–left responses (Goldman-Rakic, 1987), whereas other cells fire in anticipation of the correct motor response (Niki, 1975). In another task that presumably measures egocentric localization, namely right–left place discrimination reversal, Pohl (1973) has demonstrated that dorsolateral-prefrontal cortex lesioned monkeys are severely impaired. There is no deficit in a task that emphasizes allocentric localization, namely a landmark-discrimination reversal task. Similar deficits are seen in humans with frontal cortex damage in tasks that require the utilization of egocentric rather than allocentric space. For example, Semmes, Weinstein, Ghent, and Teuber (1963) have shown that frontal-cortex damaged subjects fail in a task requiring the touching of parts of one's body corresponding to those designated on a series of diagrams consisting of front and back views of a man. In contrast, these patients show no deficit on an allocentric spatial test requiring subjects to walk around a series of dots on the floor of a large room, guided by a plan of the room on which a route is traced. The subject carries the plan with him/her and uses it as a map. Butters, Soeldner, and Fedio (1972) have shown that frontal-cortex damaged patients have a deficit in an egocentric task (road map test used to evaluate right–left discrimination in space) but have no deficit in an allocentric task (copying two-dimensional stick patterns). A similar lack of deficit for patients with unilateral frontal lesions was found on a task that required memory for allocentric space, namely recall of spatial objects previously presented in an array (Smith & Milner, 1984).

In a final study in support of a role for the dorsolateral prefrontal cortex in egocentric spatial localization, Passingham (1978) trained monkeys on a counting task by requiring them to remember a specific number of previously made taps on a key. He found that dorsal-prefrontal-cortex lesioned monkeys were impaired in this task. This is of special interest because memory for movements requires egocentric processing of responses in specific spatial situations. Thus, in general it appears that medial prefrontal cortex is involved in coding egocentric localization, perhaps represented in the form of a spatial map.

In order to test whether the medial prefrontal cortex of the rat subserves egocentric localization functions similar to what has been described for dorsolateral-prefrontal cortex of humans, rats were tested in a task that emphasized the importance of processing and organizing egocentric localization information (Kesner, Farnsworth, & DiMattia, 1989). In this task, rats are placed at the end of a randomly selected arm in an 8-arm radial maze and trained to run to the immediately adjacent right or left arm in order to receive reinforcement. Animals first received medial prefrontal or parietal cortex aspiration lesions or served as sham-operated controls. A parietal-cortex lesioned group was included in this study, because it was assumed that this neural region would not be critical for acquiring this egocentric localization or egocentric spatial task. Following recovery from surgery, animals were familiarized with the apparatus and then given 3 trials a day with a 1-minute intertrial interval for 30 days. A trial consisted of placing the animal at the end of a randomly selected arm and allowing it to visit only 1 other arm. Visits to an adjacent arm resulted in food reinforcement. Visits to nonadjacent arms were scored as errors.

Results are shown in Fig. 12.12 as a function of blocks of trials with 9 trials within each block. The graph (Fig. 12.12) clearly indicates that control and parietal lesioned animals acquire the task easily within 90 trials. In contrast, the

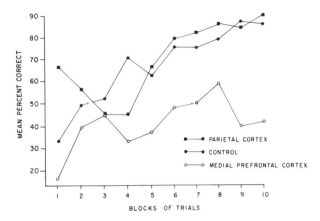

FIG. 12.12. Mean percentage of correct responses as a function of blocks of trials (9 trials per block) for animals with parietal cortex and medial-prefrontal cortex lesions or sham-operated controls.

animals with medial-prefrontal cortex lesions do not learn this task. Thus, it appears that the medial prefrontal cortex in the rat like dorsolateral cortex in humans mediates egocentric spatial information.

In conclusion, it can be stated that the medial prefrontal cortex of the rat subserves egocentric spatial and temporal information. Furthermore, the same function is mediated by dorsolateral frontal cortex of humans, suggesting that there are important parallels in frontal cortex function between rats and humans. Thus, the data provide strong support for the idea that the medial- or dorsolateral-prefrontal cortex subserves temporal and egocentric spatial cognitive maps.

MEDIAL PREFRONTAL CORTEX: EXPECTANCY- AND KNOWLEDGE-BASED MEMORY

Thus far, many studies have been presented in support of the comparative and independence assumptions, but very few studies have explicitly aimed to test whether the medial prefrontal cortex does indeed code information within the expectancy or knowledge-based memory system. Two studies are presented aimed at testing the contribution of the medial prefrontal cortex to this expectancy-based memory system. In the first study, rats were trained in an eight-arm maze with food available in four arms and no food available in the other four arms. Normally animals learn this maze by (a) not making any entries into arms that do not contain food and by (b) not making entries into baited arms that have already been visited during a given trial. Learning of the former rule is presumably based on the coding of information within the expectancy- or knowledge-based memory system. Learning of the latter rule is presumably based on the coding of information within the data-based memory system. After training, animals received medial-prefrontal cortex or sham lesions. Results indicate that medial-prefrontal cortex lesioned animals have a marked deficit in performance within the expectancy- or knowledge-based memory system as indicated by many entries into arms that do not contain food (Kesner, DiMattia, & Crutcher, 1987).

In a second study, sham-operated rats or animals with medial-prefrontal cortex lesions were tested in a task that provided an opportunity for rats to utilize retrospective and prospective memory codes, while remembering items (spatial locations) within short or long lists. More specifically, on any one trial a rat was presented with 2, 4, 6, 8, or 10 items (spatial locations) on a 12-arm radial maze followed 15 minutes later by 2 win-shift tests comprising a choice between a place previously visited and a novel place. Each animal was given a total of 20 trials with 8 tests for each point of interpolation or each list length (2, 4, 6, 8, or 10). Results are shown in Fig. 12.13 and indicate that sham-operated animals display an increase in errors as a function of point of interpolation or set size (2 to 8 items) followed by a decrease in errors with a set size of 10 items suggesting the use of both retrospective (the ability to remember the spatial locations previously visited) and prospective (the ability to anticipate the spatial locations that have not yet been visited) memory codes. In contrast, animals with medial-prefrontal cortex lesions made few errors for short list lengths, but a large number of errors for the longer list lengths, reflecting an inability to shift from a retrospective to prospective memory code.

These data suggest that the medial prefrontal cortex mediates prospective memories in a task that utilizes spatio-temporal information. Thus, there is additional support for a critical role for medial-prefrontal cortex in subserving

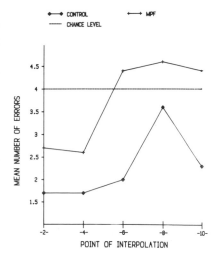

FIG. 12.13. Mean number of errors as a function of treatment (control vs. medial-prefrontal cortex (MPF) lesions) and point of interpolation of list length. Four errors represent chance performance. During the study phase rats were exposed to a variable set of 2, 4, 6, 8, or 10 spatial locations. During the test phase animals had to select of any two spatial locations, the spatial location that had not been visited during the study phase (win-shift rule) in order to receive an additional reinforcement.

critical temporal attributes within the expectancy- or knowledge-based memory system. Fuster (1985) has also suggested that dorsolateral prefrontal cortex of monkeys and humans mediates prospective functions of temporal ordering of information. Support for this possible prospective function comes from the findings that some cells in the dorsolateral-frontal cortex of monkeys show a gradual increase in their firing rate during the delay in apparent anticipation of the test phase of a delayed matching-to-sample, delayed response or delayed alternation task (Fuster, Bauer, & Jervey, 1982; Kojima, Matsumura, & Kubota, 1981; Niki, 1974a,1974b). Furthermore, Shallice (1982) has shown that left frontal-lobe damaged patients have a difficult time solving the Tower of Hanoi problem. This problem requires temporal ordering of simple moves and thus requires planning and the utilization of prospective codes.

CONCLUSION

In conclusion, data have been presented in support of a neurobiological model of an attribute theory of memory. More specifically, it has been shown that (a) the medial prefrontal cortex of rats or dorsolateral frontal cortex of monkeys and humans plays a unique role in mediating temporal and egocentric spatial cognitive maps, and (b) the prefrontal cortex appears to subserve these temporal and egocentric spatial maps within the expectancy- or knowledge-based memory system.

ACKNOWLEDGMENTS

Support for this research was provided by NIH Grant No. R01NS20771–07.

REFERENCES

Barker, D. J. (1967). Alterations in sequential behavior of rats following ablation of midline limbic cortex. *Journal of Comparative and Physiological Psychology, 3*, 453–604.

Butters, N., Soeldner, C., & Fedio, P. (1972). Comparison of parietal and frontal lobe spatial deficits in man: Extrapersonal vs. personal (egocentric) space. *Perception and Motor Skills, 34*, 27–34.

Domesick, V. B. (1972). Thalamic relationships of the medial cortex in the rat. *Brain, Behavior and Evolution, 6*, 457–483.

Estes, W. K. (1986). Memory for temporal information. In J. A. Michon & J. L. Jackson (Eds.), *Time, mind and behavior* (pp. 151–168). New York: Springer-Verlag.

Fuster, J. M. (1980). *The prefrontal cortex: Anatomy, physiology, and neuropsychology of the frontal lobe*. New York: Raven Press.

Fuster, J. M. (1984). Behavioral electrophysiology of the prefrontal cortex. *Trends in Neuroscience, 7*, 408–414.

Fuster, J. M. (1985). The prefrontal cortex, mediator of cross-temporal contingencies. *Human Neurobiology, 4,* 169–179.

Fuster, J. M., Bauer, R. H., & Jervey, J. P. (1982). Cellular discharge in the dorsolateral prefrontal cortex of the monkey in cognitive tasks. *Experimental Neurology, 77,* 679–694.

Ghent, L., Mishkin, M., & Teuber, H.-L. (1962). Short term memory after frontal lobe injury in man. *Journal of Comparative and Physiological Psychology, 55,* 705–709.

Goldman-Rakic, P. S. (1987). Circuitry of primate prefrontal cortex and regulation of behavior by representational memory (pp. 373–417). In V. B. Mountcastle, F. Plum, and S. R. Geiger (Eds.), *Handbook of physiology—The nervous system Vol. 5: Higher functions of the brain* (Part II). Bethesda, MD: American Physiological Society.

Groenewegen, H. J. (1988). Organization of the afferent connections of the mediodorsal thalamic nucleus in the rat, related to the mediodorsal-prefrontal topography. *Neuroscience, 24,* 379–431.

Hintzman, D. L., Grandy, C. A., & Gold, E. (1981). Memory for frequency: A comparison of two multiple trace theories. *Journal of Experimental Psychology: Human Learning and Memory, 7,* 231–240.

Hintzman, D. L., Nozawa, G., & Irmscher, M. (1982). Frequency as a nonpropositional attribute of memory. *Journal of Verbal Learning and Verbal Behavior, 21,* 127–141.

Hunt, M. A., Kesner, R. P., & DeSpain, M. J. (1986). The role of the hippocampus and the septo-hippocampal pathway on working (data-based) and reference (expectancy-based) memory in the rat. *Society for Neuroscience Abstract, 12,* 744.

Johnston, V. S., Hart, M., & Howell, W. (1974). The nature of the medial wall deficit in the rat. *Neuropsychologia, 12,* 497–503.

Kesner, R. P. (1980). An attribute analysis of memory: The role of the hippocampus. *Physiological Psychology, 8,* 189–197.

Kesner, R. P. (1989). *Medial prefrontal cortex lesions impair temporal strategies that mediate list learning of paired associates in rats.* (Unpublished observations).

Kesner, R. P., & Allen, M. (1989). *The effects of medial prefrontal cortex lesions impair temporal order for visual and somatosensory cues.* (Unpublished observations).

Kesner, R. P., DiMattia, B. V., & Crutcher, K. A. (1987). Evidence for neocortical involvement in reference memory. *Behavioral and Neural Biology, 47,* 40–53.

Kesner, R. P., Farnsworth, G., & DiMattia, B. V. (1989). Double-dissociation of egocentric and allocentric space following medial prefrontal and parietal cortex lesions in the rat. *Behavioral Neuroscience, 103,* 956–961.

Kesner, R. P., & Fineman, B. (1989). *Dissociation of item and order information in humans with frontal lobe damage.* (Unpublished observations).

Kesner, R. P., & Gray, M. L. (1989). Dissociation of item and order memory following parietal cortex lesions in the rat. *Behavioral Neuroscience, 103,* 907–910.

Kesner, R. P., & Holbrook, T. (1987). Dissociation of item and order spatial memory in rats following medial prefrontal cortex lesions. *Neuropsychologia, 25,* 653–664.

Kievet, J., & Kuypers, H. G. J. M. (1977). Organization of thalamo-cortical connectivity of the frontal lobe of the monkey. *Experimental Brain Research, 29,* 299–322.

Kojima, S., Matsumura, M., & Kubota, K. (1981). Prefrontal neuron activity during delayed-response performance without imperative GO signals in the monkey. *Experimental Neurology, 74,* 396–407.

Kolb, B., & Milner, B. (1981). Performance of complex arm and facial movements after focal brain lesions. *Neuropsychologia, 19,* 491–504.

Kolb, B., & Whishaw, I. Q. (1985). *Fundamentals of human neuropsychology* (2nd ed.). New York: W. H. Freeman.

Krettek, J. E., & Price, J. L. (1977). The cortical projections of the mediodorsal nucleus and adjacent thalamic nuclei in the rat. *Journal of Comparative Neurology, 171,* 157–192.

Leonard, C. M. (1969). The prefrontal cortex of the rat. I. Cortical projection of the mediodorsal nucleus. II. Efferent connections. *Brain Research, 12,* 321–343.

Lewinsohn, P. M., Zieler, J. L., Libet, J., Eyeberg, S., & Nielson, G. (1972). Short-term memory: A comparison between frontal and nonfrontal right- and left-hemisphere brain-damaged patients. *Journal of Comparative and Physiological Psychology, 81,* 248–255.

Milner, B. (1971). Interhemispheric differences in the localization of psychological processes in man. *British Medical Bulletin, 27,* 272–277.

Milner, B., Petrides, M., & Smith, M. L. (1985). Frontal lobes and the temporal organization of memory. *Human Neurobiology, 4,* 137–142.

Niki, H. (1974a). Prefrontal unit activity during delayed alternation in the monkey. I. Relation to direction of response. *Brain Research, 68,* 185–196.

Niki, H. (1974b). Prefrontal unit activity during delayed alternation in the monkey. II. Relation to absolute versus relative direction of response. *Brain Research, 68,* 185–196.

Niki, H. (1975). Differential activity of prefrontal units during right and left delayed response trials. In S. Kondo, M. Kawai, A. Ehara, & S. Kawamura (Eds.), *Symposia of the Fifth Congress of the International Primatological Society* (pp. 475–486). Tokyo: Japan Science Press.

Passingham, R. (1978). Information about movements in monkeys (Macaca Mulatta) with lesions of dorsal prefrontal cortex. *Brain Research, 152,* 313–328.

Petrides, M., & Milner, B. (1982). Deficits on subject-ordered tasks after frontal- and temporal-lobe lesions in man. *Neuropsychologia, 20,* 249–262.

Pinto-Hamuy, T., & Linck, P. (1965). Effect of frontal lesions on performance of sequential tasks by monkeys. *Experimental Neurology, 12,* 69–107.

Pohl, W. (1973). Dissociation of spatial discrimination deficits following frontal and parietal lesions in monkeys. *Journal of Comparative and Physiological Psychology, 82,* 227–239.

Pribram, K. H., Ahumada, A., Hartog, J., & Ross, L. (1964). A progress report on the neurological processes disturbed by frontal lesions in primates. In J. M. Warren & K. Akert (Eds.), *The frontal granular cortex and behavior.* New York: McGraw-Hill.

Pribram, K. H., & Tubbs, W. E. (1967). Short-term memory, parsing, and the primate frontal cortex. *Science, 156,* 1765–1767.

Rose, J. E., & Woolsey, C. N. (1948). The orbitofrontal cortex and its connections with the mediodorsal nucleus in rabbit, sheep, and cat. *Research Publication of the Association of Nervous and Mental Disease, 27,* 210–232.

Rosenkilde, C. E., & Divac, I. (1975). DRL performance following anteromedial cortical ablations in rats. *Brain Research, 95,* 142–146.

Semmes, J., Weinstein, S., Ghent, L., & Teuber, H. L. (1963). Correlates of impaired orientation in personal and extrapersonal space. *Brain, 86,* 747–772.

Shallice, T. (1982). Specific impairments of planning. *Philosophical Transactions of Royal Society of London B, 298,* 199–209.

Slotnick, B. M. (1967). Disturbances of maternal behavior in the rat following lesions of the cingulate cortex. *Behavior, 29,* 204–236.

Smith, M. L., & Milner, B. (1984). Differential effects of frontal-lobe lesions on cognitive estimation and spatial memory. *Neuropsychologia, 22,* 697–705.

Spear, N. F. (1976). Retrieval of memories: A psychobiological approach. In W. K. Estes (Ed.), *Handbook of learning and cognitive processes, Vol. 4, Attention and memory.* Hillsdale, NJ: Lawrence Erlbaum Associates.

Stamm, J. S. (1955). The function of the median cerebral cortex in maternal behavior of rats. *Journal of Comparative and Physiological Psychology, 48,* 347–356.

Underwood, B. J. (1969). Attributes of memory. *Psychological Reviews, 76,* 559–573.

13 System Properties of the Hippocampus

Theodore W. Berger
Julia L. Bassett
Center for Neuroscience
University of Pittsburgh

Multiple Memory Systems of the Mammalian Brain

One of the fundamental principles of mammalian brain function that has emerged from recent research is that learning and memory processes are not the province of a single neuronal system. Instead, several anatomically discrete systems each mediate the acquisition and/or storage of different classes of learned behaviors (Berger, Berry, & Thompson, 1986; Cohen, 1984; Desmond & Moore, 1982; Disterhoft & Segal, 1978; Gabriel et al., 1980; Gabriel & Sparenborg, 1987; Hirsch, 1974; LeDoux, 1987; Milner, 1970; Mishkin & Petri, 1984; O'Keefe & Nadel, 1975; Olds et al., 1972; Olton, Becker, & Handlemann, 1979; Squire, 1982; Thompson, Berger, & Madden, 1983) One of the most well-characterized examples of such a specialization of learning and memory function is the hippocampal formation. In humans, the hippocampus and adjacent limbic brain regions are essential for the formation of long-term memories of names and facts (i.e., "data-based" memory; Cohen & Squire, 1980; Zola-Morgan, Squire, & Amaral, 1986). In lower mammals an analogous specialization is expressed in the necessity of the hippocampus for learning higher order associations, or conditional operations (Berger & Orr, 1983; Eichenbaum, Fagan, Mathews, & Cohen, 1988; Fagan & Olton, 1986; Hirsch, 1974, 1980; Loechner & Weisz, 1987; Nadel & Willner, 1980; O'Keefe & Nadel, 1975; Port & Patterson, 1984; Ross et al., 1984.)

The hippocampus is not required for motor learning and classical conditioning of reflexes (Berger & Orr, 1983; Loechner & Weisz, 1987; Mauk & Thompson,

1987; Milner, 1970; Norman, Buchwald, & Villablanca, 1977; Oakley & Russell, 1972). That class of learned behaviors instead is dependent on the cerebellum and other brainstem regions (Berthier & Moore, 1983; McCormick & Thompson, 1984; Moore, Desmond, & Berthier, 1982; Thompson, 1986; Weisz & LoTurco, 1988). Associatively induced changes in reflexes also can occur independently of the cerebellum in the form of classically conditioned reflex facilitation (Weisz & LoTurco, 1988; Weisz & McInerney, 1988; Weisz & Walts, in press; Woody & Black-Cleworth, 1973). The anatomical substrates for associatively induced reflex facilitation have yet to be identified but are thought to involve brainstem reticular formation neurons intimately associated with the reflex pathway (Harvey, Gormezano, & Cool-Hauser, 1985; Weisz & LoTurco, 1988) and portions of the neocortex (Woody et al., 1974). An additional brain system that underlies classical conditioning of autonomic responses includes the amygdala. The results of lesion-induced behavior studies have shown that the neuronal system responsible for conditioned autonomic reflexes does not include either the hippocampus or the cerebellum (Jarrel et al., 1987; Kapp, Schwaber, & Driscoll, 1985; LeDoux & Iwata, 1987), although an interaction between amygdala and the hippocampus appears to be important for other classes of learned behaviors (Mishkin, 1978, 1982).

Functional Properties of Neurons Expressed at the System Level

The principle that information storage is distributed among several brain systems has added a qualitatively different dimension to the experimental study of the neurobiological basis of associative learning. The primary focus of research during the last two decades has been the identification of cellular and molecular mechanisms underlying learning-induced neuronal plasticity. Although impressive gains have been made in reaching this goal (for a recent review, see Byrne, 1987), no general principles have emerged that allow prediction of global system function or organismal behavior on the basis of mechanisms alone. This issue has emerged as a critical one because the same cellular mechanism may

---

[1]The term *population* is used in its traditional sense to designate a set of neurons that share a common morphology or connectivity. The term *system* is used to designate a set of populations of neurons that share a common anatomical boundary or connectivity. We define a functional property at the population level to be a relationship among the functional properties of a population of cells that provides greater predictability with respect to a stimulus and/or a behavioral response than does the activity of any one neuron of the population. We define functional property at a system level to be a relationship among the functional properties of its populations of neurons that provides greater predictability with respect to a stimulus and/or a behavioral response than does the activity of any one population of the system. The functional properties of a population can be considered equivalent to those of the system when the population consists of the projection neurons of the system (i.e., when activity of the population represents a summary measure of the activity of all other populations within the system). Further clarification of what is meant by "system property" is provided in the text.

lead to quite different changes in learned behavior depending on the memory system in which that mechanism is embedded. For this and other reasons, an intense interest has developed recently in establishing formalisms for representing and investigating the functional properties of neurons that are expressed uniquely at the levels of populations and systems[1] (Barto, 1985; Berger et al., 1988a, 1988b; Berger & Sclabassi, 1985; Burnod, 1988, Chauvet, 1988; Deadwyler, Hampson, Foster, & Marlowe, 1988; Georgopoulos, Schwartz, & Kettner, 1986; Gluck & Thompson, 1987; Grossberg, 1988; Hawkins & Kandel, 1984; Hopfield, 1982; Klopf, 1982; Kohonen, 1988; Levy, Anderson, & Lehmkuhle, 1985; Lynch, 1986; McNaughton & Morris, 1987; Moore et al., 1986; Rolls, 1986; Rummelhart & McClelland, 1986; Sclabassi, 1988; Traub et al., 1987; Zipser, 1986).

Two Classes of System Properties for Evaluating Hippocampal Function

Our own research has focused on the role of the hippocampus in associative learning and has involved studies at both the single cell and the system levels. This chapter reviews some of that research, as well as the work of others, in the context of two issues that we believe are central to understanding system properties of the hippocampus and, indeed, the system properties of any brain region. The first issue concerns the relationship between the global memory function performed by the hippocampus and the activities expressed by its intrinsic neurons during behavioral learning. The experimental strategy typically used for addressing this issue has been to formulate an hypothesis of hippocampal function on the basis of amnesia/lesion studies, design a behavioral task that maximizes the necessity of the hypothesized function, and then search for correlates of hippocampal unit activity during performance of that task. The first part of this chapter emphasizes a different strategy, one that does not attempt to define functional properties of the hippocampus based on a narrow range of testing conditions. Instead, we consider those characteristics of hippocampal unit activity that generalize from results using disparate behavioral paradigms, and that represent a convergence of findings despite differing initial hypotheses. Our assumption is that functional properties that are preserved despite such variability in testing conditions represent fundamental operating characteristics of the hippocampus at the system level and as such constitute the most appropriate foundation for further characterizations of hippocampal mnemonic function.

The second issue addressed in this chapter concerns the possibility of interactions between different memory systems, or, the extent to which the output of one memory system modifies the functioning of another. Although clinical and experimental data have demonstrated the capability for independence of memory functions associated with different brain systems (e.g., patients with bilateral temporal lobe damage can learn to solve a manual puzzle without being able to learn its name), it is unlikely that such independence characterizes the intact brain. Striking evidence exists for learned behaviors that depend on the additive and/or cooperative functioning of more than one memory system (e.g., Mishkin, 1978), and some of the more widely accepted theories of hippocampal function are based on the assertion that the learning deficits observed behaviorally after temporal lobe damage reflect the loss of hippocampal influence on other memory systems of the brain (Hirsh, 1974; Olton et al., 1979; Rawlins, 1985). From this perspective, the nature of interactions among different memory systems may be essential for understanding the functional properties intrinsic to each system, and by logical extension, for interpreting the amnesia that appears after one memory system is removed and the remaining systems interact in a different manner. In the second part of this chapter, we review studies in which we have investigated the possibility of interactions between the hippocampus and other brain systems. We feel the results strongly suggest that learning-dependent activity in the hippocampus transsynaptically modifies functioning of the cerebellum, and that it is through this interaction with the cerebellum that the hippocampus exerts an influence on learned behavior.

SYSTEM PROPERTIES OF THE HIPPOCAMPUS REVEALED BY THE ACTIVITY OF ITS INTRINSIC NEURONS

Hippocampal Pyramidal Cell Activity During Associative Learning: A Wide Range of Identified Correlates[2]

The hippocampus has been one of the most intensively studied brain systems with regard to the neurobiological basis of learning and memory (Isaacson, 1974; Isaacson, & Pribram, 1975, 1986; Lanfield & Deadwyler, 1988, Lynch, 1986; Seifert, 1983; Squire & Butters, 1984; Weinberger, McGaugh, & Lynch, 1985). One of the most consistent findings among the many studies of the hippocampus is that the activity of pyramidal neurons correlates with some aspect of learned behavior, or some aspect of the conditioned stimuli that controls learned behavior. Conditioned response (CR)- or conditioned stimulus (CS)-related pyramidal cell activity has been demonstrated to reflect primarily mnemonic aspects of the training task (though see Best & Best, 1976), and its robust appearance has been reported by many investigators despite wide differences in conditioning paradigms, motivational state of the animal, complexity of the association between

---

[2]We define *correlate* as a statistically significant increase or decrease in any parameter of spike discharge (not restricted to firing rate) that predicts the occurrence in time of (though need not be coincident with) a peripherally delivered stimulus or behavioral response. A more specific definition of the term *correlate* is offered in later sections of this chapter.

conditioning stimuli, and species (Berger, Rinaldi, Weisz, & Thompson, 1983; Berry & Oliver, 1983; Deadwyler et al., 1979, 1985; Disterhoft & Segal, 1978; Eichenbaum et al., 1987, 1989a, 1989b; Halgren et al., 1978, 1987; Holt & Thompson, 1984; Laroche et al., 1987; McNaughton et al., 1983; Muller & Kubie, 1987; Muller et al., 1987; O'Keefe, 1976; Olds et al., 1972; Olton et al., 1978; Patterson et al., 1979; Ranck, 1973; Solomon et al., 1986; Wible et al., 1986; Wiener & Eichenbaum, 1989).

The common observation of a strong correlation between hippocampal unit activity and conditioned stimuli or conditioned behavior has not been paralleled by a common interpretation: Proposed hippocampal functions inferred from these data include the formation of cognitive spatial maps, temporal patterning of learned behavior, detection of changes in environmental contingencies, and many others (Gray, 1982; Hirsh, 1974; O'Keefe & Nadel, 1975; Olton et al., 1979; Rawlins, 1985; Schmajuk, 1984). Such widely varying characterizations may indicate that the "optimal stimulus" for hippocampal neurons has yet to be identified correctly. If so, the failure has not occurred because the correlates of hippocampal unit activity are not sufficiently robust. Within the conditions of a particular experiment, the "tuning curve" of hippocampal neurons can be exquisitely narrow.

We have found this to be the case in our own recordings from antidromically identified pyramidal neurons during classical conditioning of the rabbit nictitating membrane (NM) (Berger et al., 1983), a preparation first developed by Gormezano (Gormezano et al., 1962, 1983) and adapted later by Thompson (Thompson et al., 1976) as a model system for neurobiological analyses. Our results showed that behavioral training is associated with a gradual increase in the frequency of pyramidal cell discharge during conditioning trials, but not during the intertrial intervals (Fig. 13.1). The increased discharge is time-locked to both the onset and amplitude of the behavioral response, resulting in a positive correlation between the probability of cell discharge and amplitude of the NM response (see later). Pyramidal cell firing precedes the onset of NM movement by approximately 50 ms (Berger et al., 1980a, 1983).

This learning-induced relationship between pyramidal cell activity and behavior is evident both early in training when nictitating membrane movement occurs as an unconditioned reflex (UCR) (Fig. 13.2A), and later in training when CRs are expressed during the CS-unconditioned stimulus (UCS) interval (Fig. 13.2B). As CRs develop, increased pyramidal cell activity also develops earlier in time to occur in the CS–UCS interval. Thus, the effect of conditioning is an enhancement of the within-trial firing rate of pyramidal cells, and an entrainment of activity to the amplitude-time course of the behavioral response.

These changes in hippocampal pyramidal cell activity—even the enhanced responsiveness during the UCR—reflect associative aspects of the training paradigm. They are not observed in response to explicitly unpaired presentations of the CS and UCS (Berger et al., 1976), or to paired CS–UCS presentations using

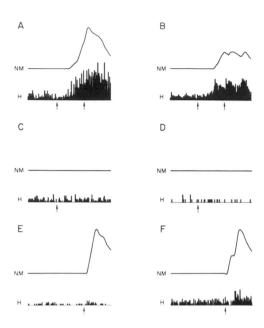

FIG. 13.1 Averaged nictitating membrane (NM) responses (top traces in all panels) and peristimulus time histograms (bottom traces in all panels) of hippocampal pyramidal cell firing during delay conditioning (A and B) and unpaired training (C–F) of the rabbit NM response. Panel A and panel B show data from two different pyramidal cells, respectively, recorded from two different animals. Panels sets C and E, and sets D and F show data from two different cells, respectively, recorded from two different animals. First arrow indicates onset of tone; second arrow indicates onset of airpuff. Interstimulus interval is 250 ms. H, hippocampus.

very short (e.g., 50 ms) interstimulus intervals that do not induce conditioned responding (Hoehler & Thompson, 1980). The fact that pyramidal cell activity during the UCR also represents an associative phenomenon is consistent with Gormezano's findings from the use of infrequent CS-alone presentations interpolated among paired trials. Using such a procedure, Coleman and Gormezano (1971) found that the first CRs to appear during training have latencies longer than the interstimulus interval, and thus are obscured by the UCR. During later phases of training when CRs are initiated during the CS–UCS interval, maximum CR amplitude is reached at the time when UCS onset would have occurred

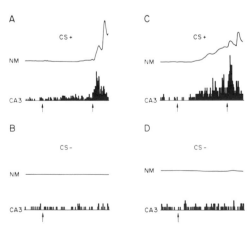

FIG. 13.2. Averaged NM responses (top traces) and peristimulus time histograms (bottom traces) of hippocampal pyramidal cell firing during early (A) and late (B) phases of two-tone discrimination conditioning of the NM response. Interstimulus interval is 750 ms.

and, thus, extend into the trial period associated with the UCR on a paired trial. Weisz also has shown recently that temporal contiguity of the CS and the UCS leads to stimulus-specific changes in the *reflex* nictitating membrane response within the first 5–10 training trials and precedes the development of CRs within the CS–UCS interval (Weisz & McInerney, 1988; Weisz & Walts, in press). Using CS alone trials presented periodically throughout the course of NM conditioning, we have found that the emergence of enhanced hippocampal pyramidal cell activity parallels both the training-induced changes in the reflex response and the development of CRs as traditionally defined within the CS–UCS interval (Berger et al., 1980a, 1983).

Specificity of Neuronal Correlates of Hippocampal Pyramidal Cells

Several aspects of our findings from use of the classically conditioned NM response paradigm provide examples of response properties of hippocampal pyramidal neurons during associative learning that have been observed by many investigators using a variety of paradigms. One such characteristic is a high degree of specificity in the environmental event with which pyramidal cell activity is correlated. Even though correlates have been identified for a wide range of stimuli and behavioral responses, only a limited subset of the total range is observed within any one experimental condition. For example, the enhanced firing of pyramidal neurons correlates highly with the amplitude-time course, or shape, of the NM conditioned response, and not with other aspects of the training procedure. This relationship is readily detectable even during individual trials (Berger et al., 1980a, 1983) and now has been observed using several different paradigms; trace conditioning (Disterhoft et al., 1988; Solomon et al., 1986), discrimination/reversal conditioning (Berger, 1984), and delay conditioning (Berger et al., 1983; Moore et al., 1982). Parameters of conditioned response shape, such as latency to peak NM amplitude, are known to be tightly coupled to the CS–UCS interstimulus interval (Schneiderman & Gormezano, 1964), and changes in the interstimulus interval result in corresponding changes in the within-trial distribution of pyramidal cell action potentials (compare Fig. 13.1A and 13.B, 250-ms interval, with Fig. 13.2A and 13.B, 750-ms interval). Consistent with this interpretation, both we (Orr & Berger, 1985) and others (Akase & Disterhoft, 1987; Port et al., 1985; Solomon et al., 1986) have shown that experimentally induced damage to the hippocampal formation is associated with an alteration in the amplitude-time course of the conditioned response (Fig. 13.3).

The same high degree of specificity characterizes the "spatial field correlates" exhibited by pyramidal neurons (typically identified as "complex spike" cells) during performance of learned optimal retrieval strategies in a maze (Deadwyler et al., 1987; Eichenbaum et al., 1987; 1989a, 1989b, McNaughton et al., 1983;

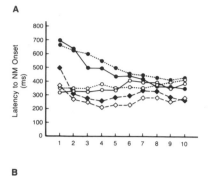

FIG. 13.3. Effects of bilateral hippocampectomy on conditioned NM response shape. Results for three parameters of response shape are shown: latency to onset (A), latency to peak amplitude (B), and integrated area of the response during the CS–UCS interval (C). Data are shown for operated control animals (OC), animals with damage to the parietal neocortex alone (CL), and animals with damage to hippocampus and overlying parietal neocortex (HL). Data have been "Vincentized" (i.e., displayed as a function of equal n^{th}'s to performance criteria.

Muller & Kubie, 1987; Muller et al., 1987; O'Keefe, 1976; Olton et al., 1978; Wible et al., 1986). Using this very different set of testing conditions, many investigators have found that the firing rate of pyramidal cells increases substantially when an animal is located only within a circumscribed portion of the maze. Although the size of the "spatial field" for a given cell can vary considerably, it is possible for large differences in firing rate to be determined by very small differences in spatial location (i.e., the boundaries of the spatial field can be well defined). A consistent finding also has been that spatial fields are remarkably stable within a particular environment and can maintain that stability for periods of days and even weeks (Best & Thompson, 1984).

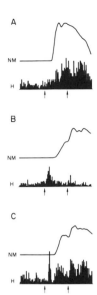

FIG. 13.4 Examples of peristimulus time histograms of three different classes of hippocampal neurons recorded during delay conditioning of the NM response: identified pyramidal neuron (A), nonpyramidal neuron (B), theta cell (C). Note that all cell types exhibit increased firing rates during the trial (trial onset indicated by the first arrow, which also indicates CS onset; second arrow indicates airpuff onset), but all have different correlates as determined by the pattern of discharge within the trial.

Results of some investigations may appear to be inconsistent with the characterization of a high degree of specificity in the correlates of hippocampal neurons. For example, Segal, Disterhoft, and Olds (1972) reported that classical conditioning led to increased CS-evoked firing rates of CA3 neurons, regardless of whether the CS predicted food reward (leading to food retrieval and consummatory behavior) or shock punishment (leading to immobility). Measurement of firing rate alone, however, often does not provide sufficient information to distinguish the appropriate correlate of a neuron, however, as illustrated by the following examples. During classical conditioning of the NM response, at least three different hippocampal cell types increase firing rate upon presentation of the CS, and yet each of their correlates is different and easily distinguishable when the within-trial pattern of firing is considered in addition to firing rate (Fig. 13.4). We also have found that differences in firing rate actually can mask a common correlate, as is true for the two theta cells shown in Fig. 13.5.

Sensitivity to Relationships Among Environmental Events

A second characteristic of hippocampal pyramidal cell firing that generalizes from a wide range of unit recording studies in the behaving animal is a remarkable sensitivity to relationships among environmental events. The firing rate of hippocampal pyramidal neurons does not change substantially when any one stimulus is presented in isolation. Instead, pyramidal cell firing rate changes primarily when two or more stimuli occur in temporal or spatial proximity to one other. As a result, one stimulus of a set can be predictive of another stimulus

FIG. 13.5. Examples of per-istimulus time histograms of two different classes of theta cells recorded during delay conditioning of the NM response. Note that both cells exhibit a periodicity in firing that corresponds to theta rhythm as determined by the within-trial pattern of discharge but display different directions of CS-induced change in firing rate (excitation for the cell shown in A; inhibition for the cell shown in B).

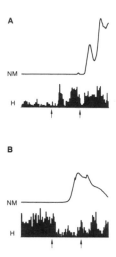

within the same set, or the entire set can be predictive of another event outside the set. In this manner, changes in the overall level of activity of pyramidal neurons are determined by the relationship between environmental events. For examples, investigations of hippocampal unit activity during NM conditioning consistently have found that CS-evoked increases in pyramidal cell activity develop only when the CS–UCS configuration is of the type that induces learned behavior. Enhanced pyramidal cell activity does not develop in response to unpaired CS and UCS events (Berger & Thompson, 1978a), and CS-alone presentations to previously trained animals leads to extinction of both conditioned responding and CS-evoked pyramidal cell activity (Berger & Thompson, 1982). Hoehler and Thompson (1980) provided a quantitative analysis of this relationship by using a range of CS–UCS intervals that included both optimal (those that lead to maximal amplitude CRs) and nonoptimal ISIs (those that support conditioned responding, but with less than maximal CRs). Their results showed that magnitude of the pyramidal cell response was highly correlated with amplitude of the CR.

When the CS–UCS configuration supports associative learning, it also has been found that changes in hippocampal unit activity occur very rapidly. For example, increases in pyramidal cell activity during NM conditioning can be detected within the first 5–10 trials, long before the 100–200 trials required for the development of conditioned responses within the CS–UCS interval (Berger & Thompson, 1978a; Berger et al., 1983). That hippocampal pyramidal neurons are among the first in the brain to respond to the particular stimulus conditions required for associative learning was first demonstrated in the rat by Olds and colleagues after a sampling of activity from a large number of brain structures (Olds et al., 1972; Segal, 1973), and by Disterhoft and Segal (1978) in their comparison of hippocampal and neocortical activity during discrimination reversal learning.

These correlates exhibited during classical conditioning represent a quantitative characterization of a commonly observed response property of hippocampal neurons in an open field or maze: the "mismatch" response, (e.g., an increase in firing rate that occurs when an animal exhibits searching behavior in the location of a previously available reward object). Although this responsiveness to differences or changes in reward first was noted in Ranck's classic study of hippocampal neuron activity during open-field exploration (Ranck, 1973), it since has been noted during performance of more explicitly trained maze behavior as well (Eichenbaum et al., 1987). Our assertion that pyramidal cell sensitivity to temporal contiguity during classical conditioning and "mismatch" responses during open field behavior represent two ends of the same continuum is supported by recent experiments of Gabriel and co-workers, who showed that hippocampal unit activity recorded from the pyramidal cell region in the rabbit exhibits the greatest magnitude change when the contingencies during avoidance conditioning are altered (Gabriel, Sparenborg, & Stoler, 1987).

When considered together, these data strongly suggest that changes in hippocampal responsiveness to peripheral stimuli do not remain static after initial acquisition, but that hippocampal neuronal response to a CS is modulated continually by the recent history of its pairing with the UCS. Deadwyler was the first to provide an elegant demonstration of such a phenomenon in a series of experiments using an instrumental discrimination conditioning paradigm with rats (Deadwyler, West, & Lynch, 1979). He and his colleagues showed that the responses of pyramidal neurons to the CS+ varied substantially depending on the number of CS− presentations that preceded it (Deadwyler et al., 1987). This "ongoing average" of the probability of CS–UCS pairings probably reflects changing synaptic bombardment from afferent sources, because short-latency CS-evoked potentials in the hippocampus (which precede the onset of unit discharge) exhibit the same exquisite sensitivity to the number of sequential CS+ and CS− occurrences in a randomly determined series of the two trial types (Deadwyler et al., 1985).

Distributed Representation:
The "Population Correlate"

Within the context of a particular learning task, the activity of the majority of pyramidal neurons is determined by the same environmental constraint (e.g., discharge rate changes upon presentation of a conditioned stimulus, upon execution of a conditioned response, or upon an animal locomoting to a specific location within a maze). Thus, the population of pyramidal neurons shares a common correlate. The activity of different pyramidal neurons, however, varies systematically in relation to different dimensions or features of that common correlate. In other words, the activity of any one neuron does not correspond to all features of a conditioned stimulus, conditioned response, or spatial location.

Conversely, the activity of different neurons corresponds to different features. This characteristic has been well documented in the case of spatial field properties of hippocampal pyramidal cells. One of the defining features of this phenomenon is that the activity of a large percentage of pyramidal cells is enhanced only when a rat is located within a particular region of the surface area of its immediate environment. Spatial field size for different cells is variable but can represent less than 5% of the total surface area (e.g., Figure 2 of O'Keefe, 1976). Although sometimes partially overlapping, the spatial fields for different pyramidal cells appear to be unique, so that the total surface area is represented by considering only the activity of a population of pyramidal neurons. In this sense, hippocampal pyramidal neurons exhibit a distributed representation of a correlate expressed uniquely at the level of population activity, or a "population correlate," in the same manner that the representation of an object or behavioral movement can be expressed optimally in the population activity of primary neocortical neurons (Georgopoulos et al., 1986).

With respect to our own research with the NM preparation, two sources of evidence support the notion of a distributed representation of the conditioned nictitating membrane response in the CS-evoked firing of hippocampal pyramidal cells. In analyses of single cell activity during conditioning, correlation coefficients were computed between the poststimulus time histogram representing the distribution of action potentials during all trials for which a cell was recorded, and the digital representation of the averaged nictitating membrane response for those same trials (Berger et al., 1983). Although many cells (68% of the total sample) exhibited a statistically significant and positive correlation with the conditioned response, different cells discharged maximally in correspondence with different components of the conditioned response. For example, Fig. 13.6B illustrates the within-trial activity pattern for one pyramidal cell that fired primarily in phase with the onset of the conditioned response; in contrast; Fig. 13.6C shows data for another pyramidal cell that fired primarily in phase with the component of the response occurring after UCS onset. Differences in the "phase relation" between the distribution of action potentials relative to the amplitude-time course of nictitating membrane extension for a large sample of pyramidal neurons ranged from $+81$ ms (enhanced unit activity precedes onset of the behavioral response) to -164 ms (enhanced unit activity follows onset of the behavioral response), indicating significant heterogeneity among neurons despite their common population correlate.

The second source of evidence comes from a comparison of the magnitude of correlation coefficients computed for averaged CS-elicited nictitating membrane responses and poststimulus time histograms generated either by single cells or small populations of cells. In all cases, the data considered were those for which the coefficient was statistically significant. For cases in which histograms were generated from recordings of single cells, the values of the coefficients ranged from 0.28–0.79. When histograms were generated from recordings of popula-

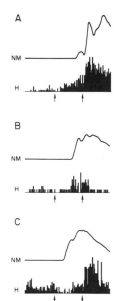

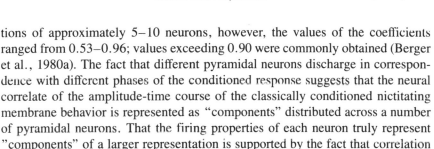

FIG. 13.6. Peristimulus time histograms showing different "phase" relations between the within-trial firing of three identified pyramidal cells and conditioned NM responses.

tions of approximately 5–10 neurons, however, the values of the coefficients ranged from 0.53–0.96; values exceeding 0.90 were commonly obtained (Berger et al., 1980a). The fact that different pyramidal neurons discharge in correspondence with different phases of the conditioned response suggests that the neural correlate of the amplitude-time course of the classically conditioned nictitating membrane behavior is represented as "components" distributed across a number of pyramidal neurons. That the firing properties of each neuron truly represent "components" of a larger representation is supported by the fact that correlation with behavior is larger when the activity of more than one neuron is considered.

Multiple "Clusters" of Neurons with the Same Population Correlate

An additional property of hippocampal pyramidal neurons expressed during performance of learned behaviors might be termed *clustering* of the correlates of single cells. The term clustering is used here to refer to the representation of apparently all major features of the population correlate by the firing of a relatively small subpopulation of pyramidal neurons. As just noted, it is not unusual for the combined activity of 5–10 neurons to exhibit a within-trial distribution of action potentials that correlates at a ≥0.90 level with the conditioned NM response shape. Furthermore, such highly correlated activity is expressed by neurons that can be recorded simultaneously from the same electrode (i.e., from a subpopulation of neurons that are in close proximity to one another).

The same property of multiple clusters also has been noted for spatial field correlates of hippocampal complex spike cells. A major proportion of the surface area of an animal's environment is well represented by the spatial fields of a small subpopulation of neurons (judging from published figures, certainly less than 50 cells). In addition, the spatial fields exhibited by adjacent cells do not relate in any obvious manner with respect to dimensions of the testing environment; investigators have reported that there is not an isomorphism between position in space and the topographic location of pyramidal cells within the hippocampus (O'Keefe, 1976; Olton et al., 1978). Instead, cells with spatial fields related to most regions of an animal's immediate environment can be found in close proximity within a localized region of the hippocampus. A quantitative investigation of the clustering of spatial fields has been reported recently by Eichenbaum et al. (1989b). Using a bundle of microelectrodes to simultaneously record the activity of several neurons within a small volume of hippocampus, Eichenbaum and co-workers found that the spatial fields of different neurons exhibited much greater overlap than would be expected on the basis of chance.

Thus, both for correlates recorded during classical conditioning and those recorded during exploration or reward retrieval in a maze, information sufficient to identify all major features of the population correlate is represented in the firing of a small subpopulation of spatially adjacent neurons. Furthermore, the size of the subpopulation is very small compared to the total number of pyramidal neurons exhibiting the same correlate, so that multiple representations of the population correlate must be distributed over many different subpopulations, or clusters, of cells. Although it remains possible that the output of each cluster varies with respect to some dimension of the population correlate, such a relationship has yet to be identified.

Context and Behavior Dependency
of the Population Correlate

The remarkable specificity that characterizes hippocampal neuronal correlates of learning suggests a high degree of invariance in the environmental stimulus (or complex of stimuli) to which pyramidal cells are most sensitive. However, the substantial body of data now available clearly indicates that, if such an optimal stimulus exists at all, it is not analogous to the "feature detection" exhibited by neurons within sensory neocortex. Sensory neocortical cells are most responsive to a set of specific features of a peripheral stimulus; the size of the set varies with hierarchical level within the visual system (e.g., the set is smaller for primary sensory cells than for neurons within secondary and tertiary regions of neocortex). Although the correlates of hippocampal pyramidal cells also are characterized by specificity and variable set size, they are distinguished from sensory neocortical cells in that the class of features contributing to the set can change as a function of the class of experimental condition.

To provide an example from research on classical conditioning, hippocampal pyramidal cell activity correlates highly with the amplitude-time course of nictitating membrane extension, but only if the ocular muscles are those activated by the UCS. When behaviors other than the nictitating membrane response are classically conditioned, hippocampal activity correlates with the amplitude-time course of the response system under CS control. This "response system" specificity of pyramidal cell correlates has been demonstrated using a behavioral preparation developed by Gormezano and associates for studying appetitive learning—classical conditioning of jaw movement in the rabbit. Using an intraoral injection of saccharin as the UCS, Smith, DiLollo, and Gormezano (1966) showed that water-deprived rabbits display a rhythmic series of jaw movements that is highly stereotypic with respect to amplitude and period. Classical conditioning of this behavior occurs readily, and as with the nictitating membrane response, can be almost purely associative in nature. Using this preparation, Berry and Oliver (1983) have shown that hippocampal neurons recorded from the CA1 pyramidal cell layer develop a within-trial increase in the frequency of spike discharge during conditioning that gradually occurs with a shorter latency from CS onset, in parallel with the development of conditioned jaw movement responses. Thus, hippocampal neurons exhibit a training-induced increase in CS-elicited firing rate during both nictitating membrane and jaw movement conditioning. The distribution of action potentials during CS onset, however, varies markedly depending on the paradigm. During jaw movement conditioning, action potentials occur with the greatest probability at the time of maximum jaw opening and thus exhibit a rhythmic bursting in synchrony with the periodicity of the behavioral response. As discussed earlier, a very different pattern of pyramidal cell discharge is exhibited during NM conditioning, which correlates with the amplitude-time course of that conditioned behavior.

Context dependency also has been demonstrated for spatial field correlates of hippocampal pyramidal cells. Perhaps the most instructive example comes from the work of Kubie and Ranck (1983), in which the activity of individual hippocampal pyramidal cells was monitored during three different behavioral settings: an elevated eight-arm maze, a smaller enclosure for instrumental conditioning of bar pressing for a food reward, and a home cage. All three settings or environments could be centered within the same observation/recording room, so that the distal spatial cues were identical. Kubie and Ranck found that a hippocampal "complex spike" cell could exhibit spatial correlates in all three different settings (i.e., mean firing rate of a neuron was highest when the animal occupied a particular location of each space). Intriguingly, however, the spatial field exhibited by one neuron also could vary substantially depending on the particular setting, to the extent that distal cues sufficient to discharge the cell in one setting could be virtually ineffective in another setting (or could be replaced by a different set of cues in another setting). Thus, as with results from studies of classically conditioned behavior, it is a *class of stimuli* that most accurately characterizes correlates of hippocampal unit activity during open-field behavior; the population correlate observed for any one experiment (i.e., a single member of the class) is determined by the specific conditions of that experiment.

The behavioral dependency of spatial field properties also has been demonstrated and, as we have noted previously (Berger, 1979), was evident in many of the initial descriptions of open-field correlates of pyramidal neurons (O'Keefe & Nadel, 1975; Ranck, 1973). McNaughton et al. (1983) have documented a direction specificity of spatial field correlates, and Eichenbaum et al. (1989b) recently have reported that the absolute firing rate within a spatial field can depend on direction, speed, and angle of turning.

Temporal Dynamics of Hippocampal Correlates

For such a wide range of highly specific correlates to be expressed within different environmental settings, the temporal dynamics governing functional properties of the hippocampus must allow the majority of pyramidal neurons to change correlates rapidly. The capability for rapid alteration in activity has been demonstrated by the sensitivity of hippocampal neurons to differences in the probability of reinforcement or UCS occurrence from the previous training session (Disterhoft & Segal, 1978) or even the previous training trial (Deadwyler et al., 1985), by the rapid changes in spatial fields of the same hippocampal neuron following changes in the testing environment (Kubie & Ranck, 1984; Muller & Kubie, 1987), and by the rapid formation of behavioral correlates during classical conditioning (Berger et al., 1983) and of spatial fields during initial exposure to a novel environment (Hill, 1978). Data that are possibly the most relevant to this issue recently were reported by Oliver and Berry (1986), who used a discrimination paradigm to classically condition NM movement to one CS and jaw movement to a second CS. When the two conditioned stimuli were delivered in a random sequence in the same training session, at least some hippocampal complex spike cells expressed different correlates (different within-trial patterns of action potential discharge) in response to each of CSs.

Many investigators have noted a rapid decay of conditioned hippocampal unit activity during extinction (Berger & Thompson, 1982; Deadwyler et al., 1979). To our knowledge, however, there is no report of a lasting or significant decay when the testing conditions are sufficient to support learned behavior. For example, neither overtraining (Kettner & Thompson, 1982) nor multiple discrimination reversals (Deadwyler et al., 1979) lead to any reduction in the amplitude of correlated unit activity. Thus, the population correlate has a duration determined only by the physical presence of the correlate, provided the context of the correlate includes the prerequisites for associative learning.

The Hippocampus as a Temporary Store
for Item-Specific Information

The findings from the studies just reviewed indicate that specific information about many different stimuli and classes of stimuli can be identified as the population correlate in the activity of hippocampal neurons. This generalization is based on observations by many investigators, a broad range of testing conditions, and substantial numbers of neurons recorded from the same general region of the hippocampus (usually the dorsal one-third to one-half). Given such a data base, it is unlikely that the qualitative differences among the many correlates identified for hippocampal pyramidal cells reflect either undersampling or sampling from nonoverlapping subpopulations of pyramidal cells. If the possibility of some systematic bias is excluded, then a collective consideration of all findings from recordings of unit activity in the behaving animal leads to the conclusion that hippocampal neurons are not "tuned" exclusively to a narrow range of stimuli or events, such as a class of testing conditions (e.g., those having stimuli that vary in time and not in space), a class of relationships among stimuli (e.g., those used to define classical conditioning and not instrumental conditioning, or those that define the organism's position in space), or a class of behaviors (those that involve movements of the whole organism and not individual reflexes). Instead, the major determinants of the population correlate are the specific features of the stimuli and/or responses defining any testing condition, provided that the testing condition also includes the necessary prerequisites for associative learning. This summary characterization of intrinsic hippocampal system properties also leads to the conclusion that the hippocampus functions as a temporary store for information about specific items relevant to ongoing learned behavior (though not necessarily being the sole determinant of ongoing behavior; see following), as suggested previously by Olton (Olton et al., 1979) and by Rawlins (1985).

Multiple, Independent, Electrophysiological Correlates of Associative Learning. This characterization of the hippocampus incorporates an important distinction between the different dimensions of hippocampal correlates that has not been integrated into past experimental strategies or theoretical discussions of hippocampal function although it is supported clearly by the electrophysiological studies outlined earlier. For example, experimental findings from classical conditioning of the nictitating membrane and jaw movement responses demonstrate that change in firing rate can reflect the number of training trials and requires temporal contiguity of the CS and UCS (compare left and right panels of Fig. 13.7). Firing pattern, on the other hand, reflects the conditioned behavioral response and is determined by the reflex pathway initiated by the UCS (compare top and bottom panels of Fig. 13.7).

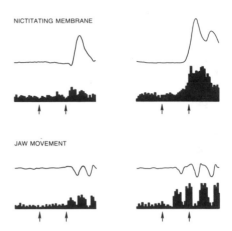

FIG. 13.7. Schematic representation of the relation between the CS-evoked rate of hippocampal pyramidal cell firing as a function of number of training trials (left: initial phase of conditioning; right: asymptotic phase of conditioning), and the relation between the pattern of pyramidal cell firing as a function of the conditioned behavioral response (top: nictitating membrane; bottom: jaw movement).

This simple distinction between firing rate and firing pattern provides a known example of the potential independence among the several dimensions of hippocampal correlates identified here. To provide a hypothetical example, the number of neurons contributing to a cluster (i.e., representing the separate features of the population correlate) may vary depending on the complexity of the population correlate and may be subject to change with conditioning as neural representations of features that share the same predictability with respect to behavior become consolidated. As another example, the extent of overlap among different clusters of neurons may vary depending on the possible relatedness of different features of the population correlate (e.g., the cells displaying spatial fields for the center of a multiarm maze may participate in several clusters or may occur in close proximity to one another), reflecting the number of permutations of arm entries relevant to guiding behavior. In contrast, cells with spatial fields representing the ends of maze arms may participate in only one cluster (or, may be located topographically distant from one another), reflecting the fact that arm ends cannot be related sequentially to an animal's behavior. These possibilities are admittedly speculative but are offered to illustrate the potential range of hippocampal correlates that have yet to be considered experimentally, and that can be readily investigated (e.g., comparing complex spike correlates recorded from animals in mazes with and without "bridges" between arm ends).

Multiple Correlates and Multiple Cellular Mechanisms. There is an important implication of the multidimensionality of hippocampal correlates: Different cellular mechanisms may underlie different learning-dependent dimensions of hippocampal unit activity. For example, mechanisms responsible for a change in the strength of synaptic drive, which would determine the magnitude of change in firing rate, may be unrelated to mechanisms responsible for the statistical distribution of spikes occurring at that altered rate (i.e., the information content of the spike train). Relevant to this issue are recent observations by Disterhoft,

Alkon, and associates (Disterhoft et al., 1986, 1988), that classical conditioning of the rabbit NM response results in a prominent reduction in the afterhyperpolarization (AHP) of CA1 pyramidal neurons. The AHP reduction requires temporal contiguity of the CS and UCS during behavioral training (is not observed in response to unpaired presentations of the CS and the UCS), and the magnitude of the reduction is proportional to the number of training trials administered. The effect is observed in approximately 60% of the CA1 neurons examined, a percentage nearly equivalent to those pyramidal neurons exhibiting a positive correlation between CS-induced firing pattern and amplitude-time course of the NM response (Berger et al., 1983). With respect to issue of cellular mechanisms, a decrease in amplitude of the AHP could account for the CS-induced increase in firing rate that occurs as a result of conditioning, as excitation-triggered spike activity will be enhanced if spike accommodation is reduced. The same mechanism cannot account in any obvious manner for the specificity in the pattern of discharge exhibited by pyramidal neurons (i.e., the correlation with amplitude-time course of the CR). The latter is irrelevant to any evaluation of the potential significance of the finding, however, because the within-trial specificity of the pattern may be determined by factors related to brain regions afferent to the hippocampus (see Berger et al., 1980a; Berger & Sclabassi, 1985) or may involve an additional mechanism intrinsic to the hippocampus that has yet to be identified. A single mechanism should not be anticipated because, as reviewed here, there is not a single correlate. When the correlate is multidimensional, it is reasonable to hypothesize multiple underlying mechanisms.

Distinction Between Correlate and Causal Factor. The extent to which correlates of associative learning are causally related to behavior remains one of the most important of the unresolved issues related to the hippocampus. As outlined in the opening sections of this chapter, robust unit activity correlates have been demonstrated for a wide range of learned behaviors. For virtually every species and training paradigm tested, it has been found that hippocampal correlates are expressed during tasks for which an intact hippocampus is not necessary (e.g., the learning of a simple association between two stimuli), such as the temporal contiguity of a CS and a UCS or the spatial contiguity of a stimulus and a food reward or an escape platform. It also has been a consistent finding that equally robust unit activity correlates are expressed during tasks for which an intact hippocampus is necessary (e.g., the learning of higher order associations such as discrimination reversals or conditional discriminations), and such as the learning of three-dimensional relationships among multiple distal cues and spatial location of a food reward or an escape platform. This remarkable inconsistency between findings of electrophysiological and lesion-behavior studies deserves restatement: Electrophysiological correlates of the output neurons of the hippocampus are expressed during the performance of all classes of learned behaviors, yet eliminating the output of the hippocampus disrupts only one class of learned behaviors—those based on higher order temporal and/or spatial relationships among environmental events.

Only one conclusion seems reasonable given these findings: Some brain system efferent to the hippocampus is responsible for the ultimate behavioral consequences of learning-related activity of hippocampal pyramidal neurons (e.g., by "gating" the activity of hippocampal pyramidal neurons to the motoneuron level). It is the activity of neurons in this as yet unidentified brain structure, and not the activity of hippocampal neurons, that should correlate differentially with higher order associations in a manner consistent with the effects of hippocampal damage. The findings from electrophysiological and lesion-behavior studies of the role of the hippocampus in learning appear to be contradictory only if it is assumed that the selective effect of a lesion should be paralleled by a selective number of stimulus conditions that lead to changes in unit activity. There currently is no experimental evidence to support this assumption. Thus, inferences concerning functional properties of the hippocampus based on lesions are unlikely to be meaningful in understanding the information content and information processing represented by the learning-related activity of intrinsic hippocampal neurons. Likewise, studies of the unit activity correlates of hippocampal neurons are unlikely to be meaningful in understanding the precise conditions under which the information represented by those correlates contributes to ongoing behavior.

SYSTEM PROPERTIES OF THE HIPPOCAMPUS EXPRESSED THROUGH ITS INTERACTION WITH OTHER MEMORY SYSTEMS

Role of the Hippocampus in the Learning of Higher Order Associations

As reviewed in the previous section, almost all current conceptions of hippocampal function assume that the structure is not necessary for rudimentary forms of learning (though see Akase & Disterhoft, 1987). There also is a substantial consensus that the hippocampus is involved in the learning of higher order associations among environmental events (Berger & Orr, 1983; Eichenbaum et al., 1988; Fagan & Olton, 1986; Hirsh, 1974, 1980; Loechner & Weisz, 1987; O'Keefe & Nadel, 1975; Solomon, 1977). For example, damage to the hippocampus results in a failure to utilize the multiple relationships among distal environmental cues specifying spatial location, though goal-directed reflexive and stereotypic movements are preserved (O'Keefe & Nadel, 1975). Likewise, learning and remembering that the temporal relationship between a tone and food depends on the relationship between the same tone and a light (i.e., a conditional discrimination) is lost upon hippocampectomy (Fig. 13.8). In contrast, nonconditional discriminations are learned and remembered readily (Loechner & Weisz, 1987; Ross et al., 1984). Conditional operations play a role in all learning

FIG. 13.8. Selective effect of bilateral hippocampectomy on conditional discriminative responding. Unoperated control rats (Group C), rats with aspiration lesions of the parietal neocortex (Group N), and rats with lesions of the hippocampus and overlying parietal neocortex (Group H) were trained using both a serial feature positive paradigm (conditional discrimination) and an auditory discrimination paradigm (nonconditional discrimination). In the conditional discrimination, a tone stimulus was followed by the delivery of food (T+) when it was preceded by a light stimulus, but not when the tone was presented alone (T−). In the nonconditional discrimination, a click stimulus was followed by the delivery of food (C+) whereas a noise stimulus was not (N−). The conditioned response was a

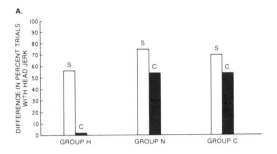

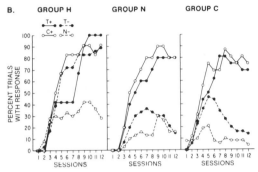

"head jerk" (see Holland & Ross, 1981). Panel A shows the difference in percentage of nonconditional (or simple, S) and conditional (C) trials in which rats exhibited a head jerk to the tone stimulus at an asymptotic point in training. Panel B shows development of conditioned responses throughout the entire course of training.

situations that demand a change in behavior in response to a change in contingencies of reward or punishment (Hirsh, 1980). Conditional operations become particularly important when the same stimuli are involved in specifying all possible contingencies, such as in the case of reversal learning paradigms (Berger & Orr, 1983; Fagan & Olton, 1986; Eichenbaum et al., 1988; Powell & Buchanan, 1980; Winocur & Olds, 1978). In such instances, cues can be sufficiently ambiguous that higher order relationships among stimuli provide the only information about response–reward contingencies.

Incompatibility of Hippocampal System Properties with Transmission of its Output via "Labeled Lines"

Because hippocampal function is the basis for a major class of learned behaviors, the activity of hippocampal output neurons ultimately must reach the level of alpha motoneurons that control striated musculature. It is unlikely, however, that hippocampal modification of motoneuron activity is accomplished through a series of point-to-point sequential connections from the hippocampus to the spinal cord. The results from electrophysiological studies of hippocampal activity in the behaving animal argue that hippocampal pyramidal neurons exhibit properties consistent with a "memory buffer" function, through which information concerning a wide range of stimuli and responses can be represented in the activity of any given pyramidal neuron. In contrast to primary sensory or motor systems, any one hippocampal pyramidal neuron does not appear to be dedicated to the representation of any one event or class of events. Instead, the activity of a given cell is determined primarily by the arbitrarily chosen stimulus conditions or response demands of each experimental task, to the extent that the majority of pyramidal neurons can discharge in association with different behaviors that are mediated by nonoverlapping motoneuron populations (e.g., Oliver & Berry, 1986).

A system with such operational characteristics obviously is not compatible with alpha motoneuron innervation of skeletal musculature, which rigidly maintains specificity of information through dedicated connectivity ("labeled lines", see Perkel & Bullock, 1968). Thus, hippocampal pyramidal neurons are most likely to exert a behavioral influence through their projection to a premotor system that could provide the interface between memory buffer and motoneuron functions. Two of the major premotor systems in the brain, the basal ganglia and the cerebellum, serve as control systems in providing on-line modification of virtually all reflexive and goal-directed movements related to striated musculature (Alexander & DeLong, 1985a, 1985b; Lisberger et al., 1987; Marshall, 1979; Pellionisz & Llinas, 1982; Rolls et al., 1983; Snyder et al., 1985). As a result, both systems are good candidates as transsynaptic targets of hippocampal output. In addition, both the basal ganglia and the cerebellum have been identified as structures essentially for conditioned reflexes and learned sequences of specific movements (Albus, 1971; Eccles, 1977; Gilbert, 1974; Ito, 1974; Marr, 1969; McCormick & Thompson, 1984; Mishkin and Petri, 1984; Moore & Berthier, 1987; Saint-Cyr et al., 1988; Thompson, 1986; West et al., 1987), raising the possibility that the hippocampus may influence motoneurons through interactions with other memory systems of the brain.

Multisynaptic Pathways Transmitting Hippocampal Output to Subcortical Brain Regions

As a first step in investigating the anatomical basis for transmitting hippocampal output to the level of the motoneuron, we have been mapping multisynaptic pathways that have the potential for connecting hippocampal pyramidal cells with subcortical premotor systems, including the basal ganglia and the cerebellum.

Subicular Projections to the Posterior Cingulate Gyrus. Our initial studies focused on the subiculum (Berger et al., 1980c), which is the target of the majority of efferents from the hippocampus. Although the subicular cortex projects to several brain regions, its reported output to the posterior cingulate gyrus

(Meibach & Siegel, 1977; Sorenson, 1980) was of particular interest in the context of the transsynaptic influence of hippocampal output on subcortical premotor structures. The cingulate gyrus provides input to both the caudate nucleus and the ventral pontine nuclei (Carman et al., 1963; Domesick, 1969); the ventral pontine nuclei are the major source of mossy fiber input to the cerebellum (Fig. 13.9).

The posterior cingulate gyrus has been subdivided into the cingulate cortex of Rose and Woolsey (1948; or the proisocortex, area 29d, of Vogt et al., 1986), and the retrosplenial cortex of Rose and Woolsey (or the periallocortex, area 29b/c, of Vogt). Using autoradiographic and horseradish peroxidase techniques, we found that the subiculum projects solely to the retrosplenial component of the posterior cingulate gyrus, terminating primarily in layer IV, with a lesser projection to layer I (Fig. 13.10); virtually no terminals were detected in the more dorsal, cingulate component. These projections to the retrosplenial arise from neurons contained only in the subiculum (and not the pre or parasubiculum), with the distribution of the cells of origin overlapping extensively with the location of terminal fields from the hippocampus.

The projection system is organized in a highly topographic manner, with neurons located near the septal pole of the subiculum projecting to more rostro-medial portions of the retrosplenial cortex; neurons located in progressively more posterior and temporal regions of the subiculum project to progressively more posterior and lateral regions of the retrosplenial. The equally topographic arrangement of intrinsic hippocampal circuitry (Andersen et al., 1971; Swanson et al., 1978), and of projections from hippocampus to the subicular cortex (Berger

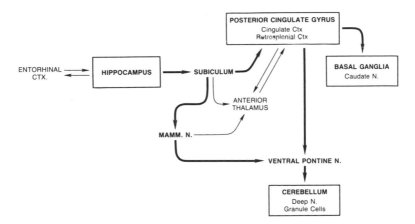

FIG. 13.9. Schematic representation of the anatomical relationship between the hippocampus/subiculum and major premotor brain systems mediated by subicular projections to the posterior cingulate gyrus, and efferent projections of the posterior cingulate to the caudate nucleus and to the ventral pontine nuclei.

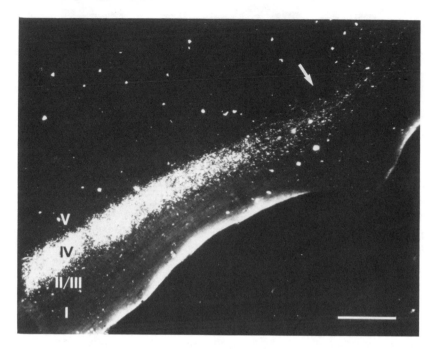

FIG. 13.10.   Example of a terminal field of subicular efferents within
the rabbit retrosplenial cortex, as demonstrated by the anterograde
transport of HRP injected into the subiculum.

et al., 1980c; Swanson & Cowan, 1977; VanGroen & Lopes de Silva, 1986),
indicates a mapping of the septo-temporal axis of pyramidal cell activity onto the
rostro-medial/postero-lateral axis of the retrosplenial cortex.

Projections from the Posterior Cingulate Gyrus to the Ventral Pons.   We
subsequently investigated the efferent systems of the posterior cingulate gyrus
and distinguished in our analysis between those arising from the retrosplenial
component and those arising from the cingulate component. Because of the
exclusive distribution of subicular efferents to the retrosplenial region, only brain
areas receiving efferents from the retrosplenial cortex could be influenced by
learning-dependent activity in the hippocampus. Although a number of different
projection sites were identified (Bassett & Berger, 1992), one of the most prominent projections was that to the ventral pontine nuclei. Of the seven ventral
pontine nuclei in the rabbit (Brodal & Jansen, 1946), the paramedian, lateral, and
the ventral gray are the primary targets of cingulate and retrosplenial efferents. In
contrast, the dorsolateral gray and nuclei reticularis tegmenti pontis receive a
lesser innervation. Although results indicated a moderate projection to the ped-
uncular and median gray, neither nucleus is well developed in the rabbit. Thus,
the majority of efferents to the ventral pons terminate within the paramedian,
lateral, and ventral nuclei.

Although studies in several species have detailed the selective distribution of efferents from each of the pontine nuclei to different regions of the cerebellum (Azizi et al., 1981; Brodal & Jansen, 1946; Kawamura & Hashikawa, 1981; Mihailoff et al., 1981), the irregular organization of retrosplenial terminals throughout multiple pontine nuclei prevents any immediate identification of cerebellar regions most likely to be influenced by hippocampal output. For example, within the paramedian, lateral, and ventral nuclei, terminals are clustered in rostrocaudally oriented columns that appear as discrete patches in coronal sections (Fig. 13.11). The patches vary greatly in their size and density; although a single patch often extends into two or three nuclei, it rarely fills an entire nucleus. Studies currently in progress are finding a highly localized distribution of ventral pontine projections to the cerebellar cortex, with fibers terminating in a "punctate" manner on selected subsets of granule cells within targeted lobules. Thus, although complex in organization, a discrete topography appears to be maintained in the successive projections from hippocampus to cerebellum.

Importantly, the cingulate subdivision was found to provide a more widespread input to the caudate nucleus than the retrosplenial cortex. Efferents origi-

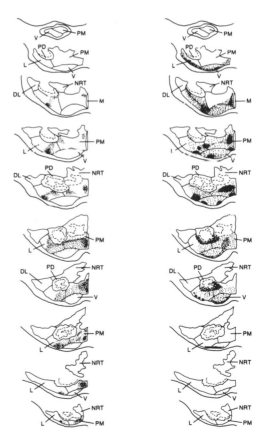

FIG. 13.11. Schematic representation of the pattern and density of terminal labeling from the rostral (top) to the caudal (bottom) extension of the ventral pontine nuclei. Labeling after ^{3}H-proline injection in the anterior retrosplenial (left), and posterior retrosplenial (right). DL = dorsolateral gray; L = lateral gray; M = medial gray; NRT = nucleus reticularis tegmenti pontis; PM = paramedian gray; V = ventral gray.

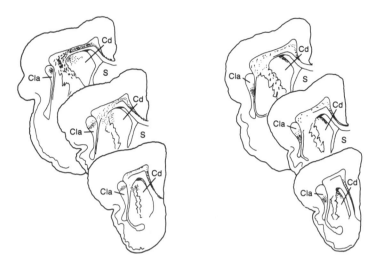

FIG. 13.12.   Schematic summary from a representative experiment of autoradiographic results showing projections from the cingulate cortex (left panel) and from the retrosplenial cortex (right panel) to the caudate nucleus (Cd) and claustrum (Cla). Note the restricted distribution of terminals from the retrosplenial cortex to the dorsomedial extent of the caudate. S, septum.

nating in the retrosplenial terminated only within a very narrow, periventricular zone (Fig. 13.12). These data suggest that the two components of the cingulate gyrus influence different subcortical motor systems, with the retrosplenial cortex providing a sparse input to a very limited region of the caudate nucleus and a substantial input to the ventral pontine nuclei. Because hippocampal output projected via connections with the subiculum reaches only the retrosplenial cortex, it is uncertain how to justify conceptions of limbic system contribution to behavior that are based on hippocampal modification of basal ganglia function (Gabriel et al., 1987; Mishkin & Petri, 1984), unless it is assumed that hippocampal/subicular output from temporal regions controls behavior through projections to the nucleus accumbens (Swanson & Cowan, 1977).

Behavioral Effect of Bilateral Lesions of the Retrosplenial Cortex.   These anatomical data suggest that successive projections to the subiculum, retrosplenial cortex, and ventral pons may provide an anatomical substrate for multisynaptic propagation of learning-related activity from the hippocampus to the cerebellum. We reasoned that if this hypothesis were correct, then interruption of transmission along the subiculo-retrosplenial-pontine pathway should result in a behavioral dysfunction similar to that observed after damage to the hippocampus.

Bilateral lesions of the retrosplenial cortex were performed using electrolytic techniques that spared the overlying neocortex and the cingulate portion of the cingulate gyrus. Using a light-tone discrimination reversal paradigm, we found that damage to the retrosplenial cortex resulted in a selective deficit in reversal learning (Fig. 13.13). Moreover, the deficit was as severe as that observed after combined bilateral damage to the hippocampus and subiculum (Berger et al., 1986b; Weikart & Berger, 1986). Solomon et al. (1986) have replicated this finding using a trace conditioning paradigm and also have demonstrated that damage restricted to the cingulum or retrosplenial cortex results in an altered

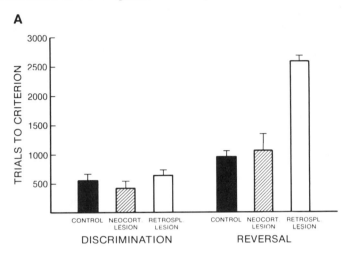

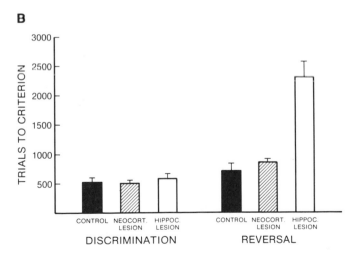

FIG. 13.13. Effects of lesions of the retrosplenial cortex (panel A) and the hippocampal/subicular cortices (panel B) on tone-light discrimination reversal conditioning of the rabbit NM response. Histograms indicate mean number of trials to performance criteria; error bars indicate S.E.M. Operated control group (CONTROL); neocortical lesion control (NEOCORT.); hippocampal lesion group (HIPPOC.); retrosplenial lesion group (RETROSPL.).

amplitude-time course of the conditioned NM response that is similar to that observed after hippocampal/subicular damage (Orr & Berger, 1985). Significantly, a recent clinical report supports the generality of an apparently similar mnemonic deficit resulting from damage to either the hippocampus or the retrosplenial cortex. Valenstein et al. (1987) described a patient who sustained hemorrhage-induced damage to the cingulum, retrosplenial cortex, and surrounding cortical areas. Hippocampal, parahippocampal, and thalamic regions previously implicated in mnemonic functions were not compromised, and only minimal damage of the fornix was found. Despite the temporal lobe regions being intact, the patient exhibited an anterograde amnesia for item-specific information identical to that observed after bilateral damage to the hippocampus.

Projections from the Subiculum and the Retrosplenial Cortex to the Anterior Thalamus.   A second prominent target of efferents originating from the posterior cingulate gyrus is the anterior thalamic complex (Bassett & Berger, 1992), a brain region that Gabriel and colleagues have demonstrated plays a central role in the development of instrumental avoidance behavior in the rabbit (Gabriel & Sparenborg, 1986). As outlined earlier, our major interest is in identifying possible multisynaptic pathways that could serve to transmit hippocampal output to the brainstem. Although the anterior thalamus receives afferents from the subiculum (Meibach & Siegel, 1977; Sikes et al., 1977; Swanson & Cowan, 1977), from both components of the posterior cingulate gyrus, and from the mammillary nuclei (Berger et al., 1980b), efferents from the anterior thalamus are distributed in a reciprocal manner to the cingulate and retrosplenial cortices (Berger et al., 1980b). As a result, the anterior thalamus is unlikely to serve as a direct link in any pathway transmitting learning-related activity from the hippocampus to the brainstem. As Gabriel has suggested, however, the anterior thalamic complex may exert a "gating" or permissive influence on transmission of information from the posterior cingulate cortex (Gabriel et al., 1980; Gabriel & Sparenborg, 1987). In such a manner, this component of the limbic system could play a role in determining the functional impact of the hippocampus on other brain systems.

Subicular-Mammillary-Ventral Pontine Projections.   The subiculum is the source of a well-known projection through the postcommissural fornix to the mammillary nuclei (Nauta, 1956; Raisman et al., 1966; Swanson & Cowan, 1975). Axons of the mammillary nuclei travel within the mammillo-peduncular pathway to terminate throughout several sites in the brainstem. Previous studies in the rat had reported the ventral pons to be one of those brainstem targets, though the relative strength of that projection had not been clear (Cruce, 1977; Guillary, 1955). We have examined the brainstem efferents of the mammillary body in the rabbit and found that projections to the ventral tegmental nuclei are far denser than those projecting to the ventral pons (Fig. 13.14). Only a very

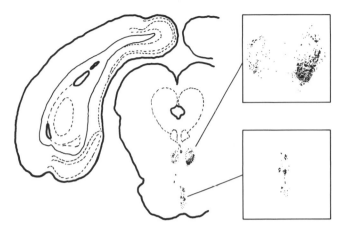

FIG. 13.14. Diagramatic representation of preliminary evidence for projections from the mammillary nuclei to the pons in the rabbit, as demonstrated by anterograde transport of WGA–HRP. Note the dense labeling in the ventral tegmental nuclei, and the much weaker labeling restricted to the medial pontine nucleus.

sparse projection to the median gray and the most medial portions of the paramedian gray were found. That these projections apparently play little role in mediating the contribution of hippocampal pyramidal cell activity to the conditioned NM response was indicated by the results of two additional experiments. First, lesions primarily of the medial mammillary nuclei have no effect on either discrimination or reversal conditioning (Fig. 13.15; Berger & Weikart, 1989), and unit recordings from either the medial or the lateral mammillary nuclei reveal no substantial CS- or UCS-related changes in firing rate or pattern, throughout the course of conditioning (Fig. 13.16; Berger & Thompson, 1978b).

FIG. 13.15. Representative example of the effects of lesions of the medial mammillary nucleus (left panel) on tone-light discrimination reversal conditioning of the NM response (right panel). Note the rapid course of both discrimination (DISCR.) and reversal phase of NM conditioning despite near-total bilateral damage of the medial mammillary nucleus. Graph shows percent conditioned response (%CR) rate as measured during the last half of each training session.

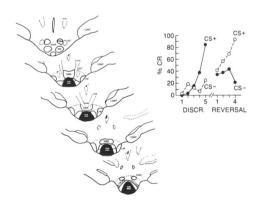

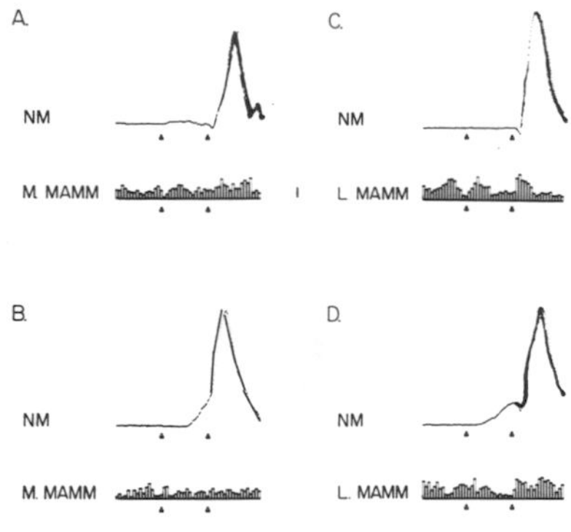

FIG. 13.16. Unit recordings from the medial (left panels) and lateral (right panels) mammillary nuclei during initial (top panels) and asymptotic (bottom panels) phases of NM conditioning.

Physiological Characteristics of the Hippocampal-Subicular-Retrosplenial-Pontine Circuit

Results of the studies outlined previously support the hypothesis that learning-induced changes in hippocampal pyramidal cell activity achieve behavioral expression through multisynaptic projections involving the subiculum and retrosplenial cortex (Fig. 13.17). The same results more definitively eliminate consideration of subicular projections to the mammillary nuclei as critical elements in such a circuit. The selective transmission of information to only one of the several projection targets of the subiculum is possible given the limited overlap that exists among the subpopulations of subicular neurons projecting to each target (Donovan & Wyss, 1981; Swanson et al., 1981). More conclusive support for the hypothesized role of the subiculum and retrosplenial, however, requires resolution of at least two additional issues. The first concerns the inference of transsynaptic propagation; that is, the assumption that hippocampal and retro-

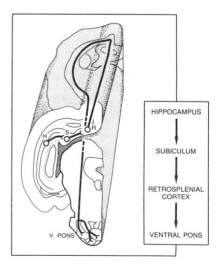

FIG. 13.17. Schematic of the proposed multisynaptic circuitry linking the hippocampus, subiculum, retrosplenial cortex, and ventral pontine nuclei.

splenial neurons share connectivity with a common population of subicular cells, such that activation of hippocampal pyramidal neurons initiates a sequential activation of subicular and retrosplenial cells. Results of the axonal transport studies reviewed earlier cannot exclude the possibility that neurons projecting to the retrosplenial cortex constitute a different population of neurons than those receiving input from the hippocampus. The disruption of discrimination reversal learning following damage to the retrosplenial cortex also cannot rule out the possibility that the posterior cingulate plays a role in reversal learning independent of the role played by the hippocampus (see Gabriel & Sparenborg, 1987).

Even if transsynaptic activation from hippocampus to the ventral pons were established, a second issue would concern the total propagation time through such a circuit. The average onset of CS-evoked increases in hippocampal pyramidal cell activity precedes the average onset of conditioned NM responses by approximately 50 ms. If conduction time through a hippocampal-subiculum-retrosplenial-pons-projection required less than 50 ms, it would be possible for learning-related hippocampal activity to play a role in all phases of the CR. A conduction time significantly greater than 50 ms would be more consistent with a contribution only to postinitiation phases of the CR. Such a finding would suggest that this circuit contributed to a reafference function (Moore, 1979), providing information that was perhaps necessary for response correction but not for "on-line" execution of the CR.

We have begun electrophysiological investigations to investigate these issues, examining the latencies to orthodromic activation of neurons in each component of the proposed hippocampus-to-cerebellum circuit after electrical stimulation of one of the proposed afferents. In addition, attempts were made to transsynaptically activate neurons in layer V of the retrosplenial cortex using electrical stimulation of the CA1 pyramidal cell field, and to antidromically and orthodromically activate single subicular neurons by stimulation of the retrosplenial cortex and hippocampus, respectively.

Results have shown that short-latency excitatory connections exist between the hippocampus and the subiculum, and between the subiculum and retrosplenial cortex. Subicular cells can be activated orthodromically within 2–3 ms of electrically stimulating the dorsal CA1 region (mean latency: 3.1 ± 1.1 ms using threshold intensity; 2.3 ± 0.8 ms using suprathreshold intensity; Fig. 13.18A). Electrical stimulation of the dorsal subiculum results within 3–5 ms in the orthodromic activation of layer V cells of the retrosplenial cortex (mean latency: 4.2 ± 1.6 ms using threshold stimulation; 3.5 ± 1.2 ms using suprathreshold stimulation; Fig. 13.18B); neurons within layer V are the cells of origin for efferents to the ventral pontine nuclei. In addition, cells in layer V of retrosplenial can be transsynaptically driven from the hippocampus at latencies (6.7 ± 2.3 ms) that are in close agreement with the additive latencies to monosynaptic activation of the subiculum and retrosplenial cortices (Fig. 13.18C). Finally, the same subiculum neurons activated orthodromically from the hippo-

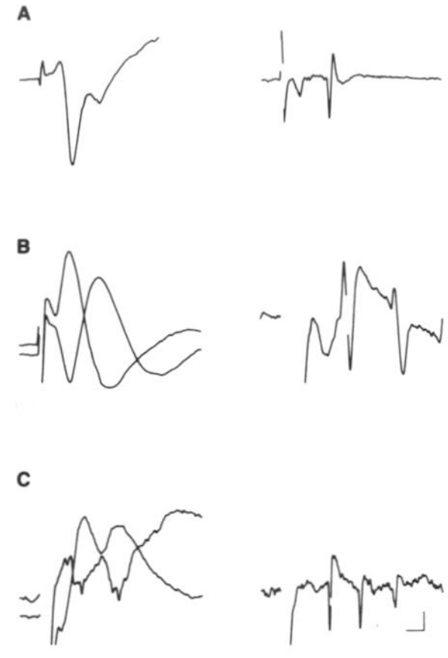

FIG. 13.18. *Panel A:* Orthodromic activation of the dorsal subiculum by electrical stimulation of the CA1 region of the hippocampus. Left: field potential negativity (calibrations, 400 uV and 1 ms); right: high-pass filtered action potential response (calibrations, 100 uV and 1 ms). *Panel B:* Orthodromic activation of the retrosplenial cortex by stimulation of the dorsal subiculum. Left: field potential negativity in layer V reverses to a positivity in the dendritic layer I (calibrations, 100 uV and 2 ms); right: high-pass filtered action potential response (calibrations, 40uV and 1 ms). *Panel C:* transsynaptic activation of layer V retrosplenial cortical neurons by stimulation of the CA1 region of the hippocampus. Left: biphasic field potential negativity (associated action potential discharges are small negative-going events at peak of field potential negativity), reverses to a positivity in layer I (calibrations, 100 uV and 2 ms); right: high-pass filtered spike responses in the retrosplenial cortex (calibrations, 40 mV and 2 ms).

campus also can be antidromically activated from the retrosplenial, indicating that at least a subpopulation of subicular cells both receives input from the hippocampus and provides output to the retrosplenial cortex (Fig. 13.19). The size of that subpopulation must be rather substantial, as disynaptic activation of retrosplenial neurons from the hippocampus was readily obtained. Preliminary characterization of retrosplenial input to the ventral pons indicates that cells within the ventral and paramedian gray can be driven orthodromically with latencies of approximately 4–7 ms.

In total, these findings suggest that learning-dependent responses of hippocampal pyramidal neurons are capable of modifying ventral pontine activity within 9–15 ms of the onset of hippocampal discharge. Such short-latency responses of pontine and cerebellar neurons to activation of hippocampal regions are consistent with previous studies in cat and rat (Grantyn et al., 1973; Saint-Cyr & Woodward, 1980). Because conduction along the subicular-retrosplenial

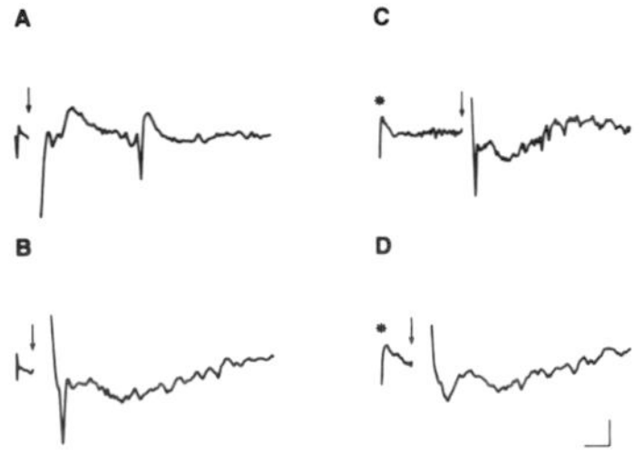

FIG. 13.19. Example of a single subicular neuron both orthodromically activated by stimulation of the CA1 region of the hippocampus (panel A) and antidromically activated by stimulation of the retrosplenial cortex (panel B). Panel C shows failure to collide a spontaneous occurring spike with an antidromically elicited spike when the interval between the two spikes is 6 ms (exceeding the latency to antidromic activation). Panel D shows collision of a spontaneously occurring spike by stimulation of retrosplenial cortex when a 1-ms interval is used (less than the latency to antidromic activation). Arrows mark stimulus onset. Asterisks mark spontaneous action potential triggering stimulation. Calibrations, 100 uV and 1 ms for A, B, & D; 100 uV and 2 ms for C.

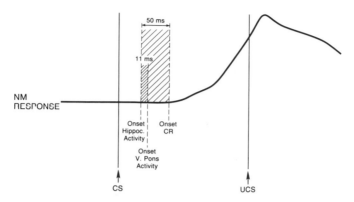

FIG. 13.20. Idealized summary of our findings regarding the relationship between the NM conditioned response the latencies to activation of hippocampal and ventral pontine neurons. Studies in awake
behaving animals have shown that the onset of conditioned hippocampal pyramidal cell activity precedes onset of the conditioned response (CR) by approximately 50 ms. Results of electrical stimulation
and recording studies in acutely prepared animals have shown that the
hippocampal-subicular-retrosplenial circuit is capable of propagating
excitatory output from the hippocampal CA1 area to the ventral pons
within 9–15 ms (latency of 11 ms shown). Thus, onset of ventral pontine activity may precede onset of the CR by approximately 35–40 ms.

pathway is rapid and powerful, and because CS-induced changes in pyramidal
cell firing rates precede NM conditioned response onset by an average of 50 ms
(though some cells precede NM onset by as much as 80 ms; see earlier), it is
possible that output from the hippocampus modifies cerebellar function in an
"on-line" manner during the expression of each conditioned response (Fig.
13.20).

Functional Significance of Limbic System Input
to the Ventral Pons

Recent findings of Thompson and colleagues and those of Solomon have provided indications as to the role of the ventral pontine nuclei in classically conditioned behavior. Both Lewis et al., (1987) and Steinmetz et al. (1986) have
shown that transection of the middle cerebellar peduncle prevents acquisition of
conditioned NM responding. Furthermore, Steinmetz et al. (1986) have shown
that electrical stimulation can serve as an effective CS for the development and
maintenance of conditioned NM responses and have reported neuroanatomical
evidence for a direct projection from the ventral cochlear nucleus to the ventral
pontine region. Koutalidis et al. (1988) have identified the circuitry underlying
visual CS information, and several of the brain sites involved also provide input
to the ventral pons. In addition, it is well established that the ventral pontine

nuclei receive afferents from a wide range of neocortical regions and are a major source of sensory input to the cerebellum (Robinson et al., 1984; Sotnichencko, 1976). Thus, output from the hippocampus may affect behavioral responding through modification of CS information transmitted to the cerebellum through the ventral pons.

Hierarchical Organization of Multiple Memory Systems

The characterization provided here of the relationship between the hippocampus and the cerebellum is consistent with findings that damage to limbic brain regions does not eliminate the capability for learning and remembering simple associations between environmental events, such as motor learning or what has been termed *procedural learning* in humans (Cohen & Squire, 1980). As outlined earlier, a consistent observation in animal studies has been that hippocampectomy disrupts learned behaviors that depend on conditional relationships among stimuli. Examples include behaviors that result from the use of serial feature-positive conditioning paradigms (Kehoe & Gormezano, 1986; Loechner & Weisz, 1987; Ross et al., 1984), or paradigms that require an animal to modify a previously learned response (see Hirsh, 1974). Within this conceptual framework, we propose that the subicular-retrosplenial-pontine projection provides the anatomical substrate for a modification of, and/or selection among, nonconditional associations (or, fundamental stimulus–response relationships) stored within the cerebellum. As has been demonstrated by others (see Thompson, 1986), output from the cerebellum initiates and/or modifies activity transmitted along reflex pathways that underlie a range of behaviors. Thus, we propose that the hippocampus alters behavior indirectly through modification of the cerebellum. In a such a manner, learned movements represent the combined contribution of several hierarchically organized memory system (Fig. 13.21).

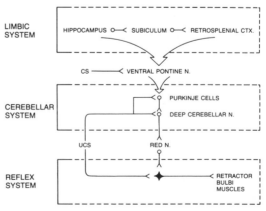

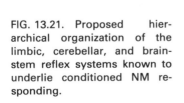

FIG. 13.21. Proposed hierarchical organization of the limbic, cerebellar, and brainstem reflex systems known to underlie conditioned NM responding.

SUMMARY

In this chapter we have attempted to define functional characteristics of the hippocampus in terms of two broad classes of system properties. The first class includes population characteristics of pyramidal neurons intrinsic to the hippocampus that are expressed during the performance of learned behaviors. Members of this class were identified as those characteristics of pyramidal cell activity that generalized with respect to several conditioning paradigms and a wide range of testing conditions. Five such system properties were identified and can be summarized as follows: (a) pyramidal cell activity exhibits a high degree of sensitivity to changes in relationships among environmental events; (b) pyramidal cell activity can correlate with many qualitatively different classes of environmental events, with the class of correlate depending on the testing conditions; (c) within a given set of testing conditions, activity of the majority of pyramidal neurons is determined by the same class of environmental event (i.e., correlates can be identified at the population level as well as the single cell level); (d) correlates expressed at the single cell level represent highly specific features of the population correlate; (e) the major features of the population correlate are expressed by subpopulations of anatomically adjacent neurons, or clusters.

The generality of these functional properties is supported by a recent analysis of unit activity recorded from depth electrodes implanted in the human hippocampus and parahippocampal gyrus (subjects were candidates for temporal lobe resection performed to treat an intractable epilepsy; Halgren, Heit, & Smith, 1987). Patients were instructed to memorize 10 different visually presented words. Half the words from the initial list of 10 items then were combined with five new words, and the new list was presented to the patients. Over 80% of the cells examined discharged preferentially upon presentation of one of the words belonging to the initial memorization list. Thus, the correlates of human hippocampal unit activity also display specificity: Cell activity was associated with only one of the total number of stimuli. Context dependency also is a major determinant: Correlates were found only for words from the initial memorization list, although all words were familiar to the subjects. Finally, each cell must be capable of expressing more than one correlate, because correlates could be found for 80% of the cells examined and yet all possible words were not tested. In addition, when a new list of words was utilized, the same cell exhibited correlates for one of the words on the new list.

The second class of system properties we considered were those related to interactions between the hippocampus and other neuronal systems of the brain in the expression of learned behavior. Our general assumption for defining this class of system properties is that learned behavior is the integrated output of all memory systems, and that the principles regulating integration between systems are likely to be fundamentally different than the principles underlying interactions among the individual elements within a system. With respect to the behavioral expression of hippocampal output, this second class of system properties must involve the process or processes through which learning-dependent information represented in the activity of hippocampal pyramidal cells ultimately is distributed to the motoneurons innervating muscles of the appropriate conditioned response. Although little is known about the interface between the hippocampus and motor systems, the available evidence suggests that such an interface is accomplished through: (a) a hierarchical organization of the brain's memory systems, whereby (b) output from the hippocampus is transmitted via projections involving the subiculum, retrosplenial cortex, and ventral pontine nuclei to modify fundamental stimulus–response relationships stored in the cerebellum; (c) output of the cerebellum then initiates or modifies activity transmitted along reflex pathways; (d) propagation time from the hippocampus to the cerebellum is sufficiently rapid to allow for a contribution of pyramidal cell output to currently executed behavior; (e) at least one of the neural structures efferent to the hippocampus (e.g., subiculum, retrosplenial cortex, anterior thalamus) may play a major role in determining whether or not learning-related activity in the hippocampus has a behavioral consequence.

In conclusion, the system properties of the hippocampus proposed here must be considered only initial characterizations in view of the very early stage of research in this area. Nonetheless, each of the properties identified represents a distillation of observations made by many different investigators using a variety of behavioral testing conditions. Together, they provide a critical set of constraints for further conceptualizations of hippocampal function, particularly those attempting a more formal characterization of hippocampal system properties through the study of network dynamics (Barrionuevo et al., 1989; Berger et al., 1989; Brown et al., 1988; Harty et al., 1992; Levy et al., 1985; McNaughton & Morris, 1987; Rolls, 1986; Sclabassi et al., 1988a, 1989; Traub et al., 1987a,b). Whatever models emerge from such research, they must incorporate properties capable of accounting for the principles of hippocampal function outlined here.

ACKNOWLEDGMENTS

This research was supported by grants from the NSF (BNS–8843368), NIMH (MH00343), ONR (N00014–87–K–0472), and AFOSR (89–0197). We also gratefully acknowledge Dr. German Barrionuevo and Dr. Donald Weisz for their helpful critiques of earlier versions of this chapter.

REFERENCES

Akase, E., & Disterhoft, J. F. (1987). Hippocampal lesions can impair memory of a short-delay eyeblink conditioned response in rabbit. *Society for Neuroscience Abstracts, 13*, 841.

Albus, J. D. (1971). A theory of cerebellar function. *Mathematical Bioscience, 10*, 25–61.

Alexander, G. E., & DeLong, M. R. (1985a). Microstimulation of the primate neostriatum. I. Physiological properties of striatal microexcitable zones. *Journal of Neurophysiology, 53*, 1401–1416.

Alexander, G. E., & DeLong, M. R. (1985b). Microstimulation of the primate neostriatum. II. Somatotopic organization of striatal microexcitable zones and their relation to neuronal response properties. *Journal of Neurophysiology, 53,* 1417–1430.

Andersen, P., Bliss, T. V. P., & Skrede, K. K. (1971). Lamellar organization of hippocampal excitatory pathways. *Experimental Brain Research, 13,* 222–238.

Azizi, S. A., Mihailoff, G. A., Burne, R. A., & Woodward, D. J. (1981). The pontocerebellar system in the rat: An HRP study. Posterior vermis. *Journal of Comparative Neurology, 197,* 543–558.

Barrionuevo, G., Harty, T. P., Bradler, J. E., Sclabassi, R. J., & Berger, T. W. (1989). *Nonlinear response properties of the in vitro hippocampal perforant path-dentate projection: Comparison with in vivo preparations.* Submitted for publication.

Barto, A. G. (1985). Learning by statistical cooperation of self-interested neuron-like computing elements. *Human Neurobiology, 4,* 229–256.

Bassett, J. L., & Berger, T. W. (1992). *Subcortical projections of the posterior cingulate gyrus in rabbit.* Submitted for publication.

Berger, T. W. (1979). Selective activation of hippocampal neurons. *Behavioral and Brain Sciences, 2,* 495–496.

Berger, T. W. (1984). Neuronal representation of associative learning in the hippocampus. In N. Butters & L. R. Squire (Eds.), *The neuropsychology of memory* (pp. 443–461). New York: Guilford Press.

Berger, T. W., Alger, B., & Thompson, R. F. (1976). Neuronal substrate of classical conditioning in the hippocampus. *Science, 192,* 483–485.

Berger, T. W., Berry, S. D., & Thompson, R. F. (1986a). Role of the hippocampus in classical conditioning of aversive and appetitive behaviors. In R. L. Isaacson & K. H. Pribram (Eds.), *The hippocampus* (pp. 203–239). New York: Plenum Press.

Berger, T. W., Eriksson, J. L., Ciarolla, D. A., & Sclabassi, R. J. (1988a). Nonlinear systems analysis of the perforant path-dentate projection. II. Effects of random train stimulation. *Journal of Neurophysiology, 60,* 1077–1094.

Berger, T. W., Eriksson, J. L., Ciarolla, D. A., & Sclabassi, R. J. (1988b). Nonlinear systems analysis of the perforant path-dentate projection. III. Comparison of random train and paired impulse analyses. *Journal of Neurophysiology, 60,* 1095–1109.

Berger, T. W., Harty, T. P., Sclabassi, R. J., & Barrionuevo, G. (1989). Modeling of neuronal networks through experimental decomposition. In V. Z. Marmarelis (Ed.), *Advanced methods of physiological system modeling.* New York: Plenum Press.

Berger, T. W., Laham, R. I., & Thompson, R. F. (1980a). Hippocampal unit-behavior correlations during classical conditioning. *Brain Research, 193,* 229–248.

Berger, T. W., Milner, T. A., Swanson, G. W., Lynch, G. S., & Thompson, R. F. (1980b). Reciprocal anatomical connections between anterior thalamus and cingulate-retrosplenial cortex in the rabbit. *Brain Research, 201,* 411–417.

Berger, T. W., & Orr, W. B. (1983). Hippocampectomy selectively disrupts discrimination reversal conditioning of the rabbit nictitating membrane response. *Behavioural Brain Research, 8,* 49–68.

Berger, T. W., Rinaldi, P., Weisz, D. J., & Thompson, R. F. (1983). Single unit analysis of different hippocampal cell types during classical conditioning of the rabbit nictitating membrane response. *Journal of Neurophysiology, 50,* 1197–1221.

Berger, T. W., Robinson, G. B., Port, R. L., & Sclabassi, R. J. (1987). Nonlinear systems analysis of the functional properties of the hippocampal formation. In V. Z. Marmarelis (Ed.), *Advanced methods of physiological system modeling* (pp. 73–103). Los Angeles: Biomedical Simulations.

Berger, T. W., & Sclabassi, R. J. (1985). Nonlinear systems analysis and its application to study of the functional properties of neural systems. In N. M. Weinberger, J. L. McGaugh, & G. Lynch (Eds.), *Memory systems of the brain: Animal and human cognitive processes* (pp. 120–133). New York: Guilford Press.

Berger, T. W., Swanson, G. W., Milner, T. A., Lynch, G. S., & Thompson, R. F. (1980c). Reciprocal anatomical connections between hippocampal and subiculum: Evidence for subicular innervation of regio superior. *Brain Research, 183,* 265–276.

Berger, T. W., & Thompson, R. F. (1978a). Neuronal plasticity in the limbic system during classical conditioning of the rabbit nictitating membrane response. I. The hippocampus. *Brain Research, 145,* 323–346.

Berger, T. W., & Thompson, R. F. (1978b). Neuronal plasticity in the limbic system during classical conditioning of the rabbit nictitating membrane response. II. Septum and mammillary bodies. *Brain Research, 156,* 293–314.

Berger, T. W., & Thompson, R. F. (1982). Hippocampal cellular plasticity during extinction of classically conditioned nictitating membrane behavior. *Behavioural Brain Research, 4,* 63–76.

Berger, T. W., & Weikart, C. L. (1989). *Effects of mammillary lesions on discrimination reversal conditioning of the rabbit nictitating membrane response.* In preparation.

Berger, T. W., Weikart, C. L., Bassett, J. L., & Orr, W. B. (1986b). Lesions of the retrosplenial cortex produce deficits in reversal learning of the rabbit nictitating membrane response: Implications for potential interactions between hippocampal and cerebellar brain systems. *Behavioral Neuroscience, 100,* 796–803.

Berger, T. W., & Weisz, D. J. (1987). Single unit analysis of hippocampal pyramidal and granule cells during classical conditioning of the rabbit nictitating membrane response: In I. Gormezano, W. F. Prokasy, & R. F. Thompson (Eds.), *Classical conditioning III: Behavioral, neurophysiological and neurochemical studies in the rabbit* (pp. 217–253). Hillsdale, NJ: Lawrence Erlbaum Associates.

Berry, S. E., & Oliver, C. G. (1983). Hippocampal activity during appetitive classical conditioning in rabbits. *Society for Neuroscience Abstracts, 9,* 645.

Berthier, N.E., & Moore, J. W. (1983). The nictitating membrane response: An electrophysiological study of the abducens nerve and nucleus and the accessory abducens nucleus in rabbit. *Brain Research, 258,* 201–210.

Best, M. R., & Best, P. J. (1976). The effects of state of consciousness and latent inhibition on hippocampal unit activity in the rat during conditioning. *Experimental Neurology, 51,* 564–573.

Best, P. J., & Thompson, L. T. (1984). Hippocampal cells which have place field activity also show changes in activity during classical conditioning. *Society for Neuroscience Abstracts, 10,* 125.

Brodal, A., & Jansen, J. (1946). The ponto-cerebellar projection in the rabbit and cat. *Journal of Comparative Neurology, 84,* 31–118.

Burnod, Y. (1988). *Cerebral cortex and behavioral adaptation: A possible mechanism.* Paris: University of Leige Press.

Byrne, J. H. (1987). Cellular analysis of associative learning. *Physiological Reviews, 67,* 329–439.

Carman, J. B. Cowan, W. M., & Powell, T. P. S. (1963). The organization of corticostriate connexions in the rabbit. *Brain, 81,* 525–562.

Chauvet, G. (1988). Correlation principle and physiological interpretation of synaptic efficacy. In J. Delacour & J. C. S. Levy (Eds.), *Systems with learning and memory abilities.* Amsterdam: Elsevier.

Cohen, N. J. (1984). Preserved learning capacity in amnesia: Evidence for multiple memory systems. In N. Butters & L. R. Squire (Eds.), *The neuropsychology of memory* (pp. 83–103). New York: Guilford Press.

Cohen, N. J., & Squire, L. R. (1980). Preserved learning and retention of pattern-analyzing skill in amnesia: Dissociation of knowing how and knowing that. *Science, 210,* 207–210.

Coleman, S. R., & Gormezano, I. (1971). Classical conditioning of the rabbit's (Oryctolagus Cuniculus) nictitating membrane response under symmetrical CS–UCS interval shift. *Journal of Comparative and Physiological Psychology, 77,* 447–455.

Cruce, J. A. F. (1977). An autoradiographic study of the descending connections of the mammillary nuclei of the rat. *Journal of Comparative Neurology, 176,* 631–644.

Deadwyler, S. A., Foster, T. C., & Hampson, R. E. (1987). Processing of sensory information in the hippocampus. *CRC Critical Reviews in Clinical Neurobiology, 2,* 335–355.

Deadwyler, S. A., Hampson, R. E., Foster, T. C., & Marlow, G. (1988). The functional significance of long-term potentiation: Relation to sensory processing by hippocampal circuits. In P. W. Landfield & S. A. Deadwyler (Eds.), *Long-term potentiation: From biophysics to behavior* (pp. 499–534). New York: Alan R. Liss.

Deadwyler, S. A., West, M., Christian, E. P., Hampson, R. E., & Foster, T. C. (1985). Sequence-related changes in sensory-evoked potentials in the dentate gyrus: A mechanism for item-specific short-term information storage in the hippocampus. *Behavioral and Neural Biology, 44,* 201–212.

Deadwyler, S. A., West, M., & Lynch, G. (1979). Activity of dentate granule cells during learning: Differentiation of perforant path input. *Brain Research, 169,* 29–43.

Delacour, J. (1982). Associative and non-associative changes in unit activity of the rat hippocampus. *Brain Research Bulletin, 8,* 367–373.

Desmond, J. E., & Moore, J. W. (1982). A brain stem region essential for the classically conditioned but not unconditioned nictitating membrane response. *Physiology and Behavior, 28,* 1029–1033.

Desmond, J.E., Rosenfield, M.E., & Moore, J. W. (1983). A HRP study of the brainstem afferents to the accessory abducens region and dorsolateral pons in rabbit: Implications for the conditioned nictitating membrane response. *Brain Research Bulletin, 10,* 747–763.

Disterhoft, J. F., Coulter, D. A., & Alkon, D. L. (1986). Specific membrane changes of rabbit hippocampal neurons measured in vitro. *Proceedings of the National Academy of Science USA, 83,* 2733–2737.

Disterhoft, J. F., Golden, D. T., Read, H. L., Coulter, D. A., & Alkon, D. L. (1988). AHP reductions in rabbit hippocampal neurons during conditioning correlate with acquisition of the learned response. *Brain Research, 462,* 118–125.

Disterhoft, J. F., & Segal, M. (1978). Neuronal activity in rat hippocampus and motor cortex during discrimination reversal. *Brain Research Bulletin, 3,* 583–588.

Domesick, V. B. (1969). Projections from the cingulate cortex in the rat. *Brain Research, 12,* 396–320.

Donovan, M. K., & Wyss, J. M. (1981). Lack of collateralization in the projections from the rat subicular cortex to the entorhinal area and the mammillary nuclei. *Anatomical Record, 199,* 72.

Douglas, R. J. (1967). The hippocampus and behavior. *Psychological Bulletin, 67,* 416–442.

Eccles, J. C. (1977). An instruction-selection theory of learning in the cerebellar cortex. *Brain Research, 127,* 327–352.

Eichenbaum, H., Fagan, A., Mathews, P., & Cohen, N. J. (1988). Hippocampal system dysfunction and odor discrimination learning in rats: Impairment or facilitation depending on representational demands. *Behavioral Neuroscience, 102,* 331–339.

Eichenbaum, H., Kuperstein, M., Fagan, A., & Nagode, J. (1987). Cue-sampling and goal-approach correlates of hippocampal unit activity in rats performing an odor-discrimination task. *Journal of Neuroscience, 7,* 716–732.

Eichenbaum, H., Wiener, S. I., & Paul, C. A. (1989a). Functional correlates of hippocampal neurons: II. Coding of spatial and non-spatial variables. *Journal of Neuroscience.*

Eichenbaum, H., Wiener, S. I., Shapiro, M. L., & Cohen, N. J. (1989b). Functional correlates of hippocampal neurons: III. The organization of spatial coding in neural ensembles. *Journal of Neuroscience.*

Fagen, A. M., & Olton, D. S. (1986). Learning sets, discrimination reversal, and hippocampal function. *Behavioural Brain Research, 21,* 13–20.

Finch, D. M., Derian, E. L. & Babb, T. L. (1984). Excitatory projection of the rat subicular complex to the cingulate cortex and synaptic integration with thalamic afferents. *Brain Research, 301,* 25–37.

Foster, T. C., Christian, E. P., Hampson, R. E., Campbell, K. A., & Deadwyler, S. A. (1987). Sequential dependencies regulate sensory evoked responses of single units in the rat hippocampus. *Brain Research, 408,* 86–96.

Gabriel, M., Foster, K. Orona, E. Saltwick, S. E., & Stanton, M. (1980). Neuronal activity of cingulate cortex, anteroventral thalamus, and hippocampal formation in discriminative conditioning: Encoding and extraction of the significance of conditional stimuli. *Progress in Psychobiology and Physiological Psychology, 9*, 125–231.

Gabriel, M., & Sparenborg, S. P. (1986). Anterior thalamic discriminative neuronal response enhanced during learning in rabbits with subicular and cingulate cortical lesions. *Brain Research, 384*, 195–198.

Gabriel, M., & Sparenborg, S. P. (1987). Posterior cingulate cortical lesions eliminate learning-related unit-activity in the anterior cingulate cortex. *Brain Research, 409*, 151–157.

Gabriel, M., Sparenborg, S. P., & Stolar, N. (1987). Hippocampal control of cingulate cortical and anterior thalamic information-processing during learning in rabbit. *Experimental Brain Research, 67*, 131–152.

Georgopoulos, A. P., Schwartz, A. B., & Kettner, R. E. (1986). Neuronal population coding of movement direction. *Science, 233*, 1416–1419.

Gilbert, P.F.C. (1974). A theory of memory that explains the function and structure of the cerebellum. *Brain Research, 70*, 1–18.

Gluck, M. A., & Thompson, R. F. (1987). Modeling the neural substrates of associative learning and memory: A computational approach. *Psychological Review, 94*, 176–191.

Gormezano, I., Kehoe, E. J., & Marshall, B. S. (1983). Twenty years of classical conditioning research with the rabbit. *Progress in Psychobiology and Physiological Psychology, 10*, 197–275.

Gormezano, I., Prokasy, W. F., & Thompson, R. F. (1987). *Classical conditioning III: Behavioral, neurophysiological and neurochemical studies in the rabbit*. New York: Academic Press.

Gormezano, I., Schneiderman, N., Deaux, E., & Fuentes, I. (1962). Nictitating membrane: Classical conditioning and extinction in the albino rabbit. *Science, 138*, 33–34.

Grantyn, R., Margnelli, M., Mancia, M., & Grantyn, A. (1973). Postsynaptic potentials in the mesencephalic and ponto-medullar reticular regions underlying descending limbic influences. *Brain Research, 56*, 107–121.

Gray, J. A. (1982). *The Neuropsychology of anxiety*. Oxford: Oxford University Press.

Grossberg, S. (1988). Nonlinear neural networks: principles, mechanisms, and architectures. *Neural Networks, 1*, 17–61.

Guillery, R. W. (1955). A quantitative study of the mammillary bodies on their connexions. *Journal of Anatomy, 89*, 19–33.

Halgren, E., Babb, T. L., & Crandall, P. H. (1978). Activity of human hippocampal formation and amygdala neurons during memory testing. *Electroencephalography and Clinical Neurophysiology, 45*, 585–601.

Halgren, E., Heit, G., & Smith, M. E. (1987). Human hippocampal neuronal firing to specific individual words and faces. *IBRO Abstracts, Neuroscience* (Supplement), *22*, S13.

Harty, T. P., Berger, T. W., Sclabassi, R. J., & Barrionuevo, G. (1992). *Nonlinear response properties of the in vitro hippocampal perforant path-dentate projection: Role of GABA$_A$ receptors*. Submitted for publication.

Harvey, J. A., Gormezano, I., & Cool–Hauser, V. A. (1985). Relationship between heterosynaptic reflex facilitation and acquisition of the nictitating membrane response in control and scopolamine-injected rabbits. *Journal of Neuroscience, 5*, 596–602.

Hawkins, R. D., & Kandel, E. R. (1984). Is there a cell-biological alphabet for simple forms of learning? *Psychological Review, 91*, 376–391.

Hill, A. J. (1978). First occurrence of hippocampal spatial firing in a new environment. *Experimental Neurology, 62*, 282–297.

Hirsh, R. (1974). The hippocampus and contextual retrieval of information from memory: A theory. *Behavioral Biology, 12*, 421–444.

Hirsh, R. (1980). The hippocampus, conditional operations, and cognition. *Physiological Psychology, 8*, 175–182.

Hoehler, F. K., & Thompson, R. F. (1980). Effects of the interstimulus (CS–UCS) interval on hippocampal unit activity during classical conditioning of the nictitating membrane response of the rabbit. *Journal of Comparative and Physiological Psychology, 94,* 201–215.

Holland, P. C., & Ross, R. T. (1981). Within-compound associations in serial compound conditioning. *Journal of Experimental Psychology: Animal Behavior Processes, 7,* 228-241.

Holt, L., & Thompson, R. F. (1984). Hippocampal correlates of instrumental behavior. *Society for Neuroscience Abstracts, 10,* 124.

Hopfield, J. J. (1982). Neural networks and physical systems with emergent collective computational abilities. *Proceedings of the National Academy of Science, 79,* 2554–2558.

Isaacson, R. L., Ed. (1974). *The limbic system.* New York: Plenum Press.

Isaacson, R. L., & Pribram, K. H., Eds. (1975). *The hippocampus* (Vols. 1 & 2). New York: Plenum Press.

Isaacson, R. L., & Pribram, K. H., Eds. (1986). *The hippocampus* (Vols. 3 & 4). New York: Plenum Press.

Ito, M. (1974). Recent advances in cerebellar physiology and pathology. *Advances in Neurology, 21,* 59–84.

Jarrel, T. W., Gentile, C. G., Romanski, L. M., McCabe, R. M., & Schneiderman, N. (1987). Involvement of cortical and thalamic auditory regions in retention of differential bradycardiac conditioning to acoustic conditional stimuli in rabbits. *Brain Research, 412,* 285–294.

Kairiss, E. W., Keenan, C. L., & Brown, T. H. (1988). A biologically plausible implementation of a Hebbian covariance algorithm. *Society for Neuroscience Abstracts, 14,* 832.

Kapp, B. S., Schwaber, J. S., & Driscoll, P. A. (1985). The organization of insular cortex projections to the amygdala central nucleus and autonomic regulatory nuclei of the dorsal medulla. *Brain Research, 360,* 355–360.

Kawamura, K., & Hashikawa, T. (1981). Projections from the pontine nuclei proper and reticular tegmental nucleus onto the cerebellar cortex in the cat. An autoradiographic study. *Journal of Comparative Neurology, 201,* 395–413.

Kehoe, E. J., Marshall-Goodell, B., & Gormezano, I. (1987). Differential conditioning of the rabbit's nictitating membrane response to serial compound stimuli. *Journal of Experimental Psychology: Animal Behavior Processes, 13,* 17–30.

Kettner, R. E., & Thompson, R. F. (1982). Auditory signal detection and decision processes in the nervous system. *Journal of Comparative and Physiological Psychology, 96,* 328–331.

Klopf, A. H. (1982). *The hedonistic neuron.* New York: Hemisphere.

Kohonen, T. (1988). *Self-organization and associative memory.* Berlin: Springer-Verlag.

Koutalidis, O., Foster, A., & Weisz, D. J. (1988). Parallel pathways can conduct visual CS information during classical conditioning of the NM response. *Journal of Neuroscience, 8,* 417–427.

Kubie, J. L., & Ranck, J. B. (1983). Sensory-behavioral correlates in individual hippocampus neurons in three situations: Space and context. In W. Seifert (Ed.), *Neurobiology of the hippocampus* (pp. 433–447). New York: Academic Press.

Kubie, J. L., & Ranck, J. B., Jr. (1984). Hippocampal neuronal firing, context and learning. In L. R. Squire & N. Butters (Eds.), *Neuropsychology of memory* (pp. 417–423). New York: Guilford Press.

Lanfield, P. A., & Deadwyler, S. A. (Eds.). (1988). *Long-term potentiation: From biophysics to behavior.* New York: Alan R. Liss.

Laroche, S., Neuenschwander-El Massioui, N., Edeline, J-M., & Dutrieux, G. (1987). Hippocampal associative cellular responses: dissociation with behavioral responses revealed by a transfer-of-control technique. *Behavioral and Neural Biology, 47,* 356–368.

LeDoux, J. E. (1987). Emotion. In F. Plum (Ed.), *Handbook of physiology, Vol. V: Higher functions of the brain* (pp. 415–459). Baltimore: Williams & Wilkins.

LeDoux, J. E., & Iwata, J. (1987). A subcortical sensory pathway mediates emotional learning. *International Journal of Neuroscience, 32,* 598.

Levy, W. B., Anderson, J. A., & Lehmkuhle, S. (1985). *Synaptic modification, neuron selectivity, and nervous system organization.* Hillsdale, NJ: Lawrence Erlbaum Associates.

Lewis, J. L., LoTurco, J. J., & Solomon, P. R. (1987). Lesions of the middle cerebellar peduncle disrupt acquisition and retention of the rabbit's classically conditioned nictitating membrane response. *Behavioral Neuroscience, 101,* 151–157.

Lisberger, S. G., Morris, E. J., & Tychsen, L. (1987). Visual motion processing and sensory-motor integration for smooth pursuit eye movements. *Annual Review of Neuroscience, 10,* 97–129.

Loechner, K. J., & Weisz, D. J. (1987). Hippocampectomy and feature-positive discrimination. *Behavioral Brain Research, 26,* 63–73.

Lynch, G. (1986). *Synapses, circuits and the beginnings of memory.* Cambridge, MA: The MIT Press.

Marek, G. J., McMaster, S. E., Gormezano, I., & Harvey, J. A. (1984). The role of the accessory abducens nucleus in the rabbit nictitating membrane response. *Brain Research, 299,* 215–229.

Marr, D. (1969). A theory of cerebellar cortex. *Journal of Physiology, 202,* 437–470.

Marshall, J. F. (1979). Somatosensory inattention after dopamine-depleting intracerebral 6-OHDA injections: Spontaneous recovery and pharmacological control. *Brain Research, 177,* 311–324.

Mauk, M. D., Steinmetz, J. E., & Thompson, R. F. (1986). Classical conditioning using stimulation of the inferior olive as the unconditioned stimulus. *Proceedings of the National Academy of Science (USA), 83,* 5349–5353.

Mauk, M. D., & Thompson, R. F. (1987). Retention of classically conditioned eyelid responses following acute decerebration. *Brain Research, 403,* 89–95.

McCormick, D. A., & Thompson, R. F. (1984). Cerebellum: Essential involvement in the classically conditioned eyelid response. *Science, 223,* 296–299.

McNaughton, B. L., Barnes, C. A., & O'Keefe, J. A. (1983). The contributions of position, direction, and velocity to single cell unit activity in the hippocampus of freely moving rats. *Experimental Brain Research, 52,* 41–49.

McNaughton, B. L., & Morris, R. G. M. (1987). Hippocampal synaptic enhancement and information storage within a distributed memory system. *Trends in Neuroscience, 10,* 408–415.

Meibach, R. C., & Siegel, A. (1977). Subicular projections to the posterior cingulate cortex in rats. *Experimental Neurology, 57,* 264–274.

Mihailoff, G. A., Burne, R. A., Azizi, S. A., Norell, G., & Woodward, D. J. (1981). The pontocerebellar system in the rat: An HRP study. II. Hemispheral components. *Journal of Comparative Neurology, 197,* 559–577.

Milner, B. (1970). Memory and the medial temporal regions of the brain. In K. H. Pribram & D. E. Broadbent (Eds.), *Biology of memory* (pp. 29–50). New York: Academic Press.

Mishkin, M. (1978). Memory in monkeys severely impaired by combined but not by separate removal of amygdala and hippocampus. *Nature, 273,* 297–298.

Mishkin, M. (1982). A memory system in the monkey. *Philosophical Transactions of the Royal Society of London B, 298,* 85–95.

Mishkin, M., & Petri, H. L. (1984). Memories and habits: Some implications for the analysis of learning and retention. In L. R. Squire & N. Butters (Eds.), *Neuropsychology of memory* (pp. 287–296). New York: Guilford Press.

Moore, J. W. (1979). Brain processes and conditioning. In A. Dickinson & R. A. Boakes (Eds.), *Mechanisms of learning and motivation: A memorial volume to Jerzy Konorski* (pp. 111–142). Hillsdale, NJ: Lawrence Erlbaum Associates.

Moore, J. W., & Berthier, N. E. (1987). Purkinje cell activity and the conditioned nictitating membrane response. In M. Glickstein, C. Yeo, & J. Stein (Eds.), *Cerebellum and neuronal plasticity* (pp. 339–352). New York: Plenum Press.

Moore, J. W., Desmond, J. E., & Berthier, N. E. (1982). The metencephalic basis of the conditioned nictitating membrane response. In C. D. Woody (Ed.), *Conditioning: representation of involved neuronal function* (pp. 459–482). New York: Plenum Press.

Moore, J. W., Desmond, J. E., Berthier, N. E. Blazis, D. E. J., Sutton, R. S., & Barto, A. G. (1986). Simulation of the classically conditioned nictitating membrane response by a neuron-like adaptive element: Response topography, neuronal firing and interstimulus intervals. *Behavioural Brain Research, 21,* 143–154.

Muller, R. U., & Kubie, J. L. (1987). The effects of changes in the environment on the spatial firing of hippocampal complex-spike cells. *Journal of Neuroscience, 7,* 1951–1968.

Muller, R. U., Kubie, J. L., & Ranck, J. B. (1987). Spatial firing patterns of hippocampal complex-spike cells in a fixed environment. *Journal of Neuroscience, 7,* 1935–1950.

Nadel, L., & Willner, J. (1980). Context and conditioning: A place for space. *Physiological Psychology, 8,* 218–228.

Nauta, W. J. H. (1956). An experimental study of the fornix system in the rat. *Journal of Comparative Neurology, 104,* 247–272.

Norman, R. J., Buchwald, J. S., & Villablanca, J. R. (1977). Classical conditioning with auditory discrimination of the eyeblink in decerebrate cats. *Science, 196,* 551–553.

Oakley, D. A., & Russell, I. S. (1972). Neocortical lesions and classical conditioning. *Physiology and Behavior, 8,* 915–926.

O'Keefe, J. A. (1976). Place units in the hippocampus of the freely moving rat. *Experimental Neurology, 51,* 78–109.

O'Keefe, J., & Conway, D. H. (1978). Hippocampal place units in the freely moving rat: Why they fire where they fire. *Experimental Brain Research, 31,* 573–590.

O'Keefe, J., Nadel, L., Keightley, S., & Kill, D. (1975). Fornix lesions selectively abolish place learning in the rat. *Experimental Neurology, 48,* 152–166.

Olds, J., Disterhoft, J. F., Segal, M., Kornblith, C. L., & Hirsh, R. (1972). Learning centers of rat brain mapped by measuring latencies of conditioned unit responses. *Journal of Neurophysiology, 35,* 202–219.

Oliver, C. G., & Berry, S. D. (1986). Hippocampal unit responses during an appetitive-aversive discrimination and reversal in rabbits. *Society for Neuroscience Abstracts, 12,* 518.

Olton, D., Becker, J. T., & Handlemann, G. E. (1979). Hippocampus, space, and memory. *Brain Behavior Science, 2,* 313–365.

Olton, D. S., Branch, M., & Best, P. J. (1978). Spatial correlates of hippocampal unit activity. *Experimental Neurology, 58,* 387–409.

Orr, W. B., & Berger, T. W. (1985). Hippocampectomy disrupts topography of conditioned nictitating membrane responses during reversal learning. *Behavioral Neuroscience, 99,* 35–45.

Patterson, M. M., Berger, T. W., & Thompson, R. F. (1979). Hippocampal neuronal plasticity recorded from cat during classical conditioning. *Brain Research, 163,* 339–343.

Pellionisz, A., & Llinas, R. (1982). Space–time representation in the brain. The cerebellum as a predictive space–time metric tensor. *Neuroscience, 7,* 2949–2970.

Perkel, D. H., & Bullock, T. H. (1968). Neural coding. *Neurosciences Research Program Bulletin, 6,* 221–348.

Port, R. L., Mikhail, A. A., & Patterson, M. M. (1985). Differential effects of hippocampectomy on classically conditioned rabbit nictitating membrane response related to interstimulus interval. *Behavioral Neuroscience, 99,* 200–208.

Port, R. L., & Patterson, M. M. (1984). Fimbrial lesions and sensory preconditioning. *Behavioral Neuroscience, 98,* 584–589.

Port, R. L., Romano, A. G., Steinmetz, J. E., Mikhail, A. A., & Patterson, M. M. (1986). Retention and acquisition of classical trace conditioned responses by hippocampal lesioned rabbits. *Behavioral Neuroscience, 100,* 745–752.

Powell, D. A., & Buchanan, S. (1980). Autonomic-somatic relationships in the rabbit (Oryctolagus cuniculus): Effects of hippocampal lesions. *Physiological Psychology, 8,* 455–462.

Raisman, W., Cowan, W. M., & Powell, T. P. S. (1966). An experimental analysis of the efferent projection of the hippocampus. *Brain, 89,* 83–108.

Ranck, J. B. (1973). Studies on single neurons in dorsal hippocampal formation and septum in unrestrained rats. I. Behavioral correlates and firing repertoires. *Experimental Neurology, 41,* 461–555.

Rawlins, J. N. P. (1985). Associations across time: The hippocampus as a temporary memory store. *Behavioral and Brain Sciences, 8,* 479–496.

Robinson, F. R., Cohen, J. L., May, J., Sestokas, A. K., & Glickstein, M. (1984). Cerebellar targets of visual pontine cells in the cat. *Journal of Comparative Neurology, 223,* 471–482.

Rolls, E. T. (1986). Theoretical analysis of response properties of single neurons in a matrix memory neuronal network. *Behavioural Brain Research, 20,* 137–138.

Rolls, E. T., Thorpe, S. J., & Maddison, S. (1983). Responses of striatal neurons in the behaving monkey. 1. Head of the caudate nucleus. *Behavioural Brain Research, 7,* 179–210.

Rose, J. E., & Woolsey, C. N. (1948). Structure and relations of limbic cortex and anterior thalamic nuclei in rabbit and cat. *Journal of Comparative Neurology, 89,* 279–347.

Ross, R. T., Orr, W. B., Holland, P. C., & Berger, T. W. (1984). Hippocampectomy disrupts acquisition and retention of learned conditional responding. *Behavioral Neuroscience, 98,* 221–225.

Rummelhart, D. E., & McClelland, J. L. (Eds.) (1986). *Parallel distributed processing,* (Vol. I and II). Cambridge, MA: MIT Press.

Saint-Cyr, J. A., Taylor, A. E., & Lang, A. E. (1988). Procedural learning and neostriatal dysfunction in man. *Brain, 111,* 941–959.

Saint-Cyr, J. A., & Woodward, D. J. (1980). Activation of mossy and climbing fiber pathways to the cerebellar cortex by stimulation of the fornix in the rat. *Experimental Brain Research, 40,* 1–12.

Schmajuk, N. A. (1984). Psychological theories of hippocampal function. *Physiological Psychology, 12,* 166–183.

Schneiderman, N., & Gormezano, I. (1964). Conditioning of the nictitating membrane of the rabbit as a function of CS–UCS interval. *Journal of Comparative and Physiological Psychology, 57,* 188–195.

Sclabassi, R. J., Eriksson, J. L., Port, R. L., Robinson, G. B., & Berger, T. W. (1988a). Nonlinear systems analysis of the hippocampal perforant path-dentate projection. I. Theoretical and interpretational considerations. *Journal of Neurophysiology, 60,* 1066–1076.

Sclabassi, R. J., Krieger, D. N. & Berger, T. W. (1988b). A systems theoretic approach to the study of CNS function. *Annals of Biomedical Engineering, 16,* 17–34.

Sclabassi, R. J., Krieger, D. N., Solomon, J., Samosky, J., Levitan, S., & Berger, T. W. (1989). Modeling of neuronal networks through theoretical decomposition. In V. Z. Marmarelis (Ed.), *Advanced methods of physiological system modeling.* Plenum Press.

Segal, M. (1973). Flow of conditioned responses in limbic telencephalic system of the rat. *Journal of Neurophysiology, 36,* 840–854.

Segal, M., Disterhoft, J., & Olds, J. (1972). Hippocampal unit activity during aversive and appetitive conditioning. *Science, 175,* 792–794.

Seifert, W. (Ed.) (1983). *Neurobiology of the hippocampus.* New York: Academic Press.

Sikes, R. W., Chronister, R. B., & White, L. E. (1977). Origin of the direct hippocampus-anterior thalamic bundle in the rat: A combined horseradish peroxidase-Golgi analysis. *Experimental Neurology, 57,* 379–395.

Smith, M. C., DiLollo, V., & Gormezano, I. (1966). Conditioned jaw movement in the rabbit. *Journal of Comparative and Physiological Psychology, 62,* 479–483.

Snyder, A. M., Stricker, E. M., & Zigmond, M. J. (1985). Stress-induced neurological deficits after injury to central dopaminergic neurons: Implications for preclinical Parkinsonism. *Annals of Neurology, 18,* 544–551.

Solomon, P. R. (1977). Role of hippocampus in blocking and conditioned inhibition of the rabbit's nictitating membrane response. *Journal of Comparative and Physiological Psychology, 91,* 407–417.

Solomon, P. R., Vander Schaaf, E. R. Norbe, A. C., Weisz, D. J., & Thompson, R. F. (1986). Hippocampus and trace conditioning of the rabbit's nictitating membrane response. *Behavioral Neuroscience, 100,* 729–744.

Sorensen, K. E. (1980). Ipsilateral projection from the subiculum to the retrosplenial cortex in the guinea pig. *Journal of Comparative Neurology, 193,* 893–911.

Sotnichencko, T. S. (1976). Convergence of the descending pathways of motor, visual and limbic cortex in the cat di- and mesencephalon. *Brain Research, 116,* 401–415.

Squire, L. R. (1982). The neuropsychology of human memory. *Annual Review of Neuroscience, 5,* 241–273.

Squire, L. R., & Butters, N., Eds. (1984). *Neuropsychology of memory.* New York: Guilford Press.

Steinmetz, J. E., Logan, C. G., Rosen, D. J., Thompson, J. K., Lavond, D. G., & Thompson, R. F. (1987). Initial localization of the acoustic conditioned stimulus projection system to the cerebellum essential for classical eyelid conditioning. *Proceedings of the National Academy of Sciences (USA), 84,* 3531–3535.

Steinmetz, J. E., Rosen, D. J., Chapman, P. F., Lavond, D. G., & Thompson, R. F. (1986). Classical conditioning of the rabbit eyelid response with a mossy fiber stimulation CS. I. Pontine nuclei and middle cerebellar peduncle stimulation. *Behavioral Neuroscience, 100,* 871–880.

Swanson, L. W., & Cowan, W. M. (1975). Hippocampo–hypothalamic connections: Origin in subicular cortex, not Ammon's horn. *Science, 189,* 303–304.

Swanson, L. W., & Cowan, W. M. (1977). An autoradiographic study of the organization of the efferent connections of the hippocampal formation in the rat. *Journal of Comparative Neurology, 172,* 49–84.

Swanson, L. W., Sawchenko, P. E., & Cowan, W. M. (1981). Evidence for collateral projections by neurons in ammon's horn, the dentate gyrus, and the subiculum: A multiple retrograde labeling study in the rat. *Journal of Neuroscience, 1,* 548–559.

Swanson, L. W., Wyss, J. M., & Cowan, W. M. (1978). An autoradiographic study of the organization of intrahippocampal association pathways in the rat. *Journal of Comparative Neurology, 181,* 681–716.

Thompson, R. F. (1986). The neurobiology of learning and memory. *Science, 233,* 941–947.

Thompson, R. F., Berger, T. W., Cegavske, C. R., Patterson, M. M., Roemer, R. A., Teyler, T. J., & Young, R. A. (1976). The search for the engram. *American Psychologist, 31,* 209–227.

Thompson, R. F., Berger, T. W., & Madden, J. IV. (1983). Cellular processes of learning and memory in the mammalian CNS. *Annual Review of Neuroscience, 6,* 447–491.

Traub, R. D., Miles, R., & Wong, R. K. S. (1987). Models of synchronized hippocampal bursts in the presence of inhibition. I. Single population events. *Journal of Neurophysiology, 58,* 739–751.

Traub, R. D., Miles, R., Wong, R. K. S., Schulman, L. S., & Schneiderman, J. H. (1987). Models of synchronized hippocampal bursts in the presence of inhibition. II. Ongoing spontaneous population events. *Journal of Neurophysiology, 58,* 752–764.

Uttley, A. M. (1979). *Information transmission in the nervous system.* New York: Academic Press.

Valenstein, E., Bowers, D., Verfaellie, M., Heilman, K. W., Day, A., & Watson, R. T. (1987). Retrosplenial amnesia. *Brain, 110,* 163–184.

VanGroen, T., & Lopes da Silva, F. H. (1986). Organization of the reciprocal connections between the subiculum and the entorhinal cortex in the cat. II. An electrophysiological study. *Journal of Comparative Neurology, 251,* 111–120.

Vogt, B. A., Sikes, R. W., Swadlow, H. A., & Weyand, T. G. (1986). Rabbit cingulate cortex: Physiological border with visual cortex, and afferent cortical connections of visual, motor postsubicular and intracingulate origin. *Journal of Comparative Neurology, 248,* 74–94.

Weikart, C., & Berger, T. W. (1986). Hippocampectomy disrupts classical conditioning of cross-modality discrimination reversal of the rabbit nictitating membrane response. *Behavioural Brain Research, 22,* 85–89.

Weinberger, N. M., McGaugh, J. L., & Lynch, G. (Eds.). (1985). *Memory systems of the brain: Animal and human cognitive processes*. New York: Guilford Press.

Weisz, D. J., & LoTurco, J. J. (1988). Reflex facilitation of the nictitating membrane response remains after cerebellar lesions. *Behavioral Neuroscience, 102*, 203–209.

Weisz, D. J., & McInerney, J. (1988). An associative process can enhance the amplitude of the unconditioned nictitating membrane response in rabbit. *Behavioral Neuroscience*.

Weisz, D. J., & Walts, C. (in press). Reflex facilitation of the rabbit NM response by an auditory stimulus as a function of interstimulus interval. *Behavioral Neuroscience*.

West, M. O., Michael, A. J., Knowles, S. E., Chapin, J. K., & Woodward, D. J. (1987). Striatal unit activity and linkage between sensory and motor events. In J. S. Schneider & T. I. Lidsky (Eds.), *Basal ganglia and behavior: Sensory aspects of motor functioning* (pp. 27–35). Toronto: Han Huber.

Wible, C. G., Findling, R. L., Shapiro, M., Lang, E. J., Crane, S., & Olton, D. S. (1986). Mnemonic correlates of unit-activity in the hippocampus. *Brain Research, 399*, 97–110.

Wiener, S. I., & Eichenbaum, H. (1989). Functional correlates of hippocampal neurons: I. Coding of stimulus and response configurations during odor discrimination performance. *Journal of Neuroscience*.

Winocur, G., & Olds, J. (1978). Effects of context manipulation on memory and reversal learning in rats with hippocampal lesions. *Journal of Comparative and Physiological Psychology, 92*, 312–321.

Woody, C. D., & Black-Cleworth, P. (1973). Differences in excitability of cortical neurons as a function of motor projection in conditioned cats. *Journal of Neurophysiology, 36*, 1104–1116.

Woody, C., Yarowsky, P., Owens, J., Black-Cleworth, P., & Crow, T. (1974). Effect of lesions of cortical motor areas on acquisition of conditioned eye blink in the cat. *Journal of Neurophysiology, 37*, 385–394.

Zipser, D. (1986). A model of hippocampal learning during classical conditioning. *Behavioral Neuroscience, 100*, 764–776.

Zola-Morgan, S., Squire, L. R., & Amaral, D. G. (1986). Hunan amnesia and the medial temporal region: Enduring memory impairment following a bilateral lesion limited to field CA1 of the hippocampus. *Journal of Neuroscience, 6*, 2950–2967.

14

Central Pathways Involved in Classical Differential Conditioning of Heart Rate Responses in Rabbits

Philip M. McCabe
Neil Schneiderman
Theodore W. Jarrell
Christopher G. Gentile

Alan H. Teich
Ray W. Winters
David R. Liskowsky
University of Miami

In recent years, a major focus of research in the area of learning and memory has been to describe the neuronal pathways involved in the integration and expression of simple learned responses. In this type of work, it is necessary to develop a paradigm that allows the investigator to have precise control over the stimuli, and that elicits a simple and clear form of associative learning (Thompson et al., 1984). Furthermore, the model system used should allow neuronal analyses (Cohen, 1974) and the neuronal activity should be related to a significant behavior (Kandel & Spencer, 1968). Thompson and colleagues (Thompson et al., 1984) have pointed out that, once a suitable preparation has been established, the first issue that must be addressed is to identify the neural structures and pathways involved in the model of learning. Using lesion, electrophysiological, and neuroanatomical techniques, it is possible to trace CNS circuitry that links sensory information, in the form of conditioned and unconditioned stimuli (CSs & USs), with motor outflow, in the form of conditioned and unconditioned responses (CRs & URs). Certainly, the CNS circuitry involved in any learned behavior is quite complex; however, through careful and systematic studies the essential neuronal pathways for a relatively simple CR may be elucidated. Once the neuronal circuitry has been identified, electrophysiological and biochemical analyses of cellular activity in the various pathways can provide further information regarding the neural substrates of learning.

The model system that we have chosen to work with is the classically conditioned heart rate (HR) response in rabbits. HR conditioning is a relatively simple model of learning that develops within a few CS–US pairings. This response is not only interesting in terms of understanding mechanisms of learning, but also it is relevant to the way in which cardiovascular responses are produced to stressful stimuli and how these responses may be learned. Although HR conditioning in other species such as pigeons (Cohen & Randall, 1984), rats (Hatton, Foutz, & Fitzgerald, 1984; Ledoux, Sakaguchi, & Reis, 1984), and baboons (Smith, Astley, DeVito, Stein, & Walsh, 1980) offer important models of learned sympathetic activation, the bradycardiac (HR slowing) response in rabbits is also important because it is similar to the HR CR seen in humans (Wood & Obrist, 1968). In addition, the rabbit model offers the advantage of allowing simultaneous conditioning of HR and the eyeblink response, a well-described model of conditioning, thereby enabling the investigator to examine differences in the CNS mechanisms mediating autonomic versus somatomotor conditioning.

Early work in the laboratory of Professor I. Gormezano at Indiana University demonstrated through appropriate control procedures that the HR CR reflected true conditioning (Schneiderman, Smith, Smith, & Gormezano, 1966). Other studies in our Miami laboratory helped to establish suitable parameters for HR conditioning (e.g., VanDercar & Schneiderman, 1967). The focus of recent work in our laboratory and in others (e.g., Gallagher, Kapp, Frysinger, & Rapp, 1980; Kapp, Frysinger, Gallagher, & Haselton, 1979; Powell, Buchanan, & Hernandez, 1985) has been on describing the putative CNS structures and pathways involved in bradycardiac responses and the integration of the HR CR. In addition, we have recently turned our attention toward the sensory side of HR conditioning, examing the role of auditory structures in differential HR conditioning.

EARLY HR CONDITIONING STUDIES

Although HR CRs in rabbits were examined in an early study by Kosupkin and Olmstead (1943), the HR CR was later studied more extensively in the experiment by Schneiderman et al. (1966). This study paired a tone as the CS with mild electric shock delivered to the pinna of the ear as the US. The original response or orienting response (OR) to the CS was in HR deceleration that habituated within 6–10 CS-alone presentations. Furthermore, it was found that a HR CR consisting of bradycardia occurred within 8–10 CS–US pairings. The onset latency of this response was less than .5 sec, and it occurred in the absence of any gross bodily movements. In addition, control groups that received the CS alone, US alone, or CS and US presented randomly failed to demonstrate bradycardiac CRs.

In a subsequent study, the US was changed to a 20 mA eyelid shock (Yehle, Dauth, & Schneiderman, 1967). The findings of this study indicated that the HR CR was, in part, secondary to blood pressure increases. However, a follow-up study (Schneiderman et al., 1969) that compared the effects of using 3 mA versus 20 mA shock found that at lower US intensities the bradycardia CR occurred in the absence of blood pressure changes. This HR CR was abolished by the cholinergic blocker atropine or bilateral vagotomy, indicating that the response was vagally mediated.

The 3 mA US was found to elicit a blood pressure UR consisting of a pressor response during shock and a depressor response immediately following shock offset. This response changed to a depressor response only after repeated presentation of the US. The HR UR was a bradycardiac response initially but changed to a biphasic response (i.e., bradycardia followed by tachycardia) after approximately 15 US presentations. Like the HR CR, this HR UR also was abolished by atropine or bilateral vagotomy. These data indicated that both the bradycardiac and tachycardiac components of the HR UR were mediated by the vagus nerves. In addition, the HR UR was, in part, secondary to the BP UR because it was attenuated by Hydergine, an alpha adrenergic antagonist.

In addition to establishing the essential US parameters, Schneiderman and co-workers also examined the optimal interstimulus interval parameters for HR conditioning (Manning, Schneiderman, & Lordahl, 1969; VanDercar & Schneiderman, 1967). VanDercar and Schneiderman (1967) demonstrated that a tone (CS+) that was previously paired with the US elicits greater bradycardiac CRs than a tone (CS−) that was not paired with the US at a variety of CS–US intervals. However, a longer CS–US interval (2.25 sec) produced larger bradycardiac responses and a greater differential response between the CS+ and CS− than a shorter interval (.75 sec). Interestingly, the .75-sec CS–US interval was better for eliciting differential eyeblink CRs. These findings are consistent with the hypothesis that the optimal length of the CS–US interval is positively correlated with response duration.

In the years that followed, the effectiveness of electrical brain stimulation as the CS and US was examined. Initial studies demonstrated that stimulation of the lateral geniculate nucleus was effective as the CS when paired with eyelid shock during simple or differential Pavlovian conditioning of bradycardia (Swadlow & Schneiderman, 1970; Swadlow, Schneiderman, & Schneiderman, 1968). Subsequent experiments demonstrated that pairing of lateral geniculate nucleus stimulation with hypothalamic, subthalamic, midbrain, or septal stimulation as the US produced decelerative HR CRs (Elster, VanDercar, & Schneiderman, 1970; Sideroff, Elster, & Schneiderman, 1972; VanDercar, Elster, & Schneiderman, 1970). In addition, these studies found that stimulation of these brain regions produced pressor and bradycardiac URs. Unlike the HR URs to eyelid shock, URs to intracranial electrical stimulation did not change their topography with repeated presentations. The bradycardiac CRs established using electrical stimulation of the brain as the US were similar to CRs obtained using eyelid shock in that they occurred independently of blood pressure changes.

Fredericks et al. (1974) examined the HR URs and CRs to intracranial electrical stimulation in detail using pharmacologic blocking agents. The HR URs to brain stimulation were abolished by administration of atropine and phenotalmine, an alpha-adrenergic blocker, indicating that the bradycardia was a reflexive vagally mediated change resulting from an increase in blood pressure. In contrast, the HR CRs conditioned using intracranial electrical stimulation were abolished by atropine but not by phenotolamine indicating that these responses consisted of primary bradycardia. These findings indicated that electrical stimulation of the brain as the US produced bradycardiac CRs that were very similar to CRs established using eyelid shock as the US.

In summary, these early studies indicated that: (a) the OR to the CS was cardiodecelerative, (b) the OR habituated within a few trials, (c) the CR also consisted of bradycardia, (d) the CR developed within 10 pairings of the CS and US, (e) the CR was not confounded by nonassociative responses, (f) the bradycardiac CR was mediated solely through the vagus nerve, and (g) the HR UR consisted of bradycardia followed by tachycardia and was mediated by the parasympathetic system. These studies established that, following repeated pairings of the CS and the US, the response to the CS was a true CR. The studies also detailed the optimal parameters for HR conditioning and laid the groundwork for later studies that began to describe the essential circuitry underlying HR conditioning. In order to establish some uniformity and allow studies to be compared across laboratories, more recent studies have used tonal stimuli for CSs and periorbital shock as the US. Some differences still exist, however, among our studies in CS–US interval, stimulus characteristics, acquisition versus retention paradigms, and the use of differential conditioning paradigms.

TRACING CENTRAL BRADYCARDIAC PATHWAYS

The fact that the HR CR and UR could be abolished by vagotomy or atropine administration suggested that these responses were mediated through the vagus nerve. In order to begin identifying the neural circuitry involved in HR conditioning, we decided to use the Sherringtonian approach of beginning at the final common outflow and tracing bradycardiac pathways back into the CNS. This work, along with studies from other laboratories (Pascoe & Kapp, 1985a; Schwaber, Kapp, & Higgins, 1980; Schwaber, Kapp, Higgins, & Rapp, 1982), has described a pathway originating in the central nucleus of the amygdala (ACE), which courses through the lateral hypothalamus (LH), lateral zona incerta (LZI), and parabrachial nucleus (PBN), before it terminates in the dorsal medulla. In the medulla, there are projections to the dorsal vagal nucleus (DVN) and nucleus tractus solitarius (NTS).

In an initial study that examined the location of vagal cardiomotor cell bodies the rabbit, Schwaber and Schneiderman (1975) determined that extracellular single neuron recordings could be obtained from the cells of origin of vagal preganglionic cardioinhibitory motoneurons in DVN of unanesthetized rabbits. Jordan, Khalid, Schneiderman, and Spyer (1982) replicated the findings of Schwaber and Schneiderman (1975) by recording from preganglionic vagal cardiomotor neurons in DVN using urethane anesthetized rabbits. In addition, recordings were also made from preganglionic vagal cardioinhibitory neurons in nucleus ambiguus (NA). Experiments in which the cervical vagus nerve has been dipped in HRP have indicated that the distribution of vagal preganglionic cell bodies in NA is far sparser than in DVN for rabbits (Ellenberger, Haselton, Liskowsky, & Schneiderman, 1983). In addition, bradycardia responses are easily elicited by low intensity (< 30 μA) stimulation in DVN and in NA.

Injection of horseradish peroxidase (HRP) into the dorsal medulla including DVN (Wallach et al., 1979) produced pronounced retrograde cell body labeling in the ACE as well as in the lateral hypothalamus. Other investigators (Schwaber et al., 1980; Schwaber et al., 1982) have reported similar findings. Furthermore, Kapp (Kapp, Gallagher, Underwood, McNall, & Whitehorn, 1982) showed that electrical stimulation of ACE produced marked bradycardia that was either abolished or markedly attenuated by intravenous injections of atropine methylnitrate. The bradycardia was shown not to be an artifact of respiratory changes or gross motor acivity, as it persisted after artificial ventilation and immobilization with Flaxedil.

A recent study by Pascoe and Kapp (1985a) examined units in ACE in awake rabbits. Most of these neurons fired at very low spontaneous rates and were unresponsive to the presentation of auditory, visual, or somatic stimuli. Furthermore, some of these ACE neurons appeared to project to the dorsomedial medulla because they were antidromically activated by stimulation in this region.

We have also found that train stimulation of the ACE nucleus in lightly anesthetized rabbits elicits bradycardia and a depressor response. This suggested to us that the bradycardia elicited by stimulation of the hypothalamus might be attributable to fibers of passage originating in ACE nucleus. Consequently, we lesioned the ACE nucleus unilaterally and then stimulated the ipsilateral and contralateral LH either 30 min or 10–14 days after the lesion (Gellman, Schneiderman, Wallach, & LeBlanc, 1981). We found that stimulation of LH only failed to elicit bradycardiac responses when the stimulation was presented ipislateral to the lesion site 10–14 days postlesion. Fibers in the hypothalamus would be expected to degenerate by 10 days after destruction of their cell bodies in the amygdala, so the results of the Gellman et al. study suggest that the bradycardia elicited by stimulation of LH is due to fibers originating in the ACE nucleus.

Moving more caudal in the diencephalon, we found that train microstimulation of LZI produced pronounced bradycardia (94 beat/min drop from an average baseline of 250 beats/min), which in turn slightly decreased blood pressure (Mean; -6mmHg; Kaufman, Hamilton, Wallach, Petrik, & Schneiderman, 1979). These changes were prevented by bilateral vagotomy. Stimulation of the medial zona incerta produced a pronounced pressor response.

Stimulation of bradycardiac producing sites in LZI activated cardiovascular-related interneurons (neurons activated by aortic nerve stimulation, but not antidromically activated by vagus nerve stimulation) in NTS, and cardioinhibitory motorneurons in DVN. Although mean onset latency of these medullary neurons to LZI stimulation was relatively short (6 msec), these units did not follow repeated stimuli faithfully. Therefore, the connection between LZI and the dorsal medulla is probably not monosynaptic. However, a short train of pulses elicited greater firing rates than single pulses did. Therefore, it is possible that some connections between LZI and the dorsal medulla may be monosynaptic but may require a high degree of temporal summation.

Another structure that showed retrograde cell body labeling in the Wallach et al. (1979) experiment after injection of HRP into the dorsal medulla was PBN. Train stimulation of either medial or lateral PBN produced primary bradycardia (mean peak change: -74 beats/min) associated with a pressor response (mean peak change: 14 mmHg) of longer latency (Hamilton, Ellenberger, Liskowsky, & Schneiderman, 1981). Injections of HRP into PBN revealed retrogradely labeled cell bodies in regions of the forebrain previously implicated in the mediation of bradycardia. These included ACE, lateral preoptic region, medial forebrain bundle, bed nucleus of stria terminalis, anterior and lateral hypothalamus, and LZI. The correspondences between these HRP findings and the results of our previous functional studies implicating the ACE nucleus, LH, and LZI in the mediation of bradycardia is quite striking. Important correspondence also exists between the results of injecting HRP into the PBN in our study and into the dorsal medulla as reported by Schwaber et al. (1980, 1982) and Wallach et al. (1979).

Although the amygdalo–vagal pathway has been well mapped out, recent studies also suggest that certain cortical structures may play an important role in bradycardiac responses. For example, electrical stimulation of insular cortex (Powell et al., 1985) or cingulate cortex (Buchanan & Powell, 1982) elicits bradycardia and depressor responses. In addition, injections of retrograde tracers into ACE produced labeled cells in agranular insular cortex and medial prefrontal cortex (Kapp et al., 1985). However, anterograde techniques verified projections to ACE from insular cortex only.

In summary, these studies have described a pathway that mediates short-latency, profound bradycardiac responses. The pathway originates in ACE and descends, either mono or oligosynaptically, through LH, LZI, and PBN before it terminates in DVN/NTS. Although there are also cardiomotor cells in NA, it has not yet been demonstrated that this region receives input from the descending pathway described.

THE ROLE OF THE AMYGDALO–VAGAL BRADYCARDIAC PATHWAY IN HEART RATE CONDITIONING

The amygdala is a complex structure that is thought to play a role in learning and memory, particularly involving aversive events (Kapp, Pascoe, & Bixler, 1984). Because electrical stimulation along the descending amygdalo–vagal pathway elicited bradycardia similar to that observed during classical conditioning, investigators were especially interested in assessing the role of the amygdala and its descending projections in HR conditioning. Studies of this nature have utilized three major techniques. First, electrolytic or chemical lesions are produced at points along the amygdalo–vagal pathway and the effects on HR conditioning are determined. Second, the response of single or multiple units are recorded during conditioning and the changes in the activity of these cells are observed and related to conditioned HR CRs. Third, pharmacological agents, either agonists or antagonists, are injected into CNS structures (particularly the amygdala), and the effects on HR conditioning are assessed.

An initial study was conducted by Kapp and co-workers (Kapp et al., 1979) that determined the effect of ACE lesions on HR conditioning. In this experiment, radio frequency lesions were made in ACE. After recovery from surgery, animals received Pavlovian conditioning or pseudoconditioning trials. These lesions attenuated the magnitude of the HR CR relative to sham lesions animals but had no significant effect on the HR OR or baseline. This study was the first demonstration that the amygdalo–vagal pathway plays an important role in the HR CR.

Using a similar strategy, we examined the role of ACE in the *retention* of differentially conditioned bradycardia (Gentile, Jarrell, Teich, McCabe, & Schneiderman, 1986a). Electrodes were implanted bilaterally in ACE or in control sites just dorsal or rostral to ACE. Two days following surgery, animals were subjected to differential conditioning in which one tone (CS+) was paired with periorbital shock and a second tone (CS−) was presented alone. Each animal received one conditioning session per day until evidence of differential HR conditioning was obtained. Bilateral electrolytic lesions were then made. Thirty minutes after lesioning, animals received an additional conditioning session. The ACE lesion group failed to demonstrate differential responses after lesioning. Furthermore, the bradycardiac CR was abolished. In both groups, lesions did not have an effect on the HR OR, magnitude of the UR, or baseline. These findings suggest that ACE also plays a role in the retention of differential Pavlovian conditioning of bradycardia in rabbits. In order to demonstrate that ACE lesions did not disrupt some general learning process, corneo–retinal potential responses (CRP) were conditioned in the same animals. The CRP, a potential change across the eye resulting from the extension of the nictitating membrane and retraction of the eyeball (VanDercar, Swadlow, Elster, & Schneiderman, 1969), is perfectly correlated with the nictitating membrane response in rabbits. ACE lesions had no effect on the CRP CR, thereby suggesting that the lesions selectively abolished HR CRs but did not affect another simultaneously conditioned response.

The role of ACE in conditioning was examined further in pharmacologic studies. Injections of the beta-adrenergic antagonist dl-propranolol into ACE impaired the acquisition of HR CRs compared to a vehicle injected control group (Gallagher et al., 1980). In addition, animals that received combined injections of dl-propranolol and the beta-adrenergic agonist l-isoproterenol did not demon-

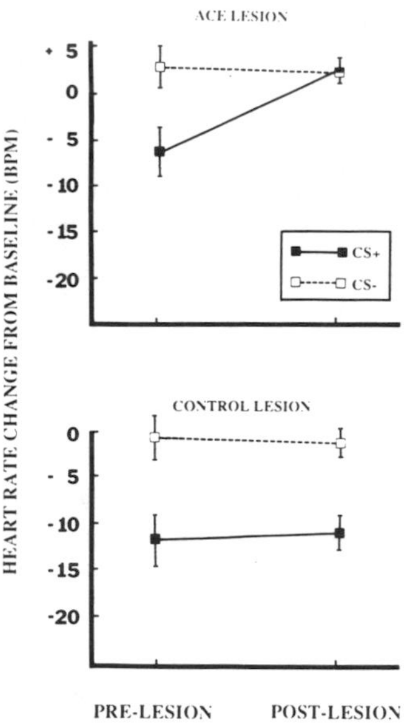

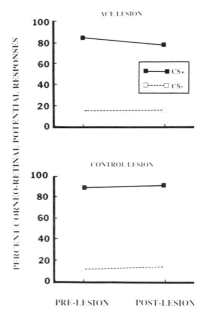

FIG. 14.1. Mean pre and postlesion heart rate changes immediately following onset of conditioned stimuli for ACE lesion and control lesion groups. Vertical bars represent the S.E.M. From Gentile et al. (1986).

FIG. 14.2. Mean pre and postlesion %CRP immediately following onset of conditioned stimuli for ACE lesion and control lesion groups. Vertical bars represent the S.E.M. From Gentile et al. (1986).

strate an impairment of the CR. Although the HR CR was impaired by beta-blockers, the HR OR and baseline were not significantly affected. These data suggest that beta-adrenergic activity within ACE contributes to HR CR acquisition.

In another experiment, Gallagher, Kapp, McNall, and Pascoe (1981) demonstrated the involvement of opioid peptides in the expression of HR CRs. Animals that received injections of the opiate agonist levorphenol into ACE demonstrated a decrement in HR CR magnitude. Conversely, injections of the opioid antagonist naloxone enhanced the CR magnitude. These data point to an ACE opioid system that can modulate the HR CR magnitude in rabbits.

Changes in unit activity in ACE have been observed during simple and differential Pavlovian conditioning procedures. In one study, multiple unit activity was recorded during simple HR conditioning (Applegate, Frysinger, Kapp, & Gallagher, 1982). It was found that there was a rapid development of short-latency increases in multiple unit activity in ACE during conditioning. In some cases, the development of increases in unit activity paralleled the development of the HR CR. In addition, these increases were significantly correlated with CR magnitude.

In another study, Pascoe and Kapp (1985b) recorded single-unit activity during differential Pavlovian conditioning. This *differential* conditioning procedure offered an advantage over the previous study because nonspecific changes in activity as a result of presentation of the CS and US could be taken into account. They identified six categories of neurons based on their spontaneous activity and responses to the CS and US. Of these, only one class of neurons (Type 1) appeared to project directly to the lower brainstem. These neurons tended to have low spontaneous firing rates (0.01 - 0.4 Hz) and demonstrated a greater decrease in firing rate to the CS+ than to the CS−. Other classes of ACE neurons (Types 2 & 3) also demonstrated changes in activity that were correlated with the HR CR. The possible role of these various neurons in the HR CR is unclear; however, Pascoe and Kapp (1985b) suggested that some of these ACE cells may influence brainstem cardioregulatory nuclei via hypothalamic regions. In light of the previous findings (Kaufman et al., 1979), that descending cardioregulatory pathways may connect oligosynaptically with the medulla, the ACE neurons without direct projections to the brainstem identified by Pascoe and Kapp (1985b) could be modulating lower cardioregulatory regions oligosynaptically.

Other studies have examined more caudal aspects of the amygdalo–vagal pathway. The role of the hypothalamus in HR conditioning was examined by Powell and colleagues (Francis, Hernandez, & Powell, 1981). Lesions of the far lateral hypothalamus produced smaller magnitude bradycadiac responses during adaptation, acquisition, and extinction. However, eyeblink CRs were relatively unaffected. This study suggests that the lesions may have selectively affected the HR responses. It should be mentioned that, in other animals, hypothalamic lesions have selectively abolished tachycardia CRs. In baboons, lesions of the perifornical area just rostral to the intrahypothalamic route of the columns of the fornix abolished the tachycardia CR but had no effect on exercise induced HR changes, on HR URs, or on lever-press response suppression (Smith et al., 1980). Similarly, in pigeons, lesions involving the terminal field of the archistriatal projection in the medial hypothalamus attenuated the tachycardia CR (Cohen & MacDonald, 1976). Both these lesions were located more medially than those described by Powell's group. It is possible that the medial region is involved in animals that develop a conditioned HR acceleration (i.e., baboon, pigeon) whereas the lateral hypothalamus mediates conditioned bradycardia in animals such as the rabbit. We have found in the rabbit that electrical stimulation of the lateral hypothalamus elicited primary bradycardia that is abolished by bilateral vagotomy (Gellman et al., 1981; Wallach et al., 1979), whereas stimulation of medial hypothalamic sites produced tachycardia accompanied by a pressor response (Gellman et al., 1981).

Other work in our laboratory indicates that lateral zona incerta (LZI) lesions in rabbits selectively abolish an existing HR CR (Jarrell, McCabe, Teich, Gentile, VanDercar, & Schneiderman, 1986c). Electrodes were implanted bilaterally in LZI or in control sites just dorsal or ventral to LZI. Two days following surgery, animals were subjected to Pavlovian conditioning or to pseudoconditioning. After a HR CR had been established, bilateral electrolytic lesions were made. These lesions did not influence either the HR OR, UR, or baseline HR. Bilateral LZI lesions, but not nearby control lesions or unilateral LZI damage, did, however, abolish the HR CR. In a follow-up experiment, both HR and CRP were recorded. Bilateral LZI lesions abolished the HR CR without affecting CRP CRs. Thus, the findings indicate that the LZI is selectively involved in the HR CR in rabbits. This study also provides evidence that the amygdalo–vagal bradycardia pathway, which passes through LZI, is the CR pathway.

Although the previous studies implicated ACE, LH, and LZI in conditioned bradycardia, it was not clear whether the results were due to destruction of cell bodies in these structures or to fibers of passage. Therefore, we undertook a study in which ibotenic acid, a substance that selectively destroys cell bodies but spares fibers of passage, was injected bilaterally into ACE, LZI, or control sites (Gentile, Romanski, Jarrell, McCabe, & Schneiderman, 1986b). After approximately 7 days of recovery, animals were exposed to differential Pavlovian conditioning. ACE, LZI, or control injections had no effect on HR baseline, HR OR, HR UR, or CRP conditioning. Animals with LZI injections of ibotenic acid or control injections showed differentially conditioned bradycardiac responses. However, animals in the group receiving ibotenic acid injection into ACE did not demonstrate differential bradycardiac responses to the acoustic stimuli. These findings indicate that cell bodies in ACE and not fibers of passage in this region play an important role in differentially conditioned bradycardiac responses but not CRP conditioned responses. In addition, it appears that the earlier finding that electrolytic lesions in LZI abolish the HR CR (Jarrell et al., 1986c) was due to the interruption of fibers of passage originating in ACE.

Despite the existence of projections from insular cortex to ACE, insular cortex does not appear to be necessary for the expression of the HR CR. Powell et al. (1985) found that lesions in anterior insular cortex slightly decreased CR magnitude, whereas lesions in posterior insular cortex tended to slightly increase the magnitude of the HR CR. Although anterior insular cortex lesions affected CR magnitude, they did not produce a decrement in response magnitude comparable to that seen after ACE lesions (Gentile et al., 1986a; Kapp et al., 1979), nor did they prevent differential conditioning. One possible explanation for these findings is that all the anterior insular cortex, a relatively large area, was not destroyed. However, anterior insular lesions decreased the magnitude of the response to the CS+ and CS−, whereas lesions in ACE only affect the response to the CS+ (Gentile et al., 1986a). Therefore, it appears that insular cortex may be involved in modulation of CR magnitude.

In contrast, cingulate cortex lesions greatly attenuated the HR CR but did not affect CRP CRs (Buchanan & Powell, 1982). Therefore, cingulate cortex may be directly involved in CR expression. It is clear that further research is necessary to clarify the role of cortical regions in the bradycardiac CR.

Powell and associates also have examined the role of the septo-hippocampal system in HR conditioning (Buchanan & Powell, 1980; Hernandez & Powell, 1981; Powell & Buchanan, 1980; Powell, Milligin, & Mull, 1982). For example, lesions of the lateral septal nucleus enhanced the HR CR magnitude (Powell, Milligin, & Mull, 1982). Similarly, lesions of the dorsal hippocampus produced an enhancement of the bradycardiac CR. Powell and co-workers have suggested that the septo-hippocampal system may be part of an inhibitory forebrain pathway that can modulate the HR CR.

Although the existing data supports the notion that a descending amygdalo–vagal pathway mediates the expression of the CR, recent studies have proposed that a descending ACE–NTS pathway may modulate the baroreceptor reflex and thereby be responsible for the CR. In fact, it has been demonstrated that the baroreceptor reflex may be important for the expression of the HR CR in rats (Fitzgerald et al., 1984; Hatton et al., 1984). To test this notion further, a recent study was conducted in our laboratory (Jarrell, Gentile, McCabe, & Schneiderman, 1986b) to examine the role of the baroreceptor reflex in differential Pavlovian conditioning of bradycardia in rabbits. Animals received aortic denervation, sinoaortic denervation, or sham denervation. After recovery from surgery, animals received one differential Pavlovian conditioning session per day over the next 6 days. Sinoaortic denervation abolished the baroreceptor reflex as assessed by intravenous injections of phenylephrine. In addition, sinoaortic denervation increased baseline HR, altered the topography of the HR UR, but did not abolish the HR OR or prevent the acquisition of bradycardiac CRs. The findings suggest that afferent barosensory input is not necessary for the expression of the HR CR in rabbits. It is likely that the discrepancy between rats and rabbits can be explained by the different nature of the blood pressure CR. In the rat, the blood pressure CR is a pressor response, whereas in the rabbit the blood pressure CR is a small depressor response (Jarrell et al., 1986c). These differences suggest that in the HR CR in rats may be, in part, reflexive to blood pressure elevations, but in the rabbit the HR CR is independent of blood pressure elevations. It should be mentioned that although the afferent limb of the baroreceptor reflex is not necessary for the acquisition of the HR CR in rabbits, this study does not rule out the possibility that the ACE–NTS pathway plays a role in HR conditioning. It has been demonstrated that ACE projects to the ventral periaqueductal grey (Hopkins & Holstege, 1978), which in turn projects to NTS (Bandler & Tork, 1987). It is possible that this pathway may be part of the CR pathway and directly contribute to CR expression via an NTS–DVN interaction.

In summary, the findings of a number of studies have revealed a descending amygdalo–vagal pathway that appears to mediate the HR CR to tones in rabbits. This pathway originates in ACE, passes through LH and LZI, and projects to the dorsomedial medulla. Although this pathway plays a role in the expression of the bradycardiac CR, it is not clear how it acts to produce HR CRs. One possibility is that this pathway is an excitatory one that acts upon cardioinhibitory preganglionic neurons in DVN and/or NA. However, there is also evidence that this pathway may provide an inhibitory input to NTS that is withdrawn during delivery of the CS.

Although ACE is an essential part of the neural circuitry for the HR CR, other telencephalic structures may also play a role in CR expression or modulation. For example, the cingulate cortex appears to modulate CR expression, whereas the septo-hippocampal region may be important in CR inhibition. The insular cortex and septo-hippocampal region may serve a modulatory function during more complex learning. Further research is necessary to establish the exact relationship of these regions to the amygdalo–vagal pathway.

SENSORY REGIONS INVOLVED IN HR CONDITIONING

Although the viceral-motor pathway that transmits conditioned information to the heart has been extensively studied, information concerning the sensory structures involved in HR conditioning has been scarce. Clearly, it is equally important to describe the pathways that mediate CS and US information as it is to detail the pathway involved in the expression of the CR. It has been suggested by Cohen and Randall (1984) that the lack of attention to sensory pathways may be due to the fact that they are not unique to cardiovascular CRs. Weinberger (1984) has provided a good rationale for studying sensory systems involved in conditioning. First, he argues that neural events related to learning may occur initially on the sensory side because the CS is the "stimulus about which something is learned" (p. 489). Second, the functions of sensory systems have been studied more extensively and are better understood than other brain systems. These features make sensory systems an attractive starting place for studying the neurophysiology of learning.

Although sensory pathways have classically been viewed as "passive" input lines for CS information during conditioning, recent evidence indicates that this is clearly not the case (Cohen & Randall, 1984). Cohen and co-workers have observed training-induced functional changes in the visual system during HR conditioning to light CSs in pigeons (reviewed in Cohen & Randall, 1984). Although the retinal output remained the same, lateral geniculate neurons demonstrated CS-evoked modifications in response as a result of conditioning. The same cells appeared to receive US information from the locus coeruleus. Based on these findings, Cohen and Randall (1984) have argued that there may be training-induced modifications at many levels of stimulus–response processing.

In addition to associative changes in the visual system, a number of studies have demonstrated a modification of units in the auditory system during differential conditioning to acoustic CSs (Birt & Olds, 1982; Gabriel, Orona, Foster, & Lambert, 1982; Weinberger, 1982). Although these studies have focused on various CRs in different species, evidence of differential conditionability has consistently been observed in the medial division of the medial geniculate nucleus (mMGN). In the rabbit, the mMGN was the only auditory region to demonstrate differential changes before evidence of differential behavioral CRs (Gabriel et al., 1982). These findings suggest that mMGN may be an important region for initial processing of stimulus significance.

In the HR conditioning paradigm that we use, tonal stimuli serve as the CSs. In order to determine an appropriate region of the auditory system to examine, in an initial study HRP was injected into ACE (Jarrell, Gentile, McCabe, & Schneiderman, 1986a). These injections produced cell body and fiber labeling in mMGN. Kapp (Kapp, Schwaber, & Driscoll, 1984) has also reported HRP labeling in this area. The role of this region in the mediation of differential conditioning of HR deceleration and CRP responses was then examined (Jarrell et al., 1986). Bilateral electrolytic lesions were made in mMGN or in control sites dorsal or rostral to MGN. Ten days following surgery, lesioned animals an unoperated control animals were subjected to 7 days (1 session/day) of differential conditioning. The 7 acquisition days were followed by 2 days of extinction in which both tones were presented alone. Each group demonstrated bradycardiac responses to both the CS+ and CS−. In the control-lesion and unoperated groups, the CS+ consistently elicited larger bradycardiac responses than the CS−. However, animals with bilateral mMGN lesions did not demonstrate differential bradycardiac responses. Bradycardiac CR magnitude was not significantly different among the three groups. Evidence of CRP differential conditioning was present in each group. These findings suggest that mMGN, or fibers passing through this region, selectively mediate HR differential conditioning in rabbits. The fact that bradycardiac responses are still present after lesions of mMGN suggests that other auditory regions may also be involved in the mediation of the bradycardiac conditioned response.

A separate study was conducted to determine whether the results of our previous experiment were due to destruction of cell bodies in mMGN or to fibers

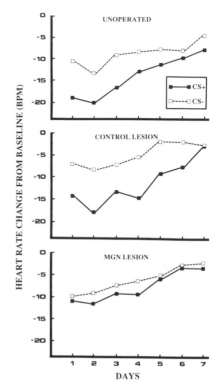

FIG. 14.3. The mean heart rate from baseline to the CS+ and CS− over 7 days of acquisition training for unoperated, control lesion, and mMGN lesion groups. Animals with lesions in mMGN failed to demonstrate bradycardia differential CRs From Jarrell et al. (1986a).

of passage (Jarrell, Romanski, Gentile, McCabe, & Schneiderman, 1986d). Injections of ibotenic acid were made bilaterally in mMGN or in control sites. In addition, control injections of pontamine sky blue were made in mMGN. After 17 days of recovery, animals were subjected to differential Pavlovian conditioning. Ibotenic acid lesions had no effect on the baseline HR, HR OR, or HR UR. In the control lesion and control injection group, the CS+ elicited a larger bradycardiac response than the CS−. However, animals with lesions in mMGN did not demonstrate differential bradycardia responses to the CS+ and CS−. In this group, bradycardiac responses to the CS+ and CS− were similar in magnitude due to a reduction in the magnitude of the response to the CS+. These data suggest that cell bodies in mMGN were responsible for the observed effect, not fibers of passage. Again, because bradycardiac responses were still present after the lesion, other auditory regions may be involved in the mediation of the bradycardiac CR.

We have recently completed another study (Jarrell, Gentile, Romanski, McCabe, & Schneiderman, 1987) that examines further the role of mMGN in bradycardiac conditioning using a retention paradigm. This experiment also examined the possible contributions of the ventral division of the medial geniculate nucleus (vMGN) and auditory cortex to differential conditioning of bradycardia

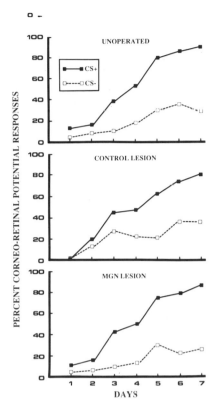

FIG. 14.4.   The mean %CRP responses to the CS+ and CS− over 7 days of acquisition training for the unoperated, control lesion, and mMGN lesion groups. Each group demonstrated evidence of CRP differential CRs From Jarrell et al. (1986a).

to tonal stimuli. Electrodes were chronically implanted bilaterally in mMGN, vMGN, or auditory cortex. After 7 days of recovery from surgery, each animal received one differential Pavlovian conditioning session. At the end of this session, electrolytic lesions were produced through the implanted electrodes. On the following day, the animals received another conditioning session. Each group of animals demonstrated differential bradycardiac conditioning during the prelesion session. During the postlesion session, animals with lesions in vMGN continued to demonstrate differential CRs. However, animals with mMGN or auditory cortex lesions failed to demonstrate differential conditioning during the postlesion session due to the fact that the postlesion response to the CS− was significantly larger. The results of this study indicate that lesions in mMGN abolish the retention of previously established differential HR CRs to acoustic CSs. The fact that either auditory cortex or mMGN lesions enhanced responses to the CS− suggests that a corticothalamic pathway may be involved in the inhibition of responses to the CS−.

It has been argued that vMGN and mMGN are part of separate auditory pathways involved in parallel processing of acoustic stimulus information. Wein-

FIG. 14.5. A representation of lesion location in coronal sections for animals with MGN lesions. Lesions were located in either the ventral division of MGN(A) or the medial division of MGN(B). Only the lesions in the medial division affected the retention of the CR. Abbreviations: MGd, dorsal division of MGN; MGm, medial division of MGN; MGv, ventral division of MGN; SC, superior colliculus; SG, suprageniculate nucleus; PT, posterior nucleus of the thalamus From Jarrell et al. (1987).

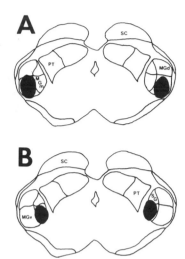

berger (1984) suggested that the secondary lemniscal system that includes mMGN may play a role in processing of stimulus significance during conditioning. Although mMGN seems to be involved in both the retention and acquisition of differential bradycardia CRs, it appears that the mechanism may be different in each case. In acquisition paradigms mMGN lesions attenuated the magnitude of the response to the CS+; however, in retention paradigms mMGN lesions enhanced the magnitude of the response to the CS−. Thus, it is possible that during

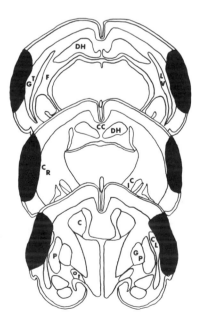

FIG. 14.6. Coronal sections showing the rostrocaudal (bottom to top) extent of cortical damage in auditory cortex lesioned animals. These lesions enhanced the response to the unpaired stimulus (CS−). Abbreviations: C, caudate; CC, corpus callosum; CL, claustrum; CR, corona radiata; DH, dorsal hippocampus; F, fimbria of the fornix; GP, globus pallidus; GT, geniculocalcarine tract; IC, internal capsule; LV, lateral ventricle; OT, optic tract; P, putamen. From Jarrell et al. (1987).

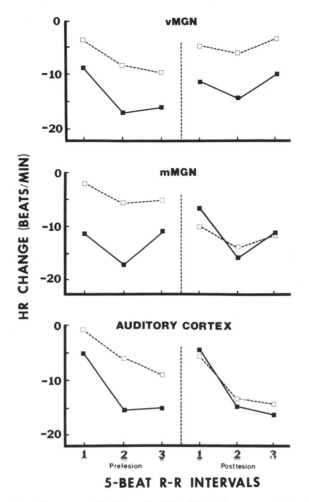

FIG. 14.7. The mean HR CRs to the CS+ (filled square; solid line) and CS− (open square; broken line) are shown for vMGN, mMGN, and auditory cortex lesion groups. Lesions in vMGN had no effect on differential HR CRs, whereas lesions in mMGN or auditory cortex enhanced the response to the CS−. From Jarrell et al. (1987).

the initial acquisition of the response mMGN may play a role in the inhibition of the response to the CS−, perhaps via a corticothalamic pathway originating in the auditory cortex. This hypothesis was tested in a recent experiment (Teich, McCabe, Gentile, Winters, Liskowsky, & Schneiderman, 1988) in which the effect of lesions of the auditory cortex on the acquisition of differential HR conditioning was examined. Lesions were made in either the auditory cortex or the visual cortex. After 7 days of recovery, animals received 7 days of differential

Pavlovian bradycardia conditioning. All animals demonstrated differential conditioning during the first 3 days of conditioning; however, on days 4–7, auditory cortex lesioned animals did not exhibit significant differential HR conditioning, whereas control lesioned animals continued to show differential CRs. The loss of differential conditioning in the animals lesioned in the auditory cortex appeared to be due to an increase in response magnitude to the CS−. These data further support the notion that the auditory cortex plays a role in differential conditioning of bradycardia to acoustic stimuli via a corticothalamic pathway involved in the inhibition of the response to the CS− after the CR has become well learned.

The existence of a corticothalamic pathway that inhibits the responses to CSs suggests the possibility that the cortex may also play a role during extinction. It has been suggested that extinction is not merely the loss of what has been learned, but rather that the organism learns a new inhibitory response (Domjan & Burkhard, 1986). Thus, the conditioned inhibition prevents the appearance of the CR. Although it has been suggested that the cerebral cortex plays a fundamental role in the inhibitory process during extinction (Konorski, 1948; Pavlov, 1927), there is no empirical evidence to support this theory.

We have recently completed a study that examined the role of the auditory cortex in the extinction of differentially conditioned HR responses (Teich, McCabe, Gentile, Liskowsky, Winters, & Schneiderman, 1989). Lesions were placed bilaterally in either auditory cortex or visual cortex. Three days after recovery from surgery, the rabbits were habituated to the tone CSs and then given one Pavlovian differential conditioning sessions (60 trials) per day for 2 days. Animals that had demonstrated reliable differential conditioning (CS+ response at least 5 beats greater than the CS− response) were placed on an extinction schedule for 7 days. The extinction schedule was identical to the differential conditioning schedule with the exception that shock never followed the CS+. The results of the study indicated that auditory cortex lesions prevent the extinction of differential bradycardiac CRs to tonal CSs. Whereas the bradycardiac responses to the CS+ quickly extinguished in the control lesion group, the auditory cortex lesion group continued to exhibit significantly larger bradycardiac HR CRs to the CS+ relative to the CS− during all 7 days of extinction. These results suggest that the animals in the auditory cortex lesioned group were unable to inhibit responses to a previously reinforced stimulus (i.e., CS+).

SENSORY CONDITIONING IN OTHER LABORATORIES

It has been reported that in the rat MGN lesions but not auditory cortex lesions significantly attenuate HR CRs (Ledoux et al., 1984). Based on this data and anatomical information, it was concluded that CS information diverges from the ascending auditory pathway at the level of MGN. At first glance, this study appears to be in conflict with work from our laboratory. The discrepant findings, however, can be explained by an important procedural difference. In the rat study, the investigators did not use a differential conditioning paradigm, whereas our studies did. Because the role of the mMGN and the auditory cortex appear to involve discrimination of stimulus significance, studies that do not employ a differential paradigm would not detect the effects of mMGN and auditory cortex lesions that we observed.

Several studies have demonstrated that neuronal activity within MGN can be modified by conditioning (Birt, Nienhuis, & Olds, 1979; Birt & Olds, 1981; Gabriel, Miller, & Saltwick, 1976; Gabriel, Saltwick, & Miller, 1975; Olds, Nienhuis, & Olds, 1978; Ryugo & Weinberger, 1978). Although primary sensory pathways were traditionally thought to provide static representations of the environment, it appears now that the associative significance of afferent information can produce functional changes in these sensory systems. Birt and Olds (1981) concluded that these neural changes are not related to general stimulus significance nor are they tightly coupled with motor activity associated with the conditioning paradigm. Instead, they viewed this modification of neuronal activity as an early stage of processing that links *specific* behaviors to *specific* stimuli. They (Birt & Olds, 1981) stated: "that although the mechanisms of learned neural changes may be quite general, the distribution of neurons exhibiting such change may be dependent both on the nature of the conditioned stimulus and the nature of the conditioned response. Thus the distribution of neurons showing conditioned change would be expected to vary as the conditioning paradigm was varied" (p. 1052).

Conditioned modulation of sensory information suggests that CS pathways may play an important role in the development of differential CRs. It is conceivable that physical changes due to association of CS and US information occur in the CS pathway. This formation of an "engram" in sensory pathways has been suggested as a possible mechanism by Olds (Olds, Disterhoft, Segal, Kornblith, & Hirsch, 1972). Gabriel et al. (1976) proposed an alternative model in which a sensory filtering process modulates the activity of neurons in primary sensory pathways. This model suggests that tonic neural input from a corticofugal pathway to sensory structures, such as MGN, may suppress the activity evoked by the CS− whereas enhancing the activity evoked by the CS+. This sensory filtering mechanism may provide the neural basis of differential conditioning, and in fact this hypothesis is supported by work from our laboratory (Jarrell et al., 1986a, 1987; Teich et al., 1988). Gabriel et al. (1976) reported that there is a close tie between MGN and behavioral discrimination, whereas MGN activity is not a precursor of behavioral responding. Studies that have *not* used *differential* conditioning paradigms have reported modulation of CS neuronal activity in dorsal cochlear nucleus (Galambos, Sheatz, & Vernier, 1955; Galin, 1965), trapezoid body (Galin, 1965), inferior colliculus (Buchwald, Halas, & Schramm, 1966; Galin, 1965), and medial geniculate nucleus (Buchwald et al., 1966). However, when *differential* conditioning paradigms *have been* employed, associative changes in CS unit activity occur only in MGN (Birt, Nienhuis, & Holds, 1979; Birt & Olds, 1981). These data are strongly supported by our finding that MGN lesions abolish the animal's ability to differentiate between CS+ and CS− but do not affect the magnitude of conditioned bradycardia (Jarrell et al. 1986a).

Work of Gonzalez-Lima and Scheich (1984) utilized the 2-deoxyglucose auto-radiographic method to map the metabolic activity of auditory nuclei in the rat before, during, and after conditioning. The results show an enhanced metabolic response to CS–US pairings in all auditory structures (i.e., dorsal cochlear nucleus, trapezoid body, superior olive, lateral lemniscus, inferior colliculus, MGN). In addition, presentation of the CS alone after conditioning produced increased metabolic activity in all structures *except* MGN. Although this study suggests that conditioning effects exist at all levels of the CS pathway, the authors have no explanation for the lack of MGN activity. The data may be explained by the fact that a differential conditioning paradigm was not used during extinction trials. Therefore, the exact role of the auditory system in HR conditioning needs further elucidation. It is not clear whether all auditory structures are involved, and if so to what extent each nucleus contributes to conditioning. Moreover, our initial data suggest that some auditory structures may only be involved in dis-crimination. It is conceivable that parallel pathways exist such that more caudal structures are involved in the expression of conditioned HR responses and more rostral structures (i.e., MGN, auditory cortex) are involved in the discrimination among various tones.

SUMMARY AND CONCLUSIONS

The circuit model in Fig. 14.8 represents a summary of the available literature relevant to bradycardia conditioning in rabbits. The CR pathway was described in some detail previously. Briefly, descending projections from ACE appear to course through LH and LZI. It is not clear, however, whether the critical fibers project directly to the cardioregulatory nuclei of the dorsomedial medulla, syn-apse in other regions (i.e., PBN), or both. It is likely that information about the US enters through the trigeminal nerve and synapses in the main sensory nucleus of V (NV) among other regions. Projections from NV to NTS and/or NA (Liskowsky, 1981) may be part of the essential US/UR pathway. In addition, barosensory inputs from the carotid sinus nerve and aortic nerve are also impor-tant for the HR UR. Although little is known about the critical pathways that carry US information, it is likely that this information is received either directly or indirectly at a number of different levels of the CS and CR pathways. The CS pathway is based on the anatomical, electrophysiological, and conditioning stud-ies reviewed previously. Although the only connections between the CS and CR pathways illustrated in this model are projections from mMGN to ACE and LZI, the CR pathway must also receive CS information either directly or indirectly

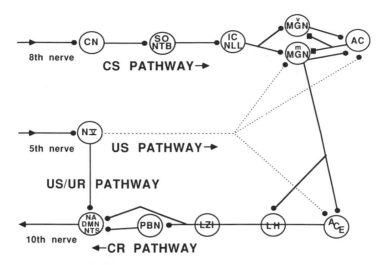

FIG. 14.8. Proposed circuit model of the conditioned stimulus (CS), conditioned response (CR), unconditioned stimulus (US), and unconditioned response (UR), pathways for classical conditioning of differential heart rate responses (from T. W. Jarrell, unpublished doctoral dissertation). Solid lines represent identified aspects of the CS and US pathways. Broken lines suggest possible US pathways. Abbreviations: AC, auditory cortex; ACE, amygdaloid central nucleus; CN, cochlear nuclei; DMN, dorsal motor nucleus of the vagus; IC, inferior colliculus; LH, lateral hypothalamus; LZI, lateral zona incerta; MGm, medial division of the medial geniculate nucleus; MGv, ventral division of the medial geniculate nucleus; NA, nucleus ambiguus; NLL, nucleus of the lateral leminiscus; NTB, nucleus of the trapezoid body; NTS, nucleus of the solitary tract; NV, main sensory nucleus of the V; PBN, parabrachial nucleus; SO, superior olivary nucleus.

from other auditory regions. This point is obvious from the fact that neither auditory cortex nor mMGN lesions totally abolish bradycardiac responses to the CSs. Injections of HRP into zona incerta produce retrogradely labeled cells in the dorsal nucleus of the lateral lemniscus in the rat (Roger & Cadusseau, 1985). However, labeling was sparse and was not present in all animals. Therefore, additional research will be necessary to determine the other auditory regions that influence the CR.

One feature of the model presented in Fig. 14.8 suggests that CS and US information are received and integrated at many different sites (e.g., ACE, mMGN, and auditory cortex). Although there may be a representation of the learned association at many sites, each region may play a different role in CR expression. For example, ACE may be capable of initiating a CR to a CS after a few CS–US pairings but may not be able to initiate differential conditioning. Projections from mMGN to ACE may begin to initiate differential conditioning by enhancing the response to the CS+. Further refinement of differential responses may then be achieved by descending inhibitiory influences on mMGN from auditory cortex neurons.

ACKNOWLEDGMENTS

The research from our laboratory described in this chapter was supported by NIH grants HL 07426 and NS 24874

REFERENCES

Applegate, C. D., Frysinger, R. C., Kapp, B. S., & Gallagher, M. (1982). Multiple unit activity recorded from amygdala central nucleus during Pavlovian heart rate conditioning in rabbit. *Brain Research, 238*, 457–462.

Bandler, R., & Tork, I. (1987) Midbrain periaqueductal grey region in the cat has afferent and efferent connections with solitary tract nuclei. *Neuroscience Letters, 74*, 1–6.

Birt, D., Nienhuis, R., & Olds, M. (1979). Separation of associative from non-associative short latency changes in medial geniculate and inferior colliculus during differential conditioning and reversal in rats. *Brain Research, 167*, 129–138.

Birt, D., & Olds, M. (1981). Associative response changes in lateral midbrain tegmentum and medial geniculate during differential appetitive conditioning. *Journal of Neurophysiology, 46*, 1039–1055.

Birt, D., & Olds, M. E. (1982). Auditory response enhancement during differential conditioning in behaving rats. In C. D. Woody (Ed.), *Representation of involved neural functions* (pp. 483–501). New York, Plenum press.

Buchanan, S. L., & Powell, D. A. (1980). Divergencies in Pavlovian conditioned heart rate and eyeblink responses produced by hippocampectomy in the rabbit (Oryctolagus cuniculus). *Behavioral and Neural Biology, 30*, 20–38.

Buchanan, S. L., & Powell, D. A. (1982). Cingulate cortex: Its role in Pavlovian conditioning. *Journal of Comparative and Physiological Psychology, 96*, 755–774.

Buchwald, J. S., Halas, E. S., & Schramm, S. (1966). Changes in cortical and subcortical unit activity during behavioral conditioning. *Physiology and Behavior, 1*, 11–22.

Cohen, D. H. (1974). The neural pathways and informational flow mediating a conditioned autonomic response. In L. V. DiCara (Ed.), *Limbic and autonomic nervous systems research*. New York: Plenum Press.

Cohen, D. H., & MacDonald, R. L. (1976). Involvement of the avian hypothalamus in defensively conditioned heart rate change. *Journal of Comparative Neurology, 167*, 465–480.

Cohen, D. H., & Randall, D. C. (1984). Classical conditioning of cardiovascular responses. *Annual Review of Physiology, 46*, 187–197.

Domjan, M., & Burkhard, B. (1986) *The Principles of Learning and Behavior*. Belmont, CA: Brooks-Cole.

Ellenberger, H. H., Haselton, J. R., Liskowsky, D. R., & Schneiderman, N. (1983). The location of chronotropic cardioinhibitory vagal motoneurons in the medulla of the rabbit. *Journal of the Autonomic Nervous System, 9*, 513–529.

Elster, A. J., VanDercar, D. H., & Schneiderman, N. (1970). Classical conditioning of heart rate discriminations using subcortical stimulation as conditioned and unconditioned stimuli. *Physiology and Behavior, 5*, 503–508.

Fitzgerald, R. D., Hatton, D. C., Foutz, S., Gilden, E., & Martinsen, D. (1984). Effects of drug-induced changes in resting blood pressure on classically conditioned heart rate and blood pressure in restrained rats. *Behavioral Neuroscience, 98,* 829–839.

Francis, J., Hernandez, L. L., & Powell, D. A. (1981). Lateral hypothalamic lesions: Effects on Pavlovian cardiac and eyeblink conditioning in the rabbit. *Brain Research Bulletin, 6,* 155–163.

Fredericks, A., Moore, J. W., Metcalf, F. U., Schwaber, J. S., & Schneiderman, N. (1974). Selective autonomic blockade of conditioned and unconditioned heart rate changes in rabbits. *Pharmacology, Biochemistry, & Behavior, 2,* 493–501.

Gabriel, M., Miller, J. D., & Saltwick, S. E. (1976). Multiple-unit activity of the rabbit medial geniculate nucleus in conditioning, extinction, and reversal. *Physiological Psychology, 4,* 124–134.

Gabriel, M., Orona, E., Foster, K., & Lambert, R. W. (1982). Mechanism and generality of stimulus significance coding in a mammalian model system. In C. D. Woody (Ed.), *Representation of involved neural functions* (pp. 535–565). New York: Plenum Press.

Gabriel, M., Saltwick, S. E., & Miller, J. D. (1975). Conditioning and reversal of short-latency multiple-unit responses in the rabbit medial geniculate nucleus. *Science, 189,* 1108–1109.

Galambos, R., Sheatz, G., & Vernier, V. G. (1955). Electrophysiological correlates of a conditioned response in cats. *Science, 123,* 376–377.

Galin, D. (1965). Background and evoked activity in the auditory pathway: Effects of noise-shock pairing. *Science, 149,* 761–763.

Gallagher, M., Kapp, B. S., Frysinger, R. C., & Rapp, P. R. (1980). Beta-adrenergic manipulation in amygdala central nucleus alters rabbit heart rate conditioning. *Pharmacology Biochemistry and Behavior, 12,* 419–426.

Gallagher, M., Kapp, B. S., McNall, C. L., & Pascoe, J. P. (1981). Opiate effects in the amygdala central nucleus on heart rate conditioning in rabbits. *Pharmacology and Biochemistry and Behavior, 14,* 497–505.

Gellman, M., Schneiderman, N., Wallach, J., & LeBlanc, W. (1981). Cardiovascular responses elicited by hypothalamic stimulation in rabbits reveal a medio-lateral organization. *Journal of the Autonomic Nervous System, 4,* 301–317.

Gentile, C. G., Jarrell, T. W., Teich, A. H., McCabe, P. M., & Schneiderman, N. (1986a). The role of amygdaloid central nucleus in differential Pavlovian conditioning of bradycardia in rabbits. *Behavioral Brain Research, 20,* 263–273.

Gentile, C. G., Romanski, L. M., Jarrell, T. W., McCabe, P. M., & Schneiderman, N. (1986b). Ibotenic acid lesions in amygdaloid central nucleus prevent the acquisition of differentially conditioned bradycardiac responses in rabbits. *Society for Neuroscience Abstracts, 12.*

Gonzalez-Lima, F., & Scheich, H. (1984). Neural substrates for tone-conditioned bradycardia demonstrated with 2-deoxyglucose. I. Activation of auditory nuclei. *Behavioral Brain Research, 14,* 213–233.

Hamilton, R. B., Ellenberger, H., Liskowsky, D., & Schneiderman, N. (1981). Parabrachial area as mediator of bradycardia in rabbits. *Journal of the Autonomic Nervous System, 4,* 261–281.

Hatton, D. C., Foutz, S. R., & Fitzgerald, R. D. (1984). Baroreceptor involvement in classically conditioned heart rate responses of restrained rats. *Physiology and Behavior, 33,* 31–35.

Hernandez, L. L., & Powell, D. A. (1981). Forebrain norepinephrine and serotonin concentrations and cardiac conditioning in normal rabbits and rabbits with septal lesions. *Brain Research Bulletin, 6,* 479–486.

Hopkins, D. A., & Holstege, G. (1978). Amygdaloid projections to the mesencephalon, pons, and medulla oblongata in the cat. *Experimental Brain Research, 32,* 529–547.

Jarrell, T. W., Gentile, C. G., McCabe, P. M., & Schneiderman, N. (1986a). The role of medial geniculate nucleus in differential Pavlovian conditioning of bradycardia in rabbits. *Brain Research, 374,* 126–136.

Jarrell, T. W., Gentile, C. G., McCabe, P. M., & Schneiderman, N. (1986b). Sinoaortic denervation does not prevent differential Pavlovian conditioning of bradycardia in rabbits. *Brain Research, 374,* 126–136.

Jarrell, T. W., Gentile, C. G., Romanski, L. M., McCabe, P. M., & Schneiderman, N. (1987). Involvement of cortical and thalamic auditory regions in retention of differential bradycardiac conditioning stimuli in rabbits. *Brain Research.*

Jarrell, T. W., McCabe, P. M., Teich, A., Gentile, C. G., VanDercar, D., & Schneiderman, N. (1986c). Lateral subthalamus area as mediator of classically conditioned bradycardia in rabbits. *Behavioral Neuroscience, 100,* 3–10.

Jarrell, T. W., Romanski, L. M., Gentile, C. G., McCabe, P. M., & Schneiderman, N. (1986d). Ibotenic acid lesions in the medical geniculate region prevent the acquisition of differential Pavlovian conditioning of bradycardia to acoustic stimuli in rabbits. *Brain Research, 382,* 199–203.

Jordan, D., Khalid, M. E. M., Schneiderman, N., & Spyer, K. M. (1982). Localization and properties of ganglionic cardiomotor neurons in rabbits. *Pflugers Archiv, 395,* 244–250.

Kandel, E. R., & Spencer, W. A. (1968). Cellular neurophysiological approaches to learning. *Physiological Review, 48,* 65–134.

Kapp, B. S., Frysinger, R. C., Gallagher, M., & Haselton, J. R. (1979). Amygdala central nucleus lesions: Effect on heart rate conditioning in the rabbit. *Physiology and Behavior, 23,* 1109–1117.

Kapp, B. S., Gallagher, M., Underwood, M. D., McNall, C. C., & Whitehorn, D. (1982). Cardiovascular responses elicited by electrical stimulation of the amygdala central nucleus in the rabbit. *Brain Research, 234,* 251–262.

Kapp, B. S., Pascoe, J. P., & Bixler, M. A. (1984). The amygdala: A neuroanatomical systems approach to its contribution to aversive conditioning. In L. R. Squire (Ed.), *Neuropsychology of memory.* (pp. 473–488) New York: Guilford Press.

Kapp, B. S., Schwaber, J. S., & Driscoll, P. A. (1984). Subcortical projections to the amygdaloid central nucleus in the rabbit. *Society for Neuroscience Abstracts, 10,* 831.

Kapp, B. S., Schwaber, J. S., & Driscoll, P. A. (1985). Frontal Cortex Projections to the Amygdaloid Central Nucleus in the Rabbit. *Neuroscience, 15,* 327–346.

Kaufman, M. P., Hamilton, R. B., Wallach, J. H., Petrik, G. K., & Schneiderman, N. (1979). Lateral subthalamic area as mediator of bradycardia responses in rabbits. *American Journal of Physiology, 236,* H471–H479.

Konorski, J. (1948). *Conditioned reflexes and neuron organization.* Cambridge: Cambridge University Press.

Kosupkin, J. M., & Olmstead, J. M. D. (1943). Slowly of the heart as a conditioned reflex in the rabbit. *American Journal of Physiology, 139,* 550–552.

Ledoux, J. E., Sakaguchi, A., & Reis, D. J. (1984). Subcortical efferent projections of the medial geniculate nucleus mediate emotional responses conditioned to acoustic stimuli. *Journal of Neuroscience, 4,* 683–698.

Liskowsky, D. R. (1981). *Descending bradycardia pathways between the parabrachial nucleus and the medulla in the rabbit.* Doctoral dissertation at the University of Miami.

Manning, A. A., Schneiderman, N., & Lordahl, D. S. (1969). Delay versus trace heart-rate classical discrimination conditioning in rabbits as a function of interstimulus interval. *Journal of Experimental Psychology, 80,* 225–230.

Olds, J. E., Disterhoft, J. F., Segal, M., Kornblith, C. L., & Hirsch, R. (1972). Learning centers of rat brain mapped by measuring latencies of conditioned unit responses. *Journal of Neurophysiology, 35,* 202–218.

Olds, J. E., Nienhuis, R., & Olds, M. E. (1978). Patterns of conditioned unit response in the auditory system of the rat. *Experimental Neurology, 59,* 209–228.

Pascoe, J. D., & Kapp, B. S. (1985a). Electrophysiological characteristics of amygdaloid central nucleus neurons in the awake rabbit. *Brain Research Bulletin, 14,* 331–338.

Pascoe, J. D., & Kapp, B. S. (1985b). Electrophysiological characteristics of amygdaloid central nucleus neurons during differential Pavlovian conditioned heart rate responding in the rabbit. *Behavioral Brain Research, 16,* 117–133.

Pavlov, I. P. (1927). *Conditioned reflexes.* London: Oxford University Press.

Powell, D. A., Buchanan, S. L. (1980). Autonomic-somatic relationships in the rabbit (*Oryctalagus Cuniculus*): Effects of hippocampallesions. *Physiological Psychology, 8,* 455–462.

Powell, D. A., Buchanan, S., & Hernandez, L. (1985). Electrical stimulation of insular cortex elicits cardiac inhibition but insular lesions do not abolish conditioned bradycardia in rabbits. *Behavioral Brain Research, 17,* 125–144.

Powell, D. A., Milligin, W. L., & Mull, P. (1982). Lateral septal lesions enhance conditioned bradycardia in the rabbit. *Journal of Comparative and Physiological Psychology, 96,* 742–754.

Roger, M., & Cadusseau, J. (1985). Afferents to the zona incerta in the rat: A combined retrograde and anterograde study. *Journal of Comparative Neurology, 241,* 480–492.

Ryugo, D. K., & Weinberger, N. M. (1978). Differential plasticity of morphologically distinct neuron populations in the medial geniculate body of the cat during classical conditioning. *Behavioral Biology, 22,* 275–301.

Schneiderman, N., Smith, M. C., Smith, A. C., & Gormezano, I. (1966). Heart rate classical conditioning in rabbits. *Psychonomic Science, 6,* 241–242.

Schneiderman, N., VanDercar, D. H., Yehle, A. L., Manning, A. A., Golden, T., & Schneiderman, E. (1969). Vagal compensatory adjustment: Relationship to heart-rate classical conditioning in rabbits. *Journal of Comparative and Physiological Psychology, 68,* 176–183.

Schwaber, J. S., Kapp, B. S., & Higgins, G. (1980). The origin and extent of direct amygdala projections to the region of the dorsal motor nucleus of the vagus and the nucleus of the solitary tract. *Neuroscience Letters, 20,* 15–20.

Schwaber, J. S., Kapp, B. S., Higgins, G. A., & Rapp, P. R. (1982). Amygdaloid and basal forebrain direct connections with the nucleus of the solitary tract and the dorsal motor nucleus. *Journal of Neuroscience, 2*(11), 1414–1438.

Schwaber, J., & Schneiderman, N. (1975). Aortic nerve activated cardioinhibitory neurons and interneurons. *American Journal of Physiology, 229,* 783–789

Sideroff, S., Elster, A. J., & Schneiderman, N. (1972). Cardiovascular classical conditioning in rabbits (Oryctylagus cuniculus) using appetitive or aversive hypothalamic stimulation as the US. *Journal of Comparative and Physiological Psychology, 81,* 501–508.

Smith, O. A., Astley, C. A., DeVito, J. L., Stein, J. M., & Walsh, K. E. (1980). Functional analysis of hypothalamic control of the cardiovascular response accompanying emotional behavior. *Federal Proceedings, 39,* 2487–2494.

Swadlow, H. A., & Schneiderman, N. (1970). Stimulus generalization and transfer of training in rabbits conditioned to electrical stimulation of lateral geniculate nucleus. *Physiology and Behavior, 5,* 841–847.

Swadlow, H., Schneiderman, E., & Schneiderman, N. (1968). Classical conditioning of a discrimination between electrically stimulated lateral geniculate bodies in the rabbit. *Proceedings of the American Psychology Association, 3,* 313–314.

Teich, A. H., McCabe, P. M., Gentile, C. G., Liskowsky, D. R., Winters, R. W., & Schneiderman, N. (1989). *Auditory cortex lesions prevent extinction of differential Pavlovian conditioned heart rate responses in rabbits.* Brain Research, *480,* 210–218.

Teich, A. H., McCabe, P. M., Gentile, C. G., Winters, R. W., Liskowsky, D. R., & Schneiderman, N. (1988). Role of auditory cortex in the acquisition of differential heart rate conditioning. *Physiology and Behavior, 44,* 405–412.

Thompson, R. F., Clark, G. A., Donegan, N. H., Lavond, D. G., Lincoln, D. G., Lincoln, J. S., Madden, J., Mamounas, L. A., Mauk, M. D., McCormick, D. A., & Thompson, J. K. (1984). Neuronal subtrates of learning and memory: A "multiple trace" view. In G. Lynch, J. L. McGaugh, & N. Weinberger (Eds.), *Neurobiology of learning and memory.* (pp. 137–164) New York: Guilford Press.

VanDercar, D. H., Elster, A. J., & Schneiderman, N. (1970). Heart-rate conditioning in rabbits to hypothalamic or septal US stimulation. *Journal of Comparative and Physiological Psychology, 72,* 145–152.

VanDercar, D. H., & Schneiderman, N. (1967). Interstimulus interval functions in different response systems during classical conditioning of rabbits. *Psychonomic Science, 9,* 9–10.

VanDercar, D. H., Swadlow, H. A., Elster, A., & Schneiderman, N. (1969). Nictitating membrane and corneo-retinal transducers for conditioning in rabbits. *American Psychologist, 24,* 262–264.

Wallach, J. H., Ellenberger, H. H., Schneiderman, N., Liskowsky, D. R., Hamilton, R. B., & Gellman, M. D. (1979). Preoptic-anterior hypothalamic area as a mediator of bradycardia responses in rabbits. *Society for Neuroscience Abstracts, 5,* 52.

Weinberger, N. M. (1982). Sensory plasticity and learning: The magnocellular medial geniculate nucleus of the auditory system. In C. D. Woody (Ed.), *Conditioning: Representation of involved neural functions.* (pp. 697–718). New York: Plenum Press.

Weinberger, N. M. (1984). The neurophysiology of learning: A view from the sensory side. In L. R. Squire, & N. Butters (Ed.), *Neuropsychology of memory* (pp. 489–503). New York: Guilford Press.

Wood, D. M., & Obrist, P. A. (1968). Minimal and maximal sensory intake and exercise as unconditioned stimuli in human heart rate conditioning. *Journal of Experimental Psychology, 76,* 254–262.

Yehle, A., Dauth, G., & Schneiderman, N. (1967). Correlates of heart rate conditioning in curarized rabbits. *Journal of Comparative and Physiological Psychology, 64,* 98–104.

15

A Cerebellar Neural Network Implementation of a Temporally Adaptive Conditioned Response

John W. Moore
John E. Desmond*
University of Massachusetts, Amherst

This chapter introduces a theory of how a neural network capable of learning and generating a temporally adaptive conditioned response (CR), the conditioned nictitating membrane response (NMR) of the rabbit, might be implemented in brainstem and cerebellar circuits underlying this behavior (Moore & Berthier, 1987; Thompson, 1986; Yeo, 1987). We characterize the conditioned NMR as temporally adaptive because its topographical features, latency and form, depend on the *timing* of the unconditioned stimulus (US) in relation to the conditioned stimulus (CS)(Gormezano, Kehoe, & Marshall, 1983). Unlike simpler CRs, such as those evinced by some invertebrate preparations, a CS for a temporally adaptive CR such as the NMR does not trigger an invariant reflexive response of fixed latency and form. Instead, it sets an occasion for a variable response that is sensitive to the temporal dimension of the task. A temporally adaptive CR can be regarded as a *skill* that requires a subtle resolution of forces (Desmond, 1988; Desmond, in press; Desmond & Moore, 1988; Moore, Desmond, & Berthier, 1989). A number of authors have previously stressed this point (Kimmel, 1965; Levey & Martin, 1968; Martin & Levey, 1965). The temporally adaptive features of the conditioned NMR encompassed by our model are listed here:

• The latency of the CR with respect to onset of a conditioned stimulus (CS) changes during training. Initially, the CR appears as an enhanced unconditioned response (UR). The nascent CR can also be detected with CS-alone probes at this stage. It next appears just prior to the onset of the unconditioned stimulus (US). At this stage of early CR acquisition, the CR anticipates the UR and tends to

*Current address: EEG Systems Laboratory, 51 Federal Street, Suite 401, San Francisco, CA 94107.

blend with it to assume a smooth unimodal form. With further training the CR emerges as a shadow of the UR cast forward in time toward CS onset. In this regard its development is analogous to the growth of a goal gradient in which the vigor of a sequence of goal-oriented actions progressively increases backward from the locus of reinforcement toward the initial segments of the sequence.

• The latency of the CR depends on the CS–US interval employed in training. If this interval is long the CR is delayed (Pavlovian inhibition of delay). Furthermore, the amplitude of the CR grows progressively (ramps) toward a peak at the temporal locus of the US, as can be demonstrated with CS-alone probes. If the temporal locus of the US changes (e.g., with the introduction of a new CS–US interval), the peak amplitude of the CR changes progressively toward the new US locus.

• In trace conditioning protocols, in which CS *offset* precedes the US, CR initiation and peak amplitude tend to occur within the trace portion of the CS–US interval (i.e., at the same temporal locus as in forward-delay conditioning protocols).

The computational model reviewed next was designed to describe these time-dependent topographical features of the conditioned NMR in a physiologically plausible manner. It has a neural network structure and assumes that adaptive modifications are computed locally by Hebb-like rules that mimic synaptic events. Ultimately, we wish to move beyond mere plausibility and use the model as a fulcrum for representing real neural events in a mathematically rigorous way. Thus, we seek models with empirically testable implications for behavior and neurobiology. The neural implementation of the model outlined subsequently illustrates this characteristic of our approach.

Our initial effort to model CR topography utilized a network consisting of a single neuron-like processing unit (Moore et al. 1986). We refer to this earlier model as the Sutton–Barto–Desmond (SBD) model because it is basically a real-time variant of the Sutton–Barto (SB) model (Sutton & Barto, 1981) as parameterized by John Desmond to yield rudimentary aspects of CR topography. Moore and Blazis (1989) proposed a cerebellar implementation of the SBD model. Although it describes an impressive array of empirical findings, the SBD model has its limitations (Blazis & Moore, 1987). Basically, the SBD model assumes that the processing unit receives a *template* of the CR whenever a CS occurs. This template resembles a CR in form, but it depends only on the CS and its duration, not on the temporal locus of the US. Consequently, it does not yield inhibition of delay or proper CR form in trace conditioning.

The model reviewed in this chapter overcomes these limitations of the SBD model by assuming the network learns not only *that* a CS predicts the US but also *when* the US is likely to occur (Desmond & Moore, 1988). The model differs from the SBD model in that it consists of two neuron-like computing units, designated V and E. The V unit computes associative *values* between CSs and

FIG. 15.1. Basic tapped delay line. Injection of CS input begins sequential propagation of signal through a delay line. Each synapse ($-$ $<$) introduces a delay; the total delay from activation of the first element in the delay line to the last element is a direct function of the number of sequential synapses. Taps from the delay-line units send timing information to higher order processing units. Copyright 1989, Springer–Verlag.

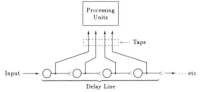

the US and generates the network output. The E unit computes the *expected* arrival time(s) of the US and reinforces computation of associative value by the V unit. Both units receive CS inputs from a *tapped delay line* that represents the temporal dimension of inputs to the network. The tapped delay line discretizes time to facilitate computation of time-dependent variables (see Fig. 15.1). For convenience, we refer to this model as VET.

MODELING CR TOPOGRAPHY WITH VET

A major underlying assumption for the VET model is that changes in CS activation initiate processes that mediate timing functions (Desmond & Moore, 1988; Moore, Desmond, & Berthier, 1989).[1] Timing is achieved by virtue of the tapped delay line architectural arrangement as illustrated in Fig. 15.1. For each CS, onset and offset of the stimulus activate separate tapped delay lines. Consequently, each element of these tapped delay lines is uniquely referenced by three indices: (a) The CS that activates it: Let i refer to the ith CS, where $i = 1, \ldots, n$; (b) whether its activation is linked to CS onset or CS offset: Let j denote whether the element is an onset ($j = 1$) or offset ($j = 0$) element; (c) a unique element number within the delay line: Let k denote the kth element in the array of elements, where $k = 1, \ldots, N$. The k index corresponds to the element's order of activation, where $k = 1$ corresponds to the first element in the delay line and $k = N$ refers to the last element. The elements are referred to as x_{ijk}, and the total number of these elements is equal to $n \times 2 \times N$.

Thus, in the VET network the timing processes initiated by the onset and offset of each CS consists of the sequential propagation of activity along elements in tapped delay lines. At any given time step, each x_{ijk} element is either in an active state [$x_{ijk}(t) = 1$] or an inactive state [$x_{ijk}(t) = 0$]. Once activated, an element remains at 1 for an arbitrary number of time steps (10 steps in the stimulations that follow) and then returns to 0. Thus, activity of the elements overlaps.

---

[1]Such changes in CS activation play an important role in Klopf's drive-reinforcement neuronal model (Klopf, 1986, 1988). However, in contrast to Klopf's model, negative changes in CS activation (i.e., CS offset) can also play a role in generating CRs.

Figure 15.2 illustrates the basic connectivity of the network. The x_{ijk} elements make modifiable "synaptic" contacts with two computational units, V and E. These synapses are designated V_{ijk} and E_{ijk}, respectively. Note that to simplify the figure only one set of x_{ijk} elements are depicted as contacting the V and E units. To fully represent the network for simulating two CSs, four such sets of x_{ijk} would have to be depicted, one set for the onset and offset of each CS. Thus, if the elements in the figure represent the onset elements for CS1, then using the notation described before they would be designated $x_{111}, \ldots, x_{119}$.

The V unit and the E unit both receive input from the US, designated $L(t)$, and the V unit also receives the output of the E unit, designated $r(t)$. These connections are not modifiable, as indicated by the open (-<) synaptic terminals in Fig. 15.2; modifiable V_{ijk} and E_{ijk} connections are indicated by the closed (-◁) synaptic terminals. The output of the network, $s(t)$, is derived from the US input and from the weighted sum of the V unit inputs and is defined as:

$$s(t) = \sum_i \sum_j \sum_k V_{ijk}(t)x_{ijk}(t) + L(t), \qquad (1)$$

where $s(t)$ is confined to the closed unit interval. Changes in the V_{ijk} weights are given by the following expression:

$$\Delta V_{ijk}(t) = c\{L(t) - \hat{s}(t)\}h_{ijk}(t)\ \bar{x}_{ij}(t)r(t). \qquad (2)$$

Equation (2) can be summarized as follows: The amount of change in a V_{ijk} weight at time t [$\Delta V_{ijk}(t)$] is determined by the difference between the US signal and the output of the network [i.e., $L(t) - \hat{s}(t)$, where $\hat{s}(t) = s(t) - L(t)$]. The rate

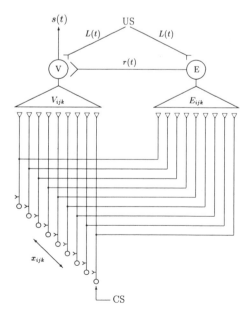

FIG. 15.2. Basic organization of the network model. Tapped delay-line elements are designated x_{ijk}. For simplicity, only 9 onset elements for a single CS (i.e., $x_{111}, \ldots, x_{119}$) are depicted; the 9 offset elements ($x_{101}, \ldots, x_{109}$) are not shown. Further details are in text. Copyright 1988, Springer-Verlag.

of change is also influenced by a learning rate constant, c. In addition, three other variables must be nonzero before any change in a V_{ijk} weight can occur: (a) the "eligibility for modification" of the synapse, $h_{ijk}(t)$, which is maximum when the synapse is activated and subsequently decays geometrically; (b) the "interstimulus interval eligibility," $\bar{x}_{ij}(t)$, which basically limits the amount synaptic change that can occur when the CS–US interval is too short or too long to support conditioning; and (c) the "expectation" of the US, $r(t)$, which is generated from the E unit by the equation,

$$r(t) = \max \{[E_{ijk}(t)\Delta x_{ijk}(t) \mid i = 1, \ldots, n; j = 0,1; k = 1, \ldots, N]$$ (3)

where:

$$\Delta x_{ijk}(t) = \begin{cases} 1 & \text{if } x_{ijk}(t) - x_{ijk}(t-1) = 1; \\ 0 & \text{otherwise,} \end{cases}$$ (4)

and E_{ijk} are the connection weights of the input elements onto the E unit. Changes in these weights are given by:

$$\Delta E_{ijk}(t) = c[L(t) - r(t)]\Delta x_{ijk}(t)\bar{x}_{ij}(t)$$ (5)

where $\Delta x_{ijk}(t)$ is defined as in Equation (4). Note that $\Delta x_{ijk}(t)$ is the E unit's version of synaptic eligibility; this term allows a much shorter period of eligibility than the $h_{ijk}(t)$ term in Equation (2). Thus, in contrast to V_{ijk} synapses, which remain eligible for several time steps after initial activation, E_{ijk} synapses are eligible for only one time step. Consequently, E_{ijk} weights can change only if the synapse is activated during US presentation.

Equations (3) and (4) indicate that an E_{ijk} weight contributes to the output signal $r(t)$ only when the corresponding x_{ijk} element is initially activated. The net effect of Equations (3), (4), and (5) is that the E unit provides discrete bursts of activity to the V unit at times of US expectation (i.e., the bursts occur at temporal loci where previous presentations of the US have occurred). It is only when these expectation signals occur that V_{ijk} synapses are allowed to change.

Basic Network Dynamics

The dynamics of the network on the second trial of acquisition training are illustrated pictorially in Fig. 15.3. Although the delay line is omitted from view and only the taps are depicted, the connectivity in this figure is identical to that depicted in Fig. 15.2. Each panel of Fig. 15.3 represents the state of the network at four different time steps. The upper right corner of each panel shows the current time step and the temporal configuration of the stimuli. The activation levels of $x_{ijk}(t)$, $L(t)$, and $r(t)$ are denoted by the "axons" carrying those signals. A solid-line axon means that the term is equal to zero. A dashed-line axon for $x_{ijk}(t)$ or $L(t)$ means that the term is equal to one; for $r(t)$ it means that $r(t) > 0$. (A

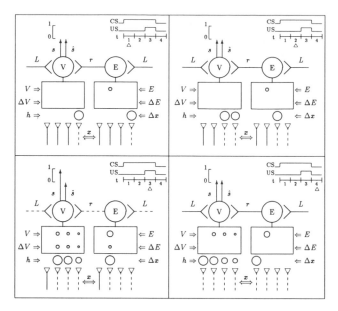

FIG. 15.3. Network dynamics during early acquisition training. See text for details. Copyright 1989, Springer-Verlag.

weak $r(t)$ signal is depicted as a single dashed line, whereas a strong $r(t)$ signal is shown as two parallel dashed lines.) Circles are used to depict relative magnitudes of other terms in the model (magnitude proportional to diameter) and whether those terms are positive (open-circles) or negative (filled-circles). The magnitudes of $s(t)$ and $\hat{s}(t)$ are represented by the lengths of the vectors emanating from the top of the V unit.

The first thing to note in Fig. 15.3 is the sequential and overlapping activation of the x_{ijk} elements for $t = 1$ to $t = 4$. The circles directly above the x_{ijk} terminals represent the degree of synaptic eligibility (h_{ijk} for the V_{ijk} weights and Δx_{ijk} for the E_{ijk} weights). For simplicity, the $\bar{x}_{ij}(t)$ term is not represented in the figure and is assumed to be equal to 1 at all time steps.

The V_{ijk} and E_{ijk} weights, along with the changes in these weights (ΔV_{ijk} and ΔE_{ijk}), are also depicted in Fig. 15.3. Note that one of the E_{ijk} weights has a small positive initial value; this value was obtained on the first training trial. None of the V_{ijk} weights changed on trial one because such changes require a positive $r(t)$ signal, which in turn requires some existing E_{ijk} weight. Thus, trial 2 is depicted in Fig. 15.3 so that the reader can observe changes in both V_{ijk} and E_{ijk} weights. As illustrated in the lower left panel of the figure, these changes occur at time step $t = 3$. It is evident that more recently activated synapses gain greater amounts of associative strength than less recently activated synapses.

Figure 15.4 illustrates network dynamics during extinction training. Note that three V_{ijk} weights and one E_{ijk} weight start out at asymptotic levels and are

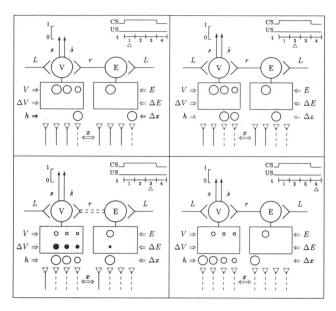

FIG. 15.4. Network dynamics during early extinction training. See text for details. Copyright 1989, Springer-Verlag.

represented in the figure by relatively large circles. At time $t = 3$, the E unit sends a strong $r(t)$ signal to the V unit, allowing changes in V_{ijk} weights to occur. Because $L(t)$ is 0 (due to the absence of the US) and $\hat{s}(t)$ is approximately equal to 1 in Equation (2), changes in V_{ijk} are negative, as depicted by the filled circles. A negative change in synaptic weight similarly occurs for the E_{ijk} synapse by Equation (5).

In the preceding examples of acquisition and extinction, only 4 r_{ijk} elements were used to generate CRs. For more realistic simulations of CR waveforms, more elements are required. In the simulations presented next, each tapped delay line is comprised of at least 50 elements.

VET Simulations

Delay Conditioning. Figure 15.5 illustrates simulated response topographies for early, middle, and late stages of acquisition and extinction training in a delay conditioning paradigm.[2] During early stages of acquisition the CRs tend to occur just prior to US onset, and from the simplified example in Fig. 15.3 it should be

---

[2]In order to simulate physiological threshold and recruitment effects at motoneurons controlling the CR, a smoothed and thresholded function of $s(t)$, designated $Y(t)$, is presented in Fig. 15.5 and in subsequent figures. $Y(t) = \sum_{i=0}^{i=2} [0.8s(t-i) + 0.2Y(t-i-1)]/3$, if $Y(t) > 0.1$; otherwise $Y(t) = 0.1$.

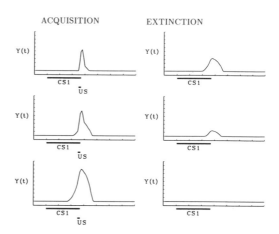

FIG. 15.5. Simulated CR to-pographies for acquisition and extinction training in a delay conditioning paradigm. Hash marks on X-axis denote 10 time steps. Simulation parameters: c = 0.05, number of x elements = 100 total, time steps/trial = 80. Early, middle, and late CR wave-forms obtained at 5, 10, and 25 trials of training, respectively. Copyright 1988, Springer-Ver-lag.

clear why this occurs: V_{ijk} synapses gain considerably more strength when acti-vated concurrently with reinforcement than they do when synaptic eligibility is allowed to decay. Thus, in early acquisition training, only those elements that are activated at or just prior to US onset will possess enough weight to drive the output above threshold level. As acquisition proceeds, elements that are acti-vated at earlier times relative to US onset become capable of generating detect-able output. This point is illustrated in Fig. 15.6, which is a learning curve over acquisition and extinction training for all the onset elements. Also evident in the acquisition phase of Fig. 15.6 is that associative strength increases over training as an S-shaped function.

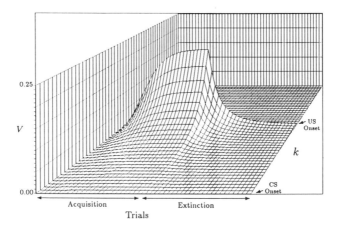

FIG. 15.6. Synaptic weight (V axis) over acquisition and extinction trials (horizontal axis) for each of the $k = 1, \ldots, N$ onset elements (remaining axis, k=1 is closest to reader). Copyright 1988, Springer-Verlag.

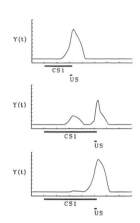

FIG. 15.7. Effects of changing US timing on CR topography. Top: In Stage 1, 25 short CS–US interval training trials are presented. Middle: In Stage 2, the CS–US interval is lengthened. After 10 trials, the short-latency CR is somewhat diminished and a longer latency CR begins to develop. Bottom: After 30 Stage 2 trials, transformation of CR topography is nearly complete. Simulation parameters for both stages: $c =$ 0.05, number of x elements = 120 total, steps/trial = 80. Copyright 1989, Springer-Verlag.

Changing US Timing. The simulation in Fig. 15.7 demonstrates the *micromolar* nature of this network. In micromolar constructs of conditioning (Logan, 1956), CRs of different latencies are considered to be *different responses*. In the network model, they truly are different responses because they are generated by different elements. Thus, a CR that develops at a short interstimulus interval, as illustrated in the top panel of Fig. 15.7, extinguishes when the interstimulus interval is lengthened. A different CR then develops independently at the new US locus. The middle and bottom panels of the figure show the gradual extinction of the short-latency CR and the establishment of the longer latency CR, a result consistent with experimental findings (Boneau, 1958; Gormezano & Moore, 1969; Leonard & Theios, 1967).

Blocking. The network model is capable of simulating the results of Kamin's blocking paradigm (Kamin, 1968). A blocking simulation is illustrated in Fig. 15.8. This paradigm is conducted in three stages. In the first stage (top panel), CS1–US trials are presented until asymptotic CRs are generated. In the

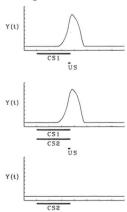

FIG. 15.8. Simulated CRs for Kamin's blocking paradigm (Kamin, 1968). See text for details. Simulation parameters: $c =$ 0.05, number of x elements = 100 total, time steps/trial = 80. Stage 1 (top) and Stage 2 (middle) CR profiles are after 25 training trials. Stage 3 testing (bottom) consists of 1 trial. Copyright 1989, Springer-Verlag.

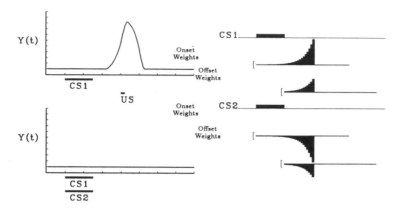

FIG. 15.9. Simulation results for conditioned inhibition. CR profiles after 30 trials for (CS1)+ and (CS1/CS2)− trial types are depicted in the upper and lower left panels, respectively. The temporal distribution of the V_{ijk} weights on a (CS1/CS2)− trial is depicted on the right side of the figure. Simulation parameters: $c = 0.15$, number of x elements = 200 total, time steps/trial = 80. Copyright 1989, Springer-Verlag.

second stage (middle panel), a different CS (CS2) is presented in compound with CS1, and the compound is paired with the US. An equal number of trials are presented in stages 1 and 2 of the simulation. In stage 3, the ability of CS2 to generate CRs is tested. In agreement with experimental results (e.g., Marchant & Moore, 1973), CS2 does not elicit a CR. The V_{ijk} for CS2 (i.e., the V_{2jk}) do not gain strength for the same reason that V does not increase in the Rescorla–Wagner (1972) model—the discrepancy between the reinforcement and the prediction is close to zero, (i.e., $L[t] - \hat{s}(t) \approx 0$ in Equation [2]), due to the large positive weights of CS1.

Conditioned Inhibition.   Simulation results for conditioned inhibition are illustrated in Fig. 15.9. In this paradigm two trial types are alternately presented.[3] For the first few type, designated (CS1) +, CS1 is paired with the US, and for the second type, designated (CS1/CS2) −, a CS1/CS2 compound is not paired with the US. The left portion of Fig. 15.9 depicts the two trial types and the predicted CRs at the end of the simulation run (after weights have reached asymptotic levels). The right side of the figure depicts the asymptotic weights for CS1 and CS2. The weights, which are depicted as solid bars, are represented at their times of initial activation (i.e., each V_{ijk} is depicted at the time step when

---

[3]In behavioral experiments the two trial types are typically presented in a random or pseudorandom sequence. In simulations, the two types are simply alternately presented. Given a large enough number of trials and equally probable trial types, the simulation results would be identical for random and alternating sequences.

the corresponding x_{ijk} element changes state from 0 to 1). Note that the weights for CS2 are negative (bars extend below the horizontal line).

Manipulations of Inhibitory Weights: Millenson et al. Simulation.   Under the network representation of conditioned inhibition, CRs are canceled out on CS1/CS2 compound trials because positive and negative weights contribute to the system's output *at the same time*. By selecting appropriate training and testing procedures, the timing of the inhibitory weights can be manipulated to either cancel or fail to cancel the effects of positive weights. This property of the model is demonstrated by simulating one experimental group from a study by Millenson, Kehoe, and Gormezano (1977). In this experiment, rabbits were trained to give conditioned nictitating membrane responses to a single tone CS in a delay conditioning paradigm; however, unlike simple acquisition training, the CS–US interval was not constant over trials and could take on either short (200 ms) or long (700 ms) values. The proportion of the short and long trial types was varied across 5 groups, with the proportion ranging from 0 to 1. The simulated group was the one designated P ½ by Millenson et al. (1977) to denote a 50:50 mixture of short and long trial types.

Simulation results for the P ½ group are presented in Fig. 15.10. CRs generated on short and long CS-alone probe trials are shown. The figure reveals that on short CS probe trials, the CR waveform is essentially unimodal, whereas a bimodal CR is generated on long CS probe trials. These two different waveforms are generated because the temporal configurations of the positive and negative weights differ on each trial type. The events occurring during this paradigm can be summarized as follows: Because the US occurs at two different interstimulus intervals, two loci of US expectation develop (i.e., for each trial, $r(t) > 0$ at two different times) and two sets of positive onset weights develop around these US expectations. Initially, these weights tend to generate bimodal CRs on both trial types. However on short trial types, the following events occur: (a) the CS terminates at the first point of US expectation, and the offset of the CS initiates the offset tapped delay line; (b) at the second point of US expectation, $r(t) > 0$ while the offset elements are active; (c) the US does not occur (i.e., $L[t] = 0$); and (d) CR output is generated around the second US expectation (i.e., $\hat{s}[t] > 0$). By Equation (2), the latter conditions lead to negative changes in $\Delta V_{ijk}(t)$ for the

FIG. 15.10. Simulation results for group P 1/2 of the Millenson et al. (1977) study. CR topographies for short CS (top panel) and long CS (bottom) CS-alone test trials are depicted. Copyright (1988), Springer-Verlag.

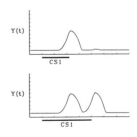

offset elements. Over a number of presentations of the two trial types, negative offset weights continue to develop until they ultimately cancel the positive onset weights on short CS trials. On long CS trials, the offset tapped delay line is initiated after the excitatory weights have contributed to the CR and, thus, the negative weights do not cancel the second CR peak.

The experimental results for Millenson et al. (1977) are shown in Fig. 15.11, which depicts averaged conditioned nictitating membrane extension as a function of time on acquisition days 3 and 10 for short (left column) and long (right column) CS-alone probe trials. The results for the P 1/2 group are found in the middle row of this figure. Notice that the experimental and the simulated CR

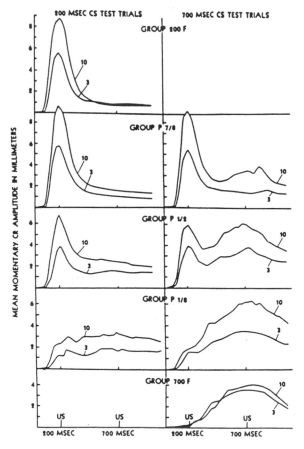

FIG. 15.11.   Experimental results of Millenson et al. (1977) study. The waveforms represent group mean nictitating membrane movement on acquisition days 3 and 10 for short (left side) and long (right side) CS test trials. Copyright (1977), Academic Press.

waveforms are similar in that CRs on short CS trials are basically unimodal but are bimodal on long CS trials; in addition, each CR peaks at a time of US onset. Also note that the CR to the short CS displays a slight tendency for a second peak. In the network, this minute second peak is attributed to an incomplete development of inhibitory weights in the offset elements. The simulated CR to the short CS in Fig. 15.10 exhibits a small second peak due to incomplete cancellation of excitatory and inhibitory weights. With extended training inhibitory weights completely cancel excitatory weights.

CEREBELLAR IMPLEMENTATION OF VET

The network architecture for learning temporally adaptive CRs presented in the preceding section might be aligned with any of a number of brain regions and circuits. Our immediate goal is to represent rabbit NMR conditioning; therefore we are obliged to superpose this architecture onto neural circuits involving the cerebellum, as evidence continues to point to an essential role of cerebellar cortex in the expression of robust CRs (Hardiman, Glickstein, & Yeo, 1988; Lavond, Steinmetz, Yokaitis, & Thompson, 1987; Yeo & Hardiman, 1988).[4] The proposed implementation builds on the theoretical ideas of Marr (1969) and Albus (1971) and recent physiological evidence suggesting the existence of Hebbian synaptic plasticity in cerebellar cortex. It has been suggested that these synaptic changes, occurring at synapses of parallel fibers (PFs) and on the dendritic spines of Purkinje cells (PCs), mediate the acquisition and performance of CRs. The implementation of VET introduced here incorporates this assumption. In this respect the implementation of VET differs from that proposed for the SBD model by Moore and Blazis (1989), in which learning is encoded at the synaptic interface between mossy fibers (MFs) and granule cells (i.e., one synapse earlier than that of the PF/PC interface).

The Marr–Albus theory assumes that climbing fibers (CFs) carry information that reinforces associative relationships encoded in cerebellar cortex, and physiological studies by Ito and others support this possibility by showing that concurrent stimulation of PCs by PF stimulation or application of glutamate (analogous to a CS) and CF stimulation (analogous to the US) causes long-lasting depression of quisqualate (QA) receptors at the PF fiber/PC synaptic interface (Crepel & Krupa, 1988; Ito, Sakurai, & Tongroach, 1982; Kano & Kato, 1987). Consistent with these studies, our implementation of VET assumes that conjoint PF fiber

---

[4]Discrete lesions of portions of cerebellar cortex that receive tactile facial inputs from the brainstem disrupt the acquisition and expression of CRs. However, a conditioned NMR can evidently be acquired by decerebrate decerebellate rabbits (Kelly, McAlduff, & Bloedel, 1988).

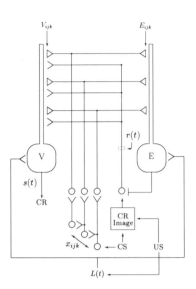

FIG. 15.12. The VET network, redepicted for the purpose of superposing the model onto cerebellar/brainstem circuits. The alignment of model architecture with that of cerebellum/brainstem is obtained by comparing this figure with Fig. 15.13. Copyright (1989), Springer-Verlag.

and CF stimulation of PCs causes a similar depression of postsynaptic receptor sensitivity. As a consequence, the pattern of PF excitation of PCs induced by a CS causes the cell to reduce its rate of firing below baseline. This reduced rate of firing disinhibits cerebellar nuclear cells and thereby initiates the CR via red nucleus (RN) and brainstem pathways that converge on motoneurons (Berthier, Desmond, & Moore, 1987).

Our implementation of VET hypothesizes that similar mechanisms for postsynaptic receptor depression exist at PF/Golgi cell synapses.[5] As in the case of PF/PC synapses, these changes are assumed to require conjoint stimulation of Golgi cell dendritic processes by PF activity induced by a CS with CF excitation induced by the US. Thus, our implementation assumes that CFs contribute to long-lasting modifications of postsynaptic receptors at PF synapses in both PCs and Golgi cells. In terms of VET, PCs are the V units and Golgi cells are the E units, as becomes clear in Fig. 15.12 and 15.13.[6]

Figure 15.12 summarizes the same ideas as Fig. 15.2 but does so in a way that hopefully facilitates superposing the VET model onto cerebellar/brainstem circuits. Figure 15.13 suggests how the network depicted in Fig. 15.12 relates to cerebellar anatomy (Ito, 1985; Llinas & Hillman, 1969). The V and E units of Fig. 15.12 are, respectively, depicted as a PC and Golgi cell in Fig. 15.13. In order to reduce crowding, the lower portion of these figures shows a CS activat-

---

[5]Apart from its plausibility in terms of cerebellar anatomy and the morphology of Golgi cells (Ito, 1984; Llinas & Hillman, 1969), we know of no direct evidence relevant to this hypothesis.

[6]Other authors have proposed models of adaptive timing in which Golgi cells play an essential role (e.g., Albus, 1971; Fujita, 1982).

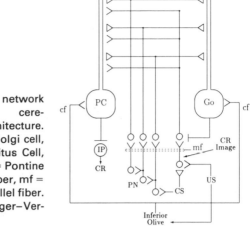

FIG. 15.13. The VET network superposed on cerebellar/brainstem architecture. Abbreviations: Go = Golgi cell, IP = Nucleus Interpositus Cell, PC = Purkinje cell, PN = Pontine nuclei, cf = Climbing fiber, mf = Mossy fibers, pf = Parallel fiber. Copyright (1989), Springer–Verlag.

ing only three tapped delay line elements, x_{ijk}, instead of nine as in Fig. 15.2. The CS-generated inputs to the dendritic process of these units are PFs arising from granule cells that comprise the neurons intervening between the tapped delay line elements, x_{ijk}, and synapses V_{ijk} and E_{ijk}. The inputs to the granule cells from the tapped delay line elements are assumed to be MFs. These MFs are tentatively aligned with the pontine nuclei, as they are one route by which information from CSs can ascend to those portions of cerebellar cortex identified in lesion studies as essential for robust conditioned NMRs. The model assumes that PCs like the one illustrated in Fig. 15.13 cause a CR by releasing inhibition from their target nuclear cells. In the case of the conditioned NMR, these nuclear cells are in the anterior nucleus interpositus (NIA). Some NIA neurons project to RN neurons that excite motoneurons in the accessory abducens nucleus, probably via elements of the sensory trigeminal system (Berthier, Desmond, & Moore, 1987).

Figure 15.13 depicts sensory input from the US, $L(t)$ in the model, as exciting the V and E units via a CF and one of its collaterals. These CFs would arise from neurons in the contralateral inferior olivary nucleus. In the case of the conditioned NMR, the olivary neurons of interest are those that respond to tactile stimulation of the eye and periorbital tissue. These cells are located primarily in the rostromedial portion of the dorsal accessory olivary nucleus (DAO) and project to the C1 and C3 parasagittal zones of the anterior and lateral cerebellar cortex encompassing hemispheral lobule VI (Yeo, 1987). Unlike the PF inputs to the V and E units, the CF input is depicted in Fig. 15.13 as acting on the "somata" of the PC and Golgi cell instead of their dendritic processes. This rendering is intended merely to capture the fact that climbing fiber processes tend to invade the large primary and secondary dendritic branches of PCs (i.e., those nearer to the soma). Collaterals of CFs that innervate Golgi cells terminate on the soma (Ito, 1984; Llinas & Hillman, 1969).[7]

The principal departure from Fig. 15.2 concerns the quantity $r(t)$, which represents the strength of the temporal expectation of the US. (The US's actual occurrence is conveyed to the V and E units by input lines labeled $L[t]$ as in Fig. 15.2.) In Fig. 15.12, $r(t)$ is not the output of the E unit but is instead the output of a "black box" labeled CR Image. We hypothesize that this CR Image is generated in the brainstem in parallel with learning in cerebellar cortex.[8] We conceive of this CR Image as being formed by Hebbian mechanisms that depend on convergent inputs from the CS and US. This is represented in Fig. 15.13 by a modifiable synapse from the CS that projects to a neuron that receives input from the US. There are any number of Hebbian rules for computing the CR Image (e.g., Klopf, 1988). Were it computed by the SB model, the CR Image would correspond to the output of neurons postsynaptic to the modifiable synapse indicated in Fig. 15.13. With training, this output would resemble a short-latency increase to a plateau of "neuronal firing" lasting as long as the time of the US.[9] If such a pattern of firing were projected directly onto motoneurons instead of being sent to the VET network in cerebellar cortex, the resulting CR would not be temporally adaptive. It would not emerge forward in time from the UR, it would not show inhibition of delay, and it could not be initiated within the trace portion of the CS–US interval in a trace conditioning procedure. The CR Image might be likened to a bolt of cloth from which the VET architecture fashions a temporally adaptive CR.

---

[7]One difficulty in assigning the quantity $L(t)$ to climbing fibers is that complex spikes in CR-related PCs may drop out as acquisition proceeds (Moore & Berthier, 1987). This could occur if PCs with a CR-related depression of firing project to NIA cells that project to DAO (Weiss, Tocco, Thompson, & Thompson, 1988). These NIA to DAO projections are likely GABAergic and therefore inhibitory (Nelson, Barmack, & Mugnaini, 1984). Because DAO cells are the source of CF input to cerebellar cortex, releasing inhibition from NIA cells during generation of a CR would not only generate a CR but would also inhibit CF input to the V and E units in response to a US. Once training becomes well established, this inhibition would cause extinction according to Equations (2) and (5). However, in their recording study of CR-related activity in PCs, Berthier and Moore (1986) reported data from one PC that exhibited the firing characteristics implied by our model. This cell inhibited its firing in anticipation of CRs and consistently responded to the US with complex spike, indicative of CF excitation.

[8]Brainstem regions where CR Image might arise include the supratrigeminal reticular formation (Desmond & Moore, 1982, 1986) and the sensory trigeminal system, especially spinal subnucleus pars oralis (Nowak & Gormezano, 1988; Schreurs, 1988). The latter is known to send projections, not only to motoneurons that control the NMR, but also to HVI of cerebellar cortex. Red nucleus, which contains neurons that evince CR related firing patterns (Desmond & Moore, 1987), is another potential source of CR Image because of reported projections to cerebellar cortex (Dietrichs & Walberg, 1983).

[9]In order to accommodate trace conditioning in the VET model, we make the additional assumption that this plateau of neuronal firing that constitutes the CR Image decays only gradually after CS offset.

By virtue of its designation as a Golgi cell, the E unit inhibits ascending activation from the CR Image until the expected time of the US, thereby bringing the quantity $r(t)$ to bear on sites of synaptic modification on the V-unit's processes. This gating by the E unit is represented in Fig. 15.13 by an inhibitory synapse on the granule cell intervening between CR Image and the V unit. The strength of $r(t)$ is proportional to the largest value of E_{ijk} active at time t, as dictated by the strength of the connections from the tapped delay lines to the E unit.[10]

In Fig. 15.12 and 15.13, each branch from the line labeled $r(t)$ is anatomically associated with each of the tapped delay line inputs from the CS to the V unit. These branches are assumed to be collaterals from the ascending axons of granule cells relaying $r(t)$ from CR Image in the brainstem. Because the V unit is assumed to be a PC, the multiple branches allow $r(t)$ to be broadcast to all local dendritic regions where it could contribute to computation of the synaptic weights, V_{ijk}s, carried by PFs. This multiple branching of $r(t)$ is not a logical necessity because one input to the V unit's "soma" as in Fig. 15.2 would suffice. It is introduced because, given the branching pattern of PC dendritic processes and likely Hebbian mechanisms of synaptic modification of PF/PC synapses, excitation from $r(t)$ ought to be "locally available" to inputs from PFs in order to change V_{ijk} connections (Alkon, 1984; Coss & Perkel, 1985). This may be particularly crucial for learning-related depression of QA receptor sensitivity at the PF/PC interface, which depends on local voltage-dependent calcium entry (Crepel & Krupa, 1988; Ross & Werman, 1987; Tank, Sugimori, Connor, & Llinas, 1988).

In terms of Fig. 15.3 and 15.4, the VET model implementation can be summarized as follows. The variables $V(t)$ and $E(t)$ may be regarded as postsynaptic to the x_{ijk} inputs arising from CS-input elements. The computation of $\Delta V(t)$ and $\Delta E(t)$ are carried out as synaptic interactions that involve local eligibility terms $h(t)$ and $\Delta x(t)$, respectively. These eligibility terms might reside in presynaptic or postsynaptic compartments (Sutton & Barto, 1981). Local membrane depolarization that would induce ionic currents essential for learning arise from CF excitation, $L(t)$, in the case of the Golgi cell E-unit, or the combination of CF and PF input from $r(t)$, in the case of the PC V-unit. Because the output of PCs and Golgi cells is inhibitory, the hypothesized mechanisms of synaptic depression are consistent with the increases of $V(t)$ and $E(t)$ during acquisition and decreases during extinction, as given in Equations 2 and 5. Figures 15.3 and 15.4 do not show the global eligibility factor, $\bar{x}_{ij}$, which influ-

---

[10]We do not wish to suggest that granule cells fed by the tapped delay lines (MFs) are not influenced by Golgi cells. Such Golgi cell modulation could play a role in implementing finer temporal resolution of CS duration, perhaps in the range of milliseconds, than might be possible with only the the tapped delay lines arising from outside the cerebellum (Braitenberg, 1967; Brand, Dahl, & Mugnaini, 1976).

ences the magnitude of weight changes according to Equations 2 and 5. This factor was introduced so that the rate of learning by the processing units be controlled by an inverted U-shaped function of the CS–US interval (ISI) employed in training. Like the other eligibility terms, it might be contributed by the input elements (Gingrich & Byrne, 1987). Desmond (1990; see also Desmond, 1988) has proposed that ISI-dependent global eligibility results from the recruitment of input elements through spreading activation and decay in a two-dimensional (planar array) representation of the CS. Alternatively, because the formation of the CR Image during acquisition would very likely depend on the ISI, the $\bar{x}_{ij}$ term in Equation 2 might be viewed as an attenuation factor imposed on $r(t)$.

CONCLUDING REMARKS

As demonstrated by the close correspondence between the simulation experiments presented previously and the results of experimental studies of conditioned responding, the tapped delay architecture of the VET model is capable of generating powerful predictions of adaptively timed conditioned responses. The VET model not only predicts well-documented features of topography but also generates novel and testable predictions of CR waveforms under various stimulus configurations (see Desmond & Moore, 1988). Given that this architecture is sufficient for generating realistic CR topography, our goal in this chapter has been to speculate how the VET model might be implemented in brain circuitry known to be critically involved in conditioning of the rabbit NMR.

We can summarize our proposed cerebellar implementation of the VET model as follows. It assumes that a CR Image is formed in the brainstem through associative processes. In the form of a CS-triggered bout of neuronal firing, this CR Image ascends to the cerebellar cortex via MFs where it is gated by the action of Golgi cells on granule cells. Through the conjoint PF and CF excitation, these Golgi cells acquire the ability to control the strength of excitation imparted to local regions on the dendritic processes of PCs where, combined with concurrent CF excitation, PF/PC synapses come to encode the topographical features of a temporally adaptive CR.

This scheme appears to account for CR-related activity that anticipates the CR in HVI PCs (Berthier & Moore, 1986; Moore & Berthier, 1987) and for the fact that CR-related neuronal firing efferent to cerebellar cortex often mirrors CR topography (Berthier, Barto, & Moore, 1988; Desmond & Moore, 1987; Thompson, Donegan, Clark, Lavond, Lincoln, Madden, Mamounas, Mauk, & McCormick, 1987). It is also consistent with the fact that lesions anywhere in the system, including DAO, disrupt or eliminate CRs (Yeo, 1987). Lesions of cerebellum also eliminate neuronal firing in the hippocampus that mirrors CR topography (Clark, McCormick, Lavond, & Thompson, 1984). Although we know of no direct evidence for the proposed cerebellar implementation of the VET model, particularly regarding the associative depression of PF/Golgi cell synapses, we believe that it is at least physiologically plausible.

Despite these successes, it is possible that the output of PCs that are the model's V-units would be insufficient to generate CRs.[11] Were this the case, the cerebellar VET network may only be required to construct a *template* of the temporally adaptive CR. This template could be fed back to cerebellar cortex through collaterals from nuclear cells (Haines, 1988). This feedback would provide input to a neural network capable of generating CRs. Such a network might resemble the one proposed by Moore and Blazis (1989) to implement the SBD model.[12]

Levey and Martin (1968) suggested that the complexities of learning a temporally adaptive CR lend credence to multistage approaches such as the three-state Markov model proposed by Theios and Brelsford (1966). Prokasy (1987) makes a similar point in support of two-stage models of CR acquisition. A two-component cerebellar network might resolve the dilemmas posed by Berthier and Moore's (1986) study of CR-related activity by HVI PCs during NMR conditioning. The firing pattern of the majority of CR-related PCs in the Berthier and Moore (1986) study can be accounted for by the Moore and Blazis' (1989) implementation of the SBD model and not by the VET implementation. Berthier and Moore (1986) observed only one PC in HVI with a firing pattern in complete accord with this scheme. It could well be the case that only a few PCs are required to generate a CR template, but many more acting in concert, as portrayed in the SBD network, are required for long-term storage of learning and the generation of robust CRs. Moore and Blazis (1989) discuss ways in which other brain systems (e.g., those involving the hippocampus) might be used to generate temporally adaptive templates for the SBD processing unit. The output of the VET network has this capability.

ACKNOWLEDGMENTS

The authors thank Diana Blazis for helpful comments on the manuscript and Neil Berthier, Diana Blazis, James Houk, and William Richards for their expertise on various aspects of the proposed cerebellar implementation of the VET model. Preparation of this chapter was supported by grants from the AFOSR and NSF.

---

[11]Llinas and Muhlethaler (1988) reported that cerebellar nuclear neurons evince high rates of firing in response release from injected hyperpolarizing currents. Thus, the possibility that CRs can be generated by the removal of weak tonic inhibition imposed on NIA neurons cannot be ruled out.

[12]Alternatively, a VET-generated template could be used to provide "error signals" for supervised learning algorithms implemented in brainstem regions afferent to motoneurons.

REFERENCES

Albus, J. S. (1971). A theory of cerebellar function. *Mathematical Bioscience, 10,* 25–61.

Alkon, D. L. (1984). Calcium-mediated reduction of ionic currents: A biophysical memory trace. *Science, 226,* 1037–1045.

Berthier, N. E., Barto, A. G., & Moore, J. W. (1988). Linear systems analysis of cerebellar deep nuclei cells during performance of classical conditioned eyeblink. *Society for Neuroscience Abstracts, 14,* 1239.

Berthier, N. E., Desmond, J. E., & Moore, J. W. (1987). Brain stem control of the nictitating membrane response. In I. Gormezano, W. F. Prokasy, & R. F. Thompson (Eds.), *Classical Conditioning III* (pp. 275–286). Hillsdale, NJ: Lawrence Erlbaum Associates.

Berthier, N. E., & Moore, J. W. (1986). Cerebellar Purkinje cell activity related to the classically conditioned nictitating membrane response. *Experimental Brain Research, 63,* 341–350.

Blazis, D. E. J., & Moore, J. W. (1987). *Simulation of a classically conditioned response: Components of the input trace and a cerebellar neural network implementation of the Sutton–Barto–Desmond model.* Technical Report 87–74.

Boneau, C. A. (1958). The interstimulus interval and the latency of the conditioned eyelid response. *Journal of Experimental Psychology, 56,* 464–472.

Braitenberg, V. (1967). Is the cerebellar cortex a biological clock in the millisecond range? In C. A. Fox & R. S. Snider (Eds.), *Progress in brain research Vol. 25. The cerebellum* (pp. 334–346). New York: Elsevier.

Brand, S., Dahl, A. L., & Mugnaini, E. (1976). The length of parallel fibers in the cat cerebellar cortex. An experimental light and electron microscope study. *Experimental Brain Research, 26,* 39–58.

Clark, G. A., McCormick, D. A., Lavond, D. G., & Thompson, R. F. (1984). Effects of lesions of cerebellar nuclei on conditioned behavioral and hippocampal responses. *Brain Research, 291,* 125–136.

Coss, R. G., & Perkel, D. H. (1985). The function of dendritic spines: A review of theoretical issues. *Behavioral and Neural Biology, 44,* 151–185.

Crepel, F., & Krupa, M. (1988). Activation of protein kinase C induces a long lasting depression of glutamate sensitivity of cerebellar Purkinje cells. An in vitro study. *Brain Research, 458,* 397–401.

Desmond, J. E. (1988). *Temporally adaptive conditioned responses: Representation of the stimulus trace in neural-network models.* Computer and Information Science technical report 88–80, University of Massachusetts, Amherst, MA 01003.

Desmond, J. E. (1990). Temporally adaptive responses in neural models: The stimulus trace. In M. Gabriel & J. W. Moore (Eds.), *Learning and Computational Neuroscience: Foundations of adaptive networks.* Cambridge, MA: MIT Press.

Desmond, J. E., & Moore, J. W. (1982). A brain stem region essential for the classically conditioned but not unconditioned nictitating membrane response. *Physiology & Behavior, 28,* 1029–1033.

Desmond, J. E., & Moore, J. W. (1986). Dorsolateral pontine tegmentum and the classically conditioned nictitating membrane response: Analysis of CR-related activity. *Experimental Brain Research, 65,* 59–74.

Desmond, J. E., & Moore, J. W. (1987). Red nucleus single-unit activity during the classically conditioned rabbit nictitating membrane response. *Society for Neuroscience Abstracts, 13,* 841.

Desmond, J. E., & Moore, J.W. (1988). Adaptive timing in neural networks: The conditioned response. *Biological Cybernetics, 58,* 405–415.

Dietrichs, E., & Walberg, F. (1983). Cerebellar cortical afferents from the red nucleus in the cat. *Experimental Brain Research, 50,* 353–358.

Fujita, M. (1982). Adaptive filter model of the cerebellum. *Biological Cybernetics, 45,* 195–206.

Gingrich, K. J., & Byrne, J. H. (1987). Single-cell neuronal model for associative learning. *Journal of Neurophysiology, 57,* 1705–1715.

Gormezano, I., Kehoe, E. J., & Marshall, B. S. (1983). Twenty years of classical conditioning with the rabbit. *Progress in Psychobiology and Physiological Psychology, 10,* 197–275.

Gormezano, I., & Moore, J. W. (1969). Classical conditioning. In M. H. Marx (Ed.), *Learning: Processes.* London: Collier-Macmillan Limited.

Haines, D. E. (1988). Evidence of intracerebellar collateralization of nucleocortical cell processes in a prosimian primate (*Galago*): A fluorescence retrograde study. *Journal of Comparative Neurology, 275,* 441–451.

Hardiman, M. J., Glickstein, M., & Yeo, C. H. (1988). Kainic acid lesions of the cerebellar cortex abolish the classically conditioned nictitating membrane response of the rabbit. *Society for Neuroscience Abstracts, 14,* 784.

Ito, M. (1984). *The Cerebellum and Neural Control.* New York: Raven Press.

Ito, M., Sakurai, M., & Tongroach, P. (1982). Climbing fibre-induced depression of both mossy fibre responsiveness and glutamate sensitivity of cerebellar Purkinje cells. *Journal of Physiology (London), 324* 113–134.

Kamin, L. J. (1968). Attention-like processes in classical conditioning. In W. F. Prokasy (Ed.), *Classical conditioning: A symposium* (pp. 118–147). New York: Appleton.

Kano, M., & Kato, M. (1987). Quisqualate receptors are specifically involved in cerebellar synaptic plasticity. *Nature, 325,* 276–279.

Kelly, T. M., McAlduff, J. D., & Bloedel, J. R. (1988). Presence of eyeblink conditioning in decerebrate and decerebellate rabbit. *Society for Neuroscience Abstracts, 14,* 169.

Kimmel, H. D. (1965). Instrumental inhibitory factors in classical conditioning. In W. F. Prokasy (Ed.), *Classical conditioning* (pp. 148–171). New York: Appleton-Century-Crofts.

Klopf, A. H. (1986). A drive reinforcement model of single neuron function: An alternative to the Hebbian neural model. In J. S. Denker (Ed.), *Neural networks for computing, AIP Conference Proceedings 151.* New York: American Institute of Physics.

Klopf, A. H. (1988). A neuronal model of classical conditioning. *Psychobiology, 16,* 85–125.

Lavond, D. G., Steinmetz, J. E., Yokaitis, M. H., & Thompson, R. F. (1987). Reacquisition of classical conditioning after removal of cerebellar cortex. *Experimental Brain Research, 67,* 569–593.

Leonard, D. W., & Theios, J. (1967). Effect of CS–US interval shift on classical conditioning of the nictitating membrane in the rabbit. *Journal of Comparative and Physiological Psychology, 63,* 355–358.

Levey, A. B., & Martin, I. (1968). Shape of the conditioned eyelid response. *Psychological Review, 75,* 398–408.

Llinas, R., & Hillman, D. E. (1969). Physiological and morphological organization of the cerebellar circuits in various vertebrates. In R. Llinas (Ed.), *Neurobiology of cerebellar evolution and development* (pp. 43–73). Chicago: American Medical Association.

Llinas, R., & Muhlethaler, M. (1988). Electrophysiology of guinea-pig cerebellar nuclear cells in the *in vitro* brain stem-cerebellar preparation. *Journal of Physiology (London), 404,* 251–258.

Logan, F. A. (1956). A micromolar approach to behavior theory. *Psychological Review, 65,* 63–73.

Marchant, H. G., & Moore, J. W. (1973). Blocking of the rabbit's conditioned nictitating membrane response in Kamin's two-stage paradigm. *Journal of Experimental Psychology, 101,* 155–158.

Marr, D. (1969). A theory of cerebellar cortex. *Journal of Physiology, 202,* 437–470.

Martin, I., & Levey, A. B. (1965). Efficiency of the conditioned eyelid response. *Science, 150,* 781–783.

Millenson, J. R., Kehoe, E. J., & Gormezano, I. (1977). Classical conditioning of the rabbit's nictating membrane response under fixed and mixed CS–US intervals. *Learning and Motivation, 8,* 351–366.

Moore, J. W., & Berthier, N. E. (1987). Purkinje cell activity and the conditioned nictitating membrane response. In M. Glickstein, C. Yeo, & J. Stein (Eds.), *Cerebellum and neuronal plasticity* (pp. 339–352). New York: Plenum Press.

Moore, J. W., & Blazis, D. E. J. (1989). Simulation of a classically conditioned response: A cerebellar neural network implementation of the Sutton–Barto–Desmond model. In J. H. Byrne & W. O. Berry (Eds.), *Neural models of plasticity: Experimental and theoretical approaches.* New York: Academic Press.

Moore, J. W., Desmond, J. E., & Berthier, N. E. (1989) Adaptively timed conditioned responses and the cerebellum: A neural network approach. *Biological Cybernetics, 62,* 17–28.

Moore, J. W., Desmond, J. E., Berthier, N. E., Blazis, D. E. J., Sutton, R. S., & Barto, A. G. (1986). Simulation of the classically conditioned nictitating membrane response by a neuron-like adaptive element: Response topography, neuronal firing, and interstimulus intervals. *Behavioural Brain Research, 21,* 143–154.

Nelson, B., Barmack, N. H., & Mugnaini, E. (1984). A GABAergic cerebello-olivary projection in the rat. *Society for Neuroscience Abstracts, 10,* 539.

Nowak, A. J., & Gormezano, I. (1988). Reflex modification (RM) and classical conditioning of the rabbit's nictitating membrane response (NMR) to electrical stimulation of brain stem structures as an unconditioned stimulus (UCS). *Society for Neuroscience Abstracts, 14,* 3.

Prokasy, W. F. (1987). A perspective on the acquisition of skeletal responses employing the Pavlovian paradigm. In I. Gormezano, W. F. Prokasy, & R. F. Thompson (Eds.), *Classical conditioning III* (pp. 287–318). Hillsdale, NJ: Lawrence Erlbaum Associates.

Rescorla, R. A., & Wagner, A. R. (1972). A theory of Pavlovian conditioning: Variations in the effectiveness of reinforcement and nonreinforcement. In A. H. Black & W. F. Prokasy (Eds.), *Classical conditioning II: Current theory and research.* New York: Appleton-Century-Crofts.

Ross, W. N., & Werman, R. (1987). Mapping calcium transients in the dendrites of Purkinje cells from the guinea-pig cerebellum *in vitro. Journal of Physiology (London), 389,* 319–336.

Schreurs, B. G. (1988). Stimulation of the spinal trigeminal nucleus supports classical conditioning of the rabbit's nictitating membrane response. *Behavioral Neuroscience, 102,* 163–172.

Sutton, R. S., & Barto, A. G. (1981). Toward a modern theory of adaptive networks: Expectation and prediction. *Psychological Review, 88,* 135–170.

Tank, D. W., Sugimori, M., Connor, J. A., & Llinas, R. R. (1988). Spatially resolved calcium dynamics of mammalian Purkinje cells in cerebellar slice. *Science, 242,* 773–777.

Theios, J., & Brelsford, J. W. (1966). A Markov model for classical conditioning: Application to eyeblink conditioning in rabbits. *Psychological Review, 73,* 393–405.

Thompson, R. F. (1986). The neurobiology of learning and memory. *Science, 233,* 941–947.

Thompson, R. F., Donegan, N. H., Clark, G. A., Lavond, D. G., Lincoln, J. S., Madden, J., Mamounas, L. A., Mauk, M. D., & McCormick, D. A. (1987). Neuronal substrates of discrete conditioned reflexes, conditioned fear states, and their interactions in the rabbit. In I. Gormezano, W. F. Prokasy, & R. F. Thompson (Eds.), *Classical conditioning III* (pp. 371–400). Hillsdale NJ: Lawrence Erlbaum Associates.

Weiss, C., Tocco, G., Thompson, J. K., & Thompson, R. F. (1988). Anatomical analysis of cerebellar-olivary projections in the rabbit. *Society for Neuroscience Abstracts, 14,* 493.

Yeo, C. B. (1987). Cerebellum and classical conditioning. In M. Glickstein, C. Yeo, & J. Stein (Eds.), *Cerebellum and neuronal plasticity* (pp. 321–338). New York: Plenum Press.

Yeo, C. H., & Hardiman, M. J. (1988). Loss of conditioned responses following cerebellar cortical lesions is not a performance deficit. *Society for Neuroscience Abstracts, 14,* 3.

16 The Essential Memory Trace Circuit for a Basic Form of Associative Learning

Richard F. Thompson
University of Southern California

Joseph E. Steinmetz
Indiana University

Some years ago we selected classical conditioning of the nictitating membrane/eyelid closure response as a model system in which to analyze the neuronal substrates of basic associative learning and memory phenomena. We adopted this paradigm and the rabbits as the experimental animal of choice for two key reasons: (a) There is an extensive literature on the properties and parameters of this form of associative learning in both humans and animals (particularly the rabbit) (Black and Prokasy, 1972; Gormezano, 1972); and (b) it obeys the basic "laws" and exhibits the fundamental phenomena of associative learning in a similar manner in humans and in other mammals.

THE CEREBELLUM AND MOTOR LEARNING

When we began this work about 18 years ago, we had no idea that we would be led to the cerebellum as the key structure that appears to store the essential memory trace. With the advantage of hindsight, it is perhaps not so surprising. The conditioned eyelid closure response is a very precisely timed movement—over CS–US onset intervals ranging from about 100 msec to over 1 sec, the learned response develops such that the eyelid closure is maximal at the time of onset of the US. In this sense it is a maximally adaptive response. (By "adaptive" we refer only to the temporal properties of the CR relative to the onset of the US and not to issues relating to reinforcement or the "law of effect"; see Gormezano & Coleman, 1973). It is also a very precisely timed "skilled" movement, perhaps the most elementary form of learned skilled movement. Our results strongly support the general spirit of earlier theories of the role of the cerebellum in motor learning (Albus, 1971; Eccles, 1977; Ito, 1972; Marr, 1969). As is noted in this chapter, this conclusion is not limited to eyelid conditioning in the rabbit but appears to hold for the learning of any discrete behavioral response learned to deal with an aversive event by mammals. Eyelid conditioning is thus a a category of associative learning and might be described as "procedural" learning (i.e., learning how).

There is general agreement that the cerebellum is involved in the production and control of movements, including skilled, learned movement, but less agreement regarding possible loci of memory storage for learned movements. On one side are the now-classic theories of how the cerebellar cortex might serve as the site for storage of memory traces that code learned movements or motor programs (Albus, 1971; Eccles, 1977; Ito, 1972; Marr, 1969). The opposing view holds that the cerebellum is a computational network involved in the control and regulation of movement, including skilled movements, but that the memory traces are not stored there (Llinas, 1981).

Evidence for the involvement of the cerebellum in learned movements is incontravertable. Particularly impressive are studies using primates trained to make highly skilled, precise movements. This literature has been reviewed in depth (Brooks & Thach, 1981; Ito, 1984). In general, when a monkey performs an "intentional" skilled movement, as in moving a lever rapidly in a particular manner following a visual or auditory stimulus, one of the earliest signs of neuronal activity is in the dentate nucleus; lateral Purkinje cells show alterations at about this time or a bit later. Next are neural changes in interpositus and in motor cortex. These statements are, of course, based on means of samples with considerable overlaps. The majority of dentate neurons fire in relation to the stimulus onset and a smaller proportion fire in relation to the onset of movement, whereas interpositus neurons, often preceding the movement in terms of onset latencies, tend to fire more in relation to the movement itself. Interestingly, the "stimulus evoked" dentate response occurs in the trained animal and *disappears* if the learned behavior is extinguished. Cooling of the dentate nucleus in monkeys trained to perform a prompt arm–wrist flexion task causes the execution of the task to be delayed by 90 to 250 msec. Furthermore, cooling of the dentate in a monkey that has just learned a new variation of an arm–wrist task reverts the animal's arm movement back to prelearning levels of performance (see Brooks, 1979; Brooks et al., 1973; Chapman, Spidalieri, & Lamarre, 1986; Meyer-Lohman, Hove, & Brooks, 1977).

A common hypothetical functional description would have the "intention" to move originate in association areas of the cerebral cortex, which activate the striatum and the pontine nuclei. Neurons in the pontine nuclei project to the cerebellum as mossy fibers. Insofar as the cerebellum is concerned, the next event is activation of dentate neurons by mossy fibers, and also activation of Purkinje neurons, which act in turn to modulate dentate neurons. The dentate neurons then activate motor cortex via the thalamus, which in turn activates descending pathways to motor neurons and also pontine mossy fibers to cerebellum. Interpositus neurons are also activated by mossy fibers and influenced by Purkinje cells, although it is not clear at exactly what points in the preceding sequence. Once behavioral movement begins, feedback from the periphery is, of course, provided to these central systems. The climbing fiber system is not thought to play a direct role in movement initiation or control because of the very slow discharge frequency of inferior olivary neurons (1–2/sec). Instead, it may play some role as a "corrective" signal when errors occur or provide some other kind of information. The motor cortex and the interpositus provide two descending motor systems, the interpositus by way of the magnocellular red nucleus and rubral pathways. This schema is, of course, greatly oversimplified; most regions that connect have reciprocal connections (e.g., the nucleocortical fibers in the cerebellum), and other neuronal systems are also involved (see Brooks & Thach, 1981, for detailed discussion). Where the motor program memory traces for such skilled movement are located in these networks is not yet known, but the possibility that they are stored in cerebellar cortex seems a reasonable working hypothesis and is not contradicted in any strong manner by current evidence.

THE CEREBELLUM IS THE ESSENTIAL SUBSTRATE FOR CLASSICAL CONDITIONING OF THE EYEBLINK NICTITATING MEMBRANE/RESPONSE AND OTHER DISCRETE BEHAVIORAL RESPONSES

We adopted the general strategy of recording neuronal unit activity in the trained animal (rabbit eyelid/nictitating membrane conditioning) as an initial survey and sampling method to identify putative sites of memory storage. A pattern of neuronal activity that correlates with the behavioral learned response, specifically one that precedes the behavioral response in time within trials, predicts the form of the learned response within trials, and predicts the development of learning over trials, is a necessary (but not sufficient) requirement for identification of a storage locus.

We mapped a number of brain regions and systems thought to be involved in learning and memory. Neuronal activity of pyramidal cells in the hippocampus exhibited all the criteria just described (Berger, Rinaldi, Weisz, & Thompson, 1983). But the hippocampus itself is not necessary for learning and memory of such discrete behavioral responses (Thompson, Berger & Madden, 1983). Nevertheless, there is recent evidence arguing strongly that long-lasting neuronal plasticity is established in the hippocampus in these learning paradigms (Disterhoft, Coulter & Alkon, 1986; Mamounas, Thompson, Lynch, & Baudry, 1984; Weisz, Clark, & Thompson, 1984). Thus "memory traces" are formed in the hippocampus during learning, but these "higher order" traces are not necessary for learning the basic association between a neutral tone or light CS and the precisely timed, adaptive behavioral response. However, the hippocampus can become essential when appropriate task demands are placed on animals, even in eyelid conditioning (Thompson et al., 1983). But the hippocampus is not a part of the memory trace circuit essential (i.e., necessary and sufficient) for basic associative learning and memory of discrete responses. Indeed, decorticate and even decerebrate mammals can learn the conditioned eyelid/nictitating membrane response (Norman et al., 1974; Oakley & Russel, 1977), and animals that are first trained and then acutely decerebrated retain the learned response (Mauk & Thompson, 1987). Accordingly, the essential memory trace circuit is below the level of the thalamus.

In the course of mapping the brainstem and cerebellum, we discovered localized regions of cerebellar cortex and a region in the lateral interpositus nucleus where neuronal activity exhibited the requisite memory trace properties—patterned changes in neuronal discharge frequency that preceded the behavioral learned response by as much as 60 msec (minimum behavioral CR onset latency approximately 100 msec), predicted the form of the learned behavioral response (but not the reflex response), and grew over the course of training (i.e., predicted the development of behavioral learning; (McCormick et al., 1981, McCormick, Clark, Lavond, & Thompson, 1981, 1982a; McCormick & Thompson, 1984a, 1984b; Thompson, 1986).

We undertook a series of lesion studies—large lesions of lateral cerebellar cortex and nuclei, electrolytic lesions of the lateral anterior interpositus-medial dentate nuclear region and lesions of the superior cerebellar peduncle. Ipsilateral to the learned response all abolished the learned response completely and permanently, had no effect on the reflex UR, and did not prevent or impair learning on the contralateral side of the body (Clark, McCormick, Lavond, & Thompson, 1984; Lavond et al., 1981; Lincoln, McCormick, & Thompson, 1982; McCormick et al., 1981; 1982a; McCormick, Guyer, Thompson, 1982b; Thompson et al., 1984). After our initial papers were published, Yeo, Glickstein, and associates replicated our basic result for the interpositus nucleus, using light as well as tone CSs and periorbital shock US (we had used corneal airpuff US), thus extending the generality of the result (Yeo, Hardiman, & Glickstein, 1985a).

Electrolytic or aspiration lesions of the cerebellum cause degeneration in the inferior olive—the lesion abolition of the learned response could be due to olivary degeneration rather than cerebellar damage, per se. We made kainic acid lesions of the interpositus—a lesion as small as a cubic millimeter in the lateral anterior interpositus permanently and selectively abolished the learned response with no attendant degeneration in the inferior olive (Lavond, Hembree, & Thompson, 1985). Additional work suggests that the lesion result holds across CS modalities, skeletal response systems, species, and perhaps with instrumental contingencies as well (Donegan, Lowry, & Thompson, 1983; Polenchar, Patterson, Lavond, & Thompson, 1985; Yeo et al., 1985a). Electrical microstimulation of the interpositus nucleus in untrained animals elicits behavioral responses by way of the superior cerebellar peduncle (e.g., eyeblink, leg-flexion), the nature of the response being determined by the locus of the electrode (McCormick & Thompson, 1984a). Collectively, these data build a case that the memory traces are afferent to the efferent fibers of the superior cerebellar peduncle (i.e., in interpositus, cerebellar cortex or systems for which the cerebellum is a mandatory efferent).

The basic interpositus lesion effect we first described—complete and permanent abolition of the CR with no effect on the UR—has been replicated in subsequent studies in our laboratory (Clark, McCormick, Lavond, & Thompson, 1984; Lavond, Lincoln, McCormick, & Thompson, 1984a; Lavond, McCormick, & Thompson, 1984b; Lavond et al., 1985; Lincoln et al., 1982; Mauk & Thompson, 1987; McCormick & Thompson, 1984a, 1984b; Steinmetz et al., 1986; Woodruff-Pak et al., 1985a) and in several studies in other laboratories (Polenchar et al., 1985; Yeo et al., 1985a).

To our knowledge, this is the first demonstration that a very discrete and localized central brain lesion can completely and permanently abolish a learned response without any effect on ability to perform the response (reflex UR) and without impinging on classical sensory systems. The effect is dramatic, as schematized in Fig. 16.1 and 16.2. Before lesion the CR is about 10 mm, using standard training conditions (e.g., 350 msec, 85 db, 1 KHz CS and a coterminating 100 msec corneal airpuff US [2.1 N/cm^2]. Following the effective lesion of the anterior lateral interpositus nucleus, the CR is completely abolished on both paired trials and CS-alone test trials (see Fig. 16.2).

The effects of partial lesions of the interpositus are particularly interesting (Clark et al., 1984). As schematized in Fig. 16.2, the CR is markedly reduced in magnitude, the onset latency is increased, and, most importantly, the frequency of occurrence of the CR is markedly reduced. The correlation between amplitude and frequency of CRs in partially lesioned animals is extremely high: $r = 0.93$.

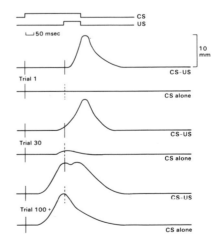

FIG. 16.1. Schematic of reflex (UR) and conditioned (CR) responses of the nictitating membrane (or eyelid). Top two traces—first trial before any learning has occurred. Upper trace, UR, bottom trace, CS-alone trial showing no response. Middle two traces, paired trial (above) and CS-alone trial (below) early in training. Bottom two traces, the same when the CR has been learned. Solid vertical lines indicate CS and US onsets, dashed lines indicate time of US onset on trials when US not presented (here and in Fig. 16.2 and 16.3).

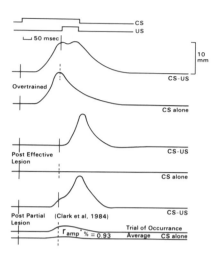

FIG. 16.2. Schematic. Top two traces, well-learned response. Middle two traces, effective lesion of the interpositus nucleus completely and permanently abolishes the CR on both paired and CS-alone trials but has no effect on the UR. Bottom three traces, effect of a substantial but incomplete lesion. Middle trace is a single trial on which a CR occurred; bottom trace is the average amplitude CR. See text for details.

Schematics in Fig. 16.2 (bottom three traces) are of an individual CS–US trial on which the CR occurs, an individual CS-alone test trial on which the CR occurs, and an average of 10 successive test trials. The much reduced magnitude of this last trace is due to the marked reduction in frequency of occurrence of the CR. The CR following partial lesion closely resembles the CR early in training (Fig. 16.1). As Gormezano (1972) showed, the CR begins to develop at about the point in time where US onset occurs within trials. Over training the CR onset latency gradually moves toward the CS onset, asymptoting at about 100 msec after CS onset. But the peak amplitude of the CR zeroes in on the time of the US onset over the range of CS–US onset intervals where learning occurs, as noted before.

This fact of permanently reduced frequency and magnitude of the CR with partial lesions has interesting implications. The lesion is causing either partial damage to the sensory afferent (CS) projection system to the memory trace, partial damage to the memory trace itself, or partial damage to the CR pathway efferent from the memory trace. But partial damage to the afferent CS pathway does not cause permanent reduction of the CR. Thus, using an auditory CS we have found repeatedly that partial lesions of the auditory pathway (e.g., lateral lemniscus) cause only temporary reduction in the amplitude and percent occurrence of the CR (Steinmetz et al., 1987). It is just as though the properties of the CS have been altered (e.g., intensity reduced). Indeed, with a marked reduction in CS intensity, additional training is required to reestablish the normal amplitude and percentage of CRs (Kettner & Thompson, 1985). Therefore, we argue that the interpositus lesion is either to the memory trace itself or to the efferent CR pathway. Recovery of CR amplitude with additional training would not be expected if the damage is efferent from the trace (i.e., beyond the site of the neuronal plasticity that codes the memory trace). By the same token, if the

FIG. 16.3. Schematic. Upper two traces, response reported by Welsh et al. (1986) following interpositus lesion and postlesion overtraining. Upper trace, trial of occurrence, lower trace, average amplitude of response. Lower two traces, response actually obtained by Welsh (1986). Compare with bottom two traces in Fig. 16.2.

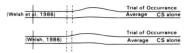

population of neurons that constitutes the trace for a particular CR is fixed, then little or no recovery from partial lesion of this population of neurons would be expected.

Welsh, Gormezano, and Harvey (1986) reported that extensive overtraining following interpositus lesions resulted in the development of a very low amplitude, infrequent, long-latency "CR."[1] To quote:

> All animals with lesions encompassing the anterodorsal D-I region [n = 15] showed a significant reduction in CRs on conditioning trials *and no evidence of reacquisition. UCRs were not affected.* [Italic's ours.] Of these 15 rabbits, nine demonstrated *responding to the tone CS that was at or below baseline levels . . .* [Italic's ours.] Analysis of test trials revealed acquisition of CRs whose response characteristics were obscured by the occurrence of unconditioned responses evoked by the UCS on paired trials. The 9 subjects that had failed to demonstrate CRs. . . . did demonstrate longer latency responses during test trials. [Latency within 250 msec after CS offset; up to 22.1% CRs; amplitude, 1.32 mm; rise time, 406 msec.] (p. 978)

The clear implication of this report is that on paired trials after lesion none of the 15 animals showed any sign of reacquisition and 9 animals showed complete and permanent absence of the CR on paired trials. By definition, CRs on paired trials are responses that occur after CS onset and before US onset (e.g., in the CS–US onset interval; Gormezano, 1972).

In sum, Welsh et al. (1986) asserted that their lesions abolished the normal short-latency CR but not a very long-latency, very weak "CR." Their reported results are schematized in Fig. 16.3 (top two traces), both for an individual test trial where the late response occurred and an average of 6 test trial (they gave 6 test trials per day) for comparison with Fig. 16.2. Note that their reported late response resembles very closely the incomplete lesion effect we described earlier (compare Fig. 16.2 and 16.3), except for its longer onset latency. One might say they are making mountains out of molehills. Their so-called "late CR" has an average magnitude of approximately 0.2 mm, compared to a normal CR of about 10 mm (i.e., only 2% of the prelesion CR)% We were puzzled by the very long onset latency of the response Welsh et al. reported and obtained their original data—Welsh's Masters Thesis (Welsh, 1986) that was supervised by J. A.

---

[1]Gormezano (personal communication) wishes to dissociate himself from that presentation.

Harvey in Gormezano's laboratory. Moreover, Gormezano (personal communication) has disavowed any affiliation or responsibility for Welsh's data analyses
or its interpretation. To our astonishment, we discovered that what Welsh et al.
(1986) reported in their abstract is not in fact what Welsh found. Because of what
this statement implies, we do not make it lightly.

Welsh et al. used an idiosyncratic training procedure: CS on for 250 msec, 35
msec of no stimulation, followed by airpuff US of 100 msec duration. A very
short trace interval separated CS offset and US onset (see Fig. 16.3). We do not
know why they used this paradigm. The reason we stress this is that in their
presentation Welsh et al. (1986) did not report whether or not there were any CRs
following lesions in the 50-msec period just prior to UR onset. This is the time
period where CRs first begin to develop in training and the time period where
markedly attenuated CRs following partial interpositus lesions occur (see Fig.
16.1 and 16.2). But these data are given in Welsh's thesis: following lesions,
animals gave up to 30% responses in this time period—exactly what we earlier
found with partial lesions (Clark et al., 1984).

Incidentally, if they had found a "late" response that developed de novo with

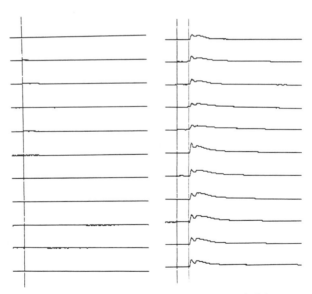

FIG. 16.4. Nictitating membrane responses recorded from a rabbit
after the left interpositus nucleus was lesioned. The 11 traces in each
column are the average responses for 11 daily postlesion sessions
(from top to bottom) during which a 350-msec tone CS (represented by
the first vertical line) was presented with a coterminating 100-msec air
puff US (represented by the second vertical line). Each trace in the left
column shows the average of 12 responses recorded on CS-alone test
trials, whereas each trace in the right column shows the average of 96
responses recorded on paired CS–US trials. The recording period for
each response was 3,000 msec.

additional training after the lesion, then it would have been absolutely essential to run a control group given unpaired CS and US presentations and interpositus lesions to determine if the responses were due to associative processes or non-associative processes (e.g., increased responsiveness as a result of the lesions). They did not run this essential control group.

But the question remains; With lesions that are complete and do completely abolish the CR in the CS–US onset interval, does any "late" response develop with extensive additional training? We have addressed this question in current work. Using our standard paradigm, animals were trained (108 trials/day every 9th trial a CS-alone test trial) to a criterion of at least 8 CRs on 9 successive trials, given 2–4 days of overtraining, then given interpositus lesions. Following 7 days of recovery, animals were trained up to 24 days. Some were trained on our paradigm and others given 10–12 days on Welsh's paradigm (the stimulus parameters were described before, see Fig. 16.3—66 trials/day; every 10th trial a

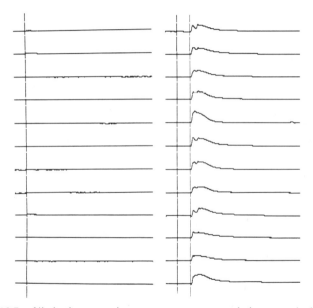

FIG. 16.5. Nictitating membrane responses recorded on postlesion days 12–23 from the same rabbit depicted in Fig. 16.4. The 12 traces in each column are the average responses for 12 daily postlesion sessions (from top to bottom) during which a 250-msec tone CS (represented by the first vertical line) was followed by a 100-msec air puff US (represented by the second vertical line) after a 35-msec delay period was allowed between CS offset and US onset (i.e., a replication of the training paradigm used by Welsh et al., 1986). Each trace in the left column shows the average of 6 response recorded on CS-alone test trials, whereas each trace in the right column shows the average of 60 responses recorded on paired CS–US trials. The recording period for each response was 3,000 msec.

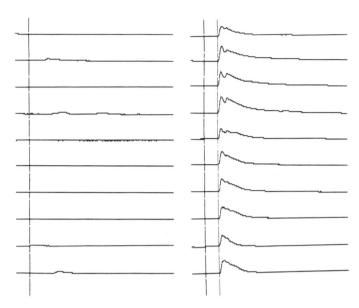

FIG. 16.6. Nictitating membrane responses recorded from a rabbit after the left interpositus nucleus was lesioned. The 10 traces in each column are the average responses for 10 daily postlesion sessions (from top to bottom) during which a 350-msec tone CS (represented by the first vertical line) was presented with a coterminating 100-msec air puff US (represented by the second vertical line). Each trace in the left column shows the average of 12 responses recorded on CS-alone test trials, whereas each trace in the right column shows the average of 96 responses recorded on paired CS–US trials. The recording period for each response was 3,000 msec.

CS-alone test trial). In all cases, data were recorded for a full 3 seconds after CS offset. In these animals (5 to date) the interpositus lesion completely and permanently abolished the short-latency CR in the CS–US onset interval. In no instance did any animal exhibit any "late" response of any kind whatsoever on test trials. Examples are shown in Fig. 16.4–16.7. An occasional spontaneous response occurred, but only on a single test trial within a given session. These very infrequent spontaneous responses had random onset latencies, as is characteristic of spontaneous responses. It must therefore be concluded that Welsh et al. (1986) are in error.

The Essential Memory Trace Circuit

The essential efferent CR pathway appears to consist of fibers exiting from the interpositus nucleus ipsilateral to the trained side of the body in the superior cerebellar peduncle, crossing to relay in the contralateral magnocellular division

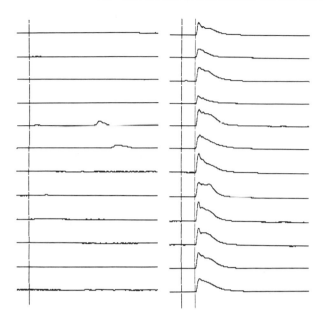

FIG. 16.7. Nictitating membrane responses recorded on postlesion days 11–22 from the same rabbit depicted in Fig. 16.6. The 12 traces in each column are the average responses for 12 daily postlesion sessions (from top to bottom) during which a 250-msec tone CS (represented by the first vertical line) was followed by a 100-msec air puff US (represented by the second vertical line) after a 35-msec delay period was allowed between CS offset and US onset (i.e., a replication of the training paradigm used by Welsh et al., 1986). Each trace in the left column shows the average of 6 responses recorded on CS-alone test trials, whereas each trace in the right column shows the average of 60 responses recorded on paired CS–US trials. The recording period for each response was 3,000 msec.

of the red nucleus, and crossing back to descend in the rubral pathway to act ultimately on motor neurons (Chapman, Steinmetz, & Thompson, 1985; Haley, Lavond, & Thompson, 1983; Lavond et al., 1981; Madden, Haley, Barchas, & Thompson, 1983; McCormick et al., 1982b; Rosenfield, Devydaitis, & Moore, 1985; see Fig. 16.8). Possible involvement of other efferent systems in control of the CR has not yet been determined, but descending systems taking origin rostral to the midbrain are not necessary for learning or retention of the CR, as noted earlier.

A somatosensory stimulus (as in our corneal airpuff US) activates both mossy fibers and climbing fibers that converge in their projection to the cerebellum. When we set out to identify the essential US pathway we decided to focus on the climbing fiber system, guided by the classic theories of cerebellar learning but recognizing that both mossy and climbing fibers are coactivated by the US. Our

FIG. 16.8. Simplified schematic of hypothetical memory trace circuit for discrete behavioral responses learned as adaptations to aversive events. The US (corneal airpuff) pathway seems to consist of somatosensory projections to the dorsal accessory portion of the inferior olive (DAO) and its climbing fiber projections to the cerebellum. The tone CS pathway seems to consist of auditory projections to pontine nuclei (Pontine N) and their mossy fiber projections to the cerebellum. The efferent (eyelid closure) CR pathway projects from the interpositus nucleus (Int) of the cerebellum to the red nucleus (Red N) and via the descending rubral pathway to act ultimately on motor neurons. The

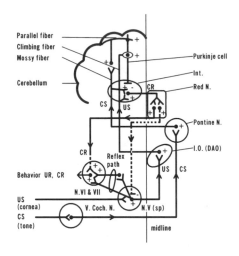

red nucleus may also exert inhibitory control over the transmission of somatic sensory information about the US to the inferior olive (IO) so that, when a CR occurs (eyelid closes), the red nucleus dampens US activation of climbing fibers. Evidence to date is most consistent with storage of the memory traces in localized regions of cerebellar cortex and possibly interpositus nucleus as well. Pluses indicate excitatory and minuses inhibitory synaptic action. Additional abbreviations: N V (sp), spinal fifth cranial nucleus; N VI, sixth cranial nucleus; N VII, seventh cranial nucleus; V Coch N, ventral cochlear nucleus. (From Thompson, 1986; Reprinted by permission of *Science,* 1986).

evidence to date argues strongly that the essential US reinforcing pathway, the necessary and sufficient pathway conveying information about the US to the cerebellar memory trace circuit, is climbing fibers from the dorsal accessory olive (DAO) projecting via the inferior cerebellar peduncle (see Fig. 16.8). Thus, lesions of the appropriate region of the DAO prevent acquisition and produce normal extinction of the behavioral CR with continued paired training in already trained animals (McCormick et al., 1985). Electrical microstimulation of this same region elicits behavioral responses and serves as an effective US for normal learning of behavioral CRs; the exact behavioral response elicited by DAO stimulation is learned as normal CR to a CS (Mauk, Steinmetz, & Thompson, 1986).

Lesion and microstimulation data suggest that the essential CS pathway includes mossy fiber projections to the cerebellum via the pontine nuclei (see Fig. 16.8). (As is noted later, approximately 60% of the Purkinje cells we have studied in the untrained animal, from H VI, Crus I, and Crus II, show clear evoked responses, usually an increase in frequency of simple spike discharge, to the tone CS stimulus.) Sufficiently large lesions of the middle cerebellar peduncle prevent acquisition and immediately abolish retention of the eyelid/nictitating membrane CR to all modalities of CS (Solomon et al., 1986), whereas lesions in the pontine nuclear region can selectively abolish the eyelid/nictitating membrane an acoustic CS (Steinmetz et al., 1986). Consistent with this result is current anatomical evidence from our laboratory for a direct contralateral projection from the ventral cochlear nucleus to this same region of the pons (Thompson, Lavond, & Thompson, 1986) and electrophysiological evidence of a "primary-like" auditory relay nucleus in this pontine region (Logan, Steinmetz, & Thompson, 1986).

Electrical microstimulation of the mossy fiber system serves as a very effective CS, producing rapid learning, on average more rapid than with peripheral CSs (although not equated psychophysically), when paired with, for example, a corneal airpuff US (Steinmetz, Lavond, & Thompson, 1985a). If animals are trained with a left pontine nuclear stimulation CS and then tested for transfer to right pontine stimulation, transfer is immediate (i.e., 1 trial) if the two electrodes have similar locations in the two sides, suggesting that at least under these conditions the traces are not formed in the pontine nuclei but rather in the cerebellum, probably beyond the mossy fiber terminals (Steinmetz et al., 1986). Finally, appropriate forward pairing of mossy fiber stimulation as a CS and climbing fiber stimulation as a US yields *normal behavioral learning* of the response elicited by climbing fiber stimulation (Steinmetz, Lavond, & Thompson, 1985b). Lesion of the interpositus abolishes both the CR and the UR in this paradigm, and backward presentation of US and CS or simultaneous presentation of CS and US produces no learning. All of these results taken together would seem to build an increasingly strong case for localization of the essential memory traces to the cerebellum, particularly in the "reduced" preparation with stimulation of mossy fibers as the CS and climbing fibers as the US.

In current work we have compared electrical stimulation of the dorsolateral pontine nucleus (DLPN) and lateral reticular nucleus (LRN) as CSs. When paired with a peripheral US (corneal airpuff), both yield normal and rapid learning (Knowlton et al., 1986). The DLPN projects almost exclusively to an intermediate region of cerebellar cortex, whereas the LRN projects in significant part to the interpositus nucleus (Bloedel & Courville, 1981; Brodal, 1975; Chan-Palay, 1977). Under these conditions, a lesion limited to the general region of cerebellar cortex receiving projections from the DLPN completely and permanently abolishes the CR to the DLPN stimulation CS but not to the LRN stimulation CS (Knowlton et al., 1986). We have thus created a situation where a relatively restricted region of cerebellar cortex is necessary for the CR, which will be most helpful for further analysis of mechanisms of memory trace formation. More generally, these results suggest that the particular region(s) of cerebellar cortex necessary for associative memory formation depend on the patterns of mossy fiber projections to the cerebellum activated by the CS. We hypothesize that the memory traces are formed in regions of cerebellar cortex and interpositus nucleus where CS-activated mossy fiber projections and US-activated climbing fiber projections coverage. This hypothesis of multiple localized cortical sites of memory trace formation is closely consistent with the organization of somotosensory projections to cerebellar cortex (Kassel, Shambes, & Walker, 1984; Shambes, Gibson, & Walker, 1978).

Recordings from Purkinje cells in the eyelid/NM conditioning paradigm are consistent with the formation of memory traces in cerebellar cortex. Prior to training, a tone CS causes a variable evoked increase in frequency of discharge of simple spikes (signaling mossy/parallel fiber activation) in many Purkinje cells (Donegan, Foy, & Thompson, 1985; Foy & Thompson, 1986). Following training, the majority of Purkinje cells that develop a change in frequency of simple spike discharge that correlates with the behavioral response (as opposed to being stimulus evoked) show decreases in frequency of discharge of simple spikes that precede and "predict" the form of the behavioral learned response, although increases in "predictive" discharge frequency also occur fairly frequently.

Prior to training, the onset of the corneal airpuff US evokes a complex spike (signaling a climbing fiber volley) in the great majority of Purkinje cells that are influenced by the US (e.g., in H VII, Crus I, and Crus II). However, the tone CS does not evoke complex spikes before or after training. These results are strongly supportive of our general hypothesis (Fig. 16.1) that climbing fibers are the essential US pathway and mossy fibers the CS pathway. After training, complex spikes are rarely evoked by US onset, a result that has interesting implications for the nature of "reinforcement" in classical conditioning (see Thompson, 1986). Thus, assume the CS–US associative strength is increased each time there is an appropriate temporal pairing of mossy fiber (CS) and climbing fiber (US) activation of Purkinje cells. Then, over the course of training the amount of associative strength added on a given trial will decrease from some maximal value at the beginning of training to some minimal value or even zero when conditioned response performance is asymptotic. This notion is strongly reminicient of the Rescorla–Wagner (1972) formulation of classical conditioning.

Conjoint electrical stimulation of mossy fibers and climbing fibers can yield normal learning of behavioral responses, as noted earlier (Steinmetz et al., 1985b). The properties of these learned responses appear identical to those of the same conditioned responses learned with peripheral stimuli (e.g., eyelid closure, leg flexion). The temporal requirements for such conjoint stimulation that yields behavioral learning are essentially identical to those required with peripheral stimuli: no learning at all if CS onset does not precede US onset by more than 50 msec, best learning if CS precedes US by 200–400 msec, and progressively poorer learning with increasing CS precedence (Gormezano, 1972). Further, normal learning occurs if the mossy fiber CS consists of only 2 pulses, 5 msec apart, at the beginning of a 250 msec CS–US onset interval (Logan, Steinmetz, Woodruff-Pak, & Thompson, 1985).

Collectively, the evidence reviewed here demonstrates that the cerebellum is essential for the category of procedural memory we have studied. It also builds a very strong case that the essential memory traces are stored in very localized regions of the cerebellum.

It is perhaps fitting to end this chapter with the following prophetic quotation from John Eccles (1977):

We can say that normally our most complex muscle movements are carried out subconsciously and with consummate skill. . . . It is my thesis that the cerebellum is concerned in this enormously complex organization and control of movement, and that throughout life, particularly in the earliest years, we are engaged in an incessant teaching program for the cerebellum. As a consequence, it can carry out all of these remarkable tasks that we set it to do in the whole repertoire for our skilled movements in games, in techniques, in musical performances, in speech, dance, song and so on. (p. 328)

ACKNOWLEDGMENTS

This chapter was supported by grants from the National Science Foundation (BNS 8117115), the Office of Naval Research (N00014-83), the McKnight Foundation, and the Sloan Foundation. We thank Dore Gormezano for his very helpful comments and suggestions.

REFERENCES

Albus, J. S. (1971). A theory of cerebellar function. *Mathematical Bioscience, 10,* 25–61.

Berger, T. W., Rinaldi, P., Weisz, D. J., & Thompson, R. F. (1983). Single unit analysis of different hippocampal cell types during classical conditioning of the rabbit nictitating membrane response. *Journal of Neurophysiology, 450,* 1197–1219.

Black, A. H., & Prokasy, W. F. (Eds.) (1972). *Classical conditioning: II. Current research and theory.* New York: Appleton-Century-Crofts.

Bloedel, J. R., & Courville, J. (1981). Cerebellar afferent systems. In J. M. Brookhart, V. B. Mountcastle, V. B. Brooks, & S. R. Geiger (Eds.), *Handbook of physiology* (Vol 2, pp. 735–829). Baltimore: American Psychological Association.

Brodal, P. (1975). Demonstration of a somatotopically organized projection onto the paramedian lobule and the anterior lobe from the lateral reticular nucleus. An experimental study with the horseradish peroxidase method. *Brain Research, 95,* 221–239.

Brooks, V. B., Kozlovskaya, I. B., Atkin, A., Horvath, F. E., & Uno, M. (1973). Effects of cooling dentate nucleus on tracking-task performance in monkeys. *Journal of Neurophysiology, 36,* 974–995.

Brooks, V. B. (1979). Control of intended limb movements by the lateral and intermediate cerebellum. In H. Asanuma & V. J. Wilson (Eds.), *Integration in the nervous system.* (pp. 321–357). Tokyo: Igaku Shoin.

Brooks, V. B., & Thach, W. T. (1981). Cerebellar control of posture and movement. In J. M. Brookhart, V. B. Mountcastle, V. B. Brooks, & S. R. Geiger (Eds.), *Handbook of physiology* (Vol. 2, pp. 877–946). Bethesda, MD: American Physiological Society.

Chan-Palay, V. (1977). *Cerebellar dentate nucleus.* New York: Springer.

Chapman, C. E., Spidalieri, G., & Lamarre, Y. (1986). Activity of dentate neurons during arm movements triggered by visual, auditory, and somesthetic stimuli in the monkey. *Journal of Neurophysiology, 55*(2); 203–226.

Chapman, P. F., Steinmentz, J. E., & Thompson, R. F. (1985). Classical conditioning of the rabbit eyeblink does not occur with stimulation of the cerebellar nuclei as the unconditioned stimulus. *Society for Neuroscience Abstracts, 11,* 835.

Clark, G. A., McCormick, D. A., Lavond, D. G., & Thompson, R. F. (1984). Effects of lesions of cerebellar nuclei on conditioned behavioral and hippocampal neuronal responses. *Brain Research, 291,* 125–136.

Disterhoft, J. F., Coulter, D. A., Alkon, D. L. (1986). Conditioning-specific membrane changes of rabbit hippocampal neurons measured *in vitro. Proceedings of the National Academy of Sciences, 83,* 2733–2737.

Donegan, N. H., Foy, M. R., & Thompson, R. F. (1985). Neuronal responses of the rabbit cerebellar cortex during performance of the classically conditioned eyelid response. *Society for Neuroscience Abstract, 11,* 835.

Donegan, N. H., Lowry, R. W., & Thompson, R. F. (1983). Effects of lesioning cerebellar nuclei on conditioned leg-flexion responses. *Neuroscience Abstracts, 9* (No. 100.7), 331.

Eccles, J. C. (1977). An instruction-selection theory of learning in the cerebellar cortex. *Brain Research, 127,* 327–352.

Foy, M. R., & Thompson, R. F. (1986). Single unit analysis of Purkinje cell discharge in classically conditioned and untrained rabbits. *Society for Neuroscience Abstracts, 12,* 518.

Gormezano, I. (1972). Investigations of defense and reward conditioning in the rabbit. In A. H. Black & W. F. Prokasy (Eds), *Classical conditioning: II. Current research and theory* (pp. 151–181). New York: Appleton-Century-Crofts.

Gormezano, I. & Coleman, S. R. (1973). The law of effect and CR contingent modification of the UCS. *Conditional Reflex, 8* (No. 1), 41–56.

Haley, D. A., Lavond, D. G., & Thompson, R. F. (1983). Effects of contralateral red nuclear lesions on retention of the classically conditioned nictitating membrane/eyelid response. *Society for Neuroscience Abstracts, 9,* 643.

Ito, M., (1972). Neural design of the cerebellar motor control system. *Brain Research, 40,* 81–84.

Ito, M. (1984). *The cerebellum and neural control.* New York: Raven.

Kassel, J., Shambes, G. M., & Walker, W. (1984). Fractured cutaneous projections to the granule cell layer of the posterior cerebellar hemisphere of the domestic cat. *Journal of Comparative Neurology, 225,* 458–468.

Knowlton, B., Beekman, G., Lavond, D. G., Steinmetz, J. E., & Thompson, R. F. (1986). Effects of aspiration of cerebellar cortex on retention of eyeblink conditioning using stimulation of different mossy fiber sources as conditioned stimuli. *Society for Neuroscience Abstracts, 12,* 754.

Kettner, R. E., & Thompson, R. E. (1985). Cochlear nucleus, inferior colliculus, and medial geniculate responses during the behavioral detection of threshold-level auditory stimuli in the rabbit. *Journal of the Acoustical Society of America, 77,* 2111–2127.

Lavond, D. G., Hembree, T. L., & Thompson, R. F. (1985). Effect of kainic acid lesions of the cerebellar interpositus nucleus on eyelid conditioning in the rabbit. *Brain Research, 326,* 179–182.

Lavond, D. G., Lincoln, J. S., McCormick, D. A., & Thompson, R. F. (1984a). Effect of bilateral lesions of the dentate interpositus cerebellar nuclei on conditioning of heart-rate and nictitating membrane/eyelid responses in the rabbit. *Brain Research, 305,* 323–330.

Lavond, D. G., McCormick, D. A., Clark, G. A., Holmes, D. T., & Thompson, R. F. (1981). Effects of ipsilateral rostral pontine reticular lesions on retention of classically conditioned nictitating membrane and eyelid response. *Physiological Psychology, 9*(4), 335–339.

Lavond, D. G., McCormick, D. A., & Thompson, R. F. (1984b). A nonrecoverable learning deficit. *Physiological Psychology, 12,* 103–110.

Lavond, D. G., Steinmetz, J. E., Yokaitis, M. H., Lee, J., & Thompson, R. F. (1986). Retention of classical conditioning after removal of cerebellar cortex. *Society for Neuroscience Abstracts, 12,* 753.

Lincoln, J. S., McCormick, D. A., & Thompson, R. F. (1982). Ipsilateral cerebellar lesions prevent learning of the classically conditioned nictitating membrane/eyelid response of the rabbit. *Brain Research, 242,* 190–193.

Llinas, R. (1981). Electrophysiology of the cerebellar networks. In J. M. Brookhart, V. B. Mountcastle, V. B. Brooks, & S. R. Geiger (Eds.), *Handbook of physiology, Vol. 2,* pp. 831–876). Bethesda, MD: American Physiological Society.

Logan, C. G., Steinmetz, J. E., & Thompson, R. F. (1986). Acoustic related responses recorded from the region of the pontine nuclei. *Society for Neuroscience Abstracts, 12,* 754.

Logan, C. G., Steinmetz, J. E., Woodruff-Pak, D. S., & Thompson, R. F. (1985). Short-duration mossy fiber stimulation is effective as a CS in eyelid classical conditioning. *Society for Neuroscience Abstracts, 11,* 835.

Madden, J., IV, Haley, D. A., Barchas, J. D., & Thompson, R. F. (1983). Microinfusion of picrotoxin into the caudal red nucleus selectively abolishes the classically conditioned nictitating membrane/eyelid response in the rabbit. *Society for Neuroscience Abstracts, 9,* 830.

Mamounas, L. A., Thompson, R. F., Lynch, G., & Baudry, M. (1984). Classical conditioning of the rabbit eyelid response increases glutamate receptor binding in hippocampal synaptic membranes. *Proceedings of the National Academy of Sciences, 81,* 2548–2552.

Marr, D. (1969). A theory of cerebellar cortex. *Journal of Physiology, 202,* 437–470.

Mauk, M. D., & Thompson, R. F. (1987). Retention of classically conditioned eyelid responses following acute decerebration. *Brain Research, 403,* 89–95.

Mauk, M. D., Steinmetz, J. E., & Thompson, R. F. (1986). Classical conditioning using stimulation of the inferior olive as the unconditioned stimulus. *Proceedings of the National Academy of Sciences, 83,* 5349–5353.

McCormick, D. A., Clark, G. A., Lavond, D. G., & Thompson, R. F. (1982a). Initial localization of the memory trace for a basic form of learning. *Proceedings of the National Academy of Sciences, 79,* 2731–2742.

McCormick, D. A., Guyer, P. E., & Thompson, R. F. (1982b). Superior cerebellar peduncle lesions selectively abolish the ipsilateral classically conditioned nictitating membrane/eyelid response in the rabbit. *Brain Research, 244,* 347–350.

McCormick, D. A., Lavond, D. G., Clark, G. A., Kettner, R. E., Rising, C. E., & Thompson, R. F. (1981). The engram found? Role of the cerebellum in classical conditioning of nictitating membrane and eyelid responses. *Bulletin of the Psychonomic Society, 18,* 103–105.

McCormick, D. A., Steinmetz, J. E., & Thompson, R. F. (1985). Lesions of the inferior olivary complex cause extinction of the classical conditioned eyeblink response. *Brain Research, 359,* 120–130.

McCormick, D. A., & Thompson, R. F. (1984a). Cerebellum: Essential involvement in the classically conditioned eyelid response. *Science, 223,* 296–299.

McCormick, D. A., & Thompson, R. F. (1984b). Neuronal responses of the rabbit cerebellum during acquisition and performance of a classically conditioned nictitating membrane-eyelid response. *Journal of Neuroscience, 4,* 2811–2822.

Meyer-Lohmann, J., Hore, J., Brooks, V. B. (1977). Cerebellar participation in generation of prompt arm movements. *Journal of Neurophysiology. 40,* 1038–1050

Norman, R. J., Villablanca, J. R., Brown, K. A., Schwafel, J. A., Buchwald, J. S. (1974). Classical conditioning in the bilaterally hemispherectomized cat. *Experimental Neurology, 44,* 363–380.

Oakley, D. A., & Russel, I. S. (1977). Subcortical storage of Pavlovian conditioning in the rabbit. *Physiology and Behavior, 18,* 931–937.

Polenchar, B. E., Patterson, M. M., Lavond, D. G., & Thompson, R. F. (1985). Cerebellar lesions abolish an avoidance response in rabbit. *Behavioral and Neural Biology, 44,* 221–227.

Rescorla, R. A., & Wagner, A. R. (1972). A theory of Pavlovian conditioning: Variations in the effectiveness of reinforcement and non-reinforcement. In A. H. Black & W. F. Prokasy (Eds.), *Classical conditioning II: Current research and theory* (pp. 64–99). New York: Appleton-Century-Crofts.

Rosenfield, M. E., Devydaitis, A., & Moore, J. W. (1985). Brachium conjunctivum and rubrobulbar tract: Brainstem projections of red nucleus essential for the conditioned nictitating membrane response. *Physiology and Behavior, 34,* 751–759.

Shambes, G. M., Gibson, J. M., Walker, W. (1978). Fractured somatotopy in granule cell tactile areas of rat cerebellar hemispheres revealed by micromapping. *Brain Behavior and Evolution, 15,* 94–140.

Solomon, P. R., Lewis, J. L., LoTurco, J. J., Steinmetz, J. E., & Thompson, R. F. (1986). The role of the middle cerebellar peduncle in acquisition and retention of the rabbits classically conditioned nictitating membrane response. *Bulletin of the Psychonomic Society, 24,* 75–78.

Steinmetz, J. E., Lavond, D. G., & Thompson, R. F. (1985a). Classical conditioning of the rabbit eyelid response with mossy fiber stimulation as the conditioned stimulus. *Bulletin of the Psychonomic Society, 23,* 245–248.

Steinmetz, J. E., Lavond, D. G., & Thompson, R. F. (1985b). Classical conditioning of skeletal muscle responses with mossy fiber stimulation CS and climbing fiber stimulation US. *Society for Neuroscience Abstracts, 11,* 982.

Steinmetz, J. E., Logan, C. G., Rosen D. J., Thompson, J. K., Lavond, D. G., & Thompson, R. F. (1987). Initial localization of the acoustic conditioned stimulus projection system to the cerebellum essential for classical eyelid conditioning. *Proceeding of the National Academy of Sciences, 84,* 3531–3535.

Steinmetz, J. E., Rosen, D. L., Chapman, P. F., Lavond, D. G., & Thompson, R. F. (1986a). Classical conditioning of the rabbit eyelid response with a mossy fiber stimulation CS. I. Pontine nuclei and middle cerebellar peduncle stimulation. *Behavioral Neuroscience, 100,* 871–880.

Steinmetz, J. E., Rosen, D. J., Woodruff-Pak, D. S., Lavond, D. G., & Thompson, R. F. (1986). Rapid transfer of training occurs when direct mossy fiber stimulation is used as a conditioned stimulus for classical eyelid conditioning. *Neuroscience Research, 3,* 606–616.

Thompson, J. K., Lavond, D. G., & Thompson, R. F. (1986). Preliminary evidence for a projection from the cochlear nucleus to the pontine nuclear region. *Society for Neuroscience Abstracts, 12,* 754.

Thompson, R. F. (1986). The neurobiology of learning and memory. *Science, 233,* 941–947.

Thompson, R. F., Berger, T. W., & Madden, J., IV (1983). Cellular processes of learning and memory in the mammalian CNS. *Annual Review of Neuroscience, 6,* 447–491.

Thompson, R. F., Clark, G. A., Donegan, N. H., Lavond, D. G., Madden, J., IV, Mamounas, L. A., Mauk, M. D., & McCormick, D. A. (1984). Neuronal substrates of basic associative learning. In L. Squire & N. Butters (Eds.), *Neuropsychology of memory* (pp. 424–442.) New York: Guilford Press.

Weisz, D. J., Clark, G. A., & Thompson, R. F. (1984). Increased activity of dentate granule cells during nictitating membrane response conditioning in rabbits. *Behavioral Brain Research, 12,* 145–154.

Welsh, J. P. (1986). *The effect of nucleus interpositus lesions on retention of the rabbit's classically conditioned nictitating membrane response.* Unpublished master's thesis, University of Iowa, Iowa City.

Welsh, J. P. Gormezano, I., & Harvey, J. A. (1986). Cerebellar lesions prevent optimal execution but not acquisition of the conditioned nictitating membrane response. *Society of Neuroscience Abstracts, 14* (No. 270.12,) p. 978.

Woodruff-Pak, D. S., Lavond, D. G., Logan, C. G., Steinmetz, J. E., & Thompson, R. F. (1985b). The continuing search for a role of the cerebellar cortex in eyelid conditioning. *Society for Neuroscience Abstracts, 11,* 333.

Woodruff-Pak, D. S., Lavond, D. G., & Thompson, R. F. (1985a). Trace conditioning: Abolished by cerebellar nuclear lesions but not lateral cerebellar cortex aspirations. *Brain Research, 348,* 249–260.

Yeo, C. H., Hardiman, M. J., & Glickstein, M. (1985a). Classical conditioning of the nictitating membrane response of the rabbit: I. Lesions of the cerebellar nuclei. *Experimental Brain Research, 60,* 87–98.

Yeo, C. H., Hardiman, M. J., & Glickstein, M. (1985b). Classical conditioning of the nictitating membrane response of the rabbit: II. Lesions of the cerebellar cortex. *Experimental Brain Research, 60,* 99–113.

Author Index

Italics denote reference pages.

Subject Index